John's Unfolding Cosmic Drama

John's Unfolding Cosmic Drama

A Literary and Theological Analysis of Revelation

DAN LIOY *and*
GEORGE COON

RESOURCE *Publications* · Eugene, Oregon

JOHN'S UNFOLDING COSMIC DRAMA
A Literary and Theological Analysis of Revelation

Resource Publications
An Imprint of Wipf and Stock Publishers
199 W. 8th Ave., Suite 3
Eugene, OR 97401

www.wipfandstock.com

PAPERBACK ISBN: 979-8-3852-5611-2
HARDCOVER ISBN: 979-8-3852-5612-9
EBOOK ISBN: 979-8-3852-5613-6

VERSION NUMBER 02/12/26

Contents

Prologue

INTRODUCTION

In John 5:45–47, Jesus rebukes the religious elites for using the writings of Moses to justify their self-serving religious system rather than recognizing the itinerant rabbi from Nazareth as the Messiah. They were so focused on legalistic details that they failed to see the big picture and purpose of Scripture, namely, to reveal Christ.

Tragically, the above scenario often occurs among those who teach and preach from Revelation. Its complex literary nature can lead to two problematic approaches. On one extreme, John's prophetic oracle has been overanalyzed in irrelevant or unhelpful ways. On the other extreme, Revelation has been either criticized, neglected, or abandoned due to the difficulty of understanding its magnificent visions and symbols.

Both approaches miss Revelation's main emphasis, that is, to highlight the glory, majesty, and identity of the risen, victorious Messiah. Attempting to decode predictive details while losing sight of the Savior is akin to the legalistic mistake of the religious elites. Also, neglecting entirely the study of the apostle's unfolding cosmic drama robs believers of its Christ-honoring purpose.

Rather than overanalysis or neglect, believers are best served by a balanced approach that keeps their gaze fixed on Jesus, especially as they seek to understand Revelation's meaning. Doing so requires humility, discernment, and a willingness to let Scripture interpret Scripture under the Spirit's guidance. When Christ remains central, John's treatise fulfills its God-intended purpose for the redeemed.

PURPOSE AND AUDIENCE

So then, what is our twofold purpose in this study? First, it is to provide an accessible interpretation of Revelation that is well-informed. Second, we aim to offer practical observations in three key areas: theological insights, ministry implications, and missional ramifications.

Concerning our intended audience, we designed this publication specifically for learners engaged in biblical, theological, and ministerial studies, especially those serving in Majority World contexts. More broadly, though, we intend our volume to be a convenient resource for Christian educators, pastors, lay leaders, and other inquisitive readers to interpret and apply responsibly John's unfolding cosmic drama to their contemporary intellectual and cultural horizons.

Though Revelation addresses end-time events, we decided early on to avoid getting entangled in endless debates over speculations about the future. Instead, we focus our discussion on the literary and theological richness of the apostle's treatise, especially by giving particular attention to its vision of the exalted, triumphant Redeemer.

STRUCTURE AND LAYOUT

We recognize that there are many insightful commentaries and theological analyses of Revelation already available. Indeed, a number of them have informed our present study. Scores of these academic works thoroughly canvass the full range of classic and contemporary scholarship on John's prophetic oracle. Admittedly, while this level of depth and precision is sometimes needed, it can frustrate readers who either lack access to such specialized resources or find such publications impractical to engage.

For the preceding reason, our volume intends to offer a distinctive contribution. On one level, it is informed by a broad range of academic works. Yet, on another level, it remains accessible to a wide readership. It is also unencumbered by the need to rehearse all that specialists have to say about every interpretive issue arising from a comprehensive analysis of the biblical text.

To further aid readers, we have included an extensive Introduction, which surveys Revelation's authorship, date, context, major themes, and theological motifs. We aim to provide a substantial yet readable synopsis of John's unfolding cosmic drama.

Along with the Introduction, the beginning of each subsequent chapter follows the same structure: learning objectives, a chapter summary, study questions, and an outline. This is followed by a concise yet illuminating explanation of the biblical text. The inclusion of informative tables helps synthesize key information at a glance. As noted earlier, toward the end of each chapter, we provide theological insights, ministry implications, and missional applications.

The volume concludes with an Epilogue, which offers guidelines for teaching and preaching through the last book of Scripture. A Glossary comes next, defining key terms, phrases, and themes essential for an informed understanding of Revelation. Finally, the Bibliography lists all publications cited in the footnotes throughout the volume.

Overall, then, our goal is to offer a publication grounded in scholarship yet accessible and applicable to a wide readership. Expressed another way, we aim to clarify Revelation's timeless message without requiring readers to navigate dense academic publications.

LITERARY ANALYSIS

The literary analysis we undertake in this volume places its focus on what John saw, heard, and felt in a trancelike, visionary state. We learn that Revelation beautifully presents the Messiah's consummation of God's end-time plan for all creation in a dramatic, picturesque symphony of prophetic oracles.

We also discover that each chapter advances the arc of Revelation's storyline. For instance, our discussion of the biblical text includes a summary of God's sobering plan of judgment for the wicked and marvelous redemption for his reborn children. Also, Jesus' admonitions for the church to persevere in faithfulness to the end are presented against the backdrop of the future events he discloses to John.

Within our explanation of each chapter, readers encounter the rich, detailed tapestry of John's unfolding cosmic drama. That said, readers also find out how each chapter contributes to the overall picture of the Messiah, as the divine Warrior, ushering in his kingdom. For believers, it is a reign characterized by righteousness, peace, and joy in the sacred, blessed, and everlasting presence of the triune God.

Moreover, within carefully curated footnotes, we place the apostle's narrative in conversation with modern sources and ancient sacred texts.

These notes include extensive references to the Hebrew Bible (Old Testament), the Apocryphal/Deuterocanonical Books, the Pseudepigrapha, and the New Testament writings.

In keeping with what we stated above, we resist the temptation to fill our citations with a plethora of cumbersome technical explanations. Instead, our goal is to showcase Revelation as a distinctive yet coherent portion of God's authoritative Word. Readers can thereby engage with the inspired text on its own terms.

THEOLOGICAL INSIGHTS

In this volume, we focus our theological insights on the person and work of Jesus Christ. Yet, in keeping with the Trinitarian nature of Revelation, we add reflections on the Father and the sevenfold Spirit.

We have also included pertinent observations dealing with the church (both militant and triumphant), spirit beings (including angels, Satan, and demons), the nature of fallen and redeemed humanity, and key aspects of the end times. Furthermore, throughout our publication, we show forth the Messiah in the execution of his righteous judgment of earth's wicked inhabitants, his worthiness to bestow covenantal blessings and curses, and his sovereign rule over God's reborn children.

We affirm that the Redeemer's manifestation at his second advent truly is a future, historic event. Yet the horizon of what John discloses in his prophetic oracle is far more extensive. Specifically, the apostle seeks to clarify and correct flawed assumptions about the Messiah.

We avoid taking rigid, theological stances on debated issues about God's future redemptive plan because we do not see the need to duplicate the elaborate discussions already in print on these issues. For this reason, our primary focus remains on Christ in all his majesty and might. In fact, he alone occupies the center stage of what we put forward in our publication about the apostle's unfolding cosmic drama.

MINISTRY IMPLICATIONS

Along with theological insights, we offer our thoughts on various ministry implications arising from this study of Revelation. We maintain that John's prophetic oracle is more focused on how the Messiah's followers, as represented by the seven churches in Asia Minor, should conduct themselves in anticipation of his imminent return.

Consider that John penned Revelation, under the Spirit's inspiration, to suffering Christians. In the apostle's treatise, he urged them to persevere in their faith, knowing that their divine Warrior would one day conquer evil and redeem the upright. This encouragement applies to the church today, especially in Majority World contexts where suffering for one's faith remains far too common.

The above perspective differs from an obsession with constructing detailed timelines or making dogmatic predictions about when specific, foretold events might occur. On the one hand, we affirm that the apostle's unfolding cosmic drama is anchored in space-time history. Yet, on the other hand, only God knows the precise time when he will bring about the consummation of the age.

For the preceding reasons, Jesus never commands his followers to be distracted by clock-and-calendar predictions about the future. Instead, the enduring ministry priority for God's reborn children is to live in an upright, virtuous manner. Also, as we note in the following section, doing so includes maintaining an active commitment to spread the gospel to people from every tribe, language, ethnicity, and nation.

MISSIONAL RAMIFICATIONS

The missional ramifications arising from this study of Revelation complete our approach in this publication. We desire that readers feel motivated to use the message of John's prophetic oracle to engage the lost with the truth of the gospel.

Admittedly, it may not seem immediately obvious that Revelation presents a missionary message. Yet we think that the apostle's treatise encourages believers to be intentional, proactive, and earnest in their engagement with the lost. After all, Jesus' mandate is for his followers to share the good news actively with all people by reaching across cultures, national boundaries, and even languages. Also, consider that in Revelation, the success of missionary outreach is represented by the worshipers in heaven being from every region of the planet.

In John's unfolding cosmic drama, we find contrasting themes, such as warning and hope, death and life, and destruction and redemption. Together these emphases showcase the two potential destinies of all humankind. In turn, this stark set of options serves as a call for all people to repent of their sin and trust in Christ for salvation.

Therefore, our volume not only recognizes these missional principles but also seeks to highlight them. We desire that readers who teach and preach from Revelation may do so with evangelistic motivation and missional fervor.

MAJORITY WORLD PERSPECTIVE

In the preceding sections of our Prologue, we stress that we are intentionally focused on believers serving in Majority World contexts. We intend to empower them to apply to their peers, among whom they live and to whom they minister, insights arising from their study of Revelation.

The reason for this unique approach is based, in part, on the history of oppression, as well as the present-day religious persecution, that prevails among Jesus' followers in regions of the developing world, especially countries in Africa, Asia, and Latin America. We maintain that for them the truths found in John's prophetic oracle are particularly applicable.

Readers of our volume discover in Revelation a repeated summons for Jesus' followers to persevere in their faith, endure hardship for the cause of Christ, and remain unwavering in their devotion to the gospel. This threefold emphasis found throughout the apostle's unfolding cosmic drama is especially meaningful in cultural contexts where believers endure shame, deprivation, and other forms of hardship.

Given the above stark reality, we regularly highlight the global context of Revelation. Yet, at the same time, we keep in view both the original recipients of the book and the needs of believers today in the West. Consequently, regardless of where God's reborn children live and minister, our publication offers them relevant, timely insights that they can apply to their lives as well as to their teaching and preaching ministries.

Our joint prayer is that the triune God may be glorified through this study of Revelation!

Abbreviations

HEBREW BIBLE / OLD TESTAMENT

Gen	Genesis
Exod	Exodus
Lev	Leviticus
Num	Numbers
Deut	Deuteronomy
Josh	Joshua
Judg	Judges
Ruth	Ruth
1–2 Sam	1–2 Samuel
1–2 Kgs	1–2 Kings
1–2 Chr	1–2 Chronicles
Ezra	Ezra
Neh	Nehemiah
Esth	Esther
Job	Job
Ps (*pl.* Pss)	Psalm(s)
Prov	Proverbs
Eccl	Ecclesiastes
Song	Song of Songs
Isa	Isaiah
Jer	Jeremiah
Lam	Lamentations
Ezek	Ezekiel
Dan	Daniel
Hos	Hosea

Joel	Joel
Amos	Amos
Obad	Obadiah
Jonah	Jonah
Mic	Micah
Nah	Nahum
Hab	Habakkuk
Zeph	Zephaniah
Hag	Haggai
Zech	Zechariah
Mal	Malachi

NEW TESTAMENT

Matt	Matthew
Mark	Mark
Luke	Luke
John	John
Acts	Acts
Rom	Romans
1–2 Cor	1–2 Corinthians
Gal	Galatians
Eph	Ephesians
Phil	Philippians
Col	Colossians
1–2 Thess	1–2 Thessalonians
1–2 Tim	1–2 Timothy
Titus	Titus
Phlm	Philemon
Heb	Hebrews
Jas	James
1–2 Pet	1–2 Peter
1–2–3 John	1–2–3 John
Jude	Jude
Rev	Revelation

APOCRYPHAL/DEUTEROCANONICAL BOOKS

Jdt	Judith
1–3 Macc	1–3 Maccabees
Sir	Sirach
Tob	Tobit
Wis	Wisdom of Solomon

PSEUDEPIGRAPHA

Apoc. Ab.	Apocalypse of Abraham
Apoc. Dan.	Apocalypse of Daniel
Apoc. El.	Apocalypse of Elijah
Apoc. Pet.	Apocalypse of Peter
Apoc. Zeph.	Apocalypse of Zephaniah
Apocr. Ezek.	Apocryphon of Ezekiel
Ascen. Isa.	Ascension of Isaiah
As. Mos.	Assumption of Moses
2 Bar.	2 Baruch (Syriac Apocalypse)
3 Bar.	3 Baruch (Greek Apocalypse)
4 Bar.	4 Baruch (Paraleipomena Jeremiou)
1 En.	1 Enoch (Ethiopic Apocalypse)
2 En.	2 Enoch (Slavonic Apocalypse)
3 En.	3 Enoch (Hebrew Apocalypse)
4 Ezra	4 Ezra
Jos. Asen.	Joseph and Aseneth
Jub.	Jubilees
LAB	Liber antiquitatum biblicarum (Pseudo-Philo)
LAE	Life of Adam and Eve
Let. Aris.	Letter of Aristeas
Liv. Pro.	Lives of the Prophets
Odes Sol.	Odes of Solomon
Pss. Sol.	Psalms of Solomon
Sib. Or.	Sibylline Oracles
T. Benj.	Testament of Benjamin
T. Dan	Testament of Dan
T. Job	Testament of Job
T. Jos.	Testament of Joseph
T. Jud.	Testament of Judah

T. Levi	Testament of Levi
T. Naph.	Testament of Naphtali
T. Sol.	Testament of Solomon

EARLY CHRISTIAN WRITINGS

1–2 Clem.	1–2 Clement
Christ Ant.	On Christ and Antichrist
Dial.	Dialogue with Trypho
Did.	Didache
Haer.	Against Heresies (Adversus haereses)
Herm.	Shepherd of Hermas
Hist. eccl.	Ecclesiastical History
Marc.	Against Marcion
Mod.	On Modesty
Noet.	Against Noetus
Praescr.	The Prescription against Heretics (De praescriptione haereticorum)
Prax.	Against Praxeas

RABBINIC LITERATURE

Lev. Rab.	Leviticus Rabba
m. ʿAbot	Pirke ʿAboth
Num. Rab.	Numbers Rabbah
Qoh. Rab.	Kohelet Rabbah

OTHER ANCIENT NEAR EASTERN TEXTS

D.P.	Dynastic Prophecy
U.P.	Uruk Prophecy
Vis. Neth.	Vision of the Netherworld

Introduction to Revelation

LEARNING OBJECTIVES

- Understand the nature and purpose of Revelation.
- Gain insight into the historical context of Revelation.
- Recognize the central role of the Messiah in Revelation.
- Explore the symbolism and imagery used in Revelation.
- Discern the relevance of Revelation for contemporary readers.

CHAPTER SUMMARY

Revelation, otherwise known as the Apocalypse, is the final book of Scripture. In this prophetic oracle, the author uses vivid symbolism and graphic imagery to describe what takes place at the end of human history. As the cosmic drama unfolds, readers encounter seven letters to seven churches, three cycles of seven judgments on wicked humanity, and the defeat of Satan and his followers. The treatise closes with a vision of a recreated heaven and earth, where God dwells with his reborn children for all eternity.

STUDY QUESTIONS

1. What do you think is the main purpose of Revelation?
2. Respond to the following statement: "The Apocalypse should be avoided because it's too difficult to understand and interpret."

3. Of the four ways to understand Revelation (preterist, historicist, futurist, idealist), which view, if any, most closely corresponds to your own prior understanding of this prophetic oracle?
4. How should/does the assurance of both judgment and blessing motivate you in (1) your personal walk with Christ and (2) your gospel witness to others?
5. Considering the assurance and hope given in the Apocalypse, what would you say to a brother or sister in Christ who is experiencing severe persecution for his or her faith?

CHAPTER OUTLINE

- Overview
- Authorship, date, place, and recipients
- Purpose, themes, and literary features
- The significance of the throne-room scenes in Revelation
- Four different ways of understanding Revelation
- Three popular views about the reference in Revelation 20:2 to one thousand years
- Women in Revelation
- Five fallacies concerning Revelation
- Three reasons for the symbolism in Revelation
- Five principles of interpretation
- The already/not-yet perspective found in the Apocalypse
- Characteristics of apocalyptic literature
- Numbers in Scripture, including Revelation
- Fulfillment motifs
- Resurrection motifs
- Son of God motif
- Son of Man motif
- The Lamb motif
- A summary of the various motifs in Revelation

- The centrality of the Messiah in Revelation
- The main purpose of Revelation
- The presence of contrasting parallels in the Apocalypse
- The use of the Old Testament in Revelation
- The relationship between Daniel and Revelation
- The influence of Revelation 1:19
- Recapitulation versus progression
- A proposed literary structure of Revelation
- Key theological insights
- Important ministry implications
- Vital missional ramifications

OVERVIEW

Revelation is an auditory, literary, and artistic masterpiece. For instance, its rhetorical strategy makes use of a distinctive Hebraic style of Greek to give expression to the book's symbolic universe. Also, the treatise skillfully brings together three types of writing: a revelation (or apocalypse),[1] a prophetic oracle,[2] and a circular letter (or epistle).[3] More information on each literary category appears later in the Introduction.

Though filled with magnificent visions and symbols that might be difficult to understand, first and foremost Revelation begins and ends with the Messiah.[4] Particular attention is given to his character, mission, and final goal of bringing every aspect of creation—including humankind (both regenerate and unregenerate)—into subjection to his Father's perfect will. Likewise, in Revelation, readers learn many truths about the Savior that they cannot find anywhere else in Scripture, especially in the amazing details about the Son's redemptive mission and everlasting rule.

Granted, a lot of mystery surrounds Revelation. For this reason, it tends to be one of the most misunderstood and least-read books in

1. See our discussion of Rev 1:1.

2. See our discussion of Rev 1:3, 19; 22:6, 7, 9, 10, 18, 19.

3. Written correspondence intended for distribution among the seven churches located in Asia Minor (the southwestern portion of modern-day Turkey); see our discussion of Rev 1:4–5, 11; 2:1—3:22; 22:21.

4. See our discussion of Rev 1:1; 22:21.

Scripture.[5] For instance, Revelation's abundant imagery and intriguing symbols have stimulated many different and conflicting explanations of its message. Furthermore, the book's unusual imagery, which is challenging to visualize and understand, has caused numerous disagreements among specialists about precise meanings. Yet, despite the mystery surrounding Revelation, hope characterizes the book more than anything else, particularly hope for believers facing a period of severe adversity. The writer eloquently declares that the Messiah would one day return to vindicate the righteous and judge the wicked.

Revelation is also known for its stern warnings. For example, throughout the unfolding cosmic drama, Jesus summons believers to live in an upright and virtuous manner. He also admonishes the unrepentant to turn away from their idolatries—including the veneration of mortal, flawed, human rulers—and to trust in him for salvation.

AUTHORSHIP, DATE, PLACE, AND RECIPIENTS[6]

There are at least five differing views concerning who wrote Revelation. These views are as follows:

1. The apostle John;
2. John the Presbyter;
3. An otherwise unknown church leader or messianic Jewish prophet named "John";
4. A so-called Johannine school, namely, a community of followers sharing the same theological perspective and church tradition to which John the apostle, John the Presbyter, and other individuals were associated; and

5. Especially as a form of protest literature that presents an alternative view of reality. Specifically, the Apocalypse often conveys a message of impending doom and divine retribution to challenge the status quo and urge earth's wicked inhabitants to repent. Moreover, Revelation depicts Jesus' marginalized, beleaguered followers petitioning the Creator to vanquish the wicked, vindicate the righteous, and replace the present fallen order with the glorious new creation that awaits God's reborn children. For an extensive examination concerning the ways in which Revelation confronts the power structures of its day and serves as a critique of Christian nationalism and imperial oppression, see Morrison, "Apocalypse as Protest."

6. What follows in our Introduction is a distillation and adaptation of the discussion appearing in Lioy, *Revelation in Christological Focus*, 1–111, which, in turn, is informed by the numerous scholarly publications cited in the footnotes of this present treatise.

5. Various anonymous editors and redactors.

Several early church fathers affirmed that John the apostle was the author of Revelation, along with the Fourth Gospel and the three Johannine letters.[7] There seems to be insufficient evidence to overturn this view. In support of the preceding conclusion are the following four observations:

1. The author refers to himself as "John";[8]
2. The author, at some level, was pastorally involved with the seven congregations located in Asia Minor;[9]
3. The author's circumstances at the time of writing agree with what reliable historical sources from the second century AD recount about John's apostolic ministry during the second half of the first century AD;[10] and,
4. The author's abundant direct and indirect references to the Old Testament[11] point to an ethnic Palestinian Jewish writer from the late first century AD, such as John.

Literary Parallels between the Fourth Gospel and Revelation		
Description	**Fourth Gospel**	**Revelation**
Affirmation concerning the validity of what the author visually witnessed	19:35; 21:24	22:8
Allusion to manna	6:31, 49	2:17
Bride and bridegroom imagery	3:29	19:7–9; 21:2, 9; 22:17
Emphasis on testifying/ witnessing (as one would do in a court of law)	1:7, 8; 2:25; 3:11; 5:31, 36, 38; 7:7; 8:13, 14; 10:25; 15:26, 27; 18:23, 37; 21:24	1:2, 5, 9; 2:13; 3:14; 6:9; 10:11; 11:3; 12:11, 17; 15:5; 19:10; 20:4; 22:16, 20

7. For example, Justin Martyr (Dial. 81), Hippolytus (Christ Ant. 36; Noet. 14), Irenaeus (Haer. 3.1.1; 3.16.5; 5.30.3), and Tertullian (Marc. 4.5; Mod. 19; Prax. 15).

8. See our discussion of Rev 1:1, 4, 9; 22:8. Unless otherwise noted, all Scripture quotations are taken from the Evangelical Heritage Version, © 2019 Wartburg Project, Inc. All rights reserved. Hereafter abbreviated EHV.

9. See our discussion of Rev 1:4, 11; 2:1—3:22.

10. See our discussion of Rev 1:9.

11. Such as Exod, Isa, Jer, Ezek, Dan, Joel, and Zech.

Literary Parallels between the Fourth Gospel and Revelation		
Description	**Fourth Gospel**	**Revelation**
Emphasis on the "beginning"	1:1	21:6
Holy Spirit	1:32–34; 3:5–8, 34; 6:63; 7:38–39; 14:16, 26; 15:26; 16:13; 20:22	1:4, 10; 2:7, 11, 17, 29; 3:1, 6, 13, 22; 4:2, 5; 5:6; 14:13; 17:3; 21:10; 22:6, 17
"I am" statements	6:35; 8:12; 9:5; 10:7–11; 10:11–15; 11:23–26; 14:1–6; 15:1–5	1:8, 17–18; 2:23; 22:16
Invitation to those who are "thirsty"	7:37	22:17
Lamb	1:29, 36	5:6, 8, 12, 13; 6:1, 16; 7:9, 10, 14, 17; 12:11; 13:8, 11; 14:1, 4, 10; 15:3; 17:14; 19:7, 9; 21:9, 14, 22, 23; 22:1, 3
Light	8:12	21:23–24
Messiah as a Shepherd	10:1–19; 21:15–17	7:17
Messiah as the temple of the redeemed	2:18–22; 4:21	21:22
Reference to Zechariah 12:10	19:37	1:7
Revealing truths from God	1:18; 5:19–20; 12:49; 17:8	1:1; 22:16
Satan / the devil	6:70; 8:44; 13:2, 27	2:9, 10, 13, 24; 3:9; 12:9, 12; 20:2, 7, 10
Source of life-giving water	4:10; 7:37–39	7:16–17; 22:1
Symbolic use of the number seven	Seven miraculous signs; seven "I am" statements	Seven beatitudes; seven churches; seven throne-room scenes; seven seal, trumpet, and bowl judgments
Word of God	1:1, 14	19:13

There are at least three different views concerning when Revelation was written, as follows:

1. Before the destruction of Jerusalem in AD 70: The main justification is the persecution under Nero (AD 37–68), who reigned from AD 54–68.

2. After the destruction of Jerusalem in AD 70: The main justification is the persecution under Domitian, who reigned from AD 81–96.
3. During the reign of Vespasian (AD 69–79): This option has enjoyed less favor than the other two.

Of those views, the second option is most likely.[12] Most New Testament scholars have concluded that John probably penned Revelation around AD 95–96.

There are at least three views with respect to where Revelation was written, as follows:

1. *Patmos.* Patmos is a small, volcanic, and mostly treeless island about 35 miles off the coast of Asia Minor and about 70 miles southwest of Ephesus in the Aegean Sea.[13]
2. *The city of Ephesus.* Ephesus was the largest city of the Roman province of Asia and a center for commerce, politics, and religion.
3. *Both Patmos and Ephesus.* Because strong cases can be made for Patmos and Ephesus, John may have spent time in both locations while penning the Apocalypse.

Regarding the third view above, John experienced his amazing vision while banished to Patmos for refusing to venerate the Roman emperor, but the text of Revelation does not specify where he wrote down his vision. While on the island or sometime thereafter, perhaps at Ephesus, the apostle faithfully recorded all that he saw and heard.

Next up for consideration are the original recipients of Revelation. In the first century AD, most ancient letters began with the name of the author, the name of the recipient, and a salutation (or greeting). The main body of the letter followed this introduction, and the letter ended with a closing greeting.

Revelation contains these same elements. According to 1:4, the sender was John, and according to verse 11, the recipients of this circular letter were "seven churches" located in the Roman "province of Asia" in the following cities: Ephesus, Smyrna, Pergamum, Thyatira, Sardis, Philadelphia, and Laodicea.[14] These towns were about 50 miles apart from

12. A view affirmed by such early church leaders as Irenaeus, Clement of Alexandria, Eusebius, and Jerome.

13. In the eastern Mediterranean.

14. See Rev 22:16.

each other and roughly formed a horseshoe-shaped circuit, starting with Ephesus and ending with Laodicea.

There are at least four views concerning why these churches were chosen:

1. The seven cities were part of a transportation network.
2. The seven cities were postal centers and judicial districts for seven different regions.
3. The choice of seven churches has symbolic relevance, namely, to signify the totality of the people of God. In this case, though John addressed his prophetic oracle to seven churches, it is argued that these congregations were representative of the entire body of Christ down through the centuries.
4. The seven churches represent seven literal periods of church history, beginning with the Ephesian congregation, which symbolized the period in which John lived, and ending with the Laodicean congregation, which symbolized the contemporary scene.

The first, second, and third views have much to commend them. In fact, none of them contradicts what the other two are asserting. For this reason, it seems plausible that all three of these options could be simultaneously true. The fourth view, however, seems considerably forced in that it imposes onto the text of Revelation an interpretive approach that cannot be directly supported by a careful study of the apostle's treatise. The subjectivity of this option coupled with the strong lack of agreement among its adherents makes it highly unlikely that John had this view in mind when he penned Revelation.

PURPOSE, THEMES, AND LITERARY FEATURES

John wrote Revelation to disclose the Creator's goal in bringing human history to its conclusion. The Father's intent was to declare the Son's victory over all the forces of evil—both physical and metaphysical—at his second coming.

During the closing decades of the first century AD, inhabitants throughout the Roman Empire, including Asia Minor, were required to offer sacrifices and prayers to the reigning monarch.[15] This worship was

15. Such as Domitian.

known as the imperial cult, especially because each emperor declared himself to be a "son of the divine,"[16] who bestowed his benevolence on his fawning subjects. Those who refused to venerate him were branded as unpatriotic and ungrateful traitors, a crime punishable by imprisonment and death.[17]

Much of John's prophetic oracle was originally intended to encourage his earliest recipients to remain loyal to the Savior, despite the persecution they endured. Even today, the book remains a source of inspiration and hope for believers around the globe who are suffering for remaining steadfast in their commitment to the Redeemer, regardless of the personal cost.[18]

Throughout John's treatise, he emphasizes that Jesus will return as the triumphant Conqueror and sovereign Ruler of the world.[19] With great power and glory, he will defeat Satan and his demonic hosts, condemn those who reject the Son, and bring the redeemed to their heavenly home.[20]

In Revelation 1:1, John used the Greek noun *apokalypsis*—meaning "to uncover," "to disclose," or "to make known," and usually translated as "revelation"—to describe the contents of his prophetic oracle. For this reason, specialists have grouped Revelation with other books of the Bible that fall within the common genre (or classification) of *apocalyptic* literature.[21] Like portions of Isaiah, Ezekiel, Daniel, and Zechariah,[22] extraordinary visions and symbols characterize Revelation. Also, like these Old Testament writers, John uses vivid imagery, promises, and warnings to describe the titanic, cosmic struggle between the Creator and his adversaries.[23]

16. Latin, *divi filius*. For a contrast between Roman imperial ideologies and Scripture's countercultural message, see the corresponding table in our discussion of Rev 16.

17. Against this historical backdrop, Revelation offered a strong polemic against (or denunciation of) the pagan, idolatrous Roman state; see our discussion of 13:4, 14–17; 14:9; 15:2; 16:2; 19:20; 20:4. For an extensive discussion of Rev as a response to the Roman imperial ideology and propaganda, along with identifying and critiquing the imperial cult in specific passages, see Thompson, *Apocalypse and Empire*.

18. Especially in Majority World contexts.

19. See our discussion of Rev 1:7; 2:25; 3:3, 11; 16:15; 19:11–16; 22:7, 12, 17, 20.

20. See Matt 19:28; 25:31; John 14:2–3; 2 Cor 5:1–5; 2 Thess 1:7–10.

21. A genre possibly having its origins in, along with representing a subcategory and intensification of, prophetic literature.

22. Along with such ancient Jewish religious writings as 1 En., 2 En., 2 Bar., 3 Bar., 4 Ezra, Jub., Apoc. Ab., Ascen. Isa., T. Levi, Herm., and Sib. Or.

23. More information dealing with the characteristics of apocalyptic literature appears later in the Introduction.

John makes both direct and indirect references to the Old Testament. He does so to indicate that the events of Revelation fulfill what the Hebrew prophets foretold centuries earlier.[24] The literary backdrop for the preceding is God's cosmic court of justice, which is presented in the form of a lawsuit.[25] Here the Lord is depicted as both the plaintiff and the judge, who summons all creation to testify against his chosen people for violating their covenant (or sacred, binding agreement) with him.

Moreover, this juridical metaphor is comparable to the Old Testament prophets' judgment oracles, in which the Creator offers forgiveness to those who repent and punishment for those who harden their hearts against him. In this role, God's spokespersons function as prosecutors who draw attention to the Israelites' failure or success in remaining faithful to their covenant with the Lord, including blessings connected with obeying the Mosaic law[26] and curses for violating this legal code.[27]

The horizon of John's prophetic oracle is dramatically scaled up from that of the Old Testament era to encompass the entire universe. Here, the accused are earth's wicked inhabitants. The charge is their violation of the Lord's righteous decrees, including the relentless persecution and systematic murder of his children. The verdict is the evildoers' guilt. The equitable punishment (or retributive justice) is the destruction of humanity's pagan, idolatrous world system, along with the present heavens and earth.[28]

24. More information regarding the use of the Old Testament in Revelation appears later in the Introduction.

25. Hence, a cosmic trial motif. Here, the Son evaluates all people according to what they have done. Likewise, he shows no partiality or favoritism in his dealings with either the church or the wicked. For more information about this theme, see the corresponding table in our explanation of Rev 21. Also, for an extensive examination concerning the ways in which the theme of cosmic conflict—portrayed as a trial between divine and diabolical forces—structures the Apocalypse's theology, see Gallusz, *Throne Motif in Revelation*.

26. Such as abundant harvests and success in battle; see Lev 26:1–13; Deut 28:1–14.

27. Such as crop failures and military defeat; see Lev 26:14–39; Deut 4:25–28; 28:15–68; 29:16–29; 32:15–43.

28. Comparable to a massive de-creation event. This represents a reversal of the original creation God brought into existence. See Gorman, *Reading Revelation Responsibly*, where he discusses the de-creation motif as part of the prophetic oracle's judgment cycles. He notes that cosmic and earthly disasters (for example, the trumpet judgments in chs. 8–9 and the bowl judgments in ch. 16) signify God's dismantling of oppressive systems (often identified with "Babylon," representing Rome and any other hegemonic power that stands against the Lord's purposes) and the corrupted aspects of creation. Gorman also emphasizes that this de-creation is not an end but a transition

Poetry in Revelation		
Category	**Biblical References**	**Description**
Songs of Worship	4:8; 5:9–10, 12–13; 7:15–17; 15:3–4	Heavenly songs of worship and praise directed to God and the Lamb, including the "holy, holy, holy" of the four living creatures and the new song of the redeemed
Words of Acclamation, Adoration, and Praise	1:7; 4:8, 11; 5:9–10, 12–13; 7:10, 12, 14–17; 11:15, 17–18; 12:10–12; 15:3–4; 16:5–6; 19:1–8; 21:6–7	Declarations of God's majesty, power, and worthiness; acclamations of victory; and expressions of adoration for God's attributes and redemptive acts
Words of Condemnation, Exhortation, and Woe	13:10; 14:7; 18:2–8, 10, 16–24; 19:17–18; 21:8; 22:10–11	Prophetic declarations of judgment against evil powers; calls to repentance and faithfulness; and pronouncements of woe upon Babylon and the wicked

THE SIGNIFICANCE OF THE THRONE-ROOM SCENES IN REVELATION[29]

The Apocalypse records seven throne-room scenes, as follows: 1:9–20; 4:1—5:14; 8:2–6; 11:19; 15:1—16:1; 16:18–21; and 19:1–10. Each of these sections has a Christ-centered function. Specifically, the throne-room scenes provide a reminder that the Son is fully just in his evaluation and judgment of humankind.[30] The Messiah first begins with the church and then targets the wicked with progressively heightened intensity.[31]

Collectively, the throne-room scenes point out that the Lamb evaluates all people according to what they have done. He shows no partiality or favoritism in his dealings with either the church or the wicked.[32]

---

to the new creation, where God's redemptive purposes are fully realized (chs. 21–22).

29. See the proposed literary structure of Revelation appearing below, which reflects the presence of the seven throne-room scenes in the Apocalypse. For an extensive discussion concerning the ways in which God's celestial dais functions as a major interpretive key to the complex structure and theology of John's prophetic oracle, see Gallusz, *Throne Motif in Revelation.*

30. See Ps 51:4; Dan 9:4–14; Rom 3:3–4.

31. See 1 Pet 4:17–18.

32. See Deut 10:17; Ps 62:12; Prov 24:12; Matt 16:27; Acts 10:34; Rom 2:6, 11; Rev 20:11–15.

Moreover, in these scenes, the outcomes of the judgments are very different for the church and the wicked.

As the upcoming chapters of the Apocalypse reveal, the Creator's throne occupies the literary center of John's prophetic oracle. God's royal seat represents his authority and power, along with his majesty and holiness. The Father's heavenly dais is the place from which the three cycles of judgment emerge as well as the point of origin for the Son's ultimate triumph of good over evil.

FOUR DIFFERENT WAYS OF UNDERSTANDING REVELATION

The four different ways of understanding Revelation are as follows:

View One: Preterists, or the "already done" (or "finished") view. This group believes the prophecies of Revelation have been fulfilled in earlier history, for example, in the destruction of Jerusalem and the temple in AD 70 as well as the fall of the Roman Empire. Advocates maintain that these sorts of events are pivotal in making sense of Revelation. This group thinks that the seven churches mentioned in chapters 1–3 were actual congregations that existed during the time when the author of the prophetic oracle lived. In this view, chapters 4–19 symbolize conditions contemporary to the writer's time, while chapters 20–22 represent heaven and the victory of good over evil.

View Two: Historicists, or the "continuing to happen" view. This group believes Revelation 6–18 offers a general chronological (or recurring) outline of the course of the church from the first century (6:1) until the return of Christ (19:11). Therefore, the prophecies in the book have been and are in the process of being fulfilled. Like the first group, this one thinks that the seven churches were actual congregations existing in the closing portion of the first century AD. Advocates regard chapters 4–19 as symbolizing the events of history. Likewise, chapters 20–22 deal with the final judgment and the eternal state.

View Three: Futurists, or the "yet to happen" view. This group believes most of the prophecies of Revelation will occur in a period of final crisis just before the return of the Messiah. Many in this group think that the seven churches were real congregations that existed during the lifetime of John, while others regard the seven churches as symbolizing seven stages of church history. In general, futurists think chapters 4–19 concern a time of upcoming tribulation. They also maintain that God will judge an apostate church, along with the antichrist and his followers. Advocates claim that this time of judgment will end with the Messiah's return.

View Four: Idealists, or the "spiritualized" (or "allegorical") view. This group believes that the symbols and prophecies of Revelation depict principles of spiritual warfare, not specific events in history. They maintain that these principles are operative throughout church history and might be repeated in numerous ways. Like the first and second groups, this one thinks the seven churches were actual congregations from the first century AD. Whereas chapters 4–19 symbolize the conflict between good and evil, chapters 20–22 are said to represent the triumph of good over evil.

In analyzing the preceding four interpretive approaches, a combination of them, in which one recognizes the potential strengths and weaknesses of each view, seems closest to the truth. This conclusion is due in part to the fact that the imagery in Revelation is colorful, intense, and capable of being understood in a variety of ways and on different levels.

To sum up, regardless of which of the above views one prefers, the practical outcome of Revelation is relatively the same. In times of conflict, humility and patience are needed. Also, maintaining faithfulness to the Messiah and a continued refusal to compromise with evil are imperative. Furthermore, amid hardship and affliction, the promise of the Father's victory over the forces of evil is assured through the Son.

THREE POPULAR VIEWS ABOUT THE REFERENCE IN REVELATION 20:1–10 TO ONE THOUSAND YEARS

There are at least three popular views concerning the reference in Revelation 20:2 to one thousand years. Specialists call this the *millennium*, a word derived from the Latin terms *mille*, which means "thousand," and *annus*, which means "year."[33]

View One: Premillennialism, meaning "before the millennium." This group believes that the kingdom age is distinct from the church age. Put differently, the millennium will be established by Jesus after his second coming.

View Two: Amillennialism, meaning "no millennium." This group believes that there will be no actual thousand-year span in which Jesus

33. Our literary and theological analysis of Rev 20 provides additional information about this topic.

rules. Instead, proponents symbolically interpret the millennium of verses 1–10 to be a reference to the church age.

View Three: Postmillennialism, meaning "after the millennium." This group believes that the Messiah will return at the end of the kingdom age, which they hold to be the present church age. It is believed that the kingdom of the Son and the church will experience much more expansion on earth before the second coming.

In thinking through the above three approaches, prudence and restraint are in order, especially when considering their respective viability and applicability. Each not only has its merits and demerits but also hinges on how prophetic texts in the Hebrew Scriptures are understood. Another layer of ambiguity centers on the fact that verses 1–10, like most of the prophetic oracle, employ language that could, at least in principle, have multiple valid fulfillments and levels of application.

Despite the above situation, the main contours of John's message remain clear. For instance, the Messiah will bring about the final defeat of Satan and his wicked subordinates. Also, the Savior will watch over his followers in their most harrowing ordeals and eternally bless them through his victorious reign.

WOMEN IN REVELATION

John's first-century readers no doubt understood more about Revelation than contemporary believers. Nevertheless, even they might have struggled with some of the complex imagery and bizarre descriptions found in his prophetic oracle. For instance, the women in Revelation are described in extremes of moral character, being filled either with virtue or with vice. These stark contrasts are typical of apocalyptic literature, which tends to be dualistic in nature. This observation, along with the unusual actions that these women take, suggest that contemporary readers should understand them as symbols rather than as literal women.

Jezebel (Rev 2:20–23): Jesus rebuked the church at Thyatira for allowing "that woman Jezebel" (v. 20) to teach people to worship false gods and to encourage immorality. In the Old Testament, Jezebel was the wife of King Ahab. Together, they were perhaps the vilest of the Israelite rulers.[34] Note that, in verse 23, Jesus said he would judge not only Jezebel, but also her children, namely, people who followed her ways.

34. See 1 Kgs 16:31; 19:1–2; 21:1–26; 2 Kgs 9:22, 30–37.

The woman giving birth (Rev 12:1–6, 13–17): This woman stands in marked contrast to Jezebel. The woman's identity has been variously interpreted. Attacked by the evil dragon, she finds protection and refuge provided by God. The dragon's attempts to destroy her, along with the "rest of her children" (12:17), might be references to Satan's attempt to destroy the people of God (Israel) and disrupt the messianic line.

Babylon, the great harlot (Rev 14:8; 16:19; 17:5; 18:2, 10, 21): Old Testament prophets[35] often referred to adulterers and prostitutes to represent people who practiced idolatry. Just as an adulteress is unfaithful to her husband, so God's people are unfaithful to him when they allow their hearts to be divided and they venerate pagan deities.

The harlot of Revelation 17 is identified as Babylon, which first-century readers would probably have identified as Rome.[36] In contrast to the new Jerusalem that descends from heaven with glory and blessing (ch. 21), Babylon is shattered and destroyed in judgment for persecuting God's people and corrupting the peoples of the earth with wickedness (ch. 18).

Babylon, a symbol of evil: In Revelation, "Babylon" (14:8) represents more than a specific city. It epitomizes an entire pagan world system in rebellion against God. The Old Testament prophets often foretold the fall of Babylon, the capital of an empire that destroyed Jerusalem, razed the temple, and carried away God's people into captivity.[37] Therefore, as the following table shows, in Revelation, Babylon becomes a fitting image for an idolatrous society that persecutes believers, yet one that God obliterates.

Babylon as a Fitting Image of an Idolatrous Society		
Biblical References	**Babylon's Condition/Action**	**Divine Judgment/ Consequence**
14:8	Made "every nation drink from the wine of her adulterous desire"	Proclaimed as "Fallen, fallen is Babylon the Great"
16:19	God remembers Babylon's ways and deeds	Given the "wine cup filled with his fierce wrath" during the seventh bowl judgment

35. For example, Hos; Ezek 16:8–58.

36. For a discussion of the history of interpretation concerning the identity of Babylon, see Schreiner, *Revelation*, 577–79.

37. See Isa 13:19–22; 14:22–23; Jer 25:12; 50:9, 41; 51:1.

Babylon as a Fitting Image of an Idolatrous Society		
Biblical References	**Babylon's Condition/Action**	**Divine Judgment/ Consequence**
17:5	Identified with the name written on her forehead	"Mystery, Babylon the Great, the mother of the prostitutes and of the abominations of the earth"
18:2	Falls from her position of power and influence	Becomes a "dwelling place for demons, and a prison for every unclean spirit, and a prison for every unclean bird"
18:10	Experiences sudden and complete destruction	Mourned by those who watch: "Woe, woe, the great city, Babylon, the strong city! For your judgment came in a single hour"
18:21	Faces final, irreversible damnation	"Will be overthrown with violence and will never again be found"

The wife (bride) of the Lamb (Rev 19:7–8): As the marriage feast of the Lamb approaches, a bride has made herself ready. The description of this woman clothing herself in righteous acts suggests that she might represent the church.

FIVE MISCONCEPTIONS ABOUT REVELATION

Misconceptions about Revelation are unfortunately commonplace. First, some assume that Revelation is a unique book, distinct from all other ancient or modern works, with its own literary genre. In reality, John's prophetic oracle aligns closely with earlier apocalyptic and end-time literary traditions. Second, many claim that Revelation focuses solely on future events. In truth, it weaves together the past, present, and future of salvation history throughout its narrative. Third, some think that only a select few can decode the obscure symbols of the Apocalypse. However, its metaphors and allusions actually draw heavily from the Old Testament and intertestamental apocalyptic texts, making them accessible to those familiar with these sources. Fourth, some argue that Revelation must be interpreted in a strictly literal manner to be understood correctly. But a purely literal, future-focused approach risks misinterpreting the text's intent. A balanced perspective recognizes that while characters and events may reflect real-world counterparts, they are depicted symbolically and require nuanced interpretation, not rigid dogmatism. Fifth, some view the Apocalypse as a disjointed collection of brief visions that lack coherence. In reality, John intentionally structured and sequenced his prophetic oracle to create a unified and orderly composition rather than a chaotic or random work. While Revelation certainly presents interpretive challenges, understanding the book's prophetic unity within its historical and literary contexts teaches faithful, discerning readers much about God's salvific work throughout the past, present, and future of human history.

THREE REASONS FOR THE SYMBOLISM IN REVELATION

First, John uses symbols to reveal, not obscure, truth. Symbols effectively illuminate, clarify, and explain profound, mysterious concepts. Second, the apostle employs vivid imagery to highlight the stakes and emphasize the moral and spiritual truths in Revelation's message with greater impact. Third, John chooses symbols to address the struggles of his persecuted fellow Christians. He wants to show them that life extends beyond physical experiences, with the spiritual realm underpinning the historical reality.

FIVE PRINCIPLES FOR INTERPRETING REVELATION

First, parallel imagery in the Old Testament and intertestamental apocalyptic literature can guide the interpretation of metaphors and allusions in Revelation. The context of a metaphor or allusion in the Apocalypse may imply a meaning different from what might initially be assumed. Second, not every detail of a symbol holds interpretive significance. The overall visual, emotional, and conceptual impact of the image likely conveys the primary message. Overemphasizing specific details may obscure the deeper truth the symbol communicates. Third, understanding the symbols in John's prophetic oracle requires considering his original intent and biblical worldview. Rather than aiming for precise, scientific propositions, the apostle uses impressionistic language to convey the surreal experience he had and its broader meaning. Fourth, the symbols in Revelation should be viewed as part of a cohesive literary work. Since metaphors and allusions appear within the narrative flow of the text, their placement and purpose carry interpretive weight. A fragmented approach to these symbols may hinder understanding. Fifth, the symbols in the Apocalypse often carry layered meanings that resist simple explanation. The richness of a metaphor or allusion lies in its evocative, textured quality. Fully grasping a symbol's impact may require reading it within the broader context of John's prophetic oracle and reflecting on its role in the book's overall message.

Diverse Objects and Entities in Revelation		
Category	**Items**	**Biblical References**
Animals (Literal)	Lion, lamb, horse, eagle, cattle, sheep	5:5–6; 6:1–8; 8:13; 18:13
Animals (Symbolic)	Dragon, sea-beast, land-beast, frogs, bear, leopard	12:3–17; 13:1, 2, 11; 16:13
Ceremonial Items	Incense, seal, lamp	5:8; 7:2; 18:23
Commerce	Balance, quart, denarius	6:5–6
Construction Items	Winepress, millstone	14:19; 18:21
Garments	Robe, sackcloth	6:11; 7:9; 11:3
Measurements	Stadia, talent (100-pound weight)	14:20; 16:21
Military Equipment	Breastplate	9:9, 17
Musical Instruments	Harp (lyre), flutes, trumpets	5:8; 8:2, 6; 18:22
Natural Phenomena	Lightning, thunder, earthquake, hail	4:5; 6:12; 8:7; 11:19; 16:21
Plants and Agriculture	Wheat, barley, olive oil, wine, fig tree, palm branches, wormwood, olive trees, grapes	6:6, 13; 7:9; 8:11; 11:4; 14:18–19
Precious Stones	Jasper, carnelian, emerald, crystal, pearls	4:3, 6; 17:4; 21:11, 19–20
Royal Regalia	Victor's wreath, crown, diadem	2:10; 3:11; 4:4; 6:2; 9:7; 12:1, 3; 13:1; 14:14; 19:12
Sacred Objects	Lampstand, throne, seven flaming menorahs, scroll, censer, ark of the covenant	1:12–13; 4:2, 5; 5:1; 8:3; 11:19
Weapons and Tools	Sword, iron staff, bow, key to the pit of the abyss, measuring rod, sickle, chain	1:16; 2:27; 6:2; 9:1; 11:1; 14:14; 20:1

THE ALREADY/NOT-YET PERSPECTIVE FOUND IN THE APOCALYPSE

In Revelation, there is a dynamic tension between reality as it presently exists (the "already") and what is prophesied to occur at the end of the age (the "not yet"). For example, consider Jesus' directive to John, which is recorded in 1:19: "So write what you have seen, both those things that are and those that will take place after this." This verse indicates that Revelation is the culmination and climax of Old Testament prophecy.[38]

Already / Not Yet in Revelation		
Theological Aspect	**Already Fulfilled**	**Not Yet Complete**
Believers' Rule	Jesus' followers reign with him in heaven (1:6; 5:10).	Reigning over the earth awaits the future kingdom age (20:1–6).
Great Tribulation	The time of great distress has started (1:9; 2:1—3:22).	The time of great distress is not yet complete (6:1—19:21).
Jerusalem/Babylon	Jerusalem's destruction has occurred (11:1–13).	Babylon's/Rome's fall is imminent, though not yet complete (17:1—18:24).
Satan's Defeat	Satan was defeated by Jesus at Calvary (12:5–12).	Satan's final banishment awaits the end of the age (20:7–10).
The Age to Come	The age to come has begun (1:1, 3, 9).	The age to come awaits completion at Jesus' return and the eternal state (1:7; 21:1—22:21).

CHARACTERISTICS OF APOCALYPTIC LITERATURE

As previously noted, Revelation is *apocalyptic* literature. This type of writing contains certain identifiable themes and features, as follows:

- The work emphasizes the divine preservation of a righteous remnant.
- The work wrestles with the philosophical and pastoral problem of evil (referred to as theodicy) and a theological interpretation of historical events.[39] Also, it views human society as fallen and corrupt.

38. On this point, see Bauckham, *Climax of Prophecy*, xi.

39. Theodicy grapples with the question concerning how the existence of evil in

- The work presents the flow of history as having a predetermined quality. Moreover, the content of the writing is prominently ethical in nature.
- The work uses symbolism to communicate God's message, especially as it relates to the course of history. Furthermore, it emphasizes numerology, in which figurative meanings are assigned to numbers.

The following table is a brief list of apocalyptic writings found within and outside of the Judeo-Christian canon. Some were penned in the centuries before and after Jesus' earthly ministry.

Apocalyptic Writings				
Old Testament Writings with Apocalyptic Elements	**Apocalyptic Jewish Writings Not Found in the Hebrew Bible**	**Babylonian, Assyrian, and Greek Writings with Apocalyptic Elements**	**New Testament Writings with Apocalyptic Elements**	**Later Apocalyptic Jewish or Christian Writings Not Found in the New Testament**
Dan	1 En.	D.P.; U.P. (ancient Babylon)	Matt 24–25; Mark 13; Luke 21	Ascen. Isa.
Isa; Ezek	4 Ezra; 2 and 3 Bar.	Vis. Neth. (ancient Assyrian)	1 Thess 4:13–18	Apoc. Pet.
Joel; Zech	Apoc. Ab.	Sib. Or. (ancient Greek)	Rev	Herm.

NUMBERS IN SCRIPTURE, INCLUDING REVELATION

As indicated in the previous section, certain numbers in Scripture seem to have representative or poetic overtones. For instance, the number one

the world can be reconciled with the idea of an all-good and all-powerful God. For a discussion of this theme in relation to the Apocalypse, see Simojoki, "Book of Revelation," 652–84. The author situates John's prophetic oracle within the broader biblical tradition of theodicy by exploring how apocalyptic literature addresses the problem of evil and divine justice. Rather than offering a detailed textual analysis of the Apocalypse, Simojoki discusses how the treatise exemplifies a shift from philosophical or sapiential (relating to wisdom) explanations of suffering (like in Job or Eccl) to an eschatological perspective in which God's ultimate justice is revealed at the end of time. In this framework, Rev does not seek to justify the Creator's ways through rational argument. Instead, the book points to the final eradication of evil and the vindication of God's righteousness through the narrative of divine judgment and the triumph of his kingdom.

often appears around the concepts of unity, independence, or uniqueness. Disunity, division, or contrast often involve the number two. When the biblical writers describe completeness or purity (or a counterfeit parody of these ideas), they frequently invoke the number three. Sacred significance appears around the number four and its multiples. Five denotes a period of incomplete or limited duration. The number seven, which finds its roots in the original seven days of creation, implies perfection, complete, or fulfillment. The number ten and its multiples serve as rounded integers of sizeable, though not always strictly literal, proportions and imply indefiniteness, ambiguity, and magnitude. The number twelve and its multiples often express the fullness of God's people. Revelation is no exception to this pattern, though it particularly emphasizes the number seven, as the following chart shows.

The Prevalence of the Number Seven in Revelation[40]	
Sevenfold mention of "Christ" (or the Messiah)	1:1, 2, 5; 11:15; 12:10; 20:4, 6
Seven solemn pronouncements of covenantal blessing (or beatitudes)	1:3; 14:13; 16:15; 19:9; 20:6; 22:7, 14
Seven churches	1:4, 11, 20
Sevenfold Spirit of God	1:4; 3:1; 4:5; 5:6
Seven occurrences of three merisms (in which two contrasting extremes refer to the entirety of a truth)	1:8, 17; 21:6; 22:13
Seven occurrences of the phrase, "Lord God Almighty" (or its equivalent variants)	1:8; 4:8; 11:17; 15:3; 16:7; 19:6; 21:22
Sevenfold emphasis on the "patient endurance" of the saints	1:9; 2:2, 3, 19; 3:10; 13:10; 14:12
Seven throne-room scenes	1:9–20; 4:1—5:14; 8:2–6; 11:19; 15:1—16:1; 16:18–21; 19:1–10
Seven gold lampstands (or flaming menorahs)	1:12, 20; 2:1
Sevenfold description of the risen and glorified Messiah	1:14–16
Seven stars	1:16, 20; 2:1; 3:1
Seven angels	1:20; 8:2, 6; 15:1, 6–8; 16:1; 17:1; 21:9

40. Table adapted from information presented in Tabb, *All Things New*, 14.

The Prevalence of the Number Seven in Revelation[40]	
Seven occurrences of the declarative phrase, "says this" (signaling that what followed was the Messiah's authoritative, solemn pronouncement or prophetic oracle)	2:1, 8, 12, 18; 3:1, 7, 14
Seven assertions of Jesus' second advent	2:5, 16; 3:11; 16:15; 22:7, 12, 20
Seven occurrences of the exhortation (originating from the risen and glorified Messiah) that "whoever has an ear, let him hear what the Spirit says to the churches"	2:7, 11, 17, 29; 3:6, 13, 22
Seven burning lamps (or torches)	4:5
Seven occurrences of the phrase, "him who sits on the throne" (or its equivalent variants)	4:9; 5:1, 7, 13; 6:16; 7:15; 21:5
Seven seals	5:1, 5; 6:1
Seven horns and eyes	5:6
Sevenfold mention of the four living creatures and twenty-four elders	5:6, 8, 11, 14; 7:11; 14:3; 19:4
Seven occurrences of the fourfold phrase, "every tribe and language and people and nation" (or its equivalent variants)	5:9; 7:9; 10:11; 11:9; 13:7; 14:6; 17:15
Seven trumpets	8:2, 6
Seven occurrences of divine preparation	8:6; 9:7, 15; 12:6; 16:12; 19:7; 21:2
Seven characteristics found in a maniacal swarm of locusts	9:7–10
Seven thunders	10:3–4
Seven heads	12:3; 13:1; 17:3, 7, 9
Seven plagues	15:1, 6, 8; 21:9
Seven gold bowls full of God's wrath	15:7; 16:1; 17:1; 21:9
Seven hills and kings	17:9–10
Two doxologies, each with seven attributes	5:12; 7:12
Three cycles of seven seal, trumpet, and bowl judgments	6:1–17; 8:1—9:21; 11:15–19; 16:1–21

FULFILLMENT MOTIFS

In Revelation 5:5, one of the twenty-four elders[41] refers to the Messiah using two fulfillment motifs—"the Lion of the tribe of Judah"[42] and "the Root of David."[43] These motifs emphasize that Jesus alone has the virtue and authority to bring human history to its conclusion. Both expressions sum up Israel's hope for the coming Messiah. God's people had called Judah—the founder of the tribe—a lion,[44] and now the elder applies the name to the greatest of all the members of Judah. The lion represented power and victory, and the risen Lord typifies these qualities. The Greek noun translated "Root" (v. 5) describes a shoot or sprout out of the main stem. As the "Root of David," the Son is identified as the Messiah who sprang from the house and lineage of Israel's greatest monarch.

Another fulfillment motif unfolds in 19:13, where Jesus, at his second advent, appears as the Warrior-King with the distinctive name of the "Word of God," which has a meaning comparable to John's usage of the phrase in the Fourth Gospel.[45] Specifically, as the supreme revelation of the One who is eternal, the Son executes the judgment that fulfills the Father's redemptive promises. In this way, the Son brings about the Father's end-time plan at the consummation of history.

RESURRECTION MOTIFS

The Apocalypse contains a cluster of motifs pertaining to the Messiah's resurrection from the dead. The first motif appears in Revelation 1:5, where the Messiah is called the "firstborn from the dead." This expression comes from Psalm 89:27 and spotlights Jesus' exalted position as head of the redeemed.[46] Because of Jesus' atoning death and resurrection, he heads (or leads, rules over) a new spiritual race of reborn people[47] who experience victory over sin and death.[48]

41. See our discussion of Rev 4:4, 10.
42. See Gen 49:9–10.
43. See Isa 11:1, 10; Jer 23:5; 33:15; Zech 3:8; 6:12; Rom 15:12.
44. See Gen 49:9.
45. See John 1:1, 14, 18.
46. See Rom 8:29.
47. See Col 1:18; Heb 12:23.
48. See 1 Cor 15:54–57.

Revelation 1:17 contains the second important motif in this cluster. Here, the Messiah refers to himself as "the First and the Last." This statement about the Savior is emphatic in the Greek, drawing attention to a truth that applies uniquely to him. Because elsewhere in Scripture this divine title refers to the Lord God,[49] its usage in Revelation 1:17 draws attention to the Son's absolute divinity.

A third noteworthy motif appears in Revelation 2:8, where the Messiah again declares himself to be "the First and the Last." Here, the motif emphasizes that no one is above or before him and that no one greater would come after him. The Messiah's assertion that he has conquered death through his resurrection highlights this important truth.

SON OF GOD MOTIF

Revelation 2:18 is the only place in the Apocalypse where the phrase "Son of God" occurs. Perhaps John's limited usage of this construction was to avoid the pagan notion that the Messiah was the physical offspring of the Father. In any case, this is a significant messianic title that finds its roots in Psalm 2:7.[50] The phrase emphasizes the special and intimate relationship that exists between the first and second Persons of the Trinity.[51]

In the original, the genitive "of God" indicates that "the Son" has the essential characteristics and nature of God. Therefore, the title indicates that the Son is to be identified with the Father and considered fully and absolutely equal to him (as well as to the Spirit).[52]

SON OF MAN MOTIF

The phrase "son of man" appears in Revelation 1:13 and 14:14. The context of the first usage is John's vision of the risen, glorified Lord, which is recorded in 1:13–16. The apostle describes the Messiah as being "one like a son of man." This title, appearing frequently in the Gospels, emphasizes Jesus' deity, humanity, messiahship, suffering, and atoning sacrifice.[53]

49. See Isa 41:4; 44:6; 48:12.

50. See Acts 13:33; Heb 1:5; 5:5.

51. See Matt 16:16; Luke 1:35; John 1:49.

52. See John 5:18; 10:30, 36.

53. See Matt 26:64; Mark 2:10; 8:31; 10:45.

Furthermore, the expression is reminiscent of the vision of the Son of Man in Daniel 7:13.[54]

As noted above, the second usage of the phrase "son of man" appears in Revelation 14:14. The apostle sees this celestial figure sitting on a white cloud, wearing a gold crown on his head, and holding a sharp sickle in his hand. Though some specialists think the preceding entity was a mighty angel under God's command, it is more likely that John saw the risen and exalted Messiah. At his second coming, he will gather the righteous and judge the wicked.[55]

THE LAMB MOTIF[56]

The Greek noun rendered "Lamb" appears throughout the Apocalypse, especially in worship passages. The term generally refers to a "sheep of any age." Some specialists have proposed that the Lamb is the central Christ-centered motif of the Apocalypse, especially in terms of this image's controlling and interpreting other major themes. Likewise, other specialists see the Lamb as playing an integral part in the visions and prophecies that were revealed to John.

In particular, the Lamb motif is a starting point for understanding the Christology of Revelation. In fact, John uses "Lamb" in a comprehensive way to describe Jesus in the totality of his person and work. Here, the focus is not on military skill and conquest but on self-giving sacrifice.

There are three literary sources worth mentioning that form the backdrop for the lamb terminology in Revelation: apocalyptic lambs, the lamb of Isaiah 53:7,[57] and Passover and sacrificial lambs. Each of these sources contributes to the dual role of the Messiah in the Apocalypse as Redeemer and Ruler/Judge.

Concerning the third of the three sources, evidence from the New Testament suggests that the early church connected the Messiah with the Passover lamb of Exodus 12:3–6. For instance, the Fourth Gospel twice refers to Jesus of Nazareth as the "Lamb of God" (1:29, 36). Also, Paul refers to Jesus as "our Passover lamb" (1 Cor 5:7). Moreover, Peter equates

54. See 4 Ezra 13:3–4; 1 En. 46:3–4; 48:2; 62:5, 7, 9, 14; 63:11; 69:27, 29.

55. See Matt 24:30–31; Mark 13:26–27; Luke 21:27–28; John 5:22; Rev 1:7.

56. For an extensive discussion about the portrayal of Jesus as the Lamb in the Apocalypse, with a particular emphasis on his divine kingship, heavenly reign, blessings to believers, and hymnic adoration, see Schedtler, *Royal Ideologies*.

57. See Jer 11:19; Acts 8:32.

the "precious blood of Christ" (1 Pet. 1:19) to that of a "lamb without blemish or spot."[58] The apostle also notes that believers have been healed by the Messiah's "wounds" (2:24).

A SUMMARY OF KEY MOTIFS IN REVELATION

The fulfillment motifs highlight the Son's unique virtue and authority to bring history to its appointed end by accomplishing the Father's redemptive plan. The resurrection motifs underscore that only the Messiah, as the risen and exalted Lord, can deliver his followers from death and grant them eternal life.

The Son of God motif emphasizes the unique, intimate relationship between the Father and the Son within the Trinity, especially by affirming the Son's full and absolute equality with the Father (and the sevenfold Spirit). The Son of Man motif primarily focuses on Christ's role as the supreme Ruler and Judge, while also highlighting his deity, humanity, messianic identity, suffering, and atoning sacrifice. Finally, the Lamb motif, which is central to the Apocalypse, portrays Jesus in the fullness of his person and work. This imagery also reveals his dual role as both Redeemer and Ruler/Judge.

THE CENTRALITY OF THE MESSIAH IN REVELATION

In the Apocalypse, everyone and everything originates from and revolves around Jesus of Nazareth. Put another way, he dominates the entire literary landscape of John's prophetic oracle, as made clear in the following two tables:

The Diverse Ways the Messiah Appears in Revelation
As the ascended and exalted Son of Man (1:12–16)
As the Sovereign of the living and the dead (1:17–18)
As the Lord of the church (chs. 2, 3)
As the "beginning," "origin," "source," and "ruler" of God's creation (3:14)
As the Lamb of God (ch. 5)
As the Monarch of the universe (11:15)
As the Lord of lords and King of kings (17:14; 19:16)
As the Word of God (or Logos; 19:13)

58. See Exod 12:5; Lev 22:17–25.

The Diverse Ways the Messiah Appears in Revelation
As the Judge of the world (ch. 19)
As the center of the new creation (chs. 21, 22)
As the everlasting God (22:12–13)

With the Son: Worship	Without the Son: Wrath
Splendor and beauty (4:2–8)	Peace gone from earth (6:4)
Praise and adoration (4:8–11)	Killing unleashed (6:5)
Access provided (5:1–8)	Death reigns (6:8)
Outbursts of worship (5:9)	Earth collapses (6:12–17)
Entitlement given (5:10)	Fires and earthquakes (8:5)
Affirmation (5:11–14)	Destructive surges (8:7–10)
Martyrs restored (6:9–11)	Many die (8:11)
Protection given (7:2–8)	Darkness pervades the earth (8:12)
Suffering ceases (7:9–17)	Woes are announced (8:13)
God's mystery completed (10:7)	Plagues torment the lost (9:2–11)
Bitter becomes sweet (10:9)	Repentance is rejected and many perish (9:18–21)

THE MAIN PURPOSE OF REVELATION

The pagan world system of John's day tried to convince Jesus' followers that they were defeated and doomed for maintaining their unwavering commitment to him. Yet, to reiterate what was previously stated, John wrote the Apocalypse, under the Spirit's inspiration and authority, to emphasize the following: the Father, through the Son, would triumph over the forces of evil, condemn the wicked, vindicate the righteous, fulfill all his promises, and accomplish his sovereign purpose in history.

In brief, Revelation narrates the Father's culmination of human history through the Son. Based on this truth, three overarching principles are discernible in the Apocalypse:

- First, faith in the Messiah is the basis for experiencing his covenantal blessings.
- Second, the Lamb's judgment of the wicked through the unleashing of covenantal curses is inevitable.[59]

59. On this point, see the substantive discussion of Stefanovic, *Revelation*, 219–23.

- Third, the Christian view of history—namely, that the Creator is moving events to a final, satisfactory consummation and the ethical values that this perspective advocates—is vastly superior to the views of fallen, pagan humanity.

In stepping back from the preceding observations, it is clear that the Apocalypse has much to say about the following key theological doctrines:

- The triune Creator;
- The Father's sovereignty, the Son's lordship, and the Spirit's revelatory work;
- Satan, sin, and death;
- Holy and fallen angels;
- Humankind, salvation, everlasting life, and eternal separation from God (that is, death); and
- The people of God.[60]

THE PRESENCE OF CONTRASTING PARALLELS IN THE APOCALYPSE

John's prophetic oracle is filled with contrasting parallels. In each instance, opposites are juxtaposed to emphasize and clarify the message.

Example #1: The travailing woman of chapter 12 and the harlotrous woman of chapter 17[61]

Travailing Woman (ch. 12)	Harlotrous Woman (ch. 17)
A mother	A prostitute
Clothed in the splendor of God's created luminaries	Adorned with brilliant yet gaudy fabrications of humanity
Not of this world (eternal)	Entirely of this world (temporal)
Gives birth to a child	Holds a cup filled with the blood of the other woman's offspring
Rescued and preserved from danger	Destroyed

60. The communion of saints from both the Old Testament and New Testament eras.

61. Connected with our discussion of Rev 2:18–29, see the table dealing with the significance of regenerate women in the early church.

Example #2: The Messiah and the sea-beast

The Messiah	The Sea-Beast
Shares power, authority, throne of God (12:10)	Shares power, authority, throne of the dragon (13:2)
Rules over every tribe, nation, people, and language (5:9)	Rules over every tribe, nation, people, and language (13:7)
The entire creation worships the Lamb (5:13)	Earth-dwellers venerate the sea-beast (13:4, 8)
Slaughtered and risen (5:6)	Mortal wound healed (13:3)
Mark of the Lamb on forehead of his followers (14:1)	Mark of the beast on the head or forehead of his followers (13:16)
Many diadems (19:12)	Ten diadems (13:1)
Wears a name—King of kings and Lord of lords (17:14; 19:16)	Wears blasphemous names (13:1)

Example #3: The two witnesses[62] and the land-beast

Two Witnesses	The Land-Beast
True prophets (11:10)	False prophet (16:13; 19:20; 20:10)
Perform signs (11:6)	Performs signs (13:13, 14; 19:20)
Receive authority from God (11:3)	Receives authority from the sea-beast (13:12)
Torment the inhabitants of earth (11:10)	Deceives inhabitants of earth (13:14)
Two olive trees; two lampstands (11:4)	Two horns (13:11)
Receive the breath of life from God (11:11)	Breathes life into the image of the sea-beast (13:15)

THE USE OF THE OLD TESTAMENT IN REVELATION[63]

As we noted earlier, the Apocalypse extensively incorporates elements from the Old Testament, particularly the Septuagint. Indeed, by some estimates, around 278 out of 404 verses in Revelation (about 69 percent) reference or allude to the Hebrew sacred writings, including phrases, lines, and entire sentences. Yet John does not employ these references mechanically or arbitrarily. Instead, he engages with them creatively and

62. Like those testifying in a court of law.

63. For an extensive discussion regarding the use of the Old Testament in Revelation, see Beale and McDonough, "Revelation," 1081–1158; Moyise, *Old Testament in Revelation*, 123–34; Schreiner, *Revelation*, 46–50.

thoughtfully by weaving their patterns of thought—images, symbols, motifs, and metaphors—into his own prophetic oracle to enhance its theological depth.

John's deep familiarity with the history, traditions, and interpretations of these sacred texts enables him to use them freely. While he remains faithful to their original contexts, he also reinterprets them through the lens of Jesus' death and resurrection. This perspective is further shaped by the emergence and growth of the early church, which, though facing persecution, expanded steadily.

The above historical and theological context informs Revelation's portrayal of salvation. No longer is the sphere of redemption limited to the people of national Israel in first century AD in Palestine. Instead, individuals from all geographical locales—regardless of their ethnicity, gender, socioeconomic status, and so on—are partakers of new life in union with the Son and heirs of his eternal kingdom.[64]

For John, the Messiah is the fulfillment of Old Testament prophecy. The apostle's frequent use of apocalyptic and intertestamental writings underscores this conviction: Jesus is the climax of divine revelation and the one in whom all prophetic promises find their completion.[65]

THE RELATIONSHIP BETWEEN DANIEL AND REVELATION[66]

The Apocalypse reflects the end-time mindset of Daniel 2 in which the prophesied kingdom of God finds its inauguration and fulfillment in the Messiah. In both books, the wicked are judged, the righteous are vindicated, and the divine kingdom is established. These correspondences are supported by the literary and thematic correlations between Daniel 9:27,[67] the Synoptic Gospels,[68] and the first six seal judgments of the Apocalypse.[69] This observation suggests that there are common end-time

64. See our discussion of Rev 5:9–10; 7:9–10.

65. See our discussion of Rev 1:2; 19:10. For a more comprehensive treatment of this theme, see Bauckham, *Climax of Prophecy*.

66. For a thoroughgoing deliberation of Old Testament segments, including Daniel's prophecy, as literary prototypes, see Beale, *The Book of Revelation*, 86–99.

67. See Dan 11:31.

68. See Matt 24; Mark 13; Luke 21.

69. See our discussion of Rev 6.

motifs among these various writings and that the Apocalypse reflects a continuing development of these themes.

Moreover, references to time appear throughout both books. There are two views concerning how to interpret these, as follows:

- Some specialists think the writer was referring to *chronological* time. In this view, the references to time should be taken literally and at face value. For instance, the expression "a time, and times, and half a time" refers to an exact period of three and a half years.[70]
- Other specialists think the writer was referring to *typological* time. In this view, the references to time should be taken figuratively. For instance, the expression "a time, and times, and half a time" symbolically refers to a limited, indefinite period with an end in sight.

THE INFLUENCE OF REVELATION 1:19[71]

Some specialists think Revelation 1:19 is an interpretive key in which the structure and content of the Apocalypse are unlocked. According to the verse, John was told to write what he had seen, what was now taking place, and what would take place later. As with prophetic passages in the Old Testament, here the emphasis was not just about predicting the future but also about faithfully proclaiming God's inspired and authoritative message. Yet, despite the uniformity of opinion concerning the importance of this verse, there is no consensus about how it should be understood.

One view says that Revelation 1:19 reflects a threefold chronological division of Revelation. The promises recorded in chapter 1 would be what John had seen. The Son's letters to the seven churches, which are recorded in chapters 2 and 3, would be what is taking place now. Finally, all that is recorded in chapters 4 through 22 would be what will take place in the future.

This view suffers from some weaknesses because each of these sections has numerous references to the past, present, and future. Also, the view does not seem to explain fully the reiteration of themes and events appearing throughout the book. Moreover, the categorical and literal way in which the view interprets Revelation tends to misunderstand the intent behind figurative motifs in the text.

70. See Dan 7:25; 12:7; Rev 12:14.

71. For an incisive discourse about the disputed significance of Rev 1:19 as an interpretive key to John's prophetic oracle, see Beale, *The Book of Revelation*, 152–70.

A second view thinks that the clause "write what you have seen" (v. 19) is Jesus' main directive and reiterates what he had commanded in verse 11, which in part says, "write what you see on a scroll." Therefore, the remaining portion of verse 19 would give further details. Expressed differently, as John wrote what he had seen, he was to comment on what now was taking place and what would take place later. Based on this view, some think that the Apocalypse follows a twofold chronological structure, with chapters 1 through 3 dealing with the present and chapters 4 through 22 dealing with the future.

Analyzing this view reveals that it suffers from some of the same weaknesses mentioned about the first view. Based on this similarity, others think that the clause under consideration in 1:19 is a general acknowledgement that both the present and the future are in view. In other words, a vision or episode might have a dual focus both on the present and the future or only on the present or the future.

A third view says that Revelation 1:19 represents the commission of John to make proclamations about all of history, including its events and their significance.[72] In this way of thinking, the wording of the verse represents a prescribed formula that inaugurates John into his prophetic task and endues his proclamations with divine authority.[73] Advocates of the third view maintain that whatever John said was applicable to the present and the future and could even transcend time and reality.

A fourth view sees Revelation 1:19, along with 1:1, 4:1, and 22:6, as an end-time expression that alludes to Daniel 2:28–29 and 45. In this view, Revelation 1:19 represents more than just a literary or historical structural marker. More importantly, it signifies the apocalyptic motif of the entire book. In brief, what seems to be anticipated in Daniel has already begun to be realized in the Apocalypse. Therefore, the appearance of similar phrasing throughout Revelation should not be interpreted narrowly to refer only to future, end-time events. Rather, the focus is on all redemptive history and its end-time implications for the past, present, and future.

72. Comparable to Ezek 2:8—3:3.

73. Comparable to Dan 10.

RECAPITULATION VERSUS PROGRESSION IN THE STRUCTURE OF REVELATION

Specialists have long debated whether the Apocalypse follows a pattern of recapitulation (repetition with variation) or progression (chronological development). According to the recapitulation view, the visions revisit the same events from different angles, with each cycle intensifying or deepening the portrayal of divine judgment. On this reading, the seal, trumpet, and bowl judgments are not successive but rather parallel depictions of the same realities, with each series offering a distinct theological or rhetorical emphasis.

In contrast, the progression view understands Revelation as a linear sequence in which events unfold chronologically toward a final climax. Here, each series of judgments builds on the last: The seventh seal introduces the trumpet judgments, and the seventh trumpet leads into the bowl plagues. This interlocking sequence suggests a telescoping structure, where each new sequence extends and elaborates on the previous one to push the narrative forward.

Both approaches face interpretive challenges. Advocates of recapitulation must account for apparent differences between the series that seem to imply distinct events. Proponents of progression, meanwhile, must explain the striking similarities between the cycles and demonstrate that they are not simply reiterations.

Ultimately, John's prophetic oracle resists rigid classification. Many interpreters now recognize that Revelation may employ both structural strategies. While the narrative moves toward an end-time consummation, it also circles back to revisit and expand earlier themes. The Apocalypse thus combines linear movement with cyclical repetition, creating a layered and theologically rich vision of divine judgment and redemption.

A PROPOSED LITERARY STRUCTURE OF REVELATION[74]

Prologue (1:1–8)

Throne-Room Scene #1 (1:9–20)

Scene of Accountability #1 (2:1—3:22)

74. See our earlier discussion about the significance of the throne-room scenes in Rev.

Throne-Room Scene #2 (4:1—5:14)

Scene of Accountability #2 (6:1—8:1)

Throne-Room Scene #3 (8:2–6)

Scene of Accountability #3 (8:7—11:18)

Throne-Room Scene #4 (11:19)

Scene of Accountability #4 (12:1—14:20)

Throne-Room Scene #5 (15:1—16:1)

Scene of Accountability #5 (16:2–17)

Throne-Room Scene #6 (16:18–21)

Scene of Accountability #6 (17:1—18:24)

Throne-Room Scene #7 (19:1–10)

Scene of Accountability #7 (19:11—22:5)

Epilogue (22:6–21)

The preceding arrangement provides a way to visualize how the literary sections in the Apocalypse might be thematically and theologically interrelated. Especially noteworthy is the placement of chapters 12 through 14 at the heart of Revelation, which implies that, because of the presence of believers with the Messiah and despite the horrors they experience from Satan and his deputies, the Lamb brings these believers safely through their ordeal. This observation emphasizes the central position which the Messiah occupies in the overall focus and literary flow of the Apocalypse.

KEY THEOLOGICAL INSIGHTS

As we noted earlier, the Apocalypse touches on several theological doctrines and reveals unique truths about them.[75] To that end, the following observations are worth considering. First, *our understanding of the work of the triune God is heightened when we consider not only what he has done in times past and present but also what we anticipate he will do in the future.* While the Creator's judgments and blessings are seen previously in biblical history, the Apocalypse gives us a higher-definition look into God's judgments and blessings that are yet to come. The judgments are

75. For a thorough description of selected theological "contributions" of the Apocalypse, see Osborne, *Revelation*, 31–49.

intense, harsh, and perhaps even extreme,[76] though always in keeping with God's holy and righteous character. The blessings endure forever and remain abundant,[77] while transcending easy description. The Creator remains who he is at all times and toward all people. Yet, in the end, all he is and does comes to a just, climactic resolution.

Second, *we see our Lord Jesus Christ in an enhanced way in the Apocalypse.* For example, we recognize his person and work. Also, while we are often drawn to a remembrance of what he has done,[78] we see him in full exaltation and complete glory. He rises victorious, in which he finally brings complete destruction to the wicked[79] and promised rest to his persevering conquerors.[80] The triumphant manifestation of *Immanuel* ("God with us") is at last realized,[81] with all the expected accompanying joy and exuberance one would anticipate from God's reborn children. Jesus is declared to be the supreme Monarch over those who reign as kings and sovereign Potentate over those who rule as lords.[82] Indeed, the very utterance of that refrain resounds throughout all creation, reaching to the highest heaven and down to the deepest depths. There is no region, people, tribe, tongue, or nation that is outside the purview of the Savior's upright reign and rule.[83]

Third, *Satan and his minions (demons), along with sin and death, are destroyed.* This truth contrasts with the presentation of Jesus as victorious and his followers as fully vindicated. Admittedly, the Apocalypse is full of descriptions involving death and destruction, plague and disaster, suffering and anguish. Yet much of this comes from God in his righteous judgments.[84] In the Apocalypse, even Satan's apparent victories—for example, the rise of the dragon (the devil), the sea-beast (the antichrist), and the

76. For example, see our discussion concerning Rev 8–9, where the trumpet judgments are repeatedly said to affect one third of all they touch, including humankind. The plagues are unleashed everywhere, not just upon one nation or people group.

77. See our discussion of Rev 22:1–5.

78. See our discussion of Rev 5:9–14.

79. See our discussion of Rev 19:11–16.

80. See our discussion of Rev 19:9.

81. See Isa 7:14; Matt 1:23; Rev 21:3.

82. See our discussion of Rev 17:14; 19:16.

83. See Eph 1:20–23; Phil 2:9–11; Col 1:15–17.

84. See our earlier discussion about the cosmic trial motif in the Apocalypse. Note that God sovereignly ordains and his emissaries dutifully execute the seal, trumpet, and bowl judgments. While Satan is aware of the death and destruction caused by these events, they are not credited to his power or plan.

land-beast (the false prophet)[85]—are found within the Creator's unassailable plan to bring final judgment and blessing to his creation. Also, in the end, Satan does nothing but play into God's hand. Ironically, the devil's grand accomplishment is his own destruction, along with those who have cast their lot with him.[86] His fallen-angel (demonic) compatriots prove to be mere appendages, that is, connected to Satan with no volition of their own independent of their evil warlord. Likewise, even sin and death, impersonal devastations as they are, meet their end.[87]

Fourth, *angels, God's obedient, celestial emissaries, play a prominent role in the events of the Apocalypse*. Their intensified activity during this time points to the battle between light and darkness. It also points to the war both now and forthcoming that encompasses the entire universe, rather than just one isolated place or people group. Angels deliver messages,[88] unleash judgment,[89] and protect God's people and plan.[90] Moreover, angels participate with his reborn children in worship,[91] as well as unite with them in praise for the Creator's glorious victory over all that stands against him. Particularly notable are the angels' aversion to receive worship, even as John becomes overwhelmed with the messenger and the message he receives.[92] At every point, these heavenly beings show us what perfect and faithful obedience to Jesus looks like, while his beleaguered followers relate to him in ways that angels can only observe.[93]

Fifth, *we learn much about humanity in the Apocalypse*. The temporal life is replaced by that which is everlasting, whether in separation from God (hell, the fiery lake filled with burning sulfur) or in perfect fellowship with the Creator in the new heaven and the new earth.[94] The division between believers and unbelievers is stark. After death, there

85. See our discussion of Rev 13.

86. See our discussion of Rev 20:7–10.

87. See our discussion of Rev 19:20–21; 20:7–10, 14–15.

88. See our discussion of Rev 1:1, 20; 10:1; 11:1; 19:9.

89. See our discussion of Rev 6:1–8; 8:5–13; 10:1–7; 14:8–10, 17–19; 16:1; 18:21; 19:17–18.

90. See our discussion of Rev 7:1–3; 12:7–9.

91. See our discussion of Rev 4:6–9; 5:6–14.

92. See our discussion of Rev 19:10; 22:9.

93. See 1 Pet 1:12. For a concise treatment concerning the topic of angels in Scripture, see the corresponding table in our discussion of Rev 1. Also, for an extensive discussion about angelology and its christological implications in the Apocalypse, see Carrell, *Jesus and the Angels*.

94. See our discussion of Rev 21:1.

are no further opportunities for repentance, grace, and forgiveness for unbelievers.[95] Their fate is sealed, and it is nothing short of complete devastation and total (spiritual) destruction.[96] For believers, a never-ending, glorified existence, free from pain and suffering, replaces the trials and tribulations of the here and now.[97] To reiterate what we noted earlier, in perfect fulfillment of *Immanuel*,[98] believers no longer need atonement, forgiveness, a mediator, or a protector.

Sixth, *the Apocalypse teaches us about the end of the age*. This refers to the culmination of God's sovereign, unfailing plan from the beginning, through its various stages of disclosure and fulfillment. The Creator's everlasting plan is to call a redeemed people for his name. It was executed in the past in his dealings with Israel,[99] is now being carried out in the present activity of the church,[100] and will be brought to fruition at the end of the age.[101] We are privileged to learn what the Creator has in store for us, which is far beyond anything we could ever think or even imagine.[102] It is in this component (namely, eschatology) where various specialists expound views about the rapture of believers, the time of tribulation, the nature of Christ's second coming, the millennial kingdom, the process of judgment for unbelievers, and the new heavens and the new earth. Yes, debates over these issues have their place. Also, one's position on these topics has implications for faith and practice. Even so, there are many components about the end times upon which people from all perspectives within biblical Christianity can agree. Likewise, it is these aspects that garner particular attention as we continue our upcoming journey through the Apocalypse.

95. See 2 Cor 5:10; Heb 9:27.

96. See our discussion of Rev 20:15; 21:8.

97. See our discussion of Rev 22:1–5.

98. See Isa 7:14; Matt 1:23. In fulfillment of all Old Testament prophecies concerning *Immanuel*, "God with us," Rev 21:3 states that the Creator establishes his "dwelling place" with redeemed humanity.

99. Note, for example, God's determination to create a people for his name in connection with his covenant with Abraham; see Gen 12:1–3; 15:7–16; 17:9–14.

100. See Acts 15:14; 1 Pet 2:9.

101. See our discussion of Rev 5:9; 7:9–10.

102. See Rom 16:25; 2 Cor 9:8; Eph 3:20–21.

IMPORTANT MINISTRY IMPLICATIONS

While we discuss more specific applications as each chapter of the Apocalypse receives our focused attention, there are several overarching points of ministry application we note here in the Introduction:

First, *the Apocalypse is universal in scope*. There is no place, region, culture, tribe, tongue, people, or nation that fails to come under some aspect of the Messiah's authority, judgment, and rescue. Any theological principles we find in the biblical text, as well as any warnings, promises, or reasons for hope and anticipation found there, are universally applicable to all of us. No individual is outside the all-encompassing reach of the Father's sovereign rule through the Son. The events described in John's prophetic oracle touch everyone, everywhere.

There are both a positive aspect and a negative aspect to the above truths. On the upside, all believers in Christ receive his eternal blessings, provisions, protections, and rewards. Economic and social statuses are flattened by God's overwhelming justice and grace. Likewise, distinctions of ethnicity, socioeconomic status, and geographical location diminish in significance when compared with our identity in Christ. Life in the church should be reflective of this equality here and now as a preview of the equality in Christ that is yet to come.[103] We can live, work, and worship together in the body of Christ because we know that our inheritance in union with the Messiah is eternally safe and secure as well as independent of those distinctions that affect our lives in the present. Imagine the powerful testimony believers have when we model this truth to the unbelieving world!

On the downside, all those rejecting Christ are equally and holistically condemned. No one can purchase freedom from judgment.[104] There is no diplomatic immunity for VIPs (that is, very important persons). Too often, we hear that the wealthy or those in privileged positions avoid criminal liability because of a bribe or an inside connection. There are also those with certain designations or political positions who prosper by exploiting loopholes in the law. Furthermore, there are reports about rampant corruption among our judges, police forces, and military

103. See Gal 3:28.

104. See our discussion of Rev 18, where, in the aftermath of Babylon's demise, those who lived lavishly, being sustained by and dependent upon their material prowess, end up losing everything in divine judgment. In the end, no one can be saved (either physically or spiritually) by the world's harlotrous and idolatrous system.

leaders. Just as distressing are the disadvantaged, oppressed, and scorned who pay for the crimes of others who are more fortunate. Yet this is not so with Christ. In him, all people are held accountable according to his unassailable character and revealed expectations.

Second, *the Apocalypse assures us of final judgment.* All are examined according to what they have done with Christ and for Christ. Admittedly, the notion of judgment is often a frightful proposition, conjuring images of divine wrath and vengeance. We naturally fear judgment because the implication is that we have done something wrong and stand ready to be punished. To be sure, there is plenty of this in the Apocalypse. Yet there is another element, less expected, that we must not overlook. Specifically, judgment is *celebrated*, especially as the Creator finally vindicates the righteous, particularly those who have given their lives for the name of Christ, even amid sorrow and martyrdom. God's judgment is upright, and the faithful long for it. Consequently, when divine retribution is finally delivered, there are cries of victory, praise, and worship.[105]

Those who, even now, reject the glorious gospel about Christ are forewarned. A day is coming when their rejection of the good news will be punished with everlasting consequences. This day should serve as motivation for congregations and individual Christians alike. Indeed, the world needs to hear the good news about Christ! As local faith communities, we must not be ashamed of the gospel. Instead, we should boldly and unapologetically declare the truth of salvation in Christ alone. We know this truth offends pagan ears and runs contrary to popular culture on several fronts. Yet it matters little when we consider that the consequences of unbelief last forever. Every believer is motivated to engage in the Father's business by proclaiming the gospel.

Relatedly, the Apocalypse has embedded within it seven letters offering reassurance to those who persevere in the faith. God's reborn children are to cling tightly to Christ and hold fast in faith, for the day of their vindication is near.[106] To those experiencing persecution for their faith, as well as suffering loss and rejection, and perhaps even the risk of being martyred, there is a comfort in the coming judgment. Ultimately, at the end of the age, the Creator of the heavens and the earth does what is right, including vanquishing all forms of evil. Right now, Christians

105. See our discussion of Rev 19:1–3, where the "immense crowd in heaven" praises God for avenging the blood of his beleaguered, martyred bondservants.

106. Note in our discussion about the Apocalypse's letters to the seven churches (chs. 2–3) the many blessings and rewards promised to those who are "victorious."

around the world are suffering for their faith. This includes some experiencing persecution from their own families, and others from the lack of religious freedom in their countries.[107] While at present evil seems to reign, the Creator pledges to vindicate the faith and faithfulness of Jesus' followers. God also promises to reward eternally those who lay their lives down for the sake of the Cross.

Third, *the Apocalypse gives assurance of God's blessings to those who persevere in their faith*. Much like the blessed hope of the Lord's judgment, true believers in Christ can look forward to an eternal reward for their forbearance. These indescribable blessings give tremendous hope for those who, perhaps not explicitly suffering for their faith, are in general struggling to persevere. Concededly, life in our fallen world is hard. The Christian life in a pagan, antagonistic society is even more challenging to maintain. And yet, God's expectation is not that those who struggle would cease doing so, though he does regularly and graciously bring his beleaguered children out of suffering. Rather, his expectation is that, by the Spirit's presence and power, those who struggle also persevere, maintain their faith-commitment, fight the good fight, and finish the race.[108] Regardless of whether their anguish is relieved, remaining loyal to the Messiah is the right choice, in all places and at all times.

Fourth, *the Apocalypse vividly describes events and circumstances that are frightening and even disturbing*. Anyone with a modicum of compassion should be moved when considering the future judgment and destruction of so many, as depicted in John's prophetic oracle. And yet, when we consider the hope that is presented for the faithful, the Apocalypse can function as a source of joy and strength, resulting in a confident expectation that heavenly blessings are assured.[109] Also, while we can experience them in part even now, we will experience them to the fullest extent in the future. Charlatans often make promises of immediate health, wealth, and prosperity. Then, tragically, these assurances often turn out to be empty and unreliable. In contrast, God has never made such pledges. Indeed, the blessings he promises to bestow are far greater

107. While there are numerous organizations and groups tracking the worldwide persecution of Christians, the work of Open Doors (opendoors.org) is noteworthy as a reliable and regularly updated source of information.

108. See 2 Tim 4:7.

109. See Schriener, *Revelation*, 72, for more on the contrast between confidence (for believers) and fear (for unbelievers) that results from understanding the judgment to come.

than what the prosperity cult communicates today. And it is in what God has *actually declared*—especially in the Apocalypse—that we find our true and enduring hope.

Fifth, *because of the assurance of God's blessing, we need not worry about our plan of escape from tribulation and persecution.* Our mentality should not be, "I can't wait to get out of here!" Rather, our thinking should be, "How can I use the time I have left to glorify my Lord and Savior?" Instead of planning to avoid hardship, we should be motivated to serve our Redeemer today with urgency and intensity. This is part of living out the hope we have in union with Christ. While we know true believers will ultimately flourish in the life to come, we do not rest on these laurels. We move with *missional* purpose by running headlong into the calling Jesus has given to each of his disciples. On one level, we spiritually repose in the assurance of our salvation. Yet, on another level, the Spirit enables us to toil, day in and day out, for the sake of the gospel. If we are motivated primarily by fear of judgment, we will do only what we believe we must to avoid whatever it is we dread. In contrast, if we are motivated by God-given hope, we will never grow weary of serving our Savior well because we have unwavering confidence in what lies ahead.

VITAL MISSIONAL RAMIFICATIONS[110]

As we briefly mentioned above, God has called us to move forward with *missional* purpose in our walk with Christ. This means to be always on mission in all places where God has placed us. Doing so can have different meanings in varying contexts. Yet biblically, operating with missional purpose is about gospel witness, namely, leading the unsaved to become united to Christ by faith. In this sense, we are all missionaries of the gospel, in which we proclaim the message of our Savior to all, especially by

110. For an exploration of how the Bible emerges from and centers on God's redemptive mission in the world, see Wright, *Mission of God.* Wright proposes that a faithful reading of Scripture demands a missional hermeneutic—an interpretive approach that examines Scripture through the lens of God's purpose to redeem and restore creation. The author argues not only that the Bible supports mission but also that mission itself constitutes the framework of Scripture's redemptive-historical narrative. For a consideration of missional themes in Revelation, especially the church's mandate and the destiny of the nations within the prophetic oracle's end-time narrative, see Morales, "Christ, Shepherd of the Nations." For an emphasis on the Apocalypse's role in understanding God's ongoing mission and the church's participation, see Flemming, *Foretaste of the Future.*

reaching across cultures, national boundaries, and even languages. The Spirit can enable us to do this in the following ways through a thoughtful and prayerful study of the Apocalypse.

First is obtaining an understanding of the context. As we noted earlier, John's prophetic oracle was written when the Roman authorities persecuted Jesus' followers, and the Apocalypse reflects the struggles and hopes of the nascent, early Christian community. This contextual understanding can help missionaries appreciate the struggles and hopes of the people with whom they are working and provide a framework for their missional work. For example, many believers in Majority World contexts do not have freedom of religion. They are unable to fight for their so-called "constitutional rights," which are enjoyed and often taken for granted by those possessing them in the Global North. Also, large numbers of believers in the Majority World struggle under systemic oppression based upon their ethnicity, economic status, or faith commitments. These believers face real and immediate spiritual and physical needs.

When missionaries share the gospel within these contexts of religious persecution and physical oppression, unbelievers receive a message of hope and resilience, just as the original audience of the Apocalypse did. Missionaries must be willing to enter the context of the community they serve and identify with the sufferings of those in that community, even if the missionaries do not directly experience the same sorts of sufferings. They must move toward the people they are seeking to reach with empathy and compassion, especially by living out genuine care and concern for the plight of the underprivileged. In this way, missionaries can earn the right to speak God's truth into the lives of the lost.

Second is recognizing the importance of symbolism. After all, the Apocalypse is rich in figurative imagery, and the motifs it employs are derived from a variety of ancient sources.[111] Understanding the vivid language of John's prophetic oracle is important for interpreting its message. This insight can help missionaries appreciate and use the local culture's symbols and motifs to communicate the gospel in a way that is relevant and meaningful to the people.

For instance, by employing the motif of "Ubuntu" (variously translated as "I am because we are") in African contexts, missionaries can engage a valuable cultural concept while connecting it to what Scripture teaches about the necessity of church unity and the responsibility we

111. As we noted earlier, these ancient sources include the Old Testament and intertestamental apocalyptic literature.

have for one another as loyal followers of Christ. Moreover, the Apocalypse introduces us to faith communities that need to bolster their commitment to endure and persevere together for the common good of one another. As the church militant[112] here on earth, the need for unity in the ongoing, persevering fight is paramount. These examples are just two of many where missionaries can employ concepts and symbols of a given culture or people group, find a connection point in the Apocalypse, and provide a ground or basis for sharing the gospel.

Third is appreciating the tension between the present and the future (along with the past). The Apocalypse portrays a dynamic tension between the present and the future, between the world as it is and the world as it will be. The prophetic oracle expresses this tension through its emphasis on the inauguration of God's kingdom and the defeat of evil in all its forms. By properly understanding and applying the vision of the Creator's future victory, missionaries can help those struggling in the present to cast their own vision toward the future, where the full consequences of the Messiah's triumphal kingdom are realized.

To reiterate what we observed earlier, the prosperity cult is one of the most insidious enemies of the biblical understanding and application of the already/not-yet paradigm. Health and wealth preachers have led many astray with their notion that the full benefits of God's kingdom are available now if we just *claim* what is rightfully ours. This heretical notion often affects the poor and marginalized most deeply, where sincere believers are manipulated into deep impoverishment because of an empty promise from a charlatan posing as a messenger of God.[113]

The Apocalypse does promise God's kingdom benefits. Yet these are often experienced only after this life and, potentially, after the suffering that might come for the sake of the good news. Missionaries must emphasize the transformative power of the gospel, both in the lives of individuals and in the world around them. This life-changing power brings a present, spiritual blessing while also opening the eyes of believers to the eternal inheritance yet to come. In addition, the message of the Apocalypse can provide missionaries with a vision of the ultimate goal of their

112. The church militant is a reference to Jesus' followers on earth during the present age who are engaged in an ongoing spiritual battle against the forces of darkness. In contrast, the church triumphant is a reference to the ultimate victory that Jesus' followers experience over the forces of darkness at the end of the age. For an extensive discussion about the church militant and triumphant in the Apocalypse, see Brighton, *Revelation*, 188–97, 199–201, 367–68, 370–71, 373–75, 616.

113. See 2 Cor 11:14.

work for Christ and motivate them to persevere in the face of opposition and adversity.

Fourth is affirming the necessity of worship.[114] The Apocalypse includes numerous scenes of corporate worship and praise, which are central activities in the heavenly realm. This insight can enable missionaries to emphasize the importance of worship and encourage the people with whom they work to join them in praising God. Missionaries can labor with confidence, knowing that the work they do is part of the Creator's plan for people of every tribe, language, ethnicity, and nation to be present before his glorious throne in jubilant praise. The Apocalypse gives missionaries a glimpse of the result of their efforts, especially as God gathers a diverse, unified people for his name, all of whom will glorify him and enjoy his presence forever. There can be no greater motivation for missionary work than to know that the Lord is using us to populate his heavenly choir with his reborn children![115]

114. For an astute analysis concerning how the veneration of the Messiah emerged within early Christian apocalyptic traditions (especially Rev and Ascen. Isa.), see Bauckham, *Worship of Jesus*.

115. For a recent work that explores the missional dynamics of the Apocalypse as a primary interpretive framework, see Urga, Smither, and Naylor, *Reading Revelation Missiologically*. That volume structures the theology of John's prophetic oracle around three interrelated questions: missionary motives (why God's people move toward the nations), missionary messages (what Revelation proclaims), and missionary methods (how worship and witness shape practice). Collectively, the essays contend that Revelation functions as a missionary manifesto designed to prepare and equip the church for global worship. In contrast, the present study provides a sequential literary and theological analysis that incorporates dedicated sections on vital missional ramifications. Rather than adopting mission as the overarching hermeneutical key, this volume treats missional engagement as the inherent and necessary outgrowth of a Christ-centered reading of the Apocalypse. This approach emphasizes perseverance under persecution, the universal scope of redemption, and the church's witness to the Messiah, themes that are particularly resonant within Majority World contexts.

Revelation 1

The Risen and Glorified Messiah

LEARNING OBJECTIVES

- Recognize the blessing that comes from the study of Revelation.
- Cultivate a deeper sense of awe and worship toward the Creator.
- Appreciate more fully the truth about the second advent.
- Gain insight into the divine nature, power, and authority of the risen and glorified Messiah.
- Explore the spiritual and emotional impact of encountering the risen and glorified Messiah.

CHAPTER SUMMARY

Revelation 1 introduces John's prophetic oracle, which he received from the risen and glorified Messiah while exiled on the island of Patmos. The apostle writes to seven churches in Asia Minor about Jesus' supreme authority and enduring presence among them. John's unfolding cosmic drama emphasizes the Father's eternal existence and the Spirit's sevenfold presence, along with the Son's sacrificial death and resurrection. Finally, we encounter Jesus' command for John to write messages of praise, rebuke, and instruction to the original recipients of his treatise.

STUDY QUESTIONS

1. What are some of the key symbols and themes in Revelation 1?

2. What does it mean that those who read (and hear) this prophetic oracle aloud are "blessed"?
3. What does the image of the Messiah with hair white as wool and eyes like blazing fire reveal about his divine nature, power, and authority?
4. How does the truth about God's greatness and majesty encourage believers to respond to him in worship and praise, rather than with cringing terror?
5. How does the knowledge of the soon return of the Messiah provide motivation in gospel witness to the lost?

CHAPTER OUTLINE

- John's introduction (1:1–4)
- John's greeting (1:4–8)
- John's circumstance (1:9–11)
- Jesus' glorious appearance to John (1:12–16)
- Jesus' instructions to John (Rev 1:17–20)
- Key theological insights
- Important ministry implications
- Vital missional ramifications

JOHN'S INTRODUCTION (1:1–4)

About six decades had passed since John last saw Jesus of Nazareth crucified, buried, resurrected, and ascended into heaven. After all those years, while the apostle was exiled on the "island called Patmos" (v. 9), he suddenly once more encountered the Messiah. This time, however, Jesus appeared quite different than he did when John leaned against the Savior at the Last Supper (John 13:23). Now the Son of God was exalted and radiant in appearance (Rev 1:12–16).

John begins his prophetic oracle by stating that it is a "revelation" (v. 1). As noted previously, here the apostle uses the Greek noun *apokalypsis* (meaning "to uncover," "to disclose," or "to make known") to describe what he is about to convey. For this reason, specialists have called John's work the Apocalypse. In brief, it is an unveiling or disclosure of truths about the Creator's universal judgment of humankind, followed by the introduction of a new era of everlasting righteousness, peace, and joy.

The apostle states that the Father gave the prophetic oracle to his Son. As the Lamb who was slain, he alone is "worthy" (Rev 5:9)[1] to bring to completion God's end-time plan of redemption. In turn, the Son uses an "angel" (or heavenly messenger; 1:1) to make the Creator's will known to John (22:16). Because the communication originated with the Father,[2] it carries his inspiration and authority. Likewise, the apostle is a fully credentialed spokesperson (or prophet, seer) for the triune God.

The active conveyance of the revelation John received is often translated as follows: "Christ communicated these things by sending them" (1:1). "Communicated" renders the Greek verb *semaino*, which means "signified" or "indicated." It is the cognate of the noun *semeion*, which means "sign." The Fourth Gospel uses *semeion* to indicate that Jesus' miracles[3] functioned as tangible *symbols* pointing to his divine authority and power. This observation, along with Revelation's repeated emphasis on vividly showing, seeing, hearing, and testifying, incentivizes translating 1:1 as follows: "Christ expressed this revelation by means of symbols sent."[4]

John's visions disclose previously hidden and inscrutable truths about the Creator, along with the ultimate course of physical and metaphysical history. Out of divine necessity, the apostle's prophetic oracle, including the unfolding of heralded events, must be consummated without delay. The declaration about "things that must soon take place" does not necessarily mean that whatever is recorded would occur in John's near future. Given the passage of almost two millennia, the apostle is most likely stressing that when the Father begins to fulfill what is written, it is certain to take place swiftly.[5]

The above observation recalls statements recorded in Daniel 2:28–30 and 45–47 about what would assuredly "happen in the latter days."[6] This is an example of typological fulfillment or prophetic foreshadowing

1. The Greek adjective rendered "worthy" (Rev 5:9) refers to that which is spiritually fit and ethically deserving.

2. Through the Son by an angel; essentially a multistage disclosure process.

3. The miracles Jesus performed were actual events occurring within space-time reality.

4. See the EHV.

5. See our discussion of Rev 3:11; 16:15; 22:6, 10, 12, 20.

6. See 2 Bar. 10:3; 1 En. 1:1–2; T. of Job 1:4; 47:9.

found throughout Revelation. Specifically, an Old Testament reference establishes a corresponding pattern for a more heightened (or escalated) and profound fulfillment in the Apocalypse. This interpretive approach is not unique to Revelation. It also reflects an ancient Jewish way of reading the Hebrew sacred writings, including how to think about history, especially by connecting a series of chronologically displaced events or prophecies in a typological manner.[7]

John stresses his role as a humble "servant" (1:1)[8] and faithful "witness" (v. 2) in resolutely declaring the Father's saving message (namely, the "word of God"). This especially includes the "testimony" from and about the Son (6:9; 19:4). In short, the apostle steadfastly communicates, as one would do in a court of law, all that he saw in his visionary experience. The Savior, of course, is the preeminent and faithful witness.[9] Also, he summons all believers to testify openly concerning him, even if it means being martyred by the forces of Satan for maintaining an unwavering allegiance to the Messiah.[10]

"Blessed" (v. 3) translates the Greek adjective *makarios*. The term means more than being superficially happy. It conveys the idea of being the privileged recipient of the Creator's life-giving kindness, fruitfulness, and abundance.[11] Here, readers find the first of seven beatitudes, or pronouncements of covenantal blessing, appearing in the apostle's prophetic oracle.[12]

The Apocalypse is unique in that it pledges not only the covenantal curse of everlasting death on the wicked[13] but also the promise of eternal life on the regenerate, who read, hear, and obey what John has penned. After all, from the Father's perspective, the "time" is "near" for the impending crisis and for the fulfillment of the apostle's prophetic oracle.[14] Noteworthy is the emphasis on hearing the contents of the treatise being

7. See our discussion in the Introduction about the use of the Old Testament in Revelation.

8. Literally "slave."

9. See John 1:18; 18:37; 1 Tim 6:13; Rev 1:2, 5; 3:14.

10. See our discussion of Rev 12:11.

11. See Ps 1:1; Matt 5:3–11; Rev 4:11.

12. See our discussion of Rev 14:13; 16:15; 19:9; 20:6; 22:7, 14. Also, for a discussion about the literary and symbolic function of the number seven and the form of the beatitudes in the Apocalypse, see Stefanovic, *Revelation*, 55.

13. See our discussion of Rev 2:11; 20:6, 14; 21:8.

14. See Ps 90:4; 2 Pet 3:8.

publicly read. After all, people living throughout the Roman Empire in the first century AD were primarily hearing-dominant, rather than text-dominant, in the way they acquired and transmitted important information.[15]

Angels in Scripture		
Aspect	**Description**	**Biblical References**
Biblical Frequency	Mentioned dozens of times in Revelation alone, encompassing both holy and fallen angels	Rev 1:1, 20; 2:1, 8, 12, 18; 3:1, 7, 14; 4:8; 5:2, 11; 7:1–2, 11; 8:2–8, 10, 12–13; 9:1, 11, 13–15; 10:1, 5, 8–10; 11:1, 15; 12:7, 9; 14:6, 8–10, 15, 17–18; 15:1, 6–8; 16:1, 3–5, 8, 10, 12, 17; 17:1, 7, 15; 18:1, 21; 19:9, 17; 20:1; 21:9, 12, 17; 22:1, 6, 8, 16
Characteristics	Mighty, powerful, and wise; typically invisible to humans unless divinely revealed	Ps 103:20; 2 Sam 14:20; 2 Kgs 6:17; 2 Thess 1:7
Key Biblical Roles	Delivered the Law at Mount Sinai; announced Jesus' conception and birth to Joseph, Mary, and the shepherds; proclaimed Jesus' resurrection	Matt 1:20; 28:2–7; Mark 16:5–7; Luke 1:26–27; 2:8–9; 24:4–7; John 20:12–13; Acts 7:38, 53; Gal 3:19; Heb 2:2
Mortality	Immortal beings who do not marry, reproduce, or die; their number is fixed	Matt 22:30; Luke 20:36
Nature and Origin	Spirit beings created by God and dwelling in heaven; not humans who died	Matt 22:30; Heb 1:14
Organization	Structured in a hierarchy with various ranks	Eph 6:12; Col 1:16
Physical Form	Human-like appearance; not all have wings, despite common belief	Isa 6:2; Dan 9:21; Luke 24:4

15. See Neh 8:2; Luke 4:16; Acts 13:15; Col 4:16; 1 Thess 5:27. Also, see the extensive discussion of Walton and Sandy, *Lost World*. The authors explore the oral nature of ancient cultures and its impact on biblical texts. They argue that: (1) ancient Near Eastern societies were primarily hearing-dominant, relying on oral communication; (2) much of Greco-Roman literature preserved elements of this hearing-dominant culture; (3) Jesus lived in a predominantly nonliterate, oral society; (4) Jesus proclaimed truth through oral forms and instructed his followers to do the same; (5) the New Testament emphasizes spoken words over written texts; and, (6) New Testament genres, including the Apocalypse, are more closely tied to orality than textuality.

Angels in Scripture		
Aspect	**Description**	**Biblical References**
Primary Duties	Serve God by protecting, guiding, and assisting humans as his messengers and agents	Ps 91:11; Dan 6:22; 10:13; Acts 8:26; Heb 1:14

JOHN'S GREETING (1:4–8)

As we noted in our Introduction, Revelation blends three types of writing. It is a revelation (or apocalypse),[16] a prophetic oracle,[17] and a circular letter (or epistle).[18] Many ancient communiques began with the name of the author, the names of the recipients, and a salutation. This formula was followed by the main body of the letter and then a closing farewell. In Revelation, readers find these same literary elements.

For instance, the sender is "John" (v. 4), and his recipients are the "seven churches" in the Roman province of "Asia."[19] The traditional salutation of "grace"[20] and "peace"[21] is expanded into a confession about the Father's eternal and sovereign reign, along with the Son's supreme and unending lordship.[22]

In John's opening greeting, he draws attention to all three members of the triune Godhead. Specifically, the prophetic oracle originated from the Father, the Son, and the Spirit.[23] The apostle stresses the Father's ev-

16. See our discussion of Rev 1:1.

17. See our discussion of Rev 1:3, 19; 22:6, 7, 9–10, 18–19.

18. See our discussion of Rev 1:4–5, 11; 2:1—3:22; 22:21.

19. That is, Asia Minor or the southwestern portion of modern-day Turkey.

20. Referring to God's unmerited favor and undeserved kindness.

21. Denoting harmonious relations with God and others.

22. See our discussion of Rev 17:14; 19:16.

23. For an examination of the Apocalypse through a pro-Nicene, Trinitarian framework, see Smith, *Trinity in Revelation*. He argues that while John's prophetic oracle is not explicitly Trinitarian, it consistently emphasizes the Father on the throne, the slain Lamb, and the sevenfold Spirit as revealer and speaker. Also, while the three are portrayed as distinct persons of the Godhead, they remain unified in their essence, purpose, and actions. Smith analyzes the imagery, titles, and worship scenes of Rev, along with showing how all three persons are jointly involved in creation, redemption, and judgment. Moreover, Smith highlights John's strategic use of Old Testament allusions (for example, Exod, Isa, Ezek, and Dan) to connect the Trinity's roles with the God of Israel and thereby reinforces their shared divinity. Smith concludes that the theological vision of the Apocalypse is inherently Trinitarian and offers a cohesive depiction of how the Father, Son, and Spirit work together in salvation history.

erlasting existence and faithful presence with his beleaguered children and reminds them that the Creator, who governs all time[24] from his cosmic royal seat (or "throne"; 1:4),[25] would never abandon them.

Here, the reference to God as the one "who is, who was, and who is coming" embodies a restatement of the divine name recorded in Exodus 3:14.[26] The Hebrew phrase rendered "I AM WHO I AM" comes from a verb that means "to exist" or "to be." The preceding forms the basis for the proper noun *Yahweh* which is translated "LORD" in verse 15.[27]

Yahweh is God's unique, deeply personal name[28] that carries implications for the abiding covenant relationship between himself and the people of Israel. Verse 14 is the only place in the Hebrew sacred writings where the significance of the divine name is highlighted. Specifically, the Creator is the self-existent, eternally present, and ever-caring Father. He never came into being at any point in time, for he always existed.[29]

Some specialists think that the mention of the "seven spirits" (Rev 1:4) is a reference to seven angels who stand before the Creator's sacred "throne."[30] Most likely, however, John is symbolically referring to the perfection of the Spirit, along with his abundant presence and dynamic ministry.[31]

24. Including the past, present, and future.

25. As we previously noted, the Creator's throne occupies the literary center of John's prophetic oracle.

26. Particularly the Septuagint rendering (an ancient Greek translation of the Old Testament); see Isa 41:4; 43:10; 44:6; 48:12.

27. *Yahweh* appears 6828 times in the Old Testament.

28. Referred to as the *Tetragrammaton* or the four-letter name YHWH.

29. A theme repeatedly emphasized throughout the Apocalypse; see 1:8; 4:8; 10:6; 11:17; 15:7; 16:5. In Exod 3:14–15, God reveals two names to Moses: "I AM" (*ʾehyeh*) and "LORD" (*yhwh*), both derived from the Hebrew verb, *hayah* ("to be"), suggesting meanings like "I am" and "he is" (or "he exists"). Some specialists interpret *yhwh* as a declaration of God's aseity—his self-existence and independence from creation. However, in the context of Exod, the name emphasizes the Creator's active presence and steadfast commitment to redeeming Israel, rather than solely the abstract, objective truth of his reality. This focus is evident in the pillar of cloud and fire (13:21–22) and Moses' plea for God's abiding presence (33:14–15). Thus, while *yhwh* may etymologically mean "he is," its primary significance in Exod is the Creator's redemptive presence with Israel. For an extensive discussion of the use of the divine name in the Apocalypse, see Bauckham, *Theology of Revelation*, 28–30.

30. See Ps 104:4; Tob 12:15; Rev 8:2.

31. See Isa 11:2; Zech 4:2–10; Rev 3:1; 4:5; 5:6. Also, see in our discussion of the letter to the church in Smyrna (Rev 2:8–11) the table concerning the Holy Spirit in the Old Testament. Additionally, see in our discussion of the letter to the church in Sardis (3:1–6) the table concerning the sevenfold Spirit in the Apocalypse.

In keeping with what was noted earlier, during the Son's earthly sojourn, he faithfully bore "witness" (v. 5) to the Father. Even in Jesus' sacrificial death on the cross, he never compromised declaring and living by the truths of Scripture. The Father vindicated the Son by raising him as the "firstborn" from the "dead," which means that he would never again die.[32] Moreover, as the ascended and sovereign Lord, Jesus was exalted as "ruler"[33] over earth's potentates.[34]

Appropriately, John praises the Savior for loving his followers continually and without fail.[35] This truth is particularly evident in his freeing (or releasing) believers from bondage to their "sins" by shedding his "own blood" at Calvary.[36] The redemption Jesus purchased through his sacrificial death was the basis for his appointing believers to serve *collectively* as a "kingdom" (v. 6), as well as "priests," to God the Father.[37]

For the above reasons, John praises the Creator for his eternal "glory" and "power." Both terms in the doxology are accented in the original language by the definite article "the" to indicate totality—namely, *all the* "glory" and *all the* "power."[38] This was literally true "to the ages of the ages."

The interjection rendered "Amen"[39] is transliterated from a Hebrew adjective that literally means "let it be so."[40] In 1:7, it is followed by the interjection rendered "Yes." Together, the preceding utterances emphasize and confirm the validity of John's assertions. They also point to the liturgical context and worship setting of the apostle's prophetic oracle.

John follows his overt expression of praise with a description about the second coming of the Messiah as the divine Warrior, which is a major theme in Revelation.[41] In 1:7, the apostle echoes two prophetic passages

32. See Ps 89:27; Rom 1:4; 1 Cor 15:20, 23; Col 1:18.

33. Namely, being foremost in rank and power.

34. See Pss 2:6–9; 89:27, 35–37; Dan 2:47; Matt 28:18.

35. See Rom 8:35–39; Gal 2:20; Eph 5:2, 25.

36. See Ps 30:8; Isa 40:2; 53:10–12; Heb 7:26–27.

37. See Exod 19:5–6; Isa 43:10–13; 61:6; Jub. 16:18; Odes Sol. 20:1; 1 Pet 2:5, 9; Rev 5:10; 20:6; 22:5. For an overview of the New Testament teaching about believers' reigning with Christ, see Middleton, *New Heaven and New Earth*, 145–47.

38. On this point, see Brighton, *Revelation*, 36, who notes that throughout the Apocalypse, "Most of the doxologies include the definite article before the qualities ascribed to God and/or the Lamb."

39. See our discussion of Rev 3:14; 5:14; 7:12; 19:4; 22:20, 21.

40. Implying "May it happen in this way."

41. See our discussion of Rev 2:25; 3:3, 11; 19:11–16; 22:7, 12, 17, 20. For a development of the concept of the divine Warrior in Scripture, see Longman and Reid, *God Is*

from the Old Testament. First, in an expansive vision, Daniel sees "one like a son of man" (7:13) making his approach to the "Ancient of Days," surrounded by the "clouds of heaven."[42] Second, Zechariah records the Lord's words: "'They will look at me, the one they have pierced.' They will mourn for him" (12:10).[43]

At Jesus' second coming, none will doubt his sovereign rule as Lord and Judge. People will lament (or weep loudly), in part because of the sins they committed and because of the judgment that is about to fall on them.[44] As noted above, Revelation 1:7 solemnly affirms these truths with the twin declaration "Yes. Amen."

Three New Testament Greek Nouns for the Second Advent		
Greek Term	**Meaning and Significance**	**Biblical References**
Apokalypsis	To uncover, disclose, make known; the unveiling of the Messiah at his second coming; emphasizes the suddenness of his return and the dramatic revelation of previously hidden truth	1 Cor 1:7; 2 Thess 1:7; 1 Pet 4:13
Epiphaneia	Appearing, appearance; the glorious, visible manifestation of Christ's divine nature; emphasizes his majestic splendor with a spectacular, unmistakable divine appearance	Titus 2:13; 2 Thess 2:8
Parousia	Presence, coming; the physical arrival of the Son at a divinely appointed time; emphasizes his actual presence (not a phantom) and an official, ceremonial arrival with divine authority	1 Thess 4:15; 2 Thess 2:8

Revelation 1:8 contains the first occurrence in the Apocalypse of the phrase "Lord God." In the Septuagint, "Lord God" is the equivalent of the Hebrew phrase "Adonai Yahweh."[45] Likewise, some variant of "Lord

a Warrior. In particular, the authors examine the biblical theme of God as a warrior, showing how Yahweh fights for his people in the Old Testament and how Christ fulfills this role in the New Testament. The authors trace the development of divine warfare from Exodus to Revelation, highlighting its theological and redemptive significance. Through this exploration, the authors elucidate how the warrior motif shapes a deeper understanding of God's character and his covenant relationship with humanity.

42. See Num 11:25; Ps 104:3; Isa 19:1; 1 En. 1:3–9; Jub. 1:28; Matt 16:27; 24:30; Mark 13:26; 14:62; Luke 21:27; Acts 1:9.

43. See Zech 12:12, 14; John 19:34, 37.

44. See Matt 25:31–33; Rev 18:9.

45. See Amos 3:13; 4:13.

God" appears elsewhere in John's prophetic oracle.[46] When combined with the Greek noun rendered "Almighty" (*pantokrator*), the essential meaning is that of "sovereign Master."

In 1:8, the supreme Monarch of the universe declares himself to be "the Alpha and the Omega." *Alpha* and *omega* are the first and last letters of the Greek alphabet. The preceding expression is a figure of speech called a *merism*, in which two contrasting parts draw attention to the full scope of a broader idea. Succinctly, this merism signifies that the Creator is the beginning and the end of all things.[47]

The above truth is emphasized by the restatement of the phrase appearing earlier in verse 4, namely, the "one who is, and who was, and who is coming." This also refutes a similar claim made in a popular hymn to Zeus,[48] the sky and thunder god in Greek mythology. Furthermore, revisiting what was noted earlier, "Almighty" (v. 8; *pantokrator*) stresses that the Creator's lordship encompasses the past, the present, and the future.[49] In the Septuagint, *pantokrator* was the common word used for the Hebrew name *Yahweh Sebaoth* which means "Lord of armies."[50]

JOHN'S CIRCUMSTANCE (1:9–11)

As previously observed, verses 9–20 are the first of seven throne-room scenes in Revelation.[51] Each highlights some aspect of the triune God's holiness, righteousness, glory, sovereignty, and might. Furthermore, while the second coming of the Messiah is a major focus of the Apocalypse, the "suffering" (v. 9) of believers is also an important concern. John says that the pagan, idolatrous Roman authorities exiled him to "Patmos" because he faithfully proclaimed the Creator's redemptive truths (the "word of God") and bore witness to the Messiah.[52]

46. See our discussion of Rev 4:8, 11; 6:10; 11:8, 15, 17; 14:13; 15:3, 4; 16:7; 17:14; 18:8; 19:6, 16; 21:22; 22:5–6, 20–21.

47. See Isa 41:4; 43:10; 44:6; 48:12; 2 Bar. 21:9.

48. Namely, the one "who was and who is and who will be."

49. A major theme appearing throughout the Apocalypse; see our discussion of 4:8; 11:17; 15:3; 16:7, 14; 19:6, 15; 21:22.

50. See 2 Sam 5:10; Jer 5:14; Hos 12:5; Amos 3:13; 4:13; 9:5; Nah 3:5; Zech 10:3.

51. The other six throne-room scenes appear in Rev 4:1—5:14; 8:2–6; 11:19; 15:1—16:1; 16:18–21; 19:1–10.

52. As one would do in a court of law.

Decades earlier, Jesus experienced abuse as the promised Redeemer.[53] Likewise, John's readers were patiently enduring maltreatment for their faith and for their commitment to the Father's kingdom. Similarly, the apostle was persecuted for openly identifying with the Son and refusing to participate in the veneration of Rome's emperor.

As noted earlier, Patmos is a small, volcanic, and mostly treeless island about thirty-five miles off the coast of Asia Minor and about seventy miles southwest of Ephesus in the Aegean Sea.[54] Patmos is ten miles long from north to south and six miles wide along the northern coast. The island was an ideal spot for a Roman prison colony. The government routinely banished dissidents there to work in the mines.

The writings of Irenaeus,[55] Eusebius,[56] and Tertullian[57] indicate that the authorities exiled John to Patmos around AD 95, which was during the reign of Domitian.[58] The government then released the apostle from the island and returned him to Ephesus in AD 96, when Nerva became emperor.[59] Irenaeus wrote that John lived into the reign of Trajan[60] and served as the leader of the church at Ephesus.[61]

John says that he was in the Spirit "on the Lord's Day" (v. 10). Some specialists think that the apostle is referring to the end-time day of the Lord, when God would bring judgment on the wicked. Most likely, however, John is referring to Sunday, the first day of the week. Early within church history, believers gathered on Sunday to worship the Father and celebrate the Son's resurrection from the dead.[62] This contrasted sharply with pagans who designated a specific day to venerate the Roman emperor.

The phrase "in the Spirit" probably refers not to John's human spirit but to his being under the control of the Holy Spirit in some special way, perhaps in a trancelike, visionary state.[63] The Spirit enabled the apostle

53. See 1 Pet 2:21.
54. In the eastern Mediterranean.
55. Hacr. 5.30.3.
56. Hist. eccl. 3.18.1–3; 3.20.8.
57. Praescr. 36.
58. AD 81–96.
59. AD 96–98.
60. AD 98–117.
61. Haer. 3.3.4.
62. See Matt 28:1; Acts 20:7; 1 Cor 16:2; Did. 14:1.
63. See 1 Kgs 18:12; Ezek 2:2; 3:12–15, 24; 11:5, 24; 37:1.

to witness[64] the unfolding events of Revelation from various distinctive vantage points.[65] For instance, John remembers hearing behind himself a "loud voice" that sounded like a "trumpet." Most likely, he heard the intense, penetrating speech of the risen Savior.

Jesus directed John to inscribe on a "scroll" (v. 11) the entirety of what he witnessed.[66] This document was probably a roll of papyrus or leather. Then the apostle was to dispatch the prophetic oracle to "seven churches" located in Asia Minor. As previously noted, the cities were about fifty miles apart from each other and roughly formed a horseshoe-shaped circuit, starting with Ephesus and ending with Laodicea.

It is unclear why Jesus chose these specific congregations, for there were others in the region of somewhat equal importance—for example, Troas, Colossae, and Hierapolis. Some specialists think that the seven cities were part of a transportation network, while others maintain that they were postal centers for seven different regions. Though John addresses his prophetic oracle to seven churches, his message is still applicable to believers today.

JESUS' GLORIOUS APPEARANCE TO JOHN (1:12–16)

When John turns around to "see" (v. 12) who is speaking to him, he spots "seven" golden "lampstands." This is an adaptation of Zechariah's fifth vision[67] of a lampstand and two olive trees.[68] The flaming menorahs used in the Jerusalem temple[69] typically had a sturdy base, a central shaft, three branches on each side, and bowls on top of each branch, as well as on top of the central shaft, for a total of seven bowls. Presumably, the "lampstands" in John's vision are similar in appearance.

The apostle also sees the risen and glorified Redeemer, as the divine Warrior, standing among the "lampstands," which verse 20 says represent the "seven churches." Jesus is there to walk among his followers in times of hardship, to guide them in times of uncertainty, and to discipline them in times of moral laxity.

64. Through the senses of seeing and hearing.
65. See Jer 30:2; Hab 2:2; Rev 4:2; 17:3; 21:10.
66. See Exod 17:14; Isa 30:8; Jer 36:2; Hab 2:2.
67. Recorded in chap 4 of Zechariah's prophetic oracle, especially vv. 2, 3, and 10.
68. See Exod 25:31–40; 37:18–21; 1 Kgs 7:49; 1 Chr 28:15; 2 Chr 4:7, 20.
69. Specifically, before the temple's destruction in AD 70.

As chapters 2 and 3 reveal, not even believers can escape their accountability to the Son.[70] In the Messiah's bestowal of covenantal blessings and curses, he first begins with the church and then scrutinizes the wicked with progressively heightened intensity.[71] This means that at the Father's cosmic court of justice, the Son evaluates all people according to what they have done. Likewise, he shows no partiality or favoritism in his dealings with either the church or the wicked.[72]

John refers to the Messiah as being "like a son of man" (1:13). This phrase, which alludes to Daniel 7:13–14,[73] is the title Jesus most often used in the Gospels to refer to himself. It emphasizes his deity, messiahship, suffering, redemptive work, and humanity.[74]

The apostle sees the Redeemer wearing the single, full-length "robe" (Rev 1:13) of a high priest.[75] A "sash" was fastened to his "robe" and made from unalloyed "gold," which was appropriate for the exalted, imperial Lord.[76] The "head" (v. 14) and "hair" of the Son were "white," comparable to the pristine color of pure "wool" and newly fallen "snow." This imagery possibly symbolizes his infinite virtue, majesty, and wisdom.[77] The radiance of Jesus' "eyes" like "blazing flames" might denote his penetrating, exhaustive insight as well as his intense opposition to his adversaries as the divine Warrior.[78]

The Redeemer's "feet" (v. 15) glow like white-hot, "polished bronze" and likely spotlight his stability, strength, and radiance.[79] His "voice" thunders like the "roar" produced by an enormous waterfall or crashing ocean waves,[80] perhaps reflecting his awe-inspiring power and authority.[81] These symbols were appropriate for the one who judges all evil and

70. See Rom 14:10–12; 2 Cor 5:10; Heb 4:12–13.

71. See 1 Pet 4:17–18.

72. See Deut 10:17; Ps 62:12; Prov 24:12; Matt 16:27; Acts 10:34; Rom 2:6, 11; Rev 20:11–15.

73. See 1 En. 46:3–4.

74. See Matt 26:64; Mark 2:10; 8:31; 10:45; John 1:51; 3:14; 8:28. Also, see the discussion about this theme in Osborne, *Revelation*, 29, 35–36, 249.

75. A sign of dignity and rank; see Exod 28:4; 29:5–9; 39:29; Lev 8:7; Zech 3:4.

76. See Dan 10:5; Apoc. Zeph. 6:12; 1 Macc 10:89; 14:44.

77. See Isa 1:18; Dan 7:9; 1 En. 46:1; 71:10; 106:2; 2 En. 1:5.

78. See Dan 10:6; 2 En. 1:5; Jos. Asen. 14:9; Rev 2:18; 19:12.

79. See Apoc. Zeph. 6:12.

80. Such as the waves pounding the shoreline of Patmos.

81. See Ezek 1:24; 43:2; Dan 10:6; Apoc. Ab. 17:1; 4 Ezra 6:17.

stands before God's cosmic court of justice on behalf of those who trust in him for eternal life.[82]

John says that the Messiah grasps "seven stars" (v. 16) in his "right hand," which verse 20 states are the "messengers" (or angels) of the "seven churches."[83] In ancient times, the right hand was a symbol of authority, might, and control.[84] Also, in Roman times, stars appeared on coins as a symbol of imperial power. The imagery of verse 16 suggests that the Savior, not the Roman emperor or any other evil entity (such as Satan and his demonic cohort), exercises absolute control over believers and their eternal destinies. Likewise, the Savior is their Defender and Protector[85] as well as their source of "righteousness and sanctification and redemption" (1 Cor 1:30).

The apostle notes that a long, "sharp" (Rev 1:16), double-edged "sword" emerges from the "mouth" of the Redeemer. This seems to be a symbol of both the Word of God and divine judgment.[86] The glory of the risen Lord is evident from the appearance of his entire countenance, which beams more intensely than the full force of the "sun" when it "shines" at noon.[87] In fact, the light of Jesus' glory, as the divine Warrior, is so radiant (or brilliant) that no one can approach it.[88]

Parallels between Daniel 10:5–6 and Revelation 1:13–16[89]		
Physical Feature	**Dan 10:5–6**	**Rev 1:13–16**
Arms and Feet	"his arms and feet were like polished bronze"	"his feet were like polished bronze"
Clothing/Sash	"around his waist he was wearing a belt made from gold of Uphaz"	"around his chest he wore a gold sash"
Eyes	"his eyes were like burning torches"	"his eyes were like blazing flames"

82. See John 5:26–27; 1 Tim 2:4–5; Heb 2:17; 4:14–16; 9:11–14; 1 John 2:1.

83. See 1 En. 18:13; 21:3.

84. See Ps 110:1; Matt 26:64; Heb 1:3.

85. See John 10:28.

86. See Isa 11:4; 49:2; 1 En. 62:2; Heb 4:12; Rev 2:12, 16; 6:8; 19:15, 21.

87. See Ps 84:11; Isa 60:19–20; 2 En. 1:5; 19:1; 4 Ezra 10:25; Jos. Asen. 14:9; Matt 17:2; Rev 21:23.

88. See 1 Tim 6:16.

89. Table adapted from information presented in Beale, *The Book of Revelation*, 208–9.

Parallels between Daniel 10:5–6 and Revelation 1:13–16[89]		
Physical Feature	**Dan 10:5–6**	**Rev 1:13–16**
Face	"his face looked like lightning"	"his face was shining as the sun shines in all its brightness"
Voice	"the sound of his words was like the sound of an army"	"his voice was like the roar of many waters"

JESUS' INSTRUCTIONS TO JOHN (REV 1:17–20)

As John stands before the Messiah, the apostle drops to his knees "like a dead man" (v. 17). Numerous Old Testament and New Testament saints had similar responses when suddenly exposed to the glorified, sacred presence of the sovereign Lord.[90] With his "right hand," the risen and exalted Savior touches John, perhaps to strengthen him physically, comfort him emotionally, and commission him for his witness-bearing, prophetic ministry.[91]

Jesus tells the apostle to discontinue being "afraid," for the Savior is "the First and the Last."[92] The preceding is a divine title that appears elsewhere in Scripture in reference to the Creator.[93] It means essentially the same thing as the title "the Alpha and the Omega" (v. 8).[94] As noted earlier, at the time John wrote Revelation, the pagan, idolatrous Roman government was pressuring believers to renounce the Messiah and declare the emperor to be their supreme ruler and god. Jesus' words to John stress why it was wrong to do so.

After all, every human authority is mortal and limited, whereas the Savior is immortal and infinite in power. The idols venerated by Rome were lifeless, whereas Jesus is the "Living One" (v. 18). This means that his core being, like that of the Father and the Spirit, was characterized by everlasting life.[95] Not even the grave could hold the Savior. Though he

90. See Josh 5:14; Isa 6:5; Ezek 1:28; Dan 8:17–18; 10:7–9, 15; 1 En. 14:14; 3 En. 1:7; 4 Ezra 10:30; Matt 17:6; Acts 26:14.

91. See Acts 6:6; 8:17–19; 13:3; 1 Tim 4:14; 5:22; 2 Tim 1:6; Heb 6:2.

92. See Gen 15:1; Dan 10:10, 12; Luke 1:30.

93. See Isa 41:4; 44:6; 48:12.

94. See our discussion of Rev 2:8; 22:13.

95. See Josh 3:10; Ps 42:2; Hos 1:10; Matt 16:16; Acts 14:15; Rom 9:26.

died on the cross and was buried in a tomb, the Messiah rose from the "dead" and now, like the Father and the Spirit, lives "forever and ever."[96]

Jesus' victory through his resurrection enables him to control "keys" of the twin, evil forces of "death" and Hades.[97] In ancient times, keys were symbols for power and control.[98] Also, death and Hades were considered places where people were bound and held captive. Jesus wants his followers to know that he alone has the supreme authority to free them from the shackles of death and give them eternal life.[99] Indeed, because the Redeemer exercises "all authority" (Matt 28:18), both in "heaven" and on "earth," he can commission his followers to be his faithful witnesses to a lost and dying world (v. 20).

The Messiah, in commissioning John to his witness-bearing, prophetic ministry, communicates specific instructions to him. Perhaps as an allusion to Revelation 1:4 and 8 in connection with the eternal Creator ("the one who is, and who was, and who is coming"), the apostle is directed to record the prophetic oracle he has seen, what is now taking place, and what will take place later (v. 19).

As previously noted, some specialists find in the above verse a possible threefold chronological division of John's treatise. According to this view, the promises and vision of the risen Messiah recorded in chapter 1 would be what the apostle had seen. Jesus' letters to the seven churches, which are recorded in chapters 2 and 3, could be what is taking place now. Moreover, all that is recorded in chapters 4 through 22 would be what will take place in the future.

A more likely possibility is that the clause "write what you have seen" (1:19) is the Savior's main directive and reiterates what he had commanded in verse 11. The remaining portion of verse 19, then, would give further details. Expressed another way, as John writes about all he has seen, he is to comment on what is now taking place and what will take place later.[100]

Whether Revelation 1:19 contains a basic outline of the book remains a matter of debate. What is clear, however, is that *each portion of the prophetic oracle deals with issues relating to the past, the present, and*

96. See Deut 32:40; Dan 4:34; 12:7; 1 En. 5:1; Sir 18:1.

97. The realm of the dead; the Greek equivalent of the Hebrew noun *Sheol*; see 1 En. 63:10; 4 Ezra 4:41; 8:53; Odes Sol. 15:9.

98. See Isa 22:22; Matt 16:19.

99. See John 5:25–29; 1 Cor 15:54–57; Heb 2:14–15.

100. See Isa 48:3–6; Dan 2:28–29, 45; 2 En. 39:2.

the future. From this observation, it is unmistakable that the treatise has continuing relevance for believers.

In verse 20, the Messiah explains the "mystery" behind the "seven stars" and the "seven gold lampstands." The Greek noun translated "mystery" does not refer to what is inexplicable or incomprehensible. Instead, it signifies divine truths that, in times past, had been hidden, but that now the Savior has made known.[101]

Jesus reveals that the "seven stars" represented the "messengers" of the "seven churches." The Greek noun rendered "messengers" could also be translated as "angels." The preceding observation has given rise to at least three different interpretations of what Jesus meant. The entities represent either earthly messengers,[102] heavenly emissaries,[103] or the prevailing spirit of each congregation.

The Savior also reveals that the "seven lampstands" represent the "seven churches." In Bible times, lampstands were used to provide light in dark areas. Additionally, in Scripture, light was often a metaphor for moral purity, truth, and wisdom. Given this information, the "lampstands" might symbolize the "seven churches" in their light-bearing or witness-bearing functions.[104] That the flaming menorahs are made of "gold" points to the priestly, regal nature of believers who testify about the Savior to a pagan and idolatrous world. They are to be his ambassadors to those who need to hear the saving message of the gospel.[105]

KEY THEOLOGICAL INSIGHTS

There are several theological truths worth reviewing from our discussion of Revelation 1, and they are all connected to the person and work of Christ. First, we note that *Jesus is the conveyor and the content of God's revelation* (vv. 1–2). Whatever themes and concepts might be addressed in the Apocalypse, the content inevitably points us to the Messiah. After all, he receives the revelation, communicates the revelation, and *is* the

101. See Dan 2:47; 1 En. 51:3; 4 Ezra 14:5; Matt 13:11; Rom 11:25; 16:25–26; 1 Cor 2:7; Eph 3:3–9; Col 1:26–27; 2 Thess 2:7; Rev 10:7; 17:5, 7. Also, in our discussion of Rev 10, see the table listing New Testament references to "mystery."

102. Such as the elders or pastors of the churches.

103. Such as guardian angels of the churches.

104. See Matt 5:14–16; Rev 2:1, 5; 11:4.

105. See 2 Cor 5:20.

revelation.[106] As John was a faithful witness of the living Word of God in his first advent,[107] so too in this opening chapter, we find the apostle entrusted with communicating the revelation about and from the Messiah in anticipation of his future, soon return.

Second, while the revelation Jesus communicates is the central theological motif of the Apocalypse, this is not to the detriment of the *all-encompassing presentation of the triune God.* John's greeting begins with a beautiful confession about the three persons of the Godhead, who are all involved in this unfolding cosmic drama. For instance, the Father is presented as the eternal one who bestows grace, peace, and blessing to those who are rightly related to his Son (v. 4). The sevenfold Spirit is depicted as being present before heaven's sacred throne and involved at every point of apocalyptic fulfillment (v. 4). Then, at the apex of John's presentation about the triune God, it is the Son's atoning work on the Cross which provides the centerpiece of revelation (vv. 5–6).[108]

Third, within and among all the components of eschatology[109] found in the Apocalypse, *the return of the Messiah is the central feature* (v. 7). Just as the first advent includes Jesus' virginal conception, his birth, his sinless life of obedience, his sacrificial death, his burial, his resurrection, and his ascension, so too the second advent incorporates all that surrounds the Messiah's return, including the period of great tribulation over all the earth, the defeat of all forces which are against our Lord, the earthly kingdom, the final rebellion, the final judgment, and the recreation of the new heavens and the new earth. Some of these components of eschatology present challenges to contemporary interpreters of the Apocalypse.[110] Despite the wide range of positions and debates, unity can be found in keeping the second coming of Jesus as the central focus of all end-time investigations.

106. See the discussion in Schreiner, *Revelation*, 69–70, concerning Jesus' unique, dual-role of both recipient and giver of "the Revelation."

107. See John 1:1–14.

108. See our discussion of Rev 5 for a portrayal of the Lamb as the centerpiece of divine disclosure.

109. Eschatology refers to the study of beliefs and theories concerning the end of the world, the judgment of the wicked, and the vindication of the upright, as well as the destiny of nations, history, and the universe.

110. Such as whether there is a rapture of the church before or during the great tribulation, the length of the tribulation period (seven years or an unspecified amount of time), the proper way to understand the thousand years of Rev 20, and the nature of the new heavens and new earth of ch. 21.

Fourth, the Messiah is depicted in a way that is previously unseen in Scripture.[111] In earlier portions of the biblical narrative, we encounter Christ victorious in his resurrection[112] and vindicated by the Father in the Son's ascension.[113] While we also find the preceding emphasis in the Apocalypse, these characteristics of the Messiah are not the complete, new vision John witnesses. *The new vision about Christ is the confluence and culmination of all aspects of his exaltation.* We encounter this vision in graphic description, knowing that this is the risen and exalted Jesus of Nazareth.[114] It is here, in the Apocalypse, that the apostle's portrayal of the glorified Son of Man is now replete with the understanding that this One is none other than the Messiah. He is shown to us as supremely royal, all-powerful, infinitely wise, and absolutely triumphant (vv. 12–16).

Fifth, along with the above breathtaking picture of the Messiah in his exaltation, we see *that Christ is with and for his church* (v. 13) *and that he addresses the Apocalypse to his church* (v. 11). The notion of Jesus as head of the church[115] takes on heightened significance and intensity, especially as he tells John to address the content of the Apocalypse to seven churches located in Asia Minor. We say more later about the doctrine of the church and how the Apocalypse informs us concerning it. Yet, for now, we note that Jesus, as our bridegroom,[116] desires that his bride know and understand his intensions for his church and, flowing out from there, his intentions for all of creation.

IMPORTANT MINISTRY IMPLICATIONS

Given the above vivid depiction of the Messiah, there are lessons we can apply to a diverse array of ministry circumstances, especially within Majority World contexts. First, those who undertake leadership roles in

111. For a detailed treatment of the Christology of the Apocalypse, see Lioy, *Revelation in Christological Focus.*

112. See 1 Cor 15:20–28, 54–57; Phil 2:9–11.

113. See Eph 4:8–10; Heb 1:3–4; 10:12; 12:2; 1 Pet 3:22; Rev 3:21.

114. Daniel's vision (Dan 10) is about the risen and exalted Messiah. Yet, we only know this because of later New Testament revelation. Daniel pictures something that is yet to come, whereas John depicts something both present and future (1:13–16; see also 19:10–12). Thus, what John witnessed was a fulfilled, and thereby a more complete, vision of Christ. For further reflection on this point, see Beale, *The Book of Revelation*, 152–70.

115. See Eph 5:23; Col 1:18.

116. See John 3:29.

local churches *must include the Apocalypse in the preaching and teaching schedule*. Regrettably, many avoid John's prophetic oracle because of its difficult-to-interpret content. As we noted earlier, end-time issues have given occasion for division within congregations and among church leaders. Be that as it may, Revelation should not be avoided but rather engaged, studied, preached, and even publicly read. This does not mean that the Apocalypse should dominate the teaching ministry of the church.[117] Yet this portion of Scripture advances and completes our understanding of Christ in his exaltation, especially by providing necessary instruction and benefit for us in our walk of faith.

Second, we must lead our churches with confidence that *victory is assured for those rightly aligned with the Messiah*. Currently, as we noted in the Introduction, many believers in Christ, especially in the Majority World, are experiencing suffering, persecution, and perhaps even seeing their own circumstances in the tribulation-like descriptions found in the Apocalypse. Yet here, Jesus is revealed to us as completely sovereign, powerful enough to execute the duties of his kingly office with righteousness and justice (vv. 12–16). All this is done in accordance with the Father's will and in partnership with the sevenfold Spirit (v. 4). Our congregants need to know that the Redeemer they serve is the victorious One. As we challenge parishioners to give their lives for Christ's sake, we can bring them this message of security and assurance of ultimate victory.[118]

Third, we are challenged to have the right vision of Christ, which is to *perceive the Messiah in his complete and all-encompassing nature*. This includes understanding that he has perfectly accomplished the Father's will through the power of the Spirit, has been granted lordship over all things, and now, as the divine Warrior, has been positioned for his glorious return.[119] We tend to emphasize the picture of Christ that fits a specific focus we have at a particular time. For instance, during Advent season, we reflect on Jesus' birth. He was born to bring hope into the world in fulfillment of the messages which the Old Testament prophets declared. Next, we focus on Christ's earthly life and ministry, in which

117. Contrary to those who have become so obsessed with clock-and-calendar speculations about the end-times that they have missed the central point of the message itself, namely, the exaltation of Christ.

118. See our discussion of Rev 22:5.

119. For a helpful treatment of "the glorified Christ" in Rev 1:13–16, see Osborne, *Revelation*, 88–93.

we encounter his teaching and preaching and his performing miracles, challenging the religious establishment, and setting forth the plan for his kingdom. Then, in the observance of Lord's Table during corporate worship, we see Christ on the cross, suffering and dying, paying the price for our sin, and taking upon himself, in our place, the righteous wrath of God. Finally, upon celebrating Christ's resurrection and ascension, we catch a glimpse of our Lord's victory and vindication, especially as he conquers death and returns to the Father in heaven to serve as our great High Priest.

Fourth, all the above portrayals of the Messiah convey fundamental truths that serve as the foundation of our faith and fidelity. Yet in this first chapter of the Apocalypse, *we encounter Christ as he stands ready for his return.* This vision fulfills and completes all others. Thus, we are called to align ourselves with the Son and to live before him in a worshipful, pleasing way. For unbelievers, this vision of Christ gives rise to fear, disdain, denial, and rejection.[120] Yet for true followers of the Messiah, this vision motivates us to announce his glory as the One who is strong to judge, condemn, save, and redeem.

VITAL MISSIONAL RAMIFICATIONS

The missional ramifications we present here stem from our consideration of the vivid descriptions of the exalted imagery of Jesus' majesty and authority. These serve to motivate believers to spread the message of repentance and salvation found in the gospel to all corners of the world.

First, as we noted in the Introduction, *the Apocalypse presents an urgency for Christ's followers to be on mission*, especially to proclaim the gospel to the lost, both near and far. The urgency can be seen in the opening paragraph of the first chapter, where John states that these events must "soon take place" (v. 1) and that the "time is near" (v. 3). Of course, this is not a guarantee that Jesus' return happens within our lifetime or even in the next several lifetimes.[121] What it does mean is that nothing further must happen for the events of the Apocalypse to unfold in rapid succession. We must be prepared for Jesus' return, and part of being

120. See our discussion of Rev 9:20–21, for example, where even amid intense suffering, the wicked still refuse to give up their sin and repent.

121. For more on how to understand "soon" and "near" in Rev 1:1, 3, see Schreiner, *Revelation*, 72–73.

prepared is living with the same urgency for the proclamation of the gospel that underlies the opening paragraph of John's treatise.[122]

Second, there is missional significance to what the apostle says in verse 3, namely, that we are blessed when we read the words of "this prophecy" aloud in corporate worship settings. Doing so demonstrates that *the Apocalypse is meant for public proclamation*, especially to reach those who either do not know about Christ or who do not know about his soon appearing. While most of today's people groups enjoy at least moderate levels of literacy and while many can read Scripture for themselves, there is value in the oral proclamation of John's unfolding cosmic drama.[123] Particularly in cultures that remain hearing-dominant, such as many people living in the Majority World, the public reading of the Apocalypse remains an effective way to reach the lost for Christ. Added to this cultural observation is the apostle's promise of blessing (or divine favor) to those who read and hear aloud his prophetic oracle. We can herald this promise to the unsaved and affirm its expectation, especially as we engage with and minister in cultures that have affinity toward oral presentation.

Third, there is missional significance to Christ's words in verse 18. He alone has the "keys" to "death and hell." This declaration, perhaps, engenders a genuine fear of the Son's judgment. Yet even more, it ought to create compassion in our hearts for those who are not united to Christ by faith in salvation. After all, this is a reality with implications for this life and consequences following death. Thus, *the Apocalypse is a wonderful missions motivator* for those who take up this challenge to proclaim the saving message about Christ. We go into all the world and confront every culture and religion, including those from our own context, that do not submit to the exclusivity of the Son as the only way to the Father.[124] While we can show a certain level of respect and appreciation for traditional religions, we must not affirm their legitimacy apart from a true recognition of Christ as Lord of the beginning and the end of all things.

122. See John 9:4, where the Son expresses a sense of urgency for the work the Father sent the Son to do.

123. See Rom 10:14.

124. See John 14:6.

Revelation 2

The Seven Churches of Revelation (Part 1)

LEARNING OBJECTIVES

- Understand the historical and cultural contexts of each church.
- Examine the strengths and weaknesses of each church.
- Explore the warnings and promises given to each church.
- Evaluate the significance of the symbols and metaphors used in the letters to the four churches.
- Discern the implications of each letter for the early church and for the church today.

CHAPTER SUMMARY

Revelation 2 contains a series of messages from Jesus to four of the seven churches in Asia Minor (Ephesus, Smyrna, Pergamum, and Thyatira). In these solemn pronouncements, Jesus commends the congregations for their positive qualities and actions. Also, aside from the congregation in Smyrna, Jesus addresses their shortcomings and warns about the potential consequences for failing to address these issues. Moreover, the chapter emphasizes the importance for believers to hear and heed Jesus' commands as well as his promise of eternal blessing to those who are victorious.

STUDY QUESTIONS

1. What are some common characteristics among Jesus' various commendations and censures of the churches he addressed?

2. How does the concept of "first love" apply to the church in Ephesus?
3. What is the significance of the "hidden manna" and the "white stone" mentioned in verse 17?
4. From the set of commendations and censures Jesus gives to the four churches, which ones would you say are characteristic of your own local church?
5. Using Jesus' instructions to the four churches, how might you, in your own local parish, positively influence people toward greater faith and faithfulness to the Savior?

CHAPTER OUTLINE

- Introductory observations
- The letter to the church in Ephesus (2:1–7)
- The letter to the church in Smyrna (2:8–11)
- The letter to the church in Pergamum (2:12–17)
- The letter to the church in Thyatira (2:18–29)
- Key theological insights
- Important ministry implications
- Vital missional ramifications

INTRODUCTORY OBSERVATIONS

Chapter 1 indicates that the original recipients of John's prophetic oracle were seven churches located in Asia Minor (v. 4). At the time the apostle authored his treatise, the Roman government was persecuting believers for refusing to participate in the imperial cult (v. 9). In the Savior's messages to the seven churches, he encourages and exhorts his followers to remain loyal to him, despite the oppression they were suffering. Chapters 2 and 3 reveal that these congregations—with their differing economic, social, and political circumstances—responded in different ways.

The Redeemer's authoritative, solemn pronouncements to the seven churches are a foretaste of the final judgment of believers at the end of the age. As previously noted, the literary backdrop is God's cosmic court of justice, which is presented in the form of a lawsuit.[1] The preceding is comparable to the Old Testament prophets' judgment oracles, along with the covenantal treaty structure found within the Hebrew sacred writings, particularly Deuteronomy. This is another example of typological fulfillment or prophetic foreshadowing in the Apocalypse.[2]

The Covenantal Treaty Structure of Deuteronomy		
Deuteronomy follows the literary format of ancient Near Eastern international treaties from the second millennium BC, making it primarily a covenant-renewal document. These sacred, binding agreements typically contain six essential elements:		
Literary Element	**Description**	**Biblical References**
Preamble	Introduces the overlord, including titles and attributes	Deut 1:1–5
Historical Prologue	Describes the historical relationship between the parties leading to the agreement	Deut 1:6—3:29
Covenantal Stipulations	Outlines the obligations imposed by the overlord and accepted by the vassal	Deut 4–26
Provision for Deposit	Specifies storing the treaty in the shrine and periodic public readings for the vassal nation	Deut 31:9–13, 24–26
List of Witnesses	Identifies deities as witnesses to the covenant, akin to legal contract witnesses	Deut 30:19; 31:19–22
Covenantal Curses and Blessings	Lists benefits for faithfulness and penalties for disloyalty to the agreement	Deut 28

The Covenantal Treaty Structure of Revelation 2–3		
Literary Element	**Description**	**Biblical References**
Introductory Messenger Formula	Opening identification of the speaker	Rev 2:1, 8, 12, 18; 3:1, 7, 14
Preamble	Description of the Messiah's introduction of himself	Rev 2:1, 8, 12, 18; 3:1, 7, 14

1. Hence, a cosmic trial motif.

2. For an extensive discussion of the covenantal treaty structure of Rev 2–3, see Graves, "Ancient Near Eastern Vassal Treaties." In his abstract, he states the following: "John's messages are hybrid prophetic oracles incorporating the covenant lawsuit message of the prophets, structured after the covenant schema found in the Torah. The treaty scheme was not some amorphous idea of treaty but the covenant treaty of the Torah found throughout the OT" (Old Testament).

The Covenantal Treaty Structure of Revelation 2–3		
Literary Element	**Description**	**Biblical References**
Prologue	The Messiah's relationship with each congregation, including commendation and censure	Ephesus: 2:2–4, 6 Smyrna: 2:9 Pergamum: 2:13–15 Thyatira: 2:19–24 Sardis: 3:1, 4 Philadelphia: 3:8–9 Laodicea: 3:15–17
Covenantal Stipulations	Commands and expectations given to each church	Ephesus: 2:5 Smyrna: 2:10 Pergamum: 2:16 Thyatira: 2:25 Sardis: 3:2–3 Philadelphia: 3:10–11 Laodicea: 3:18–20
Covenantal Curses	Warnings of judgment for disobedience	Ephesus: 2:5 Pergamum: 2:16 Thyatira: 2:22–25 Sardis: 3:2–3 Laodicea: 3:16, 18–19
Covenantal Blessings	Promises of reward for faithfulness	Ephesus: 2:7 Smyrna: 2:11 Pergamum: 2:17 Thyatira: 2:26–28 Sardis: 3:5 Philadelphia: 3:10, 12 Laodicea: 3:21
The Spirit's Witness	Concluding formula emphasizing the Spirit's testimony	Rev 2:7, 11, 17, 28; 3:6, 13, 22

To expand on the above observations, Scripture reveals that after Jesus' return, he will preside over the judgment of humankind.[3] This includes

3. See 1 Cor 4:5.

holding the members of Christ's body accountable for their deeds.[4] At that time, each believer's thoughts and actions will be scrutinized in the Lord's purifying and cleansing fires.[5] The issue will not be about the spiritual status of believers (whether they are saved or lost)[6] but will rather be about the bestowal of eternal rewards (or covenantal blessings).

The Son will conduct the investigative process in a fair and impartial manner. Whatever is done contrary to the Father's will will be regarded as worthless and will not be rewarded. In contrast, whatever is accomplished through the power of the Spirit will be regarded as worthy of praise and rewarded.[7]

Literary Structure of Jesus' Messages to the Seven Churches[8]		
Literary Element	**Description**	**Churches Addressed**
Command to Write	Directive to write a prophetic oracle (in letter form) to the messenger/angel of each congregation	All seven churches
Christ's Self-Description	Christ identifies himself with specific attributes relevant to each church.	All seven churches
Divine Knowledge	Christ demonstrates a comprehensive awareness of and insight into each congregation's condition.	All seven churches
Commendation	Praise for faithful actions, endurance, or spiritual qualities	Ephesus, Smyrna, Pergamum, Thyatira, Philadelphia
Censure	Rebuke or correction for failures, sins, or spiritual deficiencies	Ephesus, Pergamum, Thyatira, Sardis, Laodicea
Exhortation	Urgent appeal to persevere in faith or repent amid trials	All seven churches
Call to Heed	Summons for believers to listen and obey the Spirit's message	All seven churches
Promise to Overcomers	Assurance of eternal blessings for believers victorious through trials	All seven churches

4. See Rom 14:10–12; 2 Cor 5:10; Heb 4:12–13; 1 Pet 4:17–18.

5. See Deut 4:24; Heb 12:29; 2 Pet 3:7, 10–13.

6. See 1 Thess 1:10; 5:9–10; 2 Thess 2:13–14.

7. See 1 Cor 3:10–15.

8. Table adapted from information presented in Aune, *Revelation 1–5*, 119–24. Also, for a comprehensive examination regarding each of the seven letters to the seven churches in the Apocalypse (including their respective historical contexts and

THE LETTER TO THE CHURCH IN EPHESUS (2:1–7)

In Revelation 2:1, Jesus' opening, authoritative, and solemn pronouncement is to the "messenger" (or "angel") of the "church in Ephesus." During the first century AD, the city was past its prime, due in part to soil erosion and the silting of its harbor along the Casper River. Nevertheless, Ephesus was the site for the temple of Diana,[9] which was considered one of the seven wonders of the ancient world. Moreover, Ephesus had a marketplace and shrines to the goddess Roma[10] and to several Roman emperors[11] as well as gymnasiums, public baths, a large theater, and a library.

Against the preceding cultural and historical backdrop, the Messiah portrays himself as the one who grasps the "seven stars" (v. 1) in his "right hand." This imagery implies that he has firm and absolute control over the congregations and their leaders. The Savior also says that he walks among the "seven gold lampstands" or churches. This probably means that he is intimately familiar with their dealings, whether positive or negative, and that he uses these as the basis for his objective and equitable assessment.[12]

Jesus declares that he is fully aware of everything the believers in the Ephesian church have done, including their hard work and the way they have patiently endured difficulties. The Son also praises them for their intolerance of wicked individuals and false teachers (v. 2), including those who, though claiming to be "apostles,"[13] were outright "liars."

corresponding theological analysis), see Weima, *Sermons to the Seven Churches*.

9. Or Artemis, the goddess of the moon, childbirth, wild animals, and hunters.

10. A female personification of Rome and the Roman state.

11. Such as Claudius, Hadrian, and Severus.

12. See our discussion of Rev 1:20. As we noted in our analysis of vv. 12–20, this passage presents John's inaugural vision of the risen and glorified Messiah. By instructing the apostle to write to the seven churches, Jesus asserts his authority and all-knowing presence. Also, as the one who walks among the congregations, he oversees and assesses their spiritual condition.

13. Used in a general, rather than a restricted, technical sense.

Who Were the Apostles?		
In the New Testament, the term "apostle" refers to God's special envoys or messengers. Specialists debate whether apostleship was restricted to those who had seen Jesus with their own eyes or whether the office had a broader meaning.		
Apostle/Group	**Biblical References**	**Description**
The Twelve	Mark 6:30; Luke 6:13	The core group of disciples chosen by Jesus
Paul	Rom 1:1	Called himself an apostle, though not part of the Twelve
James	Gal 1:19	Likely James, the brother of Jesus
Barnabas	Acts 14:14	Paul's missionary colleague
Silas and Timothy	1 Thess 1:1; 2:6	Coworkers with Paul in ministry
Andronicus and Junia	Rom 16:7	Possibly apostles (interpretation debated)
Church Representatives	2 Cor 8:23; Phil 2:25	Itinerant messengers/representatives from churches

Veneration of the Roman emperor was prominent in Ephesus. The city was also a breeding ground for numerous pagan religions. Yet despite the incessant pressure felt by the believers in Ephesus to compromise their faith, they remained loyal to the "name" (v. 3) of Christ. Even amid dire circumstances, they did not weaken in their commitment to the truth about him.

Nonetheless, the Son raises a troubling concern. Despite the congregation's sound teaching and moral purity, they have abandoned their affection for the Son, his followers, and the redemptive implications of the gospel, including sacrificial service to others.[14] "Forsaken your first love" (v. 4) could also be rendered "you have lost the love you had at first."

Jesus exhorts the church in Ephesus always to recall and recognize the high "state" (v. 5) of devotion from which they had "fallen." He also urges the believers to "repent" from their atrophied spiritual condition.[15]

14. The Reformers of the sixteenth century understood the gospel as the joyous proclamation that sinners are justified by grace alone, through faith alone, and in Christ alone—entirely apart from human merit or works. This teaching stood in stark contrast to the prevailing medieval Catholic view, which held that righteousness before God required a cooperative process involving divine grace, the sacraments, and good works. For a more comprehensive explanation of the preceding observations, see Horton, "Reformation Gospel," 63–85.

15. In other words, to undergo a complete change in one's thoughts, attitudes, and actions.

Moreover, the congregants need to acknowledge their calloused (though doctrinally correct) hearts. Likewise, they need to turn away from their coldness and rekindle their original ardent commitment to the Savior and their fellow believers.[16]

If the church fails to "repent," Jesus warns that he will manifest his sacred presence among them as the risen and exalted Messiah. He also will "remove" their "lampstand from its place." The preceding could mean that the Son will blot out the Ephesian church as a Christian community. Another possibility is that the Savior will cause the congregation no longer to be effective in its light-bearing and witness-bearing ministry. Either option points to a potentially serious and lamentable consequence.

The Messiah follows up his admonition with another expression of approval for the way in which the Ephesian believers have detested the practices of the "Nicolaitans" (v. 6).[17] This attitude reflects the Lord's own hatred for what this heretical group is doing.[18] Some specialists think that a man named Nicholas was the original leader of the group and that he was a Jewish convert from Antioch who later became a Christian. Then he was appointed by the Jerusalem church as one of its seven deacons.[19] However, there is no certain connection between this individual and the one named in verse 6.

What remains clear is that the Nicolaitans had compromised their faith to justify their participation in the idolatrous practices lauded by Roman society. Likewise, members of the spurious group claimed their spiritual freedom allowed them to indulge in sexual immorality. Some specialists think similar groups in Pergamum and Thyatira were aligned with the Nicolaitans.[20]

The Son challenges members of the Ephesian congregation to "hear" (v. 7) and heed what the Spirit declares to the "churches" located in Asia Minor.[21] By remaining united to the Savior, their "first love" (v. 4), his followers, as the church militant, will be "victorious" (v. 7) as the church triumphant.

16. See John 13:34–35; 15:13; 1 John 3:14; 4:20.

17. A name that means "victory people."

18. As reflected in the group's priorities, ways of thinking, and actions.

19. See Acts 6:5.

20. See our discussion of Rev 2:15, 20.

21. See Isa 6:9–10; Jer 5:21; Ezek 3:27; 12:2; Matt 11:15; 13:9, 43; Mark 4:9, 23; Luke 8:8; 14:35.

Jesus promises his followers that he would give them the "privilege" to "eat" from the fruit of the life-giving "tree" in God's magnificent "garden." Genesis 2:9 is the first place that mentions the "tree of life."[22] In Revelation, it symbolizes the believers' unlimited access to the Lord's covenantal blessings.[23]

Similarly, the "paradise of God" (2:7) depicts heaven as an enclosed orchard filled with luscious, fruit-bearing trees. Here, the redeemed enjoyed an everlasting place of refuge, peace, and rest in the Lord's sacred presence.[24] All believers anticipate experiencing perpetual contentment and delight with the triune God in the eternal state.[25]

THE LETTER TO THE CHURCH IN SMYRNA (2:8–11)

The "church in Smyrna" (v. 8)[26] struggled against a heathen population that favored emperor worship. Smyrna was a seaport city on the west coast of Asia Minor. The locale had an excellent harbor, well-planned streets, and a fertile frontier. The city boasted of having a famous school of medicine and a theater that could seat 20,000. In the first century AD, around 200,000 people made their home in Smyrna.

Against the preceding cultural and historical backdrop, the Savior consoles his beleaguered followers by reminding them about their eternal rewards in heaven. He begins his authoritative and solemn pronouncement to the "messenger" (v. 8; or "angel") of the congregation with a reminder that he is the "First" and the "Last." By this, Jesus means that there is no one above or before him and that no one greater will come after him.[27] The Messiah also reminds his disciples about his sacrificial death at Calvary. Despite this seemingly tragic event, the Son rose from the "dead" and lives forevermore.[28]

Evidently, many believers in Smyrna came from the lower classes of society, including a considerable number of slaves. Additionally, these

22. See Prov 3:18; Apoc. Ab. 21:6–7; 1 En. 24:4—25:6; 60:7–8, 23; 61:12; 70:4; 2 En. 8:3; 9:1; 32:3; 4 Ezra 8:52; T. Levi 18:11.

23. See our discussion of Rev 22:2, 14.

24. See Ezek 28:13; 31:8–9; 2 En. 8:1–2; Jos. Asen. 16:14; Odes Sol. 11:16; 20:7; T. Dan 5:12.

25. See Luke 23:42–43; 2 Cor 12:4; Rev 21:3–4; 22:3–5.

26. Modern Izmir.

27. See Isa 44:6; 48:12; Rev 1:17; 22:13.

28. See our discussion of Rev 1:5, 18.

Christians had become the targets of attack from those who embraced falsehoods propagated by "Satan" (v. 9).[29] The Son refers to these antagonists as a "synagogue," perhaps to disparage their false, slanderous claims ("blasphemy") to be Torah-observant "Jews."

Here, John is not demonizing his fellow, ethnic Jews, but rather censuring those who deride the Messiah's true, loyal followers.[30] Indeed, Scripture reveals that Christians—namely, everyone worshiping and serving the Father by the power of the Spirit[31]—are the true "circumcision" (Phil 3:3) and the real people of God.[32] This includes both believing Jews and Gentiles.

It is possible that unruly crowds assaulted believers in Smyrna, destroyed their homes, stole their possessions, and brought spurious charges against them in the local Roman court. Despite the affliction and destitution experienced by the Christians in Smyrna, they were rich in faith.

The Redeemer's admonition in verse 10 ("do not fear anything") is intended not only to forewarn the Smyrnans about the hardship which is about to overtake them but also to foster their courage as they face various trials. Specifically, the "Devil"[33] will bring upon them imprisonment, persecution, and possibly "death." In turn, the commitment of these believers will be severely "tested," and they will be oppressed for "ten days," which is likely a symbolic reference to a limited time.[34]

Despite his followers' anguish, the Savior urges them to remain (or prove themselves) "faithful," even if it results in martyrdom. Furthermore, he will "crown"[35] them with eternal "life" as their reward. Then, once again, Jesus challenges his disciples to "hear" (v. 11) and heed what the "Spirit" declares to the "churches." Those who, as the church militant,

29. The adversary, archenemy, and opponent of believers; see Job 1:6–12; John 8:37, 44; Rev 2:13, 24; 3:9; 12:9; 20:2, 7.

30. The antagonists, by denouncing and spurning Christians, were also doing the same to their risen and glorified Savior. See the extensive discussion in Aune, *Revelation 1–5*, 162–65, 237. He argues that 2:9 and 3:9 refer to specific, localized conflicts between early Christians and certain Jewish groups in Smyrna and Philadelphia, rather than constituting a broad anti-Jewish polemic against Judaism as a whole.

31. See John 4:23–24.

32. See Rom 8:28–29; Gal 3:6—4:7.

33. The slanderer and accuser of believers; see Rev 12:9, 12; 20:2, 10.

34. See Dan 1:12, 14.

35. Referring to a victor's laurel wreath; see Apoc. El. 1:8; 2 Bar. 15:8; Jub. 16:30; T. Benj. 4:1; T. Job 4:3.

refuse to compromise their faith, even though it result in their sacrificing their lives, are "victorious" as the church triumphant.

The overcomers, by remaining united to the Messiah, will never experience the "second death."[36] This term refers to unending separation from the Creator as well as eternal torment in the "Lake of Fire."[37] Here, the first death would be the termination of a person's temporal, earthly existence. From a theological perspective, death represents the removal and exile of humans from God, themselves, others, creation, and life. Indeed, death is an anti-creational act resulting from sin.

The Holy Spirit in the Old Testament		
While it is commonly assumed that the Spirit's activity is primarily limited to the New Testament, the evidence shows the Spirit was equally active in the Old Testament era. The main difference was that the Spirit came upon selected individuals for specific purposes in the Old Testament, whereas the prophets anticipated and the New Testament fulfilled a broader outpouring of the Spirit to all believers.		
Spirit's Activity	**Biblical References**	**Description**
Creation	Gen 1:2	The Spirit participates in the creation of the world.
Divine Conviction	Gen 6:3	The Spirit strives with sinners, convicting them of their wrongdoing.
Empowerment for Service	Num 27:18; Judg 3:10; 1 Sam 10:9–10	The Spirit empowers judges and warriors for specific tasks and service.
Future Outpouring	Isa 32:15; 59:21; Joel 2:28–29	The prophets anticipate a time when God's Spirit will be given more broadly.
Holy Living	Ps 143:10	The Spirit stirs people to live in a holy and an upright manner.
Life-Giving	Ps 104:29–30	The Spirit imparts life to humanity and other creatures.
Messianic Promise	Isa 11:2	The Spirit of the Lord will rest upon the coming Messiah.
Pentecostal Fulfillment	John 14:16; Acts 2:14–21	The Old Testament hope is fulfilled on the day of Pentecost.
Prophetic Inspiration	2 Sam 23:2; Ezek 2:2	The Spirit gives prophetic utterance to selected individuals.

36. See our discussion of Rev 20:6, 14; 21:8.

37. See our discussion of Rev 20:6, 14; 21:8.

THE LETTER TO THE CHURCH IN PERGAMUM (2:12–17)

In 133 BC, Pergamum[38] became the capital of the Roman province of Asia and remained the seat of government for four centuries. The city was also the residence of nobles, scholars, and priests. Moreover, people assembled in Pergamum from distant places to venerate the following pagan deities: Asklepios, the god of healing;[39] Zeus, the chief of the Olympian gods; Dionysius, the god of vegetation; and Athena, the patron goddess of Athens. Likewise, Pergamum was a center for the veneration of Caesar.

In 29 BC, residents erected their first temple to Augustus for imperial worship. Likewise, the heathen living in "Pergamum" (v. 12) consistently pressured the believers residing there to renounce their faith. Pagans also labeled Christians who refused to participate as unpatriotic and subversive members of Roman society. At times, life must have seemed unbearable.

Against the preceding cultural and historical backdrop, Jesus, in an authoritative and solemn pronouncement, identifies himself to the "messenger" (or "angel") of the church in "Pergamum" as the divine Warrior who had the "sharp," two-edged "sword."[40] The implication is that not even the resident governor, who wields the blade of justice for Rome,[41] has greater power and authority than the Son to bring about retributive judgment.[42]

The references to where Satan has his "throne" (Rev 2:13), or imperial seat, and to Pergamum as the place where the devil lives were likely denoting the evil one's influence in the city.[43] Put differently, his power is great, for the locale is a site of political authority and heathen religious influence.

A believer named "Antipas" was martyred, perhaps by a crazed mob, for being a Christian. Yet, even then, the believers in Pergamum remain faithful to Jesus' sacred "name,"[44] especially by refusing to idolize pagan deities and participate in emperor veneration. Aside from what verse 13

38. Modern Bergama.
39. Represented in the form of a serpent.
40. See Wis 18:15–16; Rev 1:16; 19:15.
41. Latin, *ius gladii*, or the "right of the sword."
42. See Isa 11:4; 27:1; Matt 10:34; Rom 13:4.
43. T. Job 4:4.
44. Including all for which Jesus' name stood.

states, nothing more is known about Antipas. Possibly earlier in the reign of Domitian this "faithful witness"[45] was murdered.

Despite Jesus' praise for the unwavering commitment of the believers in Pergamum, his solemn pronouncement also carries a strong rebuke. Some in the church embraced the false teachings promoted by "Balaam" (v. 14) and the "Nicolaitans" (v. 15). Centuries earlier, Balaam encouraged the Israelites to eat food that had been "offered to idols" (v. 14),[46] as well as to indulge in "sexual immorality."[47] Both heretical groups encouraged becoming liberated from moral constraints, especially by taking part in pagan religious activities.

Jesus commands the frauds in Pergamum to "repent" (v. 16). Otherwise, the Son promises to come and do battle with them as the divine Warrior by using the "sword" coming out of his "mouth." This is a reference to his Word, which is the supreme expression of God's truth.[48]

Once again, Jesus challenges his disciples to "hear" (v. 17) and heed what the "Spirit" declares to the "churches." The Messiah pledges that those among his followers who refuse, as the church militant, to compromise with worldliness will receive some of the "hidden manna" to eat. The preceding reference recalls the manna which the Lord miraculously provided to the Israelites during their forty years of wandering in the wilderness.[49] The Son's eucharistic promise of eternal, spiritual provisions is especially fitting for those tempted to join in festivities in which food "offered to idols" (v. 14) is consumed.

Jesus also pledges to give those who are "victorious" (v. 17) as the church triumphant a "white stone." Among the many views concerning the significance of this object, two are worth mentioning. First, some specialists think that the object implies a vote of innocence and acquittal, in which the color white often symbolizes purity and righteousness.[50] Second, other specialists maintain that the object signifies tokens of

45. Like someone testifying in a court of law.

46. Especially at pagan banquets.

47. Particularly at heathen celebrations; see Num 22:1–2, 5; 25:1–4; 31:16; LAB 18:14; Jude 1:11.

48. See our discussion of Rev 19:13, 15.

49. See Exod 16:15, 31, 33, 35; Num 11:6, 7, 9; Deut 8:3, 16; Josh 5:12; Neh 9:20; Ps 78:24–25; 2 Bar. 6:5–10; 29:8; LAB 19:10; 2 Macc 2:4–8; Num. Rab. 11:2; Qoh. Rab. 1:9; John 6:31, 49; Heb 9:4.

50. Whereas a dark stone implies guilt and condemnation.

permission to enter the messianic banquet to be held at the end of the age.[51] In either case, the Father, based on the Son's atoning sacrifice, accepts repentant, believing sinners. Jesus enables them to triumph over sin,[52] to become the special object of God's favor, and to enjoy intimate communion with him.

The Redeemer states that he will write a "new name" (v. 17) on the "white stone," a "name" known only to the recipient of the object. Perhaps this "name" will serve to commend the life of devotion that Jesus' followers displayed. Their personalized "new name" serves as a reminder that they remained unwavering in their devotion to the Son, despite the intense opposition they faced from unbelievers.[53]

THE LETTER TO THE CHURCH IN THYATIRA (2:18–29)

The ancient town of "Thyatira" (v. 18)[54] had a diverse population. Some residents were aristocrats, while others were either skilled workers or slaves performing backbreaking labor. Moreover, in earlier times, Thyatira was a military outpost, standing like a sentinel to guard the entrance from the Caicus Valley to the Hermus Valley.

The city later became a center of trade and manufacturing. Indeed, ancient records indicate that a greater number of trade guilds existed in Thyatira than in any other city in western Asia Minor. Guild meetings often included immoral and idolatrous activities. Undoubtedly, these were a source of temptation for Christians who had to attend the gatherings.

The residents of Thyatira venerated the god Tyrimnos,[55] along with the Roman emperor. Supposedly, these two entities were sons of Zeus (mentioned earlier). Against the preceding cultural and historical backdrop, Jesus declares to the "messenger" (or "angel"; v. 18) of the Thyatiran congregation that he alone rules in majestic splendor as the true "Son of God."[56]

51. See our discussion of Rev 19:9.

52. By the power of the Spirit.

53. See Isa 62:2; 65:15.

54. Modern Akhisar.

55. Tyrimnos was a local Lydian deity, likely associated with solar imagery, who was at times, especially in the region of Thyatira, identified as or conflated with Apollo—the Greek god of music, poetry, archery, prophecy, medicine, and the sun.

56. A title appearing only here in the Apocalypse; see John 1:34; 48; 20:31.

Furthermore, in Jesus' authoritative and solemn pronouncement,[57] his description of himself as having "eyes" (2:18) like "fiery flames" and "feet" comparable to "polished bronze" repeats ideas appearing in 1:14 and 15.[58] These are also an allusion to Daniel's vision of the celestial messenger in 10:6 and 16. Jesus' flaming "eyes" (Rev 2:18) might suggest his power, as the divine Warrior, to peer through the lies that people spread.[59] Also, his "feet" like burnished "bronze" conveys the ideas of strength, stability, and splendor, as well as the ability to crush all forms of defiance against his rule.

The Savior commends the Thyatiran church for its "love" (v. 19), "faith" (including faithfulness), caring ministry to others, and steadfast patience. He is mindful not only of their good "works" but also of the increase in their godly virtues. Expressed differently, Jesus recognizes that they are doing more now than when they first trusted in him.

Next, the Son censures the believers in Thyatira for allowing (v. 20)[60] a woman named "Jezebel" to mislead some of Jesus' bondservants.[61] They were erroneously taught that they could participate in "sexual immorality" as well as consume food sacrificed to "idols."[62] One view is that "Jezebel" (Rev 2:20) is the woman's real name. A more likely option is that it is the name given to her to identify her with the notorious wife of Ahab, the ninth-century BC king of Israel. This wicked queen encouraged God's people to venerate Baal, the supreme deity of the Canaanites.[63]

The infamous woman in the Thyatiran church calls herself a "prophetess," for she wanted others to think that she, as a representative of God, spoke the truth. In reality, "Jezebel" is a spiritual fraud. Jesus condemns

57. The longest of the seven letters in Revelation.

58. See our discussion of Rev 19:12.

59. See our discussion of Rev 19:12.

60. Literally to permit or consent to.

61. See in our Introduction the discussion about the travailing woman of Rev 12 and the harlotrous woman of ch. 17. Also, see the extensive discussion of Beale, *The Book of Revelation*, 260–63. He clarifies that the gendered imagery in Rev 2:20 (and related passages) should not be interpreted as misogynistic. After all, the prophetic oracle employs symbolic figures to convey spiritual and moral truths, not to denigrate women as a class. Furthermore, as shown in our accompanying table below on regenerate women in the early church, Scripture affirms the equal dignity of all people before God (Gen 1:27; 5:2; Joel 2:29; Gal 3:28).

62. See Acts 15:29; 1 Cor 8:1.

63. See 1 Kgs 16:31–32; 18:4; 19:1–2; 21:1–26; 2 Kgs 9:22, 30–37.

this woman for deceiving his followers with her heretical teaching. Indeed, the Son has given "Jezebel" sufficient opportunity to "repent" (v. 21); yet, she refuses to abandon her harlotries and idolatries. The idiomatic expression translated "throw her onto a bed" (v. 22) refers to a place of severe illness and distress. Such a terrible fate awaits this Jezebel-like figure along with those who committed "adultery" with her.

Though Jezebel's time of repentance has passed, those who adhere to her apostate teachings still have a chance to abandon their evil ways. Yet if her spiritual offspring refuse to "repent," the Son promises that "death" (v. 23), perhaps due to a debilitating and contagious plague, will be the result of their sickness.

Evidently, Jezebel has made a name for herself among the believers living in nearby cities. When the Messiah, as the divine Warrior, punishes this wicked woman and her disciples, other "churches" will realize that he probes the "hearts and minds" of all people.[64] Likewise, the Savior repays everyone according to what their actions deserve.[65]

Next, Jesus speaks to the other members of the Thyatiran congregation. They have not adopted the errant teachings of the false "prophetess" (v. 20). Also, they refuse to learn and adopt what some allege to be the "deep" (v. 24) secrets originating from Satan.

While Jezebel's followers imagine she is teaching them mysterious, profound, and wonderful truths from God, they are, in fact, embracing demonic doctrines and practices.[66] A less likely view is that Jezebel urges believers to enter the devil's stronghold, encounter the full force of evil, and learn from experience how God's grace could sustain them. For instance, by participating in heathen guild feasts, Christians allegedly could prove that Satan has no power over them.

In either case, the Son admonishes the untainted believers in Thyatira to refrain from idolatry and immorality. Also, he pledges not to add any further burdens on them than to remain faithful to him and their fellow believers. Accordingly, Jesus urges his followers to hold firmly to the teaching they have received from him (v. 25). Eventually, he will return for them and bring them to their heavenly home. In the meantime, as the church militant, they are to stand their ground and resist every new assault from the enemy.

64. Including everyone's thoughts, feelings, and intentions.

65. See Pss 7:9; 62:12; 139:1–2, 23; Jer 11:20; 17:10; Matt 16:27; Rom 2:6; 8:27; Heb 4:12.

66. See 1 En. 65:6.

The Savior makes two promises to those who are "victorious" (v. 26). These are disciples who continue to submit to his will until the "end" of their earthly sojourn. First, to such overcomers, as the church triumphant, Jesus pledges to give "authority over the nations." By remaining in union with the Savior and faithful to his teachings, believers will be "victorious" over all enticements to sin and validate Jesus' decision to let them share in his rule over the Gentiles.[67]

Verse 27 is a loose citation of Psalm 2:9.[68] Jesus' "rule" (Rev 2:27) is characterized as a royal scepter made of "iron." The imagery is of a shepherd using a metal "staff" to ward off attacks from savage beasts.[69] Shattered "clay pots" further emphasize the absolute power the Lord will use to defeat his foes. Ultimately, the Son's "authority" (v. 28) comes from his heavenly "Father."[70]

The Messiah's second pledge is to give his faithful, triumphant disciples the "morning star." Four interpretations of this enigmatic phrase are worth mentioning. It could be a reference to the Son,[71] who, as the divine Warrior, ensures that a new day of salvation will dawn.[72] Other options include the Holy Spirit (especially in guiding and illuminating the path of salvation), the immortality of the redeemed (particularly the eternal life and glory that await believers in God's sacred presence),[73] or the resurrection of the righteous at the end of the age (including the promise of a new beginning and ultimate victory over death). In any case, Jesus once again exhorts his children to "hear" (v. 29) and heed what the "Spirit" declares to the seven "churches."

The Significance of Regenerate Women in the Early Church	
Assist other church leaders, such as Paul (including the delivery of his letters to designated congregations)	Rom 16:2
Host congregational meetings in their homes	1 Cor 16:19
Imprisoned for the faith with other believers, such as Paul	Rom 16:7

67. See Ps 149:5–9; Isa 60:14; Dan 7:14, 18, 27; Matt 5:5; 19:28; Luke 22:30; 1 Cor 6:2–3; 2 Tim 2:11; Rev 1:6; 3:21; 5:10; 20:4, 6.

68. Based on the Septuagint rendering.

69. See 1 En. 90:18; Pss. Sol. 17:23–24.

70. See Ps 2:7.

71. Based on Rev 22:16, which in turn alludes to Num 24:17.

72. See Jos. Asen. 14:1; T. Jud. 24:1; T. Levi 18:3.

73. See Dan 12:13.

Minister in the church (possibly as deacons)	Rom 16:1
Prominent and highly respected among the apostles	Rom 16:7
Prophesy	Acts 21:9
Share in Paul's struggle to proclaim the gospel to the lost	Phil 4:2–3
Show hospitality to itinerant missionary-evangelists	Acts 16:14–15, 40
Teach, disciple, and mentor new converts to the faith	Acts 18:24–28
The first to reach the empty tomb and announce Jesus' resurrection	Matt 28:1–10; Mark 16:1–8; Luke 23:55—24:10; John 20:1–2, 11–18

KEY THEOLOGICAL INSIGHTS

The theological highlights of Revelation 2 center on Christ and his church. These emphases clarify the profound relationship between Jesus' lordship over and pastoral guidance of his beleaguered followers.

First, we see that the *Messiah possesses and executes divine authority to render judgment and pronounce covenantal blessings and curses.* On the one hand, Jesus has always possessed this authority. He is God incarnate,[74] the agent of creation,[75] the King of kings and Lord of lords.[76] He has authority to judge simply because he is the Son of God. Yet on the other hand, we see throughout Jesus' life that he did nothing apart from the Father's plan and that the Son executed the Father's plan in the power of the Holy Spirit.[77] Everything Jesus did was according to the Father's will.[78] Then, after Jesus' resurrection and prior to his ascension, he proclaimed that all authority throughout the entire universe was his.[79]

Second, in addition to the Messiah's supreme authority, *he judges his followers with all-knowing insight.* For instance, Jesus repeatedly tells the churches in Asia Minor, "I know . . ." (2:2, 9, 13, 19). Because Christ is the

74. See Ps 2:7; Isa 9:6–7; Mic 5:2; Matt 1:23; John 1:14.

75. See John 1:3; Col 1:16–17; Heb 1:4.

76. See our discussion of Rev 17:14; 19:16.

77. See Matt 3:16; Matt 12:18; Luke 4:21 (as fulfillment of Isa 61:1–2); John 3:34; Acts 10:38.

78. See John 14:10, 24, 31; 15:10; 17:4.

79. See Matt 28:18; Acts 1:7–8.

head of the church, which is his spiritual body, he has full knowledge of her deeds.[80] Jesus has direct and unlimited experience with every local manifestation of his church. There is nothing hidden from his sight. He can see what is happening concerning his church both externally and internally. We must not think we can hide or cover ourselves by trying to keep our sins a secret[81] or by masking our inward condition with external "whitewashing."[82]

Third, flowing from the notion of Jesus' authority and all-knowing insight is the fact that the *Messiah is sovereign over and within his church.* His ability to bestow blessings and pronounce curses, even to the point of removing the lampstand of those congregations that continue in non-repentance, shows that he is in complete and absolute control (v. 5). He holds the stars in his right hand (v. 1); he is the conqueror of death (v. 8); he brandishes a double-edged sword with which to strike (vv. 12, 16); and he is fixed in stability and steadiness to carry out his purposes (v. 18). In all this, the church still bears responsibility and culpability for her actions, thoughts, and attitudes. While the Son maintains all authority, knowledge, and power, he also obligates us to obey his commands in accordance with the Father's will.

Fourth, having considered the Messiah's complete authority, knowledge, and sovereignty, we now examine *how* he executes his judgment. Specifically, his *judgment is impartial.* The Messiah does not favor one faith community over another. He does not discriminate based on ethnicity, geographical location, or socioeconomic status. This truth can encourage Christians in Majority World contexts, especially those who have been influenced to think that, to be evaluated positively, they must look more like the developed and institutional churches characteristic of Christianity in the Global North. On the contrary, the impartiality of our Savior assures that his evaluation of the church is unbiased.[83]

Fifth, *while the truth about the Messiah's impartiality is an encouragement, it is also a warning.* When the Son comes to judge his church,

80. See Rom 12:4; 1 Cor 12:12–26; Eph 1:22; 4:12–16.

81. Such as when Adam and Eve attempted to hide from God by covering themselves with fig leaves in the garden of Eden after their fall into sin (Gen 3:7–8); see also Luke 12:1–4.

82. See Matt 23:27–28.

83. See Mark 12:41–44 and Luke 21:1–4, where Jesus assessed the value of the widow's offering (about 1/64 of a day's wage) based on his ethical standards and not those of fallen, pagan humanity. Jesus commended the widow for giving all that she had from her impoverished condition, which demonstrated her sacrificial heart.

he does so with an objective standard that does not consider power or privilege from a worldly perspective. Nor does the Messiah's standard capitulate to the excuses we might offer. Whether we have prospered or have gone without, whether we have faced or escaped persecution, whether we have had limited or unlimited resources, we are evaluated according to Jesus' ethical standard and not ours.[84] This truth should bring a sobering consideration of how we live in service to our Lord. We are evaluated objectively, according to the Messiah's righteous expectations of us.

Sixth, the *Messiah's judgment is in accordance with his character*. The one who moves freely and sovereignly among the lampstands has authority and power to remove them (vv. 1, 5). He who conquers death, as well as Satan and sin, and now lives is also the one who has the power to grant eternal life to the faithful (vv. 8, 10). The one who bears the double-edged sword is willing to use it to wage war against those who pollute the church with their immorality and doctrinal deviance (vv. 12, 16). The one who has eyes like blazing flames and feet like polished bronze, symbolizing omniscience, royalty, and authority, is the one who uses all of this to render covenantal blessings and curses according to the deeds done by those in his church (vv. 18, 22–23, 26–27). The character of the Messiah relates directly to how he brings judgment, whether it results in blessings or curses.

IMPORTANT MINISTRY IMPLICATIONS

There are at least four implications for ministry leaders arising from this chapter, corresponding to the letters written to each church, as follows. First, *church leaders must be careful in their ministry endeavors to emphasize both doctrinal fidelity and affection for Jesus*. The Ephesian church was lauded for her faithfulness to sound doctrine, yet she was sharply rebuked and warned over abandoning her "first love." The Messiah calls churches to have both, not either one or the other.[85] Some pastors are strong in expositional preaching and teaching, exceptional in their academic abilities, and true to the faith "delivered to the saints once and for all."[86] Yet they lack a true affection for the Lord and a passion for the

84. See 2 Cor 10:12.

85. See 1 Tim 4:16.

86. See Jude 1:3.

edification of their flock. We must be careful in church leadership not to neglect our own relationship with Jesus and our need to grow in ongoing affection for him, and we must then pass along our true fervent affection to those under our pastoral care.

Second, *church leaders should guide their congregation to remain steadfast in faith, even amid challenging circumstances.* The believers in Smyrna had many excuses at their disposal to apostatize, yet they are lauded for their faithfulness in and through the trouble they faced. Even beyond this, they are called to persevere,[87] knowing that further persecution and martyrdom await them. We need to exemplify this type of courageous, persistent faithfulness and call other believers to the same disposition, regardless of the enemies of the faith around us. We must also remind our parishioners that the crown of life awaits those who are faithful until death. In church contexts where there is suffering and persecution, the call to the saints must be a summons to endure rather than to avoid the anguish to come. This call is seen in one such Majority World setting where church leaders, under religious persecution, have asked their Global North ministry partners *not* to pray for an end to persecution.[88]

Third, *congregational leaders must struggle for doctrinal integrity within the church.* We might be tempted to think that our love for Christ is more important than doctrinal purity. After all, Jesus is so disapproving of the Ephesians' departure from their first love that he threatens to remove them altogether from among his witnesses! It is also understandable when congregational leaders do not want to get preoccupied with the fine points of doctrine, especially at the expense of zealous passion.[89] Yet as Christianity in the Global North becomes known for its (sometimes) cold, heartless religiosity, those in Majority World contexts often point to the passion and fervor that characterize the present expansion of Christianity in their regions. While this observation might be valid, it

87. For an insightful description of "perseverance" as a key theme in the Apocalypse, see Osborne, *Revelation*, 42–46.

88. Though specific details need to remain anonymous, the statement made from the persecuted brothers and sisters in Christ was that those of us praying for an end to persecution were actually "hurting" them because we were asking God to take away the very thing he was using to build his church.

89. This is often an argument made by leaders of experience-based churches who see a "coldness" in the practice of more "word-based" churches. While all churches should avoid such "coldness" and maintain genuine vitality, this priority must not come at the expense of theological depth and rigor.

does not negate the fact that doctrine *does* matter. Additionally, while we must not allow our faith to collapse into a thoughtless, rigid routine, we must also stand for biblical truth.

Fourth, along with the struggle for doctrinal purity within the church, so too *congregational leaders must extol the virtues of sexual purity within our parishes*. Christ warned the church in Pergamum that he would fight against them for their idolatrous sexual expression. Likewise, he warned the church in Thyatira about a death blow to Jezebel's offspring due to the tolerance of sexual immorality within the congregation. These stark and sobering warnings should motivate congregational leaders to watch their own moral behavior and to exhort those under their pastoral care to do the same. Regardless of cultural norms and expectations that might endorse promiscuity, we must not capitulate to cultural pressure to tolerate promiscuous behavior among our parishioners.[90]

Significant examples of the above, from a Majority World perspective, are the issues of polygamy and premarital sex. In many cultures, polygamy is normal, and perhaps even celebrated, as a symbol of God's blessings and favor. Furthermore, the pressure on young people to have sexual relations before marriage, often to *prove* their manhood or womanhood, is intense.[91] Admittedly, congregational leaders face tremendous challenges in these areas, both personally and corporately. These issues can feel like losing battles, particularly as more and more people, even believers, give in to such self-destructive choices. Yet the Messiah expects the church to live in ethical purity while enduring pressures from the surrounding world and overcoming them through the power of the Spirit.[92]

VITAL MISSIONAL RAMIFICATIONS

The above ministry implications are characterized by an internal focus, especially as congregational leaders are encouraged to shepherd God's flock with the promises and warnings of these letters in mind. Turning

90. See 1 Cor 5 and note Paul's pointed, harsh rebuke of the Corinthians for their tolerance of such immoral conduct in the church.

91. Of course, sexual temptation and pressure is everywhere, in all cultures and among all people. Yet particularly in Majority World contexts (for example, many in Africa and Asia), the pressure to indulge in this activity is often justified as a demonstration of being blessed by God with the ability to reproduce.

92. See 1 Cor 6:18–20.

now to a more outward, missional focus, we find helpful the following principles to guide us in our evangelistic efforts.

First, *spiritual fervor, while always present in the beginning, will tend to erode over time.* As the lost come to faith in Christ, they are initially filled with passion, emotion, and strong desires to learn and grow in their spiritual walk. Many of them experience a wonderful, dramatic change of life. Also, the corresponding affections that accompany this change are faith-affirming. Yet, over time, that fervor tends to diminish. The challenge for those in missionary contexts is not to allow our converts to become dependent on feelings and emotions alone but rather to encourage them to maintain affection for Jesus and his church. For this reason, evangelism must be coupled with discipleship, where the missionary walks through the journey of the Christian life with those who come to saving faith.[93]

Second, *we must remember that God can use persecution*[94] *to grow or strengthen the church.* Those living and working in missional settings need to realize that the Creator uses tribulation to deepen the commitment of his children. Further, Jesus offers himself as the premier example of endurance to persevere through the Spirit's abiding presence and power. In sharp contrast, the prosperity gospel in all its insidious forms is not the solution. We do not serve the church or the world by perverting the true gospel to win large numbers of converts and gather large crowds of naïve followers. True believers are expected to persevere in and endure difficult circumstances, and the Messiah promises to reward them eternally for their faithfulness (vv. 7, 10–11, 17, 26–29). To be sure, we can pray that those persecuting God's people will be stopped. Yet perhaps the greater prayer and possibly the most important path of discipleship is to ask God to deepen and strengthen the faith of Jesus' followers, especially those who are facing persecution for the sake of his name.

Third, *missionaries must not capitulate to an unbiblical, syncretistic*[95] *approach to bring the gospel to the lost.* On the one hand, cultural sensitivity is essential, and a gracious approach to cross-cultural gospel ministry

93. Note Jesus' directive in the Great Commission that his followers were to teach new "disciples" to "keep all the instructions" he had given (Matt 28:18–20).

94. See Keener, *Revelation*, 120–21, for a moving description of having to endure persecution for the gospel.

95. Syncretism is the merging of different belief systems, religious practices, cultural traditions, or philosophical ideas into a new unified whole. It happens when distinct traditions or elements are combined to form a synthesis that incorporates elements from each original source.

is appropriate. Yet, on the other hand, the true teaching of Christ, mediated by the Spirit through the Word, stands above any cultural sensitivities or preferences we might encounter. Today, many are rehearsing the missteps and abuses committed by missionaries in the past (or even present) toward Majority World cultures. To be sure, learning from these past mistakes and abuses is necessary, especially as the hub of missionary activity shifts from the Global North to the Majority World.[96] Nonetheless, the challenge to those involved in missional activity, from either the Majority World or Global North contexts, is neither to destroy culture nor capitulate to it. At one point or another, the clear teaching of God's Word challenges and condemns all pagan, secular cultures. Therefore, when we consider the command to maintain both doctrinal integrity and moral purity in the church, we must also take this same concern to the mission field, regardless of what cultural barriers or sensitivities we may face.

96. Note the examples we give in the Introduction about recent attempts to critique and correct the missteps of efforts made by missionaries from the Global North, particularly in Africa and Asia.

Revelation 3

The Seven Churches of Revelation (Part 2)

LEARNING OBJECTIVES

- Understand the historical and cultural contexts of each church.
- Examine the strengths and weaknesses of each church.
- Explore the warnings and promises given to each church.
- Evaluate the significance of the symbols and metaphors used in the letters to the three churches.
- Discern the implications of each letter for the early church and for the church today.

CHAPTER SUMMARY

As a continuation of Revelation 2, chapter 3 contains a series of messages from Christ to three of the seven churches in Asia Minor (Sardis, Philadelphia, and Laodicea). Aside from Laodicea, Jesus' solemn pronouncements to the congregations in Sardis and Philadelphia record his commendation for their positive qualities and actions. Also, aside from the congregation in Philadelphia, the Messiah addresses the other two churches' shortcomings and warns them about the potential consequences for failing to address these issues. Moreover, the chapter stresses the need for Jesus' followers to hear and heed his commands and his promise of eternal blessing to those who are victorious.

STUDY QUESTIONS

1. In what ways does the historical and cultural background of each church aid in understanding how the Messiah addresses the three congregations?
2. What is the significance of Jesus' reference to the "Book of Life" (v. 5) for the believers in the church at Sardis?
3. What do you think Jesus means when he censures the church at Laodicea for being neither "cold" (v. 15) nor "hot"?
4. How do you think verse 20 relates to the work of missionary outreach in Majority World cultural contexts?
5. In one sentence, how might you summarize the overall thrust of Jesus' commendations and censures to the seven churches?

CHAPTER OUTLINE

- The letter to the church in Sardis (3:1–6)
- The letter to the church in Philadelphia (3:7–13)
- The letter to the church in Laodicea (3:14–22)
- Key theological insights
- Important ministry implications
- Vital missional ramifications

THE LETTER TO THE CHURCH IN SARDIS (3:1–6)

Sardis[1] was located northeast of Ephesus in the Hermus River valley. The older section of Sardis was built on the rock ridge of Mount Tmolus. An impressive acropolis overlooked this city with its massive temple to Artemis.[2] The town also had a gymnasium and a Jewish synagogue. Early on, residents of Sardis discovered gold and silver in the sandy bed of the nearby Pactolus River. The government soon issued gold and silver coinage, and this made the city affluent. In fact, some specialists think the earliest coins were minted around 700 BC.

1. Modern Sart.
2. Or Diana, the goddess of the moon, childbirth, wild animals, and hunters.

On the surface, the church in "Sardis" (v. 1) seems to be religious and to perform virtuous deeds. Yet against the preceding cultural and historical backdrop, Jesus reveals in his authoritative and solemn pronouncement to the "messenger" (or "angel") that the congregants are inwardly corrupt. Jesus also reminds the congregants at Sardis that he holds the sevenfold Spirit of God along with the "seven stars." As in 1:4, 4:5, and 5:6, the phrase rendered, "seven spirits," symbolizes the manifold presence and power of the Holy Spirit. Likewise, as in 1:20, the "seven stars" are the "messengers" (or "angels") of the "seven churches."

The city of Sardis rested on its past reputation without doing anything noteworthy in the present. Jesus declares that the church suffers from the same problem. Specifically, the believers might have gone through the motions of faith, yet despite their "reputation" (literally "name") for being spiritually "alive," they are actually "dead."

Tragically, the pious deeds of the believers in Sardis are incomplete, since they fall short of what the Creator expected (v. 2). Metaphorically speaking, the church is like a comatose human body nearing the point of death. Yet because the Savior loves the members of this congregation, he urges them to revitalize the dying vestiges of their faith ("wake up").[3] Jesus warns that they needed to act quickly, for even what little vitality remains is about to expire.

This congregation has no excuse for its deplorable condition. After all, these believers know the truth about the Messiah, along with once believing and obeying the saving message about him. Consequently, the Savior urges the believers in Sardis to return to the basics of their faith ("what you received and heard"; v. 3). The outcome would be abandoning their sinful ways ("repent") and holding firmly to the gospel.

At first glance, the fortress of Sardis seemed impregnable. However, on at least two occasions,[4] invaders were able to capture the citadel by surprise. The Son warns that a similar experience awaits the church in Sardis. If the believers fail to heed his counsel by waking up from their stupor, he, as the divine Warrior, will bring judgment (or covenantal curses) on them suddenly, just as a "thief" would strike unexpectedly in the night.[5]

The major industry of Sardis was dyeing woolen garments. Jesus might be alluding to this when he describes most believers in the city

3. See Rom 13:11; 1 Cor 16:13.

4. In 546 and 214 BC, respectively.

5. See Matt 24:42–44; Luke 12:39; 1 Thess 5:2; 2 Pet 3:10; Rev 16:15.

as wearing "clothes" (v. 4) that have been soiled by evil deeds, such as idolatry and immorality. The Messiah also describes a minority of believers (literally a "few names") as "worthy" of wearing "white" garments (or robes), which symbolize virtue, integrity, and triumph over evil.[6] Because they remained faithful to him, he will allow them to enjoy the sweet fellowship of his sacred presence.

In verse 5, the Savior declares that any of his followers who are "victorious"[7] will also be adorned in "white clothing." Despite whatever hardships they had to endure (as the church militant), they will eternally abide with the Son in purity and be clothed with his righteousness (as the church triumphant).

Moreover, Jesus assures the believers in Sardis that he will never "erase" (or expunge) from the "Book of Life" the names of his devoted disciples.[8] Evidently, the Savior is referring to a heavenly list containing the names of his followers. Jesus is not ashamed to claim openly these "victorious" believers as his own ("acknowledge his name") in the presence of his "Father," along with the "angels" in heaven.[9]

Once more, the Messiah directs his attention to those who have a heart open to understand what he declares. They are to "hear" (v. 6) and heed what the Spirit reveals to the seven "churches."

The Sevenfold Spirit in the Apocalypse		
Role/Function	**Description**	**Biblical References**
Community Witness	Authorizes and empowers the testimony of John's faith community	22:17
Divine Nature	All-knowing	1:4; 3:1; 4:5; 5:6
End-Time Ministry	Active in bringing about the Father's judgments on the wicked while sustaining the faithful	Throughout the Apocalypse
Member of the Trinity	Equal and active participant in the triune Godhead, working alongside the Father and Son	1:4, 10; 2:7, 11, 17, 29; 3:1, 6, 13, 22; 4:2, 5; 5:6; 14:13; 17:3; 21:10; 22:6, 17
Prophetic Inspiration	Prompts and guides John's end-time prophetic oracle	1:10; 2:7, 11, 17, 29; 3:6, 13, 22; 22:6–7, 9–10, 16, 18–19

6. See 1 En. 62:15–16; 90:32; 2 En. 22:8–9; 4 Ezra 2:39–40.

7. By remaining united to the Son through faith.

8. See Exod 32:32–34; Ps 69:28; Isa 4:3; Dan 12:1; Mal 3:16; Apoc. Zeph. 3:7; 9:2; 2 Bar. 24:1; 1 En. 47:3; 89:68; 108:3; 2 En 52:15; 3 En 18:24; Jos. Asen. 15:4; Jub. 30:20, 22; 36:10; 104:1; Luke 10:20; Heb 12:23; Phil 4:3; Rev 13:8; 17:8; 20:12, 15; 21:27.

9. See Matt 10:32; Mark 8:38; Luke 9:26; 12:8; 1 John 2:23.

THE LETTER TO THE CHURCH IN PHILADELPHIA (3:7–13)

Philadelphia[10] occupied a strategic position between the coast and the interior of Asia Minor. Because of this, the ancients thought of the city as the guardian of the gateway to the plateau beyond. Moreover, the region around Philadelphia was volcanic, and the entire area was subject to earthquakes. For example, in AD 17, an earthquake destroyed this outpost of Hellenic culture. After the residents of Philadelphia rebuilt their city with help from Rome, the town became part of the empire.

The believers in the church at "Philadelphia" (v. 7) struggle to cope with overwhelming circumstances, which Satan exploits to undermine their faith. Against the preceding cultural and historical backdrop, the Son, in his authoritative and solemn pronouncement to the "messenger" (or "angel") of the congregation, encourages his followers to remain unwavering in their commitment and promises to bring them through their ordeal.

Furthermore, in Jesus' message to the church in Philadelphia, he declares himself to be the "Holy One" (v. 7) as well as "true." By this, the Savior means that he is absolutely pure and infinitely greater than and entirely set apart from anything in fallen creation. Also, he is genuine, upright, and faithful in his character.[11]

The Messiah tells his followers that he holds the "key of David." In ancient times, keys symbolized authority. Jesus is saying that he, the one who also holds the "keys" (1:18) of "death" and Hades, is both sovereign and supreme. The reference to "David" (3:7) places the entire matter within an imperial, messianic context. The Redeemer possesses the undisputed right to the Davidic royal line.[12] Therefore, when the Son opens the door to his eternal kingdom, no one can shut it. Likewise, when he closes the door, no one can open it.[13]

The Messiah intimately knows the deeds of the small and beleaguered church in Philadelphia. Also, he has placed an "open door" (v. 8) for them to enter his everlasting sacred realm.[14] According to other views, the reference to an "open door" is an opportunity for believers to

10. Modern Alashehir.

11. See Isa 1:4; 37:23; 40:25; Hab 3:3; 1 En. 1:2–3; 10:1; 14:1; 25:3; 37:2; 84:1; 93:11; Mark 1:24; Luke 1:35; 4:34; John 6:69; Acts 3:14; 1 John 2:20; 1 Clem. 23:5.

12. See Isa 22:22; Matt 1:1, 17; Luke 1:32; 3:31; Rev 5:5; 22:16.

13. See Job 12:14; Odes Sol. 17:9, 11; 42:17.

14. As epitomized by Jesus' reference to the "new Jerusalem" in Rev 3:12.

evangelize the outlying regions of their city,[15] a chance for prayer, or an abrupt entrance into God's presence through martyrdom.

At times, due to external threats, the spiritual vigor of the Philadelphian congregation has waned ("you have little strength"). Yet despite being scorned and marginalized by their peers, they have obeyed the Savior's teachings ("kept my word"), courageously identifying themselves as his followers ("not denied my name").[16]

The church in Philadelphia also contends with the menacing reality of legalists, whom Jesus calls the "synagogue of Satan" (v. 9). Regardless of their claims to be Torah-observant "Jews," the Son indicates that they are liars. Specifically, what the dogmatists teach contradicts the gospel of grace and deserves condemnation.[17] Jesus' followers, in obedience to the truth, resist the intrusion of false religion and, in this way, overcome demonic attacks to corrupt the church.

The Savior will compel the antagonists to kneel at the "feet" of believers in Philadelphia. Some think that this could mean that the legalists will become Jesus' disciples. More likely, however, the agitators will give grudging homage to the Son as King. Amazingly, his faithful followers will be on hand to see the spectacle,[18] which will prompt Jesus' antagonists to "realize" that the redeemed are the true objects of his compassion and care.[19]

The Savior teaches his children to persevere steadfastly despite maltreatment, and they staunchly have obeyed his admonition ("kept my word about patient endurance"; v. 10). In turn, he promises to keep them safe from a time of suffering to come upon the entire "inhabited world." Jesus will use this period of trial to "test"[20] the priorities of those who live on the "earth."[21]

Specialists debate in what way the Son will keep his followers from the "hour of testing." He promises either to deliver them from the ordeal

15. See Acts 14:27; 1 Cor 16:9; 2 Cor 2:12; Col 4:3.

16. See Matt 10:32–33.

17. See Gal 1:6–9.

18. See Isa 45:14; 49:23–26; 60:3–6, 14.

19. "I have loved you" is emphatic in the original; see Isa 43:3–4.

20. Namely, assess and disclose.

21. Throughout the Apocalypse, an emphasis is placed on earth's unregenerate inhabitants, who venerated pagan deities; see Rev 6:10; 8:13; 11:10; 13:8, 12, 14; 14:6; 17:2, 8.

or to preserve them through it.[22] Regardless of which view is taken, the believers in Philadelphia remain loyal to the Messiah despite anguishing circumstances and trust that he will eternally reward them with covenantal blessings.

Jesus reminds his children that he, as the divine Warrior, is "coming soon" (v. 11).[23] The emphasis is not that the second advent will occur in a short period of time. Instead, it is that the Son's return is certain. Once the appointed moment has arrived, nothing will delay or prevent his appearing.

The Savior urges his followers to hold firmly to their faith, especially by being good stewards of what he has entrusted to their care. For instance, Jesus has given the believers in Philadelphia a variety of spiritual gifts, along with opportunities for service. Regardless of the circumstances, the Messiah's children are to remain unwavering in their commitment.

If the believers heed this admonition, no one will take away the "crown"[24] he will graciously give as a reward for their steadfast service. Conversely, those in the Philadelphia congregation who are unfaithful will forfeit eternal rewards at the judgment seat of Christ. To prevent this tragic outcome, they need to persevere in using their gifts, abilities, and resources to the glory of God.

In ancient Philadelphia, officials would honor a magistrate by placing a pillar, in his name, in one of the pagan shrines in the city. Jesus promises that he will make believers who are "victorious" (v. 12), as the church militant, to be a "pillar" in God's "temple" (or inner sanctuary), as the church triumphant. The preceding metaphor symbolizes permanence and stability. The Messiah is stating that, even if his faithful followers endure being shunned and excommunicated from the local synagogue, they will have an enduring place in the Lord's heavenly sanctuary.

In Old Testament times, the name of God was written on the front of the high priest's turban.[25] Jesus declares that one day he will inscribe the "name" of "God" on each of his loyal children. This distinctive identity will indicate the Father's ownership and protection of them, along with their unending dedication to worship and serve only him.[26] The Savior

22. See John 17:15; 2 Pet 2:9.

23. See our discussion of Rev 1:7; 2:25; 3:3; 19:11–16; 22:7, 12, 17, 20.

24. A victor's laurel wreath.

25. See Exod 28:36–38.

26. See Num 6:27; Deut 28:10; Isa 43:7; 62:2; Ezek 48:35; Dan 9:18–19; Apoc. El.

also reveals that he will place on his followers the "name" belonging to the Creator's eternal "city." This promise looks forward to the "new Jerusalem," where the Father will allow the redeemed to enter and dwell eternally in his sacred presence.[27]

In ancient times, people believed that their names reflected their moral character and attributes. The Messiah's "new name" represents all that he is, including his virtue, uprightness, and redemptive work. Jesus' inscribing his "name" on his baptized, faithful children indicates that they will be the recipients of his everlasting covenantal blessings.[28] This promise, along with his previous pledges, incentivizes all the members of the seven churches to "hear" (v. 13) and heed the truths the Spirit discloses to them.

THE LETTER TO THE CHURCH IN LAODICEA (3:14–22)

Laodicea[29] stood at the intersection of three highways, which gave the city a strategic geographic position. This location made Laodicea enormously wealthy. The city was also the residence of bankers, merchants, and financiers. Its school of medicine was famous for its eye salve and nard, which physicians used to treat ear infections. The city had a stadium, several theaters, numerous temples, and a public fountain.

A major deficiency was Laodicea's inadequate water supply. Nearby Hierapolis had hot water, and Colosse had cold water. Yet by the time the mineral-rich water reached Laodicea over a Roman-built aqueduct from the hot springs of Denizli,[30] the water had cooled significantly and became lukewarm.

The believers in the church at "Laodicea" (v. 14) struggle with spiritual apathy. They respond to severe life circumstances by becoming halfhearted, nominal Christians. The congregants have also become calloused and self-sufficient, leading to idleness. Furthermore, rather than take a bold stand for Christ,[31] they are willing only to follow him marginally.

1:9.

27. See Ezek 48:35; Jos. Asen. 17:6; T. Dan 5:12; Gal 4:26; Heb 11:10; 12:22; 13:14; Rev 21:2, 10.

28. Including pardon from sin and the abiding presence of the sevenfold Spirit.

29. Modern Eskihisar.

30. About six miles south.

31. Like an eyewitness testifying in a court of law.

Against the preceding cultural and historical backdrop, the Messiah begins his authoritative and solemn pronouncement to the "messenger" (or "angel") of the church in Laodicea by declaring himself to be the "Amen" (v. 14).[32] Put another way, the Son guarantees the certainty of whatever he declares, especially as the divine Warrior. He is the Father's "yes" to the believers' hope of salvation.[33]

Jesus is also the "faithful and true witness."[34] As such, he reveals to the Christians in Laodicea that they have major problems which they need to correct. The Greek noun *arche* can be translated as "beginning," "origin," "source," or "ruler." Together, these terms emphasize that the Son brought all things into existence and sustains them, including the believers in Laodicea.[35] Consequently, they belong to him and are obligated to obey him.

While the Philadelphian assembly receives no reproof from the Messiah, the Laodicean congregation receives no praise. Jesus knows they are apathetic and complacent as well as impotent and ineffective. In a withering indictment, the Son states that the congregants' deeds are neither refreshing like cold water nor medicinally healing like a hot spring (v. 15). Instead, like the tepid water they drink, their "lukewarm" (v. 16), ambivalent demeanor leaves them tasteless. The church's broadmindedness and tendency to appease all parties so disgusts the Redeemer that he feels nauseous. For this reason, he promises to vomit the congregants out of his "mouth."

The Christians at Laodicea incessantly brag about their affluence, which they seem to idolize. They are "rich" (v. 17) in everything except what matters most.[36] Likewise, the parishioners enjoy a surplus of gifted people and possessions. Yet, the irony is that they are spiritually bankrupt (namely, "miserable, pitiful, poor, blind, and naked") without being aware of it.

Self-satisfaction and independence characterize the Laodicean church. Its members think that they do not need any assistance. Here, the assembly of believers resemble the city of Laodicea. After all, Laodicea was the only city that refused monetary assistance from Rome when an earthquake in AD 60 leveled the town.

32. See our discussion of Rev 1:7; 3:14; 5:14; 7:12; 19:4; 22:20–21.

33. See Pss 41:13; 106:48; Isa 65:16–17; 2 Cor 1:18–20.

34. See 1 Tim 6:13; Rev 1:5.

35. See John 1:1–3; Col 1:15–18; Heb 1:2–3.

36. See Hos 12:8.

The Laodiceans were experts in trade. Accordingly, Jesus invites the believers in the city to carry out spiritual transactions with him.[37] For instance, like their peers, the Savior's followers at Laodicea take pride in the quality of their "gold" (v. 18). He urges them to acquire from him a distinctive kind of precious metal, namely, one that had been "refined by fire." Most likely, this is a metaphorical reference to the "proven character of their faith" (1 Pet 1:7), which is being tested and purified by "various kinds of trials" (v. 6).[38]

While the Christians living in Laodicea revel in their prosperity, Jesus promises them greater and more enduring covenantal blessings (Rev 3:18). Furthermore, the congregants reside in a city that had attained fame for manufacturing glossy black wool. Jesus freely offers to clothe them in the "white" robe of his righteousness and purity.[39] In turn, his declaration of pardon will eliminate the "shame" of their "public" spiritual nakedness.

Because Laodicea also produced ointments for eye diseases, the Messiah admonishes the congregants in the city to apply spiritual remedies to the "eyes" of their understanding, thereby enabling them once again to "see" what eternally matters. Despite their pathetic spiritual condition, Jesus still personally loves his children in Laodicea. Therefore, he not only rebukes but also disciplines them (v. 19).[40]

The Son's intent is twofold: he wants the parishioners at Laodicea both to "repent" and to renew their zeal for him. The Redeemer pictures himself as standing and repeatedly knocking at the door to the Laodicean assembly. Instead of forcing an entry, he seeks a voluntary response from each congregant.

Even if the congregation ignores the Messiah's summons, some individuals may hear and heed him. Intimate table fellowship with the Savior will be the experience of all within the Laodicean assembly who welcome him. Together they will enjoy a leisurely time of feasting in his sacred presence (v. 20).[41] Here, Jesus is specifically addressing the churched, not the unchurched. Nevertheless, it remains generally true

37. See Isa 55:1–3.

38. See Job 23:10; Prov 27:21; Pss. Sol. 17:43.

39. 1 En. 62:16; 2 En. 22:8–9; Ascen. Isa. 4:16.

40. See Deut 8:5; Job 5:17; Ps 94:12; Prov 3:11–12; 13:24; Pss. Sol. 10:1–3; 14:1; 1 Cor 11:32; Heb 12:5–8.

41. See 1 En. 62:14; Matt 26:29; Luke 22:29–30; Rev 19:9.

that, through the means of grace, he welcomes entering the life of every receptive individual.

In the ancient world, double thrones existed. Similarly, the Messiah promises those who are "victorious" (as the church militant; v. 21) that in the coming age, they will take their place beside him on his royal "throne" (as the church triumphant), just as he won the victory at the cross and rules with his heavenly "Father" on his imperial "throne."[42] Expressed another way, Jesus will allow his faithful followers to share in his future reign.[43]

Along with the preceding six messages revealed by the "Spirit" (v. 22), Jesus' solemn pronouncement to the church at Laodicea is worthy of being heard and heeded. To do otherwise will bring the covenantal curses of shame and regret to the unrepentant.

Strengths and Concerns Associated with the Seven Congregations[44]		
Congregations	**Strengths**	**Concerns**
Ephesus	Accurate teaching and moral purity	Lack of affection for the Son and his followers
Smyrna	Remaining faithful despite persecution	Facing the prospect of martyrdom
Pergamum	Unwavering commitment	Beginning to compromise morally
Thyatira	Patient demeanor and virtuous behavior	Led astray by heretical teachings
Sardis	Presence of pious deeds	At the point of spiritual death
Philadelphia	Remaining obedient to the Son; courageously identifying as his followers	Waning spiritual strength
Laodicea	None mentioned	Spiritually apathetic, complacent, and indecisive in commitment

KEY THEOLOGICAL INSIGHTS

Because Revelation 3 is a continuation of the letters to the seven churches in Asia Minor which John began in chapter 2, we briefly review the

42. See Ps 110:1; Matt 22:44; Acts 2:34–35; Eph 1:20; Phil 2:9; Col 2:15; Heb 1:3; 8:1; 10:12–13; 12:2; Rev 11:15; 22:1, 3.

43. See Matt 19:28; 2 Tim 2:12; Rev 1:6; 5:10; 20:4; 22:5.

44. Table adapted from information presented in Brighton, *Revelation*, 58.

theological insights given in the previous chapter and then proceed to offer four additional insights into Jesus, his church, the nature of the Messiah's judgment, and the role of the Holy Spirit. Previously, we affirmed that Jesus has every right to judge us as his church. This prerogative flows from his divine authority,[45] and it is enacted against the backdrop of his full knowledge of his church and his sovereign power in creating, sustaining, and preserving the members of his spiritual body.[46] The Messiah is unlike any other judge, for his character is beyond reproach. We need not fear corruption on his part because the One who made us and is strong enough to safeguard us is also in the best position to render his judgment of us.

When we consider the way in which the Son carries out his judgment, we remember his impartiality and his consistency. The Messiah judges by his own righteous, indiscriminatory, ethical standard; and that standard belongs to him, in accordance with the Father's revealed will. We cannot manipulate, change, or subvert this holy standard. In addition, the judgment made by Christ is consistent with his own character. The way in which he is revealed corresponds to the way in which he executes judgment. This is a comfort for those who live in persevering obedience to his commands, while it is a point of dread for those who rebel against the Messiah's equitable and upright expectations.[47]

Now, with respect to Revelation 3, we first note that *Jesus continues to judge according to how he is revealed*. The One who holds the sevenfold Spirit of God discerns what lies beneath the surface of each believer, in which the Son probes the true condition of those under his evaluation (vv. 1–2). As such, he judges the church in Sardis according to this perception, seeing the believers' comatose state (despite their "reputation for being alive") and warning them that if there is no repentance, he comes against them like a thief (vv. 2–3).

Jesus' presence in judgment is comparable to the indeterminacy of the Spirit, who, like the wind, comes and goes as he pleases.[48] Furthermore, the One who possesses all authority to open and shut doors promises to open the door to spiritual opportunity and blessing, especially

45. See Wall, *Revelation*, 82–83, for further consideration of Christ's divine authority to render judgment, specifically the catastrophic judgments described in the Apocalypse.

46. See Eph 1:20–23; 2:19–22.

47. See our discussion of Rev 2:5–7, 10, 16–17, 22–23, 26–29.

48. See John 3:8.

by granting to faithful believers entrance into and participation in his everlasting kingdom and, ultimately, the new Jerusalem (vv. 7–8, 12). Finally, the One who is the "Amen" (the "yes") of God extends his "yes" to those who repent of their useless religion as well as seek renewal and restoration in union with the Savior (vv. 14, 19–21). Here, we discern that the character of Christ informs how he judges his followers.[49]

Second, *we acknowledge that Jesus' followers are engaged in a spiritual battle as the church militant and are striving toward the blessed day when they will become the church triumphant.* This struggle is filled with temptation, fear, suffering, persecution, and even physical death. More generally, the fight for the soul of the church challenges her doctrine, belief, ethics, morality, and ongoing commitment to Christ. While the church pictures the kingdom of God on earth, and while it moves forward in the confidence that the "gates of hell" will not prevail,[50] this victorious march is replete with struggle.[51] No single local church is perfect. All are continuously at risk. Faithfulness and devotion can give way to compromise and abandonment. Likewise, affection and zeal for the glory of the Lord can give way to a lukewarm, hypocritical, going-through-the-motions duty that serves no God-glorifying purpose (vv. 1, 15–16).

Third, we note that *the judgment made by Christ always comes with an offer of restoration to the repentant.* To be sure, there is an end-time, final judgment coming where opportunities for forgiveness will be gone forever.[52] Yet here, as the Messiah challenges his church to greater commitment and loyalty to her Master, he does so in love, by offering the opportunity for his children to turn to him afresh.[53] In short, Jesus calls his bride to revival and renewal (vv. 3, 18–19).[54] Individual local churches may experience progress and decline in their purity and fidelity to Christ. Yet the Savior desires that they overcome, endure, persevere, and ultimately live out their commitment to him and in these ways demonstrate

49. The relationship between who the Son is and what he does (specifically, how he judges) reflects the way the Father reveals himself to Moses, especially when God declares the fulness of his name to the lawgiver. A prime example is Exod 34:6–7, where Yahweh discloses his name ("the LORD"). Yet in doing so, God moves from his proper name to his attributes to the way he bestows either blessings or curses on the Israelites.

50. See Matt 16:18.

51. See Eph 6:10–20.

52. See our discussion of Rev 19:20–21; 20:11–15.

53. As Wall, *Revelation*, 87, notes, the meal-offer of Jesus represents his "loving response to the one who is earnest and repents," symbolizing a "restoration of fellowship."

54. See our discussion of Rev 2:5, 16, 21–22.

the genuine status of their discipleship. This truth should encourage us to remain vigilant[55] as well as to press always forward in pursuit of the everlasting prize.[56]

Fourth, *the Holy Spirit plays a key role in Jesus' communication to the churches*. The Messiah's words are carried by the Spirit, mediated through John as the human emissary, and ultimately given to the churches as the Word of the almighty, sovereign Creator-God. Given the force of this Trinitarian authority, the message to each church is meant to be heard and heeded without qualification or evasion (vv. 6, 13, 22).[57] Today, we also have the Spirit-inspired and authoritative Word to guide and direct our lives, both individually and within the context of our churches.[58] Similarly, just as each of the seven churches in Asia Minor is instructed to take the Word of God seriously, we too must wholeheartedly embrace the Spirit's clear teachings as revealed in and through Scripture.

IMPORTANT MINISTRY IMPLICATIONS

As we did in our discussion of Revelation 2, here in our consideration of chapter 3, we identify ministry implications that correspond to the letters written to the churches. First, *congregational leaders must seek spiritual discernment to look beneath the surface of pressing issues*. Appearances can be deceiving, and even seasoned ministers of the gospel can fall prey to the deceit of outward impressions, forgetting that there may be death on the inside.[59] Ministers must seek true spiritual growth and vitality that endures and proves to be genuine as each year passes. This means spending quality time with people, getting to know them, and not assuming spiritual growth too quickly. Sadly, there is pressure to impress others with external results. Yet this pressure must be avoided in favor of what God says is the nature of real spiritual vitality. Also, congregational

55. See 1 Cor 15:58.

56. Namely, God summoning his reborn children to eternal life with him in heaven; see Phil 3:12–16.

57. See our discussion of Rev 2:7, 11, 17, 29.

58. See 2 Tim 3:16–17.

59. Note Jesus' declarations of calamity to the scribes and Pharisees recorded in Matt 23:13–36. Each "woe" depicts a situation in which the hypocrites receiving Jesus' condemnation had deceived themselves, their fellow religious leaders, and their audiences with an outward appearance of godliness. Jesus exposed the corruption, rot, and death present within the elitists and pronounced judgment on them.

leaders must be vigilant in their own journey of faith with the Lord to avoid leading others astray on a deceptive path. Regular self-evaluation, accountability to fellow ministers, and continual time in God's holy presence are key to preserve the spiritual liveliness that should characterize under-shepherds of Jesus' flock.[60]

Second, *congregational leaders must lead believers in patient endurance, even in times of weakness.* The church in Philadelphia is a wonderful model for churches in the Majority World. This parish remained faithful to God's Word and boldly confessed the name of Christ, even with "little strength" (vv. 8, 10). The weakness they experienced did not hinder their shining testimony for the gospel (v. 11). Many ministers in Majority World churches can identify with the diminished vigor of the Philadelphian church. Resources are often scarce, even if the numbers of attendees seem robust. Impact in the culture is sometimes muted by the external threats of persecution, corrupt national governments, and the lack of religious freedom. Leading churches in these situations can be trying and even exhausting. Yet having "little strength" outwardly is no indication of the potential for spiritual power and effectiveness.[61] In all situations, congregational leaders must exemplify patient endurance and faithfulness to the gospel so that their parishioners can be encouraged, invigorated, and emboldened for witness in the world.

Third, *congregational leaders must avoid complacency and entitlement on both individual and ecclesiastical levels.* Of all seven churches addressed, the Laodicean congregation is probably the most notorious.[62] Genuine parish ministers would universally agree that we should avoid the dreaded apathy and insipidness that we observe in this ancient faith community. Yet this is easier said than done. When pastoral endeavors appear to be going well, the devil can tempt congregational leaders to imagine that they have achieved much and need not maintain their own walk with Christ through the Spirit's presence and power. If ministers get to this point of complacency, the entire faith community will soon follow. And if smugness becomes the norm, a sense of entitlement usually takes over. Such congregational leaders and parishioners rely on

60. See 1 Pet 5:1–5. Note especially v. 3, in which Peter exhorts his fellow pastor-shepherds to prioritize being humble, godly "examples," rather than grasping for power and control.

61. See 2 Cor 8:1–5.

62. For a description of how the Laodicean congregation is typically evaluated in the present day, see Kistemaker, *Exposition of Revelation*, 166–68.

past successes, historical achievements, and legacy reputations.[63] The assumption is that since Jesus has prospered the church at one stage, he will continue to do so, regardless of whether we "grow in the grace and knowledge of our Lord and Savior Jesus Christ" (2 Pet 3:18). However, this sort of thinking proves to be devastatingly deceptive. That is why we must lead our fellow believers in an ongoing, never-satisfied pursuit of God's will across the spectrum of their ministry pursuits.

VITAL MISSIONAL RAMIFICATIONS

From the letters to the three churches recorded in Revelation 3, there are three vital principles for missional engagement that are worthy of consideration, as follows. First, *our Savior is seeking those who will genuinely believe in him*. The message of the gospel is a call to die to one's sinful self and evidence an inward spiritual transformation and renewal, rather than merely an outward conformity to a dead religious system. In missions-speak, we often discuss making converts to the Christian faith. Missional activity does seek conversion of the lost. Yet true missional work seeks not just outward conversion but genuine repentance, resulting in a complete change of life for those who come to saving faith. Too often, however, we settle for external results rather than internal ones. There is pressure on missionaries to perform and demonstrate external, numerical success. Often, the financial support for such missionaries is tied to these so-called results. Under this insidious pressure, the temptation is great to shortcut the biblical process of disciple-making. Yet when the true gospel of God's grace is proclaimed, it includes a call not just to add Jesus to our lives but also to submit to his lordship in every area of our existence.[64] For missions, this truth implies that we must reject the pressure to achieve immediate results and engage the long, arduous yet rewarding process of true discipleship.

63. See 1 Cor 1:10–13; 3:1–4; 4:8–21. The Corinthian church is a premier example of a faith community that seems to have rested on its impressive list of leaders (mostly past) and the work of the Spirit (again, mostly past) that had characterized the believers' walk with Christ. By identifying with their favorite celebrity pastors rather than moving forward in Spirit-led edification ministry, the parishioners invited conflict, a soiled reputation, a tolerance of sin, flippant worship, and the misuse of the many diverse special abilities the Spirit graciously bestowed on them.

64. See Matt 16:24–26; Luke 9:23–25. Hence, the language of *death* and *denial of self* found in Jesus' own explanation of the gospel.

Second, by taking a cue from Jesus' address to the Philadelphian church, *those involved in missional work must seek open doors of opportunity and boldly walk through them.* As we noted earlier, the situation in Philadelphia was overwhelmingly difficult, resulting in congregants who possessed "little strength" (v. 8). Despite this, the Father has prepared a way for the believers there to engage in testifying about the Son and the salvation he freely offers. Missional-minded believers should ask the Spirit for discernment and wisdom to recognize the open doors of gospel opportunity and for the courage to walk boldly through them.[65] Sharing the gospel in unreached areas and making disciples in regions where religious freedom is limited or persecution is common, such as in many Majority World contexts, can feel like a task beyond our strength. Yet the call to be God's witness in every corner of the earth is an ongoing mandate that must be neither ignored nor excused away. Regardless of the underlying or even prohibitive circumstances, the mission remains the same. The Lord of the harvest continues to seek workers for his harvest fields.[66]

Third, *in the pursuit of missional work, it is imperative to recognize that open doors of opportunity can manifest in diverse and unexpected ways.* Just as the church in Philadelphia faced challenges, modern-day missionaries encounter various barriers and difficulties in their evangelistic paths. It is important to acknowledge that the concept of an open door might not always be straightforward. Sometimes, it requires a perceptive and adaptable approach to discern the potential for meaningful impact. This adaptability is crucial in today's complex global landscape, where the need for spreading the gospel extends beyond geographical boundaries to encompass digital realms and virtual communities. As such, missional servants of Christ should be prepared not only to step through physical doors but also to navigate virtual doors, language barriers, and cultural nuances, all while relying on the Spirit's guidance. The mission is one of both conviction and flexibility, and it requires an unwavering commitment to share the message of salvation, even when the path ahead seems daunting. Missional work involves boldly entering unfamiliar regions, always aiming to reflect Christ's love and truth to a world in great need, despite the challenges that may emerge.

65. See 1 Cor 16:9; 2 Cor 2:12.

66. See Matt 9:37–38; John 4:34–38.

Revelation 4

John's Vision of the Creator

LEARNING OBJECTIVES

- Identify the imagery and symbolism John sees in his vision of God's throne room in heaven.
- Describe the attributes of God that John emphasizes, such as the Creator's holiness, majesty, power, and honor.
- Evaluate the significance of the 24 elders and 4 living creatures who continually worship God.
- Consider the hope for the future that John's vision gives to God's children.
- Explain how John's vision encourages believers to live in a holy and virtuous manner.

CHAPTER SUMMARY

Revelation 4 recounts John's profound vision of the Creator seated on his royal throne. The scene, which radiates his holiness and majesty, fills the senses with awe-inspiring sights and sounds. Here, a resplendent rainbow arcs through the air, while a glistening sea of glass captivates the eyes. In addition, John beholds twenty-four elders and four living creatures who offer God unending praise. This episode is a potent reminder that God remains sovereign, even amid the hardships his reborn children face. John's vision also reassures them that they will dwell with the Creator forever in heaven.

STUDY QUESTIONS

1. What stands out to you about John's portrayal of the Creator seated on his royal throne in heaven?
2. What do you think the rainbow around God's throne symbolizes?
3. What similarities or differences do you see between the praise offered by the four living creatures in verse 8 and that of the twenty-four elders in verse 11?
4. What is the significance of the twenty-four elders' casting their crowns before the Creator's throne?
5. In the ups and downs of daily life, how does John's vision of God's power and honor challenge your perception of the Lord?

CHAPTER OUTLINE

- Introductory observations
- The throne of the Creator (4:1–6a)
- The worship of the Creator (4:6b–11)
- Key theological insights
- Important ministry implications
- Vital missional ramifications

INTRODUCTORY OBSERVATIONS

Revelation 2 and 3 brought to light the temptations and persecutions that Christians faced toward the close of the first century AD (1:9). Some broke under pressure and compromised their faith, while others refused to waver in their commitment to the Lord. Throughout Jesus' solemn pronouncements to the seven churches in Asia Minor, he reveals that he will hold his followers accountable for their actions.[1] Furthermore, he promises to vindicate the upright and one day bring them to a place of eternal rest.

The above observations lead to the throne-room scenes appearing in chapters 4 and 5 of the Apocalypse, which together form a gateway to

1. See Rom 14:10–12; 2 Cor 5:10; Heb 4:12–13; 1 Pet. 4:17–18.

the rest of the book. The literary context is the book's cosmic trial motif, which, as previously noted, bears a resemblance to the prophetic judgment oracles recorded in the Hebrew sacred writings. There the Creator's spokespersons function as prosecutors. They not only censure the Israelites for their failure to heed the covenant stipulations recorded in the Mosaic law but also present a scathing condemnation of earth's wicked rulers.[2]

John, like his spiritual predecessors, concerns himself primarily with the rationale for God's judicial verdict of bringing three devastating judgment cycles on the world's ungodly inhabitants.[3] In this regard, Revelation is an example of theodicy, namely, a defense of the Creator's sovereignty and goodness amid the widespread presence of evil among the world's human inhabitants. Four sets of observations are worth noting, as follows:

- *First*, John's prophetic oracle discloses that the basis for the Lord's unleashing his wrath (or covenantal curses) is his absolutely holy character and will.[4]
- *Second*, as the supreme Monarch of the universe,[5] God is warranted in holding everyone accountable to his perfectly righteous moral standards.[6]
- *Third*, from the time of the first human parents, earth's inhabitants rebelled against their Creator.[7] They were also guilty of systematically murdering his children, who were martyred for remaining faithful to the Messiah.[8]
- *Fourth*, even in the wake of increasingly lethal cycles of destruction,[9] the wicked refuse to repent.[10] Consequently, the Father is equitable

2. See Isa 13:1—23:18; Jer 46:1—51:64; Ezek 25:1—32:32; Joel 3:1–16; Amos 1:3—2:3; Obad 1:2–14; Nah 1–3; Hab 2:2–20; Zeph 1:2–18; 2:4–15; Zech 9:1–8; 12:1–9.

3. As we explain in our discussion of the upcoming chapters of Rev.

4. See Isa 6:3; Rev 4:8.

5. See Pss 95:3; 97:9; 145:10–13; 1 Chr 29:11–12; Dan 4:3; 1 Tim 6:15–16; Rev 17:14; 19:16.

6. See Exod 34:6–7; Rom 2:16; Rev 11:17–18; 16:5–6; 20:11–13.

7. See Eccl 7:20; Rom 1:18–32; 3:9–18; 1 John 1:8.

8. See our discussion of Rev 2:10, 13; 6:9; 7:14–15; 12:11; 13:7; 14:13; 16:6; 17:6; 18:20, 24; 20:4.

9. As unveiled in the Apocalypse.

10. See our discussion of Rev 6:15–17; 9:20–21; 16:9, 11, 21.

and upright in bringing widespread ruination and death to every corner of the globe.[11]

In a manner of speaking, the planet's destruction is comparable to a massive de-creation event, or a reversal of the original creation God brought into existence.[12] At the end of the age, he will replace the entire universe with a "new heaven" and a "new earth."[13]

The preceding observations clarify one of John's theological intents for including the twofold throne-room scenes narrated in Revelation 4–5, along with the remainder of the throne-room scenes appearing throughout the apostle's prophetic oracle.[14] As we noted in our Introduction, each throne-room scene provides a defense against any accusations made by earth's wicked inhabitants that their Creator is wrong to judge them for their iniquities. Indeed, as the moral Governor of the universe, it is his solemn responsibility to hold evildoers accountable[15] and to vindicate his children for remaining steadfast in their devotion to him.

Accordingly, while chapter 4 spotlights the Father's receiving worship as the sovereign Lord of all existence, chapter 5 shifts the focus to the risen and glorified Son, to whom innumerable angels sing hymns of praise. These emphases clashed sharply with the adulation officials gave to their Roman emperors at their imperial court.[16]

The Threefold Fulfillment of the Lord's Prayer in Revelation		
Petition Offered	**Revelation Fulfillment**	**Theological Significance**
"Our Father in heaven, hallowed be your name" (Matt 6:9).	Heavenly worship scenes reveal God's holiness and majesty (Rev 4–5). His name is vindicated and glorified before all creation.	God's holiness is universally acknowledged. His name, desecrated on earth, is exalted by all in heaven and on earth.

11. See Deut 32:4; Pss 36:6; 51:4; 67:4; 145:17; Rev 15:3–4; 16:7; 18:4–8; 19:1–2, 11.

12. See Gen 1; John 1:3; Col 1:16–17; Heb 1:2; 11:3; 2 Pet 3:5.

13. See Isa 65:17; 66:22; 2 Cor 5:17; 2 Pet 3:7, 10–13; Rev 21:1. Also, see our discussion of the de-creation motif in our Introduction.

14. See our discussion of Rev 1:9–20; 8:2–6; 11:19; 15:1—16:1; 16:18–21; 19:1–10.

15. An example of retributive justice.

16. Including chanting hymns in veneration of the alleged divine-redeemer status of the enthroned human ruler.

The Threefold Fulfillment of the Lord's Prayer in Revelation		
Petition Offered	**Revelation Fulfillment**	**Theological Significance**
"Your kingdom come" (Matt 6:10).	"The kingdom of the world has become the kingdom of our Lord and of his Christ" (Rev 11:15). Christ reigns forever.	God's reign is consummated. Evil is overthrown, fulfilling the prayer's expressed longing for divine rule.
"Your will be done on earth as it is in heaven" (Matt 6:10).	God's sovereign will unfolds through judgments (seals, trumpets, and bowls) and final restoration (Rev 21–22).	God's will is enacted in judgment and renewal, uniting heaven and earth in obedience and restoration.

THE THRONE OF THE CREATOR (4:1–6A)

In the unfolding cosmic drama, John witnesses a "door" (4:1) standing "open in heaven." This door allows him, by the sevenfold Spirit,[17] to enter the celestial realm[18] and catch a glimpse of the "splendor and majesty" (Ps 96:6) that fills the Father's sacred abode.[19] The apostle hears the penetrating "voice" (Rev 4:1) of the exalted Messiah,[20] which sounded like a "trumpet."[21] He directs John to "come up" to God's throne room and receive special revelation concerning what the Creator decrees will take place in the future.[22]

Some think Jesus' invitation is a symbolic reference to the rapture of the church. More likely, John's experience parallels that of other believers in Scripture—for example, when Moses went up to Mount Sinai, or when Paul was caught up to heaven to receive special revelations from God.[23]

The Greek phrase rendered "what must happen after these things" echoes similar wording found in 1:19, in which the Savior gives John specific instructions. The apostle is fulfilling his commission to write what he has seen, including what is now occurring and what will happen as the prophetic oracle unfolds before him (v. 11).

17. See our discussion of Rev 1:10; 4:2.

18. See our discussion of Rev 17:3; 21:10.

19. See Exod 15:11; Isa 6:1; Ezek 1:1, 26–28; Dan 7:9–10; Matt 3:16; Acts 10:11.

20. See our discussion of Rev 1:12–13.

21. See our discussion of Rev 1:10; 4:1.

22. See Ezek 3:12; 8:1–3; 11:1, 5; 2 Bar. 10:3; 22:1; 23:6; 1 En. 14:8, 15, 18; 2 En. 20:1; Ascen. Isa. 6:6; T. Levi 2:6; 5:1.

23. See Exod 19:3, 20; 24:1–2; 2 Cor 12:2.

The phrase recorded in 4:1 might be an indication that chapters 6 through 20 of Revelation concern the final great conflict between the Creator and the forces of evil. Satan and his demonic cohorts will neither immediately nor voluntarily surrender to the Messiah. Nevertheless, Jesus of Nazareth will be victorious in his divine mission of defeating the devil and condemning him to the eternal Lake of Fire.[24]

In the unfolding cosmic drama, the Spirit "immediately" (4:2) takes control of John, perhaps by putting him into a trancelike, visionary state. The apostle sees the divine "throne" outstretched before him in heaven, as well as the Lord of glory on his royal seat. In ancient times, thrones were symbols of power, sovereignty, and majesty. Unlike the thrones of Satan and the sea-beast,[25] the throne of the Father radiates his magnificent presence and, as previously noted, occupies the literary center of John's prophetic oracle.[26] Indeed, the Creator's imperial court is comparable to a series of concentric rings. At the center is the supreme Monarch of the universe, who in turn is surrounded by circular spirals of various entities.

The Concentric Rings of Various Entities around the Creator's Throne[27]		
Ring Position	**Description**	**Biblical References**
Center	The dual throne of the Father and the Son	Rev 4:3; 5:6
First Concentric Ring	A gleaming circle of light (rainbow) like an emerald	Rev 4:3
Second Concentric Ring	The four living creatures	Rev 4:6–9
Third Concentric Ring	The twenty-four elders seated on thrones	Rev 4:4, 10–11
Fourth Concentric Ring	Myriads of angels	Rev 5:11–13

In keeping with Jewish custom, 4:3 does not describe the details of God's appearance. This omission is a reminder that the Creator's greatness and glory are beyond anyone's ability to comprehend as well as fully articulate with human language. First Timothy 6:16 reveals that

24. See our discussion of Rev 19:11–21.

25. As well as Rome's pagan emperors; see Rev 2:13; 13:2.

26. See 1 Kgs 22:19; Ps 47:8; Isa 6:1–4; Ezek 1:26–28; 10:1; Dan 7:9; As. Mos. 6:2; 1 En. 25:3; 2 En. 20:3; Sir 1:8; T. Levi 2:9.

27. Table adapted from information presented in Hendriksen, *More Than Conquerors*, 82–83.

the Father dwells in such intense, majestic splendor that no human can approach him. As the eternal and holy God, he neither has been nor can be seen by the naked eye.

Perhaps the preceding truths explain why John describes his vision of the Lord by referring to the appearance of precious stones (Rev 4:3). During the Old Testament era, gemstones embroidered onto the chestpiece worn by the high priest likewise served as a reminder of the Lord's infinite purity and magnificence.[28]

John first mentions a "jasper stone" and a "ruby" (or carnelian). Jasper is usually green or clear, while rubies are typically deep red or reddish white. The apostle also describes seeing the glow of an "emerald" (light green) encircling the Creator's throne like a "rainbow." Perhaps what John observed was a gleaming circle of light, akin to a resplendent halo.[29] The picture was one of a transparent jewel radiating the eternal Monarch's splendor.[30]

In ancient times, a king would permit vassal rulers, such as tribal judges, to sit on thrones next to his. In John's vision, he sees twenty-four "thrones" (v. 4) surrounding God's royal seat and twenty-four "elders" on these "thrones." The elders wear "white garments," which represent purity, uprightness, and immortality. On their "heads" are "gold crowns,"[31] which symbolize honor, splendor, and triumph.

These "elders" might be an exalted order of angels who serve the Lord in his celestial court, or they could be glorified saints in heaven. Some specialists think that the number twenty-four is a symbolic reference to the twelve tribes of Israel in the Old Testament and the twelve apostles in the New Testament. If so, this suggests that all the redeemed of all time[32] are represented before God's throne and worship him in his heavenly sanctuary.[33]

John witnesses "flashes of lightning" (v. 5) and roars of "thunder" originating from the Creator's royal seat. These storm phenomena symbolize his power and majesty. The episode recalls the natural disturbances

28. See Exod 28:15–21; 39:10–14.

29. See Gen 9:13–17; Ezek 1:27–28; 1 En. 14:14–22.

30. Compare John's description in Rev 21:11 of the new Jerusalem, which is the eternal, sacred domicile of the redeemed.

31. A victor's laurel wreath.

32. Both before and after the Messiah's sacrificial death and resurrection.

33. See Matt 19:28; Heb 12:23; Rev 21:12, 14.

that occurred on the summit of Mount Sinai three months after the Israelites departed from Egypt.[34]

In front of the celestial "throne" stand "seven burning lamps" (or torches), which are engulfed in flames and represent the "seven spirits of God." The "lamps" symbolize the perfection, completeness, and fullness of the Holy Spirit.[35] He works through the redeemed in their various churches to shine the light of the gospel to a lost and dying world.

As previously noted, 1:4 also contains a reference to the "seven spirits." Some think that this is an allusion to seven angels who stand before the Creator's royal seat.[36] Most likely, though, John is symbolically referring to the totality and purity of the Holy Spirit and his life-imparting ministry.[37] This especially involves convicting the "world about sin, about righteousness, and about judgment" (John 16:8).

In front of the heavenly dais, John sees something that resembles a sprawling "sea" (Rev 4:6) made of transparent glass. Indeed, it is clear and sparkling like rock or ice "crystal." Elsewhere in Revelation, the sea is a vile and chaotic vortex;[38] yet here, the "glassy sea" is tranquil and resplendent.[39] In New Testament times, glass was a rare item, and transparent glass was virtually impossible to find. The vast celestial ocean in John's vision possibly symbolizes God's magnificence, purity, and sacredness.

THE WORSHIP OF THE CREATOR (4:6B–11)

In the unfolding cosmic drama, John sees "four living creatures" (v. 6). These remarkable, otherworldly beings are in the "middle" of the area occupied by the celestial dais, as well as both "near" and "around" God's throne. Each creature has "eyes" covering the "front" and "back" of their bodies. This image could indicate their unceasing watchfulness and acute sagacity.[40]

34. See Exod 19:1, 16; 20:18–19; Job 37:2–5; Ps 18:12–15; Ezek 1:13; Jub. 2:2; LAB 11:5; Heb 12:18; Rev 8:5; 10:3; 11:19; 16:18.

35. See Ezek 1:13; Zech 4:2–3, 6.

36. See our discussion of Rev 8:2.

37. See Isa 11:2.

38. See our discussion of Rev 13:1; 16:3; 21:1.

39. See Ps 148:4; Ezek 1:22, 26; 10:1; 2 En. 3:1–3; Rev 15:2.

40. See Ezek 1:18.

Elsewhere in Scripture, the number four denotes the entire created realm.[41] This observation suggests the possibility that the entities in John's vision represent the totality of every being in heaven worshiping the Creator. A more likely option, however, is that John sees a regal order of angels, perhaps like the cherubim of Ezekiel 1 and 10 or the seraphim of Isaiah 6. John sees the "four living creatures" (Rev 4:6) guard the Father's throne, proclaim his holiness, and lead others in worship.

It is also possible that these angelic beings, which are individually described in verse 7, portray various aspects of divine grandeur. Another option is that they collectively symbolize all the creatures of the earth, every one of whom belongs to the Creator. For instance, the first "creature" has the form of a "lion," possibly representing either agility or majesty. The second "creature" has the form of an "ox" (or young male bull), perhaps symbolizing either strength or faithfulness. The third "creature" has a human "face," possibly representing wisdom and discernment. The fourth "creature" has the form of an "eagle" with its wings spread out as though in flight, perhaps symbolizing either speed or control.[42] Moreover, each of the "living creatures" (v. 8) has "six wings."[43] Also, the entire surface of their "wings," including their undersides, is covered with "eyes," which suggests alertness and intelligence.[44]

Day after day and night after night, "without pause," the angelic beings that John sees repeat the chorus, "Holy, holy, holy, the Lord God Almighty, who was and who is and who is coming."[45] In Scripture, triple repetition often stresses the certainty of a truth. On one level, the angels' threefold repetition of "holy" stresses the fact that God is sinless in the absolute sense of the word. Yet, on another level, there is an emphasis on his utter uniqueness as the source of life and flourishing throughout the entire universe. After all, he alone has the ability to fill the cosmos with beauty and dynamism as well as to endue it with functional integrity.[46]

Moreover, the angels' refrain stresses that unlike temporal, earthbound rulers, such as the emperors of Rome, the Creator is the

41. See Jer 49:36; Rev 7:1.

42. See Ezek 1:5–10; Apoc. Ab. 18:5; 2 En. 12:1; T. Naph 5:6.

43. See Apoc. El. 5:2; 2 En. 19:6.

44. See Ezek 1:18; 10:12.

45. Called the *Trisagion*; see Isa 6:3; 1 En. 39:12; 40:3; 2 En. 21:1; 2 Bar. 51:11; Rev 1:8; 10:6; 11:17; 15:3; 16:7, 14; 19:6, 15; 21:22.

46. See Pss 19:1–2; 33:9; Isa 40:28; 45:18; Rom 4:17; Eph 3:9; Col 1:16; Heb 11:3; Rev 3:14; 10:6; 14:7.

all-powerful Monarch of the cosmos. Likewise, the refrain indicates that he is not restricted by the limitations of time, even though he involves himself within its confines.

Roman Imperial Titles Applied to the Father and Son in Revelation		
Title	**Biblical References**	**Description**
Almighty	4:8	Divine omnipotence
Glory	4:11; 5:12, 13	Divine majesty and honor
Holy	4:8	Divine purity and sanctity
Lord and God	4:11	Supreme authority and power
Power	4:11; 5:12	Divine strength and dominion
Worthy	4:11; 5:9, 12	Deserving of adoration and praise

During John's vision, he sees that the "living creatures" (v. 9) unceasingly praise, honor, and thank the Father, who sits reposed in regal splendor as the "LORD of armies" (2 Sam 6:2).[47] Noteworthy is the repeated emphasis on the truth that God alone lives "forever and ever" (Rev 4:9).[48]

In ancient times, it was customary for court officials to lie stretched out on the ground in the presence of a ruler. Similarly, John noticed that the twenty-four "elders" (v. 10) prostrate themselves in homage before the everlasting Creator's "throne" and place their "crowns"[49] at the base of his royal seat. These are fitting acts of humility, devotion, submission, and "worship" to the one who controls all time and all people.

Whereas the "living creatures" (v. 9) praise the Father for his supreme holiness, the twenty-four "elders" (v. 10), in an antiphonal (or alternating) response, laud him for his creative acts (v. 11).[50] Unlike Roman emperors such as Domitian,[51] who required their subjects to extol the potentate's worthiness as "lord and our god,"[52] only the true "Lord and God" is "worthy" of praise.

As is the case in 1:6, so also in 4:11 each term in the doxology is accented in the original language by the definite article "the" to indicate

47. See Exod 25:22; 1 Kgs 22:19; Pss 80:1; 99:1; 132:14; Ezek 1:26–27; Sir 1:8.

48. See Isa 6:1; Dan 4:34; 7:9; 12:7; 1 En. 5:1.

49. A victor's laurel wreath.

50. See As. Mos. 1:12; 1 En. 9:5; 25:7; 36:4; 81:3; 3 Macc 2:3; Sir 18:1; Sib. Or. 3:19–20; Wis 1:14.

51. Domitian reigned from AD 81–96.

52. Latin, *Dominus et Deus noster.*

totality—namely, *all the* "glory," *all the* "honor," and *all the* "power." The idea is that God is perfect in every way, and so he deserves unlimited adoration from his creatures.[53] The idea is not of some superhuman creature[54] who statically props up the world. Rather, it is of the Creator who maintains the universe's existence and bears it along to its divinely ordained conclusion. He can do so because the entire cosmos originated with him and derived its ultimate meaning and purpose from him.

A Comparison of Revelation 4, Isaiah 6, and Ezekiel 1[55]		
Element	**Revelation 4**	**Isaiah 6 and Ezekiel 1**
Eyes	Each living creature covered with eyes all around (v. 8)	Ezek 1: Rims of wheels, full of eyes all around (vv. 17–18)
Living Creatures	Four living creatures resembling a lion, an ox, a man, and a flying eagle (v. 7)	Ezek 1: Four living creatures, each with the face of a man, lion, ox, and eagle (vv. 5, 10)
Solemn Declaration	Each living creature repeating "holy, holy, holy" (v. 8)	Isa 6: Seraphim calling to one another "holy, holy, holy" (v. 3)
Throne-Room Vision	Four living creatures positioned in the center and around the throne (v. 6)	Isa 6: The Lord seated on a throne (v. 1)
Wings	Each living creature having six wings (v. 8)	Isa 6: Seraphim, each with six wings (v. 2)

KEY THEOLOGICAL INSIGHTS

In Revelation 4, we are taken into the sacred and sublime presence of the Creator. Here, John conveys what he heard and saw regarding the worship of the Father. The resulting theological insights lead us to reflect on what we learn about God[56] from this riveting account.

First, *we see God's indescribable majesty and glory*. The Spirit inspires John to pen a heartfelt description of the One who was "sitting on the

53. See Gen 1:1; Neh 9:5–6; Pss 95:5; 146:6; 148:5; Isa 37:16; 40:26; 45:12; Jon 1:9; 1 En. 9:4; 22:14; 90:40; Acts 4:24; Rom 1:25; Rev 10:6.

54. Such as the pagan Greek deity Atlas.

55. Table adapted from information presented in Aune, *Revelation 1–5*, 284–86.

56. For a similar consideration of what we learn about God from Revelation 4, see Keener, *Revelation*, 179–82.

throne" (v. 2). Yet even with the Spirit's help, human language is incapable of fully capturing the Creator's resplendent being.[57] Scripture is replete with expressions about God as indescribable and incomprehensible.[58] From Job's regular affirmations of God's being beyond our understanding[59] to the Psalter's reflections on how God exceeds our capability to comprehend,[60] we find repeated examples of the Creator's majesty and glory. Before we attempt any description of God, we must understand that the Lord, as he truly is, can never be captured in mere words.

Second, *we encounter the holiness of God.* The unending, repetitive cry of the "four living creatures" (v. 8) conveys two related yet distinct notions. First, to be "holy" means to be morally pure, untainted with sin, and perfect in righteousness. Most contemporary uses of "holy" emphasize this part of the definition. If someone is considered holy, it typically means that he is morally superior in some way. God fits this description to an infinite degree, having moral character that is beyond reproach.[61] Second, God's holiness means that he is completely unique, the supreme *other* who has no rival and no equal.[62] The *otherness* of God does not negate his direct involvement in his creation. Rather, it is the Creator's uniqueness that makes our existence possible and what gives our lives meaning and purpose.

Third, *we witness the eternality of God.* Previously, in 1:4, we encountered John's greeting to the seven churches with the statement about the Father "who is, who was, and who is coming." In 4:8, we find the comparable statement about the Creator "who was and who is and who is coming." This statement indicates that he cannot be encapsulated by time constraints. Like his holiness, the Lord's eternality highlights two important truths. First, God transcends time. Theologians, philosophers, and even scientists have long considered the possibility that God exists outside of time.[63] Yet we lack adequate language to describe this kind of

57. Hence, as we mentioned above, John describes the appearance of the Lord by referring to the outward form of precious stones, signifying a magnificence that cannot be directly described.

58. See Eccl 3:11; 11:5; Isa 40:28; 55:8.

59. See Job 9:10; 11:7; 36:26; 37:23.

60. See Pss 92:5; 104:1; 139:4–6; 145:3.

61. See 2 Sam 22:31; Ps 18:26; Zeph 3:5; Jas 1:13.

62. See Exod 15:11; Isa 40:25; 44:6.

63. This subject has been a regular focus of theology and philosophy from the time of the Greek philosophers, through the early church's eras of speculative and mystical theology, continuing in the works of many medieval theologians, through theology's

transcendence fully. Still, as the sovereign Creator of all things, God is not limited by anything he has made—including time itself. Second, God is ever-present in time. Though he transcends time, he also engages with his creation at every moment. Nothing happens apart from his knowledge or outside of his sovereign rule. He is continually and attentively involved with all that he has made.

Fourth, *we see the worthiness of God.* As the worship continues, the twenty-four elders join in. Along with their participation in worship, we observe their casting their crowns before the Creator's sacred, royal throne, which shows complete deference to the One who alone is to be praised (v. 10). While there is more to say about God's worthiness in the next chapter of John's prophetic oracle, here the theological point is that the Lord, as the sovereign Creator, has every right to execute blessing and judgment within and over his creation.[64] God does not earn worthiness by having an impressive record of virtue measured by his actions. He is worthy because of who he is. Earth's wicked inhabitants may indeed question or even deny the Creator's worthiness, but all efforts to undermine the supreme authority of the righteous Judge ultimately fail.[65]

Fifth, *we encounter the power of God.* This is most clearly evidenced by his creative activity in speaking all things into existence.[66] The Lord's power is inseparably tied to his will. It is never blind, random, uncontrolled, or unpredictable. God's power is expressed in accordance with his sovereign plans and purposes (v. 11). Furthermore, as noted above, the Father sustains his creation according to his sovereign grace. When we realize our creatureliness, and God's complete omnipotence[67] in creation, we are confronted with his glory and majesty. We then realize that

---

encounter with Enlightenment philosophy, and even today in the works of leading Christian apologists and analytic theologians.

64. Recall from our discussion of Rev 2–3 the Messiah's right both to commend and to censure his churches because of his transcendent, all-knowing lordship; see also Exod 34:6–7; Job 34:17–30; Acts 17:31.

65. See Rom 1:28–32, where those "handed over" to their sin not only deny (ignore, disbelieve) God's justice, but also "approve of others who continue to commit such sins"; see also Rev 16:5.

66. See the repeated refrain in the account of creation "and God said . . . and it was so" (Gen 1:3, 6, 7, 9, 11, 14, 15, 20, 24).

67. God's omnipotence refers to his unlimited and all-encompassing power. This indicates that he possesses the ability to accomplish anything and everything without constraint, as well as according to his supremely good, just, and perfect will.

his power is for our temporal and eternal good.[68] Likewise, all the glory and blessing we experience is returned directly to him.

IMPORTANT MINISTRY IMPLICATIONS

Revelation 4 contains several important ministry implications worth considering. These encompass our limited ability to verbalize our knowledge about the Creator, the importance of expressing gratitude in worship, and necessity of being filled with genuine humility while doing so.

First, those who communicate the Father's glory and majesty must be cognizant *of the limitation of our words to communicate adequately what we know about God*. We should be careful, not flippant, when speaking about the Creator.[69] Our theologizing and analyses of who the Lord is and how best to describe his ways must be done with the realization that, regardless of the words we choose, they always prove to be insufficient. And yet, ministers of the church are required to speak about God, expected to extol his virtues, and privileged to proclaim the awesomeness of his glory.[70] Admittedly, it can feel intimidating to contemplate teaching and preaching about the Creator, especially when we know that we will never perfectly execute those tasks. Yet rather than shy away from speaking about God, we should embrace our calling, asking for his grace to accompany us and for his truth to be found in every word we speak.

Second, it is important for us to consider *how* the Father is worshiped by the "twenty-four elders" (v. 4) and the "four living creatures" (v. 6) around the throne. *God's true worshipers faithfully praise the Creator with a grateful attitude*. The faithfulness of the four living creatures is seen as their worship continues "day and night, without pause" (v. 8). The point here is not that the worship lasts a long time but that it is continual, because the praise and honor due to our great God is limitless.[71] As well, the living creatures give glory and honor with a disposition of

68. See Josh 4:24; Isa 45:11–13; Jer 32:17–23; Rom 4:21.

69. This is particularly true when invoking God's holy name; see Exod 20:7; Pss 66:2; 105:1–3; Isa 48:1; Mal 1:6–8; Matt 6:9.

70. See Rom 10:14–15; 2 Tim 4:1–5.

71. Note in Isaiah's vision of God that the "train of his robe filled the temple" (Isa 6:1). The length of the "train" (or "hem") of a royal garment was to be proportionate to the status of the one wearing the garment. A garment that would "fill the temple" represents limitless glory, splendor, and majesty. That being so, the praise due to God would also be limitless.

thankfulness (v. 9). The spirit in which worship is given matters. True worship is not mindless chanting or a programmed activity of emotionless automatons. Like the living creatures, we are called to lead believers in worship that both offers fitting praise to the Creator and flows from a heart of gratitude.[72]

Third, when we note the "twenty-four elders" (v. 4), *we see the humility of God's true worshipers.* The elders represent God's chosen, redeemed, and set-apart children. They have been given a privileged position encircling the Father's sacred throne, and they wear crowns signifying rewards for their faithful service to the sovereign King. And yet, their posture is one of falling prostrate before the one seated on the "throne" (v. 10). They offer their rewards, which the Father graciously gives them, to demonstrate his exclusive worthiness (vv. 10–11). Tragically, such humility in worship is a lost trait in many churches today. Performance-based, human-centered worship is increasingly employed to keep the church relevant to a modern culture where entertainment is on-demand and all the time.[73] Worship leaders must avoid performative praise that elevates people instead of, or alongside, God. The Father's glory is completely and solely his. Thus, it is shared with no one, and we must ensure that our congregants express this truth in their worship.

VITAL MISSIONAL RAMIFICATIONS

Earlier, we presented a table comparing Revelation 4 with Isaiah 6[74] and Ezekiel 1.[75] This comparison showed that John's vision not only echoes the sights and sounds experienced by Isaiah and Ezekiel but also brings their prophetic encounters to their fullest expression. Now, as we return

72. See Col 3:15–17. As Paul gives instructions for how the congregants at Colossae were to act toward each other in corporate worship, he repeats the need for thankfulness within each imperative he gives. In particular, v. 16 connects thankfulness with worship, as seen in Rev 4:9.

73. Most of these human-centered, performance-based styles of worship that began a few generations ago in the Global North have been exported throughout the globe, influencing many developing churches in Majority World contexts. While worship styles vary between and among cultures, there must always be a push from God's true worshipers to keep directing *all* the praise, *all* the glory, and *all* the honor to him alone.

74. See Keener, *Revelation*, 180, for further comment on this comparison.

75. For an added consideration of how Daniel 7 informs the structure of Revelation 4 and 5, see Beale and McDonough, "Revelation," 1098–99.

to Isaiah 6 and Ezekiel 1, we do so to deepen our understanding of the missional significance of Revelation 4.

For instance, much like John's initial vision, the one Isaiah experiences (6:1–3) is followed by the Lord's asking, "Whom shall I send? Who will go for us?" (v. 8). The prophet then does what is surely his only option, namely, to offer himself humbly ("Here I am. Send me!"). Isaiah's intent was for God to use his spokesperson in faithful service.[76]

Likewise, the scene recounted in Ezekiel 1 shares key similarities with John's vision. While we do not find the same cry from the creatures (for example, the threefold declaration of "holy"; Rev 4:8), we do see similarities concerning the living creatures, their specific appearances, and the beings with eyes all around. As with Isaiah, God's call upon Ezekiel's life is what follows from this gloriously terrifying vision (Ezek 2:1–8). In the prophet's account, he does not speak and sign up for missionary service. Yet the divine summons and commission are comparable to what Isaiah received. Therefore, following Ezekiel's encounter with God, the prophet is sent to the rebellious house of God's people to make him known and to call them to account.[77]

Admittedly, in Revelation 4, we do not find that John receives an explicit missional call. He received a prophetic summons earlier in 1:19. Yet given the similarities of the vision between the apostle and his Old Testament counterparts, it is valid to identify a few missional principles from chapter 4.

First, *a true vision of God should motivate us to sacrificial service.* Consider that Isaiah and Ezekiel did not receive a marvelous vision to begin motivational speaking tours or to become religious celebrities. Instead, like the vision John received, God used Isaiah and Ezekiel's profound encounters with him to commission them to proclaim his message to the wayward and ignorant. Also, like them, we are not called simply to know ("see") God and keep him to ourselves. If we truly understand

76. Note that the service to which God calls Isaiah would not be a successful mission (at least based on worldly standards), nor would it be one that would gain the prophet favor with his audience. God assures the lack of success by promising Isaiah that his audience would neither hear, see, nor understand what he proclaimed (Isa 6:9–13).

77. See Ezek 2:5–8; 3:9, 26–27, where seven times (!) God refers to Israel as a "rebellious house." Much like Isaiah, the task to which Ezekiel is called would not be successful by worldly standards, especially since those living in exile would, in large measure, refuse to hear the word of the Lord.

the Creator we serve, then we recognize that serving him is our only option.[78]

Second, *there is an exclusivity concerning God that must accompany our missional outreach and evangelistic message.* The object of our worship is not a God who shares his glory and majesty with multiple lesser deities. We are not sent to encourage people to add the Christian God to their lives or place him among their illustrious ancestors as one of many deified options.[79] People who have been brought up in polytheistic religions or worldviews often struggle to come to accept and believe in God's exclusivity. Many missions-minded servants of God in Majority World contexts, where polytheism is common, are aware that, even prior to hearing the saving message about Jesus, people need to be convinced about the holiness (uniqueness) of God as a first point of entry. Our mission is to proclaim the one and only Lord of all, namely, the God "who was and who is and who is coming" (4:8).[80]

Third, building upon the exclusivity of God, *the missional call does not allow us to alter the gospel to placate our audience's sensitivities.* Just as the Lord who discloses himself is unique in his worthiness, power, glory, and honor, so too the message about our Creator is direct, at times confrontational, and damning to all who would reject it.[81] Consider that at the beginning of this chapter, we noted the purpose for John's encounter with God was to assure the apostle's readers that the Creator's coming judgment is rightly executed, fully authoritative, and final. Similarly, the message we bring to a lost and dying world might not please those who hear it. Nevertheless, it is the only God-given truth that can change their lives.

78. See Gal 2:20; Phil 1:21–26.

79. In some Majority World contexts, particularly in Africa and Asia, ancestors are considered godlike, even if they are not said to be equal with the one, true, and living God. In light of this, some Christians have tried to justify the veneration of ancestors because they still reserve the best or highest worship and praise for the God of Israel. However, the Lord's exclusivity does not mean he is the best or highest deity among many within a vast pantheon. Rather, it means that the Creator *alone* is God, and no others are either like him or worthy to be compared to him; see Deut 6:4; Ps 86:10; Act 14:15; 1 Cor 8:4–6; 10:19; Gal 4:8; Eph 4:6; 1 Tim 2:5.

80. See Exod 3:14.

81. See John 3:18–21; 1 Cor 1:18, 22–25; 2:14.

Revelation 5

John's Vision of the Lamb

LEARNING OBJECTIVES

- Explain the significance of the scroll with seven seals.
- Consider the reason why John weeps when no one is found worthy to open the scroll.
- Contrast the portrayal of Jesus as both a stately lion and a slain lamb.
- Identify the main aspects of the worship scene around God's royal throne.
- Gain insight into the future of the church because the Lamb breaks the seals on the scroll.

CHAPTER SUMMARY

Revelation 5 describes a scene in heaven where God is seated on his royal throne and holds a scroll secured with seven seals. At first, no one is found worthy to break the seals, open the scroll, and unleash a series of divine judgments on the earth. Then John learns that Jesus, the Lion from the tribe of Judah, has triumphed and is worthy to break the seals. Next, Jesus, now portrayed as a slain Lamb, approaches the throne. When he takes the scroll from God's right hand, a magnificent chorus erupts with praise to God and to the Lamb for fulfilling their plan of salvation.

STUDY QUESTIONS

1. Why was it impossible for anyone other than the Lamb to break the seals on the scroll?
2. What is significant about the fact that the Lamb is both a stately lion and a slain lamb?
3. What does the new song which appears in Revelation 5:9–10 teach us about the salvation of God's people?
4. What do you think it means that all creation worships God and the Lamb, and how should believers respond?
5. How does this chapter help us better understand the missionary heart of God?

CHAPTER OUTLINE

- Introductory observations
- The scroll with seven seals (5:1–4)
- The worthiness of the Lamb (5:5–10)
- The worship of the Lamb (5:11–14)
- Key theological insights
- Important ministry implications
- Vital missional ramifications

INTRODUCTORY OBSERVATIONS

To recap what we previously observed, the major literary segments of Revelation have an introductory throne-room scene which lays the foundation for the verses that follow. For instance, the vision of the exalted Messiah recorded in 1:9–20 is a preface to the messages to the seven churches found in chapters 2 and 3. Likewise, the throne-room scene recorded in chapters 4 and 5 is a prelude to the seal judgments. The first six of these are recorded in chapter 6, followed by an interlude in chapter 7, and ending with the seventh seal in 8:1.

The material found in 8:2—11:18 follows a similar pattern. The introduction unfolds in 8:2–6, followed by the unleashing of seven trumpets in 8:7—9:21. An interlude appears in 10:1—11:14, followed by the blowing of the seventh trumpet in 11:15. Each of the introductory sections has a Christ-centered aim. Specifically, as noted earlier, each serves as a continual reminder that the Lamb is fully just in his evaluation and judgment of humankind.[1]

THE SCROLL WITH SEVEN SEALS (5:1–4)

In the unfolding cosmic drama, John saw that the Creator, while reposed on his royal seat,[2] was holding a "scroll" (5:1) in his "right hand." This roll of papyrus, leather, or parchment had writing on the "front" and the "back,"[3] and it was "sealed" in "seven" different places. The seals made it inaccessible and impossible for an unauthorized person to open.

Scrolls usually had writing on only one side and were sealed in one place. Writing covering both sides indicates that the divine decrees recorded on the scroll were extensive. Indeed, the number "seven," representing completion or perfection, indicates how thoroughly the contents of the scroll were sealed for secrecy.[4]

There are varying views about the contents of this wax-sealed scroll, including God's covenant, his law, his promises, and a legal will. The close parallels with Isaiah 8:16 and 29:11, Ezekiel 2:9—3:3, and Daniel 12:4,[5] however, suggest that the scroll of Revelation 5:1 contains God's end-time plan for the future. Most likely, the document reveals how the Lamb will bring the present fallen era to a close.

The preceding observation aligns with the declarations made by the Old Testament prophets. Judgment is the fate of those who reject the Creator, while eternal life is the destiny of those who remain steadfast in their devotion to him. The idea is that unless the "seals" of the "scroll" are broken, God's purposes will not be accomplished. This includes the Messiah's bringing covenantal curses on the wicked and bestowing covenantal blessings on the upright. In chapter 6 of John's prophetic oracle, the seals are opened.

1. See Ps 51:4; Dan 9:4–14; Rom 3:3–4.

2. As we previously noted, the Creator's throne occupies the literary center of John's prophetic oracle; see 1 Kgs 22:19; Isa 6:1; Ezek 1:26–27; 1 En. 47:3; 2 En. 20:3; Sir 1:8.

3. Literally "on the inside and outside"; technically called an *opisthograph*.

4. And so remaining inscrutable.

5. See 1 En. 47:3; 81:1–3; 106:19; 107:1.

Next, the apostle sees a powerful "angel" (5:2) herald with a "loud voice" for someone to come forward and break the "seals." In doing so, the scroll's contents will be disclosed. Intriguingly, the celestial being does not ask who is capable, influential, or powerful enough to do so. Rather, he asks who is sufficiently "worthy" to perform the task.

The Greek adjective rendered "worthy" refers to that which is spiritually fit and ethically deserving. In this context, it denotes the virtue, ability, and authorization to execute the Creator's end-time plan for the consummation of the ages. Only someone who is morally perfect can fulfill the divine will. Yet no one in all of God's creation—whether in "heaven" (v. 3) or on the "earth" or even beneath the "earth"—responds to the angel's summons.[6]

John is so caught up in the cosmic drama that he starts to "weep bitterly" (v. 4) when no one is located who is sufficiently "worthy" either to "open the scroll" or to "look" inside it.[7] Evidently, the apostle's intense emotional response is due to his sensing the urgent significance of the document.

THE WORTHINESS OF THE LAMB (5:5–10)

Amid John's anguish, one of the twenty-four "elders" (v. 5) seated around the Creator's sacred throne tells the apostle to "stop weeping." Lamenting is unnecessary, for there is someone who has the virtue and authority to bring human history to its conclusion. In ancient times, a monarch would permit lesser rulers, such as tribal judges, to sit on adjacent thrones. Previously, in 4:4, John notes that he saw twenty-four thrones surrounding God's royal seat with twenty-four elders on these thrones.

The elder mentioned in 5:5 reveals the person who is worthy to take the "scroll" from the Creator's hand and open its "seven seals." It is the "Lion" from the "tribe of Judah." He is also the "Root of David." The preceding metaphors are familiar Old Testament titles and together sum up Israel's hope for the coming Messiah.[8] God's people had called Judah—the founder of the tribe—a lion, and now the elder applies the name to the greatest of all the members of Judah. A lion represents

6. See 1 En. 61:10.

7. See Isa 22:4; Jer 9:1; 1 En. 90:41; 2 En. 1:3.

8. See Gen 49:9–10; Isa 11:1, 10; Jer 23:5; 4 Ezra 12:31–34; T. Jud. 24:5; 4 Ezra 11:37; 12:31–32; Rom 15:12.

power, dominion, and victory, and these are typified in the risen Messiah as the divine Warrior.

The Greek noun translated "Root" describes a shoot or sprout out of the main stem. As the "Root of David," Jesus is identified as the Messiah who sprang from the house and lineage of David.[9] Furthermore, the Greek verb rendered "triumphed" means "to win a victory," "to be a victor," or "to overcome." It stresses the Messiah's completed victory as the divine Warrior on behalf of the redeemed, which he achieved through his atoning sacrifice and resurrection.[10] Also, the verb translated "open" reinforces the truth that only the Son has the virtue and authority to bring about the fulfillment of the Father's end-time plan for the future.

John next fixes his gaze on an unusual entity appearing at the "center" (v. 6) and "near" the area of the celestial dais. Also surrounding the platform are the previously introduced "four living creatures" and the twenty-four "elders." John does not see a mighty lion but rather a "Lamb" that looks as if it had once been slaughtered. This shocking image portrays sacrificial death. In this way, it links the Messiah to the slaughter of the Passover (Paschal) lamb, which preceded Israel's exodus from Egypt.[11]

The above is another example of exodus typology or prophetic foreshadowing appearing in the Apocalypse. To reiterate earlier observations, through the exodus, the Creator freed his chosen people, the Israelites, from their enslavement in Egypt. Prior to this epochal event, the Lord worked through Moses to unleash ten devastating plagues on Egypt and in this way humiliate the powerless and lifeless idols venerated by the nation's inhabitants.[12]

A lamb is a gentle, guileless animal and so suggests one who is approachable. Also, a lamb is a sacrificial animal and so suggests salvation and forgiveness. The "Lamb" in John's vision,[13] who bears the marks of death, also possesses the symbols of divine power, intelligence, and

9. See Matt 1:1, 14; Mark 12:35–37; Luke 1:31–33; John 7:42.

10. See Col 2:13–15.

11. See in the Introduction our discussion about the Lamb motif in Revelation.

12. See Exod 12:5–6; Isa 53:4–8, 10–12; John 1:29, 36; Acts 8:32; 1 Cor 5:7; 1 Pet 1:18–19. Also, for an extensive discussion of the exodus typology in the Apocalypse, see Casey, "Exodus Typology in Revelation." He notes that "John unambiguously points forward to Jesus' death as that of the new Paschal lamb, whose blood marks the redemption of God's people from slavery" (141).

13. A major theme throughout Revelation; see our discussion of 5:8, 12, 13; 6:1, 16; 7:9, 10, 14, 17; 12:11; 13:8, 11; 14:1, 4, 10; 15:3; 17:14; 19:7, 9; 21:9; 21:14, 22, 23; 22:1, 3.

wisdom. For instance, his "seven horns" might represent consummate strength.[14] Likewise, the Lamb's "seven eyes" might indicate his infinite awareness, understanding, and discernment.[15]

John explains that the seven eyes are the "seven spirits of God that have been sent into all the world." This reference recalls what the apostle previously mentioned in 4:5, namely, the "seven spirits of God."[16] The parallel reference in 5:6 is also to the sevenfold perfection of the Holy Spirit.[17] His essential ministry, which encompasses every region of the planet, exalts the Son as the divine Warrior, probes the minds and hearts of the unsaved, and makes the Savior alive and real to all who trust in him.

As John witnesses the unfolding cosmic drama, he sees the "Lamb" (v. 7) approach the Creator's royal seat and take the "scroll" from his "right hand." By allowing this action, the Father authorizes his Son to carry out his end-time plan for the world.[18] Next, the "four living creatures" (v. 8), along with the twenty-four "elders" around the throne "bowed down" in worship before the "Lamb." They play harps, or lyres, the instruments traditionally used in Bible times to accompany the singing of psalms.[19]

The "gold bowls full of incense" symbolize the "prayers" of the "saints."[20] The reference here is not to a privileged group of elite, exceptional believers but to all the Creator's reborn, holy children.[21] Most likely, these are petitions for the full and final realization of the kingdom of God. This includes judgment of the wicked (namely, the covenantal curses) and vindication of the righteous (namely, the covenantal blessings).[22]

14. See Deut 33:17; 1 Sam 2:10; 2 Sam 22:3; Pss 75:10; 89:17, 24; 92:10; 112:9; 132:17; 148:14; Dan 7:7, 20, 24; 8:21–22; 1 En. 90:9, 37; Sir 47:5, 7, 11; 49:5; T. Jos. 19:8–9.

15. See Zech 4:2, 10.

16. See our discussion of Rev 1:4.

17. See Isa 11:2; John 3:34.

18. See Dan 7:13–14.

19. See 1 Sam 16:16; 1 Chr 25:1–6; 2 Chr 9:11; Neh 12:27; Pss 33:2; 43:4; 57:8–9; 71:22; 81:2; 92:3; 98:5; 108:2; 147:7; 150:3; Rev 14:2–3; 15:2–3.

20. See Exod 30:1, 7–8, 34–36; 1 Chr 28:18; Ps 141:2; 3 Bar. 11:9; 4 Bar. 4:3–4; Jdt 9:1; Tob 12:15; Luke 1:9–10; see also our discussion of Rev 6:9–10; 8:3–5; 9:13; 14:18; 15:7; 16:3, 7.

21. See Acts 9:13, 32; 26:10; Rom 1:7; 15:25, 26, 31; 16:2, 15; Eph 1:1; Phil 1:1.

22. See Gen 9:6; 17:7, 13, 19; Lev 26; Deut 28; Isa 55:3; 61:8; Ezek 37:26; 3 Bar. 11:8–9; 1 En. 47:1–2; T. Levi 3:7; Matt 26:28; Heb 13:20.

The participants begin singing a "new song" (Rev 5:9), for the Lord is about to inaugurate the distinctly superior, righteous order of his kingdom.[23] The worshipers sing this hymn to the Lamb as Redeemer.[24] Such a public acknowledgement draws attention to his royal investiture, that is, his formal appointment, inauguration, and coronation to his regal office.[25]

As with the Father (4:11), the worshipers also praise the Son for his worthiness to "take the scroll" (5:9), and to "open its seals." After all, the Messiah was "slain" on the cross, and he shed his "blood" to purchase the redemption of repentant, believing sinners.[26] The fact that the Lamb was slaughtered for the iniquities of the entire world is reflected in the declaration that the redeemed would come from "every tribe and language and people and nation."[27] The result is that the Son appoints his regenerate, baptized followers to be a "kingdom" (v. 10) and "priests," who in turn will faithfully worship and serve their Creator.[28]

Here is evidence of the success of missionary work.[29] Even in a time of such harrowing distress as described by the apostle in Revelation, people in large numbers from all over the globe respond in faith to the proclamation of the gospel. The Savior will be the rightful Monarch, and the redeemed will compose his sovereign realm. They will "reign" with him forever, not just in heaven but also on the "earth."[30]

Sources of Imagery in Revelation[31]		
Category	**Examples**	**Description**
Human Life and Activity	Commerce, warfare, idolatry, childbirth, prostitution, agriculture, medicine, government, building construction	Draws from ordinary human experience to depict profound spiritual realities
Nature	Horse, lamb, lion, locust, scorpion, eagle, tree, harvest, sea, rivers, earth, sky	Uses natural imagery to convey cosmic and end-time events

23. See Pss 33:3; 40:3; 96:1–2; 98:1–2; 144:9–10; 149:1; Isa 42:9–10; Rev 14:3.

24. See Matt 20:28; Mark 10:45; Acts 20:28; 1 Cor 6:20.

25. See 1 Chr 29:11.

26. See 1 Cor 7:23; Rev 1:5; 14:3–4.

27. See Dan 3:4, 7, 29; 7:14; 1 John 2:1–2.

28. See Exod 19:6; Jub. 16:18; Odes Sol. 20:1–4; 1 Pet 2:5; Rev 1:6; 20:6; 22:5.

29. A theme emphasized elsewhere in the Apocalypse; see 7:9; 15:4; 21:24, 26.

30. See our discussion of Rev 3:21; 20:4–5.

31. Table adapted from information presented in Mounce, *Book of Revelation*, 4–5, 42, 95–96, 104–5, 121, 196.

Sources of Imagery in Revelation[31]		
Category	**Examples**	**Description**
Old Testament	Babylon, Jerusalem, Jezebel, Egypt, Sodom, Tyre, temple and furnishings, manna, life-giving tree and water, Jesus as Lamb, Lion, Root	Reflects continuity with Israel's history and prophetic/apocalyptic language
Subterranean Regions	The abyss, Hades, Lake of Fire	Denotes realms of judgment, death, and demonic forces

THE WORSHIP OF THE LAMB (5:11–14)

As the cosmic drama unfolds, it is not difficult to imagine how John feels overwhelmed with emotion, especially as he sees and hears myriads upon myriads of "angels" (v. 11) singing around God's "throne," along with voices of the "living creatures" and twenty-four "elders." The heavenly choir encircling the sovereign Monarch's royal seat of power gives adoration to the Lamb for his worthiness.[32]

It is fitting for the Messiah to be given a comprehensive list of praises.[33] Indeed, with a thundering chorus, the incalculable multitude of worshipers piles on one accolade after another, including "power" (v. 12), "riches," "wisdom," "strength," "honor," "glory," and "blessing" (or "praise").[34]

Expressions of Praise (Doxologies) in Revelation	
Recipient	**Biblical References**
To the Father	4:11; 7:12; 14:7; 19:1
To the Son	1:6; 5:12; 19:7
To the Father and the Son	5:13; 7:10; 12:10

Next, John hears "every creature" (Rev 5:13) throughout the universe—all who were in "heaven," on "earth," "under the earth," and "in the sea"—singing hymns in adoration to the Father and the Son. The idea

32. See Deut 33:2; Job 25:3; Pss 68:17; 89:7; Dan 7:10; Apoc. Zeph. 4:1–2; 2 Bar. 48:10; 1 En. 14:22–23; 40:1; 60:1; 71:8; 4 Ezra 8:21–22.

33. Seven all together, which are joined by the presence of the article after the first noun in the series.

34. See 1 Chr 29:10–12; Luke 11:22; John 1:14; Rom 15:29; 1 Cor 1:24; 2 Cor 8:9; Phil 2:9–11; Eph 3:8.

is that the entire created realm—physical and metaphysical, human and nonhuman, animate and inanimate—unites all voices to give unending praise to the one who reigns supreme, along with the Messiah.

As in Revelation 1:6 and 4:11, so too in 5:13 each term in the doxology is accented in the original language by the definite article "the" to indicate totality—namely, *all the* "blessing," *all the* "honor," *all the* "glory," and *all the* "might." Likewise, each of these ascriptions applies equally to the Father and the Son "forever and ever." The "four living creatures" (v. 14) affirm this all-encompassing praise by declaring "Amen," which literally means "let it be so."[35] The twenty-four "elders" respond appropriately by humbly prostrating themselves in worship before the throne.

Admittedly, we live in uncertain times and there are days when the future seems bleak. That said, we should not lose hope, for the Lamb is worthy to take the scroll and open its seals. As observed earlier, this means that the Father authorized the Son to carry out his divine, end-time plan for the world. The future is not in doubt, for the Savior will bring to pass all that the Creator has decreed for the wicked and righteous, respectively.

The Equality of the Father and the Son in Their Divinity (John 10:30)[36]		
Divine Attribute	**The Father (Rev 4)**	**The Son (Rev 5)**
Divine Role	Creator (v. 11)	Redeemer (who inaugurates the new creation; v. 9)
Eternality	"who was and who is and who is coming" (v. 8)	"forever and ever" (v. 13; implying eternality and immortality)
Glory and Honor	"glory, honor, and thanks" (v. 9); "the glory and the honor and the power" (v. 11)	"power and riches and wisdom and strength and honor and glory and blessing" (v. 12); "blessing and honor and glory" (v. 13)
Holiness	"Holy, holy, holy" (v. 8)	"You are worthy" (vv. 6, 12; implying holiness)
Throne	sitting on the throne (vv. 2–3)	sitting on the throne (v. 13)
Worthiness	"worthy" (v. 11)	"worthy" (vv. 9, 12)

35. See our discussion of Rev 1:7; 3:14, 7:12; 19:4; 22:20, 21.

36. Table adapted from information presented in Gorman, *Reading Revelation Responsibly*, 83.

KEY THEOLOGICAL INSIGHTS

As we have noted, the focus of Revelation 5 moves from the Father to the Son, this time with the emphasis on the worthiness of the Lamb and the actions and attributes that follow. As such, the theological insights we present center on the person and work of the Messiah.

First, *we note our Lord's worthiness.* This is a crucial theme in the law-court setting in which we find ourselves. As John hears the question, "Who is worthy?" the concern is that there might not be anyone with the inherent virtue to break the seals and open the judgment scroll (vv. 2–4). In the upcoming chapters of the apostle's prophetic oracle, he narrates the worthiness—related directly to the judgment—for which heaven's inhabitants are desperately seeking.[37] The worthiness sought results from having the suitable qualification(s) to render judgment, and we see that the Messiah alone possesses such worthiness.

Second, *we note a striking symmetry between the Lion and Lamb designations for the Messiah.* On the one hand, Jesus is the stately Lion from the tribe of Judah, the conquering King, as well as the undisputed sovereign, with the proper character, lineage,[38] and position with which and from which to rule. Yet while John's attention is directed at the Lion, the apostle actually sees the Lamb,[39] who, as we noted above, is a symbol of meekness, humility, and sacrifice. Our Lord is at once the Savior and the slain, the victor and the vanquished. This truth ran against the prevailing notions of what the Messiah must be like for the people of Israel.[40] Yet, as we find elsewhere in Scripture, the kingdom of Christ is "not of this world,"[41] and his designation as the Lamb of God makes it possible for him to triumph as the Lion. Put another way, the stately Lion conquers *as* the slain Lamb. In God's kingdom, reality contradicts conventional wisdom. Jesus calls his followers to humility, brokenness, repentance, and

37. This desperation is due, in part, to the desire of heaven's inhabitants to see the vindication of the saints, particularly those who had been martyred for their belief in the Messiah.

38. The "Root of David" designation in Rev 5:5 demonstrates that the Lion from the tribe of Judah is the fulfillment of God's covenant with David.

39. For a helpful reflection on the contrast between what John hears (Lion) and what he sees (Lamb), see Morris, *Revelation*, 94–95.

40. A striking example of misplaced messianic expectation can be seen in Matt 16:21–23 where Peter, the leading disciple among the original Twelve, declares that Jesus' impending death must never happen.

41. See John 18:36.

death to self.[42] When they follow this summons, victory is assured. The slaying of the Lamb was necessary to pave the way for the resurrection of the glorified, and now exalted, Lion from the tribe of Judah.

Third, *we note that in terms of the worship designations attributed to the Lamb of God, he shares equality with the Father and the sevenfold Spirit*. For instance, as the Father is extolled with glory, honor, power, worthiness, and much more, the Son is also praised for having the same sorts of attributes.[43] This speaks to the deity of the Son. He is not some type of *Ubermensch*,[44] who merely attains more favor with God than anyone else before or since. Rather, the Son and the Father are one.[45] The Son is coequal and coeternal with the Father and the Spirit,[46] though the Son is unique in his incarnation. As the God-man, the Messiah alone, through his person and work, can completely accomplish the Father's will, and having done so, is now worthy to render judgment in light of the Son's completed task.

Fourth, with the bulk of emphasis on the exaltation of the Father and Son in Revelation 4 and 5, *we must not miss the all-important role of the sevenfold Spirit*. The Lamb is depicted as having "seven horns" (5:6), symbolizing all power, and "seven eyes," which are the "seven Spirits of God." As we stated above, this refers to the Spirit. Here, the Son dispatches the Spirit into all the world to testify about the Messiah. This truth resonates with what John recorded that Jesus said at the Last Supper, namely, that he would send the Spirit into the world, not to bring attention to himself but to bring attention to the Messiah.[47]

Fifth, *we see the praise of all creation*. There is nothing throughout the entire universe that fails to cry out in praise to God.[48] Of course, not everyone sees the Lord's creation in this way. Those whom God has given over to their sin misunderstand and misapply the praise offered by

42. See Matt 16:24–26; Luke 9:23–25.

43. Compare Rev 4:11 with 5:12–13.

44. The German term *Ubermensch* is often translated as "Superman" or "Overman." The philosopher Friedrich Nietzsche in his work *Thus Spoke Zarathustra* used this concept to describe an idealized individual who surpasses the limitations of ordinary human beings and embraces humanity's full potential.

45. See John 8:58; 10:30.

46. See John 1:1–3; Col 1:15–17; Heb 1:2–3. Also, note the terminology used about Christ in early church confessions, such as the Nicene Creed and the Chalcedonian Creed.

47. See John 15:26–27; 16:13–14.

48. See Pss 19:1–6; 66:4; 96:11–13; 148:1–14.

creation. These reprobates find something to be venerated in creation, rather than recognizing creation as an indication of the One who alone is worthy of worship.[49] Yet in John's unfolding cosmic drama, all creation praises God and the Lamb endlessly and abundantly (v. 13). Moreover, those rightly related to the Father through faith in the Son recognize this truth and join the chorus of worship.

IMPORTANT MINISTRY IMPLICATIONS

As with Revelation 4, the actions of the worshipers we encounter in chapter 5 offer guidance for how believers should respond to the Father and the Son and how ministers can lead people in this proper response.

First, *we again see the humility of those engaged in worship*. The action of bowing down in adoration is mentioned twice (5:8, 14), conveying an emphasis on the submissive posture of those around God's royal throne. Even the four living creatures are said to bow down when the Lamb takes the scroll (v. 8), indicating that only he is worthy to execute God's judgment faithfully. The humility we encounter does not negate the joy and celebration that rightly accompanies our worship.[50] Rather, true humility ensures that the joy and celebration of worship are directed to the Father and the Son alone.

Second, *in our worship, we must place a proper emphasis on the Messiah—both his person and work*. Throughout the New Testament, the key question facing the church is her view of Christ.[51] The seven churches in Revelation 2 and 3 are either praised or censured based on their love for Christ, their obedience to Christ, and their beliefs about Christ. True worship, therefore, centers on Christ. The Father affirms the Son's worthiness to break the seals and open the scroll (vv. 7–8). The Spirit's mission is to draw attention to the Messiah, just as he promised the Spirit would do. Church leaders must faithfully direct their congregants to the person and work of the Messiah, whether in worship, devotion, discipleship, or doctrine.

49. See Rom 1:18–32.

50. Exuberance in worship is found throughout the Apocalypse, not only in praising God for who he is but also in celebrating his judgment upon the wicked and his vindication of the saints; see our discussion of Rev 11:17–18; 15:3–4; 16:5–7; 18:2–8, 19–20; 19:1–5. For a helpful explanation of worship in the Apocalypse, see Osborne, *Revelation*, 46–49.

51. See 1 John 2:22–23; 4:1–6, 14–15; 5:1, 6–12, 13; 2 John 7–11.

Third, *those who provide spiritual direction to the church must demonstrate in their own lives the impact of the majesty, glory, worthiness, and lordship of the Messiah.* We must be willing to ask ourselves whether the spectacular vision of the Messiah recorded in Revelation 5 is the one that guides us in our ministry efforts. Do we truly see Christ in this exalted position? Does this slain Lamb of God, who takes away our sin, and this stately Lion from the tribe of Judah, who conquers according to the will of the Father and in the power of the Spirit, at times render us speechless? It is worth pondering whether we have become too familiar with the Messiah and, if so, whether we have lost the sense of awe and amazement when we behold him and when we communicate him to others.[52] We must fight against the tendency to lose our heartfelt admiration for Christ. We must also embrace the portrayal of our Lord as John describes the Messiah and carry that depiction with us as we work in and for the church.

VITAL MISSIONAL RAMIFICATIONS

In our discussion of Revelation 4, we explored Isaiah 6 and Ezekiel 1 to inform our observations about relevant missional applications. In John's vision, he witnesses the Father's glory and splendor, followed by the adoration offered to him. Although John receives no explicit missional command, the vision implicitly inspires missional activity through a deeper understanding of what it means to behold God's majesty and the glorious praise he receives. Likewise, in Revelation 5, there is no explicit missional directive for John. Yet, as in the previous chapter, there is implicit motivation for missional activity. This is especially true when we consider the apostle's vision of the Lamb as well as the activity and identity of the vast, diverse throng of worshipers around God's royal throne.

First, *missional motivation is found in the display of worship.* Missions has everything to do with worship. As John Piper notes, "Missions exists because worship doesn't."[53] His point was that the *everlasting* product of missional activity, which continues forever, is the pure, untainted worship of the Father, for his glory and the Son's exaltation.[54] Church planting, evangelism, and gospel-centered community-upliftment efforts

52. Or, for example, to ponder whether we have lost our "first love"; see our discussion of Rev 2:4.

53. John Piper, *Let the Nations Be Glad*, 11.

54. Piper, *Let the Nations Be Glad*, 11.

are aspects of missionary activity. Yet what remains after the consummation of all things is the unending worship of the Father and the Son. One day, local churches will no longer be the centerpiece of God's program, though the church will continue to participate in timeless worship. Evangelistic efforts will someday cease, even though the celebration of our salvation will continue, as we unceasingly declare the worthiness of the Lamb who has redeemed us for himself. Gospel-centered efforts to uplift communities will end when such support is no longer needed. That said, for those who come to faith in the Messiah because of these endeavors, there will be a joyful celebration of the spiritual blessings they have received by God's grace, and the celebration will last forever. Indeed, the work of missions *culminates* in God-glorifying, Christ-exalting worship.

Second, *missional motivation is found in considering the multifaceted identity of the worshipers.* John sees the culmination of missions in Revelation 5, which likewise equates to the fulfillment of the Great Commission, where the message about the Messiah has gone into all the world.[55] The new song that John records reflects this global evangelistic effort, as the Lamb is praised for his redemption of people from *every* tribe, language, people, and nation (vv. 9–10). This diverse, inclusive congregation demonstrates that mission work will ultimately succeed. Jesus assures his disciples that the church will triumphantly overcome the gates of hell by rescuing from a Christless eternity people from every corner of the world.[56] This outcome also shows us the heart of the Lamb, who redeems the lost for God's glory. In the Father's redemptive work through the Son, there are no favored nations or preferred ethnicities. All are invited to repent, believe, and be saved.[57] Given this truth, it is unfathomable that any true follower of Christ would refuse to be part of such a magnificent undertaking.

Third, for at least two centuries, the so-called missions movement was based in the Global North and in the so-called Christianized West, with outreach being targeted to unreached people groups. *Ironically today, churches in the Majority World are emerging as a homebase for missionary activity.* As the global center of Christianity shifts to the "south" and "east," the Spirit is summoning believers in these areas to be part of missionary work in fresh, creative ways. They regard themselves as the conduit to reach places that have previously been unavailable or closed

55. Matt 28:18–20; Mark 16:15; Luke 24:46–48; Acts 1:8.

56. See Matt 16:18.

57. See John 3:16; 16:8–11; Acts 17:30; 1 Tim 2:4; Titus 2:11.

to Western missionaries.[58] This development is encouraging, especially since the establishment of outward-focused missions from the Majority World has the potential to advance the global cause of missions with increasing effectiveness. And so, as the global effort continues, from all corners of the planet, we should unite with our spiritual brothers and sisters in Christ to carry out this mission of God and to gather for him a people consisting of all tribes, languages, and nations.

58. For a compelling example of this mindset and effort, see Paul Hattaway, et al, *Back to Jerusalem*. Though the accounts in this book were given decades ago, this attitude among believers in many Asian countries today remains as strong as ever. Also, while current names, places, and strategies must remain anonymous, there is a concerted effort within Majority World churches to take the gospel to the "hard places," particularly the Middle East.

Revelation 6

John's Vision of the Seven Seals

LEARNING OBJECTIVES

- Identify the four horsemen and what each entity represents.
- Analyze the symbolism behind the opening of the first six seals.
- Contrast the fate of those who have God's seal on their foreheads with those who do not.
- Consider the validity of God's judging pagan, idolatrous humanity.
- Discuss the implications of Revelation 6 for the work of missions in cross-cultural contexts.

CHAPTER SUMMARY

Revelation 6 spotlights the first six seal judgments. The Lamb's opening of the first four seals unleashes four horsemen, who represent military conquest, bloodshed in armed conflict, famine, and death, respectively. The fifth seal pictures the souls of martyred believers at the base of a celestial altar, and these martyrs cry out for justice and vengeance against their persecutors. The sixth seal brings about earthquakes, eclipses, and darkening of the sky, all of which foreshadow God's impending judgment on pagan, idolatrous humanity.

STUDY QUESTIONS

1. What do you think the four horsemen in Revelation 6 symbolize and why?

2. What does the appearance of martyred souls under the celestial altar reveal about these martyrs' situation and their plea to God?
3. How do the cataclysmic events connected with the sixth seal relate to the concept of God's judgment?
4. What does the attempt of pagan, idolatrous humanity to hide from God's wrath suggest about their reaction to impending judgment?
5. What does Revelation 6 teach us about God's sovereignty and justice?

CHAPTER OUTLINE

- Introductory observations
- The first and second seals (6:1–4)
- The third and fourth seals (6:5–8)
- The fifth seal (6:9–11)
- The sixth seal (6:12–17)
- Key theological insights
- Important ministry implications
- Vital missional ramifications

INTRODUCTORY OBSERVATIONS

The Apocalypse contains three series of seven judgments: the seal judgments of chapter 6, the trumpet judgments of chapters 8 and 9, and the bowl judgments of chapter 16. Also, each group of covenantal curses divides into four interrelated calamities,[1] followed by three interconnected catastrophes.[2] There are three primary views concerning the relationship among the seal, trumpet, and bowl judgments:

- *First*, as noted earlier, according to some specialists, the judgments occur simultaneously, with the sevenfold seals, trumpets, and bowls occurring in a chronologically parallel fashion, implying a recapitulation of events. Also, the repetition signifies the intensification of

1. Such as the four apocalyptic horsemen recounted below.
2. That is, a four and three literary pattern.

each judgment. In this case, the second and third series of judgments repeat the earlier ones.

- *Second*, other specialists think the judgments unfold in a successive sequence. In this case, the sevenfold seals, trumpets, and bowls are consecutive, with one calamity following the preceding ones, for a total of twenty-one judgments.
- *Third*, still other specialists think one series of judgments contains the next series in a telescopic or dovetailing fashion. For instance, the seventh seal judgment contains and introduces the seven trumpet judgments. Similarly, the seventh trumpet contains and introduces the seven bowl judgments.

Regardless of which of the above options is preferred, the Creator accomplishes at least three objectives:

- *First*, by sending the three series of covenantal curses on earth's wicked inhabitants, the Creator shows that he is the sovereign, all-powerful Lord as well as the one true and living God.
- *Second*, the Creator demonstrates to pagan, idolatrous humanity his unwavering concern for his persecuted, reborn children.
- *Third*, just as God did long ago in Israel's exodus from Egypt, the Creator, by proving himself to be infinitely superior to earth's heathen deities, provides the unsaved with sufficient reason to abandon their wicked ways and turn to him in saving faith.[3]

THE FIRST AND SECOND SEALS (6:1–4)

Previously, Revelation 5 disclosed that the destiny of the world was not left to random circumstances. Instead, the Father and Son, along with the sevenfold Spirit, remained in absolute control of the universe. This reality was welcome news for believers in the early church, especially as they struggled to survive intense persecution for refusing to participate in the imperial cult of ancient Rome.[4] Just when all hope seemed to be lost, the Messiah announced that he would judge the wicked with covenantal curses and vindicate the upright with covenantal blessings.

3. For a comparable analysis of the first six seal judgments, see Brighton, *Revelation*, 160; Osborne, *Revelation*, 120–22; Schreiner, *Revelation*, 262.

4. See our discussion of Rev 1:9; 2:9, 10, 13; 3:10.

The preceding theme of the triumph of the Lamb over the forces of evil resonates throughout chapter 6. Only he is sufficiently worthy to unleash the seven seal judgments on all humankind, which in turn, will bring war, conquest, famine, and disease.[5] Despite this grim picture and in keeping with the cosmic trial motif of John's prophetic oracle, the Creator will remain upright and holy in his character and sovereign over the unfolding series of events.[6] Moreover, he will preserve the redeemed and bring them safely through their harrowing ordeals into his eternal kingdom.

In the unfolding cosmic drama, the apostle witnesses the "Lamb" (6:1) breaking the "first" of the scroll's "seven seals," which were introduced in chapter 5. The Son's prominent role is a reminder that he alone has the authority and power to initiate the covenantal curses originating from the Father's celestial dais. Put another way, only the Messiah is qualified to unlock the future course of history and bring it to its preordained conclusion.

One of the "four living creatures" (6:1) positioned near God's royal seat[7] says in a "voice" that boomed like the sound of "thunder," "Come!" This might also be translated, "Go!" The preceding observation suggests that the command is meant for the four riders and their respective horses, not for either the Lamb or his bondservant, John. Therefore, as the Savior opens each of the first four seals, a distinctive "horse" (v. 2) and "rider" appears to journey throughout the earth.

The four riders mounted on horses of different colors are the Creator's judicial agents, whom he sends to inflict punishment on the world. The imagery is reminiscent of Zechariah 1:8–10 and 6:1–8. The colors of the four horses, like those of the horses in Zechariah's prophetic oracle, most likely represent a unique aspect of their respective characters.

Some specialists think that the calamities associated with the first four seal judgments symbolize an indefinite period before the Messiah's return. In this case, the disturbances occurring in the later years of the Roman Empire and throughout the history of the church were reflected in the catastrophes recorded in Revelation 6:1–17. Other specialists view these calamities as a foretaste of the final judgments to come. From this perspective, John was viewing the last period of history, in which the

5. See our discussion of Rev 5:4–5, 9, 12.

6. See our discussion of Rev 15:3–4; 18:4–8; 19:1–2.

7. As we previously noted, the Creator's throne occupies the literary center of John's prophetic oracle.

Creator chastens a sinful and rebellious world. According to this view, while those believers present might need to endure hardship during this time, the Savior will watch over them and bring them safely through their affliction.[8]

Returning now to the main flow of chapter 6, John witnesses that the "horse" (v. 2) unleashed by the first seal is "white." Its "rider" carries a "bow," wears a "crown,"[9] and wins many victories in battle.[10] Based on this information, numerous specialists think that the "rider" on the "white horse" represents the spirit of military conquest and victory. Less likely possibilities are that the "rider" symbolizes either the antichrist, the Messiah, or the triumphant advancement of the gospel down through the centuries.

After the Lamb breaks the "second seal" (v. 3), John hears the "second living creature" shout, "Come!" Then a "rider" (v. 4) mounted on a "fiery red" (or flame-colored) horse appears. The "rider" is given a large "sword." The dagger-like blade on this weapon[11] is long and effective in butchering its victims.

The combatant also receives authority to remove "peace" from the planet. He thus brings about intensified forms of warfare and "slaughter." Based on this information, the "rider" and "horse" symbolize bloodshed and death in armed conflict. A comparison of verses 2 and 4 suggests that the "rider" on the "white horse" provokes invasions of one nation against another, while the "rider" on the flame-colored "horse" provokes insurrection within individual nations.

THE THIRD AND FOURTH SEALS (6:5–8)

It is instructive to note that in Jesus' Olivet Discourse, he describes the signs that would signal the approach of the end-times.[12] His prophesies about distant events closely parallel and find their fulfillment in the seal judgments of Revelation 6. For instance, Jesus declares that the last days will be characterized by false messiahs, wars, famine, plagues, earthquakes, and death. As the time of the end drew closer, there will also be

8. See our discussion of Rev 7; 14:1–5.
9. A victor's laurel wreath, which was a symbol of regal authority and power.
10. Literally "conquering and in order to conquer."
11. Different from that mentioned in Rev 6:8.
12. See Matt 24; Mark 13; Luke 21.

unimaginable suffering and anguish. Amid all this calamity, the Messiah will return in great power and glory.[13]

Parallels between Jesus' Olivet Discourse and the Seal Judgments[14]		
Category	**Jesus' Olivet Discourse (Matt 24; Mark 13; Luke 21)**	**Seal Judgments (Rev 6)**
Cosmic Signs	Solar and lunar eclipses, falling stars, and shaking of the heavenly powers	Eclipse of the sun, moon becoming like blood, falling stars, people calling on rocks to fall on them, and shaking of the heavenly powers
Natural Disasters	Earthquakes and famines	Earthquakes, famine, and pestilence
Religious Persecution	Persecutions of believers	Persecutions of the faithful
Warfare	Armed conflict and international strife	Armed conflict and international strife

The above observations indicate that the Creator is not obligated to provide humankind with temporal blessings endlessly, especially since much of the world lives in rebellion against him.[15] Whatever he provides is based solely on his grace. That said, as Revelation 6:5–8 discloses, a time is coming when the Lord will replace food, joy, and good health with famine, anguish, and death.

For example, when John sees the Lamb opening the "third seal" (v. 5), the "third living creature" shouts "Come!" The apostle spots a "rider" on a "black horse" while holding a pair of scales in his hand. This agent of divine judgment represents intense, widespread famine because in ancient times, merchants used a balance scale to weigh their merchandise.

Next, John hears what sounds like a "voice" (v. 6) originating from among the "four living creatures." It announces that a "denarius" would buy either a "quart of wheat" or "three quarts of barley." The Greek noun translated "denarius" refers to a Roman silver coin that was equivalent to a manual laborer's average daily earnings. The noun rendered "quart" denotes a unit of dry measure that was commonly used in ancient times.

13. See 2 Thess 1:7–10.

14. Adapted from information presented in Stefanovic, *Revelation*, 224.

15. A major theme in the Apocalypse.

Due to extremely inflated prices,[16] a "quart of wheat" would be enough to feed only one person, rather than an entire family. Meanwhile, three "quarts of barley"—which was lower in quality and less nutritious than wheat[17]—would barely be adequate to feed a three-person family. In each case, a laborer's entire wages will be used to purchase food. The same "voice" declares that neither the olive "oil" (and their groves) nor the "wine" (and their vineyards) are to be harmed.[18] Though the rider on the horse could ruin everything, the Lamb graciously limits the extent of the destruction he permits.

The famine John witnesses in his vision could be caused by a severe drought. If it lasts for a only short period, the deep roots of olive trees and grapevines would enable these plants to survive the effects of the water shortage. In ancient times, food shortages were often caused when greedy merchants hoarded what they had so that they could obtain higher profits. This suggests that sparing the olive oil and wine left the wicked rich with enough resources to continue to indulge themselves.

When the Lamb opens the "fourth seal" (v. 7), John hears the "voice" of the "fourth living creature" shout "Come!" Next, a "rider" (v. 8) mounted on a "pale green" (or ashen) "horse" appears. The image resembles the pallid, gray color of a corpse. This probably symbolizes the effects of disease that are often associated with bloodshed and famine, which implies that each of the four seal judgments adds to and intensifies the devastation caused by the preceding covenantal curses.[19]

The "rider" on the fourth horse is named "Death." Following closely behind is the "Grave" (or Hades) to retrieve the putrid cadavers left in Death's wake. In Revelation, these two malevolent entities are often personified and represent the end of life and the realm of the dead, respectively, over which the Lamb supremely reigns.[20] It is unclear whether Hades is walking, mounted on a separate horse, or riding on the same horse as Death. In any case, the devastation that occurs is unmistakable.

The Lamb gives Death and Hades authority to wreak havoc over one fourth of the "earth" (v. 8), specifically by allowing people to be killed

16. Around ten to twelve times the normal amount.

17. And often fed to domestic work animals.

18. Such as through dilution or adulteration.

19. See Deut 32:24–26; Jer 24:10; Ezek 14:21.

20. See our discussion of Rev 1:18.

by swords,[21] famines, plagues,[22] and "wild animals."[23] The Son could allow the entire human race to be eliminated. Yet perhaps he limits the onslaught of covenantal curses to give unbelievers time to abandon their iniquities and trust in him for eternal life.

Here, one finds at work the holiness and the grace of the Creator. Because he is just, he must punish the wicked. Yet because he is merciful, he gives people another opportunity to turn to the Messiah in repentance and faith before the final series of divine judgments falls upon pagan, calloused humankind.

THE FIFTH SEAL (6:9–11)

In the unfolding cosmic drama, verses 9 through 11 depict the redeemed as waiting for the Creator to bring justice to bear on the wicked. Even though he will vindicate his martyred children, he will do so only in his time and in his way.

Verse 9 discloses that after the Lamb breaks the "fifth seal," John focuses his attention on an "altar" in the heavenly temple.[24] This platform reminded the apostle of either the golden altar of incense or the altar of burnt offering, both of which once existed in the Jerusalem shrine complex before it was destroyed in AD 70. The high priest routinely slaughtered an animal and poured out its blood at the base of the platform.[25]

John sees the "souls" of martyrs at the base of the celestial altar, not the blood of animals. The wicked "slaughtered" these believers for their steadfast "testimony"[26] to the gospel (the "word of God") and their unwavering loyalty to the Messiah.[27] During Jesus' earthly ministry, he tells his disciples that the pagan, idolatrous world system will persecute them.[28] Paul also teaches that unbelievers would mistreat those who belonged to the Son.[29]

21. Here, a large thrusting weapon different from that mentioned in Rev 6:4.
22. Or pestilence; literally "death."
23. See Lev 26:22; Ezek 14:15.
24. See Ps 18:6; Hab 2:20; T. Levi 18:6.
25. See Exod 29:12; Lev 4:7; 17:11.
26. Like an eyewitness in a court of law.
27. See our discussion of Rev 1:2, 9; 20:4.
28. See Mark 13:9–13; John 15:18–21.
29. See Phil 2:7; 2 Tim 4:6; 3:12.

Altars in Bible Times[30]		
Altar Type	**Materials/Construction**	**Key Features and Biblical Context**
Bronze Altar	Bronze sacrificial platform	Located in Solomon's temple court; dimensions were "thirty feet long, thirty feet wide, and fifteen feet high" (2 Chr 4:1); featured horns at the corners for asylum seekers (1 Kgs 1:50–51; 2:28–29)
Golden Altar	Made of gold	Positioned inside the temple, before the holy of holies; used for incense offerings (Exod 30:1–3; 1 Kgs 7:48)
Mud Brick / Dirt Mounds	Made of mud brick or simple mounds of dirt.	Used by nomadic people; oldest type of altar; temporary, portable structures for those with little need for permanence
Stone Altars	Single massive stones or stacked uncut stones	Most frequently mentioned in the Bible; uncut stones used to avoid defilement (Exod 20:25); no steps permitted in order to preserve priestly modesty (v. 26); distinguished from Canaanite stepped altars (Judg 6:20–21; 1 Sam 14:33–35)

While the unsaved might harass believers for their faith, this pales in comparison with the persecution of Christians that will occur in the period shortly preceding the Redeemer's second advent. During this time, people will discard biblical values for sinful and selfish ways of living. Vices such as greed, arrogance, irreverence, rebellion, and cruelty will flourish.[31]

John hears the righteous dead cry out with a "loud voice" (v. 10) to the supreme Monarch of the universe, whom they laud as being "holy and true." His martyred children ask "how long" he will wait before he exacts "justice" upon earth's pagan and idolatrous inhabitants[32] who persecuted and murdered these believers.[33]

30. Table adapted from information presented in Aune, *Revelation 6–16*, 405–6.

31. See 1 Tim 4:1–5.

32. As we previously noted, throughout the Apocalypse, an emphasis is placed on earth's unregenerate inhabitants, who venerated pagan deities; see our discussion of Rev 3:10; 8:13; 11:10; 13:8, 12, 14; 14:6; 17:2, 8.

33. See Pss 6:3; 13:1–2; 35:17; 74:10; 79:4–6, 10; 80:4; 89:46; 90:13; 94:3; Isa 6:11; Dan 12:6; Hab 1:2; Zech 1:12; 1 En. 22:5–7; 47:2, 4; 97:3–5; 99:3, 16; 104:3; 4 Ezra 4:33–37; Jub. 23:23; Sib. Or. 3:312–13.

At first it might seem odd that believers—even martyred ones—would petition the Creator to avenge and vindicate their faithfulness.[34] After all, Scripture teaches that Jesus' followers are to love their enemies and pray for those who persecute them.[35] Likewise, Christlike love is known for its patience, kindness, and willingness to forgive others.[36]

Yet further reflection indicates that the martyred believers are not motivated by either selfishness or a bitter longing to get even with their tormentors. Instead, Jesus' followers seek vindication for remaining faithful to him. Expressed differently, these Christians want to see their all-powerful "Lord"[37] fully establish and display his justice by unleashing the covenantal curses. They do not take matters into their own hands but leave to "God" the righting of all wrongs.[38]

John notes that each of the redeemed under the heavenly "altar" (v. 9) receives a long "white robe" (v. 11), which represents the joy, purity, and victory of their existence in the Creator's sacred presence.[39] Though they are eager for him to exonerate them, they are told to "rest a little longer" until the full number of their "fellow" bondservants[40] has been martyred.[41]

Based on Revelation 6:11, some think that the Lord is waiting for a certain number of Christians to be "put to death" before he brings the present age to a close. A second option is that believers must first complete or fulfill their God-given mission on earth, particularly through martyrdom. A third option is that the Creator remembers all those who suffered and died for their faith. Here, the idea is that he pledges never to forget all the anguish and hardship they endured for the cause of Christ, including their refusal to venerate mortal, flawed, human rulers.

34. See our discussion of Rev 5:8; 8:3–5; 9:13; 14:18; 15:7; 16:3, 7.

35. See Matt 5:44.

36. See 1 Cor 13:4–5.

37. Or "Master"; Greek *despotes.*

38. See Deut 32:35; Luke 18:7–8; Rom 12:17–21.

39. See our discussion of Rev 3:4–5.

40. Or "slaves"; namely, their redeemed brothers and sisters.

41. See 2 Bar. 23:4–5; 30:2; 1 En. 47:1–4; 4 Ezra 2:40–41; 4:35–37.

THE SIXTH SEAL (6:12–17)

In the unfolding cosmic drama, verses 12 through 17 spotlight how wicked people on earth responded to the sovereign Monarch of the universe. Scripture refers to this impending calamity in the grim period leading up to the Messiah's return as the day of the Lord. At that time, the Creator will shine the light of judgment on a world engulfed in spiritual darkness. Indeed, the series of calamities unveiled in the Apocalypse represent the culmination of the woe pronouncements (or covenantal curses) appearing in the Old Testament.[42] Tragically, earth's inhabitants from every walk of life try to hide from God.

The Day of the Lord		
Testament/Period	**Key Characteristics**	**Biblical References**
Old Testament	God's decisive intervention in history; execution of divine wrath upon the ungodly; time of judgment and reckoning; universal scope of God's judgment	Isa 13:6, 9; Jer 46:10; Ezek 30:3; Joel 1:15; 2:1, 11; 3:14–16; Amos 5:18–20
New Testament	Connected to the Messiah's return; for the wicked: covenantal curses and wrath; for the righteous: the full realization of redemption in union with Christ and covenantal blessings; dual nature of judgment and salvation	1 Cor 1:8; 2 Cor 1:14; Eph 4:30; 1 Thess 5:1–3; 2 Pet 3:10
Key Theological Themes	*Continuity*: Divine judgment emphasized in both Testaments *Development*: The New Testament introduces the redemptive aspect through Christ *Dynamic Tension*: Wrath for unbelievers and blessing for believers *Timing*: Scholarly debate regarding the duration and sequence of events	

John sees that when the Lamb breaks the "sixth seal" (Rev 6:12), a severe "earthquake" occurs. Then, the apostle witnesses several other cosmic disturbances. For instance, the appearance of the "sun" resembles "black," hair-covered "sackcloth." Sackcloth was a rough, dark-colored

42. See Exod 19:18; Isa 2:19; 5:8–9; Ezek 16:23; Amos 6:1–2; Hab 2:9–10; Hag 2:6; As. Mos. 10:4–5; 2 Bar. 70:8; 1 En. 1:6; 4 Ezra 5:8; LAB 11:5; Sib. Or. 3:81–83; 8:230, 233, 413.

fabric made from goat or camel hair and worn in times of intense trouble or sorrow.[43]

The apostle notes that the "entire moon" turns blood-red and that the "stars" (v. 13) in the "sky" plummet to "earth" like "unripe figs" thrashed by a fierce, unrelenting windstorm. The "sky" (v. 14) is also "removed" (or "receded") like a "scroll being rolled up," before all the planet's mountains and islands are dislodged from their foundations. These types of cosmic disturbances are foretold elsewhere in the Old Testament, where they anticipate the Messiah's return.[44] Likewise, in the New Testament, the advent of the Son of Man follows soon after extraordinary phenomena involving the sun, moon, and stars.[45]

Amid the onslaught of covenantal curses, all earth's inhabitants will reel in dread. Regardless of whether they are monarchs or slaves, wealthy or poor, high-ranking military officers or civilians, all will make desperate attempts to hide themselves from the Creator (v. 15).[46] The mention of seven types of people suggests that the scope of God's judgment will be comprehensive.

Perhaps at one time, earth's inhabitants felt safe from harm, even though they lived in rebellion against the sovereign Lord. Yet amid his judgment, not even the "mountains" (v. 16) and "rocks" of the planet can shield them from the Lamb's "wrath." Indeed, apart from his grace, no one can withstand the impending destruction.

Furthermore, the "wrath" shown by the Father and the Son is a familiar phenomenon appearing throughout Scripture, including the Apocalypse.[47] Previous occurrences of divine condemnation and punishment serve as reminders that the Creator will one day judge the wicked for all their evil deeds. Tragically, rather than abandon their iniquity and turn to the Redeemer in repentance and faith, many will try in vain to avoid him.

43. See Gen 37:34; 1 Kgs 21:27; Lam 2:10; Apocr. Ezek. frag. 2.

44. Especially, as we noted above, the end-time day of the Lord; see Isa 13:9–13; 29:6; 34:4; Ezek 32:6–8; 38:19; Joel 2:10, 28–31; 3:15–16; Amos 2:16; Hab 2:6, 11; Zeph 1:14–15.

45. See Matt 24:29–30; Mark 13:8, 24–26; Luke 21:25–27; 2 Pet 3:12–13.

46. See Isa 2:19–21; Hos 10:8; Apoc. Dan. 2:15; Apoc. Zeph. 12:6; 1 En 10:2; 102:3.

47. See Pss 2:12; 18:7; 97:5; Isa 5:25; Jer 4:24; Ezek 38:20; Nah 1:5–6; Joel 2:11, 31; Zeph 1:14, 18; 2:2; Mal 3:12; 4:5; Apoc. Zeph. 12:5; As. Mos. 10:3; 1 En. 91:7; Luke 23:30; Rom 1:18; 2:5; 2 Thess 2:5–10; Rev 11:18; 14:10, 19; 15:1, 7; 16:1, 19; 19:15.

God's Desire for the Wicked to Repent		
Theme	**Biblical References**	**Key Message**
A call to repentance and transformation	Ezek 18:31–32	God urges everyone to abandon his rebellious ways, repent, and receive a new heart and spirit.
A universal desire for salvation	1 Tim 2:4	God desires all people to be saved through faith in Christ and to know the truth.
God's desire for life, not death	Ezek 18:23	God takes no pleasure in the death of the wicked, but he wants them to repent and live.
God's patience for repentance	2 Pet 3:9	The Lord is forbearing, not wanting anyone to perish, but for all to come to repentance.

KEY THEOLOGICAL INSIGHTS

Revelation 6 showcases a dramatic shift[48] from the joyful, victorious, and celebratory worship of the Creator and of the Lamb seen in the previous two chapters. The Lamb begins to open the seven seals, and in so doing, he dispenses covenantal curses upon earth's wicked inhabitants, specifically in the form of war, famine, pestilence, and various cosmic catastrophes. As we consider these calamities, we learn much about the Lamb as Judge and the purpose for his righteous judgment.

First, *we see the Lamb display his limitless power over all creation.* When we consider God's power, we often think in terms of his *ability* to do what no one else can do. In theological nomenclature, we use the term *omnipotence* (all-powerful) to assert that the Creator can do anything he wills in accordance with his holy and righteous character. Also, while omnipotence is a well-attested attribute of God in the history of Christian theology,[49] the picture in Revelation 6 goes beyond a demonstration of the Lord's ability and shows us his sovereign *control* over the entire universe.

48. Morris, *Revelation*, 100, describes the opening of chapter 6 as "surprisingly grim," in contrast to the exuberant, worshipful content and tone of chapter 5.

49. Omnipotence, along with "omniscience" (all-knowing) and "omnipresence" (everywhere present), is considered a *great-making* attribute of God. This means that for God to be the *greatest possible being*, he must possess power beyond all would-be rivals or competitors. These *omni* attributes have attestation in all eras of Christian theology, most notably in the philosophical-theological musings of the Middle Ages (for example, Augustine, Anselm, and Aquinas).

In unleashing the covenantal curses, the worthy Lamb is not having some sort of divine temper-tantrum, replete with raw aggression, uncontrolled rage, or a parade of brute strength. Of course, God's wrath is exhibited in the events depicted here, and this exhibition is shocking. Yet the Messiah has a plan by which he judges the world; and in the execution of this judgment, he is never out of control. His judgment fulfills the promised[50] conventual curses to be experienced by those who have rejected the Messiah and his disciples, who have scoffed at his divine authority, and who have sought to destroy his regenerate followers.

Second, *we see the Lamb's grace in restraining his wrath, even amid judgment*. In the description of the four "horsemen," as we noted above, the judgments that come at their hands have an intensifying, escalating effect (vv. 2–8). If the horsemen were allowed to continue unchecked, there would be no end to the death and destruction they bring. Verse 8 indicates that these covenantal curses have a restriction, namely, a sovereignly ordained scope that spares most of earth's wicked inhabitants from their much-deserved punishment. John tells us that the horsemen were "given" (vv. 2, 8) the ability to perform their tasks, that they were permitted to bring calamity (v. 4), and that they were restricted at some points in their execution of divine wrath.[51] Thus, the Lamb sets limits on the authority of the agents of judgment. As we noted above, this restraint likely signifies the Messiah's allowance for the wicked to repent before it is too late. Scripture confirms that the Creator does not delight in the demise of the wicked.[52]

Third, *we see the Messiah's compassion and commitment to those suffering for his name*. Within the seal judgments described in Revelation 6, the fifth seal stands out as unique,[53] with its focus on the souls of the martyrs (vv. 9–11). Amid their plea for God's justice and vengeance,[54] they are told to "rest a little longer," but eventually, their cries will be

50. See Matt 24:3–13; Mark 13:3–13; Luke 21:10–19.

51. See our discussion of Rev 6:6, where the "oil" and the "wine" are unharmed, even while inflation runs rampant due to the lack of food; see also v. 8, where Death and Hades are given authority to strike down only a "quarter of the earth." While this is undoubtedly catastrophic, it would be far worse without the restrictions which the Creator set forth.

52. Note our table about God's desire for the wicked to repent; see especially Ezek 18:23–32.

53. Morris, *Revelation*, 105, observes that while the first four seals depict happenings on earth, we are "transported to heaven" for the disclosure of the fifth seal.

54. Much like a song of lament, as seen in Pss 6, 10, 13, 38, and 130.

answered. The cry of the martyrs, along with the sovereign Lord's assurance, reminds us that God neither forgets nor forsakes his reborn children. While we observe their waiting for their vindication, we note the Creator's sovereign control of all things, his unwavering plan of redemption, and even his grace in bringing yet more of the lost into his eternal kingdom.[55] Those who have faithfully given all to follow Jesus are remembered, vindicated, avenged, and rewarded.

IMPORTANT MINISTRY IMPLICATIONS

From the theological reflections we present above, we note several related implications for ministry proclamation and practice. First, *congregational leaders must affirm that the Lamb is justified in his judgment.* We should remind our parishioners that the Lamb is worthy to open the scroll, which includes his absolute right to execute judgment.[56] In Revelation's unfolding cosmic drama, the judgments given in chapter 6 and the resultant calamities are preceded by the repetitive affirmation of the Creator and Lamb as the worthy, righteous judiciary (chs. 4 and 5). Those receiving God's wrath are not suffering gratuitously or unjustly. On the contrary, the suffering unleashed by the Creator is a direct and promised consequence for those who persist in rebellion against the Messiah. Too often, we try to hold God to our own self-serving standards concerning right and wrong. We think we can evaluate whether the Lord is doing good by us, according to our own perspectives of what it means to be righteous, just, or loving.[57] Yet we must not place the Creator under our own scrutiny. He is not to be critiqued and put on trial. He alone is the one to judge according to his righteous ethical standards.

Second, *we must teach our parishioners that we can depend upon the Lamb to judge perfectly.* In our present day, with political gamesmanship and corruption prevalent around the globe, we have learned to mistrust those who are given the authority to judge. Often, those who render

55. While in this verse God seems to be waiting for the number of martyrs to be "complete," he is also giving more time for the proclamation of the gospel.

56. See our discussion of Rev 5:5–8.

57. We often see this in phrases such as the following: "A loving God wouldn't do (this or that)"; "Well, that's not the God I know and believe in!"; or, "If this is what a loving God is supposed to be like, then I don't want to follow him!" Incidentally, in our recent counseling sessions, all these sentiments have been expressed by confessing believers who are frustrated by what they see as a lack of God's "fairness" during times of difficulty.

judgment are targets for bribery, coercion, threats, and manipulation. In a culture increasingly suspicious of those who judge or enforce justice, many—even within our churches and among professing believers—harbor a fear that God might somehow make a mistake in his judgment. We need not fall prey to these fears. After all, the Creator is not subject to temptation; he is unable to do wrong; and he is not entrapped by the schemes the wicked concoct.[58] As Abraham boldly proclaimed (to Yahweh), "the Judge of all the earth should do right, shouldn't he?"[59] Even when God's righteous judgment does not make sense to us, there is great comfort for those who, by faith, rest confidently in the assurance that he does right each time he renders judgment.

Third, *we must warn our congregants that rejection and persecution are to be expected for those who live for Christ.* As we noted above, Jesus promises this to his disciples,[60] as did Paul to Timothy.[61] Persecution ought to be anticipated for those who take a determined stand in the world today against the onslaught of paganism and idolatry. This is a present reality for many believers in Majority World contexts, especially those who struggle with ongoing threats of persecution and even martyrdom. Ultimately, the Messiah sees, notices, remembers, and vindicates those who take a stand for him at great personal cost. Pastors and other congregational leaders in these contexts can encourage their parishioners to persevere in the faith, look beyond the present circumstances, and trust in the glorious victory yet to come.[62]

VITAL MISSIONAL RAMIFICATIONS

The dramatic scene of judgment in Revelation 6 offers several missional principles that can guide our work in proclaiming the gospel. First, *ministers of the gospel must be honest with their hearers about the reality of divine judgment.* The death and devastation portrayed in chapter 6 is both a present and forthcoming reality.[63] John's message is that as the

58. See Num 23:19; Hab 1:13; Jas 1:13.

59. See Gen 18:25.

60. See John 15:18–27; 16:1–4.

61. See 2 Tim 3:12.

62. See Heb 11:32–40.

63. One can detect vestiges of these judgments from Rev 6 in the world today (specifically, wars, famines, economic devastation, and widespread death). However, though these can be and have been seen throughout human history, there is also a

final consummation approaches, we can expect real judgment from God. For those who belong to the Messiah, namely, those who have aligned with the sovereign Lord by faith, the anticipation of God's judgment can bring a sense of relief, satisfaction, and even joy. Yet for those who have rejected Christ, or for those who have not yet realized the need to repent of their sin and trust in the Savior, the future is grim. Too often, we want to share only the appealing part of the gospel and sugarcoat the sad reality of sin and its consequences, such as judgment from God. Focusing on the Messiah's atonement for our iniquities and the offer of salvation given to those who repent and believe in him is certainly good news that must be shared. However, if we neglect to proclaim God's judgment—the "bad news," we fail in our responsibility to present the gospel in a complete and accurate way.[64]

Second, *evangelizing the lost concurs with the fact that God desires people to turn from their wicked ways, repent, believe in Jesus, and be saved.* As long as there are lost people, God's missional program is in effect. At the end of Revelation 6, earth's wicked inhabitants are aware that the wrath they are experiencing comes from God and the Lamb (vv. 15–17). Rather than repent, cry for mercy, or recognize that the judgment overtaking them is deserved, they long to die (v. 16). What a tragic reality! As seen in our world today, people are so entrenched in their rebellion against the Creator that they would simply long for death rather than repent. If indeed God is not willing that any should perish and if it is true that he calls and uses believers today as instruments of witness,[65] we should be motivated to answer this divine summons and take the gospel into all corners of the earth. This especially includes boldly proclaiming that the sovereign Creator and spotless Lamb stand ready to forgive, redeem, and spare the lost from impending judgment.

Third, *the kingly Lamb of God is above and before all pagan deities.* As we noted earlier in this chapter, the covenantal curses poured out on earth's wicked inhabitants demonstrate God's victory and power over

futuristic component of an intensification of these catastrophes, particularly as the second coming of the Messiah draws near.

64. The failure to present the sobering component of the gospel can be seen in contemporary expressions such as "God loves you and has a wonderful plan for your life!" Also, consider the currently popular adage of "living your best life now." Such shallow and pandering statements fail to capture the depth of our sinfulness, our desperate need for a Savior, and the sobering truth that, in our lost condition, we are counted as enemies of God.

65. See Ezek 3:16–27; Rom 10:14–15.

all potential competing pagan rulers and deities. It is here that we are moved to confront all cultures (including our own!) with the truth that the Messiah has absolute power and supreme authority over the entire planet, including any deified competitors venerated within pagan religious systems. As we carry this message forward, we must take the news about God's judgment, as well as the message about his saving grace, to all peoples, nations, and cultures. Here, we are declaring the Creator's all-sovereign and all-encompassing power over any humanly made idol or religious system.[66]

66. When we think about bringing the message of salvation to all nations and individuals, our minds often turn to unreached people groups—especially in Majority World regions—where the presence of the gospel is minimal or entirely absent. However, we must also recognize the need to evangelize within so-called Christian contexts, where many are lost while relying on a cultural version of religion. This kind of spirituality often drifts toward subtle forms of pagan idolatry that are not easily recognized.

Revelation 7

The Reborn Children of God

LEARNING OBJECTIVES

- Identify the significance of the four angels who restrain the four winds of judgment.
- Contemplate the identity of the 144,000 sealed bondservants.
- Describe the great multitude of the redeemed who praise God and the Lamb.
- Reflect on the Creator's unconditional acceptance of his reborn children in his presence.
- Consider how heaven is a starkly different place for believers than on earth, where they experience anguish.

CHAPTER SUMMARY

Revelation 7 describes John's vision of four angels who restrain the four winds of judgment, along with God's sealing of 144,000 bondservants. He chooses them from the twelve tribes of Israel and protects them from harm during an upcoming series of judgments. Next, the apostle sees a vast multitude of every nationality and ethnicity clothed in white robes. As they stand before the royal throne of God and the Lamb, the throng offers praise and worship. Despite being persecuted and martyred, they are redeemed, cleansed, and pardoned by the Lamb as they experience rest and relief from their pain.

STUDY QUESTIONS

1. Why are the four angels restraining the four winds of judgment?
2. What is the primary purpose of God's sealing the 144,000?
3. On what basis do the people dressed in white robes come to be in the presence of God and the Lamb?
4. In what ways does John's vision give believers hope for the future?
5. What insights for the work of missions can be drawn from John's vision of the vast number of worshipers?

CHAPTER OUTLINE

- The sealing of the 144,000 (7:1–8)
- The vast number of worshipers (7:9–12)
- The identity of the worshipers (7:13–17)
- Key theological insights
- Important ministry implications
- Vital missional ramifications

THE SEALING OF THE 144,000 (7:1–8)

Revelation 6 began with conquest, war, famine, and death brough to earth by the four apocalyptic horsemen. The chapter ended with the opening of the sixth seal and the vain attempt by all earth's wicked inhabitants to hide themselves from the "wrath of the Lamb" (vv. 15–16). The opening of the seventh seal was dramatically delayed so that the Creator could reassure his reborn children that he was fully aware of their persecution and martyrdom by Satan and his demonic cohorts.[1] As the interlude of chapter 7 reveals, the Lord promises to care for and watch over the redeemed amid their calamities, and he pledges to bring them through every ordeal.[2]

1. See our discussion of Rev 2:10, 13; 6:9; 7:14–15; 12:11; 13:7; 14:13; 16:6; 17:6; 18:20, 24; 20:4.

2. Just as God did long ago in Israel's exodus from Egypt.

In the unfolding cosmic drama, John sees "four angels" (v. 1), with each standing on one of the earth's "four corners." This reference does not imply an outdated view of the earth's shape. Instead, the phrase was used in the apostle's time similarly to the way we refer to the four cardinal directions of a compass today.[3] The identities of the "four angels" remain unclear. Some specialists think that they are the "four living creatures" mentioned in chapters 4 through 6, while others think that they are four previously unidentified celestial beings. In either case, they function as the Lord's agents of destruction.

The "angels" use their God-given strength to restrain the "four winds" of judgment from blowing diagonally across the planet. As a result, not a leaf rustles in the trees, and the "sea" becomes as smooth as glass. The mention of "four winds" is reminiscent of similar expressions found elsewhere in Scripture. For instance, in Jeremiah 49:36, the "four winds" symbolize military might. Additionally, in Ezekiel 37:9, the "four winds" represent every region of the earth.[4]

Next, in John's prophetic oracle, he witnesses a different "angel" (Rev 7:2) arising from the "east." This phrase is more literally rendered "ascending from the rising of the sun." It suggests that the sun's rays are illuminating the celestial being as it makes its journey skyward. The angel holds the "seal of the living God."

In antiquity, documents written on papyrus or parchment were often rolled or folded and then secured with a cord. To protect the contents and verify authenticity, a lump of clay was pressed over the cord or knot and stamped with a seal—typically made with an engraved cylinder or a signet ring. By the first century AD, the use of seals was widespread. Rulers authenticated official documents with their seals, which also served as symbols of authority for various governmental offices. Merchants used seals to mark goods in transit, indicating ownership and safeguarding against tampering.

The preceding background information suggests that when the supreme Monarch of the universe places his "seal" on his bondservants,[5] he identifies them as his own. Furthermore, as 1 Peter 1:5 declares, the Creator guarantees their protection and preservation to inherit eternal life, even as the time of distress intensifies, including the possibility of

3. See Isa 11:12; Ezek 7:2; Rev 20:8.

4. See Ps 68:33; Isa 19:1; 66:15; Jer 4:11–12; 49:36; 51:1–2; Dan 7:2; 8:8; 11:4; Zech 6:5; Matt 24:31; Mark 13:27.

5. Literally "slaves."

martyrdom. Likewise, in Ephesians 1:13–14, Paul says that when the lost were saved, the Father marked them with a seal, namely, the Holy Spirit.[6] This means that the regenerate belong to God and are members of his family.[7]

Concerning the "four angels" (Rev 7:2), the Lord gives them "power to harm" earth's lands and seas. That said, the Creator prevents these celestial agents of destruction from acting until his angels place a "seal" (v. 3) on the "foreheads" of his bondservants. God's ability to bring his covenantal curses to a halt indicates that he is ultimately in control. Circumstances will never become unmanageable, for the Lord will accomplish his purposes despite what seems to be utter chaos.

Ezekiel 9:4–6 reveals that centuries earlier, the Lord's "cross mark" of ownership, care, and protection on his people was the Hebrew letter *tav*.[8] Revelation 3:12, 14:1, and 22:4 indicate that in the time of the end, the Creator's sacred name is the visible imprint he places on the foreheads of his bondservants.[9] God's seal is the exact opposite of the mark of the sea-beast mentioned in 13:16.[10] These imprints place the people of the world in two distinct categories—those whom the Lord owns and those whom Satan controls—both in action and attitude.

Throughout history, Scripture has divided people into two broad groups—those who worship and serve the Creator and those who, in contrast, idolize and gratify themselves in slavish imitation of the devil. Through the gift of faith,[11] the Son frees baptized, Spirit-filled, and Spirit-empowered believers from the kingdom of darkness and makes them citizens of the kingdom of light.[12]

Revelation 7:4–8 states that God will place his seal on the foreheads of 144,000 people from the various tribes of Israel. The Lord chooses 12,000 people from each tribe. This numbering recalls the military censuses of Israelite warriors, whom God used to conquer Canaan. The ancient tallies were recorded in Numbers.[13] Also noteworthy is that the

6. See 2 Cor 1:22; Eph 4:30.

7. See 2 Tim 2:19.

8. Which, in turn, was the source of the lowercase English letter "t."

9. See Apoc. El. 1:9; 5:4; 4 Ezra 2:38; 6:5; Jub. 15:26; Pss. Sol. 15:6.

10. See our discussion of Rev 13:17; 14:9, 11; 16:2; 19:20; 20:4.

11. See Eph 2:8–9.

12. See 2 Cor 4:6; Col 1:12–13.

13. Particularly, Num 1:3, 18, 20, 26; 26:2, 4; 31:1–6, 14, 48, 52, 54; see 1 Chr 27:23; 2 Chr 25:5.

tribes of Ephraim and Dan are omitted from the list in Revelation 7:4–8, perhaps due to their tendency toward harlotrous and idolatrous behavior.[14] In their place, the tribes of Levi and Joseph are added.[15]

The identity of the 144,000 saints remains debated. Some think that they are a select, restored remnant from the literal twelve tribes of Israel and that they will evangelize the lost during a future seven-year great tribulation. Others claim that they are a specific number of believers whom the Lord will in some way shield during a final period of distress. Most likely, 144,000[16] is a symbolic number for the fullness of the people of God.[17] In other words, the Creator will bring all his reborn children safely to their eternal home with him in heaven.[18]

In fulfillment of God's covenant promises to Abraham,[19] the Lord will protect this messianic, multiethnic cohort by giving them the strength they need to endure persecution and remain loyal to him. A less likely option is that God will remove (or rapture) them from the earth before a time of severe distress at the end of the age.

The Occurrence of Twelve and Its Multiples in Revelation[20]	
Twelve angels	21:12
Twelve apostles	21:14
Twelve foundations for the city's walls	21:14
Twelve gate-sized pearls in the new Jerusalem	21:12, 21
Twelve kinds of fruit from the Tree of Life	22:2
12,000 stadia for the city's length and width (12 times 1,000)	21:16
Twelve stars in the woman's crown	12:1
Twelve tribes of Israel	21:12

14. See Judg 17:1–13; 18:1–7, 18, 29–30; 1 Kings 12:29–30; Hos 4:17–19; Amos 8:14; T. Dan 5:6.

15. Though neither of these tribes are included in the lists of Num 1–2. For an extensive discussion of the ordering of the twelve tribes listed in Rev 7:4–8 with the ordering of the twelve tribes in the Old Testament, see Beale, *The Book of Revelation*, 416–23; Schreiner, *Revelation*, 293–99; Stefanovic, *Revelation*, 262–68.

16. Calculated by using twelve as a multiple of twelve times one thousand.

17. See Rom 2:29; Gal 3:29; 6:16; Phil 3:3; 1 Pet 2:9; Rev 14:1, 3.

18. In this way, God will transform his reborn children from the church militant to the church triumphant.

19. See Gen 12:2; 13:16; 15:5; 17:4, 16; 22:17–18; 26:4; 32:12; Hos 1:10; Jub. 13:20; 14:4–5; Heb 11:12.

20. Table adapted from information presented in Tabb, *All Things New*, 103.

The Occurrence of Twelve and Its Multiples in Revelation[20]	
144 cubits for the city's wall (either its thickness or height; 12 times 12)	21:17
144,000 (12 as a multiple of 12 times 1,000) sealed followers of the Lamb	7:4–8; 14:1, 3

THE VAST NUMBER OF WORSHIPERS (7:9–12)

In the unfolding cosmic drama, John witnesses a vast crowd in heaven that is too large to "count" (v. 9).[21] Certainly, the depth of their unity far exceeds any earthly counterpart. Like the 144,000 described in verses 4–8, this comparable multiethnic throng is composed of people from "every nation, tribe, people, and language" (v. 9). They all stand before the "throne" of the Creator and before the "Lamb," who is in the middle, near the royal seat (v. 17).[22]

Many ideas have been suggested regarding the identity of this host of believers. They could be the saved of all the ages, only Gentile believers, or martyrs killed during a final period of great distress, to name three common views. In any case, John is impressed by the widespread representation of this cohort. No people group is excluded. As with 5:9, 7:9 shows evidence of the success of missionary work.

One remarkable aspect of the celestial scene John witnessed is the position of countless believers before the Creator. While the earth is about to feel the full force of his wrath (namely, covenantal curses), these saints are standing in his sacred presence, apart from all harm, feeling safe and secure (namely, covenantal blessings). The Lord accepts and honors them as his true bondservants.

The early readers of Revelation might have associated "white" clothing with the garb of Roman generals, who dressed in this fashion when celebrating their triumphs. The long, flowing, "white robes" worn by the saints in heaven represent the purity, righteousness, and glory of the Messiah, all of which they received by faith.[23]

John notes that the multitudes he sees in heaven are holding "palm branches," which they use to pay homage to the Messiah. The early

21. See 4 Ezra 4:40–42.

22. As we previously noted, the Creator's throne occupies the literary center of John's prophetic oracle; see our discussion of Rev 5:6; 22:1, 3.

23. See Ps 51:7; Isa 1:18; 2 En. 22:9; 4 Ezra 3:39–40; 1 John 1:7; Rev 22:14.

church regarded palm branches as a symbol of Jesus' victory over death. Moreover, they represented complete triumph and unending joy.

In ancient times, people used palm branches in a variety of ways. For instance, returning Roman conquerors wore garlands fashioned from palm branches. Also, Greek athletes received wreaths made from palm branches for winning important events. Furthermore, the Jews used palms to build shelters during the Festival of Tabernacles as an occasion to express their joy at God's deliverance and preservation of them during their exodus from Egypt.[24]

Everything about the heavenly scene John witnesses points to the unconditional acceptance of God's reborn children in his presence. They are celebrating victory in a place of honor before the Creator and the "Lamb" (v. 9). The truths disclosed here are reflected in the chorus shouted by the multitudes in heaven, perhaps as they continuously wave their palm branches in front of God's "throne" (v. 10). They acknowledge that "salvation" comes only from God the Father, who sits in supreme repose on his royal seat, along with his Son, the "Lamb," who offered his life as an atoning sacrifice for humanity's sins.[25]

John notes that "all the angels" (v. 11) who "stood around" the Creator's "throne" kneel before it with their "faces" to the ground. Likewise, the twenty-four "elders" and the "four living creatures" kneel with the "angels." This vast group "worship[s]" the Creator and sings a chorus of praise to him (v. 12). The liturgical utterance "Amen" introduces the sevenfold doxology, and "Amen" closes it.[26] The heavenly choir first uses "Amen" to register approval of the cry of the multitude. Similarly, the respondents shout, "Amen," at the end to affirm the reliability of each quality belonging to God.

The "angels" (v. 11), twenty-four "elders," and "four living creatures" ascribe seven different attributes to the Creator. As was the case in 1:6, 4:11, and 5:13, so too in 7:12 each term in the doxology is accented in the original language by the definite article "the" to indicate totality—namely, *all the* "blessing," *all the* "glory," *all the* "wisdom," and so forth. The idea is that the Father and the Son, along with the sevenfold Spirit, are perfect in every way, and so they deserve exclusive and unlimited praise from their creatures.

24. See Lev 23:40–43; Neh 8:13–17; Zech 14:16; 1 Macc 13:51–52; 2 Macc 10:5–8; T. Naph. 5:4; John 12:12–13.

25. See Exod 15:2; Ps 3:8; Rev 12:10; 19:1.

26. See our discussion of Rev 1:7; 3:14, 5:14; 19:4; 22:20, 21.

THE IDENTITY OF THE WORSHIPERS (7:13–17)

In the unfolding cosmic drama, John seems curious about the identity and origin of the vast number of people who are "clothed" (v. 9) in long, flowing, "white robes" and standing before the supreme Monarch's royal seat. If so, one of the twenty-four "elders" (v. 13) discerns his interest and rhetorically asks the apostle about the multitude.[27] John, rather than trying to bluff his way through an inaccurate response, humbly admits that he does not know the answer to the elder's question. The apostle looks to the speaker, whom John literally addresses as "my lord," for clarification (v. 14).

Based on the elder's response, some identify the "great tribulation" with a final period of intense persecution shortly before the Messiah's return.[28] Others, however, note that believers have endured affliction and grief throughout history, so the entire church age could be seen as encountering periods of severe distress.[29] Perhaps John intends to console and comfort both first-century Christians as well as God's children living during a time of final crisis. If so, this aim is reinforced by mentioning that the saints' "robes" (v. 14) are "washed" and whitened in the "blood of the Lamb."

The people in this vast throng, like all believers,[30] are redeemed, cleansed, and pardoned because of the Messiah's sacrificial death on the cross.[31] The disputed identity of this group does not alter the hope John conveys in his prophetic oracle. Through faith in the Son, we too can find acceptance before the Father and will someday experience his glory. In Romans 5:2, Paul likewise notes that through the gift of faith in the Son, we are recipients of the Father's grace and rejoice in the confident expectation of sharing in his glory.

The elder discloses to John that throughout eternity, the redeemed will worship the Creator. Indeed, as a regenerate, baptized priesthood, they will minister (or offer praise) "day and night" (Rev 7:15) before his sacred "throne" within his heavenly "temple."[32] Yet labor for the Lord will be a delight, performed without the fatigue and boredom that so often mark

27. See Jer 1:11, 13; 24:3; Amos 7:8; 8:2; Zech 4:5; 4 Ezra 2:44.

28. See Dan 12:1; Matt 24:21.

29. See John 15:20; 16:33; Acts 14:22; 2 Thess 1:5–6; 2 Tim 3:1, 12.

30. Including those mentioned in Rev 7:4–8.

31. See 1 Cor 6:11; Heb 9:14, 24; 1 John 1:7.

32. Or inner sanctuary; see Ps 134:1; 1 Chron 9:33; 23:30.

activities in this life. Scripture does not reveal what that service would entail, but surely it will involve continuous adoration and praise.

The Greek verb translated "spread his tent" has a rich Old Testament heritage. It conveys the notion of dwelling or taking up residence and was used for God's sacred presence with Israel in the tabernacle and later in the Jerusalem temple.[33] The term refers to the Creator's sheltering and protecting his children. In eternity, the Lord's glorious presence will never fade away from the redeemed as it did from Israel.[34]

The scene John witnesses in heaven tells suffering believers that their struggles (as the church militant) are worth the effort. Their oppressors might think that they are the winners. Yet in actuality, these victims are the real champions. Moreover, Jesus' beleaguered disciples can look forward to celebrating a tremendous victory (as the church triumphant) in God's holy presence. In contrast, the persecutors will face the Creator's wrath, especially for maltreating and murdering the redeemed.

Verses 16 and 17 present a dramatic contrast to the covenantal curses of death, famine, war, and sorrow in chapter 6. The Christians who endure hardship and martyrdom as the Messiah's faithful followers will find rest and relief from their pain.[35] The sorrows of earth will be utterly eclipsed by the glory of heaven for every believer.[36]

Specifically, the redeemed will no longer experience either hunger or thirst. Also, the Creator will shield them from any form of "scorching heat" (7:16), especially that produced by the "sun."[37] The Bible does not tell us all that we might like to know about the nature of life in eternity. But from what Scripture does say, we learn that the Creator takes care of our every need. In the Lord's sacred presence, we experience grace, joy, and comfort.

As seen in Genesis 3:22–24, God expelled (or exiled) Adam and Eve from the primordial garden's sacred enclave so that they would not eat the fruit produced by the Tree of Life. After all, the Creator did not want the couple to live forever in their sinful state. The following table delineates the theme of *exile* in Scripture. It is a prime example of typological fulfillment or prophetic foreshadowing. Specifically, the symbolism of

33. See Exod 13:21–22; 25:8; 29:45; 40:34–38; Lev 26:11–12; Deut 12:5, 11; 2 Chr 7:1–3; Isa 4:5–6; Ezek 37:24–28; Zech 2:10; 8:3; John 1:14.

34. See our discussion of Rev 21:3; 22:3–4.

35. See Ps 121:5–6; Apoc. El. 1:9; 5:6; 1 En. 48:1; Matt 5:6; John 4:14; 6:35; 7:37.

36. See our discussion of Rev 21:4, 6; 22:2.

37. See our discussion of Rev 22:5.

the exile involves identifying and recalling patterns of earlier historical events that are mirrored in and correspond to later episodes recorded in the Bible.[38]

The Theme of Exile in Scripture		
Figure/People	**Nature of Exile**	**Biblical References**
Adam and Eve	Expelled from the Garden of Eden	Gen 3:22–24
Cain	Banished from God's presence after murdering Abel	Gen 4:11–14
Abraham and Sarah	Called to leave their homeland in Ur	Gen 12:1, 4; Heb 11:8
Abraham and Sarah	Journey to Egypt during a famine	Gen 12:10
Hagar	Banished from Abraham's household	Gen 21:10, 14
Jacob	Fled to Haran to escape Esau's anger	Gen 27:43; 28:2, 5, 10
Joseph	Sold into slavery and taken to Egypt	Gen 37:28, 36; 39:1; Acts 7:9
Jacob and his family	Relocated from Canaan to Egypt	Gen 45:28; 46:3–4, 6–7, 26–27; Acts 7:15
Moses	Fled from Pharaoh to Midian	Exod 2:15; Acts 7:29
Naomi and her family	Relocated to Moab as foreigners	Ruth 1:1–2
David and his men	Sought refuge in the wilderness	1 Sam 23:14, 24–25, 29; 24:1
Northern kingdom of Israel	Exiled to Assyria	2 Kgs 17:6, 18, 20, 23
Manasseh	Taken captive to Babylon	2 Chr 33:11
Southern kingdom of Judah	Exiled to Babylon	2 Kgs 25:11, 21; 2 Chr 36:20
Jesus and his parents	Fled to Egypt to escape Herod	Matt 2:13–15
Jesus	Descended to the realm of the dead	Acts 2:24, 31; Eph 4:9–10; 1 Pet 3:18–19

38. For an extensive discussion of the exile motif in the Apocalypse, see Pattemore, *The People of God*. He maintains that John's prophetic oracle reinterprets Old Testament covenant language to present the Christian community as the true heirs of Israel's promises, even as they endure suffering and exile in the present age. He notes that like Israel in Babylonian exile, the churches in Rev 2–3 are portrayed as scattered among the nations. Also, he observes that the new Jerusalem (chs. 21–22) functions as the promised restoration, reversing the spiritual and political exile of the redeemed.

Unlike Adam and Eve's exile from Eden, in Revelation 7:17, the "Lamb," who is positioned at the "center" of the supreme Monarch's celestial dais, uses his royal scepter to show the redeemed the way to streams flowing with life-giving "water." The imagery is that of a shepherd who leads and guides his sheep to a clear, pristine spring in the desert.[39] Salvation from the death that sin brought into the world will be complete. In heaven, the righteous will enjoy abundant covenantal blessings, including everlasting existence.

The elder tells John that the Creator will "wipe away" all "tears" from the "eyes" of his reborn children. Here, we find an allusion to Isaiah 25:8.[40] In heaven, the redeemed will never again experience pain, suffering, sickness, grief, or death. Moreover, in the coming age, the Lord will never allow their pasts to bring them remorse.

Having taken believers to heaven, the Lord will not abandon them. His sacred presence will always be with them, bringing them unimaginable delight. Also, in eternity, the Father will provide for the needs of his Son's faithful followers. Those who are about to be martyred at the hands of pagan, earthly authorities, including the Roman emperor and his subordinates, can take heart at this vivid glimpse of the glory that awaits them. Similarly, a vast number of Christians throughout history have received courage to face life's trials by meditating on the truths John discloses in his prophetic oracle.

Shepherding in Biblical Times		
Aspect	**Responsibilities**	**Features and Benefits**
Daily Care	Lead the flocks to good pasturelands with adequate grazing; guide sheep to ample water supplies for daily hydration; provide continuous supervision and guidance	Ensures sheep are well-fed and hydrated; prevents wandering and potential injury; maintains flock health
Defense against Predators	Ward off attacks from savage animals (lions, bears, wolves); use rod and staff for protection and control; fight predators with primitive weapons	Protects the flock from harm; shepherd risks personal safety for the flock's security

39. See Ps 23:1–2; Isa 40:8–11; 49:8–10; Jer 2:13; Ezek 34:11–16, 23; John 4:14; 6:35; 7:38–39; 10:11; Heb 3:20; 1 Pet 2:25; 5:4.

40. See our discussion of Rev 21:4.

Shepherding in Biblical Times		
Aspect	**Responsibilities**	**Features and Benefits**
Flock Management	Maintain flock unity and prevent scattering; count and account for each sheep regularly; tend to injured or sick animals	Ensures all sheep are accounted for; promotes flock health and cohesion
Nighttime Security	Maintain vigilant watch throughout the night; position themselves as barriers against threats; multiple shepherds may combine flocks for safety	Prevents sheep from wandering away; enhances flock safety during vulnerable hours
Personal Sacrifice	Willingness to risk their own lives for the sheep; endure harsh weather conditions alongside flock	Demonstrates dedication to the flock's well-being; ensures the flock's survival under challenging conditions
Sheepfold Structure	Construct protected enclosure with single entrance; use branches or stone walls for enclosure; design with strategic single entrance for control	Blocks wild animals from entering; allows communal use by multiple shepherds; provides physical barrier against threats
Shelter Provision	Find adequate shelter for weather protection; ensure safe resting places during travel; plan routes with appropriate stopping points	Protects from harsh weather conditions; ensures safe resting during travel

KEY THEOLOGICAL INSIGHTS

The natural expectation at the end of Revelation 6 is that we would encounter the seventh seal judgment. After all, the first six seal calamities have been swiftly described, leaving the reader, or listener,[41] in awe of God's overwhelming judgment of earth's wicked inhabitants. Yet as we noted above, when we come to chapter 7, we see a dramatic delay in the unleashing of the seventh calamity. From the perspective of the reader, or listener, this pause offers a reprieve from the weightiness of divinely imposed catastrophes. Within this interlude we find a glorious picture of God's salvific intentions for his reborn children.

First, *we note that salvation is entirely the work of God.* He delays widespread judgment to set apart his faithful bondservants. In this way, the Lord demonstrates his supreme authority—both over the forces of

41. See our discussion of Rev 1:3.

destruction (including the natural disasters they bring) and over those who receive his mercy (vv. 1–3). Later, as we encounter the celebration offered by the redeemed, we do not find them either praising themselves or taking credit for their perseverance in the faith. To be sure, there is a faith response on the part of those who believe.[42] And yet, the saints' faith and faithfulness are not a work that merits God's favor. Rather, these are a grace-enabled response[43] to what the Creator has done for them. Therefore, the song of the redeemed is directed toward the loving Father and the worthy Lamb with the proclamation that "salvation comes from our God" (v. 10).

Second, *we observe that God's reborn children are "sealed"*[44] *by him*. As we noted above, we learn elsewhere in Scripture that this sealing is brought about by the Holy Spirit, assuring us that God's elect will see the fulfillment of his salvific work, resulting in everlasting life. The indwelling presence of the Spirit is God's gift to believers, signifying a deposit that guarantees their spiritual inheritance of eternal life and its rewards.[45] That we are sealed "for[46] the day of redemption"[47] is the Father's gracious work through the Spirit. It demonstrates that God's plan will be accomplished, regardless of appearances to the contrary, such as the pain, suffering, and even martyrdom of his reborn children.[48]

Third, *God's placing his "seal" on us means that we are "owned" by him*. We are his "bondservants,"[49] marked (sealed) in a way that reveals that we are God's possession. The notion of "ownership" (of people)—and

42. This faith response is observed when one of the twenty-four elders indicates that the multitude praising God have "washed their robes . . . in the blood of the Lamb" (7:14).

43. As such, even our faith is rightly said to be a gift from God; see Eph 2:8–10.

44. In this portion of Revelation, John uses both the noun (Rev 7:2) and various verbal forms (vv. 3, 4, 5, 8) of the Greek term rendered "seal" as points of repeated emphasis to describe what God is doing. From a literary perspective, it seems that the reader is called to careful reflection on what it means to be imprinted (that is, authenticated and confirmed) with the seal of God.

45. See Eph 1:13–14.

46. The preposition "for" typically indicates purpose, but it can also express time or destination. Thus, the phrase "sealed for the day of redemption" could also be translated as "sealed to" or "unto the day of redemption." In this context, the emphasis is on the enduring nature of the seal. It will remain in effect until the day when our redemption is fully realized.

47. See Eph 4:30.

48. See 2 Cor 4:17–18.

49. As we noted above, literally "slaves."

even more so, "slavery"—is highly offensive in our present day, and for good reason. Almost as far back as human history itself, people of various tribal and ethnic groups were subjected to slavery and sold as pieces of property, without any individual rights or dignity bestowed upon them. Even now, while the institution of slavery is denounced worldwide, there are pockets of it around the world, manifested in human trafficking, indentured servitude, forced marriage, and other means of reducing human beings to tradeable commodities.[50] It makes sense that some may recoil at the notion that the Creator "owns" us or that we are his "bondservants."

However, God's ownership of us is not oppressive, unjust, or immoral. The King of all creation is justified to enact his lordship over those whom he claims as his own. He does not owe us an explanation;[51] nor is he accountable to our notions of human rights to which we might think we are entitled. Yet rather than owning us to our detriment, the Creator asserts his lordship over us for our temporal and eternal benefit.[52] The issue is not so much that we *must* submit to his possession of us. Instead, it is that we *get* to be his possession. To belong to our loving Father and gracious Redeemer is to be in the best of all possible places. We have received his merciful rescue from sin and spiritual death, having been purchased by the shed blood of the Lamb (v. 14).[53]

Fourth, *God's seal of ownership renders us secure in our salvation.* We need not fear that the Creator is somehow unable to watch over us in his saving grace. He promises to do so, and that protection is assured in accordance with God's holy character. His seal, which is the indwelling Spirit, shows that we are safe in the Father's almighty hand, from which

50. While some first-century Christians kept slaves, the New Testament provides indications that institutional slavery is evil and should be abolished (for example, Paul's brief letter to Philemon). During the centuries since the Messiah's birth, Christians in Europe and America not only reassessed their views on slavery but also sought to limit and abolish it. For instance, one of the most powerful arguments Christian abolitionists used against slavery was that all human beings are created in the image of God and have inherent dignity and value. Accordingly, Christians sought to replace all systems of cruel and inhumane bondage and forced labor with the principles of equality, individual rights, and self-determination for all people in society, regardless of their ethnicity, gender, socioeconomic status, and so on. For a sobering, even shocking, picture of modern slavery, with particular emphasis in Majority World contexts, see walkfree.org.

51. See Job 38:1—42:6.

52. A notable temporal benefit is that believers are preserved from the "demonic influences" of the antichrist. See Charles, *Commentary on Revelation*, vol. 1, 194–96.

53. See 1 Cor 6:19–20.

no entity in all creation can ever remove us.[54] While some may see this notion of security as a license to luxuriate in sin, true believers do not flippantly apply God's unmerited favor to themselves.[55] Our security in the Messiah does not lead to unrestrained sinful behavior. Instead, it provides the foundation, reason, and motivation for our wholehearted pursuit of Christlike holiness.

IMPORTANT MINISTRY IMPLICATIONS

From the theological insights we present in the preceding section, along with a consideration of the worship offered by the saints, we can ascertain principles for ministry that are applicable across diverse local church contexts. First, when considering God's sealing his bondservants, *we see the glaring contrast between those suffering on earth in the time of judgment and those under God's protective hand, who worship him and the Lamb around the royal throne.* As we indicated earlier, all people in all places and at all times are distinguished as those who are redeemed and those who are not. This differentiation represents a theological and spiritual reality, and it also offers a point of application for ministry. Communicators of the gospel must be honest and straightforward about this dichotomy. Many in our world today bristle at the thought of God's being exclusive or selective, and many may turn away from notions of divine demands or expectations.[56] Yet those called to preach the truth of God's Word must never avoid the reality that while the Creator desires all to come to repentance and faith,[57] in the end, not everyone will receive the salvation he freely offers in Christ.[58]

54. See John 10:27–29; Rom 8:38–39; 1 Pet 1:3–5.

55. See Rom 6:1–14.

56. Such as the call to recognize one's sinfulness, repent, die to self, forsake all to follow Christ, and pursue holiness and righteousness. Many popular televangelists and promoters of the prosperity gospel often avoid the more difficult demands of the Christian message to attract the widest possible following. Frequently, the only burden they place on their audience is the expectation of generous financial contributions to their ministries. This deception has had a particularly harmful impact in Majority World contexts, where people are urged to give sacrificially from their limited resources with the false promise of material blessings in return. When the gospel of Christ is distorted in this way, the consequences are inevitably tragic.

57. See 1 Tim 2:4; 2 Pet 3:9.

58. See our discussion of Rev 20:15.

Second, *we can assure our fellow believers that their salvation will be brought to completion*. At the consummation of the age, God will surely fulfill all his promises. The pains, sorrows, struggles, and trials of the present will end, and they will pale in comparison to the glory revealed when we see Christ face-to-face.[59] We can encourage our parishioners to find rest in this comforting truth. We can also help them withstand the devil's attacks and influences, who seeks to rob our joy and destroy our confidence in the Messiah's guarantee of final victory (vv. 15–17). To minister in this way is a distinct blessing, especially as we share this truth with God's reborn children.

Nonetheless, the assurance of salvation can sometimes feel distant, especially when we fall into sinful thoughts, words, or actions. Yet our security in Christ remains an objective reality, grounded not in our feelings or performance but in God's unchanging character and promises—chiefly his justifying work in Christ. The subjective sense of assurance we experience may waver, often influenced by our conscience and emotions. When we persist in unrepented sin, our hearts become dulled to the comfort of the gospel, and we may no longer feel the assurance that remains ours in union with Christ.[60] Therefore, church leaders should exhort the faithful to daily repentance and the pursuit of godly living—not as a condition for salvation but so that believers may more fully enjoy the present and eternal comfort of the grace already given to them in Christ.

Third, *congregational leaders have the privilege of guiding faith communities in heartfelt worship of God*. The sevenfold doxology in verse 12 vividly illustrates the Lord's worthiness and the worship he deserves. Similar proclamations have been made by worshipers surrounding the royal throne,[61] as we noted earlier. Observing such worship teaches us valuable lessons. Therefore, we should think about whether our own worship reflects the same depth of praise and adoration described in verse 12.

For example, in our corporate worship,

- Do we offer praise (*blessing*) to God for who he is?
- Do we extol (*glory*) God's virtues to make him known?
- Do we assert God's all-knowing and skillful working (*wisdom*) in our lives?

59. See Rom 8:18; 1 John 3:2–3.

60. See 1 John 3:19–21.

61. See our discussion of Rev 4:8, 11; 5:9–10, 12–13.

- Do we express our gratitude (*thanksgiving*) for what God has done for us?
- Do we acknowledge (*honor*) God's holiness and righteousness in a spirit of reverence?
- Do we declare God's omnipotence (*power*) as the almighty Creator?
- Do we affirm God's ability (*might*) to do all that he has promised in and for us through the glorified and exalted Lamb?

VITAL MISSIONAL RAMIFICATIONS

The missional ramifications we discuss here in connection with our exposition of Revelation 7 arise from understanding the identity and character of those whom God has sealed and gathered to worship him and who ultimately find rest in his gracious provision and protection. First, we consider the 144,000 (vv. 4–8). As we noted above, there are various views about the identity of this multitude, along with the specific reasons John mentions them here. Whether this number represents the fullness of the people of God or whether it represents a Jewish remnant, *we see that God is at work in calling out a people for his name, even in times of distress and tribulation*. The Creator delays judgment to allow his reborn children to be sealed (vv. 1–3), which occurs because they are redemptively united with the Messiah. Furthermore, union with him can happen only when the gospel is proclaimed, heard, understood, believed, and received.[62]

In our missionary efforts, we must not look for times of comfort and convenience to share the good news. We should not waste opportunities and resources waiting for the perfect situation to present the message of salvation. We can expect to experience difficulty and encounter resistance.[63] In some Majority World contexts where religious persecution is severe, believers may face suffering and even martyrdom. In these moments of intense hardship, God calls us to rely on him, trust in his providential care, and continue our mission for the sake of his name.[64]

Second, we consider the innumerable multitude (v. 9). Just as in 5:9, here in 7:9 we see people from every nation, tribe, people, and language.

62. See Rom 10:14–15.

63. See John 15:18–20.

64. See Rom 1:5.

When we think about the global diversity of our present day and the tens of thousands of languages and dialects spoken by various people groups, we are overcome with awe at all the people whom God loves. He does indeed care for humankind to this infinite extent![65] Yet while we stand amazed at the Creator's lovingkindness, we must remember that *verse 9 is a future scene, namely, a display of the abundant fruit of missionary efforts throughout the earth, as well as an affirmation of the indisputable power of the gospel.*

Third, *God's redemptive promises and plans are fulfilled with remarkable success*, which naturally draws our attention. People are often attracted to success—whether in taking on projects they believe will succeed, investing in businesses with strong potential for profit, or surrounding themselves with accomplished individuals in hopes of sharing in their success. Even in ministry, we are often captivated by people and places that have a proven track record of spiritual fruitfulness. While an excessive focus on success can be harmful, this inclination is understandable and can be channeled for both earthly and eternal good when aligned with God's purposes.

As God's reborn children, we have the immense privilege and responsibility to participate in his mission of witness to the world. This includes sharing his message with those in our immediate vicinity, like a neighbor across the street, as well as those in distant lands. Given this profound calling, we should consider whether our commitment to missions aligns with the success[66] God has ordained for his glory and our good. Let's wholeheartedly embrace our part in God's grand design and strive to carry out his Great Commission faithfully. We can be confident that through our faith and faithfulness, empowered by the Holy Spirit, the Lord's redemptive purposes will be accomplished and his name will be glorified.

65. See John 3:16.

66. Wall, *Revelation*, 120, reminds us that this success arises out of suffering and tribulation that, in many cases, the faithful are called to endure.

Revelation 8

The Trumpet Judgments (Part One)

LEARNING OBJECTIVES

- Identify the significance of the opening of the seventh seal and the resulting silence in heaven.
- Understand the connection between the prayers of the saints and the unfolding of God's judgments.
- Analyze the meaning of the seven trumpets and the devastating plagues they bring.
- Explain the eagle's warning of even direr calamities to come.
- Consider why earth's wicked inhabitants refuse to repent.

CHAPTER SUMMARY

Revelation 8 begins with the Lamb's opening the seventh seal, which is followed by silence in heaven. Then an angel with a censer offers the prayers of the saints on the golden altar in front of God's royal throne. Next, the angel takes the censer, fills it with fire from the altar, and hurls it to the earth. This action is followed by seven trumpet blasts that unleash a series of devastating plagues. The first four include hail and fire; a huge, burning mountain which falls into the sea; a great star's falling and poisoning a third of the rivers; and the darkening of a third of the sun, moon, and stars. Finally, an eagle calls out in a loud voice for sinners to repent before it is too late.

STUDY QUESTIONS

1. Why is there silence in heaven after the seventh seal is broken?
2. What do the prayers of the saints represent?
3. What do the four trumpet judgments symbolize?
4. How does the eagle's threefold declaration of woe introduce the remaining trumpet judgments?
5. How do the trumpet judgments stress the importance of repentance and redemption as well as our responsibility to warn unbelievers?

CHAPTER OUTLINE

- The seventh seal and the golden censer (8:1–5)
- The first four trumpet judgments (8:6–13)
- Key theological insights
- Important ministry implications
- Vital missional ramifications

THE SEVENTH SEAL AND THE GOLDEN CENSER (8:1–5)

The marking of God's bondservants takes place between the opening of the sixth and seventh seal judgments (7:3). In this way, the Creator pledges to watch over those whom he set apart with his "seal." He will bring them to heaven, where they will dwell with him for all eternity. Meanwhile, chapter 7 of John's prophetic oracle provides a long interlude in the sequence of opening the seals.

As the narrative moves to chapter 8, the unfolding cosmic drama resumes. The "Lamb" (6:16) is about to unleash a huge firestorm of his "wrath" (or covenantal curses) on the wicked of the earth. Only those who abandon their evil ways (namely, repent) and trust in the Messiah have any hope of redemption. John then witnesses that about thirty minutes of "silence" throughout "heaven" follow the opening of the "seventh seal" by the "Lamb" (8:1).[1] This eerie quiet stands in sharp contrast to

1. See 4 Ezra 6:39; 7:30; Let. Aris. 95; LAB 60:2; Wis 18:14.

the thundering chorus of worshipers who previously sang praises to the Father and Son.[2]

One possibility is that the "silence" functions as a dramatic prelude to unleashing the trumpet judgments.[3] Another possibility is that the supreme Monarch of the universe calls for "silence" so that all can see how he will respond to the "prayers" (v. 3) of his martyred children, who have endured hardship at the hands of earth's wicked inhabitants.[4] A less likely option is that the great hush symbolizes the believers' eternal rest in God's sacred presence.

Next, John witnesses "seven angels"[5] (v. 2) who stand before the Creator.[6] Also, one of his courtiers gives each of the "angels" a trumpet. John sees these celestial beings use their respective "trumpets" to signal the launching of a series of covenantal curses. These curses are more intense than the seal judgments of chapter 6 but not as severe as the bowl judgments of chapter 16.

The Greek noun rendered "trumpets" (8:2) might refer to a long, straight musical instrument made from bronze, iron, or silver. In ancient times, such an object had a conical or bell-shaped bore with a mouthpiece made from animal horn. Trumpets produced a clear, distinct, and high-pitched tone. People used such instruments to announce the beginning of festivals, signal a call to battle, proclaim a victory celebration, and inform people about dramatic events.[7]

Next, John witnesses an "angel" (8:3), different from the previous seven, coming to position himself at the heavenly "altar" of incense. He holds a "censer" made from "gold." During the Old Testament era, the censer would have been a small shovel or ladle made from either bronze or gold. Temple priests used censers to carry hot coals to the altar to burn incense, which produced a sweet aroma that drifted upward.[8]

2. See our discussion of Rev 7:9–11.

3. See Hab 2:20; 3:3–6; Zeph 1:7–8, 14, 18; Zech 2:13—3:2.

4. See our discussion of Rev 6:10.

5. The identity of the angels remains anonymous.

6. See 1 En. 20:2–8; Jub. 2:1–2; Tob 12:15.

7. See Exod 19:13, 16, 19; Lev 23:24; 25:9; Num 10:1–10; Josh 6:4, 8; 1 Sam 13:3; 2 Sam 6:15; 1 Kgs 1:34, 39; 1 Chr 15:24; 2 Chr 5:12; Neh 12:41; Pss 47:5; 98:6; Isa 27:13; 58:1; Jer 4:5; 20:16; 51:27; Zech 9:14–15; Apoc. Ab. 31:1–3; 4 Ezra 6:23; LAE 22:1–2; Matt 24:31; 1 Cor 15:52; 1 Thess 4:16.

8. See Exod 30:1–10; 40:26; Lev 6:12; 16:12–13; Num 16:46; 1 Kgs 7:50; Ps 141:2; Luke 1:8–10; Phil 4:18; Heb 9:4.

In keeping with the preceding observations, the apostle witnesses the receipt by the "angel" of a huge quantity of "incense." The celestial being offers this incense, along with the "prayers" of "all the saints," on the "gold altar" in front of the Creator's royal seat.[9] Then the incense-laced smoke and the petitions of God's holy people billow up to him (v. 4). Most likely, the redeemed entreat the Lord to judge earth's wicked inhabitants by unleashing the covenantal curses and to inaugurate his kingdom quickly.[10] In turn, he honors the requests of his children for justice to prevail.

Next, God has the "angel" (v. 5) fill the "censer" with "fire"[11] obtained from the "altar" and heave its contents down to the "earth."[12] This dramatic action signals the end of the silence in heaven and the onset of seven covenantal curses associated with the blowing of seven trumpets. "Crashes of thunder" and "rumblings" followed by "flashes of lightning" and an "earthquake" dramatically signal this turning point in John's prophetic oracle.[13]

THE FIRST FOUR TRUMPET JUDGMENTS (8:6–13)

In the unfolding cosmic drama, when "seven angels" (v. 6) blow their respective "trumpets," the wicked on earth experience God's retributive justice. Specialists have noted that the trumpet calamities somewhat resemble the various plagues that the Creator brought upon Egypt through Moses.[14]

As we previously noted, the preceding correlation is sometimes referred to as exodus typology or prophetic foreshadowing. It serves as a sign of the Creator's active, sovereign involvement throughout salvation history, including the three cycles of judgment recorded in the Apocalypse. This correlation also serves to heighten the ominous and devastating significance of the adversities to follow, in which the Lord brings about a new exodus for his regenerate children. Just as he showed his

9. As we previously noted, the Creator's throne occupies the literary center of John's prophetic oracle.

10. See 3 Bar. 11:8–9; 1 En. 9:2–3, 10; 47:2; 99:3; T. Dan 6:5; T. Levi 3:5–7; Tob 12:12; Rev 5:8; 6:9–10; 9:13; 14:18; 15:7; 16:3, 7.

11. Most likely, the "fire" (Rev 8:5) is produced by burning coals.

12. See Ezek 10:2–7.

13. See Exod 19:16–20; 20:18–19; 2 Sam 22:8–10; Pss 18:12, 14; 29:7; Isa 13:13; Ezek 1:13; Nah 1:5; Hag 2:6; Heb 12:18; Rev 4:5; 10:3; 11:19; 16:18.

14. See Exod 7–11.

disgust for the idolatries of Egypt, so too at the end of the age, he reveals his abhorrence for the harlotries of earth's wicked inhabitants.

The Continuing Relevance of the Exodus Event		
Theme	**Biblical References**	**Significance**
Jesus' Transfiguration	Luke 9:28–31	Jesus discusses his "departure" (Greek *exodos*) with Moses and Elijah, thereby linking the Messiah's passion to Israel's exodus. This symbolizes liberation from slavery to Satan, sin, and death.
Redemption Parallel	Exodus narrative; New Testament Christology (for example, Rom 3:24; Col 1:13–14)	God redeems Israel from physical bondage through Moses. Christ redeems lost humanity from spiritual bondage through his atoning sacrifice, thereby establishing a new and greater exodus.
Typology of the Passover Lamb	Exod 12; John 1:29, 36; 1 Cor 5:7; 1 Pet 1:18–19	The Passover lamb's blood signifies divine deliverance. Jesus, as the "Lamb of God," fulfills this type by taking away the world's "sin," thereby surpassing the original Passover.

As we previously noted, the trumpet judgments divide into four interrelated calamities, followed by three interrelated ones.[15] For instance, the plagues associated with the first four covenantal curses affect the four major regions of the planet, namely, land, sea, fresh water, and sky. These calamities, however, are only partial, for they destroy just one-third of the land and the sea (including their lifeforms), along with one-third of the celestial bodies (Rev 8:6–12). The Creator will use the first four bowl judgments to further devastate these same regions.[16]

Consequently, when the first angel blows his "trumpet" (v. 7), he unleashes on "earth" a torrent of "hail" and "fire," all of which is "mixed with blood." In ancient Rome, people considered blood's raining from the sky as an omen indicating the anger of their pagan deities. In this case, it is a sign of God's wrath on those who are iniquitous.

John notes that one-third of the globe and its "trees" are consumed by flames. Likewise, "all the green grass" is incinerated. The hail, fire, and

15. That is, a four and three literary pattern.

16. See our discussion of Rev 16:1–9.

blood correspond to the thunder, hail, and fire of the seventh Egyptian plague in Exodus 9:22–26, as well as to the fourth and seventh bowl judgments in Revelation 16:8–9 and 21.[17]

Some specialists think the trumpet judgments should be taken at face value as describing what will occur on earth in the end times. Others, however, think that John is using graphic language of a symbolic nature. In either view, the implications of the first trumpet calamity are staggering.

When the "second angel" (Rev 8:8) blows his "trumpet," what appears to be an enormous, fiery "mountain" crashes into the "sea."[18] As a result, one-third of the water in the "sea" turns into "blood," one-third of the sea "creatures" (v. 9) perish, and one-third of all the "ships" plying the world's oceans are totally obliterated. This covenantal curse is like the first Egyptian plague, where the Nile River turned into blood.[19] The catastrophe is also comparable to the second bowl judgment in Revelation 16:3.

When the "third angel" (8:10) blows his "trumpet," an enormous "star," which blazes like a "lamp" (or torch), plummets from the "sky."[20] This fireball impacts one-third of the planet's "rivers" as well as one-third of its "springs." The Greek noun rendered "lamp" denotes a stick of wood with a twist of rope (for instance, flax or hemp) tied to its end. This torch was dipped in oil and ignited. In ancient times, such a blazing object served as a poetic symbol of terror and judgment.

John explains that "Wormwood" (v. 11) is the "name" given to the "star." This designation also refers to the bitter-tasting leaf of an aromatic herb,[21] which was used medicinally to eliminate intestinal worms. "Wormwood" is an appropriate name, for the "star" makes one-third of earth's water "bitter" or foul. Because the water is unfit for human consumption, many of the planet's wicked inhabitants perish after drinking it.[22]

When the "fourth angel" (v. 12) blows his "trumpet," an unidentified divine agent strikes one-third of the "sun," "moon," and "stars" with a forceful impact. Consequently, one-third of these celestial bodies

17. See Pss 78:47; 105:32; Isa 9:5; Ezek 21:32; 38:22; Joel 2:30–31; Sib. Or. 5:377; Sir 39:29; Wis 18:22; Acts 2:19.

18. See Jer 51:25; 1 En. 18:13; 21:3; Sib. Or. 5:158–59.

19. See Exod 7:20–25; Ps 78:44.

20. Perhaps comparable to a meteorite; see 1 En. 86:1.

21. *Artemisia absinthium.*

22. See Deut 29:17–18; Prov 5:3–4; Jer 9:15; 23:15; Lam 3:15, 19; Amos 5:6–7.

become "dark," causing one-third of the "day" and "night" to be deprived of "light." This covenantal curse is reminiscent of the ninth Egyptian plague.[23]

Revelation 8:12 could mean that the light produced by the sun, moon, and stars will be reduced in potency by one-third. Another possibility is that the twenty-four-hour cycle of day and night will, in some way, be shortened to sixteen hours. In either case, the onslaught of darkness signifies the intensity and gloom of God's judgment.

Next, as John witnesses the unfolding cosmic drama, he spots a lone "eagle" (or vulture; v. 13) traveling directly overhead in the "middle of the sky."[24] This predatory creature repeatedly shouts a threefold "woe" to earth's inhabitants, who are about to feel the withering force of God's wrath.[25] It stands in contrast to the "four living creatures" (4:8), who repeat the chorus, "Holy, holy, holy," in the presence of the "Lord God Almighty."

The Greek interjection translated "woe" (8:13) is often used in Scripture to announce the arrival of divine judgment on the planet's wicked residents.[26] Here, the three declarations of impending disaster correspond to the final three trumpet calamities, which unleash an additional series of cosmic de-creation events. The third woe consists of the seven bowl plagues described in chapter 16.[27]

As we previously noted, the series of covenantal curses unveiled in the Apocalypse represent the culmination of the judgment oracles appearing in the Old Testament, particularly Deuteronomy. Also, the solitary "eagle" (8:13) moving overhead may represent an angelic creature. If so, its purpose is to strike terror in the hearts of earth's wicked inhabitants in anticipation of the coming horrors when the final "three angels" blew their "trumpets."[28]

23. See Exod 10:21–23; Isa 13:10; Ezek 32:7–8; Joel 2:2, 10, 31; 3:15; Amos 5:18–20; 8:9; 1 En. 17:6; 63:6; 102:2; 2 En. 7:1; Jub. 5:14; LAE 36:2–3; Matt 24:29; Mark 13:24–25.

24. The placement of the creature enables it to be seen readily and heard easily.

25. As we previously noted, the Apocalypse continually emphasizes earth's unregenerate inhabitants, who venerate pagan deities; see our discussion of Rev 3:10; 6:10; 11:10; 13:8, 12, 14; 14:6; 17:2, 8.

26. See Ezek 16:23; 24:6; Matt 11:21–24; 18:7–9; 23:13–36; Mark 14:21; 1 Cor 9:16; Jude 1:11.

27. See our discussion of Rev 9:12; 11:14.

28. See our discussion of Rev 3:10; 6:10; 11:10; 13:8.

The Trumpet Judgments as a Series of Cosmic De-Creation Events[29]		
Creation Day	**Original Creation (Gen 1)**	**Cosmic De-Creation (Rev 8–9)**
Day 1	God separates light from darkness (vv. 3–5).	Fourth trumpet: A third of the sun, moon, and stars are struck, darkening a third of the day and night (Rev 8:12).
Day 2	God makes the sky (expanse; vv. 6–8).	Fifth trumpet: Smoke from the abyss darkens the sky; demon-like locusts torment humanity (Rev 9:1–12).
Day 3	God gathers the waters, revealing dry land, and creates vegetation (vv. 9–13).	First trumpet: Hail and fire mixed with blood burn a third of the earth, trees, and all green grass (Rev 8:7).
Day 4	God creates the sun, moon, and stars to govern the day and night (vv. 14–19).	Fourth trumpet (again): A third of the celestial lights are darkened (Rev 8:12).
Day 5	God fills the waters with living creatures and the sky with birds (vv. 20–23).	Second trumpet: A blazing mountain is thrown into the sea; a third of the sea becomes blood, a third of sea creatures die, and a third of ships are destroyed (Rev 8:8–9). Third trumpet: A blazing star ("Wormwood") falls on rivers and springs, making them bitter; many die (Rev 8:10–11).
Day 6	God creates humanity to rule over all creation (vv. 24–31).	Third trumpet (continued): People die from the bitter waters (Rev 8:11). Sixth trumpet: Four angels lead a cavalry of 200 million to kill a third of humanity with plagues of fire, smoke, and sulfur (Rev 9:13–18).

KEY THEOLOGICAL INSIGHTS

Following the interlude of Revelation 7, chapter 8 introduces a vivid depiction of divine judgment, more intense than any described earlier in John's prophetic oracle. As the seventh seal calamity opens to the seven

29. Table adapted from information presented in Beale, *The Book of Revelation*, 486.

trumpet judgments, we note the following theological insights that aid our understanding.

First, as we discussed in chapter 6, *we see God's power and restraint in his judgment, as well as the justification for it.* The trumpet judgments of chapter 8 demonstrate that the supreme Monarch of the universe has complete power and authority over all creation, including natural disasters and cosmic disturbances.[30] There is no time in which the occurrence of these judgments are outside the Almighty's control. However, despite the cataclysmic destruction depicted in these events, the wreckage is limited to a third of what could have been demolished (vv. 7–12). To be sure, seeing one-third of the earth's natural environment ruined is sufficiently devastating. Yet even here, the righteous Judge shows gracious restraint, because the entire planet has come under his condemnation. In addition to his power and restraint, we remember that the worthy Lamb is justified in unleashing the covenantal curses.[31] He does not answer to our sense of fairness or justice. The sovereign Lord judges according to his perfect will, and the outcomes of his judgment are always right.

Second, when we ponder the "silence in heaven for about half an hour" (v. 1) at the onset of the seventh seal, we see that *God's judgment, though fearful to behold, inspires awe in those who witness it.* One can imagine the shock at what was observed when the first six seals were opened. Hence, the anxious anticipation for what the seventh seal might bring is reflected in the quietness among the worshipers before the Creator's sacred throne. Silence is appropriate when contemplating the work of the Almighty.[32] For example, when Habakkuk hears what God had prepared for the wicked Chaldeans (Babylonians), the judgment ends with a declaration that the Lord is in his "holy temple" and that all the earth should "be silent" in his presence.[33] The all-powerful hand of the Creator inspires wonder in its working.

Third, *we are reminded that God is faithful to hear and answer the prayers of the saints.* As we noted above, another possibility for the silence in heaven involves the anticipation of how God responds to the petitions of his reborn children. Most likely, these prayers are the same

30. See Job 26:10; 37:6; 38:8–11; Pss 89:9; 127:9; 148:8; Jer 5:22; 10:13.

31. See our discussion of Rev 4:11; 5:2–5, 9–11.

32. See Zeph 1:7.

33. See Hab 2:6–20. This concluding "demand for silence" at the end of the "woes" to the Chaldeans (v. 20) is juxtaposed with the idol-maker who screams for his own lifeless creation to awaken.

ones offered earlier with a particular emphasis on the vindication of those martyred for their faith in and faithfulness to the Messiah.[34] As the hushed onlookers wait with confident expectation, they see that the Creator is trustworthy. He fulfills his promises to care for his own, and he completes his redemptive plan, including judgment on earth's wicked inhabitants.

Fourth, *we note the significance of the de-creation resulting from these judgments*. God as Creator is the basis upon which all his acts are reasoned and purposed.[35] The covenantal curses unleashed in chapter 8 harm God's good creation, which in turn brings calamity on earth dwellers. As the table above shows, each judgment here corresponds to an act of creation (though in reverse) and to one of the plagues God brought against Egypt prior to the exodus, further affirming that the natural order is under his sovereign control and care. This makes the devastation especially disturbing, because God seems to be defacing what he had originally called "good."[36]

People coming from a Majority World context tend to be keenly aware of the sacredness of their ancestral homelands. Many of these cultures articulate a belief that they are somehow connected to God through the environment itself. On the negative side, that belief can degenerate into the worship of creation rather than the Creator,[37] which would go against God's intentions. However, on the positive side, there is something valuable and commendable about respecting the world that God has made and seeing our connection to him through it. After all, he has charged humanity to steward his property,[38] and that charge remains in effect to this day. Furthermore, God's charge of stewardship has more to do with caring protection and preservation, as well as seeing his invisible qualities (both his eternal power and divine nature) revealed in it, rather than a concern for the environment to exploit what we can get out of it.[39] We must see these judgments for what they are: an awful undoing of something beautiful and good.

34. See our discussion of Rev 5:8; 6:9–11.

35. Hence, as Rev 4 and 5 depict the scene in the throne room of heaven, John initially sees the worship of God the Father as Creator. Then, the vision shifts to the worship of the worthy Lamb and the recognition of his salvific work.

36. See Gen 1:10, 12, 18, 21, 25, 31.

37. See Rom 1:25.

38. See Gen 1:28; 2:15.

39. See Rom 1:20. Some, perhaps from a more Western perspective, might read

IMPORTANT MINISTRY IMPLICATIONS

Arising from the theological reflection we present above, we see some helpful implications for those in ministerial leadership. First, much like what we said in our discussion of Revelation 6, we discern from our exposition of chapter 8 that *ministry leaders must be prepared to answer objections to God's impending judgment of those who have rejected the Messiah*. The Creator's judgment is neither blind nor random. When he initiates his covenantal curses on sinful humanity, his actions are controlled and targeted.[40] He is just to punish the wicked, and he has given ample warning about the consequences for those who choose to persist in blaspheming his holy name.[41] Nevertheless, while we expect accusations of unfairness from the lost, believers also struggle to accept that the Lord follows through on his promises to judge and punish.

The above indicates a larger cultural ethos in the Global North wherein we emphasize love, forgiveness, acceptance, and tolerance to the extent that justice, punishment, and confrontation are portrayed as unloving, harsh, and even cruel. While there is always a need to call out abuse of power and reckless vengeance,[42] when it comes to God's judgment, we must commit ourselves to affirm the righteousness of it, rather than explaining it away. As shepherds of the Messiah's flock, the sheep he entrusts to our pastoral care must learn that the Lord's justice is appropriate and does not diminish his love and offer of forgiveness. Admittedly, this is a difficult task, especially since we are all susceptible to fashion the Creator in our own image and capitulate to the prevailing cultural preferences around us.

Second, *we should cherish moments of silence in God's sacred presence*. In an age where worship is often driven by spectacle and entertainment, pausing to reflect quietly on the Creator's mighty deeds can

---

the account of earth's destruction from a business/property/economic perspective, bemoaning the fact that all these resources are destroyed. The perspective here is utilitarian rather than reverential, which unfortunately takes focus away from the primary reason God created our earthly dwelling: to display his glory and to provide us with the ability to do the same.

40. See our discussion of Rev 9:4, where only those not having "God's seal on their foreheads" are targeted for torture.

41. See our discussion of Rev 6:15–17. The response of the wicked to the calamity of the sixth seal implies that they know who is bringing the scourge and that they are aware of impending judgment.

42. Especially when we, as fallen, sinful creatures, attempt to take matters that are God's alone into our own hands. See Rom 12:19–21.

deepen our reverence of and connection with him. We need to "be still, and know that [he is] God."[43] One of the greatest blessings of the ministerial calling is the opportunity to summon people away from the hectic, overwhelming busyness of life to a quiet, reverential reflection on the Father's majesty, the Lamb's worthiness, and the Spirit's consoling presence. It is worth asking ourselves whether we, as congregational leaders, are willing to bracket times of silence in our own lives before we invite others to do the same.

Third, *parish ministers must reassure their congregants that God answers their prayers, and he highly values the petitions they offer in faith.* What a glorious sight it must have been for John to witness the offering of incense, along with the prayers of the saints, that arises from the altar of God in the heavenly temple (vv. 4–5)! The imagery inspired by this event is rich with meaning, and it shows us the care with which the Creator engages our petitions.[44] Earlier in Revelation, we encountered the prayers of the saints, yet here we see a fuller picture of how God perceives these petitions. As overseers, we can both model and encourage fervent prayer to the Lord[45]—the kind of prayer that prioritizes the holiness of his name and corresponding reputation.

VITAL MISSIONAL RAMIFICATIONS

Whereas Revelation 5 and 7 show the success of mission work, chapters 6 and 8 give us grim pictures of forthcoming divine judgment. What we noted in the missional ramifications for chapter 6 also applies here. Rather than repeat what we stated previously, we focus specifically on the notion of divine *warning* in missional activity and the way in which we are to alert others.

First, *we warn people with authentic conviction.* Gospel witness is not a sales pitch to sign people up for a movement or cause. Because we are convinced about the truth of future, divine judgment, our warning to the lost comes with a presentation of that truth embedded in our own personal faith. We respond to objections, and we give reasoned answers to concerns, not to win arguments but to guide others gently to see

43. See Ps 46:10.

44. See Wall, *Revelation*, 123. These petitions are motivated by a longing for God to give "evidence" of his vindication of those who remain faithful to him.

45. See Jas 5:16.

what we have come to see and to partake in that in which we ourselves participate.[46]

Second, *we warn people with genuine concern*. In 2 Corinthians 5:11, Paul states that we "persuade"[47] people to come to a saving knowledge of the truth. We do this in light of our understanding of the "fear of the Lord." The sobering realization of judgment should not paralyze us, especially if we are rightly related to the Messiah by faith. Yet for those who are perishing, the fear of judgment should be present, and it should motivate them toward belief in the Redeemer.

Third, *we warn people with fervent urgency*. While specialists debate how literally or figuratively we should understand the judgments recorded in the Apocalypse, nearly all agree that the time of judgment is real. Likewise, there is nothing preventing God from initiating the covenantal curses upon the earth. His judgment will happen in the time appointed, not sooner or later. Also, though we cannot know precisely when all these events will take place, we are called to witness to the world with expectancy about the time of the end.[48] We are reminded to remain faithful, while actively fulfilling our God-given purpose and awaiting the culmination of the Creator's redemptive plan.

46. See Col 4:6; 1 Pet 3:15–16.

47. See also Acts 18:4.

48. See our discussion of Rev 5:8; 6:9–11.

Revelation 9

The Trumpet Judgments (Part Two)

LEARNING OBJECTIVES

- Understand the symbolism of the smoke and locusts emerging from the bottomless pit.
- Consider the implications of the restrictions God places on the locusts as to whom they may harm.
- Analyze the symbolism of fire, smoke, and sulfur coming from the mouths of the fiendish-looking horses.
- Discern how the plagues unleashed on horses by the demons represent divine retribution for wicked humanity's evil deeds.
- Appreciate the importance of responding to God's Word in repentance and faith, rather than with a hardened heart.

CHAPTER SUMMARY

Revelation 9 spotlights the fifth angel sounding his trumpet, a star falling from heaven to earth, and the opening of a bottomless pit. Locusts resembling horses emerge prepared for battle and have the power to torment earth's inhabitants for five months. When the sixth angel sounds his trumpet, four angels are released, leading a vast army of demons riding on fiendish-looking horses to slaughter a third of humankind. Rather than repent, the remainder of earth's inhabitants continue to murder one another, practice witchcraft, commit sexual immorality, and steal.

STUDY QUESTIONS

1. How does the star falling to earth serve as an agent of God's destruction?
2. Why does God allow a horde of demons resembling a locust plague to torture earth's wicked inhabitants?
3. What is the connection between the sixth trumpet judgment and the prayers of God's martyred children?
4. Why do earth's surviving inhabitants continue to spurn the Creator and venerate idols?
5. How might the traumatic events described in Revelation 9 inform the faith and actions of believers?

CHAPTER OUTLINE

- The fifth trumpet judgment (9:1–12)
- The sixth trumpet judgment (9:13–21)
- Key theological insights
- Important ministry implications
- Vital missional ramifications

THE FIFTH TRUMPET JUDGMENT (9:1–12)

In the unfolding cosmic drama, when the "fifth angel" (v.1) blows his "trumpet," John witnesses a "star" that has "fallen" to the "earth" from the sky. Whereas the "huge star" in 8:10 is part of the phenomena associated with the third trumpet plague, the "star" in 9:1 seems to be an angel (possibly demonic) who serves as God's agent of destruction.[1]

Some entity (perhaps another angel) gives the "star" the "key" to the shaft of the "abyss." "Abyss" translates a Greek noun that refers to a well-like, bottomless "pit" that serves as the place of confinement for a cast of villainous characters.[2] When the "star" opens the underground chasm,

1. See Judg 5:20; Job 38:7; Isa 14:12–14; 1 En. 20:1–7; 86:1, 3; Luke 10:18; Jude 1:13; Rev 20:1.

2. Such as Satan, demons, and the antichrist; see 1 En. 10:4–6; 18:11–16; 21:6–10; 88:1; 90:22–27; 2 En. 28:3; 42:1; Jos. Asen. 15:12; Jub. 5:10–11; Sib. Or. 5:155–59; Luke

"smoke" (v. 2) pours out as though from a "huge furnace" and causes the sunlight and "air" to turn dark. In ancient times, thick darkness was often associated with ominous circumstances and so served as a fitting sign of the covenantal curses to follow.[3]

Next, a horde of "locusts" (v. 3) emerges from the "smoke" onto the "earth." These short-horned, winged creatures have the ability to sting like "scorpions." The Old Testament uses locusts as symbols of invading armies who are intent on bringing about widespread destruction.[4] For instance, Exodus 10:12–20 records a locust plague. Also, Joel's prophetic oracle describes a scourge of locusts as foreshadowing the time of final judgment (1:2–4; 2:1–11, 25).

Most likely, the "locusts" of Revelation 9:3 are a horde of demons whom the Creator allows to torture earth's wicked inhabitants.[5] Even then, the maniacal swarm remains under the Creator's authority, for he does not permit them to "harm" (v. 4) any of the planet's vegetation. Thousands of years earlier, the Lord shielded the Israelites from various plagues that he brought upon Egypt.[6] This foreshadowed his preventing the fiendish entities spotlighted in verse 3 from assaulting his reborn children. God permits the marauding hive to attack only those who do not have on their "foreheads" (v. 4) the "seal" of his ownership and protection.[7]

Normally, a locust swarm would remain in one place for a few days before continuing its destructive advance throughout the five-month dry season of the Middle East.[8] In John's unfolding cosmic drama, the creatures are permitted only to "torture" (v. 5), not to "kill," their hapless victims for five months. The tail of these demonic agents produces such an agonizing sting in its victims[9] that the injured long for death, yet death repeatedly eludes them (vv. 6, 10).[10]

8:31; 10:18; Rom 10:7; 2 Pet 2:4; Jude 1:6; Rev 12:9; 17:8; 20:1, 3.

3. See Gen 19:28; Exod 10:22; 19:18; 4 Ezra 7:36.

4. See Deut 28:42; 1 Kgs 8:37; 2 Chr 7:13; Ps 78:46; Jer 51:27; Nah 3:15.

5. Perhaps in part as the just reward for the maltreatment and murder of God's reborn children; see our discussion of Rev 6:9–11; 16:6; 18:6.

6. See Exod 8:20–24; 9:4–7, 26; 10:21–23; 11:7; 12:13; Wis 18:1.

7. See 4 Ezra 6:5; Pss. Sol. 15:6; Rev 7:2–3.

8. Namely, April through August.

9. Even more intense than that caused by scorpions, including swelling, restricted breathing, and nerve damage.

10. See Job 3:21; Jer 8:2–3, 16–17; Apoc. El. 2:5, 32.

John notes that the "locusts" (v. 7) resemble war "horses" prepared for "battle." These creatures wear on their heads something that appears to be "crowns"[11] made of "gold." Also, they have human-looking "faces," antennae like long, wavy, feminine "hair" (v. 8), and jaws resembling large, sharp, lion-like "teeth." Moreover, the torsos of these vicious creatures are covered with something comparable to "breastplates" (or body armor; v. 9) made of "iron."[12] Also, their "wings" roar like an army of countless horse-drawn "chariots" rushing into "battle."[13]

Verse 10 reiterates, for rhetorical emphasis, the essential information appearing in verse 5. The unmistakable impression is that these hideous creatures are intelligent, fearsome, ruthless, and invincible. Moreover, John explains that the horde's "king" (v. 11) is the "angel of the abyss."[14] While some specialists think that this entity is either Satan or the antichrist, it seems more likely to be an otherwise unknown hellish figure.

The apostle reveals that this oppressor's Hebrew name is "Abaddon," whereas in Greek it is "Apollyon."[15] Both terms mean "destroyer" or "destruction." These are fitting titles for this tormenting, ruinous creature, who is associated with the first of the three "woes" (or covenantal curses; v. 12) introduced in 8:13 of the Apocalypse.

Four Views of the Locust Plague in Revelation 9:1–12		
View	**Description**	**Historical or Theological Context**
Already Done	The locusts symbolize the fall of the Roman Empire, which was fulfilled in history.	Preterist: Views Revelation as addressing events near the time of its writing
Continuing to Happen	The locusts represent the Islamic conquest of Western Europe (AD 612–762).	Historicist: Sees Revelation as depicting unfolding church history
Spiritualized	The locusts symbolize the self-tormenting, destructive nature of wickedness within the human soul.	Idealist/Allegorical: Emphasizes spiritual truths over historical or future events
Yet to Happen	The locusts are supernatural, demonic forces unleashed by God in the end-times before Christ's return.	Futurist: Interprets Revelation as events immediately preceding Christ's return

11. A victor's laurel wreath.
12. Possibly the Roman *lorica segmentata* or *lorica lamminata*.
13. See Job 39:19–25; Jer 51:14, 27; Joel 2:4–5.
14. Or well-like, bottomless pit.
15. See Job 26:6; 28:22; Ps 88:11; Prov 15:11; 27:20.

THE SIXTH TRUMPET JUDGMENT (9:13–21)

In the unfolding cosmic drama, when the "sixth angel" (v. 13) blows his "trumpet," John hears a solitary "voice" speaking from the "four horns" of the golden "incense altar," which is in the Creator's sacred presence.[16] The reference to the "altar" suggests that the prayers of God's martyred, reborn children to vindicate their faith and faithfulness are still in mind.[17]

The "sixth angel" (v. 14) is directed to set free "four" fallen "angels," who are tied up beside the "Euphrates River." During the Old Testament era, the Euphrates symbolized the northern boundary from beyond which the enemies of Israel originated.[18] Also, in the first century AD, Rome dreaded an attack of the Parthians[19] from beyond the Euphrates, which was the eastern border of the empire. The horrors of such an invasion pale in comparison to what the apostle witnesses in his "vision" (v. 17).

Verse 15 discloses that the Creator has "prepared" the "four angels" for the appointed time ("this hour, day, month, and year") when they will slaughter one-third of humankind. Previously, one-fourth of humanity died during the fourth seal plague.[20] Together, these two covenantal curses destroy over one half of the world's population. The "four angels" are evil and lead a vast army of demons on horses. It is less likely that the mounted troops are a literal army of either 200 million soldiers or demon-possessed humans (v. 16).[21]

In the unfolding cosmic drama, John notices that the "riders" (v. 17; and possibly their horses) wear "breastplates." Their appearance is like the colors of an intensely burning inferno—"fiery red," "hyacinth blue," and "sulfur yellow." It remains unclear whether each piece of the protective chest armor is a mixture of these colors or whether the items are solid in color.[22]

Regardless, the colors match the "fire," "smoke," and "sulfur" coming from the "mouths" of the "horses," which have lion-like "heads."

16. See Exod 30:1–10; 37:25.

17. See our discussion of Rev 5:8; 6:9–10; 8:3–5; 14:18; 15:7; 16:3, 7.

18. See Isa 7:20; 8:5–8; 14:31; Jer 1:13–15; 4:5–6; 6:1, 22; 10:22; 13:20; 25:9, 26; 46:2, 4, 6, 10, 20–24; 47:2; Ezek 26:7; 38:6, 15; 39:2.

19. Especially involving archers armed with bows while riding on horseback; see 1 En. 56:5; Sib. Or. 5:93–94.

20. See our discussion of Rev 6:7–8.

21. Literally "two myriads of myriads," or an incalculable number times two; see Ps 68:17.

22. With some being red, some blue, and some yellow.

Sulfur is a yellowish mineral that burns at low temperatures to produce a colorless gas and that is common in volcanic eruptions. People in ancient times often used the image of burning sulfur (or brimstone) to depict the horrors of a catastrophe and judgment.[23]

The "horses" (v. 17) have powerful "mouths," for the "fire" (v. 18), "smoke," and "sulfur" which these creatures discharge represent "three" different "plagues," which kill one-third of humankind. The "tails" (v. 19) of these demonic creatures are also powerful, for they resemble poisonous "snakes" with serpent-like "heads" that bite and injure their hapless victims.[24]

In the first century AD, many pagan religions involved demon and idol worship. This will remain true during the terrors associated with the sixth trumpet judgment. During the exodus episode, just as the heart of Pharoah remained hardened and obstinate,[25] the survivors of the "plagues" (v. 20) refuse to "repent" and instead spurn the Creator. They also continue to venerate lifeless and powerless objects.[26] Furthermore, earth's wicked inhabitants refuse to "repent" (v. 21) or abstain from murdering one another, practicing witchcraft, being sexually immoral, and stealing.[27]

Not all specialists think the fulfillment of the trumpet judgments awaits a final period of crisis at the end of the age. Some interpret John's visions of covenantal curses as having been fulfilled both through natural disasters and through corresponding spiritual disasters agonizing the souls of the wicked. According to this view, the natural world and human beings will continue to experience periods of distress until the time when the Creator renews all things. Then, at the Son's second coming, the Father will destroy the material universe[28] and judge the unrepentant.[29]

23. Such as associated with the destruction of Sodom and Gomorrah; see Gen 19:24, 28; Deut 29:22–23; Ps 11:6; Isa 30:33; Ezek 38:22; Luke 17:29; Jude 1:7.

24. See Num 21:6–7; 1 Cor 10:9.

25. See Exod 7:13, 14, 22; 8:15, 19, 32; 9:7, 12, 34, 35; 10:1, 20; 11:9–10; 14:4.

26. See Deut 4:28; 27:15; 32:16–17; 1 Kgs 18:27–29; 2 Kgs 19:18; Pss 96:5; 106:36–38; 115:4–8; 135:15–18; Isa 2:8; 17:8; 40:18–20; 41:7, 29; 44:18; 46:5–7; Jer 1:16; 7:5–11; 10:1–5; 25:6–7; Dan 5:4, 20, 23; Mic 5:13; 1 En. 99:7; Jos. Asen. 2:3; 9:2; Jub. 11:4; Sib. Or. 3:13; 5:77, 80–84; 1 Cor 10:19–20.

27. See 1 En. 19:1; Wis 12:3–6; Rev 21:8, 27; 22:11, 15.

28. A massive de-creation event.

29. See Rom 8:18–25; 2 Pet 3:7, 10, 12.

A Comparison of the Three Lists of Iniquities in Revelation		
Revelation's three lists of iniquities catalogue the various ways pagan, fallen humanity has rebelled against the Creator's holy will. Together, the lists serve as a warning that earth's inhabitants must abandon their wickedness or face eternal ruin for refusing to do so.		
9:20–21	**21:8**	**22:15**
	All liars	Everyone who loves and practices falsehood
Murderers	Murderers	Murderers
Practice sorcery	The sexually immoral	The sexually immoral
Refuse to repent of the works of their hands	The cowardly	
	The unbelieving	
Theft	The vile, detestable, and abominable	Dogs (morally impure persons)
Venerate demons and idols (made of gold, silver, bronze, stone, and wood)	Idolaters	Idolaters

KEY THEOLOGICAL INSIGHTS

Revelation 9 continues the trumpet judgments that began in chapter 8. Here, we see the first two of three promised woes called out by the eagle at the end of the fourth trumpet judgment.[30] These covenantal curses further heighten the intensity of the unfolding catastrophes, with a particular emphasis on the fate of those living in rebellion against the Messiah. Consequently, the following theological insights relate to God's power over the forces of evil, his use of various calamities to bring punishment, and the reality of sin and its dire consequences.

First, *we observe that God's power extends over Satan and his demonic cohort.* At the sounding of the fifth trumpet, the Creator employs the agency of a fallen angel (9:1) to release a torturous plague over the earth (vv. 2–6). Whereas previously the conduit of destruction was a series of natural disasters or cosmic disruptions, now God empowers demonic beings[31] to bring suffering and pain upon unrepentant, wicked human-

30. See our discussion of Rev 8:13.

31. Some argue that the fallen "star" of Rev 9:1 represents Satan, whose casting out from heaven is further described in 12:7–9.

ity. Yet as we noted above, the ability given to the horde of locusts[32] is limited. They are not permitted to destroy the environment, and they may harm only those who do not have "God's seal on their foreheads" (v. 4). These limitations demonstrate that the Creator exercises complete lordship over all things, even the spirit beings directly opposed to him and his purposes.[33] Though they exercise tremendous power in their wicked deeds, they cannot do anything apart from God's allowance.

Second, *we note the sinful condition of fallen humanity*. Given the severity of God's judgment, including the torment experienced by numerous people, one would expect those enduring such pain and suffering to cry out to the Creator for relief. We might also imagine that even unbelievers would *eventually* humble themselves, admit defeat, and beg God for mercy amid their suffering. However, this is the opposite of how the wicked react (vv. 20–21). They purposefully, knowingly, and willingly choose to remain under torturous condemnation, rather than forsake their sinful ways and turn to the Lord. This gives us insight into what the Scriptures consistently say concerning sin: it blinds people's eyes and hearts, leaving them in total darkness, completely unable to free themselves from its power.[34] Sin overtakes the entire being, leaving the lost incapable of redeeming even the smallest part of their lives.[35]

Third, *we see that willful persistence in sin results in hard-heartedness and foolishness*. The wicked are not ignorant about what is happening to them during these judgments.[36] They are also aware of the One who is punishing them for their sin. It seems, by implication, that they are acquainted with the notion that God can respond in grace to repentant, believing sinners. So then, this elicits the question of *why* the rebellious refuse to turn away from their sin and repent. Their anger toward the Creator for bringing the promised covenantal curses prompts them to choose to suffer eternal death rather than admit that they are wrong, sinful, lost, and hopeless.[37]

32. Most likely demonic beings.

33. See Job 1:6–12; Matt 8:28–34; Mark 1:34.

34. See Isa 59:10; Lam 4:14; Zeph 1:17; John 3:19; 8:34; 9:39–41; 12:37–41; Rom 6:15–18.

35. See Eph 2:1–3, where Paul states that prior to our salvation, we were "dead in . . . trespasses and sins" and existed apart from the Father's grace given to us through faith in the Son.

36. See our discussion of Rev 6:16–17.

37. See our discussion of Rev 16:9, 11.

While we should never rejoice in anyone's destruction, the persistent grip of sin reveals a tragic pattern of stubbornness and folly.[38] Sin hardens the heart, blinding individuals to the Creator's offer of forgiveness[39] and leading to irrational anger against him. This stubbornness breeds foolishness, stripping away spiritual discernment and sound reasoning.[40] Consumed by raw emotion and base instincts, the unrepentant become like senseless beasts. This lethal blend of defiance and folly culminates in the catastrophic judgment foretold in John's prophetic oracle.

IMPORTANT MINISTRY IMPLICATIONS

Revelation 9 is replete with examples of sin's consequences for those who persist in rebellion against the Messiah. One might imagine that because these judgments are reserved only for unbelievers, there is no application to those who belong to Christ. However, although believers need not fear these specific covenantal curses, parish ministers should be diligent in leading their congregants away from sin and toward holiness.

First, *we must remind our church members that believers, though safe from everlasting damnation, do suffer the temporal consequences of their sin.* The same God who unleashes covenantal curses upon the wicked also evaluates the faithfulness of those who belong to Christ and his church. We need only recall the letters to the seven churches located in Asia Minor[41] to note that the Creator takes iniquity seriously and confronts all who are guilty of committing it. Sinfulness robs us of joy, peace, and unhindered fellowship with God.[42] Immorality hinders our testimony to those outside the faith, and the presence of vice thwarts our ability to grow in Christlikeness. We must be neither casual nor apathetic in how we teach or preach about sin. As we communicate the doctrine of sin, our congregants will be stirred to refrain from continuing in it.

Second, *we can proclaim God's grace to motivate our congregants to live opposite of what is depicted in Revelation 9.* Along with clear instruction concerning sin, we must provide a vibrant depiction of the Father's

38. Morris, *Revelation*, 132, focuses on "those who refuse the call to repentance and prefer impotent deities." Those who insist on the veneration of useless idols display a particularly nonsensical brand of folly.

39. See Exod 8:15–32; Isa 6:10; Jer 16:12; 18:12; Rom 2:5.

40. See Prov 12:1; 14:16–18; 15:21; Isa 44:18; Jer 10:8; Rom 1:21–22.

41. See our discussion of Rev 2 and 3.

42. See Pss 32:3–4; 51:10–12; 1 John 1:3, 6.

grace and forgiveness offered in the Son as well as God's expectations for us to live out this grace in our Christian lives.[43] We are not called merely to avoid sin and stop sinning. We are also called to replace sinfulness with virtuous living, which is uniquely possible because of the Creator's grace. There are several lists of vices in Scripture, such as those encountered in this chapter. Yet often there is an opposite list of moral virtues close by.[44] These juxtaposed lists demonstrate that we cannot stop doing what God says is wrong apart from doing what he declares is right. Congregational leaders should first effectively live out this principle in their own lives and then teach it to the flocks under their pastoral care.

Third, *repentance must be an ongoing activity for those seeking to grow in Christ.* While repentance leading to salvation is often seen as a one-time occurrence, repentance is a daily necessity, especially as the Spirit regularly convicts us of our need to forsake our sin.[45] As leaders of Jesus' church, ongoing repentance must characterize our lives, and that attitude should find itself reproduced in the lives of our parishioners. A body of believers who see no need to confess sin and repent from wickedness will inevitably be unhealthy. Perhaps for this reason, in John's first epistle, he warns readers that a denial of the presence of sin and a refusal to confess and repent from it are sure signs of unbelief.[46]

VITAL MISSIONAL RAMIFICATIONS

In the missional reflections we offered concerning Revelation 8, we examined the role of warning as an essential element of gospel proclamation. Now, as we turn our attention to chapter 9 of the Apocalypse, we explore the issue of repentance, especially its essential place in calling sinners to turn to Christ in faith and receive the salvation freely offered by the Father through the Son.

First, *repentance requires an acknowledgment of one's sinfulness, and this is precisely where our presentation of the good news begins.* When it comes to gospel witness on the mission field, the notion of repentance

43. See Eph 2:1–10.

44. Note especially Paul's lists of vices and virtues found in the contrast of works of the flesh and Spirit (Gal 5:16–26); the contrast between the "old self" and "new self" (Eph 4:17–32); and the contrast between what to "put off" and what to "put on" (Col 3:5–17).

45. See 2 Cor 7:9–10.

46. See 1 John 1:8–10.

is often seen as the necessary *"bad news"* component that we must rush through to get to the *"good news"* aspect we are eager to share. Yet repentance, though seemingly a harsh concept, brings direct benefit to the sinner. Those sharing the true gospel do not shrink back from challenging their hearers with it.

Sometimes the truth hurts, especially about ourselves. However, Scripture is clear that we are all, apart from Christ, lost in our sin.[47] In our modern age, this is a difficult concept to accept, especially as we are routinely told to trust ourselves, be true to ourselves, go with our instincts, and more. Even so, as we noted in previous chapters, we must not be swayed by cultural opinion or political correctness. Scripture calls sinners to acknowledge their iniquity, abandon it, and turn to Christ in faith. After all, no one can experience the miracle of God's saving grace apart from a recognition of their sin. Indeed, as missionaries, when we share the gospel with the lost, we need to be courageous in broaching the subject of sin and the need for repentance.[48]

Second, *we must realize that when repentance enters the conversation, this is often the point at which the lost reject the gospel.* Revelation 5 and 7 show the success of missionary work, but here in chapter 9, we see that those who have confirmed themselves in unbelief ultimately persevere in their rebellion and sin. As we noted above, they would rather be tortured, suffer immense pain, and ultimately die separated and alienated from God than pass through the corridor of repentance (vv. 20–21). It is important for those involved in missionary work to understand that repentance does not come about due to our cleverness of speech or winsome rhetoric.[49] It happens only as the Spirit works in the heart of the sinner, effecting inward change that leads to salvation. Admittedly, the proclamation that sinners need to repent is often the point at which we lose our audience. Yet this possibility should neither discourage nor deter us in the proclamation of the gospel, for Scripture assures us that Satan and his demonic cohort can never thwart what we do for Christ.[50] That said, we should not be surprised when people persist in rebellion out of pride and self-centeredness, as well as reject their need for repentance.

Third, *as missionaries, our task is not to force repentance upon unwilling hearts but rather to present faithfully the message of salvation.* We

47. See Rom 3:10–18, 23.

48. See Rom 1:16–17.

49. See 1 Cor 2:1–5.

50. See Matt 16:18; 1 Cor 15:58.

affirm that the Spirit's transformative power can penetrate even the most hardened hearts. Indeed, the concept of persistence and patience in missionary work finds its foundation in these truths. As we noted above, we navigate the challenging terrain of proclaiming a message that can provoke discomfort and resistance among the lost, yet we realize that we are not alone in this endeavor. Just as John and his beleaguered peers faced resistance and rejection from unbelievers, we too are called to endure, trusting that the evangelistic seeds we sow through the faithful proclamation of the gospel will find fertile ground in due time. The reality that some people refuse to repent should serve as a reminder that we, as missionaries, are Jesus' messengers, not manipulators. Here, our role is to convey faithfully the good news of salvation, leaving the work of conviction and transformation to the Spirit.

Revelation 10

The Little Scroll and the Two Witnesses (Part One)

LEARNING OBJECTIVES

- Understand the symbolism of the powerful angel and the small, open scroll.
- Consider the significance of the seven thunders in relation to God's end-time plan.
- Analyze the meaning of the angel's oath that God would no longer delay his judgment of earth's inhabitants.
- Explore the theological implications of John's consuming the small scroll.
- Ponder how John's experience can guide believers in their own lives and ministries.

CHAPTER SUMMARY

In Revelation 10, John sees a powerful, glorious angel descending from heaven and holding a small, open scroll, which represents the message of judgment John is to proclaim. The angel, while placing his feet on the sea and land, shouts, and the noise sounds like a growling lion. A voice from heaven prohibits John from writing down what he hears. Instead, the angel declares that nothing will further delay God's fulfilling his end-time plans. Finally, John eats the scroll, which symbolizes his commission to declare God's judgment oracles to earth's inhabitants.

STUDY QUESTIONS

1. What do the characteristics of the mighty angel signify?
2. What does the small scroll held by the angel represent?
3. Why do you think John is instructed not to record what the seven thunders say?
4. What is the mystery of God that the angel says is about to be fulfilled?
5. What can believers learn about the Word of God in light of John's eating the scroll?

CHAPTER OUTLINE

- The angel with a little scroll (10:1–7)
- John's commission to prophesy (10:8–11)
- Key theological insights
- Important ministry implications
- Vital missional ramifications

THE ANGEL WITH A LITTLE SCROLL (10:1–7)

Revelation 8 and 9 detailed the anguish and devastation caused by the first six trumpet judgments. Between the sixth and seventh of these covenantal curses was an interlude with two dramatic scenes. Both episodes dealt with the role of God's martyred children and the nature of their testimony during a time of great distress.

As the cosmic drama continues to unfold, John witnesses another mighty "angel" (10:1) descending from "heaven." A "cloud" envelops his body (like a garment), perhaps to emphasize his luminous, celestial origin.[1] A "rainbow" appears above the angel's "head" like a multicolored headdress, possibly as a reminder of the Creator's merciful pledge never again to use a cataclysmic flood to destroy the earth.[2] Even so, God remains at liberty to use other means to judge earth's wicked inhabitants.

1. See Ps 104:3; Dan 7:13; Acts 1:9; Rev 1:7.
2. See Gen 8:22; 9:8–17; Isa 54:8–9.

The angel's "face" beams with the intensity of the "sun," which suggests majesty and glory. The creature's "feet" (and his legs) resemble stately columns engulfed in flames, perhaps evoking the pillars of cloud and fire that the Lord used to guide and protect the Israelites in the wilderness after the exodus event.[3]

Disputed Identity of the Powerful Angel in Revelation 10:1		
Proposed Identity	**Supporting Evidence**	**Challenges/ Counterarguments**
Michael the Archangel	Involved in cosmic warfare against demonic powers; protector of Israel; Dan 10:21; 12:1	No direct textual connection; speculative based on general role similarities
Same angel from Rev 5:2	Both angels make a loud proclamation; both described as imposing in appearance and strength; similar language used in Rev 18:21	Different contexts and purposes; no explicit identification linking the two entities
The Messiah	Dazzling, radiant appearance described in Rev 1:13–16 and 10:1; supernatural characteristics	Jesus is never called an "angel" in the Apocalypse; the entity in 10:1 is specifically called "another powerful angel"; no worship is shown to this being, in contrast to 5:12–14

The angel holds a "little scroll" (Rev 10:2) in his "hand," which he apparently has unrolled and will later give to John to eat (vv. 8–11). This document, though small, is exceedingly important. Most likely, even though it was different from the large scroll of 5:1, which had been fastened with seven seals, the compact document conveys the same essential, end-time prophetic information.

Next, the celestial being places his "right foot" (10:2) on the "sea" and his "left foot" on the "land." The immense height of the angel suggests that his pronouncements are divine in origin and so authoritative. Moreover, the position of his body suggests that his declarations concern the future of the entire world.

When the angel shouts, his "voice" (v. 3) sounds like the striking yet terrifying roar of a "lion," which suggests that it, along with the entity's

3. See Exod 13:20–22; 14:19–20, 24; 40:34–38; Neh 9:12, 19; 1 En. 1:5; 19:1; 38:4; 39:7; 104:2; Jos. Asen. 14:9; 18:9.

colossal stature, catches the attention of all who hear it.[4] Thunder (personified) then reverberates "seven" times in response. In Scripture, peals of thunder are often a prelude to the unleashing of God's extensive covenantal curses on the wicked. This seems to be the case in verse 3.[5]

The message the "seven thunders" (v. 4) proclaim is sufficiently clear and detailed for John to understand. Yet as he is preparing to "write" down the pronouncement, a "voice from heaven" commands the apostle to "seal up" the declaration. This means the message must remain a secret[6] until the divinely appointed time which God has sovereignly established.[7]

The enormous angel lifts his "right hand" (v. 5) to "heaven," where the supreme Monarch of the universe sits reposed on his royal seat.[8] The celestial being swears (v. 6) an oath in the name of the Lord,[9] whom John describes as being eternal in his existence and the Creator of all things.[10] The angel declares that God will no longer "delay" in unleashing his covenantal curses on earth's wicked inhabitants. Verse 7 anticipates a time when the Lord will fulfill his redemptive plan for all history (signified by the blasting of a "trumpet" by the "seventh angel"). The Greek verb rendered "completed" can also be translated as "accomplished," "concluded," "executed," or "finished."

In the past, the Creator revealed various portions of his everlasting will to numerous Old and New Testament "prophets," who were his bondservants.[11] Nevertheless, there were some aspects of God's plan that remained a "mystery," which means undisclosed to humankind.[12] Nonetheless, as the cosmic drama unfolds, the Lord makes "this good news known."[13] Specifically, John learns that the Creator will triumph over

4. See Jer 25:30–38; Hos 5:14; 11:10; Amos 1:2; 3:7–8.

5. See Exod 19:16–19; 20:18–19; Ps 29:3–4; Isa 29:6; John 12:28–29; Heb 12:18; Rev 4:5; 8:5; 11:19; 16:18.

6. Or concealed and thus inscrutable.

7. See Dan 8:26; 12:4, 9; 4 Ezra 14:5–6; 2 Cor 12:4.

8. As we previously noted, the Creator's throne occupies the literary center of John's prophetic oracle; see Isa 57:15.

9. See Gen 14:22–23; 22:15–16; Exod 6:8; Deut 32:40–41; Isa 62:8; Ezek 20:5, 15, 23, 42; Dan 12:7; Heb 6:13–18.

10. See Gen 14:19, 22; Exod 20:11; Neh 9:6; Ps 146:6; 1 En. 101:8; 2 En. 24:2; 48:5; T. Job 2:4; Rev 1:4, 8; 4:8–10; 7:2; 11:17; 15:7; 16:5.

11. See 2 Kgs 17:13, 23; Jer 7:25; 25:4; Ezek 38:17; Dan 9:10; Amos 3:7; Heb 1:1.

12. See 1 Pet 1:10–12.

13. Rev 10:7 is literally rendered "preached the gospel."

Satan and his evil subordinates in a final confrontation. God, who is in sovereign control of the entire process, will defeat the wicked, vindicate the righteous, and reign forever.[14]

New Testament References to "Mystery"		
Mystery	**Biblical References**	**Description**
Christ's supremacy over all creation	Eph 1:9–10	God's plan to unite all things in heaven and earth under Christ's authority
God's completed plan	Rev 10:7	God's redemptive plan fulfilled when the seventh angel sounds the trumpet
God's hidden wisdom and Christ's crucifixion	1 Cor 2:7–8	God's wisdom, hidden from worldly rulers and revealed through Jesus' sacrificial death at Calvary
Mystery Babylon	Rev 17:5, 7	The mystery of Babylon the Great and the beast that supports her
The believers' transformation	1 Cor 15:50–54	Christians are radically altered at the resurrection; not all die, but all are changed.
The mystery of godliness	1 Tim 3:16	The incarnation: God manifested as a human in Christ.
The mystery of lawlessness	2 Thess 2:1–8	The hidden work of lawlessness, leading to the revelation of the "man of sin," the "son of destruction"
The partial hardening of Israel	Rom 11:25	Israel's temporary spiritual blindness until the full number of Gentiles is saved
The seven stars and gold lampstands	Rev 1:20	The seven stars (messengers/angels) and seven flaming menorahs (churches) explained
The unity of Jews and Gentiles in Christ	Eph 3:3–6	Saved Gentiles become fellow heirs with believing Jews in Christ's spiritual body.

14. See our discussion of Rev 11:15.

JOHN'S COMMISSION TO PROPHESY (10:8–11)

Next, the "voice" (v. 8) from "heaven" that John heard earlier begins again to speak. The apostle is directed to take the opened, miniature "scroll" from the "hand" of the powerful, authoritative angel who straddles the "sea" and the "land." When John does as he is instructed, the celestial being tells the apostle to "eat" (v. 9) the document. The text literally means to "eat it down." The implication is that he is to devour the scroll completely and, in doing so, both embrace and internalize its written contents.

The angel explains that at first the tiny "scroll" will taste as "sweet as honey" in John's "mouth." Yet when he has swallowed the document, it will turn "bitter" (that is, acidic or sour) in his "stomach." The apostle notes that this happens when he eats the document (v. 10).[15] By consuming the diminutive "scroll," John symbolically accepts the prophetic mission and message the Creator has given the apostle. In general, what he declares includes words of both law (threats of judgment) and gospel (promises of grace).

More specifically, the experience of a sour stomach suggests that the scaled-down "scroll" contains news about future calamity—such as the persecution of God's children—that is difficult for John to bear. He also faces the likelihood of experiencing opposition from antagonists for heralding the divine oracle. Even so, the sweet taste might point to something so delicious that it is immediately swallowed. Another possibility is that regardless of the severe nature of the divine message,[16] it will enable believers to have fellowship with the Creator and experience his everlasting goodness. In any case, there will no longer be any delay in the fulfillment of God's eternal plans.

Part of John's ongoing, sacred commission includes heralding prophecies concerning "many peoples, nations, languages, and kings" (v. 11). Put another way, the apostle will make declarations[17] about the unleashing of covenantal curses that will affect all earth's inhabitants, regardless of their ethnic, social, cultural, economic, or political status.[18] The Creator will use his bondservant to reveal that the demise of evil and the inauguration of his righteous, eternal kingdom are drawing near.

15. See Pss 19:7–10; 119:13, 103–4; Jer 15:15–18; Ezek 2:8—3:4.

16. For example, one involving solemn pronouncements of judgments.

17. Like an eyewitness testifying in a court of law.

18. See Jer 1:5, 10.

KEY THEOLOGICAL INSIGHTS

Revelation 10:1—11:14 offers a captivating interlude between the sixth and seventh trumpet judgments. Chapter 10's portion unveils an assurance of the coming prophetic, end-time events, as well as a provocative challenge within the peculiar incident of John's eating the "little scroll." From this passage emerge the following theological insights.

First, from the spectacle of the "powerful angel" (vv. 1–2) who has one foot in the sea and one on land, we see that *God's pronouncement of impending judgment covers the entire world*. We previously noted this truth,[19] yet it bears repeating here. No peoples, nations, or regions are exempt from the future accounting that all must give regarding their acceptance or rejection of the Messiah. While the narrative of end-time events in the Apocalypse draws attention to the ancient Near East,[20] all regions are affected by the covenantal curses unleashed on the earth. Not only are all geographical locales involved, but all designations of people are also touched. The covenantal curses are not limited to the wealthy, such that the impoverished are vindicated simply because they are poor. Nor are the judgments restricted to the underprivileged, as if society's elites somehow escape divine reckoning because they have managed to evade hardship in the present. Humanity's standing before God has always been and will always be demarcated according to the distinction between those who are savingly united to Christ by faith and those who are not.[21]

Second, when the angel swears "by the one who lives forever and ever" (vv. 5–7), we are reminded that *God's promise of judgment is certain*. It will be fulfilled without delay, and its purpose will be accomplished at the appointed time. Many deny the eventuality of God's judgment. They have difficulty accepting that a loving Father would or could act with such cataclysmic consequences toward the earth's inhabitants, whom he

19. See our discussion of Rev 6:12–17; 8:7–13; 9:1–6, 13–21.

20. For example, the seven churches are located in Asia Minor (Rev 2–3); the 144,000 are from the tribes of Israel (7:4–8); Jerusalem is the focus of the antichrist's corruption (11:8); Babylon, as a symbol of the pagan world system, is prominent in the pursuit and persecution of Messiah's followers (16–18); the great battle of Armageddon is located in Israel (16:14–16); and the new Jerusalem is the name given to the heavenly city that descends to the new earth (21:10–14). These are just some of numerous examples that could be cited. Yet they sufficiently demonstrate not only an ancient Near Eastern but also a Middle Eastern focus in the Apocalypse.

21. See John 3:17–21; 1 John 4:1–6; 2 John 9; Rev 20:11–15; 21:7–8, 14–15.

created. Admittedly, the thought of the Creator's bringing such destruction challenges more palatable notions of love, grace, and forgiveness.[22] Hence, the idea that he would unleash punishment may not seem to fit his gracious character. Yet as we have previously noted, the worthy Lamb is righteous in all his judgments,[23] and the assurance of this is seen in the oath the angel declares. Divine judgment has and will happen. Moreover, God does not hold himself accountable to any person or so-called "higher power" in the execution of his sovereign will.

Our third theological insight arises from a unique and especially puzzling aspect of Revelation 10, namely, when John is told to consume the "little scroll" (vv. 9–10). This incident shows us that *God's revelation produces one of two very different effects, either bitterness or sweetness.* John's experience pictures the effect of God's Word on all people. This incident is unexpected in the prophetic oracle, since to this point in the Apocalypse, John has been used to reveal the content of what the scroll contains,[24] not digest the scroll itself. Yet this seemingly absurd event is in keeping with what God instructed Ezekiel[25] to perform during his commissioning to his prophetic ministry.[26] While various opinions abound concerning the exact symbolism of John's consumption of the diminutive scroll, it cannot mean less than the fact that the apostle, as a willing instrument of God's revelation, embraces and internalizes his Word. Also, the content of his Word results in the experience of both joy and sorrow.

IMPORTANT MINISTRY IMPLICATIONS

From the preceding observations, we can identify several implications for those serving in ministry contexts, specifically those connected to local church settings. First, *we must warn our parishioners against apathy when considering our Lord's coming evaluation.* For genuine believers in Christ, their salvation is secure.[27] Also, while this is a wonderful blessing,

22. See the *ministry implications* section in our discussion of Rev 8.

23. See our discussion of Rev 4:11; 5:9, 12–13.

24. See our discussion of Rev 6, where John is allowed to record the events proceeding after the worthy Lamb (5:4–8) breaks the seals and opens the scroll.

25. For more on the connection between Ezek 2:8—3:3 and Rev 10:9–10, see Beale and McDonough, "Revelation," 1117–18.

26. See Ezek 2:8—3:3. For other strange, performative prophecies that God commanded in the Old Testament, see Isa 20:1–4; Jer 13:1–11; Hos 1:2–3; 3:1–3.

27. See John 10:27–30; Rom 8:38–39; Phil 1:6.

a dangerous spiritual apathy can arise from a misunderstanding of our security. Given that the covenantal curses are targeted toward those who do not believe, we may imagine that the only application of this to our lives is for us to be grateful that these calamities do not happen to us. However, while it is true that those united to Christ by faith need not fear everlasting condemnation and separation from God,[28] there is a day of reckoning to come, even for those who believe. We ought to be sobered by the reality of this coming judgment. One day we will all appear before the judgment seat of Christ,[29] and that truth should motivate us toward godliness, as well as care and concern for those coming under divine condemnation.

Second, *an associated danger is functional unbelief*. This is where we give mental assent to the reality of God's forthcoming judgment yet we live as if it will never happen to us. Jesus warns his disciples about such an irreligious way of living, especially as he describes the attitude of people at the time of his return.[30] This truth should motivate us to live in reverence of the Lord, with a sober-minded approach in the presence of our sovereign King and a determination to undertake what is of eternal significance in all that we do. Then, with our hearts and minds aligned with God's perfect will, as well as characterized by awe and devotion toward him, we commit ourselves fully to his service. The parishioners in our churches must first see this disposition in their leaders and then follow the call to exemplify the same in their own lives.

Third, *we should encourage our parishioners to internalize God's Word by embracing its teachings and allowing it to transform their lives.* John's act of eating the scroll illustrates the profound impact Scripture can have when it is faithfully preached and taught in the church. We can encourage our congregants to consume the scroll in a symbolic way, knowing that there will be elements of both sweetness and bitterness. The Holy Spirit, working in and through the teaching of the Word, encourages, strengthens, edifies, and uplifts us. He also convicts, rebukes, admonishes, and corrects us in our thinking and behavior.[31] As believers, we need the complete transforming power of God's Word to shape every area of our lives.

28. See Rom 5:1; 1 Thess 5:9.

29. See 2 Cor 5:10–11.

30. See Matt 24:37–39.

31. See John 16:7–8; 1 Cor 2:6–16; 2 Tim 3:16–17.

Fourth, *as congregational leaders, we must apply Scripture in a way that gives equal emphasis to both the sweetness and the bitterness of its message.* On the one hand, we must not focus exclusively on what brings feelings of positivity and affirmation, for doing so leaves our parishioners encouraged yet never confronted or challenged. Put another way, this approach renders our church members anemic, in which they survive on spiritual junk food that stunts their growth and opens the door to feebleness, illness, and even death.[32] On the other hand, we must not resort to an exclusive emphasis on the bitterness of the message, wherein we bombard our listeners with legalistic rants passed off as sermons. While our parishioners need to be confronted with the truth of their sinfulness, we cannot abuse them and expect genuine spiritual flourishing to occur. We must remember that the love of Christ is supposed to permeate our exhortations.[33] Church members deserve a complete and faithful presentation of God's Word—one that faithfully proclaims both its challenging truths and its comforting promises.

VITAL MISSIONAL RAMIFICATIONS

From the preceding theological insights and ministry implications, we can discern the following missional ramifications. First, based upon the reality that God's judgment includes all lands and peoples, *we must be mindful of those who have not yet heard the message of salvation.* This imperative should be a driving motivator for missionary work and gospel witness to the lost. We cannot forget that our commission is to seek the lost, wherever they may be, and boldly share with them the good news of redemption through faith in Christ. By some estimates, over three billion people have not yet heard about the Messiah's love for them and their need for a Savior.[34] Most of these people are in remote or restricted-

32. See 1 Cor 11:27–30. Prosperity-gospel proponents use the tactic of exclusively positive messages, whereby people are misled to believe that Christ came to enrich his disciples physically and materially in the present life and that they should not expect trials, suffering, or persecution. This view is destructive to their faith, as believers eventually realize that life in a fallen world involves difficulty. Then they often turn away from God in discouragement and disillusionment because it seems that his promises are unfulfilled.

33. See Eph 4:15; 2 John 4–5.

34. See Global Frontier Missions (globalfrontiermissions.org) for regular updates concerning the "least reached people groups of the earth" and ongoing efforts to proclaim the gospel to them.

access areas within Majority World locations. While missionary activity is needed everywhere, a particular burden for the unreached should characterize those who genuinely believe in the Creator's global rule, reign, and judgment.

Second, since God's judgment could commence at any time, *we should carry out our mission knowing that our time to do so is short*. The angelic oath (vv. 5–7) reminds us that once these covenantal curses begin, the unfolding catastrophe will be swift. Furthermore, nothing prevents the Creator from immediately unleashing these judgments, other than his longsuffering kindness and love.[35] Yet we must not presume upon God's grace and ignore our missional calling as if the lost have unlimited time and opportunities to repent and believe. We ought to live with an urgency to explain the message of warning and hope to those who need the redemption the Father freely offers in the Son. The urgency we sense is not because the salvation of the lost depends on us, as if we can force spiritual awakening to happen. Rather, it arises from our commitment to be obedient to the Messiah's call to make disciples of all nations.[36]

Third, as we noted in previous chapters, *our evangelistic appeal contains both bitter and sweet elements*. We are commissioned to share the full message of the gospel, including an honest presentation of our ungodliness, a clear description of our desperate condition under sin, and the horrific consequences of our iniquity. Moreover, we are summoned to share the good news about Christ, including his birth, sinless life, sacrificial death on our behalf, resurrection, and ascension. The call to preach the gospel to all people is also a mandate to proclaim the entire message.[37] Too often, we become intimidated by the importance to share with people their need to repent and believe. Yet this fear must not become an excuse for our failing to testify concerning Jesus. We should not hold back from declaring the whole truth, in love, to all whom the Spirit of God brings across our path.

35. See Exod 34:6–7.

36. See Matt 28:18–20; Luke 24:45–47; Acts 1:8.

37. See Matt 24:14. Jesus' prophecy that the gospel would be "proclaimed throughout the whole world" is set within the context of his warning about coming, end-time judgment.

Revelation 11

The Little Scroll and the Two Witnesses (Part Two)

LEARNING OBJECTIVES

- Analyze the significance of the temple measurements and what they symbolize.
- Understand the prophetic role of the two witnesses in God's end-time program.
- Consider the implications of the pair's ministry for believers as they engage society today.
- Describe the amazing events that take place after the two witnesses are killed.
- Draw connections between the scene of heavenly praise and the way believers worship God in local church settings.

CHAPTER SUMMARY

Revelation 11 opens with a description of two witnesses, whom God commissions to prophesy for 1,260 days. The pair have supernatural power to stop the rain and call down plagues. Though the beast from the bottomless pit executes the two witnesses, three days later they are resurrected and summoned to heaven. An enormous earthquake follows, which destroys a tenth of the great city, Jerusalem. Finally, after the seventh angel sounds his trumpet, John hears a chorus of praise and sees the heavenly temple being opened and the ark of the covenant being revealed.

STUDY QUESTIONS

1. Why do you think the temple is depicted as being measured and protected?
2. In what ways are the two witnesses powerful spokespersons for God?
3. Which view do you favor for the symbolic significance of the 1,260 days?
4. Why would God allow the two witnesses to be executed by the beast?
5. What can believers learn from the two witnesses' faithfulness and courage in the face of persecution?

CHAPTER OUTLINE

- The introduction of the two witnesses (11:1–6)
- The death and resurrection of the two witnesses (11:7–14)
- The sounding of the seventh trumpet (11:15–19)
- Key theological insights
- Important ministry implications
- Vital missional ramifications

THE INTRODUCTION OF THE TWO WITNESSES (11:1–6)

In the unfolding cosmic drama, John notes that someone (possibly an angel) gives him a "measuring rod" (v. 1),[1] which resembles a "staff." In a vision reminiscent of Ezekiel 40:3, 5, and Zechariah 2:1–5, the apostle is told to "stand up" (Rev 11:1) and use the small, lightweight object to calculate the dimensions of the "temple of God" and the "incense altar" as well as to count the number of people who worship there.

The Greek noun rendered "temple" denoted the inner shrine of the central sanctuary, rather than the entire sacred complex. To clarify further, before the Roman's destruction of the Jerusalem temple in AD 70, the sanctuary comprised the most holy place, the holy place, and the

1. Literally a hollow "reed."

altar of incense. In front of this structure were the court of the priests, the court of the Israelites (or men), the court of the women, and the court of the Gentiles. Evidently, the worshipers present in the "temple" were in the court of the Israelites.

Solomon's Temple		
Aspect	**Details**	**Biblical References**
Construction and materials	Built in the tenth century BC using gold, precious stones, and cedar wood, along with an elaborate design; considered the most significant structure in Israel	1 Kgs 5–6; 1 Chr 28; 2 Chr 3–4
Demolition	Destroyed by the Babylonians in 586 BC; the entire shrine complex was demolished, treasures looted, Jerusalem razed, and city walls torn down	2 Kgs 25:1–21; 2 Chr 36:15–21
Significance	Symbolized Israel's national identity; served as the central hub for religious, cultural, political, and economic activities for the twelve tribes	Deut 14:22–29; 16:16; 2 Sam 6; 1 Kgs 8:13; 2 Kgs 23; 2 Chr 6:6; Neh 10:37–38; Ezra 6:17
Temple structure	Comprised three main sections: the outer courtyard; the inner courtyard (holy place), used by the priests for their duties; and the holy of holies, which only the high priest could enter annually, and which housed the ark of the covenant with the Ten Commandments	1 Kgs 8:9; Heb 9:1–7

John is directed to "exclude" (v. 2) the sanctuary's "outer court" (or court of the Gentiles) from being measured. The reason for this prohibition is that the area outside the "temple" had been given to the Gentiles.[2] In turn, they would be permitted to overrun ("trample") the "holy city" (namely, Jerusalem) for forty-two months, or three and a half years.[3]

There are two primary ways of understanding the preceding verses. Some specialists think that John is referring to an actual stone-and-mortar temple that a remnant of believing, ethnic Jews would rebuild in Jerusalem during the first half of a seven-year period of tribulation. In this interpretation, at the midpoint of the cycle, the antichrist exalts

2. Or "heathen"; namely, antagonistic unbelievers.

3. See Ps 79:1; Isa 63:18; Dan 8:9–14; Zech 12:1–5; Luke 21:20–24.

himself to be venerated. Then a swarm of unbelieving Jews and Gentiles seize control of the Holy City and ruthlessly persecute God's children.[4]

Other specialists think the temple symbolizes the sacred presence of God on earth through his church. Likewise, the altar and worshipers are a symbol of the praying and witnessing church,[5] whom the Creator seals, claims, and spiritually protects, especially during a time of severe affliction.[6] According to this view, John's measurement of the sanctuary represents the Lord's personal knowledge and spiritual preservation of his children. In contrast, the Gentile control of the outer court and oppression of the Holy City symbolize the physical attacks by the wicked against Jesus' followers.[7]

In either of the above interpretive options, God continues to watch over the redeemed.[8] The prospect of their martyrdom on earth (as the church militant) does not prevent the Lord from rewarding their faith and faithfulness by reserving a place for them in heaven (as the church triumphant).

John learns that God will "commission" (v. 3) and empower "two witnesses" to proclaim his authoritative message of judgment and repentance[9] for 1,260 days, or three and a half years.[10] The "two witnesses" are "clothed in sackcloth"[11] to emphasize the seriousness of the covenantal curses they announce.[12] One view sees the 1,260 days as a literal period of time. In this case, it is characterized by great distress and intense conflict between God's children and their opponents before the Messiah's return.

Another option, from a symbolic perspective, is that three and a half years could represent an entire period of suffering cut short by half. In this case, the time reference concerns a limited period of tyranny, whether recurring throughout church history or in the closing days

4. See Dan 7:25; 12:7, 11–12; 2 Thess 2:4.

5. See our discussion of Rev 5:8; 6:9–11; 8:3–4.

6. See 1 Cor 3:16–17; 6:19; 2 Cor 6:16; Eph 2:19–22; Heb 3:6; 1 Pet 2:4–5.

7. Perhaps in response to Satan's prompting.

8. Including when God's reborn children refuse to venerate mortal, flawed, human rulers.

9. Again, like someone testifying in a court of law.

10. See Num 35:30; Deut 17:6; 19:15; Matt 18:16; John 8:17; 2 Cor 13:1–2; 1 Tim 5:19.

11. A coarse, burlap-like material made of goat's hair.

12. See 1 Chr 21:16; Esth 4:1; Dan 9:3; Jonah 3:5–8; Zech 13:4; Ascen. Isa. 2:10; Jos. Asen. 10:14–15; Matt 11:21.

preceding the second advent. The idea is that the Creator will bring a definite end to the reign of terror.

John explains in verse 4 that the two spokespersons are the "two olive trees," as well as the "two lampstands," that stand before the "Lord," who rules the entire "earth." The imagery is reminiscent of Zechariah 4:3, 12, and 14, where the two anointed ones are Joshua, the high priest, and Zerubbabel, the governor. These religious and civil leaders (respectively) overcome obstacles by the Spirit's power and the Father's grace.

The exact identities of the "two witnesses" (Rev 11:3) remain debated. If they are two literal human beings, they could be unnamed Christian prophets who were martyred shortly before the fall of Jerusalem in AD 70. Or they could be two prophets who will appear shortly before Jesus' return.

It is also possible that the "two witnesses" are symbolic figures for God's reborn children. The two might represent Christians alive and testifying during a final period of crisis before the second advent. If so, they adopt the prophetic mantle of Moses and Elijah to summon the unregenerate to abandon their iniquities and trust in the Messiah for salvation. Or the two might symbolize credible, witnessing believers throughout the history of the church.

In the unfolding cosmic drama, the Creator gives the "two witnesses" amazing supernatural abilities, especially against those who try to "harm" (v. 5) them. For instance, by divine decree, they incinerate their enemies with "fire" flashing from their "mouths."[13] Also, during their time of service, the two spokespersons have the "authority" (or "power"; v. 6) to prevent "rain" from falling. Moreover, they have the "authority" (or "power") to turn water into "blood" and to cause a multiplicity of plagues to afflict the planet whenever they choose.[14]

The preceding powers bear a strong resemblance to those of Moses and Elijah. As we previously noted, this is an example of exodus typology or prophetic foreshadowing appearing in the Apocalypse. For instance, Moses uses his staff to turn the waters of Egypt into blood.[15] Additionally, Elijah brings drought-like conditions on the land of Israel.[16] Regardless of whether verses 5 and 6 are taken literally or symbolically, it remains clear that the supreme Monarch of the universe works powerfully through his

13. See 1 Kgs 18:24, 38; 2 Kgs 1:9–12; Jer 5:14; 2 En. 1:5; Sir 48:1.

14. See 1 Sam 4:8.

15. See Exod 7:14–21.

16. See 1 Kgs 17:1; 18:1, 4–45; Sir 48:2–3; Luke 4:25; Jas 5:17.

bondservants to bring his covenantal curses on unrepentant, idolatrous humanity.

Parallels between the Old Testament and the Two Witnesses in Revelation 11[17]		
Thematic Element	**Old Testament Parallel**	**Revelation 11 Fulfillment**
Beast's victory	"That horn made war against the saints and prevailed over them" (Dan 7:21).	"The beast that comes up from the abyss will fight against them, conquer them, and kill them" (v. 7).
Consuming fire	"If I am a man of God, let fire fall from the sky" (2 Kgs 1:10). "I will make my words in your mouth a fire" (Jer 5:14).	"If anyone wants to harm them, fire is going to come out of their mouths and consume their enemies" (v. 5).
Drought authority	"There will be no dew or rain during the coming years, except at my word" (1 Kgs 17:1).	"These two have the authority to shut the sky so that no rain falls during the days when they are prophesying" (v. 6).
Gold lampstand	"I see a lampstand, made entirely of gold" (Zech 4:2).	"The two lampstands" (v. 4)
Legal testimony	"A case is to have standing only on the testimony of two or three witnesses" (Deut 19:15).	"I will commission my two witnesses" (v. 3).
Olive trees	"Two olive trees" (Zech 4:3, 11)	"The two olive trees" (v. 4)
Resurrection power	"I am about to make breath enter you so that you will live" (Ezek 37:5). "Breath entered them, and they came back to life. They stood on their feet" (Ezek 37:10).	"After three and a half days the breath of life from God came into them. They stood on their feet" (v. 11).

17. This is another example of typological fulfillment or prophetic foreshadowing in the Apocalypse. Table adapted from information presented in Tabb, *All Things New*, 100.

Parallels between the Old Testament and the Two Witnesses in Revelation 11[17]		
Thematic Element	**Old Testament Parallel**	**Revelation 11 Fulfillment**
Time period	"So the saints will be given into his hand for a time, times, and half a time" (Dan 7:25). "It would be for a time, times, and half a time" (Dan 12:7).	"Forty-two months" (v. 2) "1260 days" (v. 3)
Water to blood	"With the staff that is in my hand, I will strike the water in the Nile, and it will be turned to blood" (Exod 7:17).	"They also have authority over the waters, to turn them into blood" (v. 6).

THE DEATH AND RESURRECTION OF THE TWO WITNESSES (11:7–14)

In the unfolding cosmic drama, John observes that when the "two witnesses" (v. 3) finish declaring God's message, an archenemy named the "beast" (v. 7), emerges from the "abyss,"[18] and wages war against the Creator's two bondservants.[19] This brute-like, predatory ogre is also permitted to "conquer" and murder the two witnesses. The origin of the "beast" suggests it is demonic in character. That said, specialists debate whether this creature represents a wicked person[20] or an evil government.[21] In either case, the devilish entity opposes God, his representatives, and the message they proclaim.[22]

After executing the "two witnesses" (v. 3), the "beast" (v. 7) defiles and humiliates their corpses by leaving them unburied and exposed on the main boulevard of Jerusalem.[23] This once "great city" (v. 8) and capital of Israel is where the religious and civil authorities "crucified" the Lord Jesus. In the era of distress, Jerusalem will become enemy territory,

18. Or well-like, bottomless pit.

19. See our discussion of Rev 9:11.

20. Such as the antichrist or another diabolical figure, including the sea-beast described in Rev 13:1–10.

21. Such as Rome or some other pagan, idolatrous, and tyrannical state.

22. See Dan 7:21, 25.

23. See Isa 5:25; Apoc. El. 4:13; Pss. Sol. 2:27.

being figuratively[24] comparable to the city of "Sodom" and the country of "Egypt." In ancient times, both regions were notorious for their immorality, oppression, and idolatry.[25]

When John experienced his visions, the Romans had already destroyed Jerusalem, burned the temple, and slaughtered countless numbers of Jews.[26] Rome also played a significant role in executing the Messiah. Because of this, the "great city" could be a symbolic reference to Rome. Additional options include Babylon or some other infamous metropolis.[27] In a broader sense, ancient cities such as Jerusalem, Rome, and Babylon could represent the pagan world system in its ability to entice people away from true worship. Even modern cities can promote immorality, wickedness, and false religions. Despite humanity's attainments,[28] people are still in rebellion against the Creator.

As a further outrage against the "two witnesses" (v. 3), no one would "permit" (v. 9) their corpses to be buried in a "tomb." For "three and a half days," people from all walks of life glare at the cadavers,[29] exchange "gifts" (v. 10), and rejoice over the demise of these "two prophets," who vexed the wicked with declarations of God's truth. These malevolent responses spotlight the universal prevalence of idolatry, iniquity, hatred, and sedition among the world's unregenerate inhabitants against the Creator.[30]

24. Literally "spiritually."

25. See Gen 18:20; 19:4–11, 24; Isa 1:9–10; Ezek 16:46, 55; 20:7; Jub. 13:17; LAB 8:2; T. Benj. 9:1; T. Levi 14:6; T. Naph. 4:1; Wis 19:14–15; 2 Pet 2:6.

26. Titus, as commander of the Roman legions, led the Siege of Jerusalem in AD 70, resulting in the destruction of the Second Temple. This event was a turning point in Jewish history and concluded the First Jewish-Roman War (AD 66–73). Initially, his father, Vespasian, launched the campaign to quell the Jewish revolt, but Titus took command during the fall of Jerusalem. Later, as Roman emperor (AD 79–81), Titus was honored with the Arch of Titus in Rome, which celebrated his triumph in Judea. For the most detailed primary account of the First Jewish-Roman War and the Siege of Jerusalem, see Josephus, *Jewish War*. He was a Jewish historian and eyewitness who defected to the Romans. His narrative is vivid and comprehensive, though his pro-Roman bias and relationship with Titus require critical reading. For a more recent and authoritative study of the war, which offers a critical reexamination of Josephus's narrative, see Mason, *Jewish War*.

27. See 2 Bar. 11:1; 33:2; 4 Ezra 3:1–2; 1 Pet 5:13; Rev 16:19; 17:18; 18:10, 16, 18, 19, 21.

28. Including social, cultural, economic, and political advances fostered by science and technology.

29. Apoc. El. 4:14.

30. As we previously noted, throughout Revelation, an emphasis is placed on earth's unregenerate inhabitants, who venerate pagan deities; see our discussion of 3:10; 6:10;

Indeed, regardless of whether the preceding verses are understood literally or symbolically, they reveal that many unsaved people refuse to hear and heed the truth about their sin, their need for repentance, and the somber prospect of experiencing God's covenantal curses.

The Lord terminates pagan humanity's gloating by breathing "life" (v. 11) back into the bodies of his two witnesses, who had been left in the streets to rot.[31] As they stand up on their feet, a "great fear" literally falls upon all who see them. Then, in the hearing of the onlookers, a "loud voice" (v. 12) from "heaven" commands the Lord's "two prophets" (v. 10) to "come up here." This command recalls the summoning of Enoch and Elijah to heaven.[32]

After the two messengers ascend in a "cloud" into "heaven,"[33] a severe "earthquake" (v. 13) levels a "tenth of the city."[34] This results in the death of "seven thousand" residents. The harrowing series of events so frightened the "survivors" that they acknowledge the Creator's sovereignty, at least for the moment.[35] Presumably, any sign of repentance is soon replaced by a rebellious, obstinate disposition toward God, as well as an intense hatred of his regenerate children.[36]

If the two emissaries are actual individuals, their resurrection should be understood literally. However, if the two are representative of the church, their resurrection might symbolize the triumph of faith-filled witness and missionary outreach, even after a time of intense persecution. Another possibility is that the experience of the two spokespersons closely resembles Jesus' earthly ministry, including the following parallels:

- heralding a message of repentance and judgment;
- performing miracles having symbolic importance;
- encountering hatred, shame, and death by execution;
- being resurrected after three days;

8:13; 13:8, 12, 14; 14:6; 17:2, 8.

31. See Ezek 37:5, 9–10.

32. See Gen 5:24; 2 Kgs 2:11–12.

33. See Acts 1:9, 11; 1 Thess 4:17.

34. See Ezek 38:19–23; Zech 14:4; Rev 16:18–19.

35. Literally "gave glory to the God of heaven"; see Ezra 1:2; Dan 2:17–19; 4:37; Jonah 1:9.

36. See our discussion of Rev 9:20–21; 16:9, 11, 21.

- ascending to heaven in a cloud; and
- the occurrence of a sizeable earthquake.

In any case, the Father vindicates the faith and faithfulness of his children by giving them victory through their union with the Son. Furthermore, despite the covenantal curses unleashed by the "second woe" (v. 14),[37] earth's wicked inhabitants remain unrepentant.[38] For this reason, the Creator will soon release the devastations associated with the "third woe."

THE SOUNDING OF THE SEVENTH TRUMPET (11:15–19)

In the unfolding cosmic drama, the "seventh angel" (v. 15) blows his "trumpet." What follows serves as an overture to the "third woe" (v. 14; or covenantal curses) to fall upon unregenerate humanity, particularly as seen in the seven bowl judgments recorded in chapter 16.

John witnesses a thundering chorus of unidentified worshipers announcing that the "world" (11:15) has become the "kingdom" of the Father, who is the "Lord," and of his Son, who is the "Messiah."[39] This bold declaration is in keeping with the Old Testament, which reveals that the Anointed One will one day rule the planet as the Father's coregent.[40] The heavenly ensemble prompts the twenty-four "elders" (v. 16) to leave their "thrones," fall prostrate on their "faces," and worship the Creator as he sits reposed on his celestial dais.[41] In their praise, they acknowledge that the "Lord God" (v. 17) is omnipotent and ever-living.[42]

The above emphasis on God's eternal presence possibly explains why he is referred to as the One "who is and who was." As with 16:5, missing from the assertion in 11:17 is the phrase "who is coming."[43] There is no longer any need for the phrase, especially since the Creator alone has the overwhelming "power" and authority finally to consummate his

37. See our discussion of Rev 8:13; 9:12.

38. See our discussion of Rev 16:10–11.

39. See our discussion of Rev 3:21; 22:1, 3.

40. See Ps 2:1–2, 5, 12; Isa 9:6–7; Dan 2:44; Mic 4:7; Zech 14:9; Matt 6:10; Luke 1:33; 11:2; Acts 4:26–28.

41. As we previously noted, the Creator's throne occupies the literary center of John's prophetic oracle.

42. See our discussion of Rev 1:8; 4:8; 15:3; 16:7, 14; 19:6, 15; 21:22.

43. See our discussion of Rev 1:4, 8; 4:8–10.

reign over the entire universe. The "nations" (v. 18) are enraged that the Lord will assert his right to rule over them at that time. In response, the supreme Monarch does not hold back his "anger" (or retributive justice) on the wicked.[44]

The twenty-four "elders" (v. 16) give thanks to almighty God that the appointed "time" (v. 18) has arrived for him to judge the wicked "dead," vindicate the martyred "saints," and establish his unending reign. Though earth's unrepentant evildoers refuse to submit to the Creator's rule, there is nothing that they can do to forestall the unleashing of his covenantal curses. Indeed, the twenty-four "elders" (v. 16) praise God for overthrowing those who wreaked havoc on and morally corrupted the "earth" (v. 18).

In contrast, the sovereign Lord of the cosmos will "reward" his bondservants,[45] the "prophets," as well as his holy people, from the least to the greatest,[46] every one of whom holds his sacred "name" in reverential awe. God's vindication of those who remain loyal to him, despite unrelenting persecution, include all his martyred children. He will ensure that they receive their eternal inheritance (or covenantal blessings).

As John witnesses the unfolding cosmic drama, he sees someone (perhaps an angel) open the entrance to the Creator's "temple" (v. 19)[47] in "heaven." There, before the apostle's eyes, was the "Ark" of God's "Covenant."

The Ark of the Covenant		
Aspect	**Details**	**Biblical References**
Construction and materials	Built under Moses' supervision at Mount Sinai after God ratified his covenant with the Israelites; made from acacia wood (dark, hard, durable desert wood); overlaid entirely with pure gold (refined without alloys or impurities); carried on poles inserted in rings at the four lower corners.	Exod 25:10–16

44. See our discussion of Rev 6:16, 17; 14:10, 19; 15:1, 7; 16:1, 19; 19:15.
45. Literally "slaves."
46. Apoc. El. 5:4; 2 Bar. 30:2.
47. Or inner sanctuary.

The Ark of the Covenant		
Aspect	**Details**	**Biblical References**
Contents	Contained the stone tablets with the Ten Commandments, a golden pot of manna, and Aaron's rod that miraculously blossomed and budded.	1 Kgs 8:9; Heb 9:4
Location and purpose	Housed in the most holy place of the Tabernacle; served as the meeting place between God and the Israelites; provided divine guidance; the mercy seat (atonement cover) symbolized God's presence among the Israelites.	Exod 25:17–22
Significance	During the period of the Judges, the Israelites treated the ark almost like a good-luck charm; it was taken into battle to guarantee victory. Later in Israel's history, some regarded the ark as Judah's protection against divine judgment; many believed God would never allow his dwelling place to be destroyed.	1 Sam 4:3–11; Jer 7:1–15

Like its Old Testament counterpart,[48] the "Ark" (v. 19) that became visible in John's vision of God's cosmic "temple" symbolizes his imperial throne and indescribable, holy presence. The chest also serve as a reminder that the Lord will fulfill his promises to judge the wicked and vindicate the upright.

John notes several intense storm phenomena, including "flashes of lightning," the crash and roar of "thunder," an "earthquake," and a fierce "hailstorm."[49] Together, these signal that the Creator, in all his majesty and might, will bring his covenantal curses to an end. There will be no more delay, especially as he answers the prayers of his children for the vindication of their faith in and faithfulness to the Messiah.

48. See Exod 25:40; Heb 8:5.

49. See Exod 9:22–25; 19:16, 18; 20:18–19; Jub. 2:2; Heb 12:18; Rev 4:5; 8:5; 10:3; 16:18.

The Appearance and Disappearance of God's Enemies in Revelation		
God's enemies in Revelation are portrayed through a cast of nefarious characters, including the dragon, the sea-beast, the land-beast (or false prophet), and Babylon the Great. These entities champion iniquity, idolatry, and immorality, as well as oppose the Creator and oppress his reborn children. At the end of the age, the divine Warrior defeats the antagonists and casts them into the eternal Lake of Fire.		
Entity	**Appearance**	**Disappearance**
Babylon, the harlot	14:8	17:1—19:10
Death and Hades	1:18; 6:8	20:13–14
Satan, the dragon, the devil, and the ancient serpent	2:9, 13, 24; 3:9; 12:3–6	20:1–10
Sea-beast and land-beast	11:7; 13:1–18	19:11–21

KEY THEOLOGICAL INSIGHTS

Revelation 11 continues the interlude begun in chapter 10, with a description of the work of two witnesses, a dramatic presentation of the seventh trumpet, and the victorious declaration it contains. As each of these events in John's cosmic drama unfolds, it brings our attention to the theological significance of the Messiah's preservation of his reborn children, his empowerment of the two witnesses, and the certainty of his coming kingdom.

First, *we see God's power to preserve his reborn children and watch over them, even in times of great distress, persecution, and turmoil.* In the opening verses of the chapter (vv. 1–2), as John measures the temple, we see the Lord distinguish the redeemed from the remainder of unsaved humanity, who trample the sacred city. Even though the conflict between the redeemed and their antagonists is intense, God's knowledge of the situation and his power over the conflict are never in doubt.[50] Those who belong to the Creator and are numbered among his reborn children are never alone, abandoned, or forsaken. While it may seem, in specific moments, that God has forgotten his own, we are assured that this is never really the case.[51] The power of the sovereign Lord assures us of final protection.

50. For examples of the Messiah's triumph over the wicked in the Apocalypse, specifically coming after ch. 11, see our discussion of Rev 12:7–9; 14:8; 16:5–6; 19:1–3, 15, 20–21; 20:7–10, 14–15.

51. Psalms of lament (such as Pss 2, 13, 22, and 44, among many others) are helpful

Second, *we recognize God's power to enable his witnesses to proclaim his message*. Initially, in the narrative concerning the two witnesses, we notice their special commission, as they are empowered to pronounce the Creator's judgment and call people to repentance during the 1,260 days of distress (vv. 3–6). The pair do not operate in their own strength but are instead enabled by God to accomplish his work of witnessing in the world.[52] Furthermore, they are not only enabled by the Creator to accomplish their tasks but also to experience his power in the authentication of their message. The Lord validates his message—confirming its divine authority and imminent fulfillment—through his supernatural ability to execute judgment. This practice is consistent with many instances in the Old Testament where God attests to his messengers through accompanying signs and wonders.[53]

Third, *we observe that the Creator's power is demonstrated by triumphing over death itself*. The two witnesses undergo a barbaric execution. This is followed by the shameful desecration of their bodies lying out in the open public square, further profaning the once-holy city of God (vv. 7–10). Yet the Lord miraculously raises them from the dead,[54] immediately calls them to heaven, and punishes a significant portion of the bloodthirsty mob with death caused by an earthquake (vv. 11–13).[55] Just as God enables his witnesses to carry out his mission during their testifying period, he also ensures their safe return to heaven, despite facing unimaginable suffering in the meantime. While the pair suffer and are murdered by the sea-beast, nonetheless, the Creator's ultimate power and protection are such that even death does not have the final say over his chosen ones.[56]

Fourth, turning from the second woe (v. 14) to the seventh trumpet (v. 15), *we note the power of God in the assurance of final victory*. Nothing further prevents the sovereign Lord from establishing his kingdom over what had been the realm of the world. The song of the redeemed,

---

reflections on how God can be trusted, even when, at times, we are unable to see beyond our present circumstances.

52. See Acts 1:8; Phil 2:13; Heb 13:21.

53. See Exod 4:1–9; 7:8–13; 1 Kgs 18:20–40; 2 Kgs 4–5.

54. As we noted earlier, the resurrection of the two witnesses after three days is patterned after Christ's own death and resurrection.

55. See Beale and McDonough, "Revelation," 1121–22, for further explanation concerning the many OT allusions present in vv. 11–13.

56. See Isa 25:8; John 11:25–26; 1 Cor 15:54–57.

analogous to those heard previously in the Apocalypse,[57] comprises grateful rejoicing over the fact that the Creator has now, at last, fulfilled his promises to vindicate the righteous and vanquish the wicked. John's vision of the appearance of the ark of the covenant in the heavenly temple is a reminder of God's active, omnipotent presence as Lord of the universe.[58]

IMPORTANT MINISTRY IMPLICATIONS

The preceding theological insights center on aspects of God's power. From this, we note implications for ministry that center on how, as congregational leaders, we can assure believers that God's power operates for their temporal and eternal good.

First, from the symbolism of John's measuring the temple, *we see God's care and watchfulness over the redeemed.* As parish ministers, we have an opportunity to remind our congregants about the nature of the Lord's care for us.[59] For instance, he acts on our behalf and protects us with great might. Yet he also shepherds us as his beloved sheep. Knowing that Christ shows genuine concern for his followers brings them consolation and assurance in times of intense distress and trial. We can encourage our parishioners to rest in the caring love of our heavenly Father as well as in the arms of Jesus, our eternal Shepherd.[60]

Second, alongside God's empowerment of his two witnesses, *we can console our fellow believers by highlighting the Lord's enabling presence in our lives, equipping us to fulfill his calling and endure trials for his name's sake.* The two witnesses cannot do their work apart from the Creator's special equipping, sustaining, and enabling.[61] While not everyone is specifically called to do precisely what the two witnesses do, God can still use us in amazing ways to do his work in our world. Serving the Lord in our sinful flesh will get us nowhere. Those in ministry need to be cognizant of this pivotal truth and rely on the Spirit's power working

57. See our discussion of Rev 4:11; 5:9–10, 12–13; 7:10–12.

58. Unlike the deist view of a God who creates the universe but remains detached from its ongoing affairs, John's prophetic oracle reveals the Lord as dynamically all-powerful, actively engaged, and intimately connected with his creation.

59. See Zech 10:3; 1 Pet 5:7.

60. See Ps 23:1; Isa 40:11; John 10:11; Heb 13:20; Rev 7:17.

61. See Gal 2:20; Eph 4:12; 1 Pet 4:10.

in us to do the Father's will in obedience to the Son.[62] Also, as we rest in the Creator's power for our own ministry endeavors, we encourage our fellow believers to do the same.

Third, just as the two witnesses are resurrected, so too *we can encourage our faithful parishioners to trust and act in accordance with God's promise to restore and ultimately resurrect us.* We have the assurance that no matter what we suffer or what we are called to endure in this life, even to the point of martyrdom, we can remain confident in a future resurrection, complete with glorified bodies and freedom from the presence and effects of sin.[63] As we noted in previous chapters, we have the promise of God's blessing in moving us from the church militant to the church triumphant. That promise assures us of a safe return to our Maker, even under the specter of persecution, trial, and adversity.

Fourth, as God delivers us—whether in this life or by safely bringing us into eternity, *he also assures us that he will judge the wicked.* We see this assurance not only at the ascension of the two witnesses but also at the sounding of the seventh trumpet (vv. 15–19). The coming of Christ's kingdom instills great confidence in us concerning the ultimate destiny of the world opposed to the Messiah. We can reassure our parishioners that the song of the twenty-four elders (vv. 17–18) can be ours as well, especially in anticipation of what God ultimately accomplishes. We seek vindication, for the sake of God's holy and righteous name, and we do so for his honor and glory. We want our congregants to experience the fullness of life in the present, anchored by the certain hope of their future vindication. When doubts arise or the prosperity of the wicked causes discouragement,[64] remind them that God truly sees, hears, and cares for them. His commitment to the triumph of his glory and their ultimate good is firm and unshakable.

62. Even Jesus lived and ministered in dependence upon the Holy Spirit's power; see Isa 61:1–2, fulfilled in Luke 4:21; Matt 12:18; Acts 10:38; see also Acts 2:17–18; 4:29–31; 2 Tim 1:7.

63. See 1 Cor 15:42–44; Phil 3:20–21; 1 John 3:2; Rev 21:4.

64. Ps 73 is an excellent text with which to engage believers who struggle with what seems to be the prospering of the wicked. The journey of Asaph from despair and lament to hope and praise is instructive in our own struggles with fully trusting in God's plan for our lives.

VITAL MISSIONAL RAMIFICATIONS

When we consider missionary evangelism, it's helpful to understand it through the lens of giving a testimony in a court of law. A compelling biblical example of this is found in the two witnesses of Revelation 11. Their role highlights the powerful and public nature of proclaiming God's truth.

First, we see the witnesses' eagerness to do the will of the Father. As missionaries, *we recognize that, above all else, we must do the will of our Lord*. This means that whatever task is before us, we continue in faith, confident in the outworking of the Master's plan in and through us. In our evangelistic efforts, we may be called upon to do things that put ourselves at risk, such as moving into areas that seem dangerous. People from the Majority World are taking up this calling in ways that those in the Global North often seem unwilling to do. For instance, we see believers in persecuted countries willing to give all for the cause of Christ, regardless of personal cost.[65] They labor tirelessly and courageously, because they understand God's designation of them for gospel service. Just as the two witnesses of Revelation 11 were willing to undertake unspeakably hard tasks, at great personal cost, we must be willing to do the same today as the Lord's witnesses in our broken, fallen world.

Second, we note from the two witnesses a readiness *to proclaim God's message*. Admittedly, missionaries are called to *do* hard things. Yet we are also called to *say* hard things. After all, our message is a mix of warning and hope, judgment and blessing, confrontational dialogue (at times) and consoling reassurance. In this chapter of John's prophetic oracle, the witnesses are prophesying and testifying (vv. 3, 7). The prophesying is undoubtedly related to the announcements of impending judgment. Doing so is not easy, and it often brings about ridicule and pain.[66] Yet that is part of the message. Furthermore, our proclamation includes testifying about the hope we have in Christ, who has provided the way of our salvation. The content of our testimony is the gospel, the message of redemption offered to all, in which we urge them to repent and believe.

65. The work of *The Voice of the Martyrs* (VOM; persecution.com) is especially informative for news, statistics, and matters for prayer concerning "persecuted Christians in the world's most difficult and dangerous places to follow Christ." Of note are the remarkable ways in which these believers consistently lead the effort to fulfill the "Great Commission, no matter the cost."

66. See 1 Kgs 22:23–27; Jer 11:9; 20:2; 26:20–23; 40:1; Amos 7:10–15.

For those in missional activity, we must be willing to preach faithfully the full message which God has entrusted to us.[67]

Third, from the two witnesses, *we learn the importance of dedicated service and boldly sharing the message, knowing that the ultimate outcome rests in God's sovereign hands*. This is a critical missional point that cannot be neglected. In the Old Testament era, the Lord commissioned Isaiah, Jeremiah, and Ezekiel to engage the people of Israel missionally. Likewise, all three of them were promised rejection, persecution, and stubborn hearers.[68] The two witnesses appearing in Revelation 11 encounter much the same, and even worse, especially as they are murdered and left to lie in open shame without a proper burial. Yet whether people repent and believe, whether they respond in faith to the message proclaimed to them, is ultimately not something we can coerce or manipulate. Nor can we control what happens to us as witnesses of Christ. Regardless of the circumstance, we must engage in gospel witness by faith. Part of this means trusting the Creator with the fruit of our labors.

67. See 1 Thess 2:4.

68. See Isa 6:9–13; Jer 1:4–19; Ezek 2–3.

Revelation 12

The Woman, the Dragon, and the Beast (Part One)

LEARNING OBJECTIVES

- Identify what the woman, her child, and the dragon represent.
- Analyze the nature of the cosmic conflict between God and Satan.
- Discern the ways in which the battle in heaven clarifies the nature of spiritual warfare.
- Recognize how believers can triumph over Satan and his demonic cohort.
- Consider the importance of believers' remaining faithful to God amid life's afflictions.

CHAPTER SUMMARY

Revelation 12 spotlights a woman clothed with the sun, standing on the moon, and wearing a crown of twelve stars. She gives birth to a male child, symbolizing the Messiah, who is destined to rule all nations with an iron scepter. A hideous, powerful, red dragon, representing Satan, attempts to devour the child, but he is caught up to God's throne in heaven. Next, war breaks out in heaven, where Michael and his angels defeat the dragon and his demonic cohort, all of whom are then hurled to the earth. Though the dragon continues to persecute the woman and her offspring, they triumph by the Lamb's shed blood and by the truth they proclaim.

STUDY QUESTIONS

1. What is your understanding of the symbolic identity of the woman, her male child, and the dragon?
2. What do the ways in which Satan is portrayed reveal about his character and priorities?
3. How does knowing that the woman's male child rules all the nations with an iron scepter give believers hope?
4. Why are Michael and his angels fighting the devil and his angels in heaven?
5. In what ways does God protect the woman and her offspring?

CHAPTER OUTLINE

- The dragon and the child (12:1–6)
- The epic battle in heaven (12:7–12)
- The dragon's attack of the woman (12:13–18)
- Key theological insights
- Important ministry implications
- Vital missional ramifications

THE DRAGON AND THE CHILD (12:1–6)

Toward the end of chapter 11, the "seventh angel" (v. 15) blows his "trumpet." This act, in turn, sets the stage for unleashing the seven bowl judgments, which are discussed in detail in chapters 15 and 16. In the intervening chapters (12–14), John watches an epic battle take place between the Creator and the devil. Throughout the unfolding cosmic drama, the supreme Monarch of the universe remains equitable and upright while bringing about the demise of Satan and all who join his fiendish cause.

As John turns his gaze skyward, he witnesses a "great sign" (12:1). He is referring to a remarkable, ominous event, the significance of which goes beyond the concise details of the narrative. The apostle notices a "woman" who wears the "sun" as her outer garment. This female entity stands above the "moon," and a "crown"[1] made of twelve "stars" rests on her "head." She is "pregnant" (v. 2), and as she is about to deliver her child, she screams in "pain" and "agony."

Specialists debate the identity of the "woman" (v. 1). Four prominent views are that she represents Mary, the mother of Jesus,[2] the twelve founding tribes of Israel,[3] the twelve founding apostles of the church,[4] or the new Jerusalem (personified).[5] Perhaps John uses the "woman" to symbolize all the Father's reborn and faithful children—a united, diverse, multiethnic, multicultural, and baptized messianic community whom the Son redeemed through the cross-resurrection event. Paul refers to them as the "Israel of God" (Gal 6:16). In Hebrews 12:23, they are called the "church of the firstborn" and the "righteous people who have been made perfect."

The reference to the "sun" (Rev 12:1), "moon," and "stars" are reminiscent of Joseph's dream in Genesis 37:9.[6] This observation suggests that the Creator will one day give his children glory, dominion, and preeminence in his eternal kingdom. Though the splendors of heaven await the redeemed, in the meantime they might need to experience oppression, including martyrdom.[7] The labor pains of the woman in Revelation 12:2[8] are a reminder that throughout history, and especially during the time of the end, the wicked will persecute and murder God's children.[9]

Next, John witnesses "another sign" (v. 3) in heaven. A terrifying, immense, flame-colored "dragon" becomes visible, having "seven heads," "ten horns," and a "crown"[10] resting on each of his "heads."[11] These sym-

1. Or wreath-like, regal object.

2. See Odes Sol. 19:6–7; Matt 1–2; Luke 1–2.

3. See Isa 7:14; 9:6; 26:17–19; 54:1; 66:7–10; Mic 4:9–10; 5:3; 4 Ezra 10:44–46.

4. See our discussion of Rev 21:14.

5. See Isa 66:6–11, 13; 4 Ezra 10:25; Gal 4:26–27; Rev 21:9–10.

6. See Song 6:10; Jos. Asen. 5:5; T. Naph. 5:1–7.

7. Especially for refusing to venerate mortal, flawed, human rulers.

8. Perhaps recalling the Creator's judicial oracle in Gen 3:15–16; Jub. 3:23.

9. See Isa 26:17–18; 66:7–8; Mic 4:10; 5:3.

10. Literally "diadem" or royal headband.

11. See Job 7:12; 26:12–13; Pss 74:13–14; 89:10–11; Isa 27:1; 30:7; 51:9; Jer 51:34; Ezek 29:3; 32:2–3; Dan 7:7–8, 20, 24; 2 Bar. 29:4; 1 En. 60:7, 24; 4 Ezra 6:49–52; Odes Sol. 22:1–5; Pss. Sol. 2:25.

bols of regal authority and unbridled power are counterfeit imitations of the Lamb.[12]

The repulsive, hydra-headed creature uses his "tail" (v. 4), like that of a serpentine crocodile, to hurl one-third of the "stars" (personified) of heaven to "earth."[13] Then the "dragon" brazenly places himself in a standing position directly in front of the "woman" with the cannibalistic intent of devouring her "child" the moment it is "born."[14] The "dragon" represents Satan, the archenemy of the Creator and his reborn children.[15] The creature's blood-red hue symbolizes his deranged, homicidal nature, while his other features represent his cunning, strength, and influence over nations and peoples.

Satan's Fiendish Character		
Title/Name for Satan	**Description/Meaning**	**Biblical References**
Accuser	Brings false charges against believers	Rev 12:10
Adversary; roaring lion	A predatory brute who moves about stealthily to devour believers	1 Pet 5:8
Beelzebul	The ruler of the demons; the prince of evil spirits	Matt 12:24
Belial	The embodiment of evil and opposition to God; represents wickedness or worthlessness	2 Cor 6:15
Devil	"Slanderer" and "adversary"	Rev 12:9; 20:10
False god of this age	Blinds the minds of unbelievers	2 Cor 4:4
Murderer; father of lies	Originator of death and deceit	John 8:44
Ruler of the domain of the air	Spiritual power behind worldly rebellion	Eph 2:2
Ruler of this world	Exercises dominion over fallen human systems	John 12:31; 14:30

12. See our discussion of Rev 5:6; 19:12, 16.

13. See Dan 8:10.

14. See Gen 3:15; Matt 2:16.

15. See 1 Chr 21:1; Job 1:6, 9, 12; 2:3, 4, 6, 7; Zech 3:1, 2.

Satan's Fiendish Character		
Title/Name for Satan	**Description/Meaning**	**Biblical References**
Satan	"Opponent" or "accuser"	Job 1:6–12; 2:1–7; 1 Chr 21:1; Zech 3:1–2; Rev 12:9
The great dragon; ancient serpent	Sower of chaos, discord, and confusion	Rev 12:9
The tempter	Strives to mislead believers into sin	1 Thess 3:5

The "stars" (Rev 12:4) that the "dragon" flings to the "earth" represent the legions of demons, or fallen angels, whom the devil controls.[16] Less likely is the view that the "stars" depict a meteor shower of judgment on the planet. The creature's desire to "devour"[17] the woman's "child" symbolizes Satan's repeated attempts to overthrow the Messiah and obliterate his followers.

In the unfolding cosmic drama, John notes that the "woman" gives "birth" (v. 5) to a "son," more specifically, a "male child."[18] He is destined to "shepherd" (or rule over) "all the nations" with an "iron rod" (that is, a royal scepter).[19] This is an allusion to Psalm 2:9, especially its messianic reference to the sovereign reign of the Anointed One.

John states that despite the dragon's barbaric efforts, he cannot stop the Lord from snatching up the woman's "child" (Rev 12:5) to the safety of heaven and the Creator's sacred "throne." From this imagery, there is the likelihood that the woman's "child" represents the Messiah. Indeed, many of the events described here are reminiscent of Jesus' birth, his parents' departure with him to Egypt, Jesus' resurrection, and his ascension to heaven.[20]

Then the apostle observes that the "woman" escapes into the "wilderness" (or desert) to a locale that the Lord has "prepared." For "1,260 days" he cares for and nourishes the "woman." The "wilderness" could symbolize a spiritual place of deliverance and refuge that the supreme Monarch of the

16. See Dan 8:10; 1 En. 18:13–16; 21:6; 90:24; 2 En. 4:1; 2 Bar. 51:10; Matt 25:41; 2 Pet 2:4; Rev 12:7.

17. Literally "eat down."

18. See Isa 7:14; 66:7.

19. See our discussion of Rev 2:27; 7:17; 19:15.

20. See Matt 2:13–16; John 13:3; 16:18; Acts 1:9–11; Rom 1:3–4; Phil 2:5–11; 1 Tim 3:16.

universe makes available for his reborn children.[21] If so, this implies that even in the darkest hours before the Son's return, the Father watches over the redeemed and enables them to remain faithful to him.

Some specialists think the "1,260 days," or three and a half years, refers to a literal period in which Satan, through his diabolical human agents, persecutes Jesus' followers just before his return. A more likely option is that the chronological referent is to be taken metaphorically.[22] In this case, it symbolizes the devil's limited reign of terror, which the Creator will abruptly end.

Typological Fulfillment in Revelation		
As we previously noted, Revelation employs typological fulfillment or prophetic foreshadowing, a literary technique where Old Testament objects, people, or events prefigure similar elements in the New Testament.		
Symbol/Image	**Old Testament Foundation**	**Revelation Application**
Number seven	In the Genesis creation account (chs. 1–2), God finishes his work of creating and forming the universe in seven days, symbolizing completeness and perfection.	The number seven appears throughout the Apocalypse to represent divine completeness, as seen in the seven churches (1:4), the seven seal calamities (5:1), the seven trumpet catastrophes (8:2), and the seven bowl plagues (15:1; 16:1).
Lamb of God	In the Old Testament sacrificial system, lambs were commonly offered as temporary sacrifices for the forgiveness of sins.	Christ is depicted as the superlative Lamb who provides complete and final atonement for humanity's sins (5:6, 12), fulfilling what the Old Testament lambs foreshadowed.
Woman giving birth	Isa 7:14 records a prophecy about a virgin's conceiving and bearing a son called "Immanuel" (meaning "God with us").	In Revelation, the woman who gives birth (12:1–5) to a child represents the typological fulfillment or prophetic foreshadowing of Isaiah's messianic oracle.

21. See Deut 29:5; 1 Sam 23:14; 1 Kgs 17:1–6; 19:1–4; Ascen. Isa. 4:12–13.

22. See Dan 7:25, 27.

THE EPIC BATTLE IN HEAVEN (12:7–12)

Next, in the unfolding, cosmic drama, John witnesses a fierce battle raging in "heaven" (v. 7). The clash is between the forces of good, represented by "Michael," along with the "angels" under his command, and the forces of evil, symbolized by the "dragon," along with the fallen "angels" under his command. "Michael"[23] is an archangel and protector of the redeemed.[24] God's celestial warriors ensure that Satan and his demonic cohort fail in their attempted insurrection. Indeed, because they have insufficient strength to prevail, all of them are forced out of "heaven" (v. 8) and hurled to the "earth" (v. 9).[25]

Some specialists think that this fall to earth occurred when Jesus rose from the dead and ascended into heaven.[26] Another possibility is that the Creator will defeat the "great dragon" in the middle of a time of great distress preceding the Son's return. Perhaps John has both ideas in mind when he draws attention to Satan's demise.

The apostle explains that the fiendish dragon is the "ancient serpent,"[27] otherwise known as the "Devil" and "Satan."[28] The Greek noun translated "devil" means "slanderer" and "adversary," while the noun rendered "Satan" means "opponent" and "accuser."[29] From time immemorial, the devil sowed chaos, discord, and confusion among humans. The evil one also used subterfuge and falsehood to spread darkness and disorder throughout the "whole inhabited earth."[30]

23. Whose name means, "Who is like God?"

24. See Dan 10:13, 21; 12:1; 1 En. 20:5; 40:8; 2 En. 22:6, 8–9; 33:11; Jude 1:9.

25. Possibly foreshadowed in the fall of the king of Tyre; see Isa 14:12–15; LAE 12:1; Sib. Or. 5:512–31.

26. See Luke 10:18–19; John 12:31–33; 14:30; 16:11; Col 2:15.

27. See Gen 3:1, 14–15; Isa 27:1; 3 Bar. 9:7; Wis 2:24; 2 Cor 4:4; 11:3; Rom 16:20.

28. See Rev 20:1.

29. For a substantive overview of the proper name *Satan* in the Old Testament, the Hebrew texts from the Second Temple Period, and the New Testament, see Breytenbach and Day, "Satan," 726–32. For an alternative view, see Stokes, *The Satan*. Stokes contends that the Hebrew noun *satan* originally meant "attacker" or "executioner," designating a divine agent who enforced God's judgment, rather than primarily "accuser" or "adversary" as often translated. Stokes traces the evolution of this figure from a subordinate member of the divine council in the Hebrew Bible to the malevolent and autonomous enemy of God in later Jewish and Christian traditions. In the Apocalypse, this development culminates in the portrayal of Satan as a cosmic rebel, deceiver, and persecutor, who is ultimately destined for destruction.

30. See John 8:44; 2 Cor 2:11; Eph 6:10–17; Rev 20:8.

The faultfinder, Satan, like a hostile, rogue prosecutor in a court of law, incessantly attempts to bring false charges of wrongdoing against God's children (v. 10). Yet it was the devil, his demonic cohort, and their human vassals who were on trial before the Lord's cosmic court of justice.[31] Despite the fiend's accusations, the believers' advocate, Jesus of Nazareth, always comes to their defense and enables them to remain loyal to him.[32]

Next, John hears a "loud voice" from "heaven" announce the arrival of the Creator's provision of "salvation," along with his "power" and "kingdom" rule.[33] Likewise, the Messiah's "authority" to reign is about to be established.[34] As was the case in 1:6, 4:11, 5:13, and 7:12, so too in 12:10 each term in the doxology is accented in the original language by the definite article "the" to indicate totality—namely, *all the* "salvation," *all the* "power," *all the* "kingdom," and *all the* "authority."

Jesus' followers do not overcome Satan's false accusations by either sheer willpower or physical exertion. Instead, as theologians of the cross, they prevail due to the Lamb's sacrificial death at Calvary.[35] In turn, this becomes the basis for their bold, evangelistic witness about his atoning sacrifice.[36]

Even in the "face of death" (v. 11), the martyred saints remain loyal to the Redeemer. They are willing to give up their temporal, earthly existence to spend eternity in the sacred presence of their Creator.[37] The preceding truths are the "reason" (v. 12) the "heavens" (personified), along with all their inhabitants, are commanded to "rejoice."[38] In contrast, anguish and turmoil (or "woe") await all who dwell on the "earth" and in the "sea."[39] After all, the "Devil" is about to unleash his fury on

31. See Job 1:6–12; 2:1–5; Zech 3:1–4; 1 En. 40:7; Rom 8:33; Rev 20:2.

32. See Rom 8:33–34; 1 Thess 5:9–11; 1 Tim 2:5; 1 John 2:1–2.

33. See Ps 96:10–11; Isa 44:23; 49:13.

34. See Dan 7:14.

35. See our discussion of Rev 1:5.

36. Like someone testifying in a court of law, both in word and deed, by the power of the Spirit; see Zech 4:6; Rev 1:9; 6:9; 12:17; 19:10; 20:4.

37. See T. Jud. 25:4; Matt 16:24–26; Mark 8:34–38; Luke 9:23–26; 14:26; John 12:25.

38. See Deut 32:1; Pss 19:1; 96:11; Isa 1:2; 44:23; 49:13.

39. That is, inclusive of all human and nonhuman life.

the planet,[40] especially since Satan knows that the Lord has limited the amount of "time" that the evil one can wreak havoc.

The Threefold Distinction of God's Kingdom	
God's left-hand kingdom (or the kingdom of law)	Otherwise known as the common kingdom, namely, the created order common to all life that will one day come to an end. The left-hand kingdom encompasses secular human government and its hierarchal civil institutions, along with all familial, social, political, and environmental spheres of influence. Within this temporal, earthly realm, the use of force, the threat of punishment, and the decimation of one's enemies are the primary tools to coerce people to obey. The Son primarily reigns over this realm as Creator and Sustainer.
God's right-hand kingdom (or the kingdom of grace)	Otherwise known as the redemptive kingdom, namely, the church, which awaits the consummation of the world to come at the end of the current age. The right-hand kingdom encompasses the Father's reign through the Son by means of the Spirit's indwelling believers. Within this eternal, metaphysical realm, persuasion (especially through the pastoral ministry of Word and sacrament) is the primary way of leading sinners to faith and sanctifying believers in all areas of life. The Son primarily reigns over this realm as Redeemer and Savior.
The kingdom of the devil	This encompasses the insidious schemes and diabolical machinations of Satan, especially through his demonic cohorts. The devil's incessant goal is to corrupt God's left-hand kingdom and subvert his right-hand kingdom. One fiendish approach is to sow confusion about the precise nature of the law-gospel dichotomy. A second, related tactic involves obscuring the dialectic between the kingdom of law and the kingdom of grace. A third strategy is an all-out attempt to transform the common kingdom (including the arts, economics, and government) into the redemptive kingdom. A fourth method entails employing religion to infiltrate the realm of the state and using violence to enact extremist goals (for example, religious fanatics seizing the political levers of power to establish a theocracy). A fifth way involves the state's asserting itself in realms of the conscience, the mind, and issues involving ultimate salvation (for example, atheistic radicals using religious-sounding propaganda to delude the masses into becoming sycophants of pagan, absolutizing ideologies).

40. Through the sea- and land-beasts; see our discussion of Rev 13.

THE DRAGON'S ATTACK ON THE WOMAN (12:13–18)

Throughout history, the devil has tried to harm believers, both physically and spiritually. As the time of the second advent draws closer, the serpent's attacks grow progressively more severe and maniacal (v. 13).

For instance, in the unfolding cosmic drama, when the "dragon" realizes that he is permanently banished from heaven and hurled to the "earth," he uses everything at his disposal to hunt and destroy the "woman," along with all her offspring. Yet the Creator is committed to preserving the redeemed, who remain loyal to the woman's "male child," the Messiah, even while they face martyrdom for their refusal to venerate mortal, flawed, human rulers.

God's protection of his children is symbolized by the image of the "woman" (v. 14) as she uses two huge, eaglelike "wings" to "fly" to a "place" of safety and refuge in the "wilderness" (or desert) away from the "serpent." This is reminiscent of Israel's departure from Egypt and serves as another example of exodus typology (or prophetic foreshadowing) appearing in the Apocalypse.[41]

The Lord prepares the above sanctuary in advance for the "woman," where she is "fed" (or nourished) for a "time, and times, and half a time."[42] Correlating the preceding chronological reference with verse 6 suggests a period of three and a half years (or 1,260 days).[43] Whether understood literally or symbolically, the interval emphasizes that the Creator will limit the devil's reign of terror.

Next, John witnesses the attempt by the "serpent" (v. 15) to drown the "woman" with a torrent of "water" spewing from the creature's "mouth." The "earth" (personified; v. 16), however, comes to the woman's rescue by opening its "mouth" and swallowing all the "water."[44] This, in turn, thwarts Satan's maniacal, bloodthirsty plans.

Specialists differ in their views concerning the significance of the preceding events. For instance, these could symbolize the devil's attempt to ensnare, persecute, and murder the redeemed, along with deceiving them through false teaching.[45] Alternatively, Satan's efforts may repre-

41. See Exod 14:8; 19:3–6; Deut 32:10–12; Isa 40:27–31; 1 En. 96:2.

42. See Exod 16:32; Deut 1:31; 8:2; Ps 78:52; John 6:31; Acts 7:36.

43. See Dan 7:25; 12:7.

44. Most likely, due to the Creator's prompting; see Wis 16:24.

45. See Matt 24:24; Mark 13:6; Luke 22:31; 2 Thess 2:9–10; 1 Tim 4:1–5.

sent the slanders and accusations which he and his subordinates level against God's children.[46]

In either case, the reaction of the "dragon" (v. 17) remains the same. He becomes so enraged over what has happened to the "woman" that the creature declares all-out "war" against the woman's offspring.[47] John clarifies that he is referring to those who—in their priorities and values, along with their attitudes and actions—obey the Father's decrees, openly acknowledge that they belong to the Son, and hold steadfast to their "testimony about Jesus."[48]

The above observations indicate that Jesus' followers (as the church militant) are in an intense, prolonged spiritual battle of titanic proportions.[49] Though the war continues to rage, the Creator's defeat of Satan and his demonic cohort is assured. With the Spirit's help,[50] God's children can remain unwavering in their commitment to the gospel. The exposition of verse 18, which is thematically connected with chapter 13 of John's prophetic oracle, is discussed in that presentation.

KEY THEOLOGICAL INSIGHTS

As we noted above, Revelation 12–14 represents another interlude as the seventh trumpet judgment has sounded (11:15–19) and as the reader anticipates the coming bowl judgments (chs. 15–16). Specifically, within chapter 12, we encounter several truths about our arch adversary—the enemy, the devil, and Satan—who opposes the Creator at every turn.

First, *we note Satan's diabolical intention to destroy God's reborn children.* While there are various views as to the identity of the woman (v. 1), especially noteworthy is the possibility that she represents an Israeli-related entity[51] that births, along with the Messiah,[52] the true believers in Christ and particularly those conquerors who participate in the defeat

46. See Ps 144:7–8.

47. See Gen 3:15; Liv. Pro. 12:13.

48. Like eyewitnesses in a court of law; see Rev 1:2, 9; 14:12; 20:4.

49. See 1 Cor 10:13; Eph 6:10–17; 1 Pet 5:8–9.

50. Especially through the means of grace.

51. Options include, as we mentioned earlier, Mary, the mother of Jesus; national Israel; the church (built on the foundation of the prophets and apostles; see Eph 2:20); and the new Jerusalem as the "mother" of the heirs of the promise (see Gal 4:26; 6:16).

52. For a cogent argument that the woman must be connected to the "birthing" of the Messiah, see Thomas, *Revelation Exegetical Commentary*, vol. 2, 117–21.

of the dragon (vv. 10–11). In whatever way the details of the woman and male child are to be understood, the underlying intentions of the adversary are clear. He seeks the total obliteration of not only the Messiah but also those who represent him in their beliefs and behavior.[53] The dragon's destruction extends beyond its malevolent influence on individuals. It encompasses not only spiritual ruin but also physical devastation,[54] vividly illustrated by its gruesome attempt to devour the male child immediately after his birth.

Second, *we see that Satan is permanently ousted from God's sacred presence, where the evil one is no longer able to accuse believers falsely.* While the adversary is active and constantly at work to destroy all that the Creator undertakes, Satan will never be victorious in the end. He is neither all-powerful nor any match for the supreme Monarch of the universe.[55] The scene depicted in verses 7–9 represents a second dismissal of the archenemy from heaven.[56] The ancient serpent had already transgressed God's holiness and was banished from his heavenly position.[57] Even so, Satan still maintains access to God in order to accuse Jesus' followers of their sinfulness and unworthiness.[58] When the devil finally succumbs to defeat at the hands of Michael and his celestial warriors, the nefarious entity becomes powerless to bring any more false accusations against the saints.

Third, *we observe that Satan continues to seek the obliteration of God's reborn children, even though the devil is a defeated foe who awaits certain doom.* The adversary's ousting from heaven as accuser marks a decisive victory for the Lamb (vv. 7–9). That said, Satan refuses to relinquish his mission to attack and destroy the woman and her children (v. 17). Today, the devil continues to accuse the saints falsely, despite his decisive defeat at the cross.[59] Similarly, at the end of the age, Satan attempts to carry on

53. See Luke 22:31; 1 Pet 5:8.

54. For more on the devil as a destroyer of physical life, see John 8:44; Heb 2:14.

55. In Job 1–2, we find that while God allows Satan to do terrible things to Job, Satan needs divine permission to unleash his fury. From this observation, we realize that even though Satan is powerful, he is far from being omnipotent.

56. For an accessible overview of various perspectives on the "time" of the warfare depicted in verse 7, see Thomas, *Revelation Exegetical Commentary*, vol. 2, 128–29. Thomas's own view is that the war is an "end-time event, occurring midway through Daniel's seventieth week."

57. See Isa 14:12–20; Ezek 28:11–19.

58. See Job 1–2; Zech 3:1.

59. See Col 2:15.

his homicidal onslaught, even though he has lost his position to accuse the saints before God. The dragon knows that his time is short (v. 12), and he is fully aware of the everlasting destruction that awaits him in the end.[60] Yet he refuses to accept his final defeat. Until he is ultimately cast into the fiery lake filled with burning sulfur, he will bitterly pursue his heinous mission.

IMPORTANT MINISTRY IMPLICATIONS

The mighty work of the Creator and the faithfulness of true believers in Christ counterpoint each of the above theological insights concerning the devil. These contrasts offer significant ministerial direction for those in congregational leadership, especially as we equip our parishioners to stand against the onslaught of the enemy.

First, *while Satan persistently uses nefarious schemes to bring about the destruction of the saints, God provides them with protection and deliverance*. Physical protection is not always the Messiah's chosen path, as God's reborn children indeed suffer at times, even to the point of martyrdom.[61] Yet the Creator protects them from the adversary, always spiritually and often physically. For this reason, we can encourage our parishioners to turn to our Lord in times of distress, particularly when the enemy's pursuit is oppressive and overwhelming. Frequently, we give too much credence to Satan and his ability to subvert believers. While we know theologically that God is greater than our adversary,[62] in practical terms, we sometimes wallow in fear and dread. This is unnecessary for true believers in Christ. Accordingly, we must admonish our parishioners to look to our Master with the eyes of faith to overcome the evil one.[63]

Second, since the enemy is unable to accuse believers falsely forever, *we can reassure our parishioners that God has and will overcome the dragon's lies and accusations*. In verse 13, we read that Satan is thrown down.

60. See Matt 8:29.

61. In Rev 12:11, those who overcome are lauded for loving the Lamb, even to the extent that they are willing to sacrifice their lives in service to him; see Matt 10:39; 16:25; 24:9; Acts 7:54–60; Rev 6:9–11.

62. See 1 John 4:4.

63. See Matt 6:13; 2 Thess 3:3. Scripture is clear that our ability to overcome the devil is due only to the Spirit's presence and power. We are instructed neither to rebuke the devil nor to declare him bound. Likewise, we have no divine authorization either to speak directly to the devil or frivolously about him, as if we are the ones in control of the spiritual battle; see also Jude 1:8–9.

While this victory belongs to the Creator, we also discover that Satan is defeated by the testimony of the overcomers, namely, those who hold fast to the Word of God. As church leaders, we can exhort our congregants to live out this characteristic of being victorious in the face of Satan's false accusations against them. To be truly victorious, we must pursue lives of holiness and faithfulness, especially since God, who has called us, is holy.[64] We must challenge our fellow believers to give the enemy nothing with which to accuse them.

Third, though Satan continues to pursue the woman during the short time that is left to do so, *we can encourage the faithful to trust in God's ongoing protection and provision for his reborn children.* For every move or tactic made by the dragon in pursuit of the woman and her offspring, there is a countermove made by God (vv. 13–16). In light of this truth, our parishioners need to know that the Creator is neither distant nor detached. Likewise, he is not standing afar off and waiting to see how we will handle the onslaught of temptation and destruction that Satan unleashes on us.[65] Instead, our Lord is actively at work, equipping us to stand against the devil's attack. God is also fighting with us through the presence of the Spirit to ensure that we stand firm in our faith until the end.[66]

VITAL MISSIONAL RAMIFICATIONS

In our discussion of Revelation 11, we focused on the notion of testifying for Christ, especially as we learned about the two witnesses and their perseverance in bringing the gospel to the lost. Now, as we consider missional lessons to be gleaned from chapter 12, our attention shifts to the notion of opposition, specifically the resistance we experience from Satan and his demonic cohort when we share the good news about Christ with others.

First, *when we engage in gospel witness, we can expect the enemy to thwart our efforts.* As we noted above, while there are various views concerning how to understand the woman and the male child, most interpreters agree that there is a symbolic representation of God's plan at work, the purpose of which Satan seeks to extinguish immediately. The

64. See Matt 5:16, 48; 1 Pet 1:15–16; 2:9–12.

65. The description of God's protection of the woman (Rev 12:12–16) counters any deistic view of the Creator that is promoted in contemporary theology. God is, and always has been, directly involved with his creation at every moment; see Col 1:17.

66. See Eph 6:10–20.

dragon is pictured as ready and waiting to strike at the first opportunity to destroy what the Creator intends (v. 4). In mission work, we can anticipate opposition, especially when entering uncharted territory, breaking new ground, or launching a fresh initiative. This opposition can especially be seen in efforts to carry the good news about Jesus into unreached areas within Majority World contexts. Missionaries have given numerous testimonies of trial and difficulty, particularly as they undertook pioneering work in restricted-access countries.[67] Here, we recognize that the enemy's most effective strategy is to destroy the gospel's witness before it can take root.

Second, *opposition from Satan demonstrates that we are in a spiritual battle beyond mere human ability to wage*. Involving oneself in missions requires submission to God's sovereign will and a full reliance on his strength to accomplish the task he has set before us. Of all the works of God that Satan wishes to prevent, the salvation of the lost is paramount. Those endeavoring to bring people to faith in Christ can rest assured that he will aid in their mission.[68] Nonetheless, there will be spiritual battles that rage in and around all missional activity. Frequently in mission work, people will be friendly and receptive to the good deeds we do within their community, and they are often receptive to the positive, morally upright teachings we bring. Yet when it comes to their need to repent of sin, die to their sinful selves, and follow Christ, the increase in resistance and opposition is profound.[69] In this regard, missionaries around the world have testified to intense spiritual warfare which accompanies their proclamation of the gospel. Those engaged missionally should anticipate the enemy's seeking to remove gospel seeds before they have a chance to germinate or take root in the soil of human hearts.[70]

67. Though specifics need not be mentioned here, it is often the case that missionary families who venture into unreached territory are inundated with difficulty during their preparation for ministry in their chosen field. For instance, family health issues, visa delays, and unexpected financial hardships frequently accompany those who seek to be agents of gospel witness in these places.

68. See Matt 16:18.

69. See Matt 16:24–26. In addition, see Jesus' call to discipleship in John 6:35–71, where many of his initial followers abandon him due to the difficult demands of laying down one's life for the sake of Christ. Just as Jesus lost much of his audience at that time, so too can we expect difficulty when calling people to authentic repentance and true discipleship.

70. See Matt 13:1–23; Mark 4:1–20; Luke 8:4–15.

Third, *the opposition we face in mission work is not limited to the salvation of the lost*. Expressed differently, it goes beyond the moment of conversion and manifests throughout the lifelong discipleship process we seek to foster among those who come to faith in Christ. Even though Satan loses much when the unsaved trust in the Messiah, the devil attempts to sabotage the spiritual growth of Christians, cripple their walk, and silence their witness. As we make disciples of all nations, in faithful obedience to the Great Commission, we can expect the enemy to be on the attack throughout the lives of our converts. Those in missions should avoid becoming satisfied with external professions of faith. Instead, they should commit to safeguard the journey with those who believe, with the goal of leading them into spiritual maturity, so that they too can become effective witnesses for Christ.[71]

71. See Matt 28:18–20, where the goal of the Great Commission is that Jesus' disciples be taught to obey all he commands. More than just seeking professions of faith, the process of discipleship strives to lead followers of Christ to spiritual maturity.

Revelation 13

The Woman, the Dragon, and the Beast (Part Two)

LEARNING OBJECTIVES

- Describe the characteristics of the sea-beast and the land-beast.
- Understand the significance of the two predatory brutes within the context of Revelation.
- Consider what the pair of hideous creatures reveal about the forces of evil that oppose God and his children in the end-times.
- Discern how believers can resist the temptation to venerate satanically inspired people and organizations.
- Deliberate the meaning behind the number 666 associated with the sea-beast.

CHAPTER SUMMARY

Revelation 13 focuses on two predatory brutes, the first originating from the sea and the second arising from the land. The dragon gives his power, throne, and vast authority to the sea-beast, who resorts to homicidal acts to exterminate God's reborn children. In turn, the land-beast exploits the same authority to force earth's inhabitants to venerate the sea-beast. Moreover, the land-beast performs astounding miracles to deceive fallen humanity and undermine the faith of believers.

STUDY QUESTIONS

1. Who or what do you think is the sea-beast?

2. Why does the dragon give his power, throne, and vast authority to the sea-beast?
3. Why do earth's inhabitants venerate the dragon and the sea-beast?
4. Who or what do you think is the land-beast?
5. Why does the land-beast work so hard to deceive earth's inhabitants?

CHAPTER OUTLINE

- The beast emerging from the sea (13:1–10)
- The beast coming out of the earth (13:11–18)
- Key theological insights
- Important ministry implications
- Vital missional ramifications

THE BEAST EMERGING FROM THE SEA (13:1–10)

Several modern translations demarcate the sentence "and [the dragon] stood on the shore of the sea" as 12:18.[1] However, given the strong thematic connection between it and 13:1, other translations incorporate the sentence as part of that verse. Therefore, in a vision reminiscent of the four creatures described in Daniel 7,[2] John witnesses a hideous, predatory "beast" (Rev 13:1) gradually emerging from the "sea." In ancient times, people often associated evil with the sea, for its depths appeared mysterious and eerie.[3]

1. For descriptions in ancient Jewish literature of incredibly powerful and terrifyingly devilish sea creatures, such as Behemoth and Leviathan, which promote wickedness, foster chaos, and incite rebellion against the Creator, see Isa 27:1; 2 Bar. 29:4; 1 En. 60:7; 4 Ezra 6:49–52; 11:1. For a discussion of Behemoth in Scripture, see Batto, "Behemoth," 165–69. Also, for a discussion of Leviathan in Scripture, see Uehlinger, "Leviathan," 511–15.

2. Along with the animal visions recorded in Dan 7–12.

3. On this point, see Stolz, "Sea," 740–42. Also, see Pss 18:15; 29:3; 32:6; 46:3; 65:7; 74:13; 77:16; 93:3–5; 107:23–30; Isa 57:20–21; Jer 5:22; 6:23; 49:23; Dan 7:2–3; Nah 1:4; Hab 3:15; Rev 12:12.

Parallels between Daniel 7 and Revelation 13[4]		
Theme	**Daniel 7**	**Revelation 13**
Beasts Described	Four beasts: a lion with eagle's wings, a bear, a leopard, and an ogre with iron teeth and ten horns (vv. 3–7)	A dragon (12:3), a beast from the sea with seven heads and ten horns (13:1), and a beast from the earth with two horns like a lamb but speaking like a dragon (v. 11)
Divine Judgment and Deliverance	The Ancient of Days judges the beasts, and the kingdom is given to the saints (vv. 9–14, 26–27)	Implied through the faithfulness and perseverance of the saints; ultimate victory unfolds later in the Apocalypse (14:1–5; 19:11–21)
Oppression of God's People	The fourth beast wages war against the "saints of the Most High" and seeks to "change times and the law" (vv. 21, 25).	The sea-beast is venerated by all except true believers and makes war on the saints (vv. 7–8); the land-beast deceives and enforces the veneration of the sea-beast (vv. 12–17).
Symbolism of Beasts	Represent earthly kingdoms that oppose God's rule (vv. 17, 23)	Represent satanic powers and agents who deceive and dominate (vv. 2, 11–14)

The ogre which the apostle sees has "ten horns," with a "crown"[5] on each one. Additionally, the entity has "seven heads" with an assortment of "blasphemous names" (or titles) on each one.[6] Most likely, these are intended to slander the Creator's holy name blatantly.[7]

In ancient times, people used "horns" to symbolize the military, economic, and religious power of their monarchs. Also, people used "crowns" (or royal headbands) to represent the exalted status of their rulers. The "ten horns" and "ten crowns" worn by the hydra-headed sea-beast suggests that it is characterized by unequaled power and preeminence.

Ancient people used the head as a symbol of control and intelligence. John might be indicating that the seven-headed entity is cunning and influential. Furthermore, rulers in the first century AD[8] often

4. This is another example of typological fulfillment or prophetic foreshadowing in the Apocalypse. Table adapted from information presented in Stefanovic, *Revelation*, 410–11.

5. Literally "diadem" or royal headband.

6. Collectively indicative of the sea-beast's odious character and attributes.

7. See Dan 7:7, 20, 24; Rev 17:9, 12.

8. Such as the Roman emperor Domitian.

assumed titles of deity[9] and declared themselves to be saviors of the world. Likewise, the "beast" from the "sea" will brazenly appropriate for itself designations that the Creator reserves exclusively for himself.[10]

Though the body of the sea-beast looks like a "leopard" (v. 2; or panther), it has the "feet" (or paws) of a "bear" and the "mouth" of a "lion." In the first century AD, people associated agility with the "leopard," bone-crushing strength with the "bear," and swiftness and stealthy force with the "lion." Evidently, the sea-beast will have all these characteristics, making it extremely vicious.[11]

John explains that the "dragon" gives the sea-beast his substantial "power," "throne," and ruling "authority." Hence, this creature is a vassal and deputy of the serpent and exists to do his bidding. Also, the apostle notes that one of the sea-beast's "heads" (v. 3) has been "wounded" (by a "sword"; v. 14) beyond recovery,[12] and yet the "fatal" injury is "healed."

Some specialists think that the above is a veiled reference to the Roman emperor Nero, who committed suicide in AD 68. According to a first century AD legend,[13] he was still alive and would eventually return to Rome to regain his throne. A more likely view is that the sea-beast's recovery is a mock imitation of Jesus' resurrection.

Just as the Messiah had been slain and rose again from the dead,[14] the sea-beast will also give the impression that he has tremendous healing powers. Additionally, this creature will use his pseudo-recovery to enthrall and mislead the entire "world." The preceding should not be surprising. After all, the sea-beast, as an agent of Satan, masquerades as an "angel of light" (2 Cor 11:14) and blinds "the minds of the unbelievers" (4:4).

Parallels between the Lamb and the Sea-Beast in Revelation[15]		
Parallel Characteristic	**The Lamb (Christ)**	**The Sea-Beast (Antichrist)**
Death and Resurrection	Appears as slain but standing (5:6)	Has a fatal wound that is healed (13:3, 14)

9. Such as *Dominus et Deus noster* or "our Master and God."
10. See our discussion of Rev 17:3.
11. See Dan 7:2–7.
12. Rev 13:3 is literally rendered "slaughtered to death."
13. Known as the Nero *redivivus* or revived myth.
14. See our discussion of Rev 1:18; 5:6.
15. Table adapted from information presented in Schreiner, *Revelation*, 464–65.

Parallels between the Lamb and the Sea-Beast in Revelation[15]		
Parallel Characteristic	**The Lamb (Christ)**	**The Sea-Beast (Antichrist)**
Divine Authority	Receives authority from the Father (2:27; 3:21)	Receives authority from the dragon / Satan (13:4)
Final Outcome	Glorious return and eternal reign (1:7; 2:25; 3:3, 11; 16:15; 19:11–16; 22:7, 12, 17, 20)	Final defeat and eternal doom (19:11–21; 20:10)
Mark on Followers	Followers have God's name on their foreheads (14:1).	Followers have the beast's mark on their foreheads or hands (13:16).
Multiple Crowns/ Horns	Seven horns (5:6); many crowns (19:12)	Ten horns with ten crowns (13:1)
Universal Dominion	Rules over every tribe and nation (5:9; 7:9)	Authority over all nations (13:7); rules with ten kings (17:12)
Worship and Adoration	Receives worship from all creation (5:8–14)	Demands veneration from earth's inhabitants (13:4, 8)

Wicked humanity not only follows (Rev 13:3) the sea-beast but also prostrates in homage to him, as well as to the "dragon" (v. 4).[16] Pagan humanity will also extol the sea-beast's alleged greatness and invincibility.[17] No one can wage a successful military campaign against the dragon's deputy—not even, it is falsely asserted, the Creator.[18]

Perhaps energized by unparalleled acclaim, the sea-beast will use his "mouth" (v. 5) to speak repeatedly in an "arrogant" and slanderous manner against God's "name" (v. 6), his sacred "dwelling"[19] in "heaven," and even those who tabernacle with him for all eternity.[20] This outrageous, brazen conduct will continue for "forty-two months" (v. 5) or three and a half years.[21]

16. Possibly a veiled reference to the imperial cult that was present throughout Asia Minor.

17. Denoting counterfeit imitations of ancient Hebrew assertions about the Lord's uniqueness; see Exod 8:10; 15:11; Deut 33:26; 1 Kgs 8:33; 2 Chr 6:14; Pss 18:31; 35:10; 71:19; 86:8; 89:6, 8; 113:5; Isa 40:18, 25; 44:7; Jer 10:6; Mic 7:18.

18. See our discussion of Rev 12:7–9.

19. Literally "tabernacle."

20. See Dan 7:6, 8, 11, 20, 25; 8:10–13; 1 En. 5:4; Ascen. Isa. 4:6.

21. See Dan 7:25, 27; 8:14; 9:27; 12:7; Ascen. Isa. 4:12.

Not stopping there, the sea-beast will use his dragon-infused authority to "wage war" (v. 7) against the Creator's holy people (the "saints") and to triumph over them.[22] The serpent's deputy will also use his imperial "authority" to control individuals from all walks of life (that is, "every tribe and people and language and nation").[23] No one will be spared from the sea-beast's persecution or deceptions. Indeed, he will make every effort to crush all his opponents and delude every one of his followers.

Those belonging to the evil world system will prostrate themselves in homage to the sea-beast.[24] For this reason their "names" (v. 8) are excluded from the "Book of Life." This is the heavenly list of the redeemed, the names of whom God inscribed "from the beginning of the world."[25] Moreover, the ledger belongs to the "Lamb," whom the Creator allowed, from time immemorial,[26] to be sacrificed to atone for humanity's sins.[27]

John admonishes everyone to hear and heed the somber prophetic oracle (v. 9).[28] This includes the declaration that imprisonment and execution await some of the Messiah's loyal followers (v. 10).[29] Rather than be dismayed by such possibilities and become fatalistic, believers are to endure their trials resolutely and remain devoted to the Savior.[30] God's beleaguered children can boldly hold firm in their faith,[31] for they know that the Creator will one day punish the wicked. He will also bring his children into his sacred, everlasting presence, having pardoned them through the Messiah's sacrificial death at Calvary.

22. See Dan 7:21, 25; 8:24; 11:30–31.

23. As we previously noted, throughout the Apocalypse, an emphasis is placed on earth's unregenerate inhabitants, who venerated pagan deities; see our discussion of Rev 3:10; 6:10; 8:13; 11:10; 13:12, 14; 14:6; 17:2, 8.

24. Perhaps comparable to idolaters burning incense to a carved image of the Roman emperor.

25. See Exod 32:32–34; Ps 69:28; Isa 4:3; Dan 12:1; Mal 3:16; Apoc. Zeph. 3:7; 9:2; 2 Bar. 24:1; 1 En. 47:3; 89:68; 108:3; 2 En. 52:15; 3 En. 18:24; Jos. Asen. 15:4; Jub. 30:20, 22; 36:10; 104:1; Luke 10:20; Heb 12:23; Phil 4:3; Rev 3:5; 17:8; 20:12, 15; 21:27.

26. See As. Mos. 1:13–14; Odes Sol. 41:11–15; 1 Pet 1:19–20.

27. See Isa 53:7; John 1:29, 36.

28. See our discussion of Rev 2:7, 11, 17, 29; 3:6, 13, 22.

29. See Jer 15:1–2; 43:11; 1 En. 47:2.

30. See our discussion of Rev 1:9; 2:2–3, 10, 13, 19, 25; 3:4, 8, 10, 11; 14:12; Did. 16:5.

31. Especially by putting on the "full armor of God" (Eph 6:11).

Who or What Is the Sea-Beast?[32]		
Interpretation	**Description**	**Biblical References**
Evil World System	The embodiment of wickedness found in corrupt governmental and organizational systems. Ancient Rome serves as a historical example of a human government that endorsed the persecution of believers, the spread of immorality, and the proliferation of heretical ideas. In the end-times, another organizational entity will arise promoting these goals in an intensified manner.	1 John 2:18, 22; 4:1–4; 2 John 1:7
Individual Person	A real person commonly known as the antichrist who appears during the end times. This false messiah-like figure deceives the earth and seeks to control it through military, economic, and religious systems. While despots have existed throughout history, this individual represents the ultimate manifestation of evil leadership, persecutes Jesus' followers, and gathers the world in rebellion against him.	Dan 7:19–25; 2 Thess 2:1–10; Rev 11:7–14; 19:19

THE BEAST COMING OUT OF THE EARTH (13:11–18)

In the unfolding cosmic drama, whereas the first "beast" (v. 1) emerges from the "sea," the second "beast" (v. 11) arises from the "earth."[33] The ground might signify humbler, less mysterious origins than those of the sea. Another possibility is that John is drawing a sharp contrast between the first and second predatory brutes. If so, the apostle seeks to emphasize that though they both serve as vassals of the "dragon" (v. 2), they are different from one another in significant ways.

For instance, the sea-beast might be more of a political creature, whereas the inclinations of the land-beast are religiously oriented. A second option is that the land-beast is less imposing than the sea-beast, having "two horns" (v. 11) resembling those of the "Lamb" yet speaking

32. Table adapted from information presented in Brighton, *Revelation*, 352–53.

33. See Dan 7:17.

like a "dragon."[34] The imagery might suggest that this ogre tries to appear benign and benevolent, though it is cunning, malicious, and bloodthirsty.

The land-beast is the lieutenant of the sea-beast and uses his ruling "authority" (v. 12) to compel the world to prostrate in homage to the sea-beast.[35] In some ways, the land-beast is a mock imitation of the Holy Spirit.[36] Together, the "dragon" (12:3), the sea-beast (13:1), and the land-beast (v. 11) form an unholy, malevolent triad as a counterfeit to the triune God. In 16:13, they appear together, in which the land-beast is called the "false prophet."[37]

John notes that the land-beast continually performs astonishing signs, such as causing "fire" (13:13) to flash down from the sky to the "earth" before a throng of mesmerized onlookers.[38] The land-beast uses these fraudulent "miracles" (v. 14) to delude earth's inhabitants to venerate the sea-beast.[39]

Moreover, the land-beast convinces his sycophants to craft an "image" of the sea-beast (possibly an enormous statue), who then empowers the land-beast to make the idol appear as if it were alive and could speak. In turn, those who refuse to prostrate in homage to the sea-beast's "image" (v. 15) are ruthlessly executed.[40] In the first century AD, people thought pagan deities inhabited the statues, figurines, and images they made of their mortal rulers.[41] People also believed that these images could speak, move, sweat, and weep. In fact, charlatans would use ventriloquism to deceive spectators.

The land-beast that John sees in his vision forces all earth's inhabitants—whether regenerate or unregenerate—to have a "mark" (v. 16) of allegiance placed either on their "right hands" or on their "foreheads." This stamp or imprint is a mock replica of the seal of ownership and

34. See Dan 8:3.

35. As we previously noted, throughout the Apocalypse, John emphasizes earth's unregenerate inhabitants, who venerate pagan deities; see our discussion of Rev 3:10; 6:10; 8:13; 11:10; 13:8, 14; 14:6; 17:2, 8.

36. See John 14:26; 15:26; 16:13–15.

37. See our discussion of Rev 19:20; 20:10.

38. Reminiscent of Elijah; see 1 Kgs 18:36–39; 2 Kgs 1:10–14; Did. 16:4.

39. See Exod 7:11; Deut 13:1–4; Apoc. Dan. 13:1–13; Ascen. Isa. 4:4–10; 1 En. 54:6; Matt 7:15; 24:5–6, 23–25; Mark 13:6, 21–23; 2 Cor 11:13–15; 2 Thess 2:9–13; 2 Pet 2:3; Rev 3:10; 6:10; 8:13; 11:10; 13:8, 12; 14:6; 16:14; 17:2, 8; 19:20.

40. See Dan 3:4–5.

41. Especially as part of the imperial cult.

protection which the Creator places on his bondservants.[42] The tattoo is also a counterfeit imitation of the *Shema* recorded in Deuteronomy 6:4–8.[43] For thousands of years, this confession of faith[44] formed a key part of Jewish evening and morning prayers.

In the first century AD, small black leather pouches called phylacteries[45] contained portions of the Mosaic law written on vellum. Worshipers wore these on their foreheads or hands as a symbol of devoting their thoughts and actions exclusively to the one, true, and living God.[46] The implication was that the Creator could and should be loved above all else because of his character. Such love was with total sincerity, without reservation, and with all one's faculties.

According to Revelation 13:17, the satanic brand may include either the sea-beast's "name" or a specific "number" associated with it. Whatever the exact nature of the "mark," it will signify that those having it are controlled by the sea-beast and loyal to him. The land-beast requires that everyone have this identifying "mark" of allegiance before they can "buy" or "sell" any item, including the necessities of life. Such a sweeping edict will place tremendous economic pressure on believers to venerate the sea-beast. Refusing to do so may result in their execution.

At this point in John's prophetic oracle, he states that "wisdom" (v. 18) is needed.[47] The apostle explains that the "mark" is the name of the sea-beast in numerical form. This reflects an ancient Hebrew, Greek, and Roman practice in extrabiblical religious texts of assigning numerical values to each letter of specific words or phrases to obtain mystical insights.[48] For example, when tallied, the letters in the Greek name for *Jesus* add up to 888.

As for providing additional "understanding," John notes that the "number" is "666" and that it stands either for a person or fallen humanity (or both). The enigmatic "number" could be a code name based on the numerical value of the Greek letters. For instance, one tally of a Hebrew

42. See 4 Ezra 6:5; T. Sol. 17:4; Rev 7:3–4; 14:1; 22:4.

43. From the Hebrew verb "to hear"; see Num 15:37–41; Deut 11:13–21.

44. "Hear O Israel! The LORD is our God. The LORD is one!"

45. Or *tephillim*.

46. See Exod 13:9; Deut 6:8.

47. Referring to Spirit-provided insight and discernment; see 1 Cor 1:24, 30; 2:7; Eph 1:8, 17; Col 2:3; 3:16; Jas 1:5; Rev 5:12; 7:12; 17:9.

48. Technically referred to as *gematria*.

transliteration of the Greek letters of the Latin name Nero Caesar adds up to 666. Nero was one of Rome's most godless emperors.[49]

A second possibility is that "666" is the number of complete imperfection (or triple failure), especially since it falls short of three sevens, which is the number of absolute perfection. A third possibility is that "666" represents the unholy, malevolent triad of the dragon (the devil), the sea-beast (the antichrist), and the land-beast (the false prophet). Though specialists debate the exact significance of the above number, the prevalence of satanically inspired evil in the world is certain. It is also evident that throughout history and in the time of the end, the wicked try to slander the Father, subvert the Son's redemptive work, and destroy his faithful followers.

Who or What Is the Land-Beast?[50]		
Interpretation	**Identity and Role**	**Key Characteristics and Activities**
Deputy of the Antichrist	A real person serving as the second-in-command to a literal antichrist figure; often identified with the "false prophet" in Rev 13:11; 16:13; 19:20; and 20:10	Misleads the world through miraculous signs and prophetic declarations; compels humanity to venerate the antichrist; persecutes and oppresses those who refuse to comply; operates during the end-times as a specific individual
Imperial Priesthood System	An evil organizational entity representing the religious arm of a godless state system; acts as a counterfeit to divine authority	Functions as a sham witness to the Holy Spirit; deceives through anti-God propaganda and false religious authority; represents institutional opposition to God throughout history; continues its threat until the Messiah's return

49. The ruler's full imperial name was Nero Claudius Caesar Augustus Germanicus, whereas his birthname was Lucius Domitius Ahenobarbus.

50. Table adapted from information presented in Hendriksen, *More Than Conquerors*, 145–46, 148–49.

KEY THEOLOGICAL INSIGHTS

Whereas our discussion of Revelation 12 offered theological insights into the dragon's heinous intentions and fiendish workings, our exposition of chapter 13 introduces us to the other two members of the dragon's[51] unholy trinity, namely, the antichrist (or sea-beast) and false prophet (or land-beast).[52] The following key theological insights arise from a consideration of their identities and stratagems.

First, *we note that in the presentation of the sea-beast and land-beast, Satan intensifies his practice of counterfeiting the being and works of God, as the devil has always done.* From the beginning of his deception in the garden of Eden, the ancient serpent has been offering false alternatives of God to humanity, distorting his Word, telling plausible lies, and masquerading sin as something good and desirable.[53] It should not be surprising, therefore, that the devil has ready at his disposal his two primary emissaries for his final onslaught against the Creator. The sea-beast, representing the antichrist,[54] attempts to mimic the Messiah's power, authority, and miracle-working ability, most notably through the sea-beast's recovery from a mortal wound (v. 3). The land-beast, representing the false prophet,[55] imitates the work of the Holy Spirit in testifying to the sea-beast's alleged greatness (vv. 12–15). These diabolical mimickers demonstrate that Satan is fully invested in deceiving earth's fallen inhabitants.

Second, *we see that the power of the sea-beast and land-beast comes directly from the dragon.* Both of his lieutenants can perform various signs and wonders, and people are mesmerized by the phenomena happening before them (vv. 3–4). The works these predatory brutes perform exceed natural human ability, and their power extends throughout the earth to

51. For a succinct, convincing argument for seeing the "dragon" as the key link between chapters 12 and 13, see Kistemaker, *Exposition of Revelation*, 375–76.

52. See our discussion of Rev 16:13.

53. See Gen 3:1–5. Satan's tactic was to question God's Word ("Has God really said"), lie about God's Word ("You certainly will not die"), and impugn God's character ("God knows . . . you will be like God"). This entrenched pattern of deception can be seen in the ability of the sea-beast and land-beast to gather followers in mass numbers.

54. The specific term *antichrist* is found only in 1 John 2:18, 22; 4:3, and 2 John 1:7. In 2 Thess 2:3, Paul uses a related phrase translated "man of lawlessness" (or, according to some Greek manuscripts, "man of sin"). Later in the Apocalypse, the predatory brute originating from the sea is referred to simply as the "beast"; see our discussion of Rev 14:9–11; 16:13; 17:3, 7–8, 11–13, 16–17; 19:19–20.

55. See our discussion of Rev 19:20; 20:10.

"every tribe and people and language and nation" (v. 7).[56] In addition, the power they brandish is not limited to pseudo-miraculous signs. It is also manifested in the form of political, economic, and religious authority. The descriptions of the ogres' power imply that there seems to be nothing which they cannot and will not do.[57] Though the charade of their omnipotence ultimately falls short of reality, as the Lamb inevitably wins the cosmic conflict (19:7–18), their power is universally effective for a limited time established by the Creator.

Third, *the work of the antichrist and false prophet is characterized by deceit and coercion*. On the one hand, the initiatives the predatory brutes undertake are so effective and the words they speak are so convincing that the unsaved venerate the sea-beast and make proclamations about him that belong to God alone (vv. 5–6). Expressed differently, lost humanity gladly and willfully responds in a positive way to the deceivers' presentation and message.[58] On the other hand, the antichrist and false prophet also employ force to compel people to follow them. Specifically, the false prophet "causes" (v. 12)[59] the earth's inhabitants to venerate the sea-beast's image. His identifying mark of allegiance is needed to buy and sell (vv. 16–17). Furthermore, threats of death are given to those who refuse his message and imprint.

Fourth, *the impact of the hostile takeover by the two beasts extends to believers who are present on the earth during this time*. John clearly observes people at this point in his vision who affirm loyalty to the Messiah and refuse to venerate the sea-beast and his image. For them, the options are few and bleak. They must anticipate imprisonment or martyrdom (or both; vv. 9–10) as well as potential starvation and lack of other necessities needed to survive. While the minions of the dragon can never snatch away the souls of the believers, his underlings do whatever they can to bring about physical destruction, pain, suffering, and turmoil.[60] This

56. Set in contrast to the way in which the worship of God in heaven has participants from "every nation, tribe, people, and language" (Rev 7:9).

57. The question asked in Rev 13:4 ("Who is like the beast?") can be compared to the same question asked by Israel's prophets and poets; see Exod 15:11; Pss 35:10; 71:19; 77:13; 89:6–8; 113:5; Isa 44:7; Jer 49:19; Mic 7:18.

58. This willful response of the wicked is due either to the deception they experience or an act of rebellion against the Creator.

59. While the wicked retain a certain freedom of will in choosing to venerate the sea-beast, they are coerced through threats of punishment as well as political and economic isolation.

60. See Matt 10:28.

truth gives rise, at the midpoint of the chapter, to John's call for "patient endurance" (v. 10). Later, the exact summons is repeated in 14:12, and it serves as a restatement of Jesus' exhortation to those addressed in the letters to the seven churches who are victorious.[61]

IMPORTANT MINISTRY IMPLICATIONS

Revelation 13 presents a sobering vision of satanic deception, blasphemous worship, ruthless persecution, and oppressive control. As we encounter its ominous figures and their temporary—yet devastating—influence, even believers may feel apprehension about the trials of the last days. Yet given these truths, we can draw key lessons for ministry that can assist us in shepherding our parishioners with wisdom and reassurance.

First, *we must warn our congregants about the deception that is now present among us, along with the deception that is yet to come*. Our warning need not be one of unrelenting despair, as if failure is a predetermined outcome. After all, true believers are expected to recognize and ultimately reject the deception of the sea-beast and land-beast (v. 10). Yet the call to the redeemed for vigilance and faithfulness to the truth remains serious.[62] Jesus warns his disciples about future deception. He also says false messiahs and pseudoprophets work great miracles and signs so that, if possible, they deceive even God's chosen, reborn children.[63] Furthermore, in John's first epistle, he warns his recipients that while they anticipate the coming of the antichrist, there are many archenemies of the Messiah already present and working their deception in the world.[64] For this reason, we are duty bound, as shepherds of Jesus' flock, to warn our parishioners about the possibility of deception, expose deceit with the truth of God's Word, and lead believers into a courageous, secure affirmation of sound doctrine and upright living.

Second, *we must prepare our church members for isolation and persecution from the adversary's evil sycophants*. The key component of this preparation is to call the saints to persevere and endure, especially by

61. See our discussion of Rev 2:7, 11, 17, 26; 3:5, 12, 21.

62. See 1 Cor. 16:13; Eph 5:15–16; 1 Pet 5:8.

63. See Matt 24:24.

64. See 1 John 2:18, 22. Note the apostle's admonition that avoiding the antichrist's deception involves both correct belief and upright behavior.

holding fast to their faith in Christ. Verses 9–10 are some of the most sobering in the entire Apocalypse. As the time of the end draws near, true believers who remain on the earth face terrible calamity. During earlier judgments, God protected his reborn children by sparing them from harm. However, in this period of great distress, the antichrist and the false prophet are permitted to persecute and prevail over the saints. Since the predatory brutes cannot spiritually destroy Jesus' followers, as their names are forever written in the Lamb's Book of Life, the ogres seek to destroy believers physically. While it might be natural to call upon the Lord to remove all forms of anguish, instead the saints are called to persevere under unimaginable trial and adversity.[65] As congregational leaders, we have the somber responsibility of preparing our parishioners for maltreatment due to their faith in Christ.[66]

Third, *we can assure the faithful that their perseverance in Christ is worth the turmoil they may experience in this present life*. The death and destruction carried out by the sea-beast and land-beast are only for a limited time. Their demise is soon to come, as John's prophetic oracle later reveals.[67] Believers, through their patient endurance,[68] are clearly recognized and marked off from those who fall into the trap of the dragon's schemes, which includes venerating the antichrist and following his degenerate prophet. Our parishioners need not worry that they may unwittingly or accidentally accept the sea-beast's imprint of allegiance. Those who accept this mark instinctively recognize what it signifies and what they are doing. Remaining faithful to the Creator ensures that Satan's deception does not prevail in the hearts and lives of Jesus' true followers, since nothing can separate us from the love of Christ.[69]

VITAL MISSIONAL RAMIFICATIONS

In Revelation 12, we focused on the concept of opposition in the face of our missionary task. In our reflections on how to apply the present

65. See also Rev 14:12.

66. See 2 Tim 3:12; 1 Pet 3:13–17; 4:12–19.

67. See our discussion of Rev 19:17–21.

68. Namely, heeding the call found in Rev 13:10 by the presence and power of the Spirit.

69. See Rom 8:38–39. Kistemaker, *Exposition of Revelation*, 383, reminds us that even if some saints are called to suffer death at the hands of the beast, their eternal destiny to live and reign with Christ is secure.

chapter to the ongoing task of missionary service, we consider the notion of what is counterfeit. While there are many examples of spurious forms of Christianity that could be discussed, there are two that especially affect the work of missions today, along with a third observation regarding their evangelistic implication.

The first example of counterfeit Christianity we must avoid is syncretism.[70] As missionaries venture into cross-cultural situations to share the gospel, the key to their approach is finding similarities between indigenous religious beliefs and the teaching of Scripture for engagement on matters of faith.[71] This tactic has much to commend it, as contemporary missiologists call for us to respect (though not necessarily accept or agree with) the indigenous faith of others and to seek a starting point from which to build a bridge to gospel conversations.

Furthermore, given many of the abuses of culture[72] propagated by missionaries of past generations, we are urged to be careful in our critique of the practices and rituals that may already be in place and observed by the people we are trying to reach. Nonetheless, in a desire to maintain sociological sensitivity, we often fail to articulate a clear distinction between what is biblical and what is not concerning cultural practices or religious rituals. Examples of syncretism can be found in virtually any culture, including those places in the Majority World where the gospel has not yet had full impact.[73] Syncretism must be avoided at all costs, lest we lead people toward the deceit that comes with the spirit of antichrist.

The second example of counterfeit Christianity we must avoid is a merely cultural form of the faith. This spurious scheme of the enemy is

70. From a missiological perspective, *syncretism* refers to the merging or fusion of elements from the Christian faith and its practices with those originating from pagan religious and cultural traditions. Syncretism can manifest in various forms, including the integration of indigenous beliefs, rituals, or symbols into Christian worship, theology, or lifestyle. Missionaries are often concerned that syncretism may jeopardize the purity and integrity of the gospel message, potentially complicating the process for converts to embrace and comprehend apostolic Christian beliefs fully.

71. Such as Paul's interaction with the philosophers on Mars Hill; see Acts 17:22–34.

72. By the term "culture," we mean the set of beliefs, values, practices, customs, and behaviors that are learned, shared, and passed down from one generation to another within a particular group, community, or society.

73. Examples include the acceptance or tolerance of pagan practices, such as polygamy, underage marriage, forms of gender-based violence, ancestor worship, and bodily mutilation in religious ritual.

one that often goes unnoticed. After all, as more and more people come to saving faith in Christ, we may expect the culture to reflect the conversion experienced by individual believers.[74] Furthermore, we encourage believers to engage redemptively in all aspects of their culture by applying a biblical worldview to every discipline and societal development. Likewise, we long to see Christian values permeate our law-enforcement institutions, political structures, justice systems, and business practices. The impulse to convert culture to something *Christian* is understandable.

Nonetheless, while culture can occasionally be made to look like something genuinely Christian, too often the superficial appearance lacks any authentic substance. For example, we can deceive ourselves into thinking that a particular community has a strong Christian witness just because the Ten Commandments are displayed on the property of a municipal building. Also, we can trick ourselves into imagining that because a given town has a church on every street corner, it must be full of genuine believers. Moreover, we can incorrectly assume that because laws are passed in support of biblical values, the political leaders must be Christians.[75] Yet many times, upon deeper reflection and discernment, we discover that these are only cultural realities that lack the true substance of Christ. As we engage in the missional task, we may find ourselves seeking converts from cultural expressions of Christianity just as much as we find ourselves seeking to convert the so-called heathen to the faith.

Third, and just as importantly, both syncretism and cultural Christianity are counterfeit ploys made by the dragon, enacted by the spirit of antichrist, and affirmed by the false prophet's affirmations. Together, this satanic trio obfuscate the truth of what it means to be united by faith to Christ, and him alone, for the salvation of one's soul. The implication is that in all our evangelistic endeavors, it behooves us to guard against these counterfeiting influences and direct others away from them. In so doing, we effectively carry out our missional calling.

74. This expectation finds precedent during the First Great Awakening in England and the United States, in which jails were largely empty, taverns were closed, and the need for police officers was drastically reduced.

75. This is the perspective of many in the United States, where politicians who are otherwise despicable in their character and conduct seem to be considered "Christian" just because they pander to the wishes of Christian voters.

Revelation 14

The Bowl Judgments

LEARNING OBJECTIVES

- Explore the relationship between the 144,000 and the Lamb.
- Deliberate the nature of the everlasting gospel proclaimed by the first angel.
- Wrestle with the truth that God punishes those who luxuriate in wickedness and immorality.
- Describe the macabre details of the vision of a global harvest of fallen humanity.
- Consider how the portrayal of God's judgment and salvation impacts the work of missions.

CHAPTER SUMMARY

Revelation 14 begins with a vision of the Lamb standing on Mount Zion with a redeemed multitude, who bear the name of God and the Lamb on their foreheads. An angel flying overhead proclaims the everlasting gospel to all nations, urging humanity to fear the Creator and worship him. A second angel proclaims the imminent fall of Babylon for its wickedness, while a third angel declares that God will eternally punish those who venerate the sea-beast. Finally, a vision of a global harvest symbolizes the gathering of earth's wicked inhabitants to be trampled in the winepress of God's wrath at the end of the age.

STUDY QUESTIONS

1. What is the significance of the 144,000 standing with the Lamb on Mount Zion?
2. What is the everlasting gospel being announced by the first angel?
3. Why is the fall of Babylon the Great being proclaimed?
4. What does the description of the harvest and the winepress reveal about the final judgment?
5. How does Revelation 14 contrast the destiny of those who follow the Lamb with those who venerate the sea-beast?

CHAPTER OUTLINE

- The Lamb and the 144,000 (14:1–5)
- The announcement of impending judgment (14:6–13)
- The harvest of the earth (14:14–20)
- Key theological insights
- Important ministry implications
- Vital missional ramifications

THE LAMB AND THE 144,000 (14:1–5)

Chapter 13 ended with the spotlight on the unholy, malevolent triad of the dragon, the sea-beast, and the land-beast. In the unfolding cosmic drama, chapter 14 provides a glimpse into eternity. The reality awaiting the redeemed encourages them to endure trials and remain faithful to the Son, even in the face of martyrdom. Though the destiny of the wicked is endless separation (or exile) from the Creator,[1] his children anticipate everlasting life and joy in his sacred, heavenly presence.[2]

In the unfolding cosmic drama, John witnesses the "Lamb" (v. 1) positioned on "Mount Zion." Initially, Zion refers to the southeast hill and fortress of Jerusalem, which David captured from the Jebusites and

1. The most extreme form of covenantal curses.

2. The most profound form of covenantal blessings; see our discussion of Rev 2:7; 3:12; 21:3; 22:3–4.

made the capital of Israel.[3] Later, Zion comes to represent poetically all Jerusalem, as well as the city of God, from which the Creator rules.[4] Some specialists think that Zion in the apostle's prophetic oracle is Jerusalem on earth, namely, the future capital of the Messiah's kingdom.[5] A more likely possibility is that Zion symbolizes heaven, namely, the eternal dwelling place of the Creator and his reborn children.[6]

The Lamb Imagery in Revelation		
Symbolic Aspect	**Description**	**Biblical References**
Covenant Administrator	Bestows covenantal blessings on the faithful and covenantal curses on the rebellious	2:7, 10, 17; 3:5, 12, 21; 7:17; 19:7–9; 20:4, 6; 22:12, 14
Divine Judge	Judges all humanity, both righteous and wicked	6:16–17; 14:10; 20:11–15; 22:12
Divine Warrior	Conquering Warrior who defeats death, triumphs over evil, and vindicates the righteous	1:18; 2:8; 5:5; 6:16; 17:14; 19:11–16
Eternal King	Inaugurates, establishes, and rules over the everlasting, divine kingdom	1:6; 3:7, 21; 5:10; 11:15; 12:5; 20:4, 6; 22:1, 3
Object of Worship	All-glorious One whom the entire creation worships, serves, and honors	5:8–14; 7:9–10; 11:15; 15:3; 21:22–23; 22:3
Redemption and Salvation	Redeemer and Savior of the lost, providing eternal life through his sacrifice	1:5; 7:10, 14; 12:10; 14:4; 19:7–8; 21:27; 22:14
Resurrection Victory	Triumphantly standing due to his resurrection, demonstrating his supreme victory over death	5:6; 14:1
Sacrificial Death	Slain through his atoning sacrifice on the cross, emphasizing his role as the ultimate offering for sin	1:5; 5:6, 9, 12; 7:14; 12:11; 13:8

With the "Lamb" are "144,000" people. John last mentioned this group in 7:4, where they represented the fulness of the people of God. The presence of the redeemed with the Messiah indicates that, despite

3. See 2 Sam 5:6–7.

4. See Isa 28:16; 59:20; Obad 1:17; Mich 4:7; 4 Ezra 2:42–48; 13:35–40; Jub. 4:26; 8:19.

5. See Isa 11:9–12; 24:23; 31:4; Joel 2:32; Mic 4:6–8; Zech 14:4–5; 2 Bar. 40:1; Jub. 1:28–29.

6. See Ps 2:6; Gal 4:26; Heb 12:22–24; Rev 21:22–26.

the horrors they experience from Satan and his two brutish, predatory deputies,[7] the Creator will bring his reborn children safely through their harrowing ordeal. Permanently engraved on the "foreheads" (v. 1) of the "144,000" are the names of the Father and the Son.[8] The inscription contrasts sharply with the imprint of the sea-beast and signifies that the Creator owns and protects his children. While he might not shield them from physical harm, he ensures their safe arrival to their eternal home in heaven with Him.

As John listens, he hears (v. 2) the "144,000" (v. 3) repeatedly sing a loud, melodic chorus from "heaven" (v. 2). The "sound" they produce is comparable to the roar of a cascading waterfall or crashing ocean waves, along with the loud peal of a "thunderclap." The apostle notes that the "sound" is also like the music produced by innumerable "harpists" playing their instruments[9] in unison.[10]

Only the redeemed can "learn" (v. 3) the "new song" that the apostle hears (v. 2). After all, the melodic ode (or chant) praises the Creator for his redemption of his children from the unholy, malevolent triad ravaging earth's inhabitants. The song recalls the Lord's redemption of the Israelites from slavery in Egypt centuries earlier.[11] As previously noted, the preceding correlation is sometimes referred to as exodus typology or prophetic foreshadowing. While the multitude stands in God's sacred presence before his celestial "throne" (v. 3),[12] they are not alone. They are surrounded by the "four living creatures" and the twenty-four "elders."

John mentions three distinguishing characteristics of this heavenly choir. First, he notes that they have not been "defiled with women" (v. 4). The apostle further explains that these individuals are "virgins." Some specialists take this to mean that the "144,000" (v. 3) are an exclusive, elite group of celibate, ethnically Jewish male believers, namely, those who have never married or engaged in licentious activity. A more likely option is that John is using ancient Hebraic holy-war imagery, in which he contrasts tainted sexual behavior with the pure character of the Lamb's

7. Namely, the sea-beast and the land-beast disclosed in Rev 13.

8. See Ezek 9:4; Apoc. El. 1:9; Pss. Sol. 15:6; T. Sol. 17:4.

9. U-shaped, ten- or twelve-stringed lyres.

10. Literally "harpists harping their harps"; see Pss 33:2; 57:8; 4 Ezra 6:17.

11. See Pss 33:3; 40:3; 96:1; 98:1; 144:9; 149:1.

12. As we previously noted, the Creator's throne occupies the literary center of John's prophetic oracle.

followers.[13] Despite unrelenting coercion from a pleasure-fixated world, they remain loyal to the Messiah as his chaste bride.[14]

Second, John mentions that the redeemed "continually" (v. 4) follow the "Lamb," regardless of where he leads them. Here, the focus is on how the sacred people conduct themselves on earth. Despite the personal cost,[15] they obey their eternal Shepherd.[16] Third, the apostle notes that through the Messiah's sacrificial death on the cross, he purchases the redeemed from the evil world system.[17] The goal is to present them as "firstfruits" to the Father and the Son.[18]

The above is an allusion to an ancient Israelite practice in which God's people set apart the firstborn of all their livestock and the first portion of their harvest. In this way, they designated these items as being special and belonging exclusively to the Lord.[19] Some specialists think John is teaching that in the time of the end, the salvation of the "144,000" (v. 3) will precede the salvation of a larger group of ethnic Jews.[20] A more likely view is that the apostle is referring to all the redeemed, whom the Son saves through his shed blood as a choice offering to the Father.

In John 8:44, Jesus says that the "Devil" is a "liar" and the "father of lying." Likewise, all who hate the truth are the serpent's offspring. The opposite characterizes the redeemed. No one can accuse them of failing to tell the truth, for they are "blameless" (Rev 14:5; or faultless) in their conduct.[21] They also refuse to embrace falsehoods spread by the dragon's brutish, predatory subordinates.[22] The redeemed are genuine trophies of the Creator's grace. They bring him honor, especially as they praise him in worship while he sits in regal splendor on his sacred, royal seat.

13. The church militant on earth now transformed to the church triumphant in heaven; see Exod 19:15; Lev 15:16; Deut 20:7; 23:9–11; 24:5; 1 Sam 21:5; 2 Sam 11:8–13.

14. See 2 Kgs 19:21; Isa 37:22; Jer 14:17; 18:13; 31:4, 13, 21; Lam 1:15; 2:13; Amos 5:2; 2 Cor 11:2; Eph 5:25–27; Rev 3:4; 19:7–9.

15. Especially connected with refusing to venerate mortal, flawed, human rulers.

16. See Mark 8:34–36; John 10:3–4; Heb 13:20; 1 Pet 2:21; Rev 7:17.

17. See our discussion of Rev 1:5.

18. See Jer 2:2–3; Rom 8:23; 16:5; 1 Cor 6:15; 15:20, 23; Jas 1:18.

19. See Exod 23:16, 19; Lev 2:1–16; 23:9–14; Deut 26:1–5; Neh 10:35; Prov 3:9.

20. See Isa 2:3; Rom 11:25–27.

21. See Eph 1:4; 5:27; Phil 2:15; Col 1:22; Heb 9:14.

22. See Isa 53:9; Zeph 3:13; Sir 20:24.

THE ANNOUNCEMENT OF IMPENDING JUDGMENT (14:6–13)

In the unfolding cosmic drama, John witnesses a different "angel" (v. 6) soaring high in the "sky."[23] God gives this celestial being the "everlasting gospel" to herald to all earth's inhabitants.[24] Some specialists think that this proclamation is the saving message of Jesus' death and resurrection. More likely, the announcement recorded in verse 7 denotes the specific content of the angel's proclamation, as detailed below.

The herald shouts a threefold command for all humankind. They are to "fear," glorify (or honor), and prostrate themselves in homage to the Creator.[25] After all, they owe their existence to God, and the time for him to judge earth's wicked inhabitants has arrived. This includes bringing a series of seven final covenantal curses on the sky, land, oceans, and rivers of the earth.[26] Some specialists think that the angel's message is merely a declaration that "judgment" is imminent, without an appeal for the wicked to repent. The context, however, indicates that the Lord is making a final summons through his heavenly emissary, for the people of the world to abandon their iniquity and acknowledge him as their supreme and sole Monarch.

Next, John witnesses a second "angel" (v. 8) following the first one through the sky and announcing twice (for emphasis) that the notorious metropolis "Babylon" has met its demise. Previously, it was the location of the doomed Tower of Babel,[27] as well as the name of the mighty empire that invaded Judah, destroyed Jerusalem, razed its temple, and exiled the nation's inhabitants.[28] The celestial being in John's vision explains that "Babylon," like a filthy, brazen prostitute, has seduced "every nation" on the planet with her "adulterous" passions. Also, "Babylon" compels earth's inhabitants to swallow the noxious "wine" of her idolatry and

23. Where the angel could be easily seen and heard.

24. As we previously noted, throughout the Apocalypse, an emphasis is placed on earth's unregenerate inhabitants, who venerated pagan deities; see our discussion of Rev 3:10; 6:10; 8:13; 11:10; 13:8, 12, 14; 17:2, 8.

25. Rather than to any human ruler, such as the emperor of Rome; see Acts 14:8–18; 17:19–31; Rom 1:18–31.

26. See our discussion of Rev 15:1.

27. See Gen 11:9.

28. See 2 Kgs 25:1–21; 2 Chr 36:15–21; Jer 52:4–27; Dan 1:1–2; 4:30; 9:11–14; 2 Bar. 11:1–2; 67:7; 79:1.

immorality.[29] A detailed description of "Babylon the Great" appears in Revelation 18:2–24.[30] The reference to "Babylon" also echoes terminology found in Isaiah 21:9 and Daniel 4:30.

What Is "Babylon"?[31]		
Interpretation	**Description**	**Supporting Evidence**
Code Name for Rome	Represents Rome in the first century AD, symbolizing opposition to God and his people through the imperial cult	Isa 13:19–22; 14:20–23; Jer 25:12–14; 50:35–40; 51:24–26; 2 Bar. 11:1; 67:7; 4 Ezra 3:2; 1 Pet 5:13
Corrupt World Systems	Symbolizes corrupt political, commercial, social, and religious systems opposing God's kingdom throughout history	Universal application across time periods; represents ongoing opposition to God's everlasting rule and reign
Rebuilt Ancient City	Refers to a notorious ancient city (for example, Babylon, Rome, Tyre, or Jerusalem) rebuilt in the end-times as the capital of a world empire ruled by the antichrist	Prophetic fulfillment of ancient judgments; literal interpretation of the Apocalypse; end-times view of reality

Next, John witnesses a third "angel" (Rev 14:9) following the first two across the sky. This creature announces in a "loud voice" that those who routinely prostrate themselves in homage to the sea-beast and his idolatrous "image" (made to resemble him) will experience the Lord's covenantal curses. Likewise, those who are permanently branded on their "forehead" or "hand" with the distinctive "mark" of allegiance to the sea-beast will endure the Lord's punishment.

The apostle uses such idiomatic and descriptive phrases as the "wine of God's wrath" (v. 10) and the "cup of his anger" to refer to the Father's judgment.[32] These idioms are reminiscent of Old Testament passages that depict the Creator's intense anger as a cup of wine (or goblet filled

29. See Jer 51:6–8; 4 Ezra 15:46–47; Sib. Or. 5:143–44; Rev 17:2; 18:3.

30. See our discussion of Rev 16:19; 17:5. Also, see the discussion in our Introduction about Babylon as a symbol of evil and a fitting image of an idolatrous society. Additionally, see our exposition of chs. 17 and 18, respectively, which present a two-part exposé concerning the fall of Babylon.

31. Table adapted from information presented in Osborne, *Revelation*, 280–81.

32. See our discussion of Rev 6:16; 11:18; 14:19; 15:1, 7; 16:1, 19; 19:15.

with poison) that the wicked ingest.[33] In the ancient world, people usually diluted wine with water. Consequently, undiluted wine was regarded as being extremely potent, and it became a symbol for severe judgment.

Similarly, in Revelation 14:10, the "wine of God's wrath" is poured out in full strength[34] on earth's unrepentant evildoers. This verse contains a chilling reminder about the destiny of the wicked. Those who persecute and murder Jesus' followers will be "tormented" by the "burning sulfur" in the eternal "lake of fire,"[35] while the Creator's "holy angels," along with the "Lamb," watch.

Verse 11 reiterates truths mentioned in verse 9, adding that the sycophants of the sea-beast will never experience any "rest" (v. 11; or relief), whether during the "day" or "night," from the ruinous destiny awaiting them. Indeed, the "smoke" arising from their "torment" will continue through the endless ages of eternity.[36] It would be incorrect to conclude from the preceding observation that the Messiah and his celestial cohort will derive inordinate pleasure from the demise of the wicked. Rather, their eternal condemnation will vindicate the redeemed, who rejected the world's pagan ways. Even the possibility of martyrdom will not deter them from remaining loyal to the Savior.

John is fully aware of the anguish his Christian peers had to endure. After all, as previously noted, he is suffering for publicly identifying with the Messiah.[37] Likewise, the apostle knows that his fellow believers are tempted to compromise their faith by participating in the veneration of the Roman emperor. For this reason, John commends the Savior's followers for their steadfast "endurance" (v. 12), their heeding God's "commands," their resolute "faith in Jesus," and their single-minded devotion (or allegiance) to him. They know that they must never capitulate to the pagan world system.[38]

33. See Job 21:20; Pss 60:3; 75:8; Isa 51:17, 22; Jer 25:15–18, 27–28; 49:12; 51:7; Lam 4:21; Ezek 25:31–33; Obad 1:16; Hab 2:15–16; Zech 12:2; Pss. Sol. 8:15.

34. Literally "unmixed."

35. See our discussion of Rev 19:20; 20:10, 14, 15.

36. In answer to the prayers of the saints for the vindication of their faith and faithfulness; see Gen 19:24, 28; Job 18:15; Ps 11:6; Isa 33:33; 34:9–10; Ezek 38:22; 2 Bar. 30:4–5; 51:5–6; 1 En. 21:7–10; 48:9; 90:26; 100:9; 108:14–15; 4 Ezra 7:35–38, 61; 3 Macc 2:5; Wis 5:1–5; Luke 17:29; Rev 19:3, 20; 20:10; 21:8.

37. See our discussion of Rev 1:9.

38. See our discussion of Rev 1:9; 2:2, 3, 10, 13, 19, 24, 25; 3:4, 8, 10, 11; 13:10; 14:4–5.

Next, John hears a "voice from heaven" (v. 13) direct him to "write" that the Creator will bestow his everlasting grace upon all who remain loyal to him until the end of their earthly sojourn.[39] This is the second of seven beatitudes, or pronouncements of covenantal blessing, appearing in the apostle's prophetic oracle.[40] The sevenfold Spirit likewise affirms that the righteous, in contrast with the wicked, will one day "rest" (or experience relief) from their anguished-filled toil of serving the Lord.[41] He will eternally reward them for unrelentingly doing his will, despite the adversity and martyrdom they experience at the hands of those who are antagonistic to the gospel.

THE HARVEST OF THE EARTH (14:14–20)

In the unfolding cosmic drama, John witnesses a "white cloud" (v. 14), and sitting (or enthroned) on the "cloud" is a regal figure resembling a "son of man." This celestial being wears a "gold crown"[42] on his head and holds a "sharp sickle" in his "hand." The Greek phrase translated "son of man" recalls a similar description in Daniel 7:13.[43]

Because the phrase in Revelation 14:14 lacks the definite article, some specialists think it is a nonspecific reference to a mighty angel resembling a human being under God's command. A more likely view is that the phrase concerns the risen and exalted Messiah, who here exercises judging and ruling authority. In this case, at the end of the age, he gathers those who dwell on earth in a grisly scene of divine reckoning.

The Greek noun rendered "sickle" denoted a small, handheld tool that people used in Bible times to harvest grain and other crops. Early versions of these instruments were curved pieces of wood with jagged flints inserted in their cutting edges. Later versions were made from metal and had a wooden handle.

Next, John witnessed another "angel" (v. 15) emerge from God's heavenly "temple."[44] The celestial being speaks in a "loud voice" to direct the Messiah to use his "sickle" to bring in the "harvest." The "angel"

39. See LAB 19:12; Rev 1:11, 19; 2:1, 8, 12, 18; 3:1, 7, 14; 19:9; 21:5.

40. See our discussion of Rev 1:3; 16:15; 19:9; 20:6; 22:7, 14.

41. See Deut 12:9; Josh 21:44; 2 Sam 7:11; 1 Kgs 8:54–56; Matt 11:25–30; Heb 4:9–10.

42. A victor's laurel wreath.

43. See 1 En. 69:29; Matt 24:30; 26:64.

44. Or inner sanctuary.

announces that the crop on the "earth" is fully "ripe"[45] and is ready to be reaped. In response, the Messiah uses his "sickle" (v. 16) to harvest the crops on the "earth."

Some specialists think that the above scene symbolizes only the ingathering of God's reborn children at the consummation of the age.[46] Others, however, think that the image refers more broadly to the fulfilment of the Creator's end-time judgment on the planet's wicked inhabitants.[47] In either case, clearly, on the day of reckoning, the Son will separate the faithful from the unfaithful.[48] This will be a time of anguish for unbelievers, whereas it will be an occasion of vindication for Jesus' loyal followers.

Next, John witnesses a different "angel" (v. 17) emerge from God's heavenly "temple"[49] while holding a "sharp sickle." He is followed by another celestial being, who exercises authority over the "fire" (v. 18) of the incense "altar." The above portion of the vision suggests that the Creator's unleashing of covenantal curses on the wicked is partly in response to the prayers of martyred believers.[50] The supreme Monarch of the universe is about to honor the petition of his children for justice to prevail.

The celestial being mentioned in verse 18 declares in a "loud voice" that the "grapes" on "earth's vine" are "ripe" (that is, fully mature) and ready to be harvested. For this reason, the entity mentioned in verse 17 is directed to "swing" (v. 18) his "sharp sickle" and gather in the "grape clusters." Based on the preceding verses, some specialists think the tool in the angel's hand resembled a small, sharp pruning knife. It was the sort of instrument that farmers in Bible times used to cut clusters of grapes from vines.

At this point in the vision, John witnesses the "angel" (v. 19) swing his "sickle" across the planet. After the celestial being "harvest[s]" clusters of blood-red grapes from "earth's vine," he loads these into a larger container or trough called a "winepress." Specifically, this huge vat symbolizes "God's wrath."[51]

45. Literally "has become dry."

46. See Matt 9:37–38; 13:36–43; Mark 4:26–29; Luke 10:2; John 4:35–38.

47. See Jer 51:33; Hos 6:11; Joel 3:12–13; 2 Bar. 70:2; 4 Ezra 4:35.

48. See Matt 13:24–30; 25:31–46.

49. Or inner sanctuary.

50. See our discussion of Rev 5:8; 6:9–10; 8:3–5; 9:13; 15:7; 16:3, 7.

51. See our discussion of Rev 6:16, 17; 11:18; 14:19; 15:1, 7; 16:1, 19; 19:15.

In Bible times, people would collect harvested grapes in square or circular pits, which were either hewn out of rock or dug out of the ground, then lined with rocks and sealed with plaster. Laborers stomped on the grapes with their bare feet to extract the juice, which would flow through a duct or channel into a lower basin or tank. Verse 20 transforms the preceding activity into a macabre image of earth's wicked inhabitants' being "trampled" in the "winepress" of the Creator's "wrath" (v. 19).[52] This immensely deep container is located "outside" (v. 20) a prominent "city,"[53] because the shedding of "blood" would defile the metropolis.[54]

John observed that there was so much "blood" that it overflowed the "winepress" and turned into a river about 184 miles long.[55] Also, its depth was equivalent to the height of a horse's bit and bridle.[56] Some specialists think the above scene is a reference to Armageddon, which they claim will be the final, localized battle between the forces of the Messiah and those of the antichrist.[57] Another possibility is that John is making a symbolic reference to God's unleashing of covenantal curses on all unregenerate humankind for their idolatry and immorality.[58]

KEY THEOLOGICAL INSIGHTS

Having been introduced in Revelation 13 to the dragon's wicked deputies (the sea-beast and the land-beast), chapter 14 shifts the scene to heaven, where we encounter the exalted Lamb of God as the object of triumphal worship. Immediately following this glorious event, we come upon warnings from God's messengers along with an overview of his devastating wrath which is being unleashed on earth's rebellious inhabitants.

First, *we find the Lamb exalted in his resurrection, worshiped by those whom he has redeemed, and positioned to carry out judgment on the whole earth.* As has been the case since the opening chapter of John's prophetic

52. See Isa 5:5; 63:2–6; Lam 1:15; Joel 3:13–14; Apoc. Dan. 4:8; 1 En. 100:1, 3–4; Rev 19:15.

53. Such as Jerusalem.

54. See Zech 14:1–5; 2 Bar. 40:1–2; 4 Ezra 13:33–38; Matt 27:32; John 19:20; Heb 13:12; Rev 11:2, 8; 20:9; 21:27; 22:15.

55. Literally "1,600 stadia"; approximately the north-south length of Palestine.

56. About five feet; see 4 Ezra 15:35–36.

57. See Joel 3:2, 12; Rev 16:16; 19:17–19; 20:7–9.

58. See Isa 63:2–6; Lam 1:15. Also, on these and related points, see the extensive discussion of Bauckham, *Theology of Revelation*, 94–98.

oracle, here he expands and deepens our understanding of Christ's person and work. Specifically, we are privileged to encounter several manifestations of the Messiah in his victorious and triumphant glory as well as in his power in his righteous rule.[59] Furthermore, the contrasts are stark between the depiction of the Lamb in chapter 14 and the portrayal of the dragon's two predatory brutes in chapter 13.

For instance, the Lamb's authoritative and glorious position on Mount Zion[60] represents an everlasting rule and reign over all creation (v. 1), whereas the sea-beast and land-beast have authority for a limited season and ultimately fall under the Creator's damning judgment.[61] The Lamb's redemption of his own is secured forever (v. 4). In contrast, the dragon's two minions are unable to guarantee any kind of meaningful redemption for their followers.[62] The Lamb's judgment of the earth is a triumphal event which he executes in complete and unquestioned righteousness (vv. 14–20). Meanwhile, the judgment of the devil's two ogres is temporal and limited to those whom they have deceived and coerced.[63] These contrasts showcase the Lamb's absolute superiority, along with demonstrating his sufficiency and majesty.

Second, *we discover the joyful worship of the Lamb's followers, who are committed to him in life and death and whose lives reflect their Savior's righteousness.* Just as the contrast between the Lamb and the two predatory brutes in Revelation 13 is instructive, so too are the contrasts between Jesus' disciples and the sycophants of the sea-beast and land-beast.[64] For instance, the 144,000 are marked with an ownership of benevolence (v. 1), whereas the followers of the two predatory brutes are

59. For the elevated Christology seen in the Apocalypse prior to ch. 14, see our discussion in 1:13–18; 5:6–8; 6:1; 7:9–12; 11:15; 12:10–11. Also noteworthy is that the Lamb is the one to open the seven seals (6:1, 3, 5, 7, 9, 12; 8:1), indicating his supreme authority and righteous judgment.

60. See Beale and McDonough, "Revelation," 1131, for a brief but effective summary of the OT notion of "Zion" and its connection to verse 1.

61. See our discussion of Rev 19:20.

62. See our discussion of Rev 19:21.

63. See our discussion of Rev 13:1–8, 11–17. Note especially vv. 5–8 where the sea-beast exercises authority over "every nation, tribe, language, and people," yet his authority is limited to forty-two months and does not include those whose names are in the Lamb's Book of Life.

64. See our discussion of Rev 13:3–4, 8, 12, 14. Whereas those venerating the sea-beast and his image are forced to do so (v. 12), they also freely exercise their will and choose to capitulate, for they are in awe of his power and that exercised by his deputy, the land-beast.

marked with an ownership of manipulation. The 144,000 willfully and joyfully worship the Lamb. Also, they do so with songs of praise in deep appreciation of the love their Messiah has freely bestowed on them. In contrast, the followers of the dragon's two deputies are tricked through counterfeit miracles to offer idolatrous veneration and then coerced into swearing allegiance to the sea-beast.

Furthermore, the 144,000 are described as pure, undefiled, filled with truth, and blameless. Their salvific union with the Messiah has produced in them a righteous and holy character, reflective of their Lord's purity. Meanwhile, the captive followers of the two ogres are misled, willing to sell their souls to preserve what they have in their temporal existence, and ultimately defeated.[65] In summary, the Lamb's worshipers enjoy everlasting peace, safety, victory, and rest, whereas those who cast their lot with the unholy trinity are enthralled by the pleasures of sin for a season, even as they rush headlong to unending destruction.[66]

Third, *we learn that all those who luxuriate in political, moral, and religious corruption eventually fall and that their devastation is comprehensive.* In this chapter, we are introduced to Babylon—a pagan, harlotrous, and idolatrous entity who represents intense opposition to God and his reborn children. While more is said about Babylon later in John's prophetic oracle,[67] we note here that the lewd prostitute most likely represents both a city that serves as the headquarters for the dragon's predatory brutes and the pagan world system that stands in total rebellion against the Messiah and his righteousness. Babylon's depravity extends to the whole earth. Furthermore, her captivating and coercive sexual perversion is her chief characteristic (v. 8),[68] being manifested among those who wallow in her "adulterous desire."

65. The demise is so complete that the sycophants of the land-beast and sea-beast mourn as well as curse God for causing the great prostitute of Babylon to implode (Rev 16:19–21; 18:9–20).

66. See Heb 11:24–26. As we mentioned earlier, the Apocalypse regularly demonstrates typological fulfillment of the events of the exodus, where past events prophetically foreshadow future events. In this passage, Moses represents someone who persevered and remained triumphant, for he refused the fleeting indulgence of sin and chose to identify with God and his beleaguered people, even at great personal cost.

67. Most notably Rev 17 and 18.

68. See our discussion of Rev 17:2, 4–5; 18:3, 9; 19:2. As will be seen, sexual deviance is not the only feature of the great prostitute of Babylon. She is also known for her corruption, her materialism, her deceit, and especially her drunkenness with the blood of God's martyred, reborn children (17:6; 18:24; 19:2).

God's celestial emissary proclaims the judgment that Babylon has "fallen" from a position of prominence, influence, and authority. Moreover, those who revel in her whoredom are judged with the sickle of Lamb's retributive harvest (vv. 17–20). These observations indicate that at the end of the age, the pagan world system and those who sell their souls to it will experience eternal ruin. Nothing and no one can prevent God's justice from being served. Indeed, regardless of how hard the insurrectionists try to oppose the Creator, they are doomed to fail.

IMPORTANT MINISTRY IMPLICATIONS

Within Revelation 14, there are reassurances and admonitions that congregational leaders can bring to their parishioners. Specifically, the importance of the following four sets of observations is anchored to our saving relationship in the Lamb and the security we have by faith in the redemption he won for us through his sacrificial death at Calvary.

First, *we can reassure our parishioners that they are marked with the ownership of the Father and the Son.* We previously affirmed that the notion of ownership can feel repulsive to contemporary readers, especially given the horrors of human trafficking, slavery, and various forms of oppression experienced by many people in the Majority World. Nonetheless, here, as in Revelation 7, God's ownership of us is always and only for our eternal good.[69] Consider the 144,000, who are depicted as secure in the loving hands of the Father and the exalted, triumphant Lamb.[70] Those belonging to the Creator and the Messiah rejoice in being owned. And why? It is because they now realize the everlasting blessedness that *pursues* them into the peaceful presence of their Maker and Redeemer.[71]

Second, *we can reassure our congregants that serving the Messiah is worth all the strife and struggle they may experience in this life.* In verse 13, we find the second beatitude in John's prophetic oracle, which concerns those who "die in the Lord." The immediate context indicates that

69. See Isa 44:22; 50:2; 52:3; Pss 44:26; 107:2; Luke 1:68; Rom 8:28; 1 Cor 6:19–20; Gal 3:13; 4:5; Phil 3:12. To reiterate, as the sovereign Creator, God rightfully exercises his lordship over us without obligation to justify his authority. Yet his ownership is not oppressive. It promotes our temporal and eternal good, reflecting his loving design, both now and forever.

70. See Prov 18:10; 29:25; John 10:28.

71. See Ps 23:6, which reads, "Surely goodness and mercy will *pursue* me all the days of my life, and I will live in the house of the Lord forever" (emphasis added).

the referent is those who are martyred for their faith.[72] Throughout the Apocalypse, those who suffer physical death for following Jesus are especially lauded for their faithfulness. Yet there is an application for all believers in the present day, regardless of whether they suffer martyrdom. To "die in the Lord" includes a life that persists in faith, perseveres to the end, and remains unswervingly loyal to the Creator, even at great personal cost.[73] For believers who endure to the end of their earthly sojourn, there is a blessed, eternal reward that awaits them in heaven.

Third, in addition to these reassurances which we can offer our parishioners, *we must faithfully urge them to examine themselves and test the genuineness of their faith.*[74] Though many gather in our churches and hear God's Word proclaimed, not all truly believe. Some remain captive to unbelief and the devil's deception. As Christ's under-shepherds, we are called to awaken the complacent with the Spirit's conviction and to comfort the repentant with the certainty of grace in Christ. As we noted earlier, the deception fabricated by the unholy trinity of chapter 13 is a worldwide movement, taking in many who outwardly profess a vague notion of belief in Christ.[75] Tragically, some prove to be illegitimate children of God because they switch their allegiance to the sea-beast, receive his identifying mark, and venerate his image. As we warn our congregants about the coming judgment, we must remember that not all who profess faith have truly placed their trust in the Messiah for salvation.

Fourth, in light of the coming deception and judgment, *we must exhort our parishioners to abide in Christ, remain anchored in his Word, and trust in him alone. After all, only he, by his Spirit, sustains and preserves them in the true faith.* Revelation 14:12, in parallel with 13:10, shows us that in anticipation of the end, we must persevere in our devotion to Christ, knowing that this is what constitutes victory for God's triumphant, reborn children.[76] Our Creator realizes that during times of persecution, distress, and false manifestations of the truth, we may encounter spiritual fatigue and be tempted to succumb to the devil's

72. See our discussion in Rev 13:9–10.

73. Note Paul's description of Christlike love in 1 Cor 13:7: "It always endures, always believes, always hopes, always perseveres"; see also Matt 10:38; Rom 12:1–2; Gal 2:20; Phil 1:21; 3:12–14.

74. See 2 Cor 13:5.

75. See Jas 2:14, 19–20; 1 John 2:19.

76. See 1 John 5:4–5.

schemes. As church leaders, we must summon our congregants to look beyond their present troubles and difficulties, along with believing only in Jesus, who alone is the Alpha and Omega of their faith.[77]

VITAL MISSIONAL RAMIFICATIONS

While there are several worthwhile missional considerations that could be gleaned from Revelation 14, our focus here is on the "everlasting gospel" (v. 6) that an "angel" proclaims (as recorded in v. 7). Within this concise message, we find three ramifications for missionary activity that should inform our witness to the world.

First, *our witnessing efforts as missionaries must lead the unsaved to fear and glorify God.* The emphasis here extends beyond feeling terrified in the presence of the Lord's cosmic court of justice.[78] Of course, such a response is appropriate for those who persist in rebelling against him. Yet more importantly, fearing the Lord means to respect and honor his exalted position, universal authority, and limitless power. Furthermore, revering the Father means living in light of these realities and seeking an upright relationship with him through faith in the Son.[79] In addition to fearing the Lord, the angel summons earth's wicked inhabitants to give the Creator glory. Here, there is no room for personal promotion, self-centered comfort-seeking, or anything else that would diminish who and what God is, particularly in comparison to who and what we are. On the one hand, the gospel offers spiritual benefits and eternal blessings to those who trust in Christ for salvation. Yet on the other hand, the primary purpose for the conversion of the lost is to bring God the honor due his name.[80]

Second, *we must warn the unsaved about the judgment to come as well as point them to signs of judgment that are already upon us.* The next portion of the "everlasting gospel" (v. 6) speaks to the urgency of the

77. See Heb 12:1–2; Rev 22:12–13. As Thomas, *Revelation Exegetical Commentary*, vol. 2, 213, notes, "It is better to be killed by the beast then to suffer eternal torment with him."

78. See our discussion of Rev 11:18; 20:11–15.

79. The Old Testament wisdom literature, especially Prov, brings definition and description to "fear the LORD"; for example, see 1:7; 2:1–5; 8:13; 9:10; 14:27; 15:16; 19:23.

80. See Matt 5:16; 1 Cor 6:19–20; 10:31; 2 Cor 5:9; Phil 1:20–21; Col 3:17; 1 Thess 2:12; 2 Thess 1:11–12; 1 Pet 4:11.

hour. Time is short, and opportunities to repent and believe are fleeting. We know that the good news about Christ is set within the context of the sinners' lost condition. Yet added to the problem of personal iniquity and spiritual separation from God is the impending doom of the Messiah's decisive and devastating judgment brought upon the earth's wicked inhabitants. Part of our message, as missionaries to the lost, is the declaration that the time of judgment is imminent. We are obligated to urge people to abandon their sinful ways and place their trust in the Messiah. Also, rather than waiting for some convenient time in the future, they must urgently do so now.[81] Yes, God's provision of his saving grace is presently available. Still, one day it must give way to his judgment of the wicked. When this time of reckoning finally arrives, nothing will be able to forestall it.

Third, *we are reminded that the purpose of our missionary work and gospel witness in the world is to lead others to the true worship of the Creator.* As we noted in our discussion of Revelation 5, the everlasting promise of the gospel includes God's reborn children, before his sacred presence, extolling him as the sovereign Monarch of the universe, along with offering unending praise to the victorious Lamb. Admittedly, even if all the benefits of salvation in this life have great importance, they remain temporary. Yet what extends into eternity is that believers are privileged to offer sinless, holy, and pure worship to the Lord with inexpressible joy. Amazingly, God uses our missionary endeavors to summon the lost to saving faith so that in everlasting glory, they too can bring the sacrifice of their worship to the sacred throne of God and the Lamb.[82] What an honor and privilege it is for us to serve our Savior in this way, especially to be part of his redemptive mission to herald the good news so that everyone can trust in the Son and receive eternal life.

81. See 2 Cor 6:2; Rev 22:12–13.

82. See our discussion of Rev 4:9–11; 5:8–14; 7:9–12; 11:16–18.

Revelation 15

The Final Series of End-Time Judgments (Part One)

LEARNING OBJECTIVES

- Clarify the purpose of the seven angels who pour out the seven last plagues.
- Describe the scene where the redeemed praise the Creator.
- Identify the main message found in the song of Moses and the Lamb.
- Understand how the emphasis on God's righteous verdicts fills believers with hope.
- Consider how the seven last plagues demonstrate the Lord's power over evil.

CHAPTER SUMMARY

Revelation 15 begins with seven angels, who dispense seven plagues to bring to completion God's judgment of earth's wicked inhabitants. Next, the redeemed sing a hymn of praise to the Creator for his righteous judgments. Then the focus shifts back to the seven angels, who emerge from the heavenly temple to pour out the seven bowls of God's wrath upon the earth. Finally, the temple is filled with the smoke of his glory and power, and no one can enter the celestial sanctuary until the seven plagues are poured out.

STUDY QUESTIONS

1. What is the relationship between the seven angels and the seven last plagues?
2. What does the sea of glass mixed with fire symbolize?
3. What does the song of Moses and the Lamb represent?
4. What does the attire worn by the seven angels suggest about their divine purpose?
5. Why can no one enter the celestial temple until the seven last plagues are finished?

CHAPTER OUTLINE

- Introductory observations
- A remarkable scene in heaven (15:1–8)
- Key theological insights
- Important ministry implications
- Vital missional ramifications

INTRODUCTORY OBSERVATIONS

Chapters 15 and 16 concern the final series of end-time judgments that the Creator brings on the planet's evildoers, whose hearts remain hardened against him to the end. Corresponding to the cosmic trial motif in earlier portions of John's prophetic oracle, this segment of his treatise emphasizes that the Lord objectively and equitably judges all people according to what they have done and that he shows no partiality or favoritism in his dealings with the wicked.

The opening throne-room scene of chapter 15 is followed by the unleashing of seven last plagues recorded in chapter 16. According to 15:1 and 8, these bring "God's wrath" (or covenantal curses) to completion, likewise implying that it is finished and ended.[1] As with the seal and trumpet judgments, the last seven covenantal curses divide into four interrelated calamities followed by three interrelated ones.[2] Specifically,

1. See our discussion of Rev 6:16, 17; 11:18; 14:10, 19; 15:7; 16:1, 19; 19:15.
2. That is, a four and three literary pattern.

the initial four plagues bring destruction to the earth's land, sea, water, and sky. Then the last three calamities unleash full-scale devastation on the world's civil, economic, and military infrastructures.

A REMARKABLE SCENE IN HEAVEN (15:1–8)

In the unfolding cosmic drama, John witnesses a "sign in heaven" (v. 1) that is "great" in significance and "remarkable" in appearance.[3] Specifically, the apostle sees "seven angels" holding the "seven" concluding "plagues." Yet before these final calamities are unleashed, John notices something that resembles a sprawling "sea" (v. 2) made of "glass."

Just as in 4:6, the apostle observes in 15:2 an expanse that is clear and sparkling. Yet this time, the glassy "sea" is "mixed with fire,"[4] which serves as a reminder that the Creator is about to unleash his "wrath" (v. 1) on earth's wicked inhabitants.[5] Moreover, John notices a throng of martyred saints who had triumphed over the sea-beast, his idolatrous "image" (v. 2), and the "number" representing his "name."[6] They "won the victory" over the anti-God forces of the world by trusting in the Son, remaining loyal to him, and obeying the Father's commands.[7]

Promises in Revelation for Believers Who Overcome		
Promise	**Description**	**Biblical References**
Authority over the Nations	Exercising with Christ ruling power over the nations and divine authority	2:26–27; 20:4–6; 22:5
Hidden Manna and White Stone	Spiritual nourishment and a new identity marked by a secret name known only to the recipient	2:17
Pillars in God's Temple	Permanent, honored position in the Lord's heavenly sanctuary, bearing the names of God, Christ, and the new Jerusalem	3:12; 21:2–3, 22–23
The Morning Star	Receiving Christ as the bright morning star, representing his glorious presence	2:28; 22:16

3. Reminiscent of Rev 12:1, 3.

4. Perhaps meaning the glassy "sea" (Rev 15:2) is enveloped with flame-red, glowing streaks.

5. See 2 En. 3:3; LAE 28:4; Heb 12:29.

6. That is, "666"; see our discussion of Rev 13:18.

7. See our discussion of Rev 1:9; 2:2–3, 10, 13, 19, 24–25; 3:4, 8, 10–11; 12:11; 13:10; 14:4–5, 12.

Promises in Revelation for Believers Who Overcome		
Promise	**Description**	**Biblical References**
Throne Partnership	The ultimate honor of sharing Christ's throne and reigning with him in the eternal kingdom	3:21; 20:4–6; 22:3–5
Tree of Life	Permission to eat from the Tree of Life in paradise, symbolizing eternal life and communion with God	2:7; 22:1–2, 14, 19
Victory over the Second Death	Protection from eternal judgment and the Lake of Fire, ensuring everlasting security	2:11; 20:6, 14; 21:8
White Garments and the Book of Life	Clothed in righteousness, names permanently recorded in the Lamb's Book of Life, and acknowledgment before the Father and his angels	3:5; 19:7–8; 20:12, 15; 21:27

As these faithful followers of the Messiah stand on the transparent "sea" (15:2) in front of the Creator's majestic throne,[8] they hold multistringed "harps,"[9] which he has graciously given them.[10] While they play these instruments, they sing a chorus of praise to the "Lord God Almighty" (v. 3).[11] The worshipers declare that the deeds performed by the supreme Monarch of the universe are both "great" and astounding. Even in judging the pagan and idolatrous world system, he remains "just and true."[12]

The appropriate response is for all who are in heaven and on earth to "fear" (v. 4; or revere and honor) the Creator and to "glorify" (or praise) his awe-inspiring "name." After all, he "alone" is absolutely "holy," which includes being entirely distinct from his creation and utterly devoid of humankind's iniquity.[13] As the final series of seven covenantal curses unfolds, they serve as a disclosure of God's "righteous verdicts" (or

8. As we previously noted, the Creator's throne occupies the literary center of John's prophetic oracle.

9. Or lyres, denoting victory.

10. The Greek phrase rendered "of God" is understood here to be a genitive of agency; see Rev 5:8–9; 14:2–3.

11. See 1 En. 9:4; 25:5; 27:3; Tob 13:7, 11; Rev 1:8; 4:8; 11:17; 16:7, 14; 19:6, 15; 21:22.

12. See Pss 92:5; 111:13; 139:14; 145:17; Jer 10:6–7, 10; Amos 4:13.

13. See Exod 15:11; Deut 32:4; Pss 86:8–10; 144:17; 145:17; 1 Sam 2:2; Isa 6:3; Odes Sol. 24:13–14; 31:3–5; Rev 4:8.

equitable deeds).[14] For this reason, at the consummation of the age, all the "nations" throughout the globe will come and prostrate themselves in homage before the Creator's sacred presence.[15] As with 5:9 and 7:9, in 15:4 there is evidence of the success of missionary work.

We previously noted that exodus typology or prophetic foreshadowing is tightly woven into the literary fabric of John's prophetic oracle. Specifically, an event in the past (such as Israel's departure from Egypt) establishes a corresponding pattern for a more heightened (or escalated) and profound fulfillment in a later set of events. Consider Revelation 15:3. The phrase rendered the "song of Moses" (v. 3)[16] recalls Israel's triumphant refrain on the shore of the Red Sea. So too does the historically evocative poem that Moses delivers shortly before his death on Mount Nebo. Likewise, this same theme is emphasized in other Old Testament passages.[17]

Just as the people of God in ancient times had been victorious over their implacable foe, Egypt, the new people of God—the faithful followers of the Messiah[18]—have also triumphed over their antagonists. This observation explains why the chorus in Revelation 15:3 is called the "Song of the Lamb."[19] His sacrificial death at Calvary made victory possible for his disciples, who trust and obey him.[20] John is portraying the Son as a new, Moses-like, redemptive figure. Yet he who is infinitely greater than the famed lawgiver and bondservant of God[21] leads the newly formed Israel into an exodus-like freedom and release from the tyranny of the dragon, the sea-beast, and the land-beast.

14. See our discussion of Rev 16:7; 18:4–8; 19:1–2.

15. See Pss 46:10; 47:9; 66:4; 86:9–10; 102:15; Isa 2:2–5; 14:1–2; 19:21; 27:13; 45:23; 49:7; 60:1–3; 66:18–23; Jer 16:19; Zec 8:20–23; 14:16; Mic 4:1–5; Mal 1:11; Phil 2:9–11.

16. Or an ode originating with Moses.

17. See Exod 14:31; 15:1–18; Deut 28:59–60; 31:30—32:44; Pss 86:8–10; 98:1; 110:2–4; 111:2–4; 145:17; Jer 10:1–18; Amos 4:13.

18. See Gal 6:16.

19. Or an ode originating with the Messiah.

20. See John 15:5–10; 1 John 5:1–5; Rev 12:11.

21. See Exod 14:31; Num 12:7; Deut 34:5; Josh 1:1, 15; Ps 105:26; Heb 3:1–6.

Symbolism in the Exodus		
Exodus Type	**Historical Context and Meaning**	**Biblical Fulfillment and References**
First Exodus	God establishes the children of Israel as a nation through their departure from Egypt. The Mosaic covenant is revealed at Mount Sinai, and Israel is claimed as God's chosen people. This foundational event serves as a template for understanding the Lord's redemptive work throughout history.	*Passover Lamb Symbolism*: The substitutionary sacrifice of the Passover lamb (Exod 12) prefigures Christ as the "Lamb of God" (John 1:29, 36) and "our Passover Lamb" (1 Cor 5:7), who has been "sacrificed." *Blood of the Covenant*: The sprinkling of animal blood to ratify the covenant (Exod 24:8) is fulfilled in Jesus' blood shed on the cross (Matt 26:27–28; Heb 12:24; 1 Pet 1:2).
Second Exodus	The prophets view the first exodus as a type pointing to Israel's future redemption from Babylonian exile. This second exodus emphasizes God's faithfulness to his covenant promises and his power to deliver his chosen people from captivity once again.	*Prophetic Promises*: The prophets' pledges of restoration from Babylon (Isa 43:16–19; Jer 23:7–8) find ultimate fulfillment in the spiritual redemption available through the Messiah. The physical return from exile becomes a symbol of spiritual liberation from sin's bondage.
New Exodus	The New Testament writers, particularly John in Revelation, draw upon the promises made through the psalmists and prophets to demonstrate their ultimate fulfillment in the Messiah. This represents the climactic realization of all exodus typology.	*New Covenant*: The new covenant promised in Jer 31:31–34 is established and ratified through Jesus' sacrificial death (Luke 22:20; Heb 8:6). *Complete Redemption*: All believers experience the ultimate "exodus" from sin and death through Jesus' atoning work at Calvary (Heb 9:12). In union with him, they experience an eternal, living relationship with God (Rev 21:3–4). The physical deliverances of the past point to this spiritual and everlasting deliverance.

Parallels between the First Exodus and the New Covenant		
Aspect	**First Exodus**	**New Covenant**
Covenant Establishment	God makes a covenant with Moses and Israel at Mount Sinai (Exod 19–24).	God institutes a new covenant through the shed blood of Christ (Luke 22:20; Heb 8:6–13; 12:24).
Divine Deliverer	God raises up Moses as deliverer for the Israelites (Exod 3:10).	God sends the Messiah as the Deliverer for humanity (Luke 2:11; 4:18–19; John 3:16–17; 20:31; Acts 4:12; 13:23).
Divine Presence	God dwells among the Israelites in the tabernacle (Exod 25:8; 40:34–35).	God tabernacles among humanity through Christ (Matt 1:23; 28:20; John 1:14).
Journey to Promise	God leads the Israelites to the promised land of Canaan (Exod 13:21; Num 14:8).	God brings his reborn children to the promised inheritance of heaven (1 Thess 4:16–17; Heb 11:13–16).
Method of Deliverance	God delivers Israel from Egyptian bondage through miraculous signs and wonders (Exod 7:14—10:29; 12:29–30; 14:21–31).	God delivers humanity from sin's bondage through the cross-resurrection event (Rom 6:6–7; 1 Cor 15:3–4).
Priestly Nation	God establishes Israel as his chosen nation and kingdom of priests (Exod 19:5–6; 24:3–8).	God makes believers a royal priesthood and holy nation (1 Pet 2:5, 9; Rev 1:6; 5:10).
Recognition of Bondage	God hears the cries of the Israelites, who are enslaved by the Egyptians (Exod 3:7).	God sees humanity enslaved in bondage to sin (Rom 6:17–18).

In the unfolding cosmic drama, the apostle witnesses the opening of the heavenly inner "sanctuary" (Rev 15:5), or "Tent[22] of Testimony." The preceding phrase is an allusion to the comparable and frequently occurring expression in the Pentateuch.[23] More specifically, the term rendered "testimony" denotes the ark of the covenant, in which were placed the two stone tablets upon which God recorded the Decalogue (or Ten Commandments).[24] This testimony is a distillation of the Creator's righteous moral law, which idolatrous and pagan humanity repeatedly violates. For this reason, as decreed from the Lord's cosmic court of

22. Or "tabernacle."

23. See Exod 40:20–21; Num 17:22–23; 18:2; 2 Chr 24:6; Rev 11:19.

24. See Exod 16:34; 25:16, 21; 27:21; 31:18; 32:15; 40:24, 34; Lev 16:13; Num 1:50; 17:4, 10; Deut 10:1–2, 5; 1 Kgs 8:9; 2 Chr 5:10.

justice, his wrath (or covenantal curses) is poured out on earth's wicked inhabitants.

Accordingly, the "seven angels" (v. 6) emerge from the celestial inner "sanctuary" holding the "seven plagues," which they are about to unleash on the earth. These agents of God's retributive justice are dressed in robes made of pure "bright linen." Also, they wear around their torsos "sashes" made of pure "gold." Perhaps this attire signifies the priestly, noble, and spotless character of these "angels."[25] Previously, in 1:13, John states that his vision of the risen and exalted Messiah includes his wearing a "gold sash" around his "chest." Centuries earlier, the "sash" would have been part of the high priest's wardrobe.[26]

John notes that one of the "four living creatures" (15:7), who are stationed both "near" (4:6) and "around" God's "throne," gives each of the "seven angels" (15:7) a golden "bowl." These wide, shallow vessels overflow with the "wrath" of the Creator,[27] whom the apostle once again describes as living "forever and ever."[28]

Next, the apostle witnesses that the heavenly inner "sanctuary" (v. 8) is being "filled with smoke," which originates from the Lord's "glory" and "power."[29] This observation emphasizes the sacred and sustained nature of the bowl judgments which are coming upon earth's wicked inhabitants. Likewise, it is an additional reminder that the martyred saints' great High Priest has not ignored their prayers for the vindication of their faith.[30]

Along with verse 1, verse 8 again emphasizes that the supreme Monarch of the universe will not permit any creature to enter his heavenly "sanctuary" until the seven scourges have completely run their course.[31] This restriction confirms the dignity and solemnity of the occasion.

25. See Lev 16:4, 23; Ezek 9:2–3, 11; 10:2; Dan 10:5; 12:6–7.

26. See Exod 28:4; 29:5.

27. See our discussion of Rev 6:16, 17; 11:18; 14:10, 19; 15:1; 16:1, 19; 19:15.

28. See Deut 32:39–40; Isa 40:28; Dan 4:34–35; Rev 1:4, 8; 4:8; 7:2; 10:6; 11:17; 16:4.

29. See Exod 40:34–35; 1 Kgs 8:10–12; 2 Chr 5:13–14; 7:1–3; Isa 6:1–4; Ezek 10:2–4; 44:4.

30. See Heb 2:17; 4:14–16; 7:26–28; Rev 5:8; 6:9–10; 8:3–5; 9:13; 14:18; 16:3, 7.

31. That is, until the last series of covenantal curses is finished or ended.

KEY THEOLOGICAL INSIGHTS

In Revelation 15, we are invited into a heavenly scene of preparation for the final outpouring of the Creator's wrath (v. 1). From this celestial vantage point, we can glean several theological insights concerning the redeemed witnesses, the heavenly hosts who are readying themselves to execute God's end-time plan, and the solemnity of his judgment on earth's wicked inhabitants.

First, we note that *God's righteous judgment is every bit as praiseworthy as his work of redemption.* When considering the Creator's mercy and grace, particularly in his redemptive work on our behalf through the Messiah, a response of worship makes sense. Yet when it comes to God's wrath, worship is not typically our immediate, intuitive response. The notion of his righteous judgment's outpouring on pagan humanity can invoke within us feelings of fear and dread, especially for those who are not abiding in God's love.[32] Nonetheless, in this chapter, as the host of heaven prepare for the unleashing of the final series of covenantal curses, we are greeted with the saints' praising and worshiping the Creator (vv. 2–4).[33] The vindicated conquerors know that God's judgment is right and true and that it does not need any justification or defense. They also recognize that the wicked have willfully and rebelliously placed themselves in the position to experience the Lord's retribution for their sinful ways.[34]

Second, we observe that *the Creator's angelic emissaries are justified in bringing about the unleashing of his wrath.* The seven angels emerging from the celestial sanctuary are clothed in purity and authority, symbolized by the "bright linen" (v. 6) and "gold sashes" worn "around their chests." John's description of their appearance demonstrates their special commission by the sovereign Monarch of the universe.[35] Throughout the Apocalypse, angels have been deployed for many tasks, including heralding God's message, participating in worship, restraining catastrophe, and dispensing his judgment. Angels, who are confirmed in the

32. See 1 John 4:16–18. Here, the apostle reassures us that God's love eliminates the fear of punishment for those who are faithful believers.

33. This is also the case elsewhere in the Apocalypse; see our discussion of 11:17–18; 19:1–3.

34. See our discussion of Rev 16:9, 11, and 21, where the wicked are entrenched in their denial and rejection of God, even though they know from whom the judgment is coming; see also our explanation of 6:15–17; 9:20–21.

35. See our explanation of the angels' appearance in the above commentary.

righteousness of their actions, flawlessly and unfailingly carry out the Creator's will. These ministering spirits do not enact their own agenda, because everything they do is in accordance with the sovereign Lord's will.[36] Though they are impressive beings and at times even appear divine, they are not equal with God and should not receive the worship reserved for the Creator alone.[37]

Third, *we are confronted with God's sovereignty in executing his judgment*. The wording of verse 8 is striking: no one and nothing are allowed to enter the celestial sanctuary until the execution of the covenantal curses is complete. The image here is of the Creator's absolute holiness[38] and sovereignty. God's end-time plan is known only to himself. Likewise, he alone determines when and how the details of what he intends to do are executed.[39] The shroud of smoke in this heavenly scene, while reminiscent of the martyrs' prayers, sets forth God's power and glory.[40] This observation clarifies that the eternal Lord answers only to himself in bestowing judgment. Likewise, he is not obligated to cater to our curiosity and reveal the reasons for his actions.

IMPORTANT MINISTRY IMPLICATIONS

In our discussion of Revelation 15, we provide a table listing several characteristics of what it means for God's reborn children to experience victory over Satan and his demonic cohort. As the cosmic drama unfolds, the hymn the worshipers sing offers a portrait of their ultimate triumph amid adversity and martyrdom. Also, within this song, we discover several principles for how church leaders can encourage the faithful to think and live as the church militant on earth in anticipation of becoming the church triumphant in heaven.

First, *true victory for the saints is found in overcoming the evil one and his influences*. Recall the statement in Revelation 12:11 that Jesus' followers triumph through the Lamb's sacrificial death on the Cross, along with

36. See Heb 1:14. Also, for a concise treatment concerning the topic of angels in Scripture, see the corresponding table in our discussion of Rev 1.

37. As seen in Rev 19:10; 22:8–9, even John mistakes an angel for the Messiah and seeks to worship the celestial being rather than God.

38. As we note elsewhere, God's holiness speaks to both his complete uniqueness and impeccable moral character.

39. See Matt 24:36.

40. See our discussion of Rev 5:8; 6:9–10; 8:3–5.

bearing witness to him, even in the face of maltreatment and execution at the hands of Satan and his demonic cohort. In contrast, today we are inundated with competing ideas about what constitutes spiritual success. The me-centered focus of much of contemporary Christian teaching would have us believe that victory is inward-looking and self-exalting. Yet this is a lie concocted by the devil. The celebrating saints in chapter 15 are those who "won the victory over the beast and his image and over the number of his name" (v. 2). Put another way, they have overcome true spiritual opposition, not just their own personal challenges and difficulties. They have successfully resisted the worldly, godless system that positions itself against the Messiah and his righteousness.[41] As church leaders, we must lead our congregants beyond the self-centered teachings prominent in our day. We should also urge our parishioners to depend on the indwelling Spirit to combat evil, especially by emulating Christ's holiness and righteousness.[42]

Second, *true victory for the saints is found in the recognition of God's greatness.* While the overcomers are presented in a position of triumph, their song deflects all praise and glory to the Creator, because they know that without him, they can accomplish nothing.[43] In today's culture, we are taught to promote ourselves, highlight our own accomplishments, and bring attention to what we have done. Yet in the first part of this song of the Lamb, the victors give all accolades only to their Redeemer. Those in pastoral leadership have a unique obligation and privilege to do the same.[44] Rather than building empires of self-promotion to expand our influence and audience, we must point beyond ourselves and direct people to the exclusive praise and worship of the Creator and the victorious Lamb.

Third, *true victory for the saints is found in the awareness of the global reach of God's righteousness.* So much of our praise and worship today is filled with singing about what God has done for individual Christians, how they have been personally blessed by his grace, how Jesus has redeemed them, and so on. Of course, there is an appropriate place for the personalization of the Lord's work in each of our lives that finds relevance to us as individuals. Even so, within the hymn which the overcomers sing, there is not one personal pronoun. Instead, the focus is

41. See our discussion of Rev 18:4–8.

42. See Eph 5:1–2; Phil 2:5; 1 Pet 2:21; 1 John 2:6; Rev 12:11.

43. See John 15:5; 1 Cor 4:7.

44. In contrast to innumerable celebrity pastors who are building their own followings today; see 1 Pet 5:2–3.

outward, beyond mere individualistic concerns. It is the recognition of God's glory and righteousness manifested throughout the earth.[45] As we lead our congregants in worship and praise, we do well to broaden our perspective beyond what God has done for any of us as individuals and encourage our parishioners to praise the Creator for the worldwide extent of his righteous blessings and judgments.

VITAL MISSIONAL RAMIFICATIONS

As we reflect on the global scope of God's greatness and self-revelation, several key applications emerge for missional outreach from our discussion of Revelation 15. First, *our missional activity must point to the Lord as the King of the nations.* The global reach of God's mighty deeds must be set in the context of his universal kingship, noting that he is the supreme Monarch of all peoples and nations. This includes not only those nations that are culturally Christian but also those that have no visible recognition of the Creator's omnipotence and the Messiah's lordship.[46] God's complete sovereignty and the extent of his power over the entire universe are not truths that require our acceptance and agreement to be valid. Instead, the emphasis here is on our recognizing and acknowledging the inherent veracity of these assertions. Then, as we share the gospel with others, we ought to reflect these affirmations in our own lives, along with summoning others to do the same.

Second, *missional efforts must call people to fear the Lord and glorify his name.* The message of the gospel extends beyond individual forgiveness of sin and redemption. It includes a call for people to live in reverential submission to God and to display him in all facets of their lives. The rhetorical question at the beginning of verse 4 implies the absurdity

45. See Isa 6:3; Hab 2:14.

46. So-called "culturally Christian" nations are those where the gospel has had a long historical presence and where biblical principles have, to some extent, influenced political, legal, and social institutions. Yet even in such nations, which may publicly affirm Christian values, civil society remains part of the left-hand kingdom, in which God governs indirectly through human authorities, natural law, and the structures of civil order. By contrast, many Majority World nations have experienced little gospel influence or have actively resisted Christian teaching in their legal and political frameworks. Nevertheless, Christ's lordship is not confined by national borders or political systems. His reign as Messiah transcends all earthly rule. His right-hand kingdom advances through the preaching of the gospel, calling all people, regardless of nation or culture, to repentance and faith in him. See in our discussion of Rev 12 our table dealing with the threefold distinction of God's kingdom.

of anyone who fails to fear the Lord and give him glory.[47] For believers, the only reasonable response to who God is and his "great and marvelous . . . works" (v. 3) is faith in him alone, as well as a commitment to follow the Messiah wholeheartedly.[48] Just as we have come to respond to God in the only way that truly makes sense, namely, by fearing and glorifying his name, so too we must urge the lost to adopt this response in their lives.

Third, *our missional efforts include bringing God's righteous acts to light so that those who believe may worship him in an acceptable manner.* We previously noted that the goal of missions is to worship the Creator and the Lamb. Here, in verse 4, we see that "all the nations" eventually worship God. This truth is a great encouragement that we can use to incentivize the missional task. Yet beyond this observation, we note the reason *why* all nations worship the almighty Creator. It is because God's righteous acts have been disclosed, proclaimed, and explained.[49] In missions, we must prioritize sharing with the lost the revelation of God's mighty deeds. As we faithfully do so, we can expect that the Spirit will enable some to recognize their need for a Savior. We can also anticipate that they will believe and become savingly united to Christ. Therefore, to show forth God's righteousness, especially by declaring his mighty deeds and just dealings with humanity, is an essential component of our missionary work.

47. As seen in our discussion of Rev 16:9, 11, 21, there are indeed many who neither fear the Lord nor give him glory.

48. See John 6:68.

49. See Acts 8:30–31; Rom 10:14–15.

Revelation 16

The Final Series of End-Time Judgments (Part Two)

LEARNING OBJECTIVES

- Describe the nature of the seven bowls of God's wrath.
- Identify the targets of the sevenfold scourges.
- Understand the implications of the Creator's judgments for pagan, idolatrous humanity.
- Consider how earth's wicked inhabitants respond to the final series of calamities.
- Reflect on the hope the bowl judgments offer for believers.

CHAPTER SUMMARY

Revelation 16 chronicles the unleashing of the final seven bowls of God's wrath. The first five scourges include painful sores; turning the sea, rivers, and springs into blood; scorching heat; and engulfing the sea-beast's kingdom in total darkness. The sixth bowl involves the drying up of the Euphrates River, followed by the seventh bowl, which brings about Babylon's destruction. Despite all these calamities, earth's wicked inhabitants refuse to repent and instead choose to slander the Creator.

STUDY QUESTIONS

1. Why does the Creator unleash the seven bowl plagues on earth's inhabitants?

2. How does the final series of calamities challenge your understanding of God's justice?
3. What is significant about the three unclean spirits which come out of the mouth of the dragon, the sea-beast, and the land-beast (or false prophet)?
4. How should the Messiah's sudden, unexpected return affect the priorities that believers adopt?
5. In what sense does God remember the great city of Babylon?

CHAPTER OUTLINE

- The first five bowl judgments (16:1–11)
- The sixth bowl judgment: the battle of Armageddon (16:12–16)
- The seventh bowl judgment: widespread destruction (16:17–21)
- Key theological insights
- Important ministry implications
- Vital missional ramifications

THE FIRST FIVE BOWL JUDGMENTS (16:1–11)

As previously noted, the last seven bowl judgments divide into four interrelated calamities, followed by three interrelated ones.[1] Specifically, the initial four plagues bring destruction to the earth's land, sea, water, and sky. Then the last three calamities unleash full-scale devastation on the world's civil, economic, and military infrastructures.

Consequently, in the unfolding cosmic drama, the scene shifts to the first of the seven covenantal curses, each of which transpires in an abrupt sequence. These calamities, like the trumpet disasters of chapters 8 and 9, resemble the various plagues that the Creator brought upon Egypt through Moses.[2] As previously noted, this is an example of the exodus typology or prophetic foreshadowing that dominates the literary landscape of John's prophetic oracle.

1. That is, a four and three literary pattern.
2. See Exod 7–12.

The apostle recalls hearing a "loud voice" (16:1) declare from the Creator's "temple"[3] that the "seven angels" are to "pour out" on the planet the "seven bowls," which, collectively, contain the final installment of "God's wrath."[4] John's intent is to emphasize the cumulative severity of the seven scourges which fall one after another on wicked humanity. The preceding observations possibly explain why, in verse 5, the Creator is referred to as the "one who is and who was." As with 11:17, missing from this assertion is the phrase "who is coming."[5] That wording is no longer needed since the Lord's righteous indignation has fully arrived with the unleashing of the final series of covenantal curses.

When the first agent of destruction proceeds to dispense his scourge, those who bear the "mark" (v. 2) of allegiance to the sea-beast and prostrate themselves in homage before his "image" experience "horrible and painful sores." These ulcerations possibly resemble fungating tumors or malignant skin lesions.[6] Next, the second agent of destruction empties his "bowl" (v. 3) on the seas around the globe. In turn, the salt water they contain becomes so putrid and toxic—like the dark, coagulated "blood" of rotting corpses—that "every living creature" within the earth's oceans perishes.[7] Then the third agent of destruction dumps his calamity on the fresh "water" (v. 4) within all the "rivers" and "springs" of the planet's landmasses. All of these, too, instantly turn "into blood" and eradicate every trace of life they contained.

The Apocalypse as Persecution Literature		
Theme/Motif	**Description**	**Biblical Example**
Eschatology	End-time themes emphasize the belief that the present wicked era will eventually end and that the suffering endured by Jesus' faithful followers serves as a confirming sign of this truth.	The structure of Revelation moves from the present persecution of the church militant (chs. 2–3) to the ultimate victory of the church triumphant and its dwelling in the new Jerusalem (chs. 21–22).

3. Or inner sanctuary.

4. Or the Creator's intense anger and indignation; see Ps 69:24; Isa 66:6; Jer 7:20; 10:25; Lam 2:4; 4:11; Ezek 14:19; 22:21–22; 30:15–16; Zeph 3:8; Rev 6:16, 17; 11:18; 14:10, 19; 15:1, 7; 16:19; 19:15.

5. See our discussion of Rev 1:4, 8; 4:8–10; 11:17.

6. Corresponding to Exod 9:8–12; Deut 28:35.

7. Corresponding to Exod 7:17–24; Ps 78:44.

The Apocalypse as Persecution Literature		
Theme/Motif	**Description**	**Biblical Example**
Hope	Persecution literature emphasizes the hope early Christians maintained despite maltreatment. They believed that in the eternal state, God would honor and reward them for their suffering and that their faithfulness through the Spirit would ultimately triumph.	Revelation 2–3 contains numerous promises to Jesus' followers, such as the bestowal of the "crown of life" in 2:10.
Martyrdom	Noteworthy accounts describe the deaths of early Christian martyrs who were executed for their refusal to renounce their faith. These narratives emphasize the courage and steadfastness of martyrs in the face of death.	Antipas in 2:13 is described as Christ's "faithful witness" (or "martyr"), who was killed at Pergamum.
Resistance	Despite suffering, early Christians are portrayed as resisting pressure to renounce their faith. They stand firm in their beliefs even when faced with imprisonment, torture, and death.	The believers in the church at Ephesus are commended for their perseverance and refusal to "tolerate evil people" (2:2–3).
Suffering	Persecution literature highlights the physical, emotional, and spiritual suffering which early Christians endured for their faith. The authors use vivid imagery to convey the pain and trauma of persecution.	Various passages throughout Revelation, such as 1:9, depict the hardships faced by believers.

In stepping back from the second and third bowl judgments (or covenantal curses), it would be sensible to wonder why the Creator would bring such widespread ruination and death to every corner of earth.[8] The reason is that, as with the previous two judgment cycles, the current one was presented in the form of a cosmic trial. To reiterate earlier observations, the pagan, idolatrous world system had not only violated God's holy will but also rebelled against his righteous moral standards and systematically murdered his "saints and prophets" (v. 6). For these

8. Comparable to a series of mass-extinction events.

reasons, the supreme Monarch of the universe is justified in thoroughly punishing earth's wicked inhabitants.[9]

Consider verse 5, in which John recalls hearing the "angel" whom the Creator appointed to exercise authority over the "waters" of the earth.[10] The celestial being declares that even amid all the plagues that the Lord commanded to be unleashed on earth's inhabitants, he remains absolutely "righteous" (or just) and "holy" (or entirely distinct from and untainted by his creation).[11]

No one can charge the One who lives forever and ever with being unfair in his judicial decrees. This includes turning earth's saltwater and freshwater sources into "blood" (v. 6). After all, the planet's wicked inhabitants are guilty of shedding the "blood" of the innocent, namely, God's bondservants and spokespersons, who refused to venerate mortal, flawed, human rulers. It is only fitting that the punishment given is equal to the offense committed. Therefore, the Creator gives the members of the world's pagan and idolatrous system "blood to drink" from earth's oceans, seas, lakes, and rivers. The transgressors are "worthy" (or deserving) to ingest this rancid hellstew.[12]

Next, John hears the "incense altar" (v. 7; personified) affirm that the all-powerful, "Lord God"[13] remains "true and just" (or valid and fair) in his judicial rulings.[14] The fact that the voice originates from the "incense altar" serves as another reminder that the Creator is attentive to the prayers of his children for the vindication of their faith and faithfulness to the Lamb.[15] After this brief interlude, the narrative sequence resumes with the "fourth angel," (v. 8) who unleashes his "bowl" calamity on the "sun." This perpetual source of life-giving warmth and light discharges "fire" on earth's wicked inhabitants. In turn, they are immediately "scorched" (v. 9) by the sun's "fierce heat."[16]

9. See Deut 32:43; 2 Kgs 9:7; Pss 7:11; 9:8; 67:4; 75:2; 79:10, 12; 119:137; Isa 11:4; 49:25–26; Jer 11:20; 2 Macc 12:6; 2 Tim 4:8; Rev 6:10; 18:20; 19:2.

10. See 1 En. 66:1–3; 2 En. 19:4; Jub. 2:2.

11. See 1 En. 1:2–3; 10:1; 14:1; 25:3; 37:2; 92:2; 98:6; 104:9; Odes Sol. 24:13–14.

12. See Gen 9:6; Ps 79:3, 12; Isa 49:26; 65:6; Jer 32:18; Jub. 1:12; Sib. Or. 3:311–12; T. Job 43:13; Wis 11:15–16.

13. See our discussion of Rev 1:8; 4:8; 11:17; 15:3; 16:14; 19:6, 15; 21:22.

14. See Exod 34:6; Deut 32:4; Apoc. El. 5:22–24; Rev 15:3–4; 18:4–8; 19:1–2.

15. See our discussion of Rev 6:9–11; 8:3–5; 14:8; 15:8.

16. Perhaps due to an intense burst of electromagnetic radiation.

The divinely intended response is for the sea-beast's followers to renounce their allegiance to him, "repent" of their iniquities, and offer the Creator "praise" and honor. Instead, the evildoers slander and curse God's sacred "name," which represents his character and attributes.[17] He alone has ruling "authority" over the totality of the devastating calamities (or covenantal curses), including the remaining ones to be poured out on the planet through his celestial agents of destruction.

With that, the "fifth angel" (v. 10) unleashes his "bowl" on the "throne" of the sea-beast. In this way, the supreme Monarch of the universe overturns the temporal, earthly seat of power and control exercised by Satan's deputy. Specialists debate whether this "throne" should be understood literally or symbolically. In either case, the sea-beast's "kingdom" is plunged into darkness.[18]

The above somber turn of events, which signals the onset of the day of the Lord, only increases the agony and dread felt by the sea-beast's sycophants—so much so that they begin to gnaw their "tongues."[19] Yet even though the wicked endure such harrowing "torments" (v. 11) and "sores," they remain entrenched in their evil and idolatrous ways. Once more, instead of repenting, they blaspheme the sovereign Lord of "heaven" and earth, who alone is the source of their existence and wellbeing.

The Lord as Israel's Kinsman-Redeemer[20]		
Old Testament (First Exodus)	**New Testament (New Exodus)**	**Key Parallels and Fulfillment**
God makes the Israelites his prized possession and brings them out of Egypt to grant them the promised land.	Jesus purchases the believers' freedom through his life and sacrificial death.	Liberation from bondage: Egypt in the Old Testament versus sin, death, the law's curse, and Satan's power in the New Testament
The Israelites are "baptized" (1 Cor 10:2) as God's chosen people through the waters of the Red Sea.	Jesus makes repentant, believing sinners his own through holy baptism—the "washing of water in connection with the Word" (Eph 5:26).	Water as a means of being united with God and his redemptive work

17. See T. Levi 4:1.

18. Corresponding to Exod 10:21–23.

19. See Joel 2:1–2; Amos 5:20; Wis 17:21; Matt 8:12; 24:29; 2 Pet 2:17; Rev 8:12.

20. This is another example of John's tightly weaving exodus typology or prophetic foreshadowing into the literary fabric of his prophetic oracle.

The Lord as Israel's Kinsman-Redeemer[20]		
Old Testament (First Exodus)	**New Testament (New Exodus)**	**Key Parallels and Fulfillment**
The Lord assumes the role of kinsman-redeemer (rescuer and restorer) for Israel.	Jesus assumes the role of kinsman-redeemer by taking on human nature to rescue and restore believers.	Both act as Rescuer and Restorer of God's people.
The sacrificed lives of Egypt's firstborn males signifies the ultimate cost of Israel's release from slavery.	Jesus' life and death are the redemption price / ransom paid to secure the freedom of believers.	The death of the first-born in Egypt (along with the sacrifice and shed blood of the Pass-over lamb) prefigures Christ's atoning death at Calvary.

THE SIXTH BOWL JUDGMENT: THE BATTLE OF ARMAGEDDON (16:12–16)

In the unfolding cosmic drama, John witnesses the "sixth angel" (v. 12) unleash his "bowl" on the famed "Euphrates." This divinely ordained calamity includes drying up all the "water" the river contains so that the armies commanded by the monarchs located "east" of the Promised Land are unhindered in their brazen march westward.[21]

In Bible times, the regions located north and east of Israel were viewed as the locale where the nation's despised enemies arose.[22] Likewise, those areas were where the Romans' dreaded adversary, the Parthians, originated. Indeed, according to the myth of Nero *redivivus* (or revived),[23] the former ruler (now restored to life) would use a throng of Parthian combatants to invade and seize control of the empire.[24] It is fitting, then, in the apostle's prophetic oracle, for antagonistic hordes to emerge from this region. Nonetheless, specialists debate whether the envisioned scenario should be understood literally or symbolically.

Next, John witnesses a trio of "unclean spirits" (v. 13), which resemble "frogs," come from the mouths of the "dragon" (Satan), the sea-beast,

21. See Exod 14:21–22; Josh 3:13–17; 4:23; Isa 11:15; 44:27–28; 50:2; 51:10; Jer 50:38; 51:36; Zeph 3:8; Zech 10:11.

22. Including Assyria and Babylon.

23. A legend in the first century AD.

24. See 1 En. 56:5; Sib. Or. 4:138–39.

and the land-beast (or "false prophet").[25] The ancient Hebrews regarded loud, croaking "frogs" to be unclean, detestable creatures.[26] The hideous image points to the demonic nature of what the apostle sees. Specifically, the unholy, malevolent triad dispatches a legion of evil "spirits" (v. 14) on the monarchs of earth's inhabitants. Through the use of miraculous signs, the throng of diabolical entities lures scores of people across the globe to amass their "armies" (v. 16) for a climactic, epic "battle" (v. 14) against the Creator.[27]

The above encounter will occur on the momentous "day" of judgment previously decreed by "Almighty God."[28] John discloses that "Armageddon" is the name where the confrontation unfolds. The Hebrew form is "Har Megiddo," which means "Hill (or Mount) of Megiddo." It was the route people often used to travel through the plain of Esdraelon (or Jezreel Valley) in northern Israel. This location was also the scene where numerous battles were waged during the Old Testament era.[29]

As noted previously in 14:20, specialists debate whether this dramatic challenge to God's rule, along with the geographical reference in 16:16, should be understood literally or symbolically. Regardless of which option is preferred, there is a somber tone to John's prophetic oracle, as emphasized in verse 15. The apostle records the Lamb's declaration that he will suddenly and unexpectedly return "like a thief."[30]

Verse 15 includes the third of seven beatitudes (or pronouncements of covenantal blessing).[31] Here, the Lamb commends those among his followers who remain vigilant against the wiles of Satan and his demonic cohort. Jesus uses graphic imagery to stress his point. He directs believers to remain clothed in his righteousness,[32] rather than exposing themselves to and soiling themselves with the shameful deeds of darkness.[33]

25. Corresponding to Exod 8:1–15; Pss 78:45; 105:30.

26. See Lev 11:9–12, 41–47.

27. See Deut 13:1–2; Jer 14:14; Lam 2:14; Joel 2:11; 3:2; Matt 7:15; 2 Pet 2:1; 1 John 4:1–3.

28. See our discussion of Rev 1:8; 4:8; 11:17; 15:3; 16:7; 19:6, 15; 21:22.

29. See Judg 5:19–21; 2 Kgs 9:27; 23:29–30; 2 Chr 35:22; Zech 12:11.

30. See Matt 24:42–44; Luke 12:39–40; 1 Thess 5:2–4; 2 Pet 3:10; Rev 3:3.

31. See Rev 1:3; 14:13; 19:9; 20:6; 22:7, 14.

32. Which the Son graciously provides by faith through the means of grace; see Acts 2:38; Gal 3:27; Eph 5:26; Col 2:12; 3:10.

33. Including the temptation to venerate mortal, flawed, human rulers, such as those represented by the emperors of Rome.

Roman Imperial Ideologies	Scripture's Countercultural Message
Religious syncretism (or the merging of differing religious beliefs into one system) holds sway. All religious pathways lead to an idyllic afterlife, and no single group has the right to an exclusive claim on truth.	There is only one God, who is the Creator; and there is only one Lord, Jesus Christ, who is the Architect of the universe and the Author of life. Moreover, only through faith in the Son does anyone have access to the Father in heaven (Rom 5:1–2; 1 Cor 8:6; Eph 4:4–6).
The emperor, Augustus (whose name means "the exalted one"), is "son of the deified" (in Latin, *divi filius*) and "son of god" (in Latin, *dei filius*; that is, the adopted son of Caesar, who himself is a god).	Jesus, the messianic "seed of David," is the true "Son of God" (Rom 1:3–4; 2 Cor 1:19; Gal 2:20; Eph 4:13).
The emperor is the "Savior" and supreme ruler of the world.	Jesus is the one and only Savior of the world and the exalted Lord of the cosmos (Phil 2:9–11; 3:20; Col 2:9–10).
The emperor is to be worshiped.	Only the God of Israel is to be worshiped. All other objects of veneration constitute idolatry (1 Cor 8:4–6; Gal 4:8–11; 1 Thess 1:9–10).
The pantheon of gods and goddesses favors Rome and brings the world under Rome's control.	The Father is bringing the entire created order and the whole of history under the control of his Son (1 Cor 15:23–28; Eph 1:20–23; Phil 3:20–21; Col 1:15–20).
The Roman Empire is sovereign, a reality decreed by the chief deity, Jupiter, and actualized for endless ages to come by the three female personifications of destiny, the Fates.	Only the God of Israel is sovereign and eternal. All other claimants to sovereignty will be eliminated, and all the nations will become obedient to the Son's unending reign (see Rom 1:5; 15:12; 16:26). Accordingly, people are summoned to repent and become citizens of God's kingdom (Col 1:13; 1 Thess 2:12; 2 Thess 1:5).
The birth of a miraculous child named Augustus inaugurates a new era. It is a golden age in which Rome transforms society into a utopia characterized by universal justice and peace.	The entire universe languishes under the curse of physical decay and moral chaos. Only Jesus' life, death, and resurrection inaugurate a new era of righteousness and reconciliation between sinful humans and the justifying God (Rom 5:9–11; 8:18–23; 2 Cor 5:17–21).

Roman Imperial Ideologies	Scripture's Countercultural Message
The Roman Empire is the guarantor of tranquility, affluence, and security throughout the world.	The Messiah's atoning sacrifice at Calvary is the only basis for true harmony and everlasting blessing for redeemed humanity (Rom 15:33; 16:20; Phil 4:9; 1 Thess 5:23; 2 Thess 3:16).
The new era involves unification of the nations under the emperor's rule.	The Son brings together the nations within his spiritual body, the church (1 Cor 12:13; Gal 3:28; Eph 2:14–18; Col 3:11).
Crucifixion is one means the Roman government uses to eliminate any miscreants who threaten the imperial vision for a perfect society.	The Father raises his crucified Son from the dead and, in doing so, overturns the unjust verdict rendered by the potentates of the world (1 Cor 2:6–9).
Rome's cultural heroes are renowned for their wealth, fame, and power, which they seize by brazen self-interest, ruthless competition, and savage violence.	Jesus' followers live in ways that are cruciform in nature. Indeed, the cross is the premier expression of God's power and wisdom, both during the present age and for all eternity (Rom 6:3–8; 1 Cor 1:18–25; 2 Cor 4:10; Gal 2:20; 5:22–26; 6:14; Phil 2:1–8; 3:10; Col 2:11–12, 20).

THE SEVENTH BOWL JUDGMENT: WIDESPREAD DESTRUCTION (16:17–21)

At last, in the unfolding cosmic drama, the "seventh angel" (v. 17) empties his "bowl" into the atmosphere. Next, John hears a "loud voice" shout from the throne of God's "temple"[34] that the cycle of divine judgments (or covenantal curses) is "done."[35] Though the actual terminus does not appear until 21:6, it is anticipated and announced in 16:17. This is not problematic, for the progression of events in John's prophetic oracle is best understood as being primarily a *literary*, not a *chronological*, movement.

In imagery reminiscent of the Israelites' encounter with the Lord at Mount Sinai,[36] the seventh scourge is accompanied by a series of terrifying storm phenomena, including "flashes of lightning" (v. 18), explosive

34. Or inner sanctuary.

35. Or finished, ended.

36. See Exod 19:16–18; 20:18–19; LAB 11:5; Heb 12:18; Rev 4:5; 8:5; 10:3; 11:19.

sounds, and crashes of "thunder." Moreover, a historically monumental "earthquake" of unparalleled enormity convulses the entire planet.

The result is that the notorious, sprawling metropolis called "Babylon" (v. 19)[37] is divided into "three" separate sections.[38] Simultaneously, all cities in every nation are reduced to rubble. Together these calamitous events signal to pagan, idolatrous humanity that the Creator remains sovereign and righteous in judging the planet. Indeed, he forces the heathen world system, along with its rulers and subjects, to ingest the "wine cup" overflowing with his "fierce wrath."[39]

Next, John witnesses the vanishing of all earth's islands and the leveling of all the "mountains" (v. 20) throughout the globe.[40] Just as horrendous is the pummeling of humanity with "massive," one-hundred-pound "hailstones" from the "sky" (v. 21).[41] Yet despite experiencing a divinely sanctioned scourge, pagan, idolatrous humanity once again refuses to repent. Instead, they curse and slander the Creator, to whom they owe their existence and wellbeing.

The widespread ruination unleashed by the seventh bowl[42] signifies the utter failure of humanity's insurrection against the Lord. There can be no doubt that he reigns supreme even over those—whether human or demonic—who unite in rebellion against him, even as they experience his retributive justice.

Comparison of Egyptian Plagues and Revelation Judgments[43]		
Egyptian Plagues	**Trumpet Judgments**	**Bowl Judgments**
1st Plague: Nile water turns to blood; fish die (Exod 7:20–21).	*2nd Trumpet:* Flaming mountain falls into the sea; one-third of sea turns to blood; one-third of sea creatures die (Rev 8:8–9).	*2nd Bowl:* Poured on the sea; it turns to blood and all sea life dies (Rev 16:3).

37. Whether Jerusalem, Rome, or some other notorious city.

38. Indicating that the metropolis is completely wiped out.

39. Like a goblet filled with poison; see Rev 6:16, 17; 11:18; 14:10, 19; 15:1, 7; 16:1; 19:15.

40. See As. Mos. 10:4; 1 En. 1:6.

41. Frozen boulders literally "weighing a talent"; see Exod 9:22–25; Josh 10:11; Ezek 38:18–22; Rev 8:7; 11:19.

42. Comparable to a cosmic de-creation event.

43. This is another example of exodus typology or prophetic foreshadowing tightly woven into the literary fabric of John's prophetic oracle. Table adapted from information presented in Koester, *Revelation*, 444.

Comparison of Egyptian Plagues and Revelation Judgments[43]		
Egyptian Plagues	**Trumpet Judgments**	**Bowl Judgments**
1st Plague: Nile water turns to blood; fish die (Exod 7:20–21).	*3rd Trumpet:* Huge, blazing star ("Wormwood") falls on rivers and springs; waters become bitter (Rev 8:10–11).	*3rd Bowl:* Poured on rivers and springs; they turn to blood (Rev 16:4).
2nd Plague: Frogs invade the land (Exod 8:1–15).		*6th Bowl:* Poured on the Euphrates; river dries up; frog-like demonic spirits emerge (Rev 16:12–14).
6th Plague: Fine dust becomes festering boils on people and animals (Exod 9:8–12).		*1st Bowl:* Poured on the land; painful sores afflict those who have the beast's mark and who venerate his image (Rev 16:2).
7th Plague: Thunder, hail, lightning fall throughout Egypt (Exod 9:13–35)	*7th Trumpet:* Lightning, thunder, earthquake, and hail (Rev 11:15–19)	*7th Bowl:* Poured into the air; lightning, thunder, massive earthquake, and giant hailstones (Rev 16:17–18)
8th Plague: Swarm of locusts devour the land (Exod 10:1–20).	*5th Trumpet:* Abyss opens; smoke darkens sky; demonic locusts torment people (Rev 9:1–12).	
9th Plague: Thick darkness covers Egypt (Exod 10:21–29).	*4th Trumpet:* Sun, moon, and stars struck; one-third of their light darkens (Rev 8:12).	*5th Bowl:* Poured on the beast's throne; darkness and agony produced (Rev 16:10–11)
	1st Trumpet: Hail and fire mixed with blood fell on the land; one-third of the earth and trees burned up; all the verdant grass incinerated (Rev 8:7)	*4th Bowl:* Poured on the sun; people scorched with severe heat (Rev 16:8–9)
	6th Trumpet: Four angels released at the Euphrates River to kill one-third of mankind (Rev 9:13–19)	

KEY THEOLOGICAL INSIGHTS

In Revelation 15, we considered the scene in heaven during the preparation for the release of the seven bowl judgments. Now, in chapter 16, we see these judgments dispensed on the earth and its wicked inhabitants. From the unleashing of these covenantal curses, we gain insight into God's righteous judgment, the entrenched depravity of unbelieving humankind, and the promise of the Lamb's triumphant return.

First, we see that *God remains just and true in his judgments, regardless of how they may appear to us*. In this chapter, we encounter a furthering of the theodicy of the Apocalypse.[44] Our natural ideas of what is fair for a loving, forgiving God to do must be replaced with the declarations of the angels and the altar's (personified) praising of the Creator for the retribution he brings (vv. 5–7). In verse 6, we see the declaration that those suffering under the horrific judgment of the seven bowls are getting what they deserve.[45] Perhaps it seems excessive to our modern sensibilities that God would initiate such widespread destruction and devastation, both upon people and on the earth. Yet in emptying the seven bowls, the justification of the Lord's mighty hand of judgment comes to its fullest expression: the wicked are indeed deserving of these calamities.[46] They have brought this dire outcome upon themselves, and God is just in his righteous judgment.[47]

Second, we see that *God's enemies, left to the consequences of their sinful choices, are spiritually bankrupt, morally depraved, and persistent in their rebellion against the Creator*. Three times in this chapter we find that when the bowl judgments are unleashed, the recipients of the covenantal curses fail to repent and give glory to God (vv. 9, 11, 21). The implication is that perhaps because of the Lord's great mercy, he will listen to their

44. To reiterate what we previously noted, theodicy grapples with the question of how the existence of evil in the world can be reconciled with the idea of an all-good and all-powerful God.

45. In particular, the reason earth's wicked inhabitants deserve such awful punishment is because they slaughter God's reborn children ("poured out the blood of the saints and prophets"; Rev 16:6).

46. Kistemaker, *Exposition of Revelation*, 442, adds that the primary reason why the wicked are getting their "just deserts" is because they refuse to repent. The implication is that while God may have been willing to respond graciously to a last-minute cry for forgiveness, the stubbornness of the wicked renders God's judgment appropriate and necessary.

47. The theodicy of ch. 16 continues into chs. 18 and 19, specifically concerning the destruction of Babylon, as well as the sea-beast and land-beast.

cries of repentance and extend forgiveness and redemption.[48] Nonetheless, the wicked prefer to spend their last breaths slandering the Creator and turning their backs on him as the sovereign Monarch of the universe. And therefore, not only do wicked people get what they deserve, but they also are implicitly granted what they wish.[49] By failing to forsake their sinfulness by repenting of their wickedness and to glorify God, the unrighteous turn an opportunity for grace into a demonstration of their commitment to self-destruction. This reality strengthens the theodicy already set forth in this chapter, assuring us that the Lord is justified in his righteous judgments.[50]

Third, *we have the Messiah's promise to return, which offers assurance of victory for the saints and defeat for the wicked.* In verse 15, we encounter the third of seven declarations of covenantal blessings in Revelation. This beatitude is directed toward the faithful, and it assures God's favor on those who are ready, prepared, and watchful for Jesus' second advent. The certitude of Christ's return is one of the most agreed-upon points of eschatology amid numerous perspectives on end-time events.[51] Christians across all ages and from varied denominational perspectives affirm the literal, bodily return of Christ to the earth to carry out his judgment and rescue his reborn children. We look forward to the day when the victorious Lamb comes back to make all things right and new.[52] Related to the blessedness of this expectation is the implicit warning to those who luxuriate in unbelief (v. 15). While they continue to deny the Messiah's return, it is certain to happen in surprising fashion like a thief.[53]

IMPORTANT MINISTRY IMPLICATIONS

The above theological insights offer helpful considerations for those ministering in local church contexts. As we lead our parishioners through the difficulties of this present age, we can offer both reassurances and

48. See 1 Tim 2:4; 2 Pet 3:9; Rev 2:21.

49. Obviously, the wicked do not enjoy the pain and suffering they experience. Yet from their adamant refusal to repent, they are at least passively choosing damnation over grace. Consequently, God allows their choice to stand, and the condemnation proceeds.

50. See our discussion of Rev 15:3–4.

51. Such as opposing views about the rapture, the tribulation period, the meaning and duration of the millennial kingdom, the nature of heaven and hell, and more.

52. See our discussion of Rev 21:5.

53. See Matt 24:43; 1 Thess 5:2–3; 2 Pet 3:10.

warnings about what is coming at the end of the age. Revelation 16 helps to crystallize the blessed eternal future that awaits the saints, in stark contrast to the unending fate of those who ultimately reject the Messiah.

First, *believers need not worry about whether God's dispensing of justice is right.* We can comfort our parishioners with an assurance that the time of final judgment is an exhibition of the Creator's glorious holiness and grace to Jesus' faithful followers, rather than an uncontrolled, arbitrary outpouring of vengeance. As we previously mentioned, the voice which affirms the truth and justice of the Lord's judgments (v. 7) emanates from the celestial "altar." Here, we encounter the symbolic representation of the prayers of the saints, especially as depicted by the rising "incense."[54] While unbelievers regularly challenge Christians with accusations that God's judgment is inconsistent with his love, we can take solace in the fact that his decrees are in keeping with his holy character and consistently displayed from the beginning. Additionally, we find reassurance in his gracious consideration of the faithful and in his responses to their prayers.

Second, *we must caution our parishioners against unrepentant sinfulness and rebellion against the Creator.* Within this chapter, we see the absurdity of sinful humanity and their stubborn refusal to be brought to forgiveness through repentance. While the focus here is on unbelievers, there is a warning for believers as well. Congregational leaders must regularly preach and teach against sin and encourage our congregants to pursue the path of holiness.[55] As we have seen previously, sin renders people irrational, and even believers can still choose to behave in accordance with who they once *were* without Christ, rather than who they now *are* in union with him. The consequences of sin are foolishness, an absurd denial of truth, and ultimately everlasting destruction.[56] God commissions us to caution those under our pastoral care to steer clear of this ruinous course of thinking and behavior, regularly confess their sinfulness, and seek cleansing forgiveness from him.[57]

Third, *we are expected to warn and encourage our parishioners to be prepared for the return of the King.* Jesus is coming again! This glorious truth must have forceful impact on how we think, feel, and act. Within our local churches, we have an opportunity to equip and prepare congregants

54. See our discussion of Rev 5:8; 6:9–10; 8:3–5.

55. See Lev 11:44; 19:2; Matt 5:48; 1 Pet 1:15–16.

56. See Jas 1:14–15.

57. See 1 John 1:8–10.

for the second advent. Anticipating the Messiah's coming with power and glory, in which he vindicates his loyal followers and sets everything right, is a truly blessed prospect, especially for those who have endured suffering in the name of the gospel.[58] In contrast, for others, even in the context of the church, the notion of Jesus' return is frightful. Many fear that when Christ comes back, he will be angry and ready to punish everyone and everything he finds displeasing. While it is true that our Lord's return occurs within the context of judgment, it is also a point of blessedness for those who are found to be faithful.[59] Our parishioners need not dread Jesus' return, for he comes to rescue his disciples powerfully. We can encourage our congregants toward the faithfulness and fruitfulness that inevitably lead to rejoicing at the time of the Son's appearing.

VITAL MISSIONAL RAMIFICATIONS

In Revelation 15, we saw the inevitable success of missions, given that those who experience victory over the sea-beast and his idolatrous image represent all nations. Their victorious song of worship is instructive to our own thinking on missional activity. Now, in chapter 16, we encounter the opposite, as the perspective shifts from the triumphant ones in heaven who celebrate God's vindication of the saints to the wicked who persist in unbelief and rebellion. Within this account, the following points of missional application are noteworthy.

First, *we can expect many people to resist God's message of salvation persistently.* As we noted above, this chapter gives us insight into the depth of humankind's depravity and utter refusal to repent and believe. The implication for missions is that despite our best efforts, and regardless of the Father's gracious offer of the Son, along with the convicting ministry of the sevenfold Spirit, there remain some who staunchly reject the gospel to the end of their days.[60] They would rather be eternally doomed than admit the error of their ways and turn from sin and self. This sobering truth must not discourage our missional activity, for the Messiah indeed promises the success of missions. Yet he also warns about the resistance of those who do not and will not believe. Their opposition

58. See our previous declaration of covenantal blessing in Rev 14:13 where, in view of God's final judgments, those who have died "in the Lord" are the object of his favor and invited to rest from their labors.

59. See Titus 2:11–14.

60. See Gen 6:10; John 15:8–10.

arises regardless of how articulate we are, how skilled we are in apologetic discourse, or how passionately we communicate the gospel. Those who reject the good news will see the light only through the regenerating work of the Spirit, and we must pray that they do so.[61]

Second, *the deception that causes resistance to our missional efforts has and will encompass the entire globe.* The demonic forces within and behind the unholy trinity of the dragon (the devil), the sea-beast (the antichrist), and the land-beast (the false prophet) incentivize rejection of the gospel, along with confrontational aggression against the Messiah. Satan's wicked miscreants gather opposition to God from the whole world and are ultimately successful at assembling an army to fight the forces of the King of kings (v. 16).[62] The deception coordinated by the dragon and his sycophants reaches all nations. Countries in the Global North are not immune to the deception just because they supposedly are Christianized. Also, nations in the Majority World are equally susceptible to this deception. While they have avoided some of the pagan influences of the West, they embrace their own set of false teachings and beliefs that have infiltrated their communities and peoples. It should never surprise us that demonic deception works unceasingly to undermine our missional efforts in all parts of the globe.

Third, missionary proclamation offers the lost an opportunity to receive salvation and be reconciled to God, thereby escaping his righteous judgment. As we previously noted, part of the message of redemption to the lost is a warning of coming judgment. Just as the deception we mentioned above is worldwide, so too is God's coming judgment upon earth's wicked inhabitants. In our missional efforts, we have the wonderful privilege to communicate saving hope amid this warning.[63] We urge the lost to repent and believe, to be spared from the outpouring of the Creator's wrath. The gospel we proclaim is a message of deliverance. It is a tremendous blessing to be chosen by God for this rescue mission and to serve as messengers of the good news. After all, the Spirit can use our sharing of the gospel to save others from eternal ruin, especially as the day of judgment approaches. We should acknowledge this privilege and, with humility, spread the wonderful truth in obedience to God's call for us to fulfill our missional task.

61. See 1 Cor 1:18—2:16. Paul's long discourse demonstrates that it is only through the Spirit's convicting and enlightening intervention that unbelievers move from seeing the gospel as foolishness to experiencing its saving power in their lives.

62. See our discussion of Rev 19:19; 20:7–9.

63. See 2 Cor 5:11–21; 1 Thess 5:9–11.

Revelation 17

The Fall of Babylon (Part One)

LEARNING OBJECTIVES

- Clarify your understanding of the brazen prostitute, the scarlet beast with seven heads and ten horns, and the coalition of rulers.
- Explain the meaning behind the harlot who sits on the scarlet beast.
- Identify the ways in which the prostitute mistreats Jesus' loyal followers.
- State the interpretation you favor for the mystery of the harlot, the scarlet beast, and the coalition of rulers.
- Understand how the demise of the prostitute, the scarlet beast, and the coalition of rulers fulfills what God has decreed.

CHAPTER SUMMARY

Revelation 17 describes John's vision of a great prostitute who sits on a scarlet beast. The harlot dons attire that is purple and crimson, wears a golden crown, holds a goblet full of abominations and impurities, and is drunk from the blood of martyred saints. The prostitute represents the great city that rules over earth's rulers and leads them into immorality. Eventually, the scarlet beast turns against the prostitute and destroys her. In turn, the Lamb destroys the ogre and its coalition of monarchs.

STUDY QUESTIONS

1. What is the nature of the relationship between the prostitute and the scarlet beast?
2. What are the atrocities the harlot commits?
3. Why does the prostitute bring about the demise of Jesus' followers?
4. What is your understanding of the scarlet beast's seven heads and ten horns?
5. How can believers remain faithful to the Messiah in a world that seems increasingly hostile to Christianity?

CHAPTER OUTLINE

- The vision of the idolatrous harlot (17:1–6a)
- The significance of the vision (17:6b–18)
- Key theological insights
- Important ministry implications
- Vital missional ramifications

THE VISION OF THE IDOLATROUS HARLOT (17:1–6A)

Chapters 15 and 16 dealt with the final series of judgments (or covenantal curses) the Creator will bring on earth's wicked inhabitants. As previously noted, all three judgment cycles are presented in the form of a cosmic trial, in which John's prophetic oracle demonstrates the validity of God's decree to punish the pagan, idolatrous world system thoroughly. Chapters 17 and 18 function as an interlude to advance the narrative by vividly portraying the depraved, evil character of civilized humanity apart from the Lord. The unfolding cosmic drama reinforces the truth that the supreme Monarch of the universe is fully just in condemning and judging those who live in rebellion against him.[1]

1. Including the veneration of mortal, flawed, human rulers. The depiction of Babylon in Rev 17–18 as a corrupt, idolatrous city which persecutes God's people exemplifies John's polemical theology. Through confrontational rhetoric, the apostle upholds the truth of the gospel, condemns false worship and oppressive power, and asserts the supremacy of God's kingdom. By framing the conflict as a cosmic battle, John's prophetic oracle exhorts believers to resist temptation and remain faithful to

John begins by noting that one of the "seven angels" (17:1), who previously emptied his bowl judgment, invites the apostle to venture forth, witness, and report on what the celestial emissary discloses. Specifically, John learns that the Creator is bringing retributive justice against the sacrilegious, bloodthirsty harlot, who sits on "many waters." This phrase denotes the tumult and devastation connected with earth's wicked inhabitants.[2]

Verse 18 discloses that this hideous predator symbolizes a notorious "city" that exercises sovereignty and power over earth's monarchs. Furthermore, verse 15 reveals that the "waters" upon which the "prostitute" sits represent masses of people from all ethnicities, "nations," and "languages." The preceding information indicates that the harlot's influence over the evil world system is pervasive. The term rendered "prostitute" (v. 1) denotes not only religious apostasy but also the corrupt, idolatrous ways of supposedly enlightened, progressive, and civilized humanity. In John's day, Babylon, Tyre, Edom, Rome, and Jerusalem—as well as the nations they symbolized—were centers of heathen beliefs, sexual depravity, and commercial exploitation.[3]

Verse 2 discloses that earth's rulers practice "sexual immorality" with the harlot. Meanwhile, people around the globe become intoxicated by ingesting the "wine" of the prostitute's brazen ways.[4] Indeed, domination, decadence, and debauchery are the heathen deities the ogre promotes.[5] According to verse 3, John remains under the control of the Spirit throughout the apostle's trancelike, visionary experience in the "wilderness" (or desert).

One option is that the above locale provides the desolate backdrop for God's judgment to occur.[6] A second possibility is that, as in 12:6

God rather than capitulate to the forces of darkness. For extensive analyses of how the Apocalypse critiques Roman imperial ideology—including its claims to divine authority and oppressive structures, see Bauckham, *Theology of Revelation*; Friesen, *Imperial Cults*; Gorman, *Reading Revelation Responsibly*; Koester, *Revelation*.

2. See Pss 29:3; 93:4; 144:7; Isa 8:6–8; 17:12–14; 23:10; Jer 46:7; 47:2; 51:13, 55; Ezek 29:10.

3. See Lev 17:7; 20:5–6; Num 14:33; 15:39; Deut 31:16; Isa 1:21; 23:15–17; Jer 2:20; 3:1–3, 6–10; 13:27; Ezek 16:15–22; 23:1–49; Hos 1:2; 2:4; 4:10, 12–13, 18; 5:3–4; 6:10; 9:1; Nah 3:4.

4. As we previously noted, throughout the Apocalypse, an emphasis is placed on earth's unregenerate inhabitants, who venerate pagan deities; see our discussion of Rev 3:10; 6:10; 8:13; 11:10; 13:8, 12, 14; 14:6; 17:8.

5. See Jer 51:7.

6. See Isa 13:21; 21:1–10; 50:12; 51:43; Tob 8:3.

and 14, here the "wilderness" (17:3) represents a spiritual place of deliverance. A third option is that the desert region symbolizes a place of refuge that is detached from the pagan, idolatrous influences of the world.

Wilderness as a Symbol		
Theme	**Biblical References**	**Description**
Place of Provision and Anticipation	Matt 15:32–39; Mark 8:1–9	In a desolate region, Jesus miraculously feeds thousands, echoing God's provision of manna and foreshadowing messianic abundance and divine care.
Place of Restoration and Hope	Hos 2:14–15	God leads Israel into the wilderness for renewal, transforming it into a place of tenderness and hope, rather than punishment.
Place of Spiritual Testing and Triumph	Matt 4:1–11; Mark 1:12–13; Luke 4:1–13	Jesus is led by the Spirit into the wilderness to face temptation. Jesus' victory over the devil in this barren place symbolizes triumph over evil and affirms Jesus' divine nature.
Place of Threat and Fear	Isa 34:13–14	The wilderness embodies desolation, inhabited by wild animals and demons, symbolizing chaos and spiritual/physical danger.
Place of Wandering and Judgment	Deut 29:5; 32:15–18; Ps 107:4–6; Jer 2:6	The wilderness represents a terrifying, lifeless place, symbolizing the consequences of Israel's unbelief and disobedience. Despite the people's wandering, God provides manna and preserves their clothing, highlighting his care amid judgment.

In any case, the apostle uses his unique vantage point to witness the unfolding cosmic drama. This includes the sight of a "woman" who sits astride a "scarlet" (or crimson) "beast" to control it, perhaps through religious, political, and economic means. This appalling creature has "seven heads," along with "ten horns." Also, pejorative "names" are written all over the beast's body[7] and are used profanely against the Creator.

The "beast" is the same hydra-headed brute that, according to 13:1, emerged from the chaotic and unruly "sea." It remains unclear whether this entity is a person or nonhuman entity. In either case, the homicidal

7. Such as "Lord," "God," "Savior," and so on.

ogre is evil—opposing the Creator and determining to liquidate his reborn children.

The attire worn by the "woman" (17:4) is both stunning and bloodcurdling in appearance. Though she is lavishly adorned, she is repulsive in character. Specifically, the entity's raiment is "purple" (bluish red) and "scarlet" (crimson), embellished with "gold," "precious stones," and "pearls." All of these are symbols of opulence and royalty.[8] Moreover, this ostentatious creature holds a "gold" vessel that promises to supply an especially satisfying brew. Yet the chalice overflows with idolatrous "abominations" and the "filth" produced by her "sexual immorality."

The seemingly cryptic "name" (v. 5) emblazoned on the woman's "forehead"[9] gives further evidence of her particularly degenerate nature. She openly claims to be the renowned metropolis of "Babylon," along with the "mother" of all "prostitutes" and the detestable perversions in which earth's inhabitants luxuriate. It is best not to limit the application of verse 5 to any historical city, such as either Babylon or Rome. Instead, the woman most likely represents all forms of satanic deception, exploitation, rebellion, harlotries, and idolatries throughout history. This fountainhead of evil is responsible for the slaughter of countless believers. In fact, the woman is habitually intoxicated with the "blood" (v. 6) of God's holy people (the "saints"), including those who are martyred for their faithful witness to Jesus of Nazareth.[10]

THE SIGNIFICANCE OF THE VISION (17:6B–18)

As the cosmic drama unfolds, it is not difficult to imagine John's feeling alarmed and bewildered while he stares in astonishment at the obscene prostitute and the sea-beast (v. 6).[11] The Creator uses the "angel" mentioned in verse 1 to interpret the vision for the apostle.[12] The celestial emissary begins by affirming that there is a sense of intrigue and

8. Note the comparable description in Rev 18:16; see Judg 8:26; Esth 8:15; Dan 5:7.

9. Such as would be engraved around a diadem-like headpiece.

10. See Isa 34:5, 7; 49:26; 51:21; Jer 46:10; Ezek 39:18–19; Jdt 6:4; Rev 14:8; 16:19; 18:24. Also, see the discussion in our Introduction about Babylon as a symbol of evil and a fitting image of an idolatrous society, along with the table in our discussion of Rev 14, where we present three different views concerning the identity of "Babylon."

11. Literally "I marveled a great marvel."

12. See Dan 2:18–19, 28–30, 47; 4:9, 19; 7:15; 8:15–16.

"mystery" (v. 7) surrounding the harlot, as well as the predatory creature upon which the "woman" rides. The "angel" reiterates that the "beast" has "seven heads," along with "ten horns."

This ogre once lived but is now dead (v. 8). Also, the "beast" will emerge from the abyss,[13] reappear to pagan, idolatrous humanity, and then be banished to the Lake of Fire, where the brute will experience eternal ruin. On one level, the preceding information possibly recalls the first-century-AD Nero *redivivus* (or revived) myth that the deceased emperor would come back to life, lead a rebellious force of Parthians from the east, and return to power. On another, more significant level, verse 8 indicates that the "beast" tries to counterfeit the Messiah's death, burial, and resurrection.[14]

Similarly, the Greek phrase rendered "he existed, is no more, and he is about to come," is a parody on the divine name in 1:4. There the eternal Creator is referred to as the One "who is, who was, and who is coming."[15] Furthermore, though evil in the world might subside for a while, it always reappears. Throughout the long arc of human history and with each successive generation, new demonically inspired governments and leaders have arisen to oppose the Creator and persecute his reborn children.[16]

Next, the celestial emissary discloses to John that the hydra-headed "beast" (17:8) will captivate and deceive earth's unsaved inhabitants.[17] None of their "names" appear in the heavenly ledger containing those of Jesus' followers, a list that existed prior to the "creation of the world."[18] As chapter 13 revealed, the sea-beast's lieutenant will marshal the predatory brute's authority to compel the world to prostrate in homage to him. Indeed, the land-beast will use trickery and intimidation to force everyone across the planet to obey the sea-beast.

13. Or well-like, bottomless pit.

14. See our discussion of Rev 1:18; 2:8; 13:3, 12, 14.

15. See our discussion of Rev 1:8; 4:8.

16. See Dan 7:19, 21, 25.

17. As we previously noted, throughout the Apocalypse, an emphasis is placed on earth's unregenerate inhabitants, who venerate pagan deities. See our discussion of Rev 3:10; 6:10; 8:13; 11:10; 13:8, 12, 14; 14:6; 17:8.

18. See Exod 32:32–34; Ps 69:28; Isa 4:3; Dan 12:1; Mal 3:16; Apoc. Zeph. 3:7; 9:2; 2 Bar. 24:1; 1 En. 47:3; 89:68; 108:3; 2 En. 52:15; 3 En. 18:24; Jos. Asen. 15:4; Jub. 30:20, 22; 36:10; 104:1; Luke 10:20; Heb 12:23; Phil 4:3; Rev 3:5; 13:8; 20:12, 15; 21:27.

The angel, wanting John to have Spirit-provided insight and discernment about the significance of the vision,[19] explains that the "seven heads" (17:9) on which the harlot sits represent "seven hills." Because Rome was originally built on seven hills,[20] it is likely that the apostle and his earliest readers would have associated the celestial emissary's words with this notorious city. In the first century AD, the city, empire, and ruler of Rome were the embodiment of civilized, pagan, idolatrous humanity, especially in their rebellion against the Creator and display of hostility toward his reborn children. Similarly, other cities, nations, and rulers at additional times throughout history would embody humanity's opposition to God and persecution of the redeemed.

The angel explains that the "seven heads" of the sea-beast also represent "seven kings," which the prostitute evidently dominates, especially given the fact that she is depicted as sitting upon (or controlling) these monarchs. At the time represented by the vision, "five" (v. 10) of the rulers are dead, the sixth one is alive, and the seventh one has not yet arisen to power. Yet when the seventh monarch assumes ruling authority, he will do so for only a short while before being replaced by the sea-beast. Though this ogre was once alive and then died, he will reappear as the "eighth king" (v. 11). Then, like the preceding seven monarchs, this one is headed for "destruction." This is a reference to unending misery in the eternal Lake of Fire.

Some specialists think that the celestial emissary is referring to a *strict* succession of Roman emperors, and these interpreters have attempted to match lists of first-century rulers of Rome with John's vision. Yet the subjectivity of this approach and the lack of agreement among its adherents have led other specialists to consider alternative options. For example, some think that the "seven kings" (v. 9) are a *selective* list of Roman emperors or world empires. Others suggest that the monarchs represent all anti-God and anti-Christian governments throughout history. Still others, by taking note of the symbolic way in which John uses numbers in his prophetic oracle, maintain that the "seven heads" signify the saturation of evil and blasphemy within the pagan, idolatrous world system.[21]

19. See our discussion of Rev 13:18.

20. Namely, Capitoline, Aventine, Caelian, Esquiline, Quirinal, Viminal, and Palatine; see Apoc. Dan. 7:2, 5; 1 En. 21:3; 24:2.

21. For a detailed explanation of Rev 17:9–10, see Aune, *Revelation 17–22*, 941–50; Brighton, *Revelation*, 447–50; Schreiner, *Revelation*, 583–88.

Regardless of which view is preferred, throughout history, unregenerate humanity has been in rebellion against the Creator. Likewise, since the fall of Adam and Eve in the primordial garden, the wicked have mistreated God's children. At the end of the age, humanity's opposition against the Lord Jesus and their hatred of his followers will intensify. Then, at the second advent, the Messiah will overthrow the wicked, triumph over evil, and vindicate the redeemed.[22]

The angel discloses to John that the "ten horns" (v. 12) of the sea-beast represented "ten kings" who had not yet risen to power.[23] For a brief period ("one hour") these individuals would exercise ruling "authority" with the sea-beast. Furthermore, these subservient monarchs collectively would "share" (v. 13) the same "purpose,"[24] namely, to relinquish their "power and authority" to the sea-beast.

The sea-beast and the above vassal minions wage "war" (v. 14) against the "Lamb." Even so, the divine Warrior easily crushes their insurrection, for he remains the sovereign "Lord" and supreme Monarch of the universe.[25] His triumph vindicates the faith of his regenerate entourage, whom he has "called," chosen, and enabled to remain steadfastly loyal to him.[26]

Some specialists think that the "ten horns" (v. 12) represent a coalition of European leaders who, in the end times, are part of a revived Roman Empire in the West that is under the control of the antichrist. Reputedly, he is the final earthly ruler mentioned in verse 11. According to this view, he plays the role of a monarch and exploits all other rulers to further his homicidal cause against the Creator and his reborn children.

Other specialists think that the "ten horns" (v. 12) symbolize the entirety of pagan, idolatrous, earthly power and authority in rebellion against the Lord. According to this view, as the time of the end draws near, the satanic and human forces of evil unite to free themselves from the Messiah and obliterate his followers. Yet despite their efforts, he triumphs over his foes, as well as vindicates the faith and faithfulness of the redeemed.[27]

22. See 2 Thess 1:6–11; Rev 16:12–16; 19:11–21.

23. See Dan 7:7, 20, 24.

24. Literally "mind" or resolve, intent.

25. Also Rev 19:16, where the wording is reversed; see Deut 10:17; Ps 136:2–3; Dan 2:37, 47; 4:37; 1 En. 9:4; 63:4; 84:2; 2 Macc 13:4; 3 Macc 5:35; 1 Tim 6:15.

26. See Heb 13:20–21; 1 Pet 5:10–11; Jude 1:24–25.

27. For a detailed explanation of Rev 17:11–12, see Beale, *The Book of Revelation*,

As we noted earlier, the angel discloses to John that the "waters" (v. 15) he saw and upon which the "prostitute" sits represent her dominance over the earth's wicked inhabitants, namely, a multitude of "peoples," along with "nations" and "languages." Verse 18 adds that the filthy harlot is also a sprawling metropolis of ill repute that reigns over the world's monarchs. In brief, the "woman" is an archetype of every political, social, and religious entity opposed to the Creator throughout history.

The celestial being also reveals to John that in an apparent power struggle between competing, diabolical factions, the sea-beast and his allies (the "ten horns"; v. 16) show their intense hatred for the "prostitute." The coalition lays waste to the harlot, strips her "naked," consumes her "flesh" like crazed, ravenous animals, and incinerates her remains with "fire."[28]

Parallels between Ezekiel 23:11–35 and Revelation 17:16[29]

Theme	Ezekiel 23:11–35 (Oholibah—Apostate Jerusalem)	Revelation 17:16 (The Prostitute—Babylon)
Betrayal by Former Allies	Oholibah's lovers turn against her and treat her with hatred (vv. 22, 24, 29).	The ten horns and the sea-beast despise the prostitute and turn against her.
Judgment by Former Partners	Oholibah is judged by her lovers according to their own standards (v. 24).	The ten horns and the sea-beast bring about the prostitute's demise.
Public Shame and Exposure	Oholibah's lovers strip off her clothes, leaving her naked and exposed (vv. 26, 29).	The ten horns and the sea-beast strip the prostitute of her garments, laying bare her shame.
Physical Desecration	Oholibah suffers mutilation; her nose and ears are sliced off (v. 25).	The ten horns and the sea-beast devour the prostitute's flesh, desecrating her body.
Total Destruction by Fire	Oholibah's children and survivors are consumed by fire (v. 25, 47).	The ten horns and the sea-beast incinerate the prostitute with fire, completing her destruction.

875–79; Osborne, *Revelation*, 284–87; Stefanovic, *Revelation*, 525–26.

28. See Ezek 16:37–41; 23:11–35; 38:21; Hag 2:22; Zech 14:13.

29. This is another example of typological fulfillment or prophetic foreshadowing in the Apocalypse. Table adapted from information presented in Moyise, *Old Testament in Revelation*, 72.

None of the above grisly events happen by chance. The angel discloses to John that the Creator will place within the minds ("hearts"; Rev 17:17) of the ruling coalition to execute his "purpose."[30]

It would be incorrect to surmise from the preceding observation that God is the author of evil. Instead, in keeping with previous remarks about theodicy in the Apocalypse,[31] the Creator works through the machinations of wicked people and power structures to bring about his sovereign will, which remains "good, pleasing, and perfect" (Rom 12:2). In particular, the "ten horns" (Rev 17:16) will unanimously agree[32] to transfer their "royal authority" (v. 17) to the sea-beast. This is, in part, the way in which God's plan to unleash his covenantal curses will be "fulfilled" (or brought to completion).

One interpretation of the preceding verses is that the "woman" (v. 18) heads up a worldwide apostate church. According to this view, because the prostitute represents a threat to the political and economic authority of the antichrist, he and his allies will overthrow the harlot's powerful religious organization. Presumably, this occurs at the midpoint of a seven-year tribulation period. Another interpretation maintains that the prostitute and the sea-beast represent opposing forces of evil. According to this view, because all forms of wickedness are inherently self-serving and self-destructive in nature, it is to be expected that one fiendish entity (whether human or demonic) will turn on another to become more powerful.

In either of the above views, contrarian factions unwittingly spawn the destructive forces of chaos and anarchy. Then, as competing groups battle one another for power and supremacy, together they reduce every region of the planet to a toxic, tooth-and-claw hellscape. Also, regardless of which interpretive option is preferred, the Creator remains in control of the seemingly random plans concocted by all who are wicked. He even uses these diabolical forces to accomplish his sovereign will. Though the Lord allows depravity to exist, he will one day completely and permanently ban its presence from the new creation.[33]

30. Literally "mind" or resolve, intent.

31. Especially the observations we put forward in our Introduction about theodicy.

32. Literally "to do one mind."

33. See our discussion of Rev 21:8, 27; 22:3, 15.

KEY THEOLOGICAL INSIGHTS

At the end of Revelation 16, as the seventh angel poured out his bowl of judgment, we noted that God remembered Babylon[34] to ensure that she experienced the fury of his wrath. In chapter 17, John focuses on the identity of this powerful and corrupt entity while also previewing her impending doom. From this closer look, we gain insight into the multifaceted influence of evil, the self-destructive tendencies of the wicked, and the truth about the Creator's sovereignty over the activities of the wicked who oppose him.

First, we see that *Babylon, as representative of an evil world system, infiltrates all realms of society.* The prostitute uses deception to convince the "kings of the earth" (v. 2) to participate in her "sexual immorality." This reflects a moral deviance that is sinister and detestable. Added to the wicked prostitute's debauchery is her religious abomination (v. 3), resulting in her murderous pursuit of the saints (v. 6). This apostacy somehow succeeds in convincing earth's wicked inhabitants that God's reborn children deserve to be murdered for their unwavering allegiance to the Messiah.[35] Furthermore, the evil world system represented in Babylon infiltrates the political and military spaces. This is seen in the gathering of all nations to stand against and "wage war" with the Lamb (vv. 12–14).[36] With the moral, religious, political, and military spheres infiltrated, the deception and coercion exercised by Babylon is comprehensive in its scope, affecting "peoples, multitudes, nations, and languages," such that they all come under her mesmerizing spell.[37] The success of Babylon to penetrate each aspect of human existence and societal structure reminds us of the pervasive nature of evil. It is never satisfied until everything in its path comes to complete destruction.

Second, we see that *the evil world system eventually implodes.* One feature of the deceitfulness of sin is its ability to appear sustainable, beneficial, and perhaps even inconsequential. Yet all sinfulness is based upon

34. For a helpful summary of allusions to OT notions of "Babylon," see Beale and McDonough, "Revelation," 1137–40.

35. The religious nature of Babylon fundamentally opposes the true Christian faith, not merely differs from it, and actively resists coexisting peacefully with Jesus' steadfast followers. Here we see that Babylon is truly an anti-Christ religion that rationalizes the slaughter of God's reborn children.

36. See our discussion of Rev 16:15–16.

37. See our discussion of Rev 13:7–8.

falsehood and a distortion of reality.[38] Toward the end of chapter 17, the kings and the sea-beast betray the prostitute and oversee her destruction (vv. 16–17). Initially, while these evil forces align in solidarity to oppose the Lamb, they prove their self-serving nature by breaking their own unanimity to terminate one of their own.[39] These traitorous acts should not surprise us, since the entity these wicked beings serve, the devil, is the "father of lies."[40] It is no wonder, then, that those enslaved to the Messiah's archenemy manifest self-destructive behavior. This is a sobering reminder that those who choose the path of rebellion are actively participating in their own damnation.[41]

Third, we see that *God ultimately maintains control, even over the forces of evil*. There is a key statement in verse 17 that should not be overlooked. As the world's evil system is betrayed by the "royal authority" and the "beast," all this happens according to God's purposes.[42] He places his plans within the "hearts"[43] of his enemies, such that they eventually turn against the prostitute and her evil regime. This is done so that in the end, the "words of God are fulfilled." While the Creator does not bring about or desire evil to happen, he remains in control amid the machinations of his wicked opponents.[44] Furthermore, he ensures that every wicked act accomplishes his ultimate purposes. Yet at no time does the supreme Monarch of the universe either abandon his creation or falter in his sovereign control over what is happening within it.[45]

38. Recall our discussion of Rev 13:13–14, where we note that the signs and wonders perpetrated by the sea-beast and land-beast are a dazzling fraud, producing awe and wonder among earth's wicked inhabitants.

39. Morris, *Revelation*, 206, notes that those devoted to evil always act in "self-destructive" ways, rather than "cohesive" ones, even though they may seem to us to be united.

40. See Gen 3:4; John 8:44; Rev 12:9.

41. See Rom 1:18–32, where those who ignore the revealed truth about God in creation are ultimately "given over" to their sinfulness.

42. See Thomas, *Revelation Exegetical Commentary*, vol. 2, 304–6, for an insightful explanation of how God's sovereign purposes act as the "ultimate cause" of the monarchs' handing over their kingdoms to the beast.

43. See Prov 21:1.

44. For a better understanding of how God maintains control over the wicked, even as they deliberately rebel against him, consider how the Lord hardened Pharoah's heart as a just consequence of the ruler's hardening his own heart; see Exod 7:3–4, 13, 24; 8:15, 19, 32; 9:7, 12, 34–35; 10:1, 20, 27; 11:9–10; 14:8.

45. Contrary to deistic or open-theistic views about God and his sovereignty, which we previously mentioned.

IMPORTANT MINISTRY IMPLICATIONS

As we consider the reality of the evil world system and its global influence, we take heart that God has equipped his reborn children with everything they need to stand against the forces of wickedness. Given this truth, we note the following implications for ministry that congregational leaders can employ while shepherding their parishioners in legitimate resistance to the enemy and his deceptive devices.

First, *we must teach our fellow believers about the reality of our enemy and his forces at work in the evil world system.* In Ephesians 6:12, Paul warns his readers that the spiritual battle we face as God's reborn children goes beyond the physical and material. Our struggle is against "world rulers" and "spiritual forces of evil" in unseen realms. The apostle's observation fits well with the description of Babylon in Revelation 17. Our enemy is real, spiritual forces and influences are real, and the evil that seeks to entice us away from our fidelity to the Messiah is real. In the Global North, there is often an apathetic sanitation of the reality of Satan and his wicked minions, where even professing believers often approach demonic realities with a wink and a smirk.[46] Conversely, for many in Majority World contexts, the reality of satanic and demonic powers remains a significant part of their cosmological framework.[47] They are more apt to believe in the reality of the devil and his evil world system at work in our world. By taking biblical teaching at face value, believers in these contexts have much to teach those in the West, as they tend to face the reality of spiritual warfare in a more sobering manner.[48]

Second, given the above observations, *we must encourage our congregants toward discernment and discretion in their daily walk.* Even those who profess faith in Christ are vulnerable to being ensnared by the perilous grip of deception. Scripture is replete with examples of otherwise faithful people who were drawn into the deceptiveness of sin at some

46. One of the most damaging legacies of the Western Enlightenment—especially as it has shaped thought in the Global North—is the rise of a materialistic (or naturalistic) worldview that denies, or at least marginalizes, the reality of the spiritual and the supernatural.

47. The term "cosmological" pertains to anything connected to the study of the universe's origin, structure, and evolution.

48. Of course, church leaders in Majority World contexts face an opposite danger of overplaying the power and ability of the devil, striking paralyzing fear into the hearts of their congregants, and manipulating this fear for selfish gain.

point in their lives.[49] This truth calls for our careful discernment when considering the reality of the evil forces around us. Though Satan cannot seize our souls, he can still corrupt our character and diminish our witness.[50] We may unintentionally acquiesce to the evil world system, being influenced toward godless behavior and speech. We may also be drawn in by the allure of comfort and ease, success and recognition, only to discover later that by conforming to the surrounding pagan culture, we have rendered ourselves ineffective as witnesses for Christ. We must warn our congregants that deceptiveness is an ever-present danger to the true testimony we are called to exemplify as believers.

Third, *we must encourage our parishioners to live in a way that spurns the influence of wicked Babylon*. Being countercultural and opposing evil are essential for those who identify as the Messiah's faithful followers. We should look, act, speak, and think differently than the unsaved world around us. For instance, we are called to distance ourselves from every manifestation of evil, and we must encourage our parishioners toward holiness and godliness in all areas of life.[51] As we noted earlier, sin permeates every realm of human existence. To combat this reality, we must intentionally prioritize our loyalty to God and faithfulness to his Word in our daily lives. As we do so, we can expect conflict and opposition, perhaps even suffering and personal loss. Yet as the armies of evil seek to wage war with the Lamb, they will also eventually hate those who stand with him. As congregational leaders, we must guide our parishioners in steadfast obedience to our Lord, even in the face of a culture and society that compels us away from righteousness.[52]

49. See Gen 3:1–7; 16:1–4; Num 20:7–13; 2 Sam 11:1—12:15.

50. See Luke 22:31–34; 1 Pet 5:8.

51. See 1 Thess 5:19–24.

52. See Jas 4:4; 1 John 2:15–17. As we noted in our discussion of Rev 13, the term "culture" refers to the set of beliefs, values, practices, customs, and behaviors that are learned, shared, and passed down from one generation to another within a particular group, community, or society. In contrast, the term "society" denotes a complex and organized group of individuals who interact with one another within a shared geographical or social space. A society encompasses all individuals interacting within a specific geographical or social boundary, whereas a culture is a subset of a society, representing the distinct way of life and sense of belonging within a particular community-based context.

VITAL MISSIONAL RAMIFICATIONS

The missional implications we derive from Revelation 17 call believers to resist the corrupt world system and proclaim the gospel faithfully. The lost are urged to abandon all loyalty to the idolatrous elements of their culture and follow the Messiah wholeheartedly. As we seek the conversion of the lost, we must pursue consistent, obedient discipleship in an uncompromising way. Likewise, we must be willing to critique our own culture as well as the cultures of those to whom we witness.

First, given the pervasiveness of the evil world system, *missionaries must not compromise the gospel for the sake of cultural accommodation.* While cultural sensitivity is appropriate to avoid unnecessary barriers to gospel communication, we must not avoid critiquing any aspects of a culture that display features of the wicked prostitute. In the past, missionaries have been keenly aware of the shortcomings of the cultures in which they ministered. Yet often they have been unwilling to note the shortcomings of the cultures from which they originated. As such, much missionary activity has been perceived as a desire to force the recipient culture to look more like the sending culture.[53] Over time, this tendency has hindered the work of the gospel in many places, especially as people in recipient cultures have more recently resisted the attempts of missionaries to change them.

Second, in more recent times, *missionaries have tended to go to an opposite extreme by failing to call out sinfulness in the recipient culture.* They have tried to accommodate sinful practices in a kind of syncretism that pollutes the message of the gospel and Jesus' call to repentance and holiness.[54] Confronting sinful behavior in any culture is a necessary component of missionary work, especially as we proclaim God's holiness

53. This tendency is often described as a form of colonialism, and many missionaries and missions movements have been labeled colonialist. "Colonialism" refers to a historical practice where a powerful nation or group of people directly extends its control and influence over a weaker region or territory, often located in different parts of the world, for an extended period. Admittedly, the issue here is highly complex, requiring careful discernment on all sides. In short, not all accusations of colonialism are valid. Yet many of them are, and in those cases, the purity of the gospel message and mission have been compromised.

54. Examples of unbiblical syncretism that we mentioned previously include accepting ancestor worship in addition to the worship of the Creator, giving allowance for polygamy and sexual promiscuity, and tolerating various levels of gender-based violence in patriarchal social structures. These practices have no place among those who profess genuine faith in Christ.

and urge people to dwell in his righteousness. Just as Babylon is seated on "many waters" (v. 1), so the evil world system has influenced and corrupted all cultures to one extent or another. Good missionary practice heralds the gospel above all cultural influences, noting that no culture exists in pure righteousness.

Third, *the pervasive nature of the evil world system necessitates the presence of missionaries everywhere.* The history of missions has been predominantly shaped by individuals from the Global North, who often engaged Majority World cultures with a narrow, one-directional approach to evangelism. However, Western cultures have exhibited just as much, if not greater, moral and spiritual brokenness as the so-called "pagan" or "uncivilized" cultures they aimed to convert. Longstanding assumptions about the moral superiority of the West are gradually eroding and proving false, as evidenced by the greater faithfulness found in Majority World Christianity compared to the Global North.[55] Consequently, there is an emerging interest among Christians in Majority World contexts to pursue missionary activity in the West. This is a positive development, especially considering the urgent need for the gospel to be proclaimed in all places. Wherever the spirit of Babylon is present, the imperative for missional engagement in those places remains as strong as ever. May God find us faithful to carry out his mission in all places and to all peoples.

55. Recent divisions within mainline Protestant denominations highlight contrasting approaches to theological fidelity. Majority World representatives often exhibit greater faithfulness to Scripture by adhering closely to biblical teachings. In contrast, some Western leaders have embraced theological and moral compromises by endorsing teachings and practices that directly contradict Scripture.

Revelation 18

The Fall of Babylon (Part Two)

LEARNING OBJECTIVES

- Identify the symbolic elements and meaning of Babylon.
- Understand the reasons for God's judgment of the notorious city.
- Describe the events that accompany Babylon's sudden and sweeping demise.
- Consider the response of earth's monarchs, merchants, and mariners to the city's destruction.
- Deliberate the implications of Babylon's judgment for the work of missions.

CHAPTER SUMMARY

Revelation 18 begins with an angel's announcement of the fall of Babylon, which is depicted as a cesspool of iniquity and immorality from which Jesus' followers are urged to flee. Despite Babylon's unrivaled wealth and power, God's judgment of her is sudden and comprehensive. Earth's monarchs, merchants, and mariners, whom Babylon enriched, mourn her transformation into a desolate and uninhabitable place. In contrast, God's children, whose blood the city shed, rejoice over her demise.

STUDY QUESTIONS

1. What are the iniquities that Babylon is guilty of committing?

2. Why are Jesus' followers urged to flee from Babylon?
3. Why do earth's monarchs, merchants, and mariners lament Babylon's sudden demise?
4. What do Babylon's excesses teach believers about materialism and greed?
5. How can believers avoid being enticed by Babylon's harlotries and idolatries?

CHAPTER OUTLINE

- The announcement of Babylon's destruction (18:1–8)
- The funeral lament over Babylon's destruction (18:9–24)
- Key theological insights
- Important ministry implications
- Vital missional ramifications

THE ANNOUNCEMENT OF BABYLON'S DESTRUCTION (18:1–8)

In the unfolding cosmic drama, John witnesses "another angel" (v. 1), who has enormous "authority" (and power), descend from God's sacred throne room in "heaven."[1] The creature's splendor is so intense that it illuminates the entire planet. Moreover, because of this celestial emissary's exalted commission, his radiance reflects that of the Creator. Put another way, the angel's majesty emphasizes the divine source and universal scope of his message.[2]

The mournful chant that appears in verses 2 and 3 draws heavily upon the language of the Old Testament to herald the destruction of "Babylon."[3] This is no ordinary city or government but a worldwide center of power, affluence, harlotry, and idolatry that detests the Creator and his children.

1. As we previously noted, the Creator's throne occupies the literary center of John's prophetic oracle.

2. See Isa 24:23; 60:1–3; Ezek 43:2–3.

3. This is another example of typological fulfillment or prophetic foreshadowing in the Apocalypse; see Isa 13; 21; Jer 50–51; Ezek 25–27; Rev 14:8; 17:6.

Taunt songs, found in both the Old and New Testaments, are impassioned pleas for God to judge the wicked by enacting the covenantal curses outlined in Scripture. Though their stark language may initially seem jarring, these songs are authentic expressions of human anguish in response to profound injustice and immorality. They consistently target sources of egregious sin and oppression. The composers, under the Spirit's inspiration and authority, leave justice up to the Creator, trusting that he will always be equitable and upright in his judicial decisions.

Revelation 18:2 highlights the nature of Babylon's obliteration, whereas verse 3 explains the reason for the demise of the notorious metropolis. This is another instance where John paints the cosmic trial motif on the narrative canvas of his prophetic oracle. Babylon's collapse will be so complete that no person will inhabit her again.

Indeed, the prostitute will become the "prison" (or haunt, lair) for demonic spirits, unclean birds (such as carrion fowl), and detested beasts.[4] This is a fitting end (and prime example of retributive justice), for "Babylon" has intoxicated the world's monarchs with the "wine" (v. 3) of her idolatry and immorality. Likewise, the planet's merchants have grown "rich" (and spiritually complacent) from the "abundance" of the harlot's "luxury."[5] Another option is that John is emphasizing that earth's vendors have become satiated with the prostitute's unrestrained lust.

4. See Isa 13:19–23; 34:11–15; Jer 50:39; 51:37; Zeph 2:14–15; Tob 8:3.

5. See Ezek 27:12, 27; Rev 3:17. For a detailed analysis of the economic imagery in Rev 18—especially the list of trade goods in vv. 11–13, see Bauckham, *Climax of Prophecy*, 338–83. He argues that the chapter's imagery critiques Rome's exploitative economic system. The depiction of Babylon as a wealthy and corrupt city reflects a broader indictment of Roman imperialism and its excesses, drawing on Old Testament prophetic oracles against cities like Tyre and Babylon (for example, Ezek 27:7–25). Bauckham highlights that the list of twenty-eight luxury commodities—a multiple of four, symbolizing the world—emphasizes Rome's global economic reach and its associated moral decay.

Repeated Sets of Three in Revelation 18		
Theme	**Description**	**Biblical References**
Sixfold affirmation (a trio times two) of Babylon's demise	"This is the way Babylon, the great city, will be overthrown with violence and *will never again be found.* The sound of harpists and musicians, flutists and trumpeters, *will never be heard in you again.* No craftsman of any trade *will ever be found in you again.* The sound of a millstone *will never be heard in you again.* The light of a lamp *will never shine in you again.* The voice of bridegroom and bride *will never be heard in you again*" (emphasis added).	vv. 21–23
Threefold repetition of sudden judgments	"In a single hour"	vv. 10, 17, 19
Threefold repetition of "woe, woe"	Repeated, impassioned expressions of grief	vv. 10, 16, 19
Trio of demonic haunts	"And a prison for every unclean spirit, and a prison for every unclean bird, and a prison for every unclean and hated beast"	v. 2
Trio of innocent victims	The shed blood of the prophets, saints, and martyrs	v. 24
Trio of laments	From monarchs, merchants, and mariners	vv. 9, 11, 17
Trio of offenders	"For all the nations have drunk from the wine of her adulterous desire, and the kings of the earth committed adultery with her, and the merchants of the earth became rich from the abundance of her luxury."	v. 3
Trio of plagues	"Death, mourning, and famine"	v. 8
Trio of reasons for God's judgment of Babylon	"*Because* your merchants were the great ones of the earth, *because* your witchcraft led all the nations astray, and [*because*] the blood of prophets and saints was found in this city, along with the blood of all those who were slain on the earth" (emphasis added).	vv. 23–24
Trio of the redeemed	"Saints, apostles, and prophets"	v. 20

Repeated Sets of Three in Revelation 18		
Theme	Description	Biblical References
Trio of retributive judgments	"Pay her back even as she has paid. Pay her back double for what she has done. In the cup that she mixed, mix her a double portion."	v. 6
Trio of vaunted assertions	"I sit as a queen, I am not a widow, and I will never mourn."	v. 7

Next, John hears "another voice" (v. 4) from God's throne room in "heaven" command believers to escape from the harlot's cesspool of iniquity.[6] After all, everyone who participates in the filthy prostitute's "sins" will also share in her "plagues" (or covenantal curses).[7] Before the supreme court of the Creator's justice, Babylon deserves her guilty verdict and demise. Specifically, the wickedness of this pagan, idolatrous world system is piled higher and higher,[8] until it reaches to the heights of heaven.[9] In turn, the supreme Monarch of the universe will never forget the harlot's criminal acts (v. 5).

The "voice" (v. 4) urges the Creator to enact retribution fully on the prostitute for all her vile deeds. This is a situation in which the punishment fits the crime. Specifically, the harlot is to pay "double" (v. 6) for all she has done. Likewise, her "cup" is to overflow with a "double portion" of the toxic brew she mixes for others to ingest.

The above is a suitable consequence, especially since Babylon is guilty of exalting herself and living in "luxury" (or sensuously; v. 7). Therefore, she is to be repaid with as much (if not more) torment and misery for her unrestrained immorality.[10] Additionally, the prostitute arrogantly boasts about her imperial status as a "queen," immunity from widowhood, and exemption from disaster. Yet in a short period of time (in a "single day"; v. 8), the supposedly regal harlot will be overwhelmed

6. Particularly by withdrawing from and renouncing any affiliation with the iniquitous enclave.

7. See Isa 48:20; 52:11; Jer 50:8–9; 51:6, 45, 50; Ezek 20:41; Zech 2:6–7; 2 Bar. 2:1; Sib. Or. 5:143–44; 2 Cor 6:14–18; Eph 5:11; 1 Tim 5:22.

8. Literally "were glued together."

9. See Jer 51:9.

10. See Pss 28:4; 137:8; Prov 24:12; Isa 3:11; Jer 16:18; 17:18; 50:15, 29; 51:24; Lam 3:64; 2 Bar. 13:8; 1 Macc 2:68; Pss. Sol. 2:34; 17:8; Sir 16:12, 14.

by "mourning" and "famine."[11] Then "fire" will incinerate the prostitute's lifeless corpse.[12]

Despite the harlot's vaunted assertions, the Creator will easily bring about her downfall, for he is the all-powerful, "Lord God." As the supreme Monarch of the universe, he has the authority to enact this judicial verdict.[13] John is not being vindictive when he faithfully records the preceding taunt song. Instead, the apostle is revealing that the Creator will one day vindicate the faith and faithfulness of his martyred children by annihilating all the forces of evil in the world.

THE FUNERAL LAMENT OVER BABYLON'S DESTRUCTION (18:9–24)

Centuries before John lived, Ezekiel wrote a funeral lament over the fall of Tyre, an ancient oceangoing and trading powerhouse.[14] The Lord caused this notorious center of commerce to implode because of its hubris. Similarly, in the unfolding cosmic drama about the end of the age, earth's wicked inhabitants will bemoan God's destruction of Babylon.[15]

In the first dirge (Rev 18:9–10), the planet's rulers wail aloud and beat their chests in grief, especially as they witness the "smoke" arising from Babylon's charred remains.[16] The powerbrokers are heartbroken because they can no longer take part in the prostitute's harlotries and luxuriate in her sensual, seductive pleasures.[17] All the world's monarchs can do is "stand" (v. 10) a long way off, terrified over the prospect of sharing in the harlot's "torment." Together, they bemoan how horrible and awful is the downfall of this once-mighty metropolis, especially because the Creator's "judgment" (or covenantal curses) take place so quickly (in a "single hour").

In the second dirge (vv. 11–17a), the earth's "merchants" sob and lament over Babylon's collapse. They are particularly distressed that they

11. See Isa 47:7–11; Sib. Or. 5:170–74.

12. See our discussion of Rev 17:16.

13. See Rev 15:3–4; 16:7; 19:1–2.

14. See Ezek 26–27.

15. This is another example of typological fulfillment or prophetic foreshadowing in the Apocalypse; see Apoc. Dan. 7:1–14; Apoc. El. 2:29–38.

16. In answer to the prayers of the saints for the Creator's vindication of their faith and faithfulness.

17. See Ezek 27:33–36.

can no longer purchase the prostitute's exotic and lavish "cargo." Verses 12 and 13 detail all the diverse wares the harlot offers.[18] In addition to an extensive list of material objects, the prostitute also puts the "bodies and souls of people" up for sale. Most likely, this is a reference to an institutionalized form of slave trade.[19] The merchants shed tears over the fact that all the "fruit" (v. 14) that Babylon's "soul" craves has disappeared. Likewise, all the harlot's wealth and glamour are lost forever.[20]

Like earth's monarchs (v. 10), those who become wealthy from buying and selling what "Babylon" (v. 15) has to offer stand "far away" from her. These traders are horror-stricken over the prospect of being forced to participate in the prostitute's suffering. Similarly, as with verse 10, verse 16 records a mournful chant voiced by the planet's merchants over the demise of the once "great city."[21] As the traders recall the harlot's beauty and "wealth" (v. 17), they grieve over her lost splendor and deplore the Creator's swift destruction of the prostitute's riches (in a "single hour").

In the third dirge (vv. 17b–20), the mariners of the world cry out in despair over Babylon's demise. Like the planet's monarchs and merchants, the world's shipmasters, seafarers, and "sailors" all stand "far away" as the nightmarish scene unfolds.[22] Everyone who profited from Babylon's extensive maritime trade begins to wail in despair when they witness the "smoke" (v. 18) ascend to the Creator's sacred throne room from the harlot's smoldering, putrid carcass.[23] They realize that nothing will ever replace the once proud and prosperous "city."

Like earth's monarchs and merchants (vv. 10, 15), the planet's mariners repeatedly sob and lament. Also, as a sign of their intense grief, they throw "dust" (v. 19) on their "heads."[24] As the profiteers wail, they voice their anguish over how appalling it is for the once bustling metropolis to become a silent "wasteland" (v. 19) in such a short period of time (in

18. See Ezek 27:12–24.

19. During the first century AD, out of an estimated total population of fifty million people within the Roman Empire, between five and ten million were enslaved, including prisoners of war, those born into slavery, and those bound in penal slavery; see Num 31:32–35; 1 Chron 5:21; Ezek 27:13.

20. The underlying Greek conveys the sense of "they will never be found any longer."

21. Note the comparable description in Rev 17:4.

22. See Ezek 27:28–32.

23. Once again, in answer to the prayers of the saints for the vindication of their faith and faithfulness.

24. See Josh 7:6; 1 Sam 4:12; 2 Sam 13:19; 15:32; Job 2:12; Lam 2:10; Ezek 27:30.

a "single hour"). The prostitute now stands abandoned, with no ship-owner ever again anchoring at her ports to grow "rich" from her alluring "treasures."

In stepping back from the preceding three dirges, it is clear that those who bow the knee before the altar of the world's pagan and idolatrous system will lose everything when it implodes. In that day of retributive judgment,[25] the Lord will wipe out all that earth's wicked inhabitants have amassed, including their money, power, fame, and pleasure.

Verse 20 shifts the focus from the trio of monarchs, merchants, and mariners, who grieve over Babylon's destruction, to those who voice joyful shouts originating from "heaven."[26] Regardless of whether the threesome are the "saints," "apostles," or "prophets," the Creator's martyred children are directed to participate in celebrating the prostitute's downfall.

The spotlight is on God, who unleashes his covenantal curses against the notorious, pagan, idolatrous world system.[27] After all, it has the audacity to accuse, condemn, persecute, and murder countless believers falsely. As before, the call to celebration was not an invitation for Jesus' followers to derive pleasure over the demise of the wicked. Instead, the redeemed praised the Creator for vindicating their faith in and faithfulness to the Son, and for his bringing justice to pass.[28]

Next, in the unfolding cosmic drama, John witnesses a "mighty angel" (v. 21) lift a boulder that resembles a huge "millstone" and hurl it into one of the planet's oceans.[29] The apostle probably has in mind

25. Comparable to a massive de-creation event. The Old Testament concept of *herem*—the complete destruction or consecration of enemies and their possessions to God (for example, Josh 6:17–21)—prefigures the de-creation imagery in Rev by portraying divine judgment as the purging of evil to reestablish God's order. In the Apocalypse, the Lord's final judgment (for example, chs. 18–19) similarly entails the overthrow of corrupt powers like Babylon, leading to a dismantling of the present creation for the eradication of sin and rebellion. Both *herem* and the series of catastrophes described in John's prophetic oracle highlight the Creator's absolute sovereignty, employing destruction as a means of removing what opposes his holiness and preparing creation for cosmic renewal (21:1). Thus, *herem* serves as an early typological counterpart to the theme of de-creation in Rev, where divine wrath culminates in the obliteration of evil and inaugurates the new creation; see the relevant discussions in Aune, *Revelation 17–22*; Beale, *The Book of Revelation*; and Koester, *Revelation*.

26. See Deut 32:43; Jer 51:48.

27. See Deut 19:16–19; Dan 7:21–22.

28. See our discussion of Rev 5:8; 6:10; 8:3–4.

29. See Jer 51:63–64; Ezek 26:12, 21; Luke 17:2.

the upper stone of a donkey mill that people used in Bible times. These objects were typically four to five feet in diameter, one foot thick, and weighed thousands of pounds.

Verses 21–24 record a doom song about Babylon. To begin, the celestial being announces that the once powerful and idolatrous harlot will be thrown down and obliterated in a violent, forceful manner. All evidence of human activity and creativity will never be found again in the once-notorious metropolis. Whatever the evil world system has produced—including music, workers, machinery, light, and happiness—will permanently cease to exist.[30]

Why would the Creator be so decisive and thoroughgoing in bringing about his covenantal curses? In keeping with the cosmic trial motif found throughout John's prophetic oracle, the powerful "angel" (v. 21) declares that Babylon is guilty of enabling a cadre of moguls to exploit and oppress earth's inhabitants. Furthermore, the notorious prostitute uses "witchcraft" (or sorcery) to deceive the "nations" (v. 23).[31] Even worse, the harlot is at fault for the wholesale slaughter of innumerable people (v. 24)—especially God's "prophets" and "saints" (or holy ones), who are innocent of committing any crimes meriting the death sentence.[32]

It is appropriate, then, for all believers to rejoice over the demise of the pagan, idolatrous world system that Babylon represents. At the end of the age, the Creator will demonstrate that his children are correct in remaining faithful to him, despite all the enticements and pressures to do otherwise.

Parallels between Ezekiel 26–27 and Revelation 18[33]		
Theme/Category	**Ezekiel 26–27 (Tyre)**	**Revelation 18 (Babylon)**
Aromatic Woods	Traded "ebony" and "cassia" (27:15, 19)	Sold "every kind of aromatic wood" (v. 12)
Crafted Materials	Traded "bronze," "ivory," and "wrought iron" (27:13, 15, 19)	Sold items made of "ivory," "brass," and "iron" (v. 12)

30. See Isa 24:8; Jer 7:34; 16:9; 25:10; 33:11; Ezek 26:13.

31. See Nah 3:4; Rev 9:21.

32. See Sib. Or. 3:310–13; Rev 16:6; 17:6; 19:2.

33. This is another example of typological fulfillment or prophetic foreshadowing in the Apocalypse. Table adapted from information presented in Moyise, *Old Testament in Revelation*, 73–74.

Parallels between Ezekiel 26–27 and Revelation 18[33]		
Theme/Category	**Ezekiel 26–27 (Tyre)**	**Revelation 18 (Babylon)**
Economic Influence	Tyre "enriched the kings of the earth" (27:33).	The "kings of the earth . . . lived in luxury" with Babylon (v. 9).
Fine Textiles	Sold purple-dyed fabric and "finely embroidered . . . linen" (27:16)	Sold "fine linen" and "purple cloth" (v. 12)
Food and Drink	Sold olive "oil" and "wine" (27:17, 18)	Sold "wine" and "olive oil" (v. 13)
Gems and Jewelry	Sold "turquoise" (27:16)	Sold "precious stones" and "pearls" (v. 12)
Human Trafficking	"Traded human beings" (27:13)	Sold the "bodies and souls of people" (v. 13)
Lament over Lost Greatness	"How you have perished, . . . you city that was celebrated" (26:17).	"Who is like the great city" (v. 18).
Livestock	Traded "lambs, rams, and goats" (27:21)	Sold "cattle" and "sheep" (v. 13)
Maritime Mourning	Sailors, pilots, ship builders, and merchants "cry out bitterly," "throw dirt on their heads," and "roll in ashes" (27:27–30).	"Every ship captain and all the ocean travelers and the sailors . . . threw dust on their heads and cried out as they wept and mourned" (vv. 17, 19).
Maritime Wealth	"All the ships of the sea and their sailors were in your harbor to engage in trade with you" (27:9).	"All who have ships on the sea were made rich from her treasures" (v. 19).
Permanent Disappearance	"You will be sought but never found again" (26:21)	"Will never again be found" (v. 21)
Precious Metals	Traded "silver" and "gold" (27:12, 22)	Traded "gold" and "silver" (v. 12)
Silenced Music	The "sound of your lyres will be heard no more" (26:13).	"The sound of harpists and musicians, flutists and trumpeters, will never be heard in you again" (v. 22).
Spices and Perfumes	Traded "all kinds of expensive perfumes" (27:22)	Sold "cinnamon, spice, incense, myrrh, frankincense" (v. 13)
Total Destruction	Made into a "ruined city" (26:19)	"Such great wealth . . . made a wasteland" (v. 17)

Parallels between Ezekiel 26–27 and Revelation 18[33]		
Theme/Category	**Ezekiel 26–27 (Tyre)**	**Revelation 18 (Babylon)**
Transportation	Traded chariot "horses" and "war horses" (27:14)	Sold "horses" and "carriages" (v. 13)

KEY THEOLOGICAL INSIGHTS

In Revelation 18, we are given extensive insight into the fall of Babylon, which represents the evil world system that stands opposed to God and his reborn children. Within both the taunting declaration of Babylon's fall (vv. 1–8) and the funeral dirge of her demise (vv. 9–24), we gain further insight into the temporary pleasure of sin, the Creator's determination to overthrow all forms of evil, and the permanent result of his judgment upon the powerful and corrupt city or system.

First, we see that *while sin may offer fleeting gratification, its satisfaction is short-lived.* A key part of iniquity's deception is that—for a time—it appears to fulfill its promises to those who pursue it.[34] For example, the "kings of the earth" (vv. 3, 9), who choose to participate in the great prostitute's cult, luxuriate in seemingly boundless pleasures for a while. Similarly, merchants enjoy profitable sales of precious cargo and reap benefits of trading commodities (vv. 3, 11, 15). Likewise, seafarers realize financial gain from their industry (vv. 17, 19).

Because of this, all three groups gladly participate in the nefarious ways of the wicked prostitute, along with failing to consider the moral implications of their actions.[35] They are deceived by Babylon's attractions, which explains their dramatic cries of mourning when she implodes. From these observations, we discern that there is temporary pleasure in sin. Also, with this allure, the devil seduces and enslaves those who join the ranks of service to the great prostitute. At least for a time, the enticements of iniquity appear worth it to those who participate in Babylon's ways.[36]

Second, while sin offers short-lived delights, *God is resolved to bring about the swift destruction of the wicked prostitute.* Several times

34. See Eccl 2:1–11; Luke 15:11–16; Heb 11:25.

35. While buying, selling, and earning a living through trade are not inherently sinful, the monarchs, merchants, and mariners in Rev 18 prosper materially by participating in the sinful practices of the prostitute, which stand in clear opposition to God.

36. This perhaps explains why earlier, in Rev 16, we see that those falling under God's judgment refuse to give up their sin and repent, choosing rather to prolong their insurrection to its bitter, ruinous end; see vv. 9, 11.

throughout this chapter the fall of Babylon is described as something that happens in a "single day" (v. 8) or "single hour" (vv. 10, 17, 19). While we presently await the Creator's plan to unfold, we are assured from this description that once his judgment begins, no one and nothing can delay it.[37] This truth may seem improbable, namely, that such a powerful world system, which has set itself against God with so much apparent success, can rapidly implode. Yet the reality of Babylon's quick demise is further proof that God remains sovereign over everyone and everything. Indeed, the intentions of earth's rulers rest in the "hand of the LORD."[38] The Creator is not thwarted by wickedness as he executes his plan, nor is he weakened by evil's temporary success. He remains Lord of all. Accordingly, when God's end-time judgment unfolds, all creation will witness his absolute sovereignty and power.[39]

Third, we are assured that *at the consummation of the age, the Creator will overthrow the evil world system forever*. There is no comeback for Babylon. God's victorious judgment cannot be reversed. The vindication of his holy ones does not offer merely a limited reprieve for the faithful, persevering saints (v. 20).[40] Once the horrific prostitute is destroyed, there is no further concern that she can be revived again to oppose the Creator.[41] Babylon's primary offense is that her clothing is soaked with the blood of God's reborn children, the "saints, apostles, and prophets." They have stood faithfully for the Messiah and proclaimed his gospel, even while facing unspeakable persecution and martyrdom (v. 24). Moreover, as we have seen many times in the Apocalypse, the Father remains resolute finally to vindicate those who have suffered for the sake of the Son's name.[42] And as this vindication comes, the saints rightfully rejoice and praise God for the justice he delivers.[43]

37. For previous indications of God's swift judgment and the short timeframe left for wickedness, see Hab 2:3; Mal 3:5; Matt 24:36–42; Luke 12:43–48; Rev 12:12.

38. See Prov 21:1.

39. See our discussion of Rev 6:16–17.

40. See our discussion of Rev 14:13, where those who "die" in faithful service to the "Lord" are "blessed" because they now eternally rest (or experience relief) from their anguish-filled toil; see also our discussion of 15:2–4.

41. Note the repetitive use of "never . . . again" in 18:21–23; see also our discussion of Rev 19:1–3.

42. See our discussion of Rev 6:9–11; 8:3–5; 11:11–13, 17–18; 12:10–12; 14:12–13; 15:2–4; 16:5–7.

43. For further reflection on how the "rejoicing" of the saints at the fall of Babylon is indeed justified, see Osborne, *Revelation*, 653–55.

IMPORTANT MINISTRY IMPLICATIONS

Given the dramatic fall of Babylon—a symbol of seemingly invincible wickedness, church leaders must vigilantly warn believers not to be enticed by her corrupting influence, lest they participate in her sins and suffer the covenantal curses that overtake her. At the same time, we can properly rejoice in God's righteous judgment that brings about Babylon's destruction. This section focuses on the two messages to the saints in Revelation 18:4 and 20, particularly highlighting their threefold application to our faithful, persevering congregants.

First, *we must summon our parishioners out of Babylon* (v. 4). While believers may not live according to the evil world system, God's reborn children do find themselves within it. The temptation and influence of the prostitute is ever present, even for those who have chosen to follow the Savior faithfully. The call is for believers to separate themselves from the surrounding wickedness, even as they reside in the realm of the enemy's domain.[44] This reflects Jesus' prayer in John 17, where he asks the Father that the disciples would be kept from the "Evil One" (v. 15) while residing in the world. Jesus sends his followers into the world to fulfill his mission, while praying to the Father to protect them and keep them set apart from its corrupting influence.[45] In much the same way, congregational leaders must urge the saints under their pastoral care to distance themselves from the evil structure in which they live.[46]

Second, *the call for believers to separate from Babylon should be paired with a solemn warning about the consequences of disobedience, including suffering and divine judgment.* After all, believers are not exempt from temptation and moral failure, as much as we might imagine otherwise.[47] Neither are we free from the temporal consequences of our sinful choices. As church leaders, we are called to urge our congregants to pursue holiness, reflecting the holiness of our Lord, and to live distinctly—set apart and fully devoted to Christ in unwavering faithfulness. Previously, in the letters to the seven churches, John's prophetic oracle declared that God's judgment extends to Jesus' followers, for he shows no partiality. Though

44. See Jas 1:27; 1 John 2:15–17.

45. See John 17:15–19.

46. For a striking excursus on the ways in which we can, perhaps unwittingly, participate in the evil world system, see Keener, *Revelation*, 436–46.

47. See 1 Cor 10:12.

the Messiah's disciples need not fear everlasting condemnation,[48] it is possible for them to get caught up in the love of this world and receive his censure for their own participation in its sinful ways.[49]

Third, *we can rejoice with our parishioners in the Creator's vindication of the saints through his destruction of Babylon.* This has been a repeated ministry implication throughout our study of Revelation, yet it bears asserting once again. Admittedly, the precise way in which God allows for evil and uses it for his purposes remains mysterious to us. Yet we can rest in the truth that though the forces of wickedness have their day, the Creator's powerful judgment always prevails.[50] Even now, while we wait for God's final vindication of all things, we can be comforted that our caring Lord knows, sees, and sovereignly controls all situations in our lives and in all world events. Furthermore, according to verse 20, we can take delight in the Lamb's comprehensive and decisive victory. This is not because we gloat over the fact that people experience condemnation. Instead, it is because the Son judges in our favor, assuring us that we are on the right side of his will and plan for this age, as well as the age to come.[51]

VITAL MISSIONAL RAMIFICATIONS

The missional ramifications of Revelation 18 concern the nature of our summons to the lost, in which we urge them to escape the entrapment of the evil world system through repentance and faith in Christ alone. As we proclaim the gospel, we warn the unsaved about the dire consequences of sin. We also offer an alternative to trusting in status, power, and wealth for the attainment of salvation.

First, *missionary activity entails summoning the lost out of the world to become devoted followers of Christ alone.* Just as believers are urged to come out of Babylon—to avoid being ensnared by her sins and sharing in her judgment, so also unbelievers are called to turn from the world and its ways and follow Christ. Throughout the Apocalypse, we see that people facing God's judgment have ample opportunity to repent of their

48. See Rom 5:1; 8:1; 1 Thess 5:9–10.

49. See our discussion of Rev 2:14–16, 20–23; 3:17–20; see also 2 Tim 4:10, where Paul notes that Demas abandoned the apostle because of Demas's love of the "present world."

50. See Job 42:2; Isa 45:7–9; Lam 3:37–39; Col 1:16–17.

51. For the assurance that the Messiah's faithful followers are on the right side of God's final judgment, see our discussion of Rev 19:1–2; 20:11–15, 22–27.

sinfulness, trust in the Messiah, and experience God's gracious redemption. Sadly, amid the Creator's judgment, most unbelievers choose to remain as they are, adamantly opposed to his offer of grace and mercy.[52] Yet as we anticipate the eventual destruction of Babylon, we must faithfully herald the good news, calling unbelievers to true repentance, imploring them to forsake the seduction of the prostitute, and urging them to believe in Christ. In our gospel proclamation, we are warning about the consequences of sin and judgment as well as showing forth God's marvelous grace offered in redemption.

Second, *within our gospel witness, we must summon the lost to place their faith in the Messiah as their all-sufficient Redeemer and the only way of salvation.* Throughout this chapter, we see dramatic sadness and grief concerning the fall of Babylon (vv. 9–20). The monarchs, merchants, and mariners place their trust in Babylon. After all, this powerful and corrupt entity provides them with immense luxury, pleasure, power, wealth, status, and enjoyment. These worldly trappings become a source of security for those who venerate the prostitute. They opt to stake their future in all the temporal, material, and sensual pleasures afforded by the evil world system. Part of our missional task is to demonstrate the futility of trusting in these pagan substitutes for salvation, security, and true fulfillment in this life and in the life to come.[53]

Third, *the prosperity gospel, which has been exported from the West to the Majority World in recent decades, has caused significant harm by misleading people about where true faith should be placed.* This false teaching leads many to believe that Jesus desires his followers to pursue wealth, status, and pleasures symbolized by Babylon. This heretical preaching replaces the cross with consumerism and exchanges spiritual blessings for worldly success. The result is that people come to seek salvation in the temporal, trivial, and transient pleasures of this life. Missionary activity, particularly in Majority World contexts, must confront such an erroneous theology and replace it with the truth of salvation and security in Jesus alone as the Messiah.

52. See our discussion of Rev 6:15–17; 9:6, 20–21; 16:9, 11, 21.

53. See Matt 6:19–34.

Revelation 19

The Final Victory (Part One)

LEARNING OBJECTIVES

- Appreciate the significance of the praise that heaven's multitudes offer God for Babylon's demise.
- Discern how the Messiah is preparing his followers for the wedding supper of the Lamb.
- Consider why Jesus, as the divine Warrior, is declared to be faithful and true.
- Understand the implications for all humanity that Jesus is the sovereign King and Lord.
- Deliberate how Jesus' final victory over rebellious, pagan humanity incentivizes believers to urge the lost to trust in Christ for salvation.

CHAPTER SUMMARY

Revelation 19 opens in heaven with a multitude of angels, the twenty-four elders, and the four living creatures, all of whom rejoice over Babylon's demise. They also praise God for judging the wicked and vindicating the faithfulness of Jesus' followers. The focus then shifts to the wedding supper of the Lamb, where the bride, representing the church triumphant, is united with the Lamb. Next, the Messiah, as the divine Warrior, returns with the armies of heaven to defeat rebellious, pagan humanity. At the end of the chapter, the sea-beast and land-beast are thrown alive into the fiery lake of sulfur, where they remain for all eternity.

STUDY QUESTIONS

1. What attributes of God are emphasized in the praise chorus sung by the immense crowd in heaven?
2. What is the significance of the marriage supper of the Lamb?
3. What does the Messiah's return on a white horse communicate about his character and purposes?
4. What is the great supper of God, and who is invited to it?
5. In what ways does the judgment of the sea-beast and land-beast motivate believers to pursue holiness?

CHAPTER OUTLINE

- The song of triumph in heaven (19:1–5)
- The wedding feast of the Lamb (19:6–10)
- The divine Warrior on the white horse (19:11–21)
- Key theological insights
- Important ministry implications
- Vital missional ramifications

THE SONG OF TRIUMPH IN HEAVEN (19:1–5)

Revelation 17 and 18 concerned the diabolical nature of Babylon and the demise of the pagan, idolatrous world system represented by the notorious metropolis. Chapters 19 and 20 shift the focus to the Messiah's triumph over the forces of evil and his vindication of the righteous.

Once again, the cosmic trial motif forms the literary backdrop of John's prophetic oracle. The harlot and her sycophants transgressed the Creator's decrees, flouted his righteous standards, and maniacally attempted to exterminate his reborn children. It is appropriate for the sovereign Lord to bring about his covenantal curses, which ensure the destruction of the prostitute. Whereas legions on earth will bewail the harlot's overthrow, multitudes in heaven will rejoice when the Savior avenges the faith and faithfulness of his followers.[1]

1. See the detailed analysis of Aune, *Revelation 17–22*, 1021–28. He notes that the

In the unfolding cosmic drama, John remembers hearing what sounds like the roar of an "immense crowd" (19:1) from God's sacred throne in "heaven." The celestial throng, whether composed of angels, believers, or both, first shouts, "allelujah."[2] The preceding interjection is a Hebrew transliteration—a word whose sound has been carried over into English without interpreting its meaning. The thought behind the term was to give exuberant praise to the Creator.

Understanding "Hallelujah" in the Bible	
What Does "Hallelujah" Mean?	"Hallelujah" is a special word from Hebrew that means "Praise the LORD." It comes from two parts: *Halal*: A Hebrew verb meaning "to praise" or "to give glory." *Yah*: A short form of "Yahweh," the sacred name of God. Together, "hallelujah" is a joyful call to praise God.
Old Testament Usage	"Hallelujah" appears thirty-three times, mostly in the Psalter but also in Isaiah 62:9 and Jeremiah 20:13. In English Bibles, "hallelujah" is always translated as "Praise the LORD." Psalms 146–50 are called the "Hallelujah Psalms" because each one starts and ends with "hallelujah." In ancient times, during corporate worship, these were sung as hymns of praise.
New Testament Usage	"Hallelujah" appears only four times, all in Revelation (19:1, 3, 4, 6). This section is often called the "Hallelujah Chorus" because it describes a powerful moment of worship in heaven.
Context in Revelation	"Hallelujah" is used in a scene of heavenly worship, in which God's judgment, victory, and reign are celebrated. This moment connects the praise of the Old Testament with the worship of the New Testament, showing that God's greatness is celebrated forever.
Why Does "Hallelujah" Matter?	"Hallelujah" is more than a word. It is an invitation to praise God joyfully for who he is and what he has done. Whether in the Psalms or in Revelation, "hallelujah" reminds us to give glory to God in all times and places.

praise chorus of Rev 19:1–5 functions as a "judgment doxology" because it extols the Creator for his righteous verdict against Babylon, the great harlot who corrupted the earth. The chorus exalts God for vindicating his bondservants and avenging the martyrs' blood, transforming divine judgment into an occasion for rejoicing. The repeated "Hallelujah" highlights that the Lord's justice is not only retributive, but also inherently praiseworthy, affirming his glory and sovereignty in the destruction of evil.

2. See Tob 13:18.

After the opening shout of adoration, the heavenly choir praises the Creator for his "salvation" (v. 1). This includes the Messiah's deliverance of believers from sin and all its dire consequences. It also denotes Jesus' final victory over the principalities of the heathen world system, which crucified the Son and murdered his followers. Furthermore, the celestial throng declares that "glory and power" belong to God alone. The reason for this assertion is that his judicial rulings against the wicked are "true and just" (or valid and fair).[3]

As was the case in 1:6, 4:11, 5:13, 7:12, and 12:10, so too in 19:1, each term in the doxology is accented in the original language by the definite article "the" to indicate totality—namely, *all the* "salvation," *all the* "glory," and *all the* "power." This expression of praise is validated by the way the Lord "condemn[s]" (v. 2) and punishes the filthy "prostitute."

As a lover of harlotries and idolatries, the vixen "corrupt[s]" earth's inhabitants with her captivating, shameful deeds. Moreover, as an enemy of righteousness, the prostitute sheds the "blood" of Jesus' loyal followers ("servants").[4] Consequently, it is right for the Creator to exact retribution for his beleaguered, reborn children by making the harlot pay for her innumerable crimes.[5]

For a "second time" (v. 3), John recalls hearing the throng shout, "Hallelujah." They intensify their praise to God for overthrowing Babylon, as seen in the "smoke" which rises upward from the prostitute's charred remains "forever and ever."[6] It is possible that these worshipers are an angelic host. They also could be the redeemed of all the ages or martyrs killed during a final period of great distress on earth.[7]

As the supreme Monarch of the universe sits in repose on his glorious, sacred "throne" (v. 4),[8] the twenty-four "elders," along with the "four living creatures," prostrate themselves in homage. They shout the resounding affirmation, "Amen! Hallelujah!"[9] Then a "voice" (v. 5) which

3. See Deut 32:4; Rev 15:3–4; 16:7; 18:4–8.

4. Literally "slaves."

5. See Deut 32:43.

6. In answer to the prayers of the saints for the Creator's vindication of their faith and faithfulness; see Isa 34:8–10; Rev 14:11.

7. Namely, the church militant now transformed into the church triumphant.

8. As we previously noted, the Creator's throne occupies the literary center of John's prophetic oracle; see 1 Kgs 22:19; Isa 6:1; Ezek 1:26–27; 2 En. 20:3; Sir 1:8.

9. See our discussion of Rev 1:7; 3:14, 5:14; 7:12; 22:20, 21.

originates from the "throne" directs that all the Lord's "bondservants"[10] are to extol him for passing judgment on the notorious prostitute. Everyone who fears the Creator, both "small and great," is to offer him joyful "praise." Clearly, the members of the celestial chorus are not limited to one category. All the redeemed from every social class, ethnic group, and economic level are to join in worshiping and revering the Lord.

THE WEDDING FEAST OF THE LAMB (19:6–10)

Next, in the unfolding cosmic drama, John recalls hearing what sounded like the shout of a vast "crowd" (v. 6), the "roar" of a cascading waterfall or ocean waves, and the rumbling of a thunderclap all mixed together. The multitude shouts in unison, "Hallelujah," to the Creator for being the sovereign and all-powerful Monarch (the "Lord our God, the Almighty, reigns").[11] The heavenly choir unites in expressing exuberant joy and giving honor to the Father (v. 7).[12] After all, the time of the Lamb's "wedding" ceremony (or nuptials) has arrived, and his "bride" has prepared herself for the sacred event.[13]

Scripture teaches that the church—which consists of all true believers from the Old and New Testament eras—is the bride of Christ.[14] In a sense, the church is presently betrothed (or pledged in marriage) to the Redeemer and awaits the day when he will claim her as his "bride." At his return, he will join himself to his followers in everlasting intimacy, love, and joy. Throughout the centuries, the Savior's "bride" has been preparing herself for the day when she would meet him.

10. Literally "slaves."

11. See our discussion of Rev 1:8; 4:8; 11:17; 15:3; 16:7, 14; 19:15; 21:22.

12. Rev 19:6–8 functions as a deliverance doxology by commemorating the Lord's triumphant reign. The praise chorus declares the almighty Creator's royal power and links his sovereignty to Babylon's defeat and the saints' vindication. By shifting the focus from judgment to worship, the hymn proclaims that God's righteous acts prepare the church, the bride, for the marriage of the Lamb, which culminates in the saints' redemptive union with him. On this point, see the detailed analysis of Brighton, *Revelation*, 491–98.

13. See Isa 61:10—62:5.

14. See Isa 49:18; 50:1; 54:1–7; 61:10; 62:5; Jer 3:20; 31:32; Ezek 16:7–14; Hos 2:16–20; Odes Sol. 38:10–11; Matt 9:15; 25:1–13; Mark 2:20; Luke 5:35; 2 Cor 11:2; Eph 5:25–32; Rev 21:2, 9; 22:17; 2 Clem. 14:2.

Unlike the lurid clothing worn by the harlot,[15] Jesus' "bride" is wearing a wedding dress made of "fine linen" (v. 8). In appearance, the attire is radiant ("bright") and pure ("clean"). This garment symbolizes the upright deeds that believers perform at the Father's initiative, in the Spirit's power, and for the Son's glory.[16] All of this is the result of the Creator's "not guilty" verdict, which he "pronounce[s]" on his holy people (the "saints").

A Five-Part Hymn of Praise		
Element of Praise	**Description**	**Biblical Reference**
Opening Summons	Call to offer praise with "hallelujah"	Rev 19:6
Foundation for Praise	Recognition that "the Lord our God, the Almighty, reigns"	Rev 19:6
Threefold Response	Summons to "rejoice," "be glad," and give "glory" to God	Rev 19:7
Reason for Celebration	The "wedding of the Lamb has come" and "his bride has made herself ready"	Rev 19:7
Bridal Preparation	The bride's clothing is "bright, clean, fine linen," representing the "'not guilty' verdicts pronounced on the saints"	Rev 19:8

At the command of an "angel,"[17] John writes that the Creator's blessing rests on all whom he "invite[s]" (v. 9) to the "wedding" feast of the "Lamb." This is the fourth of the seven beatitudes, or pronouncements of covenantal blessing, appearing in the apostle's prophetic oracle.[18] The divine summons is no idle promise. What the Lord pledges concerning this joyous event is "true" (or valid) and will surely take place.[19]

The ancient Near Eastern marriage banquet is a fitting symbol of the celebration that will occur when Jesus consummates his union with the church triumphant.[20] This joyous, messianic feast stands in sharp

15. See our discussion of Rev 17:4; 18:16.

16. See Isa 61:10; 1 En. 62:15–16; 2 Cor 11:2; Eph 2:8–10; Phil 2:12–13; Titus 2:14; Jas 2:24.

17. See our discussion of Rev 17:1; 22:8–9.

18. See our discussion of Rev 1:3; 14:13; 16:15; 20:6; 22:7, 14.

19. See our discussion of Rev 21:5; 22:6.

20. See Isa 25:6–9; 2 Bar. 29:8; 1 En. 62:14; 4 Ezra 2:38–40; Matt 8:11; 26:29; Mark 14:25; Luke 13:29; 14:15; 22:18, 28–30; Rev 2:7; 22:14.

contrast to the carnage noted in chapters 17 and 18. Eternal rewards await the redeemed, whereas unending ruin is the fate of the wicked.

Ancient Near Eastern Wedding Ceremonies		
Phase/Aspect	**Details**	**Participants and Customs**
Pre-Ceremony	Held after dark at the bride's house; the groom leads friends in a procession along a planned route to the bride's home	Groom and friends, joined by others along the way; includes singing, playing instruments, and dancing
Attire and Appearance	Bride wears an ornate dress, expensive jewelry (if affordable), and a veil symbolizing modesty and the transition to marriage; groom wears a garland of flowers symbolizing celebration and joy	Attire reflects bride's social standing; her veil signifies her virtue and new role as a wife; groom's floral garland conveys jubilation and the festive spirit of the occasion
Post-Ceremony	Procession returns to the groom's or his father's home; a lavish feast lasts up to seven days; at the conclusion, the couple is escorted to a private wedding chamber	Friends sing love ballads and share stories about the couple; includes consumption of generous food and drink; marriage consummated on the first night

John, perhaps stunned by what he has seen and heard, prostrates himself in homage at the "feet" (19:10)[21] of the celestial emissary. In response, the angel stops the apostle,[22] explaining that he is also a "fellow" bondservant[23] of the Creator, as are John and his Christian peers. The preceding individuals demonstrate by their faithful and sacrificial service[24] that they hold firmly to the "testimony" the Messiah bore in his life and death. Similarly, his followers witness to others[25] about their faith in the Savior.

The angel urges John to prostrate himself in homage to the supreme Monarch of the universe. After all, the Father, due to his love for the lost, sent his Son to earth to atone for humankind's sins.[26] Indeed, the essence (or "spirit"; v. 10) of Scripture's prophetic declarations is to offer

21. See our discussion of Rev 22:9.

22. Literally by uttering the idiomatic expression "do not see to it"; see Apoc. Zeph. 6:15; Ascen. Isa. 7:21.

23. Literally "slave."

24. By the presence and power of the indwelling Spirit.

25. Again, by the Spirit, like those testifying in a court of law.

26. See John 3:16.

a lucid and vibrant "testimony about Jesus."[27] Furthermore, the message that Jesus declares is central to the gospel truth his followers proclaim with clarity and conviction to the unsaved. In contrast, angels[28] are God's bondservants whom he sends to assist his children.[29]

THE DIVINE WARRIOR ON THE WHITE HORSE (19:11–21)

In the unfolding cosmic drama, John witnesses the opening of "heaven" (v. 11) and the emergence of a Conqueror who rides a "white horse." Throughout biblical times, cavalry commanders often chose to ride on these animals because of their stately appearance, triumphant posture, and spirited disposition.[30] In this scene, Jesus is the subjugator. The image of the "white horse" implies total victory over his foes, along with the complete vindication of his followers. The Messiah, at his second advent,[31] is prepared to wage a final, consequential battle against Satan, sin, and death, as well as judge pagan, idolatrous humanity.

In keeping with the cosmic trial motif found in John's prophetic oracle, the apostle emphasizes the Savior's righteous cause. He is fully just in using a series of covenantal curses to vanquish his enemies, condemn the wicked, and avenge their persecution of God's reborn children.[32] The preceding observations explain why John calls the Son "Faithful" and "True." Expressed another way, he forever remains genuine, upright, and loyal in his character. He also guarantees the certainty of whatever he decrees.

As with John's vision of the risen and exalted Messiah recorded in 1:12–16, the apostle notes in 19:12 that Jesus' "eyes" resemble "blazing flames," a description that symbolizes his infinite majesty, power, and authority, along with his unlimited insight and wisdom.[33] The omnipotent Redeemer wears many diadem-like "crowns," after the manner of ancient

27. See Luke 24:27, 44–48; 1 Pet 1:11–12.

28. Such as the one who speaks to John; Rev 19:9.

29. See Heb 1:7, 14.

30. See 2 Macc 3:25; 11:8.

31. See our discussion of Rev 1:7; 3:11; 22:7, 12, 17, 20.

32. See Isa 11:3–5; 2 Bar. 39:7—40:4; 72:1–6; Pss. Sol. 17:21–27; John 5:27; Acts 17:31; 2 Thess 1:7–8.

33. See Dan 10:6; 1 En. 106:5; 2 En. 1:5; Rev 1:14; 2:18.

monarchs, who donned multiple royal headbands to represent their authority over scores of nations.[34]

Also, emblazoned on the Son is a "name," known only to him, which emphasizes his upright character and royal attributes. While interpretations vary regarding what the apostle means, the current passage suggests that there is much about the Messiah that believers are unable to understand completely. For example, his person and nature are so exalted that they transcend limited human comprehension.

John recounts seeing Jesus dressed in an outer "garment" (v. 13) that is permanently soaked with "blood." Some specialists think that this description refers to the Redeemer's sacrificial death. Yet in the present context, the apostle may be talking about the "blood" shed by Jesus' foes, whom he slays in battle.[35]

The Father gives the triumphant Son—who perfectly discloses, announces, and executes retributive justice—a designation that sums up everything about him: the "Word of God."[36] This name recalls John 1:1 and 14, where the Savior is unveiled as the divine, incarnate Logos. To Jesus' faithful followers, he is above all else, the supreme and ultimate revelation of the One "who is, who was, and who is coming" (Rev 1:4).[37]

John observes that the Redeemer does not return alone. Behind him are the "armies of heaven" (19:14),[38] all dressed in the finest of "white," pure "linen" and riding upon "white horses." Their attire is appropriate, especially given the majestic and regal nature of the divine Warrior they serve.[39]

In an image adapted from Isaiah 11:4 and 49:2, John notes that proceeding out of the Savior's "mouth" (Rev 19:15) is a "sharp sword."[40] This object is a fitting symbol of the Son's ability to "strike down" earth's wicked, seditious inhabitants.[41] He will "shepherd" (or rule) the "na-

34. As epitomized by the dragon and the sea-beast; see our discussion of Rev 12:3; 13:1.

35. See Exod 15; Deut 33; Judg 5; Isa 26:16—27:6; 59:15–20; 63:1–6; Hab 3; Zech 14:1–21.

36. See Odes Sol. 29:7–9.

37. See John 1:18; Heb 1:1–3; 1 John 1:1.

38. Whether angels, martyred saints, or everyone of Jesus' faithful followers.

39. See Zech 14:5; 1 En. 1:9; 2 En. 17:1; T. Levi 3:3; Matt 13:40–42; 16:27; 24:30–31; 25:31–32; 26:53; 1 Thess 3:13; 2 Thess 1:7; 2:8; Titus 2:13; Jude 1:14–15.

40. See our discussion of Rev 1:16; 2:12, 16; 19:21.

41. See 1 En. 62:2; 2 En. 32:1.

tions" with an "iron staff" (that is, a royal scepter), which is an allusion to Psalm 2:9.[42]

Moreover, like grape juice flowing out of a wine vat, the Messiah will stomp the "winepress" (Rev 19:15) filled with the all-powerful Creator's "fierce anger."[43] In this ghastly imagery, the divine Warrior crushes his foes in a trough, causing their lifeblood to pour out. This observation calls to mind how people in ancient times trampled grapes to make them into wine. The "winepress" is a symbol of the Lord's wrath (or covenantal curses).[44]

Imprinted on the Son's "garment" (v. 16), at the place covering his "thigh," is a distinctive "name." It declares him to be the sovereign "King" over all who reign as "kings," as well as the supreme "Lord" over all who rule as "lords."[45] The preceding title sums up who Jesus is in relation to the rest of the universe. In a civilization with an emperor and many lesser monarchs and aristocrats,[46] the Spirit wants all humankind to know that the Savior alone is the most powerful of all. Every human and spiritual entity is subservient to the Messiah. Also, one day his kingship will be fully exercised throughout the universe.

Next, John witnesses an "angel" (v. 17) "standing" in the middle of the "sun."[47] This imposing and ominous figure uses a "loud voice" to summon every "bird" soaring high overhead to assemble for the Creator's sumptuous banquet. As noted previously, this gruesome "supper" contrasts sharply with the joyous feast awaiting the redeemed when the Lamb returns (v. 9). Specifically, the fowl will gorge themselves on the corpses of all the wicked listed in verse 18, who were slain in battle.[48]

Prior to the above massacre, the rulers and their military forces, under the command of the sea-beast, assembled to fight against the Messiah and his "army" (v. 19).[49] However, the insurrection utterly fails.

42. See our discussion of Rev 2:26–27; 12:5.

43. See our discussion of Rev 1:8; 4:8; 11:17; 15:3; 16:7, 14; 19:15; 21:22.

44. See Isa 63:1–6; Rev 6:16, 17; 11:18; 14:10, 19, 20; 15:1, 7; 16:1, 19; 18:20.

45. See Deut 10:17; Ps 136:2–3; Dan 2:37, 47; 1 En. 9:4; 63:2, 4; 2 Macc 13:4; 3 Macc 5:35; Phil 2:9–11; 1 Tim 6:14–15; Rev 17:14.

46. Who, like the emperors of Rome, ascribed to themselves an assortment of vaunted titles.

47. Where the celestial being could be easily seen and heard.

48. It was common for spectators in John's day to see countless scavenger birds feasting on the lifeless corpses of thousands of combatants whom the Roman armies and their adversaries slaughtered in brutal, armed conflict; see Ezek 39:4, 17–20.

49. See 4 Ezra 13:33–34; T. Jos. 19:8.

First, the divine Warrior captures the sea-beast and his lieutenant, the "false prophet" (v. 20). As previously noted in John's prophetic oracle, the land-beast uses spurious "miracles" to deceive innumerable people to be branded with the sea-beast's "mark" of allegiance and to venerate his "image."

Second, Jesus casts the fully conscious, satanic pair "alive" into a fiery lake filled with burning "sulfur."[50] Then, the divine Warrior uses his sharp "sword" (v. 21) to exterminate the rest of the duo's insurrectionist army.[51] Finally, vulture-like "birds" satiate themselves on the "flesh" of the slain corpses strewn across the vast battlefield. Within the honor-and-shame culture of ancient Jewish and Greco-Roman societies, such an outcome was regarded as the most severe form of degradation and humiliation that people could experience.[52]

Based on the mention of Armageddon in 16:16, some specialists think a climactic battle will literally take place near the city of Megiddo, in the plain of Esdraelon, in northern Israel. However, others think John is making only a symbolic reference to a final struggle during the last days, in which the Messiah will emerge victorious over all the anti-God forces of pagan, idolatrous humanity.

Parallels between Ezekiel 38–39 and Revelation 19–20[53]		
Parallel Theme	**Ezekiel 38–39 (An Oracle against Gog)**	**Revelation 19–20 (Final, End-Time Battles)**
Divine Summons to Birds and Beasts	"Birds," "every winged creature," and "wild animals" are summoned to "assemble yourselves and come" to God's "sacrificial meal" (39:17).	"Birds" are summoned to "come, gather together for God's great supper" (19:17).

50. An allusion to Dan 7:11; see Apoc. Zeph. 6:2; As. Mos. 10:10; 2 Bar. 59:10; 1 En. 27:2; 48:9; 54:1; 90:26–27; 2 En. 10:1–3, 6; 4 Ezra 7:36; Ascen. Isa. 4:14; Matt 5:22; Mark 9:43.

51. See Isa 11:4; 49:2.

52. See Deut 28:26; 1 Sam 17:44, 46; 1 Kgs 14:11; 16:4; 21:24; Jer 7:33; 16:4; 19:7; 34:20.

53. This is another example of typological fulfillment or prophetic foreshadowing in the Apocalypse. Table adapted from information presented in Beale and McDonough, "Revelation," 1142–50.

Parallels between Ezekiel 38–39 and Revelation 19–20[53]		
Parallel Theme	**Ezekiel 38–39 (An Oracle against Gog)**	**Revelation 19–20 (Final, End-Time Battles)**
Divine Judgment by Fire	"I will judge him with plague and with bloodshed. I will rain down torrential rain, hailstones, and burning sulfur on him and on his troops and on the many peoples who are with him" (38:22). "I will also send fire on Magog and on those who live in security on the coastlands" (39:6).	"Fire came down from God out of heaven and devoured them" (20:9).
Feasting on Fallen Warriors	"Eat the meat of warriors and drink the blood of the princes" and "be filled with horses and charioteers" (39:18, 20).	"Eat the flesh of kings, and the flesh of military leaders, and the flesh of mighty men, and the flesh of horses and of their riders" (19:18).
Identity of the Enemy	"Gog from the land of Magog" (38:2)	"Gog and Magog" (20:8)
Invasion Description	Gog "will come up like a devastating storm. You will come up like a cloud to cover the land, you and all your troops and many peoples with you" (38:9). "You will come up against my people Israel like a cloud covering the land" (38:16). "Gog comes against the land of Israel" (38:18).	"[The nations] came up over the broad expanse of the earth" (20:9).
Multitude Like Natural Phenomena	"Many peoples . . . like a cloud covering land" (38:9, 16)	"As numerous as the sand on the sea" (20:8)
Vast Assembled Forces	A vast "horde" of "troops" materialize (38:9, 15)	Deceived "nations" assemble for "battle" (20:8)

KEY THEOLOGICAL INSIGHTS

In Revelation 19, John describes three climactic visions: God's judgment on the great prostitute (vv. 1–5); the joyous wedding feast (supper) of the Lamb with his bride, the church (vv. 6–10); and Christ's triumphant return where he defeats the armies of earth, along with their notorious leaders—the sea-beast (antichrist) and the land-beast (false prophet; vv. 11–21). From these victorious scenes, we observe the proper way to celebrate God's justice, the manifestation of the church in complete victory, and the demise of evil forces assembled against the Messiah and his faithful followers.

First, we find that *the vindicated saints, in their celebration, draw singular attention to God's glory*. In this chapter's opening portrait of victory, the eternal Creator is the sufficient and final cause of Babylon's demise (vv. 1–5). His salvation, glory, power, truthfulness, justice, vengeance, and praise compose the substance of the worship song in heaven.[54] For this reason, the multitude gives adoration exclusively to God. The saints' joy and delight are found in the fulfillment of the Creator's redemptive plan and victory. The everlasting reminder of the harlot's downfall brings joy to the worshipers (v. 3) because in this they see God's holiness and righteousness on full display.[55] While this scene of victory holds substantial benefits for the faithful,[56] its ultimate purpose is to further the glory of the Father.[57]

Second, we are assured that *the church militant becomes the church triumphant*. The next depiction of victory portrays the bride of Christ prepared to unite with her groom and adorned with righteousness and purity (vv. 7–8), ready to celebrate the Lamb's redemption of his disciples.[58] No longer must the church suffer through trials and tribulations or continue to endure pain, loss, and death. Now, at last, she is rewarded for her faithfulness to the Messiah, and she is indeed blessed.[59] Jesus

54. In Rev 17–18, Babylon's downfall is described largely from the earthly perspective, where the reason for her demise, though according to God's purpose, is also the result of betrayal of the wicked prostitute by the ten rulers and the sea-beast. Here, in ch. 19, the focus is entirely on God's bringing about Babylon's destruction due to his supreme power and righteous judgment.

55. Osborne, *Revelation*, 665, adds that the "smoke of torment" (19:20), in contrast and comparison to the "smoke of incense" (8:4; 15:8), is a key component of God's display of righteous indignation against his enemies.

56. Such as bringing an end to the physical suffering of God's reborn children, vindicating them for their faithfulness to the Messiah, and celebrating the final defeat of the detestable harlot, whose evil system sought to defile and destroy Jesus' followers.

57. See our discussion of Rev 21:10–11, 22–26, where the culmination of God's glory, including how it benefits the redeemed, is further elucidated.

58. See Eph 5:25–27.

59. As we noted above and note in the following section, this is the fourth of seven beatitudes in Rev.

proclaims that his faithful followers are saved in the end—secure in his sheepfold and unable to be separated from their Savior.[60] At this wedding feast, God's promises find their ultimate fulfillment as the church completes her earthly mission and rejoices in her eternal union with Christ, which is marked by perfect purity and holiness.

Third, we see *the victorious Lamb return to earth, hurl the sea-beast (antichrist) and land-beast (false prophet) to their demise, and obliterate all who wage war against the Lamb*. While the Messiah's appearance here (vv. 11–16) has similarities to the description in the opening chapter of Revelation,[61] there are now added elements detailed above, which deepen our wonder and awe at his glorious manifestation. The vision of the returning, sovereign King and Lord effectively communicates his divine attributes and supremacy as the incarnate Son of God. This vision also establishes his full justice and righteousness in executing God's judgment upon earth's wicked inhabitants.[62] The Redeemer, previously revealed in majesty and exaltation at the outset of the Apocalypse, now returns to earth as the conquering, divine Warrior, who fights on behalf of the Creator and his reborn children. The Lamb's victory is never in doubt, for he annihilates all opposition with the sharp sword emerging from his mouth. Through this episode, the unveiling of Jesus as the avenging hero deepens our understanding of what it means for Christ to be exalted.[63] The truth, which was previously revealed in heaven, is now executed on earth. While the outcome is a stunning victory for those who trust in and remain faithful to the Son, it is a devastating ruin for those who reject him and persist in their rebellion against him.

IMPORTANT MINISTRY IMPLICATIONS

The ministry applications arising from Revelation 19 relate directly to the theological insights we noted above. They concern how pastors can prepare their parishioners for the consummation of the church's marriage

60. See John 10:7–11, 27–30; Rom 8:38–39; 1 Pet 1:3–4.

61. See our discussion of Rev 1:12–16.

62. In continuation of the cosmic trial motif, a consistent emphasis throughout the Apocalypse; see the table in our discussion of Rev 20, which explores this thematic pattern.

63. Hence, our understanding of the person and work of Christ is further advanced from earlier depictions of the Lamb as the divine Warrior in the Apocalypse.

to the Lamb, as well as the implications of the appearance of the fully exalted, conquering Messiah at his second advent.

First, *pastors should lead their parishioners in celebrating the victory God has won for them over the evil world system*. While the opening vision focuses on a future occurrence in heaven (v. 1), the church can live in light of this forthcoming victory even now.[64] Presently, the bride of Christ, in fulfilling her calling as the church militant, faces struggle, difficulty, and at times intense opposition. Yet even as this characterizes her experience today, by faith, Jesus' followers can take time to celebrate not only what the Creator has done for them but also what he will do for them in the future as he transforms them into the church triumphant. The optimal time to observe this anticipatory celebration is when Christians gather for worship. This is the fitting occasion for congregational leaders to help parishioners shift their attention away from themselves and rest it in the victory they anticipate when the divine Warrior triumphs over the indulgent, arrogant, and idolatrous Babylon.

Second, *we must encourage our congregants toward preparedness for the wedding feast of the Lamb*. In verse 9, we encounter the fourth beatitude in Revelation, namely, the blessedness of those invited to the wedding feast (supper) of the Lamb. Those who compose the bride of Christ, the church, are clothed in fine linen, which represents their virtuous deeds. On the one hand, this purity is God's gift of grace to them. Indeed, Jesus' bride is arrayed in a holiness not of her own accomplishment.[65] Yet on the other hand, throughout Revelation, those united with Christ are called to live in accordance with their identity as his bride. This calling involves pursuing the holiness and purity befitting those who are rightly called saints. Put differently, we are to engage actively in the Spirit-led pursuit of Christlikeness.[66] As congregational leaders, we are entrusted with the task of shepherding our people to reflect deeply on their identity in Christ so that, by God's grace, they may be prepared for the consummation of the church's marriage to the Lamb at the end of the age.

64. In keeping with what we state in our Introduction, this forthcoming victory speaks to the already/not-yet character of much of the prophetic information in the Apocalypse.

65. See 1 Cor 4:7; 2 Cor 5:21; Eph 2:10; Phil 2:12–13.

66. Consider the following Pauline passages that urge believers to turn away from sinful behaviors and instead develop Christlike character through the power of the Spirit: Gal 5:16–26; Phil 2:12–13; Eph 4:22–24; Col 3:5–17.

Third, *we have the blessed opportunity of presenting the Messiah as the warrior-hero, who alone vanquishes all those opposed to him at his return.* In our discussion of Revelation 18, we noted the tendency for Christians to sanitize Satan and his demonic forces into something less than real. There is a similar tendency among believers to sanitize Jesus, such that we focus only on the kinder, gentler aspects of his saving person and work while forgetting the division and offense caused by the proclamation of the gospel.[67] As we teach the whole council of God, we must not forget, downplay, or ignore the bloody, gruesome, and devastating portrait of the Lamb that we encounter at the end of chapter 19. The once humiliated, ethnic, Palestinian Jew hanging on the cross has risen from the dead[68] and ascended to the Father and will one day return to vanquish his enemies, both human and supernatural. Admittedly, the outlook is bleak for those remaining outside of a right relationship with the divine Warrior. Nonetheless, there is no justification for our shielding our parishioners from the grim aspects of the end-time picture of the returning, conquering King.

VITAL MISSIONAL RAMIFICATIONS

In Revelation 19:10, we find John, who is feeling overwhelmed by what he sees and hears, starting to worship the angel present with him. The heavenly emissary first exhorts the apostle to stop doing so, directing him to worship God. John is reminded that the "testimony about Jesus" is foremost in priority.[69] Immediately following this episode, John offers an editorial comment that the essence of "prophecy" entails believers' testifying about their faith in the Savior. As we noted above, this suggests that the ultimate purpose for prophetic proclamation is to bear witness to Christ. From this statement, we glean the following principles for missionary work.

First, *the central focus of our missionary message revolves around the testimony about Jesus.* Simply put, for missionaries, evangelism is the

67. See Matt 10:34–39; Luke 12:49–53; 1 Cor 1:18–25.

68. It is through Christ's humiliation and exaltation that he is now qualified to return as the divine Warrior who conquers. The vindication of the saints is dependent upon and follows from the Father's vindication of the Son through the cross-resurrection event; see Rom 1:4; Phil 2:5–11; Col 2:15; Heb 12:1–3.

69. For more on the significance of the phrase "testimony of Jesus," see Kistemaker, *Exposition of Revelation*, 517–18.

essence of whatever they undertake in cross-cultural contexts.[70] At its core, the work of evangelism is a prophetic task, where we declare the message of God's Word and shed light on its Christ-centered meaning and application to individuals. The testimony, or witness, about Jesus is the spirit, substance, and content of this prophetic message. As missionaries communicate in foreign contexts, we inevitably engage in conversations that cover a wide range of topics, such as cultural customs, social expectations, philosophical worldviews, and comparative religions. While all these may be essential to build rapport, deepen relationships, and lay the groundwork for our gospel witness, the true essence of missionary proclamation is not realized until the good news about Christ is shared and understood by those who receive it.

Second, *giving a consistent, uncompromising witness to Jesus' person and work is the true indication of missional faithfulness.* After the angel halts John from worshiping him instead of God, the heavenly emissary notes that holding to the "testimony about Jesus" (v. 10) is a characteristic of those who have remained faithful to the Messiah. From this observation, we discern that the chief aspect of missional fidelity is offering a prophetic witness concerning the Lamb. Determinants of missionary success are often reduced to visible, numerical, or otherwise humanly measurable indicators. While these benchmarks have their place, in the eyes of our heavenly Father, they are insufficient standards of success. Consider the fact that well-known pioneers of missions sometimes went years without seeing converts to the faith.[71] Admittedly, from a limited, temporal perspective, their efforts may appear to be unsuccessful. Yet the Creator evaluates the fidelity of his ambassadors in proclaiming the saving message about and from the Messiah.

Third, *effective missionary communication about the Redeemer requires a complete proclamation about who he is, what he has accomplished, and what he has taught.* When it comes to sharing the saving

70. As we noted in previous chapters, the concept of missions has historically been thought of as sending people from the Global North *to* people living in the Majority World. Yet over the past few decades, the landscape has dramatically shifted such that most missionaries are now being sent *from* Majority World nations to people living in the Global North.

71. Examples include William Carey in India and Adoniram Judson in Burma, who labored seven and six years, respectively, before seeing their first converts. There are several websites that detail the lives of missionaries like Carey and Judson, including their struggles and triumphs. Noteworthy are the *Christian History Institute* (christianhistoryinstitute.org), *Desiring God* (desiringgod.org), and *The Gospel Coalition* (thegospelcoalition.org), which frequently publish articles on these topics.

message about Christ, we must not limit our teaching to what we think is palatable to our audience. Because missionaries desire to make their communication about the Messiah easy to understand and apply, we are tempted to pander to others by leaving out the complexities of Jesus' person, work, and teachings. Yet this tendency falls short of the Great Commission, where the Savior instructs his devoted followers to teach their fellow disciples everything he communicated. This is a multifaceted endeavor. For instance, it includes sharing Christ's message of redemption, his humility, his sinless character, his call for believers to follow him, his invitation for them to renounce their sinful nature, and his triumphant resurrection. Furthermore, in the context of Revelation 19, the undertaking involves heralding the truth about the Lamb's impending return as the divine Warrior, who is ready to obliterate God's enemies. Therefore, the "testimony about Jesus" (v. 10), which is central to all missionary activity, is enough to occupy us fully in our evangelistic outreach.

Revelation 20

The Final Victory (Part Two)

LEARNING OBJECTIVES

- Explain the significance of Satan's imprisonment in the bottomless pit for one thousand years.
- Evaluate different perspectives on when and how the events in Revelation 20 are fulfilled.
- Consider why Satan leads a horde in a futile attempt to exterminate God's beloved children.
- Describe the final judgment and the eternal state of the saved and the lost.
- Ponder how end-time events inform your understanding of the relationship between God and culture.

CHAPTER SUMMARY

Revelation 20 begins with a powerful angel descending from heaven. The celestial figure seizes Satan, throws him into the bottomless pit, and locks it securely for one thousand years. During this period, the Messiah's resurrected martyred followers reign with him. At the end of the millennium, Satan is released and deceives the nations to join him in eradicating God's reborn children. However, the Creator defeats the horde and casts their leader, the devil, into the fiery lake of sulfur. This victory is followed by the final judgment, where the unsaved, along with death and the grave, are thrown into the burning lake, where they remain for all eternity.

STUDY QUESTIONS

1. Why does the powerful angel imprison Satan for a thousand years?
2. For the participants in the first resurrection, what is the nature of their reign with the Messiah?
3. What happens when Satan is released after a thousand years?
4. What does the final judgment teach us about God's love and mercy?
5. How does the reality of the final judgment either challenge or encourage you in your Christian walk?

CHAPTER OUTLINE

- The thousand-year reign (20:1–6)
- The final defeat of Satan (20:7–10)
- The final judgment of humankind (20:11–15)
- Key theological insights
- Important ministry implications
- Vital missional ramifications

THE THOUSAND-YEAR REIGN (20:1–6)

Throughout history, Satan has deceived humanity and tormented God's children. At the end of the age, however, the Messiah will bring an end to the devil's reign of terror. Accordingly, in the unfolding cosmic drama, John witnesses an "angel" (v. 1) descend from "heaven." In the celestial being's hand is a "key" to the abyss,[1] along with a massive "chain" consisting of metal shackles.

The "angel" has the God-given power and authority to "seize" (v. 2) the "dragon." John reveals that this evil entity is the "ancient serpent," who first appeared in the primordial garden to tempt Adam and Eve.[2] The wicked one is also known as the "Devil," which points to him as the slanderer and adversary of believers. The diabolical fiend is also known

1. Or well-like, bottomless pit.
2. See Gen 3:1–4, 13–14; Rom 16:20.

as "Satan," drawing attention to him as the opponent and accuser of believers.[3]

The celestial being secures the devil in chains for a "thousand years." This involves hurling the wicked one into the abyss and then locking and sealing its entrance (v. 3).[4] This action will prevent Satan from further deceiving the "nations"[5] for a millennium. After this, the Creator decrees that it is necessary for the devil to be "released" for a "short" while. Some specialists think these "nations" represent people groups who refuse to wage war with the Lamb. Others think they denote the survivors among earth's inhabitants who were previously antagonistic to Christ.

There are two primary ways of understanding the binding of Satan. Some specialists think it refers to the results of the Savior's death and resurrection, which has already restricted (or curtailed) the devil's power to deceive during the present church age.[6] Other specialists associate Satan's binding with the beginning of an extraordinary future age of peace and prosperity. This view indicates that the devil is a defeated foe who, along with his demonic cohort, await certain doom at the end of the church age.[7]

As we noted in our Introduction, there are sharp differences among specialists concerning the reference to a thousand years in verse 2. Experts call this the *millennium*, a word derived from the Latin term *mille*, which means "thousand," and *annus*, which means "year." Some think John is referring to a *literal* period of one thousand years, in which the Messiah will reign on earth. Others think the apostle is speaking *metaphorically* about an indefinite interval in which the Son rules victoriously from either heaven or earth.[8]

3. See our discussion of Rev 12:10.

4. See 2 Bar. 56:13; 1 En. 10:4–6, 11–13; 13:1–2; 14:5; 18:11–16; 19:1–2; 21:3–10; 54:3–8; 88:1, 3; 2 En. 7:1–2; 42:1; Jub. 5:6; 10:7–11; T. Jud. 25:3; T. Levi 18:12; Luke 8:31; 2 Pet 2:4; Jude 1:6; Rev 9:1, 11; 11:17; 17:8; 20:3.

5. Especially by counterfeiting and corrupting the saving message about the Son.

6. And therefore, *before* the second advent; see John 12:31; Col 2:15.

7. And therefore, *after* the second advent; see 2 Cor 4:3–4; Eph 2:2; 1 Thess 2:18; 1 Pet 5:8.

8. See Isa 11:10–16; 65:20–25; Dan 7:14, 27; 1 En. 91:12–17; 2 En. 32:2—33:2; 4 Ezra 7:28.

Three Popular Views about the End Times[9]		
Premillennialism	**Amillennialism**	**Postmillennialism**
Core belief: Christ returns before the millennium to establish a literal thousand-year earthly kingdom.	*Core belief:* The millennium is symbolic of the current church age; there is no literal thousand-year reign.	*Core belief:* Christ returns after the millennium; the church age is or becomes the millennium.
Biblical foundation: literal interpretation of passages such as 1 Cor 15:52; 1 Thess 4:13–18; Rev 20:1–6	*Biblical foundation:* symbolic interpretation of Rev 20:1–6; emphasizes a spiritual fulfillment (John 5:28–29)	*Biblical foundation:* optimistic reading of Rev 20:1–6; sees the church's mission as transforming society
Current church age: The gospel is preached with a mixed response; conditions worsen until Christ returns.	*Current church age:* The millennium occurs now (symbolically); the gospel is preached to all nations while evil simultaneously increases (Rom 11:25–27).	*Current church age:* The gospel enjoys progressive success; large-scale conversions lead to societal improvement and Christian influence.
Tribulation: seven-year period of intense suffering under the antichrist	*Tribulation:* a short period (possibly seven years) of great rebellion and tribulation at the end of the church age	*Tribulation:* brief period of tribulation and rebellion at the end of the church age
Rapture: varies between pre-, mid-, or post-tribulational; believers meet Christ in the air (1 Thess 4:16–17).	*Rapture:* no separate rapture event; all believers (living and dead) rise to meet Christ at his return (1 Thess 4:16–17).	*Rapture:* no separate rapture event; all believers (living and dead) rise to meet Christ at his return (1 Thess 4:16–17).
Second Coming: Christ returns to earth with raptured believers to establish his kingdom.	*Second Coming:* Christ returns once; all the dead are raised for a final judgment (John 5:28–29).	*Second Coming:* Christ returns after the millennium for a final judgment.
Millennium: literal thousand-year reign of Christ on earth with improved conditions; believers rule with Christ (Rev 20:1–6).	*Millennium:* symbolic period representing the entire church age from Christ's first coming to his return (Rev 20:1–6)	*Millennium:* either the entire church age or its final portion, marked by widespread Christian influence

9. For a structured, comparative analysis of premillennialism, amillennialism, and postmillennialism, see Blaising, Gentry, and Strimple, *Three Views*. In this work, Blaising (premillennialism), Gentry (postmillennialism), and Strimple (amillennialism) defend their eschatological positions and respond to critiques from one another. This format fosters a robust dialogue by illuminating key differences and theological nuances among the three perspectives.

Three Popular Views about the End Times[9]		
Premillennialism	**Amillennialism**	**Postmillennialism**
Israel's role: distinct future for ethnic Israel; a literal fulfillment of Old Testament promises (Rom 11:25–27)	*Israel's role:* "fullness of Israel" refers to elect ethnic Jews throughout history (Rom 11:25–27).	*Israel's role:* "fullness of Israel" refers to a large-scale conversion of ethnic Jews during the church age (Rom 11:25–27).
Final events: final rebellion after millennium; resurrection of unbelievers; final judgment; eternal state	*Final events:* final rebellion, general resurrection, final judgment, eternal state (Rev 20:7–15; 21:1–8)	*Final events:* final rebellion, general resurrection, final judgment, eternal state (Rev 20:7–15; 21:1–8)
Resurrection: believers before or during the millennium; unbelievers after the millennium (1 Cor 15:52)	*Resurrection:* one general resurrection of all the dead at Christ's return (John 5:28–29)	*Resurrection:* one general resurrection of all the dead at Christ's return (John 5:28–29)
Judgment: interim judgment to determine millennium participation; a final judgment after the millennium (Rev 20:11–15)	*Judgment:* one final judgment for all people (Rev 20:11–15)	*Judgment:* one final judgment for all people (Rev 20:11–15)
Outlook: generally pessimistic about current age; expects deteriorating conditions until Christ's intervention	*Outlook:* mixed outlook; acknowledges both gospel success and increasing evil in the current age	*Outlook:* optimistic about the gospel's power to transform society; expects Christian influence to grow
Eternal state: Believers live eternally with God; unbelievers face eternal punishment (Rev 21:1–8).	*Eternal state:* Believers live eternally with God; unbelievers face eternal punishment (Rev 21:1–8).	*Eternal state:* Believers live eternally with God; unbelievers face eternal punishment (Rev 21:1–8).

In the unfolding cosmic drama, John sees innumerable "thrones" (Rev 20:4) located either in heaven or on earth. Also, the Creator gives the people sitting on them the "authority to judge," but the apostle does not identify the occupants of these "thrones." One possibility is that the preceding refers to a tribunal of angels. A more likely option is that the occupants are believers—whether the twelve apostles, the resurrected martyrs from a final period of distress, or the redeemed throughout history.[10] In this case, the Father allows his reborn children to exercise judgment and rule with the Son, either in heaven or on earth.

Next, John witnesses the "souls" (v. 4) of believers whom the sea-beast "beheaded"[11] for testifying about the Son[12] and proclaiming the Father's saving message (namely, the "word of God").[13] Despite the abuse these martyrs received from the forces of darkness, they refused to prostrate themselves in homage to the sea-beast and his "image." Similarly, they refused to be branded with the wicked one's "mark" of allegiance, whether on their foreheads or hands.

The Father will vindicate the faith of all the Son's loyal followers by raising them from the dead and allowing them to reign with him for a "thousand years," whether in heaven or on earth.[14] John refers to this as the "first resurrection" (v. 5). The apostle explains that the Creator will not resurrect the remainder of the "dead" until the "end" of the thousand-year period. There is no consensus among specialists as to whether the above group will be restricted to the wicked only or include both saved and unsaved.

Even among those who affirm that verses 4 and 5 refer to believers, there remain at least two primary views concerning the "first resurrection." According to some specialists, John is referring to a spiritual resurrection of believers.[15] In this case, it takes place either at the moment when believing sinners are united with the Son[16] or when a person goes to be with the Savior at the time of bodily death.[17] According to other specialists, John refers to a bodily resurrection of all believers. Therefore, when the Messiah returns, he will raise them from the dead and allow them to reign with him in his kingdom, whether in heaven or on earth.[18]

In either case, the participants in the "first resurrection" (v. 6) are particularly "blessed and holy." Put another way, they enjoy the Lord's

10. That is, the church militant now transformed into the church triumphant.

11. A common form of capital punishment in the Roman Empire in the first century AD.

12. Like someone in a court of law.

13. See our discussion of Rev 1:2; 6:9.

14. See Apoc. El. 1:8–9; 5:39; 2 Bar. 30:1; 1 En. 108:11–13; T. Jud. 25:4.

15. Namely, being born again or born from above; see John 3:3, 7; 1 Pet 1:3.

16. See Rom 6:3–5; 1 Cor 12:13; Eph 2:6; Col 3:1; Titus 3:5.

17. See John 5:24–25; 2 Cor 5:1–8; Phil 1:23.

18. See Dan 7:9–10, 18, 22, 26–27; Wis 3:7–8; Matt 19:28; Luke 14:14; 22:29–30; John 5:29; 1 Cor 6:2–3; 15:51–57; 1 Thess 4:13–18; Rev 1:6; 2:26–28; 3:12, 21; 5:10.

special favor and exist as his sacred children. Here, readers find the fifth of the seven beatitudes, or pronouncements of covenantal blessing, appearing in the apostle's prophetic oracle.[19]

John reveals that the "second death" exercises no "power" (or authority) over those sharing in the "first resurrection." As with 2:11,[20] here the "second death" (20:6) refers to unending separation and exile from God, as well as eternal, conscious torment in the "Lake of Fire."[21] Accordingly, the first death is the termination of a person's temporal, earthly existence. Verse 6 adds that those participating in the "first resurrection" will collectively serve as "priests" of the Father and Son. They will also "reign" with the Messiah in his kingdom for an entire millennium.[22]

THE FINAL DEFEAT OF SATAN (20:7–10)

In the unfolding cosmic drama, John notes that when the thousand-year period has run its course,[23] the Creator releases "Satan" (v. 7) from his "prison." Despite the long passage of time, wickedness and rebellion will still characterize the devil, along with his unregenerate human sycophants. The apostle states that the "father of lying" (John 8:44) ventures forth to "deceive" (Rev 20:8; or mislead) the "nations" scattered over the entire globe.[24] The evil one amasses a vast army with seemingly innumerable combatants (greater than the "sand" along the seashore)[25] for one last climactic "battle" against the Creator and his holy people.

The reference to the insurrectionist forces of darkness as "Gog and Magog" recalls the language of Ezekiel 38–39, where Gog was the foremost ruler of the land of Magog.[26] This allusion to the preceding person and place epitomizes a vast, wicked horde under Satan's control. Specialists debate, though, whether this allusion is literal or symbolic, as

19. See our discussion of Rev 1:3; 14:13; 16:15; 19:9; 22:7, 14.

20. See our discussion of Rev 20:14; 21:8.

21. See our discussion of Rev 20:14.

22. See Exod 19:5–6; 1 Pet 2:5, 9; Rev 1:6; 5:10; 22:5.

23. Or is ended, finished, completed.

24. As before, especially by counterfeiting and corrupting the saving message about the Son.

25. See Gen 32:12; 41:49; Josh 11:4; 1 Sam 13:5; 2 Sam 17:11; Isa 10:22; Jer 15:8; 33:22; Rom 9:27; Heb 11:12.

26. This is another example of typological fulfillment or prophetic foreshadowing in the Apocalypse; see Jub. 7:19; 8:25; 9:8; Sib. Or. 3:319–22, 512–13.

well as whether it refers to a demonic or human army. Moreover, if it is a human army, there is disagreement about the origins of these hostile "nations" (Rev 20:8). To restate one option we noted earlier, some think the "nations" denote the survivors among earth's inhabitants who were previously antagonistic to the Lamb.

In any case, the devil's malevolent horde swarms over a "broad expanse" (v. 9) of the planet. Next, these forces encircle the fortified encampment of the "saints," which is the "beloved" community of the redeemed.[27] Yet there is no confusion about the outcome of this armed conflict. Just as the evil forces brazenly march "up," the Creator sends down "fire" from "heaven" to "devour" them. The entire army is immediately and completely incinerated.[28]

The "Devil" (v. 10), now a vanquished foe, is "thrown" into a fiery "lake" filled with burning "sulfur." The arch-deceiver will not be alone, for the sea-beast (antichrist) and the land-beast (the "false prophet") are already there to greet him. For endless ages to come this unholy, malevolent triad will experience never-ending, conscious "torment."[29]

There should be no uncertainty in the minds of God's reborn children about whether they are on the right (or correct) side of history. As believers, they are victors in union with the Messiah and the recipients of his everlasting, covenantal blessings.

The Threefold Banishment of Satan in Revelation		
Stage	**Location/Destination**	**Biblical References**
First Banishment	Cast out from heaven to earth	12:7–9
Second Banishment	Bound and cast into the abyss	20:1–3
Third (Final) Banishment	Cast into the fiery lake filled with burning sulfur	20:10

THE FINAL JUDGMENT OF HUMANKIND (20:11–15)

Unlike human victories, the Lamb's triumph over his foes does not end on the battlefield. Instead, his supreme mastery over his enemies reaches a crescendo before the Father's infinitely pure and holy "throne"

27. Namely, Jerusalem or Mount Zion, the Holy City of God; see Pss 78:68; 122:6; 132:12–14; Jer 11:14–15; Zech 3:16–17; 14:1–5; Sib. Or. 3:667–68.

28. See 2 Kgs 1:9–14; Pss 46; 48; 76; Ezek 38:22; 39:6; 1 En. 56:5–8; 4 Ezra 13:5, 8–9, 25–29.

29. See Gen 19:24; Ps 11:6; Ezek 38:22; 1 En. 10:13; 2 En. 10:1–3; 3 Macc 25:1.

(v. 11).[30] This culmination brings the cosmic trial motif found in the Apocalypse to a fitting and somber conclusion.

In the unfolding cosmic drama, John recalls seeing not only the Creator's enormous, gleaming, royal seat but also that the "earth" (Rev 20:11) and the "sky" (personified) try to run away from God's sacred "presence." Yet there is "no place" for these entities to hide.[31] Some specialists think that at this time God destroys the present universe[32] and replaces it with a "new heaven" (21:1) and a "new earth."[33]

Next, John witnesses all those who have ever died, both "great" (20:12) and "small," stand in front of the Creator's "throne." No exceptional reputation or noteworthy lifestyle will exempt anyone from the Lord's searing and penetrating gaze. Likewise, there will be no human life so humble or insignificant that God will overlook it.

It remains unclear who stands before the supreme Monarch of the universe as he sits in repose on his celestial dais. Some specialists think the judgment involves only unbelievers, while others think that both saved and unsaved will appear before God at this time.[34] In either case, the Creator's assessment will be fair and impartial. Only those who trusted in the Messiah—whose genuine faith was demonstrated through a lifetime of loyalty to him[35]—will be delivered from experiencing unending covenantal curses.[36]

Likely, John sees the Lord's attending angels open several scrolls that contain a record of the deeds of every human being (v. 12).[37] These documents will be the factual and objective basis for evaluating all people according to their works, along with the bestowal of either covenantal blessings or curses.[38] This observation does not mean that salvation is

30. As we previously noted, the Creator's throne occupies the literary center of John's prophetic oracle; see Ps 11:4; Isa 6:1; Ezek 1:26–28; Dan 7:9–10, 22; 1 En. 55:4; 61:8; 2 En. 65:6; 3 En. 28:7; 4 Ezra 8:21; Ascen. Isa. 4:18; Rev 4:2–3.

31. See our discussion of Rev 6:14; 16:20.

32. Namely, a massive de-creation event.

33. See Ps 102:25–27; Isa 13:10, 13; 34:4; 51:6; Ezek 32:7–8; Joel 2:10; Rom 8:18–22; 2 Pet 3:7, 10, 12.

34. See Dan 12:1–2; John 5:28–29; Acts 24:15.

35. By the power of the Spirit and regardless of the harrowing circumstances believers encountered.

36. See Ps 62:12; Jer 17:10; 32:19; 2 Bar. 24:1; 4 Ezra 6:17–20; Matt 16:27; 25:31–46; 1 Pet 1:17.

37. See Dan 7:10; 2 Bar. 24:1; 1 En. 47:3; 90:20; 98:6–8; m. 'Abot 2:1.

38. See Pss 28:4; 62:12; Prov 24:12; Isa 59:18; Jer 17:10; Sir 16:12; Matt 16:27; Rom 14:12; 1 Cor 3:12–15; 2 Cor 5:10; 1 Pet 1:17.

based on good deeds. Instead, the implication is that the Creator kept a record of whatever people did throughout their temporal, earthly sojourns. Furthermore, only those who trusted in the Messiah will be appointed for "obtaining salvation" (1 Thess 5:9) rather than "wrath."

The apostle mentions one final scroll that God has "opened" (Rev 20:12), perhaps through his attending angels, which is called the Lamb's "Book of Life." As previously noted, this document records the names of those who put their faith in the Redeemer for eternal life.[39] Only the regenerate will be delivered from the ensuing judgment before the "great white throne" (v. 11). In contrast, for those who spurned the Son, all that remains will be for the Father to condemn them eternally. It will be a terrifying scene as he issues a final guilty verdict against the unsaved from his heavenly court of justice (v. 12).

Next, in the unfolding cosmic drama, John witnesses the oceans of the planet release the "dead" (v. 13) from within them. Likewise, "Death" and the "Grave"[40] surrender their "dead."[41] Everyone is "judged" based on one's lifetime of actions. The implication is that no one will escape the Creator's righteous evaluation.[42]

Then, John recalls seeing the sovereign Lord hurl "Death" (v. 14) and the "Grave"[43] into the fiery "lake."[44] The apostle refers to this searing, inescapable cauldron as the "second death" because it is the final state of everlasting, conscious torment.[45] The apostle notes that the scrolls which detail humanity's deeds will be a sobering witness[46] that cannot be factually refuted.

For the above reason, the Creator will forever banish from his sacred presence those who do not have their names listed in the Lamb's "Book of Life" (v. 15). Instead, the fiery "lake" will be the place of eternal

39. See Exod 32:32–34; Ps 69:28; Isa 4:3; Dan 12:1; Mal 3:16; Apoc. Zeph. 3:7; 9:2; 2 Bar. 24:1; 1 En. 47:3; 89:68; 108:3; 2 En. 52:15; 3 En. 18:24; Jos. Asen. 15:4; Jub. 30:20, 22; 36:10; 104:1; Luke 10:20; Heb 12:23; Phil 4:3; Rev 3:5; 13:8; 17:8; 20:15; 21:27.

40. Or Hades, the realm of the dead, personified.

41. See 1 En. 51:1; Rev 1:18.

42. See Ps 62:12; Matt 16:27; Rom 2:6–11; Rev 22:12.

43. Or Hades, the realm of the dead, personified.

44. Which Jesus said was originally "prepared for the Devil and his angels" (Matt 25:41); see 1 En. 10:13; T. Jud. 25:3.

45. See Isa 66:24; Dan 7:9–11; 12:2; 1 En. 27:1–2; 48:9; 54:1; 90:24–27; 108:3–4; 2 En. 10:2; Mark 9:43–48; Matt 3:12; Luke 16:19–31; Rev 2:11.

46. Comparable to objective, incontrovertible evidence of guilt being presented in a court of law.

judgment for the unregenerate. This remains true whether the imagery of everlasting torment is taken literally or symbolically and regardless of whether the location is conceived as part of a heavenly or earthly realm.

The Cosmic Trial Motif in Revelation

As we noted in our Introduction, John's prophetic oracle prominently features a cosmic trial motif. This thematic pattern is characterized by several key elements that evoke a formal legal setting:

- The text employs language and descriptions commonly associated with judicial proceedings.
- The unfolding cosmic drama bears a resemblance to the stages of a trial.
- The rewards for the righteous and punishments for the wicked reinforce the judgment theme inherent in a trial.
- The role of witnesses in a legal context is linked to the suffering and death of Jesus' beleaguered followers.
- The narrative grapples with the question of divine justice in the face of rampant injustice (theodicy), a central concern in legal and theological thought.

Scene/Element	Description	Legal/Judicial Significance
Introduction (1:1–2)	John is to bear "witness" to what he sees.	Uses legal terminology of testimony/witness which frames the entire treatise as courtroom evidence
Letters to the Seven Churches (2:1—3:22)	Christ examines, evaluates, and judges the churches.	Function as preliminary hearings with Christ as both witness and judge, promising rewards or consequences
Heavenly Throne Room (4:1–11)	Description of God's throne with twenty-four elders and four living creatures	Establishes the divine court where judgment proceeds, with the throne as the central symbol of judicial authority
The Scroll and the Lamb (5:1–14)	A sealed scroll that only the slain Lamb can open	Legal document (containing an indictment and a verdict) that requires proper authentication by an authorized figure
Fifth Seal: Martyrs under the Altar (6:9–11)	The souls of the martyrs cry out, "How long until you judge and exact justice for our blood?"	Represents victims' testimony and petition for final judgments
Temple Opened (15:5–8)	Seven angels emerge from the sanctuary with seven bowls of wrath.	Court officers prepare to execute the divine sentence.
Seven Bowls of Wrath (16:1–21)	Systematic administration of judgment on the earth	Implementation of the judicial sentence

The Cosmic Trial Motif in Revelation		
Scene/Element	**Description**	**Legal/Judicial Significance**
Judgment of Babylon (17:1–18)	Declaration of judgment on Babylon the Great	Pronouncement of the judicial decision against a major defendant
Fall of Babylon (18:1–24)	Detailed accounting of Babylon's crimes and punishment	Execution of the verdict with full documentation of charges
Heavenly Multitude Rejoicing (19:1–5)	"For his judgments are true and just"	The divine court's verdict is affirmed by celestial witnesses.
Rider on White Horse (19:11–16)	Christ "judges and makes war in righteousness."	The judge renders the final verdict and executes the sentence.
Satan Bound (20:1–3)	The devil is confined for a thousand years.	Imprisonment of a convicted criminal
Judgment Thrones (20:4–6)	Those beheaded for their testimony are given authority to judge.	Court officials (or jury) rendering verdicts
Great White Throne (20:11–15)	Final judgment with scrolls opened and the dead judged by their deeds	Comprehensive final trial with objective and irrefutable documentary evidence
New Heaven and Earth (21:1–8)	Those who overcome inherit the new creation.	Final resolution with rightful inheritance awarded to vindicated parties
Christ's Final Declaration (22:12–13)	"Look, I am coming soon and my reward is with me, to repay each one according to what he has done."	Judge's final statement affirming justice is served

KEY THEOLOGICAL INSIGHTS

Revelation 20 provides an overview of the events that unfold after the infamous battle of Armageddon. At that time, the antichrist (sea-beast) and false prophet (land-beast) meet their doom, along with their armies of rebellious opponents to the Lamb. In this chapter, we find the account of Christ's millennial reign (vv. 1–6), Satan's final rebellion (vv. 7–10), and the concluding judgment of humanity at the "great white throne" (vv. 11–15). From each of these episodes, we gain insight into the nature of the millennium, the everlasting damnation of the dragon (Satan), and the only way of escape from a future time of accountability after the millennium.

First, we see that *one day Christ will rule on the earth in perfect righteousness*. With the sea-beast and the land-beast destroyed, every form of opposition to the Lamb eliminated, and Satan cast into the abyss (vv. 1–3), the only remaining authority is the Messiah's. He now reigns supreme, shepherding the "nations with an iron staff."[47] Christ is the perfect Monarch, for he is untainted by either corruption or power-hungry manipulation. Furthermore, he is unbending in his righteous and holy standards. Added to this, the Messiah's risen, glorified, and persevering saints are blessed by the Father to rule with the Son for a thousand years (vv. 4–6).[48] During this time, the earth is at peace, since the King of kings reigns in righteousness over all creation.[49]

Second, *despite Christ's perfect government over earth's inhabitants, some persist in sin*. Even with the dragon (Satan) confined to the bottomless pit, sinful people still populate the earth. While it may be difficult for us to imagine how this could be, we must remember that people do not follow Jesus simply because he is physically present. Consider that when he ministered on earth, most of his hearers rejected his teaching and chose to rebel against him.[50] True discipleship is only possible when the Spirit brings about a genuine change of one's heart in repentance and faith.[51] After all, people are sinners by nature and by personal choice. While the external influences that lead them into temptation may be removed, the inward heart-tendency away from the Savior remains. Consequently, at the end of Christ's thousand-year reign, Satan is still able to amass a vast multitude[52] to oppose the saints (vv. 7–9). While this final rebellion is immediately squelched (vv. 9–10), it reminds us that apart from the Spirit's inward renewal, the human heart remains devious and wicked.[53]

Third, we see that, *in the final judgment, the only way to escape the Lake of Fire is to have one's name written in the Lamb's Book of Life*. The

47. See Ps 2:7–9; Rev 19:15.

48. This is the fifth of the seven beatitudes in Revelation; see our discussion of 2:26–27.

49. While there are various views as to the nature of Christ's reign (discussed above in our expositional section of Rev 20), the anticipation of the Messiah's perfect rule on earth is a feature of most eschatological systems, whether during the thousand-year period presented in this chapter or in the manifestation of the new heaven and the new earth disclosed in chs. 21 and 22.

50. See John 6:60–66.

51. See Ezek 36:26–27; 37:14; John 3:5–8; 6:63; Titus 3:5.

52. Osborne, *Revelation*, 712, notes that this multitude includes those in opposition to Christ from all nations.

53. See Jer 17:9.

great white throne judgment is an event where the Creator evaluates each person according to what he has done.[54] The singular Book of Life is opened alongside the multitude of books in which are recorded everyone's works (vv. 12–13). Only those whose names appear in the Book of Life are saved (v. 15). This grim truth indicates that ultimately salvation is by faith apart from works.[55] We cannot earn, keep, preserve, or merit our escape from the fiery lake filled with burning sulfur. The names in the Lamb's salvific ledger are there because of the believers' union with him, not for any other reason. When it comes to meriting our redemption, all our pious deeds amount to nothing, for it is by God's grace that we are redeemed through faith.[56]

IMPORTANT MINISTRY IMPLICATIONS

Building on the theological truths arising from Revelation 20, we should encourage our parishioners to remain faithful to the Messiah and urge them to persevere by trusting solely in him for their salvation. As we do so, we give them the Christ-centered focus they need to navigate their lives in relationship with the Redeemer.

First, *we must exhort our congregants to remain steadfast, knowing that those who are faithful will reign with Christ in glory*. As we noted earlier, there is widespread debate among specialists regarding not only the nature of the messianic kingdom but also who are among Jesus' coregents. Whether they are a select group of tribulation saints martyred for their faith or representative of all Jesus' true followers, their lives are marked by endurance, perseverance, and a willingness to sacrifice everything for the sake of the Messiah and his kingdom.[57] The faithfulness described in this chapter is evident in those who reject the influence of the sea-beast (antichrist) and refuse to bear his mark of allegiance and bow down in homage to his idolatrous image.[58] In that same vein, congregational lead-

54. This is yet another debated point of eschatology, namely, whether the subjects of divine judgment are all unsaved or a combination of both saved and unsaved.

55. See Hab 2:4; Rom 5:1; Gal 2:16, 21; 3:24.

56. See Isa 64:6; Eph 2:8–9.

57. Within the Apocalypse, there seems to be a particularly gracious disposition of God toward those who have given their all for the Messiah, including sacrificing their physical lives. Yet this does not mean that Christian martyrs are intrinsically better or more valuable than other believers who do not suffer in this way and to this extent for their faith.

58. See our discussion of Rev 13:7–10, 15–17; 14:12.

ers should encourage their parishioners away from the deception of the antichrist and toward greater fidelity to the Messiah.

Second, *we must encourage our parishioners with the truth that those rightly aligned with God avoid the devastating consequences of Satan's final rebellion.* Though the Apocalypse describes terrifying plagues, widespread devastation, and death, it assures Jesus' faithful followers of ultimate redemption and vindication.[59] As Satan's hordes align to make war against God and his reborn children, the fire of heaven incinerates the antagonists before they can fulfill their diabolical scheme (v. 9). In contrast, the true saints, who have remained steadfast in their obedience to the Son, are forever saved, both physically and spiritually. Here, the final rebellion runs strikingly parallel to the account of the battle of Armageddon in the previous chapter.[60] In both accounts, while it may appear that everything is stacked against Jesus' faithful and longsuffering followers, he fights for them[61] as the divine Warrior and finally destroys his enemies (v. 10). From the account of this epic, end-time battle, we can console our parishioners with the truth that they are safe in the hands of their Redeemer and that they need not fear the devil's nefarious plans against them.

Third, *we must warn our parishioners that in the final judgment, only those whose names are written in the Lamb's Book of Life escape everlasting torment.* The sobering reality is that all forms of works-based righteousness have no place in a biblical theology of salvation. As congregational leaders, we must steward our responsibility to be clear about this truth. Even those who affirm justification by faith alone can be influenced by works-based notions of salvation.[62] The fact that we cannot earn our way into heaven is both a solemn warning and a deep comfort. To those who seek to secure God's favor by adding their own works to faith, we

59. See our discussion of Rev 14:13; 16:15. For an encouraging reflection on why true believers have no need to fear Satan's present or future activities, see Keener, *Revelation*, 480–81.

60. See our discussion of Rev 19:19–21.

61. The notion of the Lamb, as the divine Warrior, fighting on behalf of his reborn children is a common thread in Old Testament narratives which recount how the Lord protected and preserved the Israelites. In addition to our discussion about this theme in our exposition of Rev 1, see Exod 14:14; Deut 20:4; 2 Chr 20:17; Pss 56:9; 68:20; 140:7.

62. Some legalistic impulses stem from a misunderstanding of the role of good works in the lives of believers. As Jas 2:12–26 indicates, good works are not what believers do to earn their salvation. Instead, good works are an essential demonstration and validation of their regenerate status.

must faithfully warn that such efforts undermine the gospel and lead only to condemnation.[63] Conversely, for those who know that salvation rests entirely in Christ—received by grace through faith, we offer the sure consolation that God's mercy is not earned but freely given in union with Christ. They can rest assured that since their names are listed in the Lamb's Book of Life, they are delivered from spending eternity away from the Creator in the fiery lake filled with burning sulfur.

VITAL MISSIONAL RAMIFICATIONS

Within the end-time events disclosed in Revelation 20, we find implicit instructions and reminders about the missional task Jesus has called us to perform. Specifically, as we proclaim the gospel, we can offer our hearers assurances of peace, restoration, salvation, and safety. We must also warn them that all those outside a saving relationship with Christ are destined to suffer everlasting damnation and separation from God.

First, the *primary objective of missions is to introduce people to the risen Lamb*. This chapter emphasizes the significance of our relationship with Christ, whether it pertains to his messianic reign on earth, the protection he provides against the forces of evil, or our union with him, as evidenced by the inscription of our names in the Book of Life. The implicit question within each episode of this chapter is this: *Where do any of us stand in relationship to the Messiah?* The reality of Christ and his call to discipleship transcends one's ethnicity, cultural background, and socioeconomic status. While we have noted this truth in our discussion of previous chapters, the specific nuance here includes the stark differences in outcome for those who belong to the Lamb and those who do not. Those united to him by faith enjoy peace, security, satisfaction, purpose, meaning, significance, and glorification. Oppositely, for those in rebellion against the Lamb, everlasting death and destruction await them. In our missional engagement, we must confront people—lovingly and with the offer of God's grace—concerning where they stand in relationship to the Messiah.[64]

Second, *in the account about these end-time events, the whole world, along with its entire population, are in view*. No one falls outside the offer of God's grace. Similarly, no one falls outside the reality of his condemnation of sinners. Whenever we encounter references to the "nations" or

63. Gal 1:6–8; 3:1–9.

64. See Acts 26:26–29; 28:23–24; 2 Cor 5:11.

"all people" in the Apocalypse, we should consider the implicit missional principles they contain.[65] Here we see that the message of the divine kingdom, the potential deceit of the enemy, and the final judgment of humanity involves everyone. What we learn about the Lamb, his final victory, his final judgment, and his unending reign are equally applicable to all people and in all places. These truths should eliminate any delusions among us about our presumed, inherent superiority or entitlement based on our ethnicity, geographical locale, economic success, political status, or any other factor that, from a human-centered perspective, grants us special privileges.

Third, *at the end of the age, there remain only two types of people, namely, those who endure everlasting torment in the Lake of Fire and those whose names are written in the Lamb's Book of Life*. An emphasis on this clear contrast must remain central to our gospel message. In our ongoing missionary efforts, we may be tempted to shrink back from the truth that there is only one way of salvation.[66] Yet by doing so, we may imply that people can choose to luxuriate in unbelief without any dire repercussions.

By downplaying the reality of God's judgment, we may convey the falsehood that the lost can ignore their responsibility of choosing either to follow the Messiah or to reject him. Nonetheless, when we consider the sobering reality that one day everyone will appear before God's enormous, gleaming, royal seat, all forms of unbelief place dissenters in opposition to the Creator. He has commissioned us, as Jesus' missionaries, to declare that at the conclusion of history, there will be no neutral, unaffected party. *All* the dead, whether small or great (v. 12), whether significant in the world's eyes or otherwise, whether rich or poor, and whether slave or free, will stand before God to be judged impartially. We must also state that our only hope is to be found by having our names written in the Lamb's Book of Life.

Therefore, our message to the nations needs to remain clear. First, we proclaim the bad news to the lost that those who refuse to trust in the Messiah are in active rebellion against him. Second, we present the good news that faith in Christ is the only way to salvation.[67] All need to know that if they reject Christ, their destiny is to be cast into the fiery lake filled with burning sulfur to experience everlasting separation from the Creator.

65. As we have delineated in our discussion of previous chapters of the Apocalypse where all humanity is in view.

66. See Acts 4:12.

67. See John 14:6.

Revelation 21

The New Heaven and the New Earth (Part One)

LEARNING OBJECTIVES

- Explore the themes of hope and redemption represented by the new heaven and the new earth.
- Consider the significance of God's dwelling with his reborn children in the new Jerusalem.
- Describe the key features of the Holy City.
- Analyze the various symbolic elements in the description of the new Jerusalem.
- Recognize who enters the Holy City and who is excluded from it.

CHAPTER SUMMARY

Revelation 21 depicts a glorious vision of a new heaven and a new earth. After the original creation disappears, John sees the new Jerusalem descend out of heaven, adorned as a bride for her husband. In the Holy City, God dwells with redeemed humanity. Death, sorrow, and pain, along with any sinful, corrupting influences, are eradicated. The eternal dwelling place radiates the Creator's glory and splendor. God and the Lamb are the city's source of light, and earth's rulers bring their glory and honor into it.

STUDY QUESTIONS

1. What do the new heaven and the new earth replace?
2. What is the implication of God's wiping away every tear from the eyes of his reborn children?
3. In what ways are the new heaven and new earth a place of perfect peace, harmony, and justice?
4. Why is there no temple in the new Jerusalem?
5. What do the new heaven and new earth teach us about the nature of sin and its ultimate defeat?

CHAPTER OUTLINE

- The new creation (21:1–8)
- The new Jerusalem (21:9–27)
- Key theological insights
- Important ministry implications
- Vital missional ramifications

THE NEW CREATION (21:1–8)

In the unfolding cosmic drama, after the final judgment of humankind,[1] John witnesses the glorious new creation that awaits God's reborn children (v. 1). This contrasts with humanity's repeated, failed attempts throughout history to fabricate innumerable utopian communities. Each stillborn effort to reproduce heaven on earth[2] was fueled by Satan-inspired optimism, greed, and hubris.

The Creator will ensure that the situation is far different for the redeemed in eternity. They will dwell in the "New Jerusalem" (v. 2) and enjoy God's radiant beauty. Moreover, those who were victorious in this life[3] will experience unbroken fellowship with the Lord of glory.

1. See our discussion of Rev 20:11–15.
2. Including social, cultural, economic, and political advances fostered by science and technology.
3. By the presence and power of the sevenfold Spirit.

The apostle recalls seeing "a new heaven and a new earth" (v. 1). The Greek adjective rendered "new" denotes the fresh essence and superlative quality of what comes into being. What John witnesses are not mere renovations (rehabilitations) of their old counterparts but total replacements of "the first heaven and the first earth," which have completely disappeared.

Evidently, God ends their existence to remove any corrupting presence or influence of sin.[4] The Lord will also eliminate the vast and mysterious "sea."[5] In the Old Testament, the sea is a symbol for the agitation and restlessness associated with evil.[6] Likewise in Revelation, the "sea" (21:1) is the source of the satanic beast and a burial site for the wicked dead.[7] Yet in the eternal state, there can be no physical or symbolic place for this liquified, primeval vortex of iniquity.

As we previously noted, John observes what is comparable to a massive de-creation event. Put another way, it is a reversal of the original creation which God brought into existence.[8] What the apostle describes is consistent with Isaiah's reference to the "new heavens and a new earth" (65:17–22; 66:22). John, however, is not thinking only about a world free of sin and hardness of heart. The apostle's end-time portrayal is about a creation new in *all* its particulars.

Heaven in Scripture[9]		
Theme	**Description**	**Biblical References**
Divine Activity	From heaven God sends blessings to his children and judgment on his foes.	Deut 26:15; Ps 11:4–7
God's Dwelling Place	Heaven is where God resides and his sanctuary is established.	Ps 102:19; Isa 63:15

4. See Apoc. El. 5:38; 2 Bar. 32:2–6; 44:12; 57:1–3; 1 En. 45:4–5; 72:1; 83:3–4; 91:16–17; 4 Ezra 7:75, 88–99; 8:51–55; Jub. 1:29; 4:26; 23:18; LAB 3:10; 32:17; T. Levi 18:5–10; Matt 5:18; 24:35; Mark 13:31; Luke 16:17; 21:33; Rom 8:19–22; 1 Cor 7:31; 15:42–44; 2 Cor 5:17; Gal 6:15; Heb 12:27; 2 Pet 3:7, 10–13; 1 John 2:17.

5. On this point, see our discussion of Rev 13:1; also see As. Mos. 10:6; Sib. Or. 5:157–59, 447; 8:236–37; T. Levi 4:1.

6. See Pss 18:15; 29:3; 32:6; 46:3; 65:7; 74:13; 77:16; 93:3–5; 107:23–30; Isa 27:1; 57:20–21; Jer 5:22; 6:23; 49:23; Dan 7:2–3; Nah 1:4; Hab 3:15; Rev 12:12.

7. See our discussion of Rev 13:1; 20:13.

8. See Gen 1; John 1:3; Col 1:16–17; Heb 1:2; 11:3; 2 Pet 3:5.

9. For an extensive discussion about the role of heaven in biblical eschatology, see Middleton, *New Heaven and New Earth*, 211–14, 219–20.

Heaven in Scripture[9]		
Theme	**Description**	**Biblical References**
God's Throne	Heaven is referred to as God's throne, highlighting his authority and sovereignty.	Ps 103:19; Isa 66:1
Means of Communication	Heaven serves as a point of origin for divine revelations and interventions.	Gen 28:12; Neh 9:13
Praise and Glory	The heavens (personified) declare God's glory, righteousness, and creativity and summon all to worship him.	Pss 19:1; 50:6; 69:34
Transience of Heaven	Though majestic, the present heaven is not eternal in its current form; it will be replaced by a new heaven.	Ps 102:25–26; Isa 34:4; 65:17; 66:22; 2 Cor 5:17; Gal 6:15; Heb 1:10–12; 2 Pet 3:7, 10–13; Rev 21:1

Next, in the unfolding cosmic drama, John's attention quickly passes from the creation to the "new heaven" (Rev 21:1) and "new earth" and to the "Holy City, the New Jerusalem" (v. 2).[10] The Creator causes the new city to descend out of "heaven." Furthermore, the Lord "prepare[s]" the sacred domicile just as, in ancient times, a "bride" would beautifully dress herself before meeting her "husband" (the groom). The implication is that the city surpasses the beauty of everything else God has made.

Some specialists think that the new Jerusalem is a symbol of the beloved, perfected Christian community in heaven.[11] Yet based on the detailed information recorded in verses 10–21, others maintain that the new Jerusalem will be a literal city where God's people dwell for all eternity. In either case, the main point is that a new world is coming and that it will be magnificent beyond imagination.

John recalls hearing a "loud voice" (v. 3) shout from the Creator's sacred, heavenly "throne."[12] The voice announces that in contrast to what took place in the primordial garden after Adam and Eve's failed insurrection,[13] the Lord is tabernacling with his reborn children. More-

10. See Isa 52:1; 1 En. 90:28–29; T. Dan 5:12; Gal 4:25–26; Phil 3:20; Heb 11:10, 16; 12:18–24; 13:14; Rev 3:12.

11. That is, the church triumphant, now faultless and glorified.

12. As we previously noted, the Creator's throne occupies the literary center of John's prophetic oracle.

13. See Gen 3:8, 24.

over, the declaration that "God himself will be with them, and he will be their God" recalls his previous covenant with the Israelites. As with that solemn, binding agreement, the Lord adopts the redeemed as his chosen people and legal heirs for all eternity.[14]

John's beatific vision[15] of the future far exceeds whatever the Israelites experienced during the Old Testament period with the tabernacle and temple.[16] In the eternal state, the Lord will permanently dwell among his children, fulfilling their long-anticipated desire.[17] The saints will be his "people" and he will be their "God." The same "voice" also discloses that five scourges of fallen, temporal, human existence will no longer persist in the eternal state (v. 4)—tears, "death," "sorrow," "crying," and "pain" (or anguish caused by incessant toil).[18] In the new, everlasting order, all these forms of covenantal curses from the past will disappear.[19]

John hears the Creator, who reigns from his sacred "throne" (v. 5) as the supreme Monarch of the universe, declare that he is "making everything new."[20] Then, the Lord tells the apostle to record what is revealed to him, for God's words are "trustworthy and true." Put another way, his children can, with assurance, anticipate spending eternity with him in heaven, for they know that the Creator's promise is accurate and reliable.

In verse 6, the phrase "It is done" can be paraphrased as "Everything is finished." The idea is that just as in the first creation event at the dawn of space-time history,[21] so too with the glorious new creation, whatever the Lord decrees is accomplished and certain to occur. This is possible because God is the "Alpha" and the "Omega." The Lord's assertion—drawing upon the first and last letters of the Greek alphabet—is emphatic in the original. It is as if the Creator is declaring, "I and no other!"

14. See 2 Sam 7:14; 1 Chr 17:13; 22:10; 28:6; Pss 2:7; 89:26–27; Jer 3:19; 31:9, 33; Rom 8:14–17, 23; 2 Cor 6:18; Gal 4:4–6.

15. The beatific vision is a reference to the believers' ultimate, direct, and unmediated experience of the Creator's glory in the eternal state. On this point, see Bauckham, *Theology of Revelation*, 140–43.

16. See Exod 25:8; 29:45; 2 Chr 6:18.

17. See Lev 26:11–12; Jer 32:38; Ezek 37:26–27; 43:7–9; Zech 2:10–13; 8:8; Sib. Or. 3:785–87; Matt 1:23; John 1:14; 1 Cor 3:16–17; 2 Cor 6:16; Eph 1:4–5.

18. See Ps 126:5–6; Isa 25:8; 30:19; 35:10; 51:11; 61:2–3; 65:10, 19; Hos 13:14; As. Mos. 10:1; 2 Bar. 73:2–3; 1 En. 10:22; 2 En. 65:9; 4 Ezra 8:53; 1 Cor 15:20–26, 53–57.

19. See Isa 42:9; Rev 7:16–17.

20. See Isa 43:19; 2 Cor 5:17.

21. See Gen 1:1—2:3; John 1:3; Col 1:16–17; Heb 1:2–3; 11:3.

God's proclamation is comparable to his saying that he is the "Beginning" and the "End." It is also comparable to the expression "the First and the Last."[22] The idea behind these statements—applied interchangeably to both the Father and the Son—is one of totality.[23] Expressed differently, God is the commencement and consummation of all things. Also, his rule encompasses the past, the present, and the future. Moreover, the Father is sovereign over all that takes place in human history and, through the Son, is directing its course to a final and proper conclusion.[24]

Next, John hears the Creator promise to give "water" (v. 6) without cost from the life-giving fountain to everyone who is "thirsty."[25] This pledge is a vivid reminder of the refreshment and contentment which believers will enjoy in heaven.[26] In eternity, God will permanently satisfy the yearnings of the believer's soul. This assurance is grounded in the Lord's infinitely pure and utterly distinctive nature.

Those who are victorious in this life[27] will receive an everlasting inheritance and an abiding relationship. They will be the eternal people of almighty "God" (v. 7).[28] Moreover, virtue and purity will characterize life for the redeemed in heaven. In contrast, the Creator will ban from his sacred presence all who are characterized by the vices listed in verse 8.[29] Their habitually wicked actions will be irrefutable evidence of their unregenerate status.[30] In turn, the Lord is justified to imprison them in the fiery lake filled with burning "sulfur" to experience unrelenting, conscious torment.[31] As before,[32] John reveals that this grim fate is the "second death," or eternal separation and exile from God.

22. See our discussion of Rev 1:17; 22:13.

23. See Isa 41:4; 44:6; 48:12.

24. See 1 Cor 15:23–28; Col 1:17; Heb 1:3.

25. See our discussion of Rev 22:17.

26. See Pss 23:2; 36:8–9; 42:1; 46:4; 63:1; Isa 12:3; 49:10; 55:1; Jer 2:13; Ezek 34:10–16; Joel 3:18; Odes Sol. 6:18; 30:1–2; Matt 11:28–30; John 4:10, 14; 6:35; 7:37–39; Rev 7:16–17.

27. By remaining united and faithful to the Lamb; see Rev 12:11.

28. See 2 Sam 7:14; Ps 2:7; Jub. 1:24; Heb 1:5.

29. Namely, the "cowardly, unbelieving, detestable, murderers, adulterers, sorcerers, idolaters, and all the liars"; see our discussion of Rev 9:21; 21:27; 22:15.

30. See Matt 7:21–23.

31. See Gen 19:24; Ps 11:6; Ezek 38:22; 2 En. 10:2, 4; 3 Macc 2:5.

32. See our discussion of Rev 2:11; 14:10; 19:20; 20:6, 14.

THE NEW JERUSALEM (21:9–27)

Two Contrasting Cities in Revelation[33]		
Comparison	**Babylon the Great (From the World Below)**	**The New Jerusalem (From Heaven Above)**
Clothing	Clothed with purple and scarlet (17:4)	Clothed with bright, clean, and fine linen (19:8)
Destiny	Woe and immediate judgment (18:10)	Blessing, cleansing, and access to the life-giving tree (22:14)
Divine Call	A heaven-sent command for the regenerate to leave Babylon (18:4)	A divine invitation for the regenerate to enter the eternal city (22:14)
Global Influence	The prideful, prosperous, and powerful city that rules over earth's pagan monarchs (17:18)	The Holy City coming down out of heaven from God (21:2, 10)
Glory	Characterized by self-glory (18:7)	Reflects the glory of God (21:11, 13)
Impact on the Nations	Nations led astray by Babylon's magic spells (18:23)	Fruit produced by the life-giving tree for the healing of the nations (22:2)
Inhabitants	A dwelling place for every unclean demon, spirit, bird, and despised beast (18:2)	Nothing that is unclean, along with no one who does what is detestable or who tells lies, ever enters (21:27).
Material Adornment	Cargo consisting of gold, precious stones, pearls, fine linen, purple cloth, silk, and scarlet fabric (17:4; 18:12, 16)	A radiant domicile consisting of crystal-clear jasper, pure gold, and exquisite pearls (21:11, 18, 21)
Moral Character	Notorious for sins and crimes (18:4–6)	Acclaimed for righteous deeds (19:8)
Relationship with the Nations	Earth's pagan rulers commit adultery with and mourn over Babylon's demise (18:9).	Earth's regenerate rulers bring their glory into the eternal city (21:24).
Vision Introduction	"Come, I will show you the judgment on the great prostitute who is sitting on many waters" (17:1).	"Come, I will show you the bride, the wife of the Lamb" (21:9).

In the unfolding cosmic drama, John draws attention to one of the "seven angels" (v. 9). He had responsibility for one of "seven bowls" filled with

33. Table adapted from information presented in Sturm, *The Ultimate Exodus*, 4.

"seven" concluding "plagues" (or covenantal curses).[34] The celestial being might be the same angel who revealed to the apostle the judgment of the brazen, filthy "prostitute" (17:1) enthroned on "many waters."

The angel summons John to see the "bride" (21:9), who is the "wife of the Lamb." Previously, in verse 2, the "New Jerusalem" is described as a "bride" who is exquisitely "adorned" for her "husband." John recalls being transported by the Spirit to a huge, majestic "mountain" (v. 10).[35] "Spirit" could also refer to John's human spirit.

In either case, the apostle seems to have been in a trancelike, visionary state as he views the "Holy City"—the new "Jerusalem"—descend out of "heaven" from the Creator.[36] This magnificent gift of grace is the final dwelling place[37] for all those who remain loyal to the Messiah throughout their earthly sojourns. In sum, the new Jerusalem denotes both a redeemed people and a sacred locale. Hebrews 11:8–10 reveals that Abraham had the preceding celestial home in mind when he began his epic journey to Canaan at the age of seventy-five.[38] By faith, he progressively made his way to a site that God had promised to the patriarch and his descendants, even though Abraham did not know his specific destination.

John is thinking about this blessed metropolis when he says that the everlasting abode of the redeemed is filled with the "glory of God" (Rev 21:11) and that its "radiance" (or brilliance) is like an extremely "precious" jewel.[39] Indeed, the "Holy City" (v. 10) is "crystal-clear" (v. 11) like prized, translucent "jasper." In biblical times, this "stone" tended to be mostly reddish in hue, though jasper also is green, brown, blue, yellow, or white in color. The gleaming of the new "Jerusalem" (v. 10) like a gemstone suggests that it radiates the infinite majesty of the Creator.

The megacity is also depicted as an enormous gold cube—the same shape as the Most Holy Place in the tabernacle and temple.[40] In ancient Israel, both the tabernacle and the temple were set apart for God and became the locale where he manifested his sacred presence among his

34. See our discussion of Rev 15:1, 5–6; 16:1.

35. See Exod 19:1–3; Deut 34:1–4; Isa 2:2; 4:1–5; Ezek 40:1–2; Mic 4:1; 1 En. 18:8; 24:1–3; 25:3; Jub. 4:26.

36. See 4 Ezra 13:35–36.

37. Signifying the uniting of heaven and earth.

38. See Gen 12:1–9; John 8:56.

39. See Isa 60:1, 2, 19; Ezek 43:5; Rev 15:8; 21:23.

40. See Exod 25:11; 1 Kgs 6:20; 2 Chr 3:4; Rev 21:18, 21.

people. Every detail of their exterior construction and interior contents were to correspond exactly with the Lord's definitive instructions.[41]

As for the eternal city in heaven, all its dimensions are multiples of twelve. This number symbolically designates the fullness and unity of God's redeemed children throughout salvation history. For instance, the new "Jerusalem" has a massive, "high wall" (v. 12)[42] with twelve "gates. Also, "engraved" on these are the "names" of the twelve "tribes" of the nation of "Israel,"[43] and there are twelve "angels" stationed at the "gates" to keep its entrances safe.

Long ago, after Adam and Eve sinned in the ancient orchard of Eden (Gen 3:8), the Creator "stationed cherubim" (v. 24) east of the sacred enclave. These angelic sentries used a "flaming sword," which moved back and forth in all directions, to "guard" the access point to the "Tree of Life." In contrast, John sees that the east, north, south, and west sides of the glorious city in his vision each has "three gates" (Rev 21:13), which permit entrance from any point on the compass.[44] Moreover, the "wall" (v. 14) of the new "Jerusalem" (v. 10) has twelve foundation stones, and on them are inscribed the twelve "names" (v. 14) of the twelve "apostles" of the "Lamb" (that is, one apostle's name per stone).[45]

The angel who is speaking with John holds a "gold measuring rod" (v. 15) so that the celestial being can determine the dimensions of the "city," along with its "gates" and "wall."[46] The "length, width, and height" (v. 16) of the "Holy City" (v. 10) are equal,[47] making it an enormous, perfectly symmetrical, and spectacular gold cube.[48] Next, the celestial being "measure[s]" (v. 17) the "wall" of the metropolis, according to "human" standards used when John lived. It is "144 cubits"[49] thick (or high), which emphasizes the immense spaciousness and security of the everlasting domicile.

41. See Exod 25:9, 40; 26:30; 27:8; 31:11; 39:32, 42, 43; 40:16, 21, 23, 25, 27, 32; Num 8:4; Acts 7:44; Heb 8:5.

42. Suggestive of divine protection and security; see Isa 26:1; Zech 2:5.

43. See Exod 28:21; Ezek 48:30–35.

44. See 1 Chr 9:24; Ezek 42:16–20.

45. See 1 Kgs 5:17; Eph 2:20.

46. See Ezek 40:3; 42:16–17.

47. "12,000 stadia" (Rev 21:16), or about 1,400 miles.

48. Larger, in fact, than the modern state of Israel; see 1 Kgs 6:20; Ezek 45:2.

49. Or about 200 feet.

The "wall" (v. 18) is also made of solid "jasper."[50] Moreover, as noted earlier, the expansive, pristine city is "pure gold," like transparent "glass."[51] The foundation stones of the "city's wall" (v. 19) are inlaid with twelve gems, which John lists in verses 19 and 20. Each of the twelve "gates" (v. 21) is made from just one massive "pearl." Also, the main "street" of the sacred domicile is made of "pure gold" and as "transparent" as "glass."

All the preceding details indicate that the stunning city John sees in his vision has a splendor and opulence reflecting the beauty and magnificence of the triune Creator.[52] Furthermore, the eternal home of all God's reborn children[53]—spanning the entire era of salvation history—is characterized by awesomeness and durability.

Next, John observes that there is no "temple" (v. 22) in the holy enclave. Indeed, a sanctuary is no longer needed, for the all-powerful Monarch (the "Lord God Almighty")[54] and the "Lamb" are now the everlasting "temple" for the redeemed.[55] Similarly, the "Holy City" (v. 10) has no need for either the "sun" (v. 23) or the "moon" to provide any light. After all, the Creator's "glory" illumines the domicile, and the "Lamb," as its "lamp," supplies it with all the light it needs for all eternity.[56]

All the "nations" (v. 24)[57] will "walk"[58] in the "light" shining upon the new "Jerusalem" (v. 10). Likewise, the monarchs throughout the planet will continuously bring their "glory" (v. 24; or splendor) into the astonishing metropolis.[59] The "Holy City" (v. 10) will truly be the center of life for the redeemed in eternity. It will be such a haven that throughout the "day" (v. 25) its "gates" will always remain open.[60] Even

50. A precious stone that varied in color, including purple, blue, green, and yellow.

51. See Tob 13:16–17.

52. See Exod 28:16–21; 39:9–14; Isa 54:11–12; Ezek 28:13–14.

53. The end-time "Israel of God"; see Gal 6:16.

54. See our discussion of Rev 1:8; 4:8; 11:17; 15:3; 16:7, 14; 19:6, 15.

55. See Isa 8:14; Jub. 1:17, 28; John 2:18–22.

56. See Isa 60:19–20; Jer 3:16–17; Hab 2:14, 16, 20; 4 Ezra 2:35; 7:39–42; Lev. Rab. 24:2; Rev 22:5.

57. Namely, the redeemed from around the globe.

58. That is, conduct daily activities.

59. See Ps 72:10–11; Isa 2:2–5; 60:3, 5, 11; Mic 4:1–5; Pss. Sol. 17:34; Sib. Or. 3:772–74; T. Ben. 9:2; T. Naph. 8:3; Tob 13:11; John 14:2–3; 2 Cor 5:1–5.

60. See Isa 60:10–11.

the "night," with all the fears and uncertainties connected with it, will be eliminated.[61]

Darkness and Light as Symbols	
Darkness	**Biblical References**
Associated with Satan as the source of ignorance, superstition, and oppression	1 John 1:5–7
Associated with wickedness, turmoil, and evil	Job 18:18; 21:17
Characterizes the unrepentant and evil at the end of the age	Rev 16:10; 18:23
Epitomizes spiritual blindness and rejection of the Messiah	John 1:4–5; 12:35
Existed before creation; associated with chaos and precreation disorder	Gen 1:2
Represents human ignorance of God's will and sin	Job 24:13–17; Isa 24:13–17
Symbolizes death and the realm of the dead (*Sheol*)	Job 10:21–22; 17:16; 38:17
Light	**Biblical References**
Brought into existence by God at creation	Gen 1:3–4
Comes from God as the essence and source of light, knowledge, and understanding	Ps 27:1; 1 John 1:5–7
Represents spiritual illumination and guidance	Ps 119:105; John 1:4–5
Symbolizes God's presence, truth, holiness, and redemptive activity	Ps 27:1; 1 John 1:5–7

The sacred dwelling will be a cosmopolitan place, where redeemed humanity in all its cultural diversity will live together in safety and tranquility. Assuredly, the "nations" (v. 26), along with all their "glory" and "honor," will stream into the new "Jerusalem" (v. 10). As with 5:9, 7:9, and 15:4, in 21:24 and 26, there is evidence of the success of missionary work.

John states that the Creator will vindicate the faith and faithfulness of his children by prohibiting any immoral or wicked people from entering the holy abode (v. 27). Such individuals include those who are idolatrous, degenerate, and unscrupulous.[62] Indeed, the inhabitants of the new Jerusalem will be only those whose names are engraved in the

61. See our discussion of Rev 22:5.

62. See our discussion of Rev 9:21; 21:8; 22:11, 15.

Lamb's scroll of the living.[63] These are Jesus' followers, who remained loyal to him, even to the point of being martyred for their faith.

Parallels between Zion's Future Splendor, Ezekiel's End-Time Temple, and the New Jerusalem[64]		
Prophetic Element	**Old Testament Vision**	**New Testament Fulfillment**
Divine Glory Filling the Temple	Isa 60:1–2, 19: "Arise, shine, for your light has come, and the glory of the LORD is dawning upon you" Ezek 43:2, 5: "Suddenly I saw that the Glory of the God of Israel was coming from the east. . . . The Glory of the LORD filled the temple."	Rev 21:11, 23: "It has the glory of God. . . . The city does not need the sun or the moon to shine on it, because the glory of God has given it light, and the Lamb is its lamp."
Gates Always Open	Isa 60:11: "Your gates will always remain open. Day and night they will not be shut."	Rev 21:25: "There is no day when its gates will be shut, for there will be no night in that place."
God's Throne among His People	Ezek 43:7: "This is the place of my throne, and this is the place for the soles of my feet" Ezek 48:35: "The LORD is There."	Rev 21:3: "Look! God's dwelling is with people."
Life-Giving Tree	Ezek 47:12: "Beside the river, on both its banks, every kind of tree will grow for providing food. . . . Its fruit will provide food, and its leaves will be for healing."	Rev 22:2: "On each side of the river was a tree of life that yielded twelve kinds of fruit. . . . And its leaves are for the healing of the nations."
Life-Giving Water	Ezek 47:1: "Water was flowing out from under the threshold of the temple toward the east."	Rev 22:1: "The river of the water of life, which was as clear as crystal, flowing from the throne of God and the Lamb."

63. See Exod 32:32–34; Ps 69:28; Isa 4:3; Dan 12:1; Mal 3:16; Apoc. Zeph. 3:7; 9:2; 2 Bar. 24:1; 1 En. 47:3; 89:68; 108:3; 2 En. 52:15; 3 En. 18:24; Jos. Asen. 15:4; Jub. 30:20, 22; 36:10; 104:1; Luke 10:20; Heb 12:23; Phil 4:3; Rev 3:5; 13:8; 17:8; 20:12, 15.

64. This is another example of typological fulfillment or prophetic foreshadowing in the Apocalypse. Table adapted from information presented in Beale, *The Book of Revelation*, 1039–1103.

Parallels between Zion's Future Splendor, Ezekiel's End-Time Temple, and the New Jerusalem[64]		
Prophetic Element	**Old Testament Vision**	**New Testament Fulfillment**
Measuring with a Rod	Ezek 40:3: "In his hand he had a linen cord and a measuring rod."	Rev 21:15: "The one who spoke with me had a gold measuring rod so that he could measure the city, its gates, and its wall."
Nations Bringing Their Tribute	Isa 60:3, 5: "Nations will walk to your light, and kings to the brightness of your dawn. . . . The wealth of the nations will come to you."	Rev 21:24, 26: "The nations will walk by its light, and the kings of the earth will bring their glory into it."
No Need for the Sun or the Moon	Isa 60:19–20: "The sun will never again be your light by day, and the moon will not shine to provide brightness for you, for the LORD will be your everlasting light, and your God will be your splendor."	Rev 21:23; 22:5: "The city does not need the sun or the moon to shine on it. . . . There will no longer be any night or any need for lamplight or sunlight."
Perfect Symmetry	Ezek 45:2—The sanctuary is a "square [measuring] five hundred by five hundred cubits" (about 875 feet by 875 feet).	Rev 21:16: "The city is laid out as a square. Its length and width are equal . . . 12,000 stadia" (about 1,400 miles).
Transported to a High Mountain	Ezek 40:2: "In visions of God, he brought me to the land of Israel and set me down on a very high mountain."	Rev 21:10: "He carried me away in spirit to a great and high mountain."
Twelve Gates Named for Israel's Tribes	Ezek 48:30–35: Gates named for the twelve tribes, with the city called "The LORD Is There."	Rev 21:12: "It has a large, high wall. It has twelve gates. Twelve angels are at the gates, and twelve names are engraved on the gates, the names of the twelve tribes of the sons of Israel."

KEY THEOLOGICAL INSIGHTS

In Revelation 21, John shifts our attention from Satan's final rebellion and the great white throne judgment to the everlasting blessedness awaiting

God's reborn children. This is because they dwell in his sacred presence with the Lamb. From this marvelous account of the eternal state, we gain insight concerning the new heaven and the new earth. Of note is the permanence of the Creator's abiding with believers, the impossibility of sin, and the splendor of their heavenly abode in its new, earthly setting.

First, *in the new heaven and new earth, the promise of Immanuel (God with us) comes to its complete fulfillment.* Isaiah is the first of the Old Testament prophets to use this expression, when he is told that a young woman (virgin) would give birth to a son. In turn, this child would signify Yahweh's protection of and provision for his people, even while the nation would endure hardship at the hand of her enemies.[65] Though this prophecy was initially fulfilled in Isaiah's own day, the fuller manifestation of Immanuel occurs when Matthew uses the term to describe the advent of the Christ-child.[66] Through his virginal conception and subsequent birth, along with his sinless life, vicarious death, triumphant resurrection, and glorious ascension, Jesus fully embodies the *Immanuel* promise.[67] Here, in John's account of the new Jerusalem, the sovereign Monarch of the universe declares that his dwelling is with mankind, forevermore tabernacling (tenting) among his reborn children (vv. 2–3). This final manifestation of Immanuel goes beyond all previous occurrences, for it is the Immanuel of both the Father and the Son, the Creator and the Messiah. Along with the sevenfold Spirit, they lift regenerate humanity out of sinfulness and suffering (v. 4), as well as bring heaven to earth in a perfect, permanent state of residing together.[68]

Second, *we see that sin, its consequences, and even its possibility are forever removed.* Because of this truth, the culmination of salvation

65. See Isa 7:14; 8:8, 10. The truth of "God with us" (Immanuel or Emmanuel) is seen throughout the biblical narrative, from the Creator's presence in the garden of Eden through the entirety of Israel's journey in covenant relationship with Yahweh.

66. See Matt 1:23, quoting Isa 7:14. At the end of Matthew's Gospel, Christ, as the true Monarch of the universe, commissions his disciples to herald the gospel to the entire world. They can do so knowing that their Immanuel will remain with them until the day he finally returns in great power and glory.

67. See Kistemaker, *Exposition of Revelation*, 557, for the connection between the promise of "Immanuel" and the Old Testament notion of God's "tabernacling" among his chosen people. This truth is brought into sharp relief in 2 Corinthians 12:9, where Paul declares that he is "glad to boast all the more" in his "weaknesses," so that the "power of Christ may *shelter*" (or tabernacle with) the apostle (emphasis added).

68. In the final "God with us" event, we have the assurance that the Creator's glory will never leave us. Also, the forces of evil will no longer conspire to disrupt and destroy what God intends for his creation.

history is indeed better than the beginning. At the dawn of time, the Creator gave our first human parents the opportunity to choose between obedience to his command or submission to the serpent's temptation and deceit.[69] Oppositely, at the consummation of the age, all sources of temptation[70] are forever removed, such that sin can no longer occur (vv. 6–8). Specifically, in the new heaven and new earth, the evil world system known as Babylon ceases to exist.[71] Similarly, the devil is finally defeated. He becomes a permanent resident of the fiery lake filled with burning sulfur, never to be seen or heard from again.[72] Moreover, the sinful flesh, representing the fallen condition in which all Adam and Eve's descendants are born, is eradicated. God gives his reborn children glorified, resurrection bodies.[73] They are now freed from experiencing any malevolent, sensuous desires, and their bodies no longer undergo decay and death. For these reasons, they rejoice in the fact that they are free never to sin again.[74]

Third, *in the new heaven and new earth, believers enjoy the beauty and splendor of their blessed Creator, the worthy Lamb, and their heaven-brought-to-earth dwelling.* The detailed account of the new Jerusalem's features[75] reflects the indescribable glory of the Creator and the unsurpassable radiance of the Lamb, as well as the beauty that surrounds them co-seated on the heavenly throne.[76] In John's description (vv. 9–21), we are meant to be overwhelmed with the jewel-endowed character of the city's construction and magnificence. This lengthy description prepares us for the depiction that follows of the almighty Lord and the triumphant Lamb (vv. 22–27). The Holy City is indeed opulent and a joy to inhabit. We are rightly impressed with the stunning picture given to us

69. See Gen 2:16–17; 3:6–7, 11–13. Adam and Eve's freedom to choose sin does not mean that God failed to create the world with functional integrity. From the beginning, he provided our first human parents with sufficient resources and incentive to obey his will.

70. Namely, the evil world system, the flesh, and the devil (Satan, the dragon); see Eph 2:1–3; 1 John 2:15–17.

71. See our discussion of Rev 17 and 18.

72. See our discussion of Rev 20:10.

73. See 1 Cor 15:42–44; Phil 3:21.

74. True human freedom finds its perfect expression not by sinning but in refusing to do so.

75. For an edifying commentary on the new Jerusalem as a manifestation of the "holy of holies," see Osborne, *Revelation*, 745–67.

76. Or perhaps a dual throne, as seems to be the case in Rev 5.

in John's end-time vision. Yet the magnificence of the Holy City is due to the Father's sacred presence and the ongoing manifestation of the Lamb in boundless glory.[77]

IMPORTANT MINISTRY IMPLICATIONS

As we noted above, the prospect of the new heaven and the new earth is a comfort and joy for God's reborn children. Those in pastoral ministry have an assuring, faith-affirming message to communicate about the truthfulness of the Creator's end-time plan, the personal renewal believers will experience with the disappearance of sin, and the safety and security they will have in the presence of their all-sufficient Lord and Savior.

First, *we must reiterate to our parishioners that the consummation of all things, as described in Revelation 21, is assured*. In verse 5, John learns that the words of the prophecy he received are "trustworthy and true." At times, it may be difficult for our congregants to accept that one day these promises will actually come to pass, especially for those suffering difficulty, along with those undergoing intense persecution for their faith. Believers can rest assured that God's promises are certain to happen, according to his volition and in his time.[78] Admittedly, as we discuss in our Introduction, the Apocalypse is filled with symbolic language, and some of Revelation's images and depictions exceed our ability to comprehend. Yet it would be incorrect to conclude that the content of John's prophetic oracle is devoid of any real meaning and significance. As congregational leaders, we can proclaim with confidence that since our loving, heavenly Father affirms the truth of his redemptive plan, then it will assuredly take place.[79]

Second, *we should motivate our parishioners toward holiness with the guarantee that in the end, all personal experiences of sin and temptation are forever removed*. One of the reasons we continue to work out the

77. In this sense, the superlative glory of the new Jerusalem is a reflection of the unimaginable, incomprehensible glory of the Creator and the Lamb.

78. See Heb 11:13, where many faith-filled saints of old died while not yet receiving in their lifetimes what God promised.

79. This message of truthfulness and trustworthiness is comparable to Jesus' often repeated phrase, "Amen, Amen, I tell you," in John's gospel, as an assurance to Jesus' disciples concerning the veracity of his declarations; see 1:51; 3:3, 5, 11; 5:19, 24; 6:26, 32, 47, 53; 8:34, 51, 58; 10:1, 7; 12:24; 13:20, 21, 38; 14:12; 16:20, 23; 21:18.

reality of our redemption with deep awe and reverence[80] is that, at end of the age, the Creator brings about the completion of our holiness. This blessed assurance of being fully sanctified is a strong motivation for us to become increasingly Christlike now in how we live. After all, through our union with Christ, we are empowered to die daily to our sinful nature and live for God.[81] Misunderstanding this truth can lead to apathy, fatalism, or a dismissive "so-what" attitude toward living out our salvation by the Spirit's power. However, when we grasp the eternal glory awaiting us in Christ—where we will be fully freed from sin's presence, we are motivated by gratitude to please our Savior in the present.[82] Church leaders can leverage this truth to encourage their congregants to pursue a Spirit-empowered walk of Christlikeness.

Third, *we must confirm to our parishioners that the Father and Son, along with the ever-present, sevenfold Spirit, are enough to satisfy our eternal longings.* With the almighty God as our resplendent temple, and the Lamb as our radiant lamp, we recognize the adequacy of their holy presence. They meet all our physical and spiritual needs.[83] This truth reminds us that when we seek God and his kingdom above all else, he provides us with everything we need. For this reason, we can rest in his loving care.[84] We must help our congregants to understand and live in light of the sufficiency offered by the Creator and the Lamb.[85] When believers seek to do so, they experience a foretaste of the promised blessings awaiting them in the eternal state. This includes the peace-giving realization of the safety and security available to them, especially as they submit every aspect of their lives to and remain dependent upon the sovereign Monarch of the universe.

80. See Eph 2:10; Phil 2:12.

81. See Rom 6:5–14.

82. See Phil 3:12–16.

83. The unending presence of light, such that there is no need for the sun, moon, and stars, represents physical provision, whereas the abiding, sacred presence of the Lord Almighty signifies the permanence of God's spiritual provision without the need for a physical temple.

84. See Matt 6:25–34.

85. Keener, *Revelation*, 510, notes that realizing this sufficiency is the "true wealth" which the faithful seek.

VITAL MISSIONAL RAMIFICATIONS

In the concluding portion of Revelation 21, there is a description of what happens within the new Jerusalem. The key feature here is the multiple references to the nations of the earth and the activities of its kings. Undoubtedly, there is a global view in John's vision of the eternal state. From this worldwide perspective, those involved in missions can invite the lost to become future inhabitants of the Creator's Holy City.

First, as we have previously noted, *no nation, people, tribe, or tongue is outside the reach of the end-time events depicted in John's unfolding, cosmic drama*. Here, at the consummation of the age, the nations bring their glory and honor into the Holy City, which is illuminated by the Lamb's splendor (vv. 24–26). The clear implication is that there presently exists an opportunity for anyone from anywhere to trust in Christ for salvation and one day join in the activity of the redeemed on the new earth. Indeed, the depiction is characterized by joy and fulfillment. It is not as if the nations are vanquished people, who, in cringing terror, endlessly serve the Messiah and his followers as punishment for failing to follow the Lamb.[86] Rather, the nations, in bringing their glory and honor into the new Jerusalem, do so with freedom and delight. From these observations, we see that our evangelistic message to the nations includes an invitation for the lost to become part of the God's eternal, heavenly dwelling.

Second, *a future day awaits when the monarchs of the earth will lead their citizens to offer their praise exclusively to their glorious Creator*. The last time the Apocalypse mentions earth's kings, they assemble in open rebellion against the warrior-Lamb at the battle of Armageddon, where he brings about their complete destruction.[87] There, the rulers are mentioned first in a list of those whose flesh is consumed by innumerable birds flying high overhead. Yet here, at the conclusion of chapter 21, the depiction is the exact opposite. Earth's monarchs are joyously worshiping the sovereign King, and they gather their citizens to participate in the activities taking place within the heavenly city. This is a depiction of governments and leaders who are free from corruption and oppression and who lead the nations of the earth with integrity. What a wonderful opportunity we have in our missional engagement to articulate to the lost

86. Those who choose opposition and rebellion to the Lamb find themselves banished from his presence, forever tormented in the fiery lake filled with burning sulfur.

87. See our discussion of Rev 19:15–18.

this magnificent vision of the future! It is characterized by the intentional and blissful submission of earth's rulers to the all-glorious Lamb, who eternally abides with them.[88]

Third, from the warning in verse 27, *we see again that only those whose names are written in the Lamb's Book of Life inhabit the Holy City.*[89] Admittedly, there is an exclusivity to this sobering statement. Yet in our missional engagement, as we proclaim the gospel, we extend an open invitation to the lost from all nations to be granted permission one day to enter the new Jerusalem. No one is either included or excluded from the cosmic ledger due to personal merit. Instead, the only basis for inclusion is being united to Christ by faith. This involves confessing the truth about his saving person and work, along with turning from sin and self to receive the Father's gift of grace. Simply put, our evangelistic message to the unsaved is an *inclusive* invitation to an *exclusive* allegiance.[90] In turn, the Spirit renders our faithful proclamation of God's Word effective when it is undertaken according to the truth he has revealed in it.

88. As so many nations today are repressed with governmental corruption and enslavement, the picture of virtuous leadership is indeed compelling.

89. See our discussion of Rev 20:11–15.

90. A leading criticism against biblical Christianity is that it is too exclusive, too prejudiced against other religious and secular belief systems. Yet the invitation to trust in Christ is *inclusive*, not exclusive. After all, everyone is welcomed to join the glorious adoration of the Creator and the Lamb for all eternity. While the way to salvation is exclusive to faith in Christ alone, the opportunity to receive God's declaration of pardon freely is open to all, regardless of ethnicity, gender, socioeconomic status, and so on.

Revelation 22

The New Heaven and the New Earth (Part Two)

LEARNING OBJECTIVES

- Consider the symbolic significance of the life-giving river and the life-giving tree.
- Take comfort in the promise that God's reborn children will worship him and reign with him forever.
- Appreciate the conscientious way that John faithfully reports the vision he received.
- Recognize that only the redeemed will dwell in the new Jerusalem with the triune God.
- Affirm the profound truths revealed through John's prophetic oracle.

CHAPTER SUMMARY

Revelation 22 records John's vision of the eternal state. He sees a river of life-giving water flowing from the throne of God and the Lamb. The Creator claims his beloved children as his own and watches over them. In turn, they worship, serve, and reign with him for all eternity. Jesus, after affirming his imminent return, contrasts those who have the right to partake of the life-giving tree with those who are banned from the Holy City. The chapter ends with a final prayer for Jesus' second coming and for his grace to remain with his followers.

STUDY QUESTIONS

1. What is significant about the life-giving river John saw?
2. What is the implication of believers' seeing God's face in the eternal state?
3. Why does Jesus emphasize the certainty of his second advent?
4. What does Jesus mean by referring to himself as the Alpha and Omega?
5. How might the hope of eternity influence the way missionaries reach the lost for Christ?

CHAPTER OUTLINE

- The life-giving river (22:1–5)
- The exhortation to remain faithful (22:6–11)
- The certainty of the Messiah's return (22:12–17)
- The apostle's final warning (22:18–21)
- Key theological insights
- Important ministry implications
- Vital missional ramifications

THE LIFE-GIVING RIVER (22:1–5)

In the unfolding cosmic drama, the same interpreting "angel" mentioned in 21:9 shows John a "river" (22:1) filled with life-giving, crystal-clear "water." The radiance (or brilliance) of the stream—which draws upon imagery found in Genesis 2 and Ezekiel 47—points to the tributary's magnificence and purity.

The "river" (Rev 22:1) pours out from the sacred, heavenly "throne" which belongs to "God" and the "Lamb." From there, the stream courses down the middle of the new Jerusalem's main thoroughfare, which, according to 21:21, is made of "pure gold" and is "transparent" as "glass." The "river" (22:1) and its "water" symbolizes the fullness of eternal life that proceeds from the sacred presence of the Creator. To those residing in parched regions (such as Palestine) in the first century AD, the above scene was a vivid image of the triune God's ability to quench the spiritual thirst of the redeemed.[1]

Noteworthy is John's repeated, joint reference to "God" and the "Lamb." It indicates that the apostle does not want believers to overlook the centrality and prominence of the Messiah in the eternal state. In this vision of the future, the Father and the Son are dual occupants of the heavenly "throne."[2] Also, the imperial role of the two is now a functional unity.[3] The fact that they share a single royal seat emphasizes the full divinity of the Son as well as his equality with the Father and the sevenfold Spirit.[4]

Next, John observes that a life-giving "tree" (v. 2) grows on each side of the vivifying "river."[5] This verdant plant, which alludes to what originally existed in the primordial garden, radiates God's creative, life-giving power.[6] Some specialists think that the Greek noun rendered "tree" should be taken in a collective sense to refer to an orchard lining both sides of the riverbank (perhaps reminiscent of Eden).

Regardless of whether the "tree" is singular or plural in reference, it produces twelve different "kinds of fruit," with a new crop appearing each "month" of the year. The "fruit" is a source of "life," and its "leaves" are used medicinally to heal the "nations." This reference does not mean that there will be illness in heaven. Rather, the "leaves" symbolize the well-being and vigor that all God's reborn children will enjoy in eternity.

Long ago, a life-giving tree existed in Eden's primordial garden, and it must have been lush. After all, in Hebrew, "Eden" means "pleasure," "luxury," or "delight." Yet after humanity's first parents sinned, the Creator banned them from eating the life-giving fruit produced by the tree.[7] In eternity, however, the all-powerful Lord will allow the redeemed to partake fully of his covenantal blessings, which are symbolized by the tree and its fresh, abundant produce.

1. See Gen 2:10; Pss 36:9; 46:4; Isa 12:3; 35:6–9; 55:1; Jer 2:13; Ezek 47:1; Joel 3:18; Zech 14:8; 1 En. 48:1; 2 En. 8:5–6; LAE 9:3; Odes Sol. 6:8, 18; John 4:10, 14; 7:37–39; Rev 7:17; 21:6; 22:17.

2. As we previously noted, the Creator's throne occupies the literary center of John's prophetic oracle; see Rev 3:21.

3. See our discussion of Rev 5:13; 6:16; 7:10; 11:15; 14:4; 20:6; 21:22.

4. See John 10:30.

5. See our discussion of Rev 2:7; 22:14.

6. See Gen 2:9; 3:22, 24; Ezek 47:12; Apoc. Ab. 21:6; 4 Bar. 9:16; 1 En. 24:3–5; 25:4–6; 2 En. 8:3–4; 4 Ezra 7:123–24; 8:52; Odes Sol. 11:16; Pss Sol. 14:3; T. Levi 18:11.

7. See Gen 2:9; 3:22, 24.

Moreover, after the Fall, God subjected all creation to a "curse" (v. 3).[8] This does not refer to some kind of magical spell. Instead, it is a deep disruption to human flourishing. It is marked by desecration, scarcity, isolation, and death, all of which reflect the brokenness sin introduced into the world. In the eternal state, however, the Lord will remove the "curse" of sin and all its effects. Likewise, the Creator will ban from the new Jerusalem all who are eternally doomed because of their iniquity.[9] This truth is another reason for the wicked to renounce their evil ways and for the upright to avoid the path of sin.

In the new creation, the Father and the Son will be seated on their joint "throne." Additionally, their bondservants,[10] the redeemed, will continually "worship" and offer priestly service to the triune Creator.[11] Admittedly, prior to the eternal state, God's reborn children know him only partially. Nevertheless, they look forward to a time when they will know him fully.

Indeed, the presence of believers with the Lord in heaven will enable them to see his "face" (v. 4).[12] It would be incorrect to infer from the preceding observation that God, who is "spirit" (John 4:24), has a literal human face. Rather, John speaks figuratively to stress that the supreme Monarch of the universe will establish direct, continual, and intimate communion with his reborn children.[13]

At the end of the age, believers not only will be like the Messiah but also will see him as he truly is.[14] Concededly, now the redeemed can view reality only imperfectly, like trying to see their reflection using an inferior mirror. Yet in the eternal state, they will understand their place in the cosmos with crystal clarity.[15] Furthermore, the apostle uses metaphorical language when he says that God's sacred "name" (Rev 22:4) will be written on the "foreheads" of the redeemed.[16] The idea is that

8. See Rom 8:18–21.

9. See Gen 3:14–19, 22–24; 5:29; Zech 14:11; Rev 22:15.

10. Literally "slaves."

11. See Isa 61:6; 1 Pet 2:5, 9; Rev 1:6; 5:10; 7:15.

12. Referring to the beatific vision of the triune God; see Exod 33:20, 23; Num 6:25; Job 33:26; Pss 17:15; 42:2; 84:7; 4 Ezra 7:91, 98; Jub. 1:28; Matt 5:8; 2 Cor 3:18; 1 Tim 6:16; Heb 12:14; Rev 22:4.

13. On this point, see Middleton, *New Heaven and New Earth*, 168–70.

14. See 1 John 3:2.

15. See 1 Cor 13:12.

16. See Exod 28:36–38; Rev 3:12; 14:1.

with this newly bestowed identity, the Creator will claim his children as his own and watch over them for all eternity.

Nighttime will no longer exist, nor will there be any "need" (v. 5) for the illumination produced by "lamplight or sunlight."[17] The reason is that the glory of the "Lord God"[18] will give copious light to the redeemed. Here, we see that the end of history will be better than the beginning, for a radiant city will replace the Edenic garden. Additionally, there will be no idleness or boredom in the eternal state, for the Creator will give his children unending ruling and priestly responsibilities.[19]

The last book of Scripture assures believers of God's final purposes. Revelation also increases their longing for fellowship with the triune Creator. What they now enjoy is only a foretaste of a grand and glorious future to come.

Creation Themes: From Genesis to Revelation[20]		
Theme	**Genesis (Beginning)**	**Revelation (Consummation)**
Creation under Curse	The earth is cursed because of sin, subjected to futility, thorns, and decay (Gen 3:17; Rom 8:20).	Creation itself is liberated from bondage to decay; a new heaven and new earth come into existence without any presence of the curse (Rom 8:21; Rev 21:1, 4–5; 22:3).
Death and Mortality	Death enters through sin, becoming the destiny of all humanity (Gen 5:5–31; Rom 5:12–14).	Death is conquered through Christ's victory in the cross-resurrection event; believers receive eternal life and reign forever (1 Cor 15:50–56; Rev 21:4; 22:1–2, 17).
Human Relationship with God	After sinning, Adam and Eve hide from God's presence in fear and shame (Gen 3:8).	The redeemed enjoy perfect, unfiltered fellowship with God face to face (Rev 21:3; 22:4).

17. See Isa 60:19–20; Zech 14:7; Rev 21:23, 25.

18. See our discussion of Rev 1:8; 4:8, 11; 6:10; 11:8, 15, 17; 14:13; 15:3, 4; 16:7; 17:14; 18:8; 19:6, 16; 21:22.

19. See Dan 7:18, 27; Matt 19:28; Luke 22:30; 1 Cor 6:2–3; 2 Tim 2:12; 1 Pet 2:5, 9; Rev 1:6; 5:10; 20:4, 6.

20. This is another example of typological fulfillment or prophetic foreshadowing in the Apocalypse. Table adapted from information presented in Brighton, *Revelation*, 623–33.

Creation Themes: From Genesis to Revelation[20]		
Theme	**Genesis (Beginning)**	**Revelation (Consummation)**
Light and Illumination	God creates the sun to give light and govern day and night (Gen 1:14–18).	The sun is no longer needed because God's glory and the Lamb provide eternal light (Rev 21:23; 22:5).
Sin and Separation	Sin enters the human race through their disobedience, bringing spiritual death and separation from God (Gen 3:1–7).	Sin is permanently expelled from the redeemed; no unclean thing enters the Holy City (Rev 21:8, 27; 22:15).
Sorrow and Tears	Human life becomes epitomized by sorrow and weeping due to sin's consequences (Job 7:3; Lam 1:16; 2:11, 18; 3:48–49; Ps 69:20; Eccl 4:1; Jer 13:17; 14:17; 16:7).	God wipes away every tear; sorrow, crying, and pain are eliminated forever (Rev 7:17; 21:4).

THE EXHORTATION TO REMAIN FAITHFUL (22:6–11)

If John has any doubts concerning the vision he received, the interpreting angel dispells them with reassuring words. After all, God's spokespersons (namely, both Old and New Testament "prophets"; v. 6) are filled with, as well as controlled and inspired by, the sevenfold Spirit. Moreover, it is the same "Lord" and "God" who dispatches his "angel" to disclose to his bondservants[21] that his decrees will "take place" in a short time.[22]

Parallels between Revelation's Prologue (1:1–8) and Epilogue (22:6–8)[23]		
Corresponding Theme	**Prologue (1:1–8)**	**Epilogue (22:6–21)**
Blessing on Faithful Readers	"Blessed is the one who reads the words of this prophecy and blessed are those who hear it and hold on to the things written in it" (v. 3).	"Blessed is the one who holds on to the words of the prophecy of this book" (v. 7).
Christ's Second Advent	"Look, he is coming with clouds" (v. 7).	"Look: I am coming soon!" (v. 7).

21. Literally "slaves."

22. See our discussion of Rev 1:1–3.

23. Table adapted from information presented in Mounce, *Book of Revelation*, 398.

Parallels between Revelation's Prologue (1:1–8) and Epilogue (22:6–8)[23]		
Corresponding Theme	**Prologue (1:1–8)**	**Epilogue (22:6–21)**
Divine Revelation through Angels	"Christ expressed this revelation by means of symbols sent through his angel" (v. 1).	"The Lord . . . sent his angel" (v. 6).
John as a Witness	"John spoke as a witness . . . to everything he saw" (v. 2).	"John . . . heard and saw these things" (v. 8).
Grace Benediction	"Grace" (v. 4)	"Grace" (v. 21)
Liturgical Affirmation	"Amen" (v. 7)	"Amen" (vv. 20, 21)
Urgency of Prophetic Events	"Show his servants the things that must soon take place" (v. 1)	"Show his servants what must soon take place" (v. 6)

The primary focus of John's prophetic oracle is the Lamb's triumph over evil and the eternal joy awaiting his steadfast followers. Indeed, whatever the Apocalypse unveils is absolutely "faithful" (22:6) and trustworthy, as well as valid and "true."[24] In this regard, one prominent, Christ-centered aspect of John's message is Jesus' return at the end of the age. At the divinely appointed moment, there will be no delay (v. 7).[25]

The certainty of the Son's future appearance comforts believers in times of hardship and motivates them to remain obedient and faithful in times of temptation. Therefore, in the sixth beatitude, or pronouncement of covenantal blessing, found in verse 7—which mirrors the first statement recorded in 1:3,[26] the upright are reminded that as a result of heeding the exhortations appearing in the apostle's prophetic oracle,[27] they will be the privileged recipients of the Father's favor.[28]

Previously, in 1:2, John affirms that the "witness" he bears concerning the Messiah.[29] The apostle reintroduces this theme in 22:8 when he declares that he personally "heard and saw" the visions recorded in the last book of Scripture. The preceding observation emphasizes that one of

24. See Dan 2:45; Rev 21:5.

25. See our discussion of Rev 1:7; 3:11; 19:11–16; 22:12, 17, 20.

26. See our discussion of Rev 14:13; 16:15; 19:9; 20:6; 22:14.

27. By faith through the power of the Spirit.

28. See our discussion of Rev 2:26; 14:12.

29. Like someone testifying in a court of law.

the apostle's Christ-centered goals is to shift the focus of believers from themselves and their hardships to the Lamb and his promised blessings.

Yet, oddly enough, John falls prostrate in homage "at the feet" of the interpreting angel.[30] In response, the angel stops the apostle.[31] The emissary adds that he is literally a "fellow slave" (v. 9), just like John's peers, namely, the rest of the "prophets,"[32] along with all those who heed what is recorded in Revelation. For this reason, the angel urges the apostle to prostrate himself in homage to the Creator. Similarly, all his children are to make him the sole recipient of their "worship" and praise.[33]

Centuries earlier, in Daniel 12:4,[34] an angel commanded the elder statesman to "seal," or close up, the vision he had received so that it would remain confidential (as well as inscrutable). Oppositely, in Revelation 22:10, the interpreting angel tells John not to "seal up," or keep secret, what is recorded in the Apocalypse. The reason for this turnabout is that the divinely appointed "time" for the fulfillment of the prophetic oracles is "near." From the Creator's eternal perspective, when he issues the decree, there will be no further delay in the actual unfolding of the cosmic drama the apostle witnessed.[35]

An improper response includes remaining entrenched in the world's idolatrous and harlotrous system, along with taking God lightly. Verse 11 draws particular attention to those who continually practice injustice and wallow in moral filth. It is fitting for them to become increasingly hardened and set in their present course of wrongdoing.[36] Oppositely, a proper response includes repenting of sin, seeking to live uprightly, and desiring to become more like the Messiah. Here, the focus shifts to those who remain "just" in their treatment of others and "holy" in their character. By the power of the Spirit, nothing and no one can dislodge them from their unwavering devotion to the Savior.

30. See our discussion of Rev 19:10.

31. Literally by uttering the idiomatic expression "do not see to it"; see Apoc. Zeph. 6:15; Ascen. Isa. 7:21; 8:5.

32. See 1 Cor 12:28; Eph 4:11.

33. In contrast to the veneration of mortal, flawed, human rulers.

34. See Dan 8:26; 12:9.

35. See Ps 90:4; 2 Pet 3:8.

36. See Isa 6:9–10; Ezek 3:27; Matt 13:13–15; Mark 4:10–12; John 12:40; Acts 28:26–27; Rom 11:8; Rev 13:10.

THE CERTAINTY OF THE MESSIAH'S RETURN (22:12–17)

Revelation 1 begins by stressing the certainty of the Messiah's return, the importance of remaining faithful to the Lord, and the authenticity of the prophecy John has received. These same themes are emphasized in the conclusion of the book and prove to be a source of pastoral consolation to the apostle and his peers as they face intense persecution. Of course, throughout history, Christians have endured abuse from enemies of the faith. For this reason, Jesus' promise of "coming soon" (v. 12) provides solace for his beleaguered followers down through the centuries.

No one can determine in advance when Jesus will return. Yet believers know that when his appearing will occur, it will take place quickly. God's children can rest assured of the second advent, for the Son, as the "Alpha" (v. 13) and the "Omega," is sovereign over all that occurs in history. Furthermore, due to his being the "First" and the "Last," as well as the "Beginning" and the "End," the Messiah's lordship encompasses the past, the present, and the future.[37]

At the conclusion of the age, Jesus will "repay" all according to their deeds (v. 12). While everlasting joy (or covenantal blessings) is the heritage of the righteous, eternal anguish (or covenantal curses) is the lot of the wicked.[38] Ultimately, then, the way people live is an indicator of whether they are regenerate or unregenerate (v. 14).[39]

Those who are "born from above" (John 3:1) by "water" (v. 5) and the "Spirit" are given the "right" (1:12) to become the Father's "children." Moreover, through the means of grace, Jesus' followers have washed their "robes" (Rev 22:14).[40] Likewise, their union with him is the basis for his granting them the "right" (authority) to "enter" the "gates" of the new Jerusalem, along with consuming the lush, delectable fruit produced by the life-giving "tree."[41]

In brief, the Creator will allow the faithful—namely, those who have not defiled themselves by the corrupt world system—to abide with him in heaven and enjoy the abundance of eternal life. Verse 14 records the

37. See Isa 44:6; 48:12.

38. See 2 Chr 6:23; Job 34:11; Pss 28:4; 62:12; Prov 24:12; Isa 40:10; 59:18; 62:11; Jer 17:10; Ezek 18:20; Hos 12:2; 2 Bar. 14:12; 1 En. 41:1; 4 Ezra 7:35, 99; 8:33; Pss. Sol. 2:16; 17:8; Rom 2:6; 14:12; 1 Cor 3:12–15; 2 Cor 5:10; 2 Tim 4:14; 1 Pet 1:17; Rev 20:12.

39. See Matt 7:15–20; 1 John 1:6–7.

40. See our discussion of Rev 7:14.

41. See Gen 2:9; Ezek 47:12; 4 Bar. 9:16; 1 En. 25:3–5; 2 En. 8:3.

seventh and final beatitude, or pronouncement of covenantal blessing, appearing in John's prophetic oracle.

The fate of the wicked is far different. God will permanently ban them from his sacred presence. Verse 15 refers to them collectively as mangy, filthy, scavenger "dogs."[42] This is the moral character of such degenerates as "sorcerers," "adulterers," "murderers," "idolaters," and all those who love and practice "falsehood."[43]

In verse 16, the Messiah reiterates what is recorded in 1:1 and 4. Specifically, "Jesus" dispatches his "angel" (or heavenly messenger) to provide John with the "testimony" he is to communicate[44] to and for the benefit of the "churches."[45] The Son can guarantee what he has declared, for he originates from the house ("Root") and lineage ("Offspring") of "David" (22:16).[46] Likewise, as the "bright Morning Star,"[47] the divine Warrior ensures that a new day of salvation will dawn.

With such magnificent promises from the Savior awaiting fulfillment, it is no wonder that both the sevenfold "Spirit" (v. 17) and Jesus' "bride" (the body of Christ)[48] invite everyone to "come."[49] Those who do so[50] are the ones whose spiritual thirst is quenched by partaking of the life-giving water (offered as a "gift") flowing from the Creator's sacred throne in the new Jerusalem.[51]

THE APOSTLE'S FINAL WARNING (22:18–21)

Revelation—like the rest of Scripture—is to be distinguished from mere human words. The divine message is so important that the Messiah promises to judge anyone who might distort what it discloses. Specifically, Jesus declares that those who add anything to what they hear read aloud will experience the various "plagues" (v. 18; or covenantal curses)

42. See Deut 23:17–18; Ps 22:16, 20; Odes Sol. 28:13–14; Matt 15:26–27; Phil 3:2.
43. A reference to every form of deceit; see our discussion of Rev 9:21; 21:8, 27.
44. Like someone in a court of law.
45. Both existing in the apostle's day and down through the centuries.
46. See Isa 11:1, 10; Rev 3:7; 5:5.
47. See Num 24:17; T. Jud. 24:1; T. Levi 18:2–4; Rev 2:28.
48. See our discussion of Rev 19:6–9; 21:9.
49. See Isa 55:1; Odes Sol. 30:1–3; Matt 11:28–30; John 7:37.
50. Through repentance and faith.
51. See our discussion of Rev 21:6.

detailed in the scroll.[52] Likewise, those who remove anything from John's prophetic oracle will no longer be allowed to have any "share" (v. 19) in the life-giving "Tree" (or covenantal blessings), along with the "Holy City."[53]

The above serves as a warning against perverting the message of Revelation. Spiritual frauds are especially guilty of doing this by making spurious declarations. In contrast to these false prophets, Jesus admonishes believers to handle all Scripture with accuracy and objectivity, as well as care and respect, and to heed what it disclosed.[54]

Jesus, who faithfully testifies to the accuracy and reliability of the entire Apocalypse, once more asserts, "Yes, I am coming soon" (v. 20).[55] Similarly, with John, all believers can solemnly affirm[56] the certainty of this wonderful promise with the interjection "Amen."[57] The phrase rendered "Come, Lord Jesus" is equivalent to the transliterated Aramaic expression, *Marana tha* in 1 Corinthians 16:22, which is rendered "Our Lord, come!"[58]

Just as John opens his prophetic oracle to the "seven churches in the province of Asia" (Rev 1:4), so too he ends it with a benediction referring to Jesus' "grace" (22:21)[59] for all God's holy people,[60] followed by the solemn affirmation of "Amen."[61] By living in union with the Messiah,[62] they can resist any temptation to compromise their faith. Then, when the Son appears in glory, his followers will be able to face him with joy and gladness.[63] At that moment, all their deepest longings will finally be fulfilled.

52. See Deut 28:15; 29:19–20.

53. A form of retributive justice, in which the punishment fits the crime.

54. See Deut 4:1–2; 12:32; Prov 30:6; Jer 26:2; 3 Bar. 1:7; 1 En. 104:9–11; 2 En. 48:7–8; Let. Aris. 310–11.

55. See our discussion of Rev 22:7, 12.

56. Like those testifying in a court of law.

57. See our discussion of Rev 1:7; 3:14; 5:14; 7:12; 19:4.

58. See Did. 10:6.

59. Namely, the abundant provision of Jesus' unmerited favor and kindness.

60. See 1 John 2:28.

61. See our discussion of Rev 1:7.

62. See John 15:4–5.

63. See 1 John 3:2–3.

The Fulness of Life for the Redeemed in the Eternal State[64]			
Description	**Old Testament Reference**	**Jesus' Pledge to the Seven Churches**	**Fulfillment of the Pledge in the Eternal State**
A distinctive identity and a holy dwelling	Isa 62:2; 65:15	Rev 3:12	Rev 21:2; 22:4
Adorned with beautiful garments	Isa 52:1; 61:10	Rev 3:5	Rev 19:7–8; 21:2
Bestowal of the hidden manna to eat at the wedding supper of the Lamb	Exod 16:31–34	Rev 2:17	Rev 19:9
Names recorded in the Lamb's Book of Life	Dan 12:1	Rev 3:5	Rev 21:27
Permanent residency in the Creator's sacred temple	Isa 56:5	Rev 3:12	Rev 21:22–27
Recipients of the Morning Star (the Messiah)	Num 24:17	Rev 2:28	Rev 22:16
Ruling authority over all the nations with the Messiah	Ps 2:8–9	Rev 2:26–27; 3:21	Rev 1:6; 22:5
Privilege of eating from the life-giving tree	Gen 2:9	Rev 2:7	Rev 22:2, 14, 19

KEY THEOLOGICAL INSIGHTS

In Revelation 22, John deepens his portrayal of the eternal state and issues final exhortations and warnings to his readers. Here, we gain greater insight into life on the renewed earth in the heavenly city, the imminent return of the Lamb, and the culmination of biblical teaching about the Messiah.

First, *in the eternal state, the Creator and the Lamb have accomplished all that is necessary for their worshipers to enjoy everlasting fellowship before the heavenly throne, as well as the fulfillment of all Scripture's promises to them*. In our discussion of chapter 21, we noted the sufficiency of God's provision, along with the safety and security of those who dwell with him

64. This is another example of typological fulfillment or prophetic foreshadowing in the Apocalypse. Table adapted from information presented in Sturm, *The Ultimate Exodus*, 27–28.

in the new Jerusalem. Now, in the opening section of chapter 22, we have a further description of the beatific vision and the covenantal blessings lived out within the Holy City (vv. 1–5). The curse is lifted, and life is abundant, full, and pleasurable.[65] The identity of God's reborn children is secure, for there is no mistaking who belongs to the Creator and the Messiah.[66] Additionally, those who dwell with God find in him not only the source of all life but also the source of all light. In the end, every blessing promised to those who have been faithful to the Messiah comes to fruition. Furthermore, since the saints reign with God forever, there is no fear that this everlasting bliss will expire.[67]

Second, *we understand the hope and warning about the Messiah's soon return*. Jesus' threefold declaration of his second advent indicates that once the appointed time arrives, it will not delay (vv. 7, 12, 20). Our Lord does not want us to make authoritative proclamations or clock-and-calendar predictions concerning when he will come again.[68] After all, Christ taught that other than the Father, no one knows the day or hour of the Son's return.[69] While the second advent may be at any time in the future, the "soon-ness" is best understood as an assurance, stamped with divine authority, that what is promised must come to pass and does not fail in its fulfillment.[70] For believers, the threefold promise of Christ's soon return gives them hope and certainty amid life's struggles, such that the Messiah's bride longs for his coming (vv. 17, 20).[71] For unbelievers, this threefold declaration serves as a somber warning. Before it is too late, they must repent of their sins and receive the Father's gracious offer of salvation in the Son.

65. See John 10:10.

66. As noted above, the imprint on the foreheads of the saints is representative of our gracious heavenly Father's ownership, in stark contrast to the sea-beast's mark of allegiance taken by those opposed to God and the Lamb.

67. In complete fulfillment and final consummation of the previous promises recorded in Rev 2:26–27 and 20:4–6.

68. As so many so-called celebrity pastors do today on television and in social media. While every generation seems convinced that theirs is the one in which the Messiah will return, the truth is that we do not know with any certainty when the second advent will take place. Yet we can rest assured that when the time comes, it will do so without delay and will be quickly manifested.

69. See Matt 24:36.

70. Keener, *Revelation*, 520, affirms that the trustworthy promises of Christ's soon coming also assure us of the final fulfillment of "God's entire purpose in redemptive history."

71. See 2 Tim 4:8.

Third, *we see that Christ affirms his equality with the Father (along with the sevenfold Spirit), in which the Son declares himself to be the Alpha and Omega.* As we noted above, this assertion indicates not only the Messiah's full divinity but also his sovereign reign throughout the entire universe (v. 13). His supremacy implies complete power, righteous judgment, and full authority over all creation. Indeed, as Paul notes, the Son's rule encompasses everything, since all things originate from him, proceed through him, and ultimately exist for him.[72] Likewise, everything has been placed under his control, and there is nothing outside the reach of his divine lordship.[73] For those rightly related to Christ by faith, there cannot be more assuring words in all Scripture. In contrast, those who persist in their rebellion against the Messiah will ultimately find their place outside the heavenly, sacred dwelling.[74]

Fourth, in addition to the Alpha and Omega, *Jesus declares himself to be the Root of David and the Bright Morning Star.* These superlative descriptions recorded in verse 16 signify the fulfillment of all Israel's covenant promises, which Yahweh gave to the nation.[75] Even more profound is the Messiah's occupying his rightful place as the One who brings to pass all the covenantal blessings and eliminates all the covenantal curses described in chapter 21.[76] With this understanding, our Christology is brought to completion. After all, John's prophetic oracle has offered us the full display of the risen, exalted, and glorified Messiah. He is the returning and conquering King, as well as the Lord of all.

IMPORTANT MINISTRY IMPLICATIONS

Within Revelation 22, we encounter the final two beatitudes of covenantal blessings for those who believe and respond in obedience to God's Word. In addition, we have a solemn warning for those who would distort or tamper with John's prophetic oracle. Furthermore, within these two beatitudes and the concluding warning of the Apocalypse, we find key principles for ministry leaders to implement in their local church contexts.

72. See Rom 11:36.

73. See Eph 1:22–23; Phil 2:9–11; Col 1:15–17.

74. Specifically, in the fiery lake filled with burning sulfur, a place of everlasting torment and separation from God.

75. See Osborne, *Revelation*, 792–93, for further reflection on the significance of these identity markers of Jesus in verse 16.

76. See our discussion of Rev 21:4–5.

First, as we have previously noted in our discussion of Revelation, *we must inform our church members that the Lamb rewards faithful, consistent obedience to him.* In 22:7, after Jesus declares his soon coming, he gives the sixth beatitude. As we noted above, this beatitude is similar to the one given in 1:3 that whoever "holds on to" (obeys, follows) the words of the "prophecy" are the recipients of covenantal blessing. This is not saying that our salvation is earned by obsessively accomplishing pious deeds, for salvation is by faith alone.[77] The point here is that those who persist in faithful obedience demonstrate the reality of their union with the Lamb. By living out their faith, they stand ready to receive God's eternal blessing upon their lives. We can encourage our parishioners that obedience to the teaching of Scripture is the fitting and expected fruit of their profession of faith.[78]

Second, *we must admonish our steadfast congregants to endure in the faith, pursue obedience, and separate themselves from the evil world system.* In doing so, they demonstrate that they are truly God's reborn children, who have access to the Holy City and the Tree of Life. Once again, this is not a matter of earning one's salvation by completing a long list of commendable activities. After all, our righteousness can never rise to the infinite standard of moral perfection that God has established.[79] The beatitude in 22:14, like the one in verse 7, is a message to believers that those who are genuinely reborn from above live in a way that is characterized by spiritual regeneration, victory over sin, and an intentional pursuit of holiness.[80] Good works do not earn us salvation; instead, they confirm the underlying reality of our reborn status. To this end, we encourage the faithful to persist in following our Lord's righteousness.

Third, *those of us who regularly teach and preach from God's Word must model faithfulness to the text and warn others about the dire consequences for failing to do so.* Verses 18–19 caution that if we add to or take away from the prophecy of Revelation, we are in danger of experiencing the Lord's covenantal curses, including being banned from the Tree of

77. See Hab 2:4; Rom 5:1; Gal 2:16, 21; 3:24.

78. A common teaching of the Reformation is that genuine faith inherently leads to good works. For example, Luther emphasizes in his "Preface to the Epistle of St. Paul to the Romans" that true faith naturally results in good works, just as heat and light are inseparable from fire (*Luther's Works*, Vol. 35, 371). Similarly, Calvin argues in the *Institutes of the Christian Religion* that while justification is by faith alone, true faith is always accompanied by good works as its evidence (3.16.1).

79. See Isa 64:6; Rom 3:23.

80. See 1 John 2:1, 15–17; 3:4–10; Jas 2:12–26.

Life. This is a warning that those who manipulate the oracles recorded in the Apocalypse show themselves to be false prophets. They are outside of a right relationship with the Lamb and face the prospect of eternal doom.

In light of this warning, we must stress to our parishioners the importance of remaining careful and accurate in the way they handle the teachings of Revelation.[81] This admonition leaves no room for those who reduce the Apocalypse to some sort of fantasy-like metaphor or allegory that carries no timeless truths. It also leaves no room for those who manipulate the details of Revelation to fit their eschatological systems, such that they claim to have figured out or resolved the mystery of God's end-time plan. In both instances, such approaches to the Apocalypse result in divine condemnation. As we handle God's Word with and for our congregants,[82] we must remain careful to treat Scripture as the inspired and authoritative revelation it is, as well as seek to apply it faithfully to the lives of our congregants.

VITAL MISSIONAL RAMIFICATIONS

Revelation 22 includes several critical declarations with far-reaching implications for the church's missionary mandate, particularly in proclaiming the gospel to the unreached. First, we note that *the nations are in view within the heavenly dwelling on the new earth*. As we noted in our discussion of chapter 21, no nation is exempt from the offer of a redemptive place in the eternal state. Given that the leaves of the Tree of Life[83] bring "healing" (v. 2), we see the final, ultimate success of missionary activity.[84] We can be encouraged to persevere in our evangelistic and disciple-making calling, especially as we proclaim, unashamedly, the gospel about Christ to the lost. We can expect our heavenly Father, through the power of the sevenfold Spirit, to work in us and in the lives of those who eventually receive by faith the saving message we proclaim. We can obey our Lord's Great Commission with confidence, not in ourselves, but in union with him who has summoned us to be instruments in his hand for the fulfillment of his marvelous plan.[85]

81. Also, by implication, the entirety of God's inspired and authoritative Scripture.

82. See 2 Tim 2:15.

83. See Beale and McDonough, "Revelation," 1157.

84. Just as we have previously noted in our discussion of Rev 5:9; 7:9; 15:4; 21:24, 26.

85. See Matt 28:18–20.

Second, *we must share the gospel as long as the Spirit empowers us because the end of the present age is near.* This means that the window of opportunity is closing for the lost to repent, trust in the Messiah, and receive the Creator's covenantal blessings rather than his covenantal curses.[86] At the consummation of the age, all humanity, without exception, will be divided between those who have sided with the mighty, worthy Lamb and those who have chosen to persist in rebellion against him.[87] We who are involved in missionary work must sense the urgency and redeem the time for fulfilling God's call in our lives to share the saving message about Jesus with the lost.

Third, *we are to appeal to the lost to respond in faith to the sevenfold Spirit's work in their lives and in this way satisfy their deepest eternal needs.* We know that left to ourselves, none of us would ever seek the Lord Jesus. We do not have a so-called "divine spark" within us that draws us to the Son. Likewise, our inherent desire is to disobey him, especially given our natural, sinful condition.[88] In 22:17, when John invites the "thirsty" to come, urging them to take the "water of life," the apostle is presenting redemption to those within whom the Spirit is working.[89]

The central task of missions is to offer salvation to the lost. It is the communication of the Father's unconditional grace in the person and work of the Son, which is made effective through the Spirit's inner, convicting power.[90] In our missionary endeavors, when we invite all to repent and believe, we trust that the Spirit goes before us and creates the thirst within the lost for Jesus, the true Living Water and Bread of Life.[91] We reach out to the unsaved with the assurance that the Spirit, who proceeds ahead of us, also leads sinners to a right relationship with

86. See Rom 11:25–26. Here, Paul speaks about a preordained time set by God for the "full number of Gentiles" to come to faith in Christ. This implies that there is a set point in time when, once all those predestined to faith have believed, the opportunity for salvation is ended. Then, at Jesus' second coming, "all Israel" (v. 26) will be "saved." One option is that Paul's statement refers to a future mass conversion of Jews. A second possibility is that this denotes an ongoing process of Jews who come to faith throughout history. A third option is that the apostle refers to the elect among Israel who will be saved. A fourth possibility is that "all Israel" is the church, composed of both Jewish and Gentile believers (see Gal 6:16; Eph 2:13–18; Heb 12:22–24).

87. See our discussion of Rev 20:11–15.

88. See Rom 3:10–18.

89. Note how this offer is free, "as a gift" (Rev 22:17), which is another indication that salvation is received by grace alone, through faith alone, and in Christ alone.

90. See John 16:7–11.

91. See John 4:10–15; 6:35–40; 7:37–39.

the Father through the redemption obtained for us by the Son. What a privilege it is for us, who are equipped with God's holy Word, to herald the message of salvation!

Epilogue

INTRODUCTION

In this volume, we have attempted to demonstrate the relevance of the Apocalypse for today. On the one hand, it includes making direct application of John's prophetic oracle to the church. On the other hand, it also involves considering the global implications of Revelation for our exegetical understanding, theological insight, pastoral assistance, and missional activity.

We maintain that the apostle's unfolding cosmic drama, while complex in many ways, is not so mysterious as to warrant setting it aside in the preaching ministry of the church. As part of God's inspired and authoritative Word, the Apocalypse is meant for Christians to read, understand, obey, and proclaim. We are convinced that Revelation offers remarkable content for our appreciation of the Messiah in his exaltation, as well as how we should live in anticipation of our Lord's soon return.

In light of the preceding observations, our intent in this Epilogue is to motivate you to engage the Apocalypse conscientiously for the edification of your parishioners. We also want to encourage you to resist the impulse to set aside Revelation due to any perceived difficulties encountered in its interpretation. Therefore, we offer the following principles and recommendations for preaching through the Apocalypse, which is perhaps the most profound disclosure about the Messiah in all Scripture.

PRINCIPLES FOR TEACHING AND PREACHING THROUGH THE APOCALYPSE

First, *keep Christ central in communicating the Apocalypse.* John's prophetic oracle is indeed the revelation from and about the Messiah. In our study, we have encountered him in his glorified, exalted state. We have also considered his messages to the saints, especially as represented in the letters to the seven churches in Asia Minor.

Furthermore, we have found the Son to be declared worthy to unleash the Father's righteous judgment on earth's wicked inhabitants. In contrast, we have considered Jesus' care of and protection for his followers, as well as the Spirit's abiding presence with those enduring tribulation and persecution throughout the history of the church. We have learned about the unfolding of John's cosmic drama according to God's sovereign will.

Furthermore, we have witnessed in the pages of Revelation the revolt of the forces of evil against the Creator and the Lamb. Specifically, various malevolent entities have sought to deceive the nations, turn them away from Christ, and redirect them to luxuriate in idolatrous, sensuous behavior. We have witnessed the harassment, persecution, and martyrdom of God's reborn children. We have also seen the wicked prosper, especially by living in unrestrained depravity, yet with no immediate consequences, at least for a season.

Next, we have beheld the destruction of the forces of evil, including the wicked. This devastation occurs from within, as Satan's malcontents turn on each other. The implosion also takes place from without, as the Lamb comes to overthrow the ungodly and establish his reign in complete power and sovereignty.

From there, the Creator and the Lamb make all things new, where sin is forever eradicated. The devil, antichrist (sea-beast), false prophet (land-beast), and all their sycophants are banished to the fiery lake filled with burning sulfur. In contrast, those united to the Messiah find themselves to be citizens of the new Jerusalem, where the sacred presence of the triune God is forever with the redeemed on the new earth. Here, the bride of the Lamb enjoys everlasting joy and fulfillment, without the possibility of experiencing hardship, pain, persecution, or injustice.

In view of the full and final exaltation of Christ, we are challenged to live with anticipation, hope, faith, and righteousness. This truth is especially poignant as we await the soon appearing of our Lord and Savior.

Indeed, at every point in John's treatise, we encounter the Messiah. Because of this, our preaching through Revelation must demonstrate a Christ-centered outlook, in which we show our congregants how each portion of the narrative discloses the majesty and glory of the risen, exalted Lamb.

Second, *do not succumb to the pressure to fit characters and events in Revelation into today's context.* After all, not every detail in the Apocalypse is meant to have a specific referent in present-day events. For instance, when we are introduced to the antichrist (sea-beast) in chapter 13, speculating about who this entity might be does not benefit our congregants. Admittedly, while many think someone will eventually emerge as the Messiah's archrival, nowhere in John's prophetic oracle are we instructed to identify that antagonist with persons alive today.

The point of the apostle's description of the antichrist—as well as the other nefarious creatures opposed to the Creator and the Lamb—is to depict the massive deception and apostasy that takes place as our world careens to its end. Consequently, engaging in futile theorizing concerning the identity of the antichrist, especially in teaching and preaching, draws congregants away from the explicit emphases of God's Word. It also invites an unhealthy preoccupation with tangential matters that ultimately dilute the effectiveness of the Spirit's work in and through the proclamation of John's unfolding cosmic drama. Our focus, then, as bondservants of Christ, is to present the truths of Revelation in a clear and accurate manner, along with faithfully applying pertinent insights to the everyday lives of our parishioners.

Throughout the history of the church, nearly every generation has considered itself as possibly the one in which the end-time events depicted in Revelation will occur. Thus, the above admonition is easier said than done. Undoubtedly, as we teach and preach through John's treatise, congregants may ask questions about what to make of this or that prominent political figure in our own time. We may also feel pressured to explain how present-day conflicts in the Middle East, particularly if they involve Israel, possibly fit into a specific future-oriented timeline.

At first, participating in the above sorts of inquiries may feel intimidating to us. Nonetheless, these must not be allowed to derail our focus on preaching from John's prophetic oracle in a contextually appropriate, Christ-centered manner that seeks relevant application for twenty-first-century believers. Speculative questions are best handled in a gracious, deferring way where we remind our congregants that the message of the Apocalypse centers on unveiling and exalting the Messiah.

Third, *remember that Revelation was written to and for the church.* Recall that in chapter 1, John is instructed to write to the seven churches located in Asia Minor. These congregations are clearly identified as the original, target audience of his unfolding cosmic drama. Then, chapters 2 and 3 record the Messiah's authoritative and solemn pronouncement to each of the seven congregations. Within each of these declarations, there are various challenges to the church. These include warnings against unbelief, apathy, idolatry, and immorality along with hopeful encouragements toward holiness, faithfulness, endurance, and perseverance.

Next, chapters 4 and 5 depict the company of believers, as represented by the twenty-four elders, gathered around the throne of the Creator and Lamb in worship. We are graced with a vision of the church triumphant, unhindered by sin and suffering, enjoying the bliss of offering unending praise to the Creator. From these observations we deduce that sermons taken from the opening five chapters of John's prophetic oracle should easily find relevance to the body of Christ, including direct applications to her mission today.

Following chapter 5, the presence of the church is less prominent, at least until the latter part of chapter 19. Recall that in chapters 6, 8, 9, and 16, we encounter the Lamb's unleashing of covenantal curses on earth's wicked inhabitants. God's judgment falls primarily upon the lost, not believers, even though some of the Father's reborn children do consequently endure some hardships.

The preceding observation has led some specialists to argue that the church is not in view, by and large, from chapter 6 until the middle of chapter 19. Yet even within these chapters, there are regular reminders of the devil's persecution and oppression of the saints, the suffering they endure, and the call for them to persevere during seasons of anguish and deprivation.

Consequently, regardless of whether the church is present in any given chapter or passage of the Apocalypse, John's description of these calamities remains instructive for the Lamb's bride. We infer from this observation that our teaching and preaching through Revelation must be done in a way that motivates the church militant to separate herself from all manifestations of wickedness and depravity. We should also exhort our parishioners to pursue righteousness, as well as patiently endure all for the sake of the gospel and the Messiah, who alone is the giver of eternal life. Sermon applications, regardless of where one is preaching in the apostle's unfolding cosmic drama, must ultimately connect to Revelation's overall church-related purpose.

Fourth, *avoid the extremes of either overly idealistic or hyper-literal interpretations of Revelation.* Given the apocalyptic nature of what John sees and hears, we recognize that some of the signs and symbols, while having purpose and meaning, are not always meant to be taken in a crassly literal manner. Indeed, trying to force a wooden interpretation onto every depiction of a character, location, event, or proclamation in the apostle's prophetic oracle fails to appreciate the exquisite nature of the apocalyptic genre.

Yet it would be incorrect to surmise from the preceding observations that the solution is to take everything in John's treatise in an overly idealistic manner. Regardless of one's position on the specifics of what is either literal or symbolic, nearly all specialists agree that the apostle writes about a period characterized by intense adversity preceding the Messiah's second advent. Just as poignant is his return to rule on earth in righteousness.

Therefore, it is irresponsible for teachers and preachers to gloss over the truth of a final judgment. At that time, the Creator will vindicate and reward his faithful, reborn children, along with casting earth's wicked inhabitants into the fiery lake filled with burning sulfur, where they will experience everlasting separation from him. Put differently, while John may use symbolic expressions and vivid descriptions, he does so to instruct the church regarding actual, historical events that compose the consummation of all things at the end of the present age.

There is a twofold implication arising from the above points concerning teaching and preaching from the Apocalypse. On the one hand, if we err on the side of an overly idealistic interpretation, our efforts are reduced to a series of moralistic tropes that one can find in any pagan myth or allegory that addresses the perennial battle between good and evil. Most likely, our teaching and preaching will also overlook the uniqueness of Revelation's compelling and riveting content, as well as the sense of urgency associated with end-time events.

On the other hand, if we err on the side of a hyper-literal interpretation, we subject our congregants to a comparably great injustice. After all, our sermons will ignore the homiletical point of each passage and degenerate into opinion-laden speculation, fanciful musings, and a failure to apply the unfolding cosmic drama responsibly to the lives of twenty-first century parishioners (especially in Majority World contexts). For instance, some teachers and preachers have tried to pinpoint which nations will become Gog and Magog. Others endeavor to identify who supposedly is the present-day antichrist. Still others speculate about precise times and dates when Jesus will return. In each instance, there is a failure to edify believers in their journey toward becoming more Christlike.

In essence, one's interpretive stance has direct implications for how one teaches and preaches from John's prophetic oracle. Accordingly, we must remain mindful of this as we proclaim to our congregants the truths found in the Apocalypse.

Fifth, *teach and preach the message of Revelation with a global view toward God's redemptive work*. One of the key facets of apocalyptic literature is its universal reach to all peoples in all places. In this regard, John's treatise is no different, as there are numerous examples, both positive and negative, about the global extent of what he discloses.

For instance, all nations are included in the worship of the Creator and the Lamb. Oppositely, all nations are included in the worldwide deception of the unholy trinity (the dragon or devil, the sea-beast or antichrist, and the land-beast or false prophet), who stand opposed to God. On the one hand, all nations are judged for their rebellion against the Messiah, and all are held accountable for their deeds. On the other hand, all nations are represented in those who compose the new Jerusalem. Here, redeemed humanity enjoys everlasting freedom from sin, and dwells forever in the sacred presence of the triune God.

In each major event of the Apocalypse, the entire creation and all her inhabitants are in view. This is why Revelation's message not only includes everyone but also is meant for everyone. Consequently, when teaching and preaching through John's prophetic oracle, we are encouraged to maintain this worldwide perspective.

Moreover, all peoples and nations come under God's judgment. Likewise, all are urged to repent of their sins and turn to Christ in faith. Accordingly, teaching and preaching through the apostle's unfolding cosmic drama should include regular exhortations toward outreach, witness, and evangelism. When we consider who the Messiah is and as we anticipate his soon return, we are incentivized to encourage and admonish the saints.

That said, in our teaching and preaching, we also call believers to a global view of God's mission. Specifically, we summon our congregants to obey faithfully Jesus' mandate for his followers to reach the lost with the saving message of the gospel. Further motivation to do so is found in the truth about the Creator's just evaluation of all humankind at the end of the age. Therefore, as we deliver messages anchored in the Apocalypse, we must motivate our parishioners to take advantage of the remaining time to fulfill God's purposes for our lives, both individually and collectively.

SUGGESTIONS FOR TEACHING AND PREACHING THROUGH THE APOCALYPSE

We offer the following table to help you in teaching and preaching through the Apocalypse. This includes making important connections between the content of each chapter (exegetical summary), the key point concerning the Creator and/or the Lamb that arises from each chapter (theological principle), and a recommended applicational point for each chapter (homiletical exhortation). Keep in mind that the information below is mainly intended as a series of suggestions. Therefore, as you proclaim eternal truths arising from John's prophetic oracle, be sure to do so in your own words, especially as you make pertinent applications to your specific ministry context.

Exegetical Summary	Theological Principle	Homiletical Exhortation
Chapter 1: John introduces the resurrected, glorified Messiah, who, along with the Father and the sevenfold Spirit, possesses divine authority to render judgment and blessing.	Christ is exalted and victorious in his resurrected, glorified state as well as coequal with the Father and the sevenfold Spirit in power and authority.	We must see the Son for who he is in all his majesty and splendor, while submitting to his divine authority in all things for his glory and our good.
Chapter 2: John conveys the messages from Christ, which contain commendations and censures, to four of seven churches located in Asia Minor.	The Messiah sees the activities of his church, whether good or bad, and evaluates his followers impartially, according to his holy, righteous character.	We must return to our first love, the Son of God; persevere in our faithfulness to him; hold on to sound doctrine; and shun all forms of sexual temptation.

Exegetical Summary	Theological Principle	Homiletical Exhortation
Chapter 3: John conveys the messages from Christ, which contain commendations and censures, to the remaining three of seven churches in Asia Minor.	As the Messiah evaluates his followers, he offers rewards for their faithfulness and restoration for those who need to repent.	We must awaken to our Savior's mission, recover our usefulness in promoting God's glory, and avoid spiritual complacency and apathy.
Chapter 4: John recounts his vision in the throne room of heaven of the awe-inspiring worship of the holy, all-powerful, and righteous Creator.	The Father is completely distinct from his creation, righteous in all his deeds, and worthy to judge the earth and its inhabitants.	We must worship God in reverential awe of his power and glory, especially as we anticipate being in his sacred presence with all the saints and angels throughout eternity.
Chapter 5: John describes the worthy Lamb, who has fulfilled God's plan of salvation and who, as the Son, takes his rightful place alongside the Father as the One who breaks the seven seals of divine judgment.	The slain, risen Lamb of God is singularly worthy, coequal with the Father and the sevenfold Spirit, and rightfully worshiped by all creation.	We must offer humble worship and praise to our majestic, worthy Lamb of God, as well as recognize his redeeming work on our behalf.
Chapter 6: John spotlights the first six seal judgments, including the plagues of the four horsemen, the martyrs' cry for justice, and the series of natural disasters that foreshadow additional calamities to come.	God's judgment, executed through the Lamb, demonstrates his power over creation as well as his concern for his beleaguered, reborn children.	We must trust our Lord's righteousness in judging earth's wicked inhabitants, for we know that our vindication will come in his perfect time.
Chapter 7: John communicates his vision of the angels who restrain God's judgment, the 144,000 sealed from the tribes of Israel, and the multitude before the throne of God and the Lamb, all of whom praise the Savior for his redemption and righteous judgment.	The Creator and the Messiah remain faithful and determined to keep their redeemed, chosen people secure in their salvation, even amid cosmic trouble and turmoil.	We must rest in the safety and security of being numbered among God's reborn children, knowing that despite whatever temporal adversity we encounter, we are eternally saved.

Exegetical Summary	Theological Principle	Homiletical Exhortation
Chapter 8: John recounts the opening of the seventh seal, followed by the unleashing of the first four trumpet judgments.	The Creator's pouring out of covenantal curses inspires awe and wonder for those rightly related to him by faith, while promising doom for unbelievers.	We ensure our saving relationship with the righteous Judge by trusting in Christ so that we may avoid the coming judgment, and we urge others to do the same.
Chapter 9: John describes the unleashing of the fifth and sixth trumpet judgments, along with a specific focus on the Creator's use of demonic forces and the stubborn refusal of the wicked to repent and cry out to God for mercy.	The Creator's sovereign control of all things extends to Satan and his demonic cohort, who are willfully complicit in the destruction of creation and humanity.	We must fully recognize the deceptiveness of sin, the foolishness that results from succumbing to its temptations, and the devastating consequences of living in its grasp.
Chapter 10: John's call and commission to prophecy is renewed through the eating of a scroll which represents the divine message of judgment, in which the apostle experiences both the sweet and bitter aspects of God's revelation.	God's plans for judgment come to pass in his way and time, in which there is eternal blessing for his reborn children and everlasting doom for those who remain entrenched in unbelief.	We must internalize the entirety of God's Word by embracing the sweet-tasting portions that appeal to us and the bitter-tasting parts that we find difficult to obey.
Chapter 11: John reveals the work, martyrdom, and resurrection of two enigmatic witnesses, who proclaim God's judgment oracle to the world for 1,260 days, followed by the sounding of the seventh trumpet, which results in praise from heaven's inhabitants.	The Creator powerfully watches over those who faithfully proclaim the message from and about the Messiah, ensuring their final victory even in the face of suffering and martyrdom.	We must engage in faithful witness to the person and work of Christ, regardless of the sacrifices we may be called to make in the process.

Exegetical Summary	Theological Principle	Homiletical Exhortation
Chapter 12: John observes a woman who is giving birth to a male child, whom the dragon (representing Satan) seeks to destroy; yet the devil and his demonic cohort are defeated in heaven by Michael and his angels, while on earth the saints overcome by the blood of the Lamb and their truthful witness about him.	Despite Satan's best attempts to destroy everything that the Creator does, his sovereign plan succeeds, for he alone is the all-powerful Monarch of the entire universe.	We must live according to the assurance we have that the Creator will ultimately defeat Satan and his nefarious schemes.
Chapter 13: John introduces the sea-beast (antichrist) and the land-beast (false prophet), who heed the dragon (Satan) and mislead people from all nations to venerate the sea-beast as well as continue the devil's murderous plot against God's reborn children.	Satan convincingly counterfeits God's person and work by using deceptive means and coercive tactics.	We must beware of the fraudulent spirit of the antichrist (sea-beast), which is already at work in the world and will one day manifest itself to delude as many of earth's inhabitants as possible.
Chapter 14: John shares another vision of the 144,000, an angel declares an everlasting gospel, a second angel pronounces the imminent fall of Babylon, a third angel heralds judgment on the followers of the sea-beast (antichrist), and there is a gruesome depiction of the harvest of the wicked because of God's wrath.	The Lamb is victorious in his exalted position—worshiped by the redeemed and positioned to apply the Creator's wrath on the wicked, who persist in rebellion against him and persecute his reborn children.	We must take solace in the security we have in union with Christ so that we may neither fear the coming judgment nor succumb to the temptation to abandon our faith in times of intense suffering and persecution.
Chapter 15: John offers a glimpse into the heavenly preparation for the final series of covenantal curses to be dispensed from heaven upon the earth.	The power of the Creator and Messiah, as seen in the outpouring of their wrath, is worthy of reverential awe and adoration by those who believe in the Son for salvation.	We must praise the sovereign Monarch of the universe for his power and justice, as well as express gratitude for the safety and security that all believers have in union with the Messiah.

Exegetical Summary	Theological Principle	Homiletical Exhortation
Chapter 16: John details the final series of bowl judgments, where God's covenantal curses are poured out over all creation, with devastating consequences for both the environment and earth's wicked inhabitants.	The Creator is completely just in the outpouring of his wrath, as the planet's rebellious occupiers ultimately get what they deserve and (ironically) even what they want.	We must accept the just nature of God's wrath, even when it seems extreme from our limited human perspective, as well as warn those who are in danger of receiving the consequences of its outpouring.
Chapter 17: John portrays the great harlot (Babylon), who seduces the world with her wicked system of sensuousness, greed, corruption, and idolatry, yet who eventually suffers betrayal and defeat.	God brings about the defeat of the notorious prostitute, who represents the sinful world order that draws the unsaved to luxuriate in all manner of iniquity.	We must beware of fallen humanity's pagan ideologies and the allure of their temptations, lest we fall prey to their sensuous, idolatrous, and rebellious ways.
Chapter 18: John depicts the sudden and comprehensive fall of Babylon and the destruction of her wicked system, after which God's reborn children and the heavenly emissaries celebrate the harlot's demise.	The Creator is determined to put an end to Babylon and her sinful world order, though all earth's inhabitants are negatively affected by her implosion.	We must separate ourselves from the harlotries and idolatries of the notorious prostitute, while rejoicing in the Messiah's destruction of her as a key component of our final redemption.
Chapter 19: John completes his description of Babylon's fall, transitions to the heavenly wedding feast of the Lamb, describes his triumphant return to earth as the divine Warrior, and recounts his destruction of all the forces of wickedness gathered against him and his faithful followers.	The Lamb's bride is one day formally wedded to her bridegroom in an extravagant celebration of her redemption and in anticipation of the Lamb's return to earth as the Conqueror of the planet's evil inhabitants.	We must celebrate our union with the Lamb and rejoice in the promise of his victorious return to earth in triumphal victory over the forces of darkness arrayed against him and his faithful followers.

Exegetical Summary	Theological Principle	Homiletical Exhortation
Chapter 20: John discloses the inauguration of the Messiah's kingdom on earth for one thousand years, the last rebellion of Satan and the nations he deceives, and the final judgment, where the unsaved, death, and Hades are all cast into the fiery lake filled with burning sulfur.	The Creator's promise of the Messiah's rule over all the earth is fulfilled, after which comes the final judgment of those opposed to the sovereign reign of the triune God.	We must rejoice in the fulfilled promise of our rule and reign with the Messiah, along with the assurance of having our names written in the Lamb's Book of Life because we have trusted in him for salvation.
Chapter 21: John depicts a glorious vision of a new heaven and a new earth, the descent of the new Jerusalem in all its regal splendor, and the final, complete fulfillment of the promise of Immanuel, God with us.	The Creator and the Messiah one day remake heaven and earth so that God's reborn children finally dwell with him forever in complete freedom from all possibility and effects of sin.	We have the assurance that the final reward of our salvation is the privilege of dwelling forever in the sacred presence of the Creator, the Lamb, and the sevenfold Spirit.
Chapter 22: John concludes his prophetic oracle with a final description of life in the new creation and provides a sobering and encouraging reminder about the Messiah's soon coming, along with a restatement of the dire fate that awaits the wicked.	The Lamb's promise of his soon coming and the assurance that he will fulfill this pledge motivate us to live right now in an upright and virtuous manner.	We must dedicate our entire lives to please our Messiah in anticipation of his second coming, our vindication, and the blessing of everlasting bliss in the sacred presence of our Creator and Redeemer.

Revelation Unraveled

A Glossary of Key Terms, Phrases, and Themes

Abaddon: A Hebrew term that means "destroyer" or "destruction."

abyss: A term referring to a well-like, bottomless pit that serves as the place of confinement for a cast of villainous characters (such as Satan, demons, and the antichrist).

almighty (omnipotence): A term that refers to God's unlimited and all-encompassing power. This term indicates that he possesses the ability to accomplish anything and everything without constraint, according to his supremely good, just, and perfect will. Moreover, he exercises sovereign control over every aspect of reality, whether the past, present, or future; whether physical or metaphysical; and whether seen or unseen.

Alpha and Omega: The first and last letters of the Greek alphabet. The preceding expression is a rhetorical figure of speech known as a merism, in which two contrasting parts draw attention to the full scope of a broader idea. Here, the merism emphasizes that the Creator is the commencement and consummation of all things. Also, his rule encompasses the past, the present, and the future. Moreover, the Father is sovereign over all that takes place in human history and, through the Son, is directing its course to a final and proper conclusion.

already/not-yet perspective: A way of understanding the Apocalypse which reflects a dynamic tension between the present and future fulfillment of end-time events. This view suggests that some aspects of God's kingdom have already been inaugurated through Christ's life, death, and resurrection, while their ultimate consummation is yet to come. Moreover, this perspective emphasizes the idea that believers live in the tension of experiencing the "already" of God's kingdom, while eagerly anticipating the "not yet" of its final realization at the Messiah's second advent.

amen: An interjection transliterated from a Hebrew adjective that literally means "Let it be so" and implies "May it happen in this way."

amillennialism: A view that interprets the prophecies of Revelation, along with other apocalyptic literature in the Bible, as broader spiritual and symbolic truths, rather than as specific, future, and literal events. Adherents maintain that there will be no future, literal 1,000-year earthly reign of Christ. Instead, they contend that his reign is already happening on earth in a metaphysical sense through the church, which advances his rule through the proclamation of the gospel. Moreover, the current age will continue until the Messiah's final return and the full establishment of his eternal kingdom.

angels: Spirit beings who live in heaven, but whom the Creator sends to earth as his messengers. Angels are mighty and powerful, and they possess great wisdom. Ordinarily, they are invisible to humans, though these celestial beings have appeared to humans. Angels exist as an organized hierarchy whose duties include serving the Creator by serving humans, providing them with protection, guarding them, guiding them, and helping them.

antichrist: A false, messiah-like figure whom John describes as a hideous, predatory beast that gradually emerges from the depths of the sea (symbolizing the agitation and restlessness associated with evil). This ogre not only deceives the earth but also seeks to control it through the world's military, economic, and religious systems. While there have been despots throughout history, this maniacal, homicidal entity will appear during the time of the end to spread wickedness, persecute Jesus' followers, and gather the world in rebellion against him. The Lamb, however, emerges victorious as the divine Warrior over all the world's anti-God forces led by the dragon (the devil), sea-beast (the antichrist), and land-beast (the false prophet).

antisemitism: A form of prejudice, discrimination, or hostility directed against Jewish people based on their ethnicity, religion, or cultural background. It can take the form of harmful stereotypes, negative attitudes, and acts of violence and harassment targeting Jewish individuals and communities. It is important not to confuse antisemitism with statements appearing in the Apocalypse which censure those who allege to be Torah-observant Jews. The author is not demonizing his fellow ethnic peers but rather censuring those who deride the Messiah's true, loyal followers. Indeed, Scripture reveals that all those—whether Jew or Gentile—who trust in Jesus of Nazareth for salvation are God's reborn children.

apocalyptic literature: A genre characterized by visions, dreams, and allegories that portray catastrophic, world-ending events. These texts convey messages about divine judgment, the eradication of evil and suffering, and the renewal of the universe. Common themes include the intervention of God and his authorized emissaries, the vindication of the righteous, and the ultimate destiny of humanity. The literature encourages the redeemed to persevere as they wait in hope for the dawn of a new age characterized by justice and peace.

apokalypsis: A Greek noun meaning "to uncover," "to disclose," or "to make known" and usually translated as "revelation." It is used to describe the contents of John's prophetic oracle.

Apollyon: A Greek term that means "destroyer" or "destruction."

apostles: God's special envoys or messengers. One option is that apostleship is restricted to some of the people who saw Jesus with their own eyes. A second option is that the term does not always have such a restricted meaning and can refer to other believers beyond the original Twelve whom Jesus chose during his earthly ministry.

ark of the covenant: In the Old Testament, a sacred box or chest built under Moses' supervision at Mount Sinai. The ark was made from acacia (a dark, hard, and durable desert wood), entirely covered with pure gold, located within the most holy place of the tabernacle, and carried on poles inserted in rings at the four lower corners. Like its Old Testament counterpart, the ark in the Apocalypse symbolizes God's imperial throne and indescribable, holy presence. The chest also serves as a reminder that the Creator fulfills his promises to judge the wicked and vindicate the upright.

Armageddon: The presumed site of the climactic, epic battle between the Creator and the world's anti-God forces led by the dragon (the devil), the sea-beast (the antichrist), and the land-beast (the false prophet). The Hebrew form is "Har Megiddo," which means "Hill (or Mount) of Megiddo." Megiddo was an ancient city and key military stronghold overlooking a strategic valley. It was also the route people often used to travel through the plain of Esdraelon (or Jezreel Valley) in northern Israel. Furthermore, Megiddo was the site of numerous battles during the Old Testament era.

ascension: Jesus' return to preincarnate glory after completing his work of salvation on earth. His ascension marks his exaltation as the risen Lord, who now reigns with supreme authority at the right hand of the Father. This event assures believers that Christ intercedes for them as their eternal High Priest and prepares their heavenly dwelling place. The ascension also confirms the promise of Jesus' triumphant return in power and glory as the conquering King and Judge. This blessed hope instills God's reborn children with assurance that Christ will achieve complete victory over all the forces of evil at the end of the age.

Asia Minor: The southwestern portion of modern-day Turkey.

Babylon: A symbolic reference to a powerful and corrupt city or system (including, but not limited to, the rulers and society of the Roman Empire of the first century AD) that opposes God as well as persecutes and murders his reborn children. The portrayal of Babylon as indulgent, arrogant, and idolatrous signifies the epitome of worldly sin and rebellion against the Lamb's ruling authority. Despite the unrivaled wealth and power of this notorious metropolis, God's judgment of her is sudden, comprehensive, and irreversible.

beatific vision: A reference to the believers' ultimate, direct, and unmediated experience of the Creator's glory in the eternal state. It signifies the culmination of the salvation that God's reborn children have by faith in union with the Messiah. It also represents the ultimate goal of the

Christians' journey, one that is characterized by righteousness, peace, and joy in the sacred, blessed, and everlasting presence of the triune God.

binding of Satan: One option is that it refers to the results of the Savior's death and resurrection, which have already restricted (or curtailed) the devil's power to deceive during the present church age. A second option associates Satan's binding with the beginning of an extraordinary future age of peace and prosperity. This view indicates that the devil is a defeated foe who, along with his demonic cohort, awaits certain doom at the end of the church age.

blessed: A term that means more than being superficially happy. It conveys the idea of being the privileged recipient of the Creator's life-giving kindness, fruitfulness, and abundance. This truth is evident in John's prophetic oracle, where there are seven beatitudes, or pronouncements of covenantal blessing, to those who endure trials and tribulations. God's reborn children are reminded of the eternal rewards that await them in heaven for remaining faithful to Christ in the face of adversity and martyrdom.

Book of Life: A record in heaven containing the names of God's chosen, reborn children. They are redeemed by the Lamb's blood, which he shed on the cross to atone for their sins. The cosmic ledger is also a symbol of the Creator's unconditional love and grace, as well as a reminder that nothing and no one can separate believers from the Father's mercy and pardon in union with the Son. The heavenly list reminds Jesus' followers to live in an upright, holy, and humble manner, in keeping with their summons to salvation.

bride of Christ: A metaphorical reference to the church, which consists of all true believers from the Old and New Testament eras. In a sense, the church presently is betrothed (or pledged in marriage) to the Redeemer and awaits the day when he claims her as his bride. At his return, he will join himself to his followers in an eternal and profound bond of everlasting intimacy, love, and joy. Throughout the centuries, the Savior's bride has been preparing herself for the day when she will meet him. In Revelation, the church is depicted as wearing a wedding dress made of fine linen, and the attire is radiant and pure in appearance. This garment symbolizes the upright deeds that believers perform at the Father's initiative, in the Spirit's power, and for the Son's glory.

centrality of the Messiah: Throughout the Apocalypse, the Messiah is not just one important character among many but is rather the pivotal figure of the entire prophetic oracle. For instance, the Messiah is depicted as the Lamb of God who unleashes the seal, trumpet, and bowl judgments on wicked, pagan humanity. Also, as the divine Warrior who brings about the ultimate victory of good over evil, the Messiah's return signifies the culmination of God's plan for redemption and the establishment of his eternal kingdom.

church militant: A reference to Jesus' followers on earth during the present age who are engaged in an ongoing spiritual battle against the forces of darkness. Despite the threat of persecution and martyrdom, his disciples remain vigilant in their constant struggle against wickedness and iniquity, especially as promoted by Satan and his minions (such as the dragon, the sea-beast, and the land-beast).

church triumphant: A reference to the ultimate victory that Jesus' followers will experience over the forces of darkness at the end of the age. They will overcome their antagonists through the Lamb's sacrificial death on the cross, along with bearing witness to him, even in the face of maltreatment and execution at the hands of the devil and his maniacal, homicidal throng. God's reborn children will experience the ultimate triumph of their faith and faithfulness by dwelling in the Creator's sacred presence forever in heaven.

colonialism: A historical practice where a powerful nation or group of people directly extends its control and influence over a weaker region or territory, often located in a different part of the world, for an extended period. This control is typically enforced through military and economic domination, allowing the colonial power to exploit for its own economic gain the resources, labor, and markets of the colonized area. Colonialism has been a significant driver of global historical developments, leading to the subjugation and displacement of indigenous populations, the confiscation of their lands, the repression of their local cultures and languages, the destruction of their traditional ways of life, the violation of their human rights, the establishment of repressive colonial administrations, and the imposition of foreign cultural and societal changes.

contrasting parallels: The use of dualistic imagery, where dissimilar symbols represent opposing forces. For example, there is the contrast between the Lamb of God, representing the redemption the Messiah secured through his sacrificial death on the cross, and the sea-beast (whether a false messiah-like figure or a degenerate organizational entity), symbolizing the embodiment of wickedness found in the evil world system. These diametrically antagonistic entities highlight the cosmic battle between good and evil, with the ultimate triumph of the Lamb, as the divine Warrior, over all the forces of darkness.

cosmic trial motif: A common theme in the Apocalypse that has as its backdrop God's universal court of justice. Here, the Son evaluates all people according to what they have done. Likewise, he shows no partiality or favoritism in his dealings with either the church or the wicked. Furthermore, the charge against the wicked is their violation of the Lord's righteous decrees, including their relentless persecution and systematic murder of his reborn children. The verdict is the evildoers' guilt. The equitable punishment (or retributive justice) is the destruction of humanity's pagan, idolatrous world system, along with the present heavens and earth.

cosmology: The scientific study of the origin, evolution, and structure of the entire universe, including the galaxies, stars, planets, and other celestial objects within it. Cosmology also seeks to understand the beginning and development of the universe over time, along with its fundamental laws and properties on the broadest scales.

covenantal blessings: A sevenfold series of declarations (beatitudes) that signify the Creator's promise of favor to his faithful, reborn children. Each beatitude offers encouragement and hope to Jesus' beleaguered, martyred followers. They are reassured that God vindicates their faith in and faithfulness to the Messiah; that in union with him their redemption is secure; and that at the end of the age, they will dwell forever with the Lord in heaven.

covenantal curses: A reference to the unleashing of God's wrath on the unholy trinity of the dragon (the devil), the sea-beast (the antichrist), and the land-beast (the false prophet), along with earth's wicked inhabitants. Divine judgment unfolds through a sequence of three sets of seven devastating events known as the seal, trumpet, and bowl plagues. The basis for the Creator's unleashing these calamities is his absolutely holy character and will. Also, as the supreme Monarch of the universe, God is warranted in holding everyone accountable to his perfectly righteous moral standards. Tragically, even in the wake of increasingly lethal cycles of destruction, the unrighteous refuse to repent.

crown: A term that literally refers to a laurel wreath worn by victorious athletes and military leaders in ancient times. Symbolically, it denotes the eternal blessings which Jesus bestows on his followers, who remain faithful to him despite the threat of persecution and martyrdom at the hands of Satan and his wicked minions.

culture: The set of beliefs, values, practices, customs, and behaviors that are learned, shared, and passed down from one generation to another within a particular group, community, or society. Culture encompasses the dynamic ways people interact, communicate, and express themselves through their traditions, art, language, and ethical norms. Culture also plays a fundamental role in shaping the identity and collective consciousness of a group, especially by providing a framework for how individuals within that group understand the world and their place in it.

culture versus society: Society encompasses all individuals interacting within a specific geographical or social boundary, whereas culture is a subset of society, representing the distinct way of life and sense of belonging within a particular community-based context.

day of the Lord: An impending calamity in the grim period leading up to the Messiah's return. At that time, the Creator will shine the light of judgment on a world engulfed in spiritual darkness. Indeed, the series of catastrophes unveiled in the Apocalypse represent the culmination of the woe pronouncements (or covenantal curses) which appear in the Old Testament. One option is that the second coming, the resurrection of the dead, and the final judgment all take place in a brief span of time and together compose the day of the Lord. A second option is that the day of the Lord is a long period that begins after the resurrection of the dead and ends following the completion of the Messiah's reign on earth.

death: A term that symbolizes physical mortality and the end of earthly life. In John's prophetic oracle, death highlights the reality of human impermanence and the consequence of sin.

de-creation event: A reference to the destruction of the earth at the end of the age, which represents a reversal of the original creation God brought into existence. Here, the Lord replaces the entire fallen and corrupted universe with a new heaven and a new earth, in which righteousness, peace, and joy prevail throughout eternity for the Creator's reborn children.

deism: A system of thought that was developed by European philosophers, primarily in England and France, during the Enlightenment of the seventeenth and eighteenth centuries. It posits a deity (often referred to as the "divine watchmaker") who set the natural laws of the universe into operation yet does not actively intervene in its ongoing operation, including human affairs. Deists assert that the world can be understood through reason and empirical observation. While deists do not entirely reject miracles and revelation, they remain critical of claims that cannot be supported by factual evidence. Deists also criticize organized, institutional religion, which supposedly can be divisive and intolerant. This is said to be especially true for Christianity, due to its dogmas, rituals, and supernatural claims.

devil: The slanderer and adversary of believers. This malevolent, supernatural being is depicted as the epitome of evil, temptation, and opposition to God and his reborn children.

discipleship: Instructing both new converts and mature believers in Jesus' words and works. More specifically, discipleship involves guiding Christians on their spiritual journey, nurturing them in their faith, and equipping them to become faithful followers of the Messiah. It is not just about imparting knowledge but also about fostering a deep, personal relationship with the Savior, one that leads to the Spirit's transformation of the believers' thoughts, feelings, and actions. Through this dynamic, interactive mentoring process, Christians are encouraged not only to live out Jesus' teachings in all areas of their lives but also to spread his saving message of love, grace, and redemption to the lost. In short, the goal is to make disciples who can then go on to make more disciples.

Divine Warrior: A designation for the Messiah where he engages in a cosmic battle against the unholy trio of the dragon (the devil), the sea-beast (the antichrist), and the land-beast (the false prophet), along with earth's wicked inhabitants. This portrayal emphasizes Christ's role as the ultimate defender and champion of his faithful, beleaguered, and martyred followers. Through vivid imagery and symbolism, the Apocalypse reveals that the Son's total victory over all anti-God forces is inevitable and that he establishes his reign of justice, peace, and joy throughout the new heaven and the new earth.

dragon: A terrifying, immense, flame-colored creature with seven heads, ten horns, and a crown resting on each of his heads. These symbols of regal authority and unbridled power are counterfeit imitations of the Lamb. The dragon represents Satan, the archenemy of the Creator and his reborn children. The creature's blood-red hue symbolizes his deranged, homicidal nature, while his other features represent his cunning, strength, and influence over nations and peoples.

eschatology: The study of beliefs and theories concerning the end of the world, the judgment of the wicked, and the vindication of the upright, as well as the destiny of nations, history, and the universe.

exodus typology: An example of prophetic foreshadowing in which the Israelites' liberation from slavery in Egypt and journey to Canaan serve as a symbolic template for the end-time themes in Revelation. Here, the focus is on the Creator's deliverance of his reborn children from Satan, sin, and death through the Lamb's atoning sacrifice on the cross. This typological connection emphasizes the continuity of God's redemptive plan across the Old and New Testaments. It also offers encouragement to Jesus' beleaguered followers, whom he ultimately delivers from all forms of evil and oppression.

evangelism: The act of sharing the gospel with the lost and inviting them to trust in Christ for salvation. This endeavor requires believers to be proactive, intentional, and earnest in articulating the good news with clarity and conviction to their unsaved peers so that they can experience the blessings of eternal life, including Jesus' redeeming love and forgiveness.

evangelism versus missionary outreach: Evangelism is primarily concerned with sharing the good news about Christ with the unsaved, especially with the goal of making disciples, all within a familiar cultural context. In contrast, while missionary outreach encompasses similar evangelistic activities, it also involves reaching people from different cultures. In addition, missionary outreach may include establishing new churches, educating new believers, and offering humanitarian aid as a vehicle to share the saving message about Christ.

everlasting gospel: The phrase first appears in Revelation 14:6. One option is that this phrase refers to the saving message about Jesus' death and resurrection. A second option is that the angelic announcement denotes the specific content of the celestial being's proclamation, namely, that all humankind must fear the Creator, glorify (or honor) him, and prostrate themselves in homage to him. In this case, the Lord makes a final summons through his heavenly emissary for earth's wicked inhabitants to abandon their iniquity and acknowledge him as their supreme and sole Monarch.

fear of the Lord: This is not about harboring a cringing terror of the Creator but rather about having a deep reverence, awe, and honor for him. Here, his reborn children acknowledge his sovereign authority and judgment through their thoughts, words, and actions. The phrase emphasizes the importance of the believers' faithfulness and obedience to God, even in the face of persecution and martyrdom. Only he is righteous and just, and he alone is worthy of their worship and praise as the almighty Lord.

fearing versus loving God: Although these two concepts are important and complementary, they represent different aspects of the relationship between the Creator and his reborn children. For instance, they should love God with every aspect of their being and do so through worship, obedience, and service. In contrast, revering the Lord stems from a recognition of the truth that he is the ultimate and absolute Judge and that he has the power to reward or punish according to his sovereign, holy, and perfect will. Love without fear becomes sentimental and fails to result in obedience. Oppositely, fear without love becomes cringing terror and drives people away from an intimate relationship with the Creator. Together, love and fear produce a healthy relationship with the Lord and result in obedience to his will.

first and the last, the: A phrase used to describe the Messiah. He is portrayed as the beginning and the end of all things to signify his divine nature and eternal existence. This title also highlights Christ's omnipotence and everlasting presence, along with his being the ultimate authority and source of salvation for God's reborn children.

first death: The termination of a person's temporal, earthly existence.

firstfruits: An allusion to an ancient Israelite practice in which God's people set apart the firstborn of all their livestock and the first portion of their harvest. In this way, they designated these items as being special and belonging exclusively to the Lord.

first resurrection: An event in which the Father vindicates the faith and faithfulness of all the Son's loyal followers by raising them from the dead and allowing them to reign with him for a thousand years, whether in heaven or on earth. Some see the resurrection as occurring before the millennium, while others place the resurrection right after the start of the millennium. The Creator does not resurrect the remainder of the dead—whether restricted only to the wicked or including both the saved and unsaved—until the conclusion of this era. Even among those who claim that the first resurrection concerns all believers, one group thinks that the focus is on a spiritual resurrection. In this case, it takes place either when believing sinners are united with the Son or when a person goes to be with the Savior at the time of bodily death. A second group thinks that John has in mind a bodily resurrection of all believers. In this case, when the Messiah returns, he will raise them from the dead and allow them to reign with him in his kingdom, whether in heaven or on earth.

forty-two months, twelve hundred and sixty days, or three and a half years: One option is that these terms refer to a literal period in which Satan, through his diabolical human agents, persecutes Jesus' faithful followers just before his return. A second option is that the time duration represents a complete period of suffering cut short by half. Here, the focus is on a limited period of tyranny, whether recurring throughout church history or occurring in the closing days preceding the second advent. The idea is that the Creator brings a definite end to the reign of terror.

four angels: A group of celestial beings who are each depicted as standing on one of the four corners of the earth. One option is that these entities are the four living creatures mentioned previously in the Apocalypse. A second option is that they are four previously unidentified angels. In either case, they function as the Lord's agents of destruction, who use their God-given strength to restrain the four winds of judgment from blowing diagonally across the planet.

four horsemen: A symbolic representation of divine judgments associated with the first four seal calamities. The first rider on a white horse represents the spirit of military conquest and victory. The second rider on a flame-colored horse symbolizes bloodshed and death in armed conflict. The third rider on a black horse represents intense, widespread famine. The fourth rider (referred to as Death) mounted on a pale green (or ashen) horse symbolizes the effects of disease that are often associated with bloodshed and famine. Each of the four riders, in succession, adds to and intensifies the devastation caused by his predecessor or predecessors.

four living creatures: Remarkable, otherworldly beings located near God's sacred throne in heaven. This regal order of angels guards the Father's royal seat, proclaims his holiness, and leads others in worship. Collectively, the foursome are unceasing in their watchfulness and acute in their intelligence. Moreover, these entities possibly symbolize all the creatures of the earth, every one of whom is under the Creator's dominion.

fulfillment motif: Refers to the recurring theme of the Creator's faithfulness to his promises and sovereignty in accomplishing what he has prophesied through Scripture. Additionally, the motif emphasizes the culmination of God's plans and purposes for humanity, especially by depicting the Messiah's ultimate triumph of good over evil, his vindication of the righteous, and his establishment of the divine, eternal kingdom.

futurist view: An outlook that considers most of Revelation's prophecies as events yet to be fulfilled in time to come. These include predictions about an upcoming seven-year period of intense tribulation; the rise of an apostate world religion, government, and ruler; a literal 1,000-year reign of Christ on earth; and the ultimate triumph of God's eternal kingdom.

God's eternality: The truth that the Lord exists above and beyond the constraints of time. This concept emphasizes that the Creator of the universe is not limited by past, present, or future events. Indeed, he transcends time itself. Consequently, he does not experience time as a linear progression but rather sees all of time at once with perfect understanding. Yet rather than being detached from creation (an idea claimed by adherents of deism), God maintains a perpetual engagement with it. For instance, he sustains and governs the universe, as well as ensures that nothing occurs without his knowledge or falls outside his sovereign control. Likewise, he is fully aware of everything that has happened, is happening, and will happen, along with guaranteeing that his everlasting plan of salvation is brought to a successful and fulsome completion in the Messiah.

God's glory: The outward, radiant display of the Lord's intrinsic, divine attributes, such as his greatness, holiness, majesty, perfection, and sovereignty over creation. The glory of the triune God is often associated with his awe-inspiring presence, which evokes worship and praise, whether from innumerable angels surrounding his sacred throne in heaven or from his grateful, reborn children on earth.

God's holiness: Two fundamental truths are encompassed by this concept. First, God's holiness signifies his sinlessness in the absolute sense, along with denoting his complete freedom from moral imperfection. Second, the concept highlights the Creator's unparalleled uniqueness as the ultimate source of life and flourishing in the universe. Indeed, he alone possesses the capacity to fill the cosmos with beauty, dynamism, and functional integrity.

God's omniscience: The belief that the Creator possesses complete, infinite, and instantaneous knowledge about all things, whether past, present, or future. This attribute indicates that God is not limited by either time or space, for he transcends both. He also has a perfect apprehension of every detail about the universe, including the thoughts, actions, and intentions of all individuals. Indeed, nothing is hidden from his sight. The Creator's omniscience implies that he knows everything that is knowable, including the deepest mysteries and secrets of existence. Moreover, this concept emphasizes that his knowledge is boundless and his awareness is all-encompassing.

God's righteous verdicts: A concept that affirms the Creator's intrinsically holy and just character and stresses that his judgments are forever righteous and deserved (rather than being arbitrary and capricious). In the Apocalypse, an additional emphasis is placed on the consequences of human rebellion against God, along with the need for the wicked to repent and trust in Christ for salvation.

God's seal on believers: A symbol of the Creator's ownership and protection of his reborn children, in which he sets them apart from earth's wicked inhabitants. This seal assures Jesus' faithful followers that he safeguards them from spiritual harm (especially originating from Satan and his demonic cohort), as well as grants believers the ultimate victory over all the anti-God forces arrayed against them.

God's wrath: The Creator's righteous anger against all forms of evil, injustice, and oppression. The implication is that wicked humanity's iniquity and rebellion against God are doomed to fail. Indeed, those who oppose his just and sovereign rule bring upon themselves such calamities as environmental catastrophes, plagues, and warfare. At the end of the age, the Lord's wrath culminates in the great white throne judgment and leads to the establishment of righteousness, peace, and joy in the new creation.

Gog and Magog: A reference to insurrectionist forces of darkness that recalls the language of Ezekiel 38–39, where Gog is the foremost ruler of the land of Magog. This allusion to the preceding person and place epitomizes a vast, wicked horde under Satan's control (whether literal or symbolic, as well as whether a demonic or human army). At the end of the age, the devil will gather a cadre of antagonistic nations for a final battle against the beloved community of the redeemed. The Creator's incineration of the evil forces signifies the Lamb's ultimate triumph of good over evil.

gospel: The message of salvation through faith in Christ. Redemption is made possible by Jesus' sacrificial death on the cross, and his resurrection demonstrates his victory over Satan, sin, and death. This good news is shared with the lost so that, by faith, they receive his offer of forgiveness and new life in union with him.

grace: The Lord's undeserved favor, kindness, and compassion to those who trust in the Messiah, resulting in their being forgiven of their sins and adopted into God's family as his reborn children. This grace offers believers solace in difficult times. Even amid the chaos spawned by Satan and his demonic cohort, the Creator's love and mercy shine brightly on Jesus' faithful followers and guide them onward to their eternal, heavenly home.

Great Commission: Jesus' command for his followers to go into all the world and make disciples of all nations. This endeavor includes baptizing new believers and teaching them to obey all that he taught. The Spirit empowers Christians to fulfill the Great Commission, such as by sharing the gospel with others, volunteering in their local church or parachurch ministry, donating to missions organizations, conveying an affirming and appealing witness to the lost, and establishing faith communities where members are encouraged to remain loyal to the Messiah.

great white throne judgment: A reference to a future time of accountability after the millennium in which the Creator fairly and impartially, as well as factually and objectively, assesses the deeds of everyone, including the dragon (the devil), the sea-beast (the antichrist), the land-beast (the false prophet), and earth's wicked inhabitants. It is then that the dead, both small and great, stand before God's enormous, gleaming, royal seat. Likewise, various ledgers are opened, which contain a record of everyone's actions. One option is that this judgment involves only unbelievers, while a second option is that both saved and unsaved appear before the Creator. Those whose names are not recorded in the Book of Life are cast into the fiery lake filled with burning sulfur to experience everlasting separation from God.

Hades: A term that refers to the subterranean realm of the dead and is often associated with eternal separation from God, both physically and spiritually.

hallelujah (alleluia): An interjection used to express exuberant praise to God. The ancient Israelites joined the noun *Yah*, which is a shortened form of *Yahweh* (the covenant name for the Lord), to the verb *halal*. The combined phrase means "Praise the Lord," making it a powerful expression of worship and adoration.

harlot or prostitute: A sacrilegious, bloodthirsty entity depicted as sitting on many waters. This portrayal denotes the tumult and devastation connected with earth's wicked inhabitants. This hideous, predatory ogre symbolizes a prominent city that exercises sovereignty and power over the earth's monarchs. Furthermore, the waters upon which the prostitute sits represent masses of people from all ethnicities, nations, and languages. This observation indicates that the harlot's influence over the evil world system is pervasive. One option is that the prostitute heads up a worldwide apostate church. A second option is that the harlot and the sea-beast represent opposing forces of evil. In either case, the woman is an archetype of every political, social, and religious entity opposed to the Creator throughout history.

heaven: The dwelling place of God and the abode of his sanctuary. Heaven is not a cosmic shelter where the Creator isolates himself from the earth (an idea claimed by adherents of deism). Rather, it is the divine workplace, where he sends blessings to his people and punishment on his enemies. A time is coming when heaven will be replaced by a new heaven and a new earth.

historicist view: Regards the events and symbols described in the Apocalypse as representing a chronological and continuous sequence of historical events. These extend from the time of John's writing to the end of human history, with specific identifications of historical figures and periods in Western church history fulfilling biblical prophecy.

Holy One: When applied to the Savior, this phrase emphasizes his fully divine nature, along with his being absolutely pure and infinitely greater than and entirely set apart from anything in fallen creation (including its imperfect and corrupted aspects).

idealist view: Interprets the Apocalypse as a symbolic and allegorical representation of timeless spiritual truths and the ongoing battle between good and evil. This perspective claims that the imagery and narrative of Revelation serve as a metaphorical guide for Christians, especially by spotlighting moral and spiritual lessons, rather than emphasizing specific prophecies about future historical events (such as the end of the world, the judgment of the wicked, the vindication of the righteous, and the reign of the Messiah).

imperial cult: A state-sanctioned religious practice throughout the Roman Empire in which the reigning monarch was deified and venerated as a god. This practice played a crucial role in consolidating the emperor's power and authority, especially as it helped unite Rome's vast and culturally diverse territories under a shared religious and political identity.

Jerusalem, the great city: Previously, the capital of ancient Israel and the place where Jesus of Nazareth was crucified. In the era of intense distress, Jerusalem becomes enemy territory, being figuratively comparable to the city of Sodom and the country of Egypt, two regions once notorious for their immorality, oppression, and idolatry. Jerusalem could also be a symbolic reference to either Babylon, Rome, or some other infamous metropolis, as well as the pagan world system in its ability to entice people away from the true worship of the Creator.

Jezebel: One view maintains that this is the real name of a literal woman. A more likely option is that it is the name given to an otherwise anonymous woman to identify her with the notorious wife of Ahab, the ninth-century BC king of Israel. This wicked queen encouraged God's people to venerate Baal, the supreme deity of the Canaanites. The infamous woman in the Thyatiran church claims to be a prophetess, for she wants others to think that she, as a representative of God, speaks the truth. In reality, the woman is a spiritual fraud, whom Jesus condemns for deceiving his followers with her heretical teaching.

judgment cycles: Three series of seven calamities known as the seal, trumpet, and bowl judgments. One view is that the judgments occur simultaneously, with the sevenfold seals, trumpets, and bowls occurring in a chronologically parallel fashion, implying a recapitulation of events. A second view is that the judgments unfold in a successive sequence, with one calamity following the preceding ones, for a total of twenty-one judgments. A third view is that one series of judgments contains the next series in a telescopic or dovetailing fashion, in which the seventh seal judgment contains and introduces the seven trumpet judgments and the seventh trumpet judgment contains and introduces the seven bowl judgments. Through these judgment cycles, the Creator shows that he is the sovereign, all-powerful Lord, as well as the one, true, and living God. He also demonstrates to pagan, idolatrous humanity his unwavering concern for his beleaguered, martyred children. Moreover, he provides the unsaved with sufficient reason to abandon their wicked ways and turn to the Messiah in saving faith.

key of David: A symbol of authority, especially within an imperial, messianic context. Specifically, the Redeemer possesses the undisputed right to the Davidic royal line. When the Son opened the door to his eternal kingdom, no one could shut it. Likewise, when he closes the door, no one will be able to open it.

kingdom and priesthood of all believers: A concept that emphasizes the dual role of God's reborn children as both rulers and mediators in his redemptive plan and program. They are also affirmed in their identity and purpose as Christ's ambassadors, who faithfully proclaim the good news about him to the lost. Moreover, this theme highlights the believers' responsibility to participate in God's salvific work on earth through faithful service and compassionate ministry to whomever they encounter.

Lake of Fire: Either a literal or symbolic place of everlasting punishment for the dragon (the devil), sea-beast (the antichrist), and land-beast (the false prophet), along with earth's wicked inhabitants. From a literary perspective, the fiery lake filled with burning sulfur functions as a vivid and terrifying image that emphasizes the consequences of humankind's iniquity and rebellion. From a theological perspective, the blazing cauldron underscores the reality of the Creator's justice, in which he separates the righteous from the unrighteous, as well as highlights the seriousness of one's choices and the eternal consequences therein.

Lamb motif: Used in the Apocalypse to juxtapose the Messiah's humility and power. For instance, he is depicted as being pure, innocent, and proactive in atoning for the sins of humanity through his sacrificial death on the cross. Likewise, the motif emphasizes Christ's victorious role as the divine Warrior in defeating Satan, his demonic cohort, and earth's wicked inhabitants, along with consummating the Father's end-time plan and program. Indeed, throughout Revelation, the Lamb serves as a pivotal symbol of redemption, divine authority, and the ultimate source of hope for God's reborn children.

land-beast (false prophet): The sea-beast's lieutenant, who represents either an individual (such as the deputy of a literal antichrist) or an evil entity (such as the imperial priesthood of a godless state). If the land-beast is an individual, he misleads the world through amazing signs and prophetic declarations. If the land-beast is an evil entity, it is a counterfeit witness to the Holy Spirit and tries to deceive the world through anti-God propaganda.

Lion motif: The symbolism of the Lion, when applied to the Messiah, indicates that he alone has the virtue and authority to open the seven-sealed scroll containing the Creator's end-time judgments and to bring them to completion. After all, Jesus of Nazareth was from the tribe of Judah and sprang from the house and lineage of David. Likewise, Christ won the victory as the divine Warrior on behalf of the redeemed, which he achieved through his atoning sacrifice on the cross and resurrection from the dead.

lists of iniquities: Various catalogs of sins that emphasize the moral degradation and spiritual corruption of earth's wicked inhabitants. These lists also stress that the Creator is just in his decision to hold unrepentant sinners accountable for luxuriating in depravity, violence, and idolatry. This especially includes suffering eternal separation from God in the fiery lake filled with burning sulfur.

literary purpose of the Apocalypse: The Father, through the Son, triumphs over the forces of evil, condemns the wicked, vindicates the righteous, fulfills all his promises, and accomplishes his sovereign purpose in history. Here, faith in the Messiah is the basis for experiencing his covenantal blessings. Also, the Lamb's judgment of the wicked through the unleashing of covenantal curses is inevitable. Moreover, the Christian view of history—namely, that the Creator is moving events to a final, satisfactory consummation and the ethical values this perspective advocates—is vastly superior to those of fallen, pagan humanity.

Lord God: A phrase that, in the Septuagint, is the equivalent of the Hebrew expression "Adonai Yahweh." When combined with the Greek noun rendered "Almighty," the meaning is that of "sovereign Master," which emphasizes God's supreme authority and rule over all creation.

male child: A reference to the Messiah, who is born to a symbolic, female figure and whose destiny includes shepherding (or ruling over) all the nations with an iron rod (that is, a royal scepter). Despite the barbaric efforts of the dragon (the devil) to devour the woman's child, he is snatched up to the safety of heaven and the Creator's sacred throne. In brief, God checkmates Satan's repeated attempts to overthrow the Messiah and obliterate his followers.

mark of the sea-beast: An imprint of allegiance placed on either the right hand or forehead of earth's wicked inhabitants. This stamp is a mock replica of the seal of ownership and protection which the Creator places on his bondservants. The satanic brand includes either the sea-beast's name or a specific number associated with it and signifies that those who have it are controlled by the predatory brute and remain loyal to it.

Michael: An archangel (or chief angel) and protector of the redeemed. He is portrayed as a powerful celestial figure who leads the armies of heaven in a triumphant, epic battle against Satan and his demonic cohort, all of whom are cast out of heaven.

millennium: A word derived from the Latin term *mille*, which means "thousand," and *annus*, which means "year." One option is that the term in the Apocalypse refers to a literal period in which the Messiah reigns on earth. A second option is that John is speaking metaphorically about an indefinite interval in which the Son rules victoriously from either heaven or earth.

missional: The active commitment of Jesus' followers to spread the gospel to people from every tribe, language, ethnicity, and nation. Being missional involves the believers' intentional, proactive, and earnest engagement with the lost. Expressed differently, it entails a mindset of being on mission as a specific set of tasks to be performed. Here, Christians share the good news about the Messiah, summon the unsaved to heartfelt repentance, and demonstrate Jesus' grace through his followers' words and actions. Ultimately, being missional is about fulfilling the Great Commission, in which believers go into all the world to proclaim Jesus' redeeming love and make disciples of all nations.

missionaries of the gospel: The mandate for Christians to share the message of the Savior actively to all people by reaching across cultures, national boundaries, and even languages. Missionaries, through their words and actions, spread the good news about the cross to others, regardless of their ethnicity, geographical location, or socioeconomic status. This approach to outreach often involves evangelism, humanitarian aid (such as compassion and relief work), and living biblically in all areas of life. Ultimately, the Spirit uses this holistic approach to plant the seed of faith in the soil of unsaved hearts so that they can experience the transformative power of new life in union with the Messiah.

morning star: This phrase may be a reference to the Son, who, as the divine Warrior, ensures that a new day of salvation dawns. Three other options include the Holy Spirit (especially in guiding and illuminating the path of salvation), the immortality of the redeemed (particularly the eternal life and glory that awaits believers in God's sacred presence), or the resurrection of the righteous at the end of the age (including the promise of a new beginning and ultimate victory over death).

Mount Zion: Initially, a reference to the southeast hill and fortress of Jerusalem, which David captured from the Jebusites and made the capital of Israel. Later, Zion came to represent all Jerusalem poetically, as well as the city of God, from which the Creator rules. One option is that Zion in the Apocalypse is Jerusalem on earth, namely, the future capital of the Messiah's kingdom. A second option is that Zion symbolizes heaven, namely, the place where the Creator dwells with his reborn children and showers them with eternal blessings.

mystery: A term that does not refer to what is either odd or bizarre. Instead, it signifies divine truths that, in times past, were hidden but that now the Savior has made known to his faithful followers.

new heaven and new earth: A reference to a renewed creation, where God establishes a purified, perfected, and everlasting order that is free from the corruption and decay caused by iniquity. In this glorious vision of the future, righteousness, peace, and joy replace sin, suffering, and death, and the Creator's reborn children dwell in his sacred presence for all eternity.

Nero *redivivus* (or revived) myth: A first-century AD legend claiming that Nero, the former ruler of Rome, would come back to life and lead a rebellious force of Parthians from the east to invade and seize control of the empire.

new Jerusalem: Either a figurative or literal city coming down out of heaven to earth and signifying the union of these two realms. The metropolis, which denotes both a redeemed people and a sacred locale, is characterized by holiness, righteousness, and perfection, along with peace, love, and joy. As part of God's renewed creation, the megacity is immensely beautiful, with streets of gold and gates made of precious jewels. The stunning abode, as the culmination of the Creator's redemptive plan for humanity, is the ultimate destination of his reborn children, with whom he dwells forever.

Nicolaitans: A heretical group active in Ephesus (one of the major centers of early Christianity), whose leader possibly was a man named Nicholas. The adherents were guilty of compromising their alleged faith in Christ to justify their participation in the idolatrous practices lauded by Roman society. Likewise, members of the spurious group claimed their spiritual freedom allowed them to indulge in sexual immorality.

numbers in Scripture: These often carry symbolic and spiritual significance in both the Old and New Testaments, especially to convey deeper meanings and messages beyond their numerical value. For instance, the number seven symbolizes perfection, completeness, the Spirit of God, and the seven days of creation, while twelve represents divine governance or organization, the twelve tribes of Israel, and the twelve apostles. In Revelation, numbers like 666 symbolize imperfection or evil, while 144,000 represents the great multitude of people from all over the world whom the Creator redeems. These numerical symbols add layers of meaning and convey spiritual truths, thereby enriching the biblical narrative.

one hundred and forty-four thousand: A chosen number of people from the twelve tribes of Israel. One option is that this is a select, restored remnant from the literal twelve tribes of Israel who evangelize the lost during a future seven-year period of great tribulation. A second option is that these are a specific number of believers whom the Lord in some way shields during a final period of immense distress. A third option is that the 144,000 are a symbolic number for the fullness of the people of God. Expressed another way, the Creator brings all his reborn children safely to their eternal home with him in heaven.

open door: One option is that the phrase refers to believers entering the Messiah's everlasting, sacred realm. Other options are that the phrase denotes an opportunity for believers to evangelize the outlying regions of their city, a chance for prayer, or an abrupt entrance into God's presence through martyrdom.

open theism: A theological perspective that challenges traditional concepts of God's omniscience. It posits that God does not know everything about the future, particularly regarding human choices. Open theists also believe that the future is partly open and not predetermined, allowing for genuine human free will. This view emphasizes the relational aspect of God's interaction with humanity, suggesting that he responds to events in real time, rather than having a fixed plan for every detail of the future.

paradise of God: A phrase, reminiscent of the garden of Eden, in which heaven is depicted as an enclosed orchard filled with luscious, fruit-bearing trees. Here, at the end of the age, God's reborn children enjoy an everlasting place of refuge, peace, and rest. Indeed, all Christ's faithful followers share the hope of experiencing perpetual contentment and delight with the Creator in his sacred presence, free from the presence of evil.

parousia: A term that carries the ideas of "presence" and "coming," especially in connection with the official visit of a high-ranking dignitary. Implied is that when the Son returns at the end of the age, he is not some sort of phantom. Rather, he physically arrives at a divinely appointed place and time to consummate the Father's end-time plan and program.

peace: The ending of the hostility that once existed between sinners and God, along with denoting harmonious relations among his reborn children. This peace comes through faith in the Messiah, whose atoning sacrifice on the cross bridges the great divide between a holy God and sinful humanity. In union with the Son, believers partake of an eternal, heavenly citizenship that transcends the depraved appetites of sinful people, the sensual desires of their eyes, and their bragging about what they have and do.

persecution of believers: The maltreatment of God's reborn children spotlights the enduring faith and resilience of early Christian communities in the face of Roman oppression. The repeated references to the trials and tribulations experienced by Jesus' disciples form the backdrop for the Creator's promise to vindicate their faith and faithfulness, especially by judging the forces of darkness and establishing his eternal kingdom.

persecution literature: Ancient, sacred texts that emphasize the physical, emotional, and spiritual maltreatment believers endure for their faith. The Apocalypse uses vivid, symbolic imagery to showcase the refusal of early Christians to renounce their faith, even when faced with imprisonment, torture, and death. Furthermore, John's prophetic oracle highlights the truth that the present wicked era will one day come to an end and that in the eternal state, the Creator will bless his reborn children for their suffering.

postmillennialism: A view claiming that before the Messiah's second coming, there is a long period of spiritual, moral, and societal improvement, with the gospel spreading and the church gradually transforming the world into a godlier, righteous, and peaceful state known as the kingdom of heaven. Adherents maintain that the current messianic age of the church will transition into a golden era of peace, prosperity, and righteousness on earth.

prayers of the saints: The petitions made by God's reborn children that highlight their unwavering faith and faithfulness despite unrelenting persecution and martyrdom. Ultimately, the believers' cries for vindication and judgment lead to the unfolding of the Creator's redemptive plan, including the Lamb's final triumph of good over evil and the establishment of the new creation. Here, Jesus' beleaguered followers find reassurance in his gracious consideration of and attentive response to their prayers.

premillennialism: A view claiming that the Messiah will return to earth before a literal 1,000-year period of peace and righteousness, known as the millennium. During this time, he is believed to reign as a triumphant King, Satan's power is temporarily bound, and he has limited influence over humanity. After the millennium, the devil is released for a final rebellion before being defeated once and for all. Though premillennialists differ in their interpretations of the timing of the rapture, along with the events leading up to Christ's return, they generally anticipate a period of intense persecution of Jesus' followers before his second coming.

preterist view: Interprets the prophecies in Revelation as being fulfilled primarily in the past, especially during the first century AD. This perspective holds that the symbolism and imagery of the Apocalypse are intended to address contemporary issues faced by the early Christian community, rather than foretelling distant future events.

protest literature: Ancient, sacred texts that, by using vivid imagery and symbolism, offer a critique of corrupt political systems and pagan societal norms. In this regard, the Apocalypse often conveys a message of impending doom and divine retribution to challenge the status quo (such as that of pagan, idolatrous Rome) and to urge earth's wicked inhabitants to repent. Moreover, Revelation depicts Jesus' marginalized, beleaguered followers petitioning the Creator to vanquish the wicked, vindicate the righteous, and replace the present fallen order with the glorious new creation that awaits God's reborn children.

rapture: A term that refers to a sudden and forceful snatching or taking away. The rapture denotes a future event in which true believers are said to be instantaneously removed from the earth and transported to heaven, whether before, during, or after a period of immense distress on earth. This view is often associated with the end times and is a subject of intense theological debate within Christianity.

remaining faithful: Emphasizes the importance of the believers' steadfastness and loyalty to the Messiah amid adversity. God's reborn children are encouraged to persevere in their devotion to him, for they have his promise of being vindicated in their faith, reigning with Christ, and experiencing everlasting joy in the Creator's sacred presence in heaven.

repentance: To undergo a complete change in one's thoughts, attitudes, and actions toward the Creator and life's priorities. Repentance is part of the conversion process. Through the working of the Spirit, sinners come to the point at which they are ready to turn away from sin and place their trust in the Messiah for salvation. Tragically, within the Apocalypse, earth's wicked inhabitants not only refuse to do so but also persevere in their harlotries and idolatries. In contrast, God's reborn children regularly seek to forsake their iniquity, as well as align themselves with his upright moral standards and ethical priorities.

resurrection motif: Refers to a recurring theme throughout the Apocalypse where the wicked who have died are raised to final judgment and unending punishment in the Lake of Fire and where God's reborn children are raised to join the Messiah in his future reign. This motif symbolizes the triumph of faith over death, the ultimate victory of the righteous, and their sure hope of dwelling forever with the Creator in heaven.

Root of David: A phrase indicating that the Messiah arose, like a shoot or sprout out of the main stem, from the historical and royal lineage of King David. The implication is that the long-awaited Savior, whom the Old Testament prophets foretold, fulfills the covenant promises God made to David and his dynasty.

saints: A reference, not to a privileged group of elite, exceptional believers, but to all the Creator's reborn, holy children.

salvation: A term referring to the Messiah's deliverance of believers from sin and all its dire consequences. It also denotes the Lamb's final victory over the principalities of the pagan and idolatrous world system, which crucified the Son and murdered his faithful followers.

Satan: A reference to the opponent and accuser of believers. As the epitome of all that is evil, he embodies the cosmic spiritual battle he and his demonic cohort wage with the Creator, his angels, and his reborn children. Ultimately, at the end of the age, the Messiah brings to completion his triumph over Satan and his minions, resulting in their being cast into the Lake of Fire to experience everlasting punishment.

sea-beast: A false, messiah-like figure who symbolizes either a real person (commonly known as the antichrist) or a rogue organizational entity (functioning as the embodiment of wickedness found in the evil world system). If the sea-beast is an individual, he seeks to control the planet through the military, economic, and religious systems of the world. If the sea-beast is an organizational entity, it endorses the persecution of believers, the spread of idolatry and immorality, and the proliferation of heretical ideas.

seal of the living God: A mark placed on the foreheads of the Creator's bondservants to signify his ownership, care, and protection of them from the impending series of calamities to be unleashed on earth's wicked inhabitants. More specifically, God's name (which represents his holy character and attributes) is the visible imprint he affixes to his reborn children, who faithfully follow the Lamb, conduct their lives according to his teachings, and inherit eternal life.

second advent: The belief that at the end of the age, as prophesied in the Old Testament, the Messiah returns to earth as the divine Warrior, bringing a time of undisputed victory, judgment, and rule. These truths are meant to encourage God's reborn children to remain unwavering in their devotion to him, as well as to exhort the unsaved to abandon their iniquity and trust in Christ for salvation.

second death: A reference to unending separation and exile from the Creator, as well as eternal, unrelenting, conscious torment in the fiery lake filled with burning sulfur. Indeed, this searing, inescapable cauldron functions as an everlasting penal colony for the unregenerate.

second resurrection: An event that occurs at the conclusion of the millennium. One option is that this event is restricted only to the wicked, while a second option is that it includes both saved and unsaved.

sensory verbs: The widespread use in Revelation of such terms as "hear," "listen," and "see" to indicate awareness, understanding, and the importance of obedience among Jesus' followers. For example, sensory verbs often evoke vivid imagery and engage the readers' senses. These terms also enable believers to connect with the knowledge on a deeper level by imagining and experiencing it firsthand. Moreover, this approach invites them to pause, meditate, and consider the profound meanings behind the sensory descriptions.

seven churches: Specific congregations located in the Roman province of Asia Minor (encompassing the modern-day western part of Turkey) in the following cities: Ephesus, Smyrna, Pergamum, Thyatira, Sardis, Philadelphia, and Laodicea. These towns were about fifty miles apart from each other and formed a roughly horseshoe-shaped circuit, starting with Ephesus and ending with Laodicea. The cities were strategically positioned and could have served as crucial hubs within a larger transportation network, a postal system, or judicial districts, catering to various regions in Asia Minor. Most likely, the choice of seven churches has symbolic relevance, namely, to signify the totality of the people of God.

seven heads, seven hills, and seven kings: The seven heads of the sea-beast on which the harlot sits may initially be a reference to Rome, especially since it was originally built on seven hills. Moreover, the seven heads of the sea-beast represent seven kings, which the prostitute evidently dominates, especially since she is depicted as sitting upon (or controlling) these monarchs. One option is that this detail refers to a strict succession of Roman emperors. A second option is that the reference is to a selective list of Roman emperors or world empires. A third option is that the monarchs represent all anti-God and anti-Christian governments throughout history. A fourth option is that the seven heads signify the saturation of evil and blasphemy within the pagan, idolatrous world system.

seven lampstands: A phrase that represents the seven churches located in Asia Minor, especially in their light-bearing or witness-bearing functions about the Savior to a pagan and idolatrous world.

seven-sealed scroll: A roll of papyrus, leather, or parchment containing text on both sides, signifying the extensive and comprehensive nature of its contents. It is sealed with wax in seven different locations to safeguard its contents from unauthorized access or tampering. The scroll's content may include God's covenant, his law, his promises, and divine revelations. Most likely, the object records the Creator's end-time plan, with a particular emphasis on the Lamb's role in bringing the present fallen era to a close.

seven spirits: One option is that the phrase refers to seven angels who stand before the Creator's sacred, cosmic throne. Most likely, however, John is symbolically referring to the totality and purity of the Spirit, along with his fulsome presence and life-giving ministry.

seven stars: A symbol of the earthly messengers, heavenly emissaries, or the prevailing spirit of each of the seven churches. In Roman times, stars appeared on coins as a symbol of imperial power. The imagery of the Messiah's grasping the seven stars indicates that he, not the Roman emperor or any other evil entity (such as Satan and his demonic cohort), exercises absolute control over believers and their eternal destinies. Likewise, he is their Defender and Protector.

sharp, double-edged sword: A long metal blade emerging from the mouth of the Redeemer, symbolizing both the Word of God and divine judgment.

six, six, six: The name of the sea-beast in numerical form, which stands either for a person or fallen humanity (or both). One option is that the enigmatic number is a code name based on the numerical value of the Greek letters. For instance, one tally of a Hebrew transliteration of the Greek letters of the Latin name Nero Caesar adds up to 666. Nero was one of Rome's most godless emperors. A second option is that 666 is the number of complete imperfection (or triple failure), especially since it falls short of three sevens, which is the number of absolute perfection. A third option is that 666 represents the unholy, malevolent trinity of the dragon (the devil), the sea-beast (the antichrist), and the land-beast (the false prophet).

slavery: While some first-century Christians kept slaves, the New Testament provides indications that institutional slavery is evil and should be abolished (for example, Paul's brief letter to Philemon). During the centuries since the Messiah's birth, Christians in Europe and America not only reassessed their views on slavery but also sought to limit and abolish it. For instance, one of the most powerful arguments Christian abolitionists used against slavery was that all human beings are created in the image of God and have inherent dignity and value. Accordingly, Christians sought to replace all systems of cruel and inhumane bondage and forced labor with the principles of equality, individual rights, and self-determination for all people in society, regardless of their ethnicity, gender, socioeconomic status, and so on.

society: A complex and organized group of individuals who interact with one another within a shared geographical or social space. It is characterized by a set of norms, values, and rules that govern the behavior of its members as well as help to maintain order and cohesion. Here, various strata of individuals—from small, tight-knit tribes to large nation-states with millions of citizens—form social structures and institutions, such as families, governments, and educational systems, to fulfill various collective needs and functions. Moreover, these structures and interactions play a crucial role in shaping the culture, relationships, and overall well-being of society's members.

song of Moses: A chorus of praise recalling Israel's triumphant refrain on the shore of the Red Sea after the exodus from Egypt, along with the historically evocative poem that Moses delivered shortly before his death on Mount Nebo.

Son of God motif: This theme highlights the Messiah's divine nature and supreme authority, especially in connection with his unique relationship to the Father. The motif also stresses that only the Messiah, in his exalted glory, is deserving of adoration and praise. After all, he alone, as the victorious Warrior and ultimate Conqueror, defeats Satan and his demonic cohort and vindicates the faith and faithfulness of the righteous.

Son of Man motif: This theme offers a symbolic representation of the Messiah, with an emphasis on his supreme authority, sovereign role in judgment, and triumphant return. By drawing upon imagery from Daniel's prophecy, the imagery presents the Messiah as a powerful, heavenly figure who alone is responsible for judging the world, bringing salvation to God's reborn children, and establishing his eternal reign. This motif also highlights both Jesus' full divinity and full humanity, while stressing his unique role in the end-time events described in John's prophetic oracle.

song of the Lamb: A chorus of praise celebrating the triumph of the new people of God—the faithful followers of the Messiah—over their antagonists. The Lamb's disciples acknowledge that his sacrificial death at Calvary made victory possible for them who trust and obey him. In John's prophetic oracle, Jesus is portrayed as a new, Moses-like redemptive figure. He who is infinitely greater than the famed lawgiver and bondservant of God leads the newly formed Israel into an exodus-like freedom and release from the tyranny of the dragon (the devil), the sea-beast (the antichrist), and the land-beast (the false prophet).

soon fulfillment: The notion that the end-time events which John declares in his prophetic oracle will be brought to completion without delay. Given the passage of almost two millennia, the apostle most likely stresses that whenever the Father begins to fulfill what is written, it is certain to take place swiftly. Even Revelation's emphasis on the second advent does not imply that it occurs in a short period of time. Instead, the focus is on the suddenness and unexpectedness of the Son's return. Once the appointed moment arrives, nothing will prevent his appearing.

spiritual victory: The notion that Jesus' followers, through the Lamb's sacrificial death at Calvary, ultimately overcome any challenges to their faith that stem from satanic and worldly forces. These believers remain steadfast in following the Messiah's teachings and refuse to participate in idolatry, even if they are persecuted or martyred for their unwavering devotion to Christ. Despite the hardships they may face, at the end of the age, they are adorned with the Son's righteousness, dwell with him in purity for all eternity, and partake in his future, glorious reign.

storm phenomena: Dramatic and awe-inspiring events that signify God's wrath and power. These supernatural episodes, which include thunder, lightning, earthquakes, and hail, serve as apocalyptic symbols of upheaval, God's final judgment of humanity, and his ushering in of a new creation.

syncretism: The merging or fusion of elements from the Christian faith and its practices with those originating from pagan religious and cultural traditions. Syncretism can manifest in various forms, including the integration of indigenous beliefs, rituals, or symbols into Christian worship, theology, or lifestyle. Other pernicious examples include accepting ancestor worship along with worship of the Creator, giving allowance for polygamy and sexual promiscuity, and tolerating various levels of gender-based violence in patriarchal social structures.

ten horns: Ten kings affiliated with the sea-beast, none of whom have yet risen to power. For a brief period, these individuals exercise ruling authority with the sea-beast while remaining subservient to him. This coalition is depicted as eventually laying waste to the harlot, stripping her naked, consuming her flesh like crazed, ravenous animals, and incinerating her remains with fire. Furthermore, the sea-beast, along with his minions, are portrayed as failing in their efforts to wage war against the Lamb, for he remains the sovereign Lord and supreme Monarch of the universe. One option is that the ten horns refer to a confederation of European leaders that, in the end times, belong to a revived Roman Empire in the West that is dominated by the antichrist. A second option is that the ten horns symbolize the entirety of pagan, idolatrous, earthly power and authority in rebellion against the Lord.

Tent of Testimony: The ark of the covenant, wherein is placed the two stone tablets. Upon these are recorded the Decalogue (or Ten Commandments). This is a distillation of the Creator's righteous moral law, which idolatrous and pagan humanity repeatedly violates. For this reason, as decreed from the Lord's cosmic court of justice, his wrath (or covenantal curses) is poured out on earth's wicked inhabitants.

testifying: The notion that Jesus' followers bear witness to him, as one would do in a court of law. This testimony involves believers' proclaiming the gospel and making disciples of all nations. It also involves their remaining faithful to the Messiah, even in the face of persecution and martyrdom.

theodicy: An argument that grapples with the question of how the existence of evil in the world can be reconciled with the idea of an all-good and all-powerful God. Theodicy aims not only to acknowledge but also to defend the Creator's inherently righteous and virtuous nature, as well as his complete control over all that occurs, regardless of whether it aligns with one's understanding of goodness. In the context of the Apocalypse, readers encounter numerous instances where God's providence is reaffirmed, often accompanied by declarations of his justice, truth, and righteousness. This serves as a response to the implicit accusations made by the wicked, who argue that it is unjust and ethically questionable for the Lord to impose his covenantal curses upon them.

throne: God's sacred, heavenly, royal seat, which epitomizes his supreme authority and unrivaled power, along with his majesty and holiness. The Creator's throne occupies the literary center of John's prophetic oracle. It is the place from which the three cycles of judgment emerge, as well as the point of origin for the Lamb's ultimate triumph as the divine Warrior over the dragon (the devil), the sea-beast (the antichrist), and the land-beast (the false prophet). The throne also serves as the focus of heavenly worship, with innumerable beings, including angels and elders, constantly praising and adoring God. Moreover, the imagery of the throne provides hope for his beleaguered, reborn children by reassuring them of the promise of eternal life for remaining faithful to him, even amid persecution and martyrdom.

throne-room scenes: The vivid and symbolic passages where John describes his visionary encounters with the Creator in heaven. He is depicted as positioned on his sacred, royal seat and surrounded by countless angelic beings. Each scene highlights some aspect of the triune God's holiness, righteousness, glory, sovereignty, and might, while playing a crucial role in conveying the various messages of the apostle's prophetic oracle.

Tree of Life: A life-giving, verdant plant in the primordial garden. In Revelation, the tree is by the river flowing from God's throne in the new Jerusalem. It radiates his creative, animating power and symbolizes the believers' unlimited access to his covenantal blessings (including spiritual vitality and physical well-being). One option is that the tree collectively refers to an orchard lining both sides of the riverbank. The tree produces twelve different kinds of fruit, with a new crop appearing each month of the year. Also, the fruit is a source of life, and its leaves are used medicinally to heal the nations.

Trinity: The belief that there is one God who simultaneously exists as three distinct persons, referred to as the Father, the Son, and the Holy Spirit. These three are consubstantial—that is, of the same divine substance or essence. They are also coequal and coeternal, forming a unified

Godhead. As such, though they are distinct in their personhood, they are not divided. Moreover, the divine presence is both immanent (or present in the world) and transcendent (or beyond the world). These truths complement the emphasis in the Apocalypse on the Father as the Creator, the Son as the sacrificial Lamb and divine Warrior, and the Spirit in his sevenfold perfection, manifold presence, and fulsome ministry.

twenty-four elders: Vassal rulers seated on twenty-four thrones surrounding God's sacred, royal seat in heaven. They wear white garments, which represent purity, uprightness, and immortality. Also, on their heads are gold crowns, which symbolize honor, splendor, and triumph. The elders are possibly an exalted order of angels who serve the Lord in his celestial court, or they might be glorified saints in heaven. One option is that the number twenty-four is a symbolic reference to the twelve tribes of Israel in the Old Testament and the twelve apostles in the New Testament. If so, this suggests that all the redeemed of all time are represented before God's throne and worship him in his heavenly sanctuary.

two witnesses: A pair of spokespersons, also referred to as the two olive trees and the two lampstands, who stand before the Lord. One option is that these are two unnamed Christian prophets who were martyred shortly before the fall of Jerusalem in AD 70, or they could be two prophets who appear shortly before Jesus' return. A second option is that the two are symbolic figures for God's reborn children, such as Christians alive and testifying during a final period of crisis before the second advent. In this case, they adopt the prophetic mantle of Moses and Elijah to summon the unregenerate to abandon their iniquities and trust in the Messiah for salvation. Or the two might symbolize credible, witnessing believers throughout the history of the church.

typological fulfillment (prophetic foreshadowing): A concept that highlights Revelation's use of Old Testament references, particularly its imagery and prophecies. In the Apocalypse, these references are woven into a pattern that serves to anticipate a deeper and more profound realization in the events and symbols being described. This approach emphasizes that Revelation's prophecies extend beyond mere historical or contemporary events. They also carry profound spiritual significance and are intricately linked to God's end-time plan for the universe.

unholy trinity: A blasphemous threesome comprising the dragon (the devil), the sea-beast (the antichrist), and the land-beast (the false prophet). These hideous entities conspire to undermine the Creator's rule, persecute the Messiah's followers, and mimic/counterfeit the Spirit's work.

veneration of Satan: To give homage and adoration to the devil, whom Revelation portrays as the enemy of the Creator, as well as the adversary, archenemy, and accuser of his reborn children. Moreover, the evil one is depicted as leading astray earth's wicked inhabitants into idolatry and false worship. At the end of the age, divine judgment awaits Satan and all those who succumb to the allure of his worldly power and deception.

wedding feast (supper) of the Lamb: A fitting symbol of the celebration, based on the ancient Near Eastern marriage banquet, that occurs when Jesus consummates his union with the church triumphant. This joyous, messianic feast stands in sharp contrast to the somber destiny of the wicked at the end of the age. While eternal rewards await the redeemed in heaven, unending ruin and separation from the Creator's sacred presence are the fate of the wicked in the fiery lake filled with burning sulfur.

white stone in Revelation: One option is that this object implies a vote of innocence and acquittal, in which the color white often symbolizes purity and righteousness. A second option is that the object signifies tokens of permission to enter the messianic banquet to be held at the end of the age (often associated with the marriage feast of the Lamb).

wife (bride) of the Lamb: The teaching that the church—which consists of all true believers from the Old and New Testament eras—is the bride of the Lamb. Presently, God's reborn children are betrothed (or pledged in marriage) to the Messiah and await the day when he claims them as his beloved. Throughout the centuries, the Redeemer's bride has been preparing herself for the day when she meets him. At the Savior's return, he joins himself to his followers in everlasting intimacy, love, and joy.

wilderness (or desert): One option is that this refers to a desolate backdrop where God's judgment occurs. A second option is that the term denotes a spiritual place of deliverance (which resonates with Revelation's use of the exodus wilderness motif of salvation). A third option is that the desert region symbolizes a place of refuge that is detached from the pagan influences of the world (which aligns with the Apocalypse's dichotomy between faithfulness and idolatrous compromise).

wine of God's wrath, cup of his anger: Idiomatic references to the Father's judgment. These expressions are reminiscent of Old Testament passages depicting the Creator's intense anger as a cup of wine (or goblet filled with poison) that was poured out in full strength and that the wicked ingested. In the ancient world, people usually diluted wine with water. Consequently, undiluted wine was regarded as being extremely potent, and it became a symbol for severe judgment.

woman giving birth: A symbolic female figure portrayed as standing above the moon while wearing the sun for her outer garment and a crown made of twelve stars upon her head. Moreover, she is depicted as being pregnant and screaming in labor pains while she gives birth to her son. Four prominent views about the identity of the woman are that she represents Mary, the mother of Jesus, the twelve founding tribes of Israel, the twelve founding apostles of the church, or the new Jerusalem (personified). More generally, the woman could symbolize all the Father's reborn and faithful children—a united, diverse, multiethnic, multicultural, and baptized messianic community whom the Son redeemed through the cross-resurrection event.

Word of God: A reference to the triumphant Savior as the divine, incarnate Logos (which means "word," "reason," or "principle"). To the Lamb's faithful followers, he is, above all else, the supreme and ultimate revelation of the eternal, all-powerful, and absolutely holy Creator.

worldview: A coherent system of thought that shapes the impressions people have about reality and their interpretation of the world. More specifically, it encompasses the assumptions, values, and beliefs individuals have regarding the nature of existence, knowledge, morality, purpose, and humanity's position within the universe. Worldviews serve as guiding lenses through which people perceive events, make decisions, seek meaning, and find purpose in their lives. Furthermore, one's worldview is influenced by various factors, including culture, religion, scientific understanding, and personal experiences.

worship of God: Heavenly scenes where various creatures, along with the redeemed, offer unceasing praise and adoration to the Creator. Together, the episodes highlight his absolute sovereignty as Ruler and supreme authority as Judge. The continuous worship evokes a sense of awe, humility, and hope for God's reborn children, especially amid unrelenting adversity. They are reminded that Christ, the Lamb, is the divine Warrior who vindicates their faith and faithfulness, as well as guarantees their full and final reception of eternal life at his second advent.

Yahweh: God's unique, deeply personal name. Specifically, the Creator is the self-existent, eternally present, and ever-caring Father. His everlasting existence and faithful presence with his beleaguered, reborn children reminds them that the One who governs all time from his cosmic royal seat will never abandon them.

Bibliography

Aune, David E. *Revelation 1–5*. Word Biblical Commentary 52A. Dallas: Word, 1997.

———. *Revelation 6–16*. Word Biblical Commentary 52B. Dallas: Word, 1998.

———. *Revelation 17–22*. Word Biblical Commentary 52C. Dallas: Word, 1998.

Barr, David L. *Tales of the End: A Narrative Commentary on the Book of Revelation*. 2nd ed. Salem, OR: Polebridge, 2011.

Batto, B. F. "Behemoth." In *Dictionary of Deities and Demons in the Bible*, edited by Karel van der Toorn, Bob Becking, and Pieter W. van der Horst, 165–69. 2nd ed. Leiden: Brill, 1999.

Bauckham, Richard. *The Climax of Prophecy: Studies on the Book of Revelation*. Edinburgh: T&T Clark, 1993.

———. *The Theology of the Book of Revelation*. New Testament Theology. Cambridge: Cambridge University Press, 1993.

———. *The Worship of Jesus in Apocalyptic Christianity*. Cambridge: Cambridge University Press, 2009.

Beagley, Alan James. *The "Sitz im Leben" of the Apocalypse with Particular Reference to the Role of the Church's Enemies*. Beiheft zur Zeitschrift für die neutestamentliche Wissenschaft und die Kunde der älteren Kirche 50. Berlin: de Gruyter, 1987.

Beale, Gregory K. *The Book of Revelation*. The New International Greek Testament Commentary. Grand Rapids: Eerdmans, 2013.

Beale, Gregory K., and Sean M. McDonough. "Revelation." In *Commentary on the New Testament Use of the Old Testament*, edited by G. K. Beale and D. A. Carson, 1081–1158. Grand Rapids: Baker Academic, 2007.

Blaising, Craig A., Kenneth L. Gentry Jr., and Robert B. Strimple. *Three Views on the Millennium and Beyond*. Counterpoints Series, edited by Darrell L. Bock and Stan N. Gundry. Grand Rapids: Zondervan, 1999.

Blount, Brian K. *Revelation: A Commentary*. The New Testament Library. Louisville: Westminster John Knox, 2009.

Boring, M. Eugene. *Revelation*. Louisville: Westminster John Knox, 2011.

Bousset, Wilhelm. *Die Offenbarung des Johannes*. Augsburg: Jazzybee, 2021.

Boxall, Ian. *The Revelation of Saint John*. Black's New Testament Commentaries. Peabody, MA: Hendrickson, 2006.

Breytenbach, C., and P. L. Day. "Satan." In *Dictionary of Deities and Demons in the Bible*, edited by Karel van der Toorn, Bob Becking, and Pieter W. van der Horst, 726–32. 2nd ed. Leiden: Brill, 1999.

Brighton, Louis A. *Revelation*. Concordia Commentary. St. Louis: Concordia, 1999.[1]

Caird, G. B. *The Revelation of St. John the Divine*. Harper's New Testament Commentaries. New York: Harper & Row, 1966.

Calvin, John. *Institutes of the Christian Religion*. Edited by John T. McNeill. Translated by Ford Lewis Battles. Library of Christian Classics. 2 vols. Louisville: Westminster John Knox, 1960.

Carey, Greg. *Elusive Apocalypse: Reading Authority in the Revelation to John*. Studies in American Biblical Hermeneutics 15. Macon, GA: Mercer University Press, 1999.

Carrell, Peter R. *Jesus and the Angels: Angelology and the Christology of the Apocalypse of John*. Cambridge: Cambridge University Press, 1997.

Carrington, Philip. *The Meaning of the Revelation*. Eugene, OR: Wipf & Stock, 2008.

Casey, Jay Smith. "Exodus Typology in the Book of Revelation." PhD diss., Southern Baptist Theological Seminary, 1982.

Charles, R. H. *A Critical and Exegetical Commentary on the Revelation of St. John*. 2 vols. The International Critical Commentary. Edinburgh: T&T Clark, 1920.

Collins, Adela Yarbro. *Crisis and Catharsis: The Power of the Apocalypse*. Philadelphia: Westminster, 1984.

Corsini, Eugenio. *The Apocalypse: The Perennial Revelation of Jesus Christ*. Translated and edited by Francis J. Moloney. Eugene, OR: Wipf & Stock, 2019.

Court, John M. *Revelation*. Sheffield: Sheffield Academic, 1994.

deSilva, David Arthur. *Seeing Things John's Way: The Rhetoric of the Book of Revelation*. Louisville: Westminster John Knox, 2009.

Draper, Richard D., and Michael D. Rhodes. *The Revelation of John the Apostle*. BYU New Testament Commentary. Provo: BYU Studies, 2013.

Fee, Gordon D. *Revelation*. Eugene, OR: Cascade Books, 2010.

Flemming, Dean. *Foretaste of the Future: Reading Revelation in Light of God's Mission*. Downers Grove, IL: InterVarsity Press, 2022.

Fletcher, Michelle. "Reading Exodus in Revelation." In *Exodus in the New Testament*, edited by Seth M. Ehorn, 181–201. London: T&T Clark, 2022.

Ford, J. Massyngberde. *Revelation: Introduction, Translation, and Commentary*. The Anchor Bible 38. Garden City, NY: Doubleday, 1975.

Friesen, Steven J. *Imperial Cults and the Apocalypse of John: Reading Revelation in the Ruins*. Oxford: Oxford University Press, 2001.

Gallusz, Laszlo. *The Throne Motif in the Book of Revelation: Profiles from the History of Interpretation*. Library of New Testament Studies 487. London: T&T Clark, 2015.

Gentry, Kenneth L., Jr. *The Divorce of Israel: A Redemptive-Historical Interpretation of Revelation*. 2nd ed. 2 vols. Acworth, GA: Tolle Lege, 2024.

Giblin, Charles Homer. *The Book of Revelation: The Open Book of Prophecy*. Good News Studies 34. Collegeville, MN: Liturgical Press, 1991.

Gorman, Michael J. *Reading Revelation Responsibly: Uncivil Worship and Witness: Following the Lamb into the New Creation*. Eugene, OR: Cascade, 2010.

Graves, David E. "The Influence of Ancient Near Eastern Vassal Treaties on the Seven Prophetic Messages in Revelation." PhD diss., University of Aberdeen, 2008.

Gregg, Steve. *Revelation, Four Views: A Parallel Commentary*. Nashville: Thomas Nelson, 2013.

Hanson, Anthony Tyrrell. *The Wrath of the Lamb*. Eugene, OR: Wipf & Stock, 2010.

1. A more recent edition is also available: Brighton, Louis A. *Revelation*. Concordia Popular Commentary. St. Louis: Concordia, 2009.

Harrington, Wilfrid J. *Revelation*. Sacra Pagina Series 16. Collegeville, MN: Liturgical Press, 1993.

Hattaway, Paul, Brother Yun, Peter Xu Yongze, and Enoch Wang. *Back to Jerusalem: Three Chinese House Church Leaders Share Their Vision to Complete the Great Commission*. Downers Grove, IL: InterVarsity, 2003.

Hays, Richard P., and Stefan Alkier, eds. *Revelation and the Politics of Apocalyptic Interpretation*. Waco, TX: Baylor University Press, 2012.

Hendriksen, William. *More Than Conquerors: An Interpretation of the Book of Revelation*. Grand Rapids: Baker Books, 1967.

Hoeck, Andreas. *Worthy Lamb: An Exegetical-Spiritual Commentary on John's Apocalypse*. Catholic Theological Formation Series. St. Paul: Saint Paul Seminary Press, 2024.

Horton, Michael. "The Reformation Gospel." In *Five Views on the Gospel*, edited by Michael F. Bird and Jason Maston, 63–85. Counterpoints: Bible and Theology. Grand Rapids: Zondervan Academic, 2025.

Hughes, Philip Edgcumbe. *The Book of the Revelation: A Commentary*. Grand Rapids: Eerdmans, 1990.

Jauhiainen, Marko. *The Use of Zechariah in Revelation*. Wissenschaftliche Untersuchungen zum Neun Testament 2. Reihe 199. Tübingen: Mohr Siebeck, 2005.

Johnson, Dennis E. *Triumph of the Lamb: A Commentary on Revelation*. Phillipsburg: P&R, 2001.

Josephus, Flavius. *The Works of Josephus: Complete and Unabridged*. Translated by William Whiston. Peabody, MA: Hendrickson, 1987.

Keener, Craig S. *Revelation*. The NIV Application Commentary. Grand Rapids: Zondervan, 2000.

Kiddle, Martin. *The Revelation of St. John*. London: Hodder & Stoughton, 1946.

Kistemaker, Simon J. *Exposition of the Book of Revelation*. New Testament Commentary. Grand Rapids: Baker Books, 2001.

Koester, Craig R. *Revelation: A New Translation with Introduction and Commentary*. Anchor Yale Bible Commentaries. New Haven: Yale University Press, 2015.

Ladd, George Eldon. *A Commentary on the Revelation of John*. Grand Rapids: Eerdmans, 1972.

Leithart, Peter. *Revelation 1–11*. The International Theological Commentary. London: T&T Clark, 2018.

———. *Revelation 12–22*. The International Theological Commentary. London: T&T Clark, 2018.

Lioy, Dan. *The Book of Revelation in Christological Focus*. Studies in Biblical Literature 58. New York: Peter Lang, 2003.

Longman, Tremper, III. *Revelation*. Through Old Testament Eyes. Grand Rapids: Kregel, 2022.

Longman, Tremper, III, and Daniel G. Reid. *God Is a Warrior*. Studies in Old Testament Biblical Theology. Grand Rapids: Zondervan, 1995.

Luther, Martin. *Luther's Works*, Vol. 35, *Word and Sacrament I*. Edited by Jaroslav Jan Pelikan, Hilton C. Oswald, and Helmut T. Lehmann. Philadelphia: Fortress, 1999.

Maier, Harry O. *Apocalypse Recalled: The Book of Revelation after Christendom*. Minneapolis: Fortress, 2002.

Mason, Steve. *A History of the Jewish War, AD 66–74*. Cambridge: Cambridge University Press, 2016.

Mathewson, David L. *A Companion to the Book of Revelation*. Cascade Companions. Eugene, OR: Cascade, 2020.

McKnight, Scot, and Cody Matchett. *Revelation for the Rest of Us: A Prophetic Call to Follow Jesus as a Dissident Disciple*. Grand Rapids: Zondervan, 2023.

Metzger, Bruce M. *Breaking the Code: Understanding the Book of Revelation*. Nashville: Abingdon, 2006.

Michaels, J. Ramsey. *Revelation: A Commentary on the New Testament*. The IVP New Testament Commentary Series. Downers Grove: InterVarsity Press, 2011.

Middleton, J. Richard. *A New Heaven and a New Earth: Reclaiming Biblical Eschatology*. Grand Rapids: Baker Academic, 2014.

Morales, Jon. "Christ, Shepherd of the Nations: The Nations as Narrative Character and Audience in the Apocalypse." PhD diss., Southeastern Baptist Theological Seminary, 2016.

Morris, Leon. *Revelation: An Introduction and Commentary*. Tyndale New Testament Commentaries 20. Downers Grove: InterVarsity, 2009.

Morrison, Dan. "Apocalypse as Protest: Reading Revelation from Places of Poverty, Privilege, Power, and Persecution." PhD diss., McMaster Divinity College, 2020.

Mounce, Robert H. *The Book of Revelation*. Rev. ed. The New International Commentary on the New Testament. Grand Rapids: Eerdmans, 1997.

Moyise, Steve. *The Old Testament in the Book of Revelation*. Journal for the Study of the New Testament Supplement Series 115. Sheffield: Sheffield Academic, 1995.

Mueller, Ekkehardt. "Creation in the Book of Revelation." In *The Genesis Creation Account and Its Reverberations in the New Testament*, edited by Thomas R. Shepherd, 405–49. Berrin Springs: Andrews University Press, 2022.

Munck, Johannes. *Petrus und Paulus in der Offenbarung Johannis: Ein Beitrag zur Auslegung der Apokalypse*. København: Rosenkilde og Bagger, 1950.

Osborne, Grant R. *Revelation*. Baker Exegetical Commentary on the New Testament. Grand Rapids: Baker, 2002.

Pattemore, Stephen. *The People of God in the Apocalypse: Discourse, Structure, and Exegesis*. Society for New Testament Studies Monograph Series 128. Cambridge: Cambridge University Press, 2004.

Patterson, Paige. *Revelation*. New American Commentary. Nashville: B&H, 2012.

Paul, Ian. *Revelation: An Introduction and Commentary*. Tyndale New Testament Commentaries 20. Downers Grove: InterVarsity Press, 2018.

Piper, John. *Let the Nations Be Glad! The Supremacy of God in Missions*. Grand Rapids: Baker Academic, 1993.

Poythress, Vern S. *The Returning King: A Guide to the Book of Revelation*. Phillipsburg: P&R, 2000.

Prigent, Pierre. *Commentary on the Apocalypse of St. John*. Translated by Wendy Pradels. Tübingen: Mohr Siebeck, 2001.

Reddish, Mitchell G. *Revelation*. Smyth and Helwys Bible Commentary 30. Macon: Smyth & Helwys, 2001.

Resseguie, James L. *The Revelation of John: A Narrative Commentary*. Grand Rapids: Baker Academic, 2009.

Roloff, Jürgen. *Revelation*. Translated by John E. Alsup and James S. Curie. Continental Commentary Series. Minneapolis: Fortress, 1993.

Rowland, Christopher. *Revelation*. Epworth Commentaries. London: Epworth, 1994.

Schedtler, Justin P. Jeffcoat. *Royal Ideologies in the Book of Revelation*. Cambridge: Cambridge University Press, 2023.

Schreiner, Thomas R. *Revelation*. Baker Exegetical Commentary on the New Testament. Grand Rapids: Baker Academic, 2023.

Shepherd, Thomas R., ed. *The Genesis Creation Account and Its Reverberations in the New Testament*. Berrin Springs: Andrews University Press, 2022.

Simojoki, Anssi. "The Book of Revelation." In *Theodicy in the World of the Bible: The Goodness of God and the Problem of Evil*, edited by Antti Laato and Johannes C. de Moor, 652–84. Leiden: Brill, 2003.

Smalley, Stephen S. *The Revelation to John: A Commentary on the Greek Text of the Apocalypse*. Downers Grove, IL: InterVarsity Press, 2012.

Smith, Brandon D. *The Trinity in the Book of Revelation: Seeing Father, Son, and Holy Spirit in John's Apocalypse*. Downers Grove, IL: IVP Academic, 2022.

Stefanovic, Ranko. *Revelation of Jesus Christ: Commentary on the Book of Revelation*. 2nd ed. Berrien Springs: Andrews University Press, 2009.

Stokes, Ryan E. *The Satan: How God's Executioner Became the Enemy*. Grand Rapids: Eerdmans, 2019.

Stolz, F. "Sea." In *Dictionary of Deities and Demons in the Bible*, edited by Karel van der Toorn, Bob Becking, and Pieter W. van der Horst, 737–42. 2nd ed. Leiden: Brill, 1999.

Sturm, W. J. *The Ultimate Exodus: A Commentary on the Book of Revelation: A Futurists, Non-Pretribulational Perspective*. Enumclaw: Redemption, 2015.

Sweet, John Philip McMurdo. *Revelation*. Westminster Pelican Commentaries. Louisville: Westminster John Knox, 1979.

Swete, Henry Barclay. *The Apocalypse of St. John*. Eugene, OR: Wipf & Stock, 1998.

Tabb, Brian J. *All Things New: Revelation as Canonical Capstone*. New Studies in Biblical Theology 48. Downers Grove, IL: IVP Academic, 2019.

Thomas, John Christopher, and Frank D. Macchia. *Revelation*. The Two Horizons New Testament Commentary. Grand Rapids: Eerdmans, 2016.

Thomas, Robert L. *Revelation Exegetical Commentary*. Wycliffe Exegetical Commentary. 2 vols. Chicago: Moody, 2016.

Thompson, Leonard L. *Apocalypse and Empire*. Oxford: Oxford University Press, 1997.

———. *Revelation*. Abingdon New Testament Commentaries. Nashville: Abingdon, 1998.

Trites, Alison A. *The New Testament Concept of Witness*. Society for New Testament Studies Monograph Series 31. Cambridge: Cambridge University Press, 1977.

Uehlinger, C. "Leviathan." In *Dictionary of Deities and Demons in the Bible*, edited by Karel van der Toorn, Bob Becking, and Pieter W. van der Horst, 511–15. 2nd ed. Leiden: Brill, 1999.

Urga, Abeneazer G., Edward L. Smither, and Michael P. Naylor, eds. *Reading Revelation Missiologically: The Missionary Motive, Message, and Methods of Revelation*. Pasadena, CA: William Carey Publishing, 2025.

Wall, Robert W. *Revelation*. New International Biblical Commentary. Peabody, MA: Hendrickson, 2002.

Walton, John H. and D. Brent Sandy. *The Lost World of Scripture: Ancient Literary Culture and Biblical Authority*. The Lost World Series. Downers Grove: InterVarsity, 2013.

Walvoord, John F. *Revelation*. Revised and edited by Philip E. Rawley and Mark Hitchcock. The John Walvoord Prophecy Commentaries. Chicago: Moody, 2011.

Weima, Jeffrey A. D. *The Sermons to the Seven Churches of Revelation: A Commentary and Guide*. Grand Rapids: Baker Academic, 2021.

Wilcock, Michael. *The Message of Revelation: I Saw Heaven Opened*. The Bible Speaks Today. Downers Grove: InterVarsity Press, 1975.

Wilson, Mark W. *Revelation*. Zondervan Illustrated Bible Backgrounds Commentary. Grand Rapids: Zondervan, 2019.

Witherington, Ben, III. *Revelation*. The New Cambridge Bible Commentary. Cambridge: Cambridge University Press, 2003.

Wright, Christopher J. H. *The Mission of God: Unlocking the Bible's Grand Narrative*. 2nd ed. Downers Grove, IL: IVP Academic, 2025.

www.ingramcontent.com/pod-product-compliance
Lightning Source LLC
LaVergne TN
LVHW020517100826
845148LV00010B/1259
9798385256112